Material Change
The Impact of Reform and Modernity on
Material Religion in North-West Europe,
1780-1920

JAN DE MAEYER & PETER JAN MARGRY, EDS

MATERIAL
CHANGE

THE IMPACT OF REFORM AND MODERNITY
ON MATERIAL RELIGION
IN NORTH-WEST EUROPE, 1780-1920

KADOC Artes 19

LEUVEN UNIVERSITY PRESS

This book appears in the peer-reviewed series KADOC Artes and is the fifth volume of the sub-series 'The Dynamics of Religious Reform in Northern Europe, 1780-1920', published in the peer-reviewed series KADOC Studies on Religion, Culture and Society.

Editorial board

Timothy Brittain-Catlin, University of Cambridge
James Chappel, Duke University
Kim Christiaens, KADOC - KU Leuven
Wilhelm Damberg, Ruhr-Universität Bochum
Jean-Dominique Durand, Université Lyon
James C. Kennedy, Utrecht University
Rupert Klieber, Universität Wien
Mathijs Lamberigts, KU Leuven
Peter Jan Margry, Meertens Instituut / Universiteit van Amsterdam
Francisca Metzger, Pädagogische Hochschule Luzern
Madalena Meyer-Resende, Universidade Nova de Lisboa
Anne Morelli, Université Libre de Bruxelles
Silvia Mostaccio, Université catholique de Louvain
Patrick Pasture, KU Leuven
Isabelle Saint-Martin, EPHE Sorbonne I Paris
Joachim Schmiedl, Philosophisch-Theologische Hochschule Vallendar
J.T. (Thijl) Sunier, VU Amsterdam
Steven Van Hecke, KU Leuven

Board members of the project 'The Dynamics of Religious Reform in Northern Europe, 1780-1920' are Jan De Maeyer (KU Leuven), Joris van Eijnatten (Utrecht University), Andreas Gestrich (German Historical Institute, London), Anders Jarlert (Lund University), James Kennedy (Utrecht University), Liselotte Malmgart (Aarhus University), Peter Jan Margry (Meertens Institute Amsterdam), Keith Robbins† (University of Wales, Lampeter), Nigel Yates† (University of Wales, Lampeter), and Paula Yates (South Wales Baptist College, Cardiff).

Cover: View of the ceiling inside the Copenhagen Cathedral (Vor Frue Kirke).
[© Oliver Förstner / Alamy Stock Photo, 2016]

© 2021
Leuven University Press / Presses Universitaires de Louvain / Universitaire Pers Leuven
Minderbroedersstraat 4, B-3000 Leuven

All rights reserved. Except in those cases expressly determined by law, no part of this publication may be multiplied, saved in an automated data file or made public in any way whatsoever without the express prior written consent of the publishers.

ISBN 978 94 6270 282 0
D/2021/1869/53
NUR: 704

Contents

Comparing Perspectives in Material Change: an Introduction   9
Jan De Maeyer & Peter Jan Margry

1 THE ROLE OF 'PRESSURE GROUPS'   27

Introduction   28
Jan De Maeyer

1.1
Shaping Material Reform: 'Pressure Groups' in Great Britain and Ireland   30
William Whyte

1.2
A Varied and Remarkably Landscape of Pressure Groups: 50
a Societal Debate as a Result in Belgium
Jan De Maeyer

1.3
Pressure Groups and Networks in the Multi-Denominational Netherlands   64
Antoine Jacobs

1.4
The Institutionalisation of Christian Art and Architecture in Germany: 82
Protagonists and 'Pressure Groups'
Wolfgang Cortjaens

1.5
Church Building Societies in Scandinavia   94
Carsten Bach-Nielsen

2. SPACE AND THE FABRIC OF BUILDINGS AND CONSTRUCTIONS   113

Introduction   115
Jan De Maeyer

2.1
Land Control and Development in the Politics of the Churches   118
in the United Kingdom and Ireland
Timothy Brittain-Catlin & Roderick O'Donnell

2.2
Reconquering a Lost Visibility: Catholic Revival in Early Industrial Belgium 140
Thomas Coomans

2.3
Spatial Concepts in Religious Architecture and the Politics of Building 154
in the German Countries
Wolfgang Cortjaens

2.4
Reforming Religious Material Landscapes in Nineteenth-Century Scandinavia 184
Arne Bugge Amundsen

3. BUILDING AND FURNISHING OF RELIGIOUS ARCHITECTURE 211

Introduction 213
Timothy Brittain-Catlin

3.1
The Pugin Revolution and its Aftermath: the United Kingdom and Ireland 216
Timothy Brittain-Catlin & Roderick O'Donnell

3.2
Gothic Revival: Style, Construction and Ideology in Nineteenth-Century Belgium 244
Thomas Coomans

3.3
To Induce a Beneficial Impression in Their Souls: Church Architecture 258
and Interior Décor in the Netherlands
Wies van Leeuwen

3.4
The Dialectics of Religious Architecture and Liturgy in the German Countries 276
Wolfgang Cortjaens

3.5
The Lutheran State Churches of Denmark, Norway and Sweden and 298
Emerging Minorities
Jens Christian Eldal

4. MATERIAL REFORM IN EVERYDAY RELIGION — 315

Introduction — 316
Peter Jan Margry

4.1
Victorian Piety and the Revival of Material Religion in Britain — 322
Mary Heimann

4.2
Reform and Change in Material Expressions of Catholic Devotion in Ireland — 342
Patricia Lysaght

4.3
The Material Expression of Everyday Religion in Belgium — 360
Tine Van Osselaer

4.4
Societal Change and the Shifts in the Material Expression of Devotional Catholicism in the Netherlands — 374
Peter Jan Margry

4.5
God's Word Materialised: the Domestication of the Bible in Dutch Protestantism — 394
Fred van Lieburg

4.6
Pious Things: Popular Religiosity of the Nineteenth Century from the Perspective of Material Culture in Germany — 404
Dagmar Hänel

4.7
The Impact of Religious Reform on the Material Culture of Popular Piety in Scandinavia — 416
Anders Gustavsson

Colour Illustrations — 425
Authors — 441
Index — 443
Colophon — 448

Comparing Perspectives in Material Change
An Introduction

Jan De Maeyer & Peter Jan Margry

Material Christianity and Material Reform

The long nineteenth century (c 1780-c 1920), the timeframe of this book and at the same time the approximate era of 'modernity', could be called a 'material century', in the sense that the creation, production and possession of material culture experienced a steep rise unprecedented in the history of Europe, as well as a renewal in the forms and variety of its expressions. This development was mainly due to population increase and sharp economic growth, facilitated by political reforms, nation-building and colonialism, and by the processes of industrialisation and modernisation. Religion in its material forms, from church buildings to small devotional objects, did not escape this development. The period between 1830 and 1950 has also been characterised as the century of religion,[1] typified by confessions, confessionalisation and devotionalisation.[2] It is a period that coincides for the most part with the long nineteenth century, and so, not unsurprisingly, this material century was also the heyday of material religion.[3]

This volume analyses how various reforms in relation to the state, society and the church that were part of the process of modernisation have affected the character of material culture within Protestantism, Anglicanism, and Roman Catholicism. Although this book departs from a comparative European perspective, research was limited to a specific set of 'Christian' countries, situated in North-West Europe: Germany, Belgium, the Netherlands, the United Kingdom, Ireland and Scandinavia. The choice of this limited and debatable set was a given for this publication, the fifth and final volume of a series resulting from a long-term research project.[4]

This project, entitled *The Dynamics of Religious Reform in Northern Europe, 1870-1920*, was initiated in 2008, and its research output published in the subsequent years.[5] Now, finally, the last volume is materialised. The project in general encountered difficulty in carrying out proper comparative research within the specific set of the countries, partly due to the limited number of European countries, and partly to strong differences in the *status quaestionis* of research in the countries involved. Moreover, individual contributors to the different volumes had difficulty in applying the project's overall research question, which was formulated in 2008: "what reforms did the organised religions of Northern Europe initiate between c 1780 and c 1920 to accommodate the changing relations between church, state and society, and what was the role of church and state in these reforms?" This was the underlying question for this volume also.

The thinking behind this research question is the following. The end of the *Ancien Régime*, the late eighteenth century, was taken as a point of departure. This was a time when a relatively clear and remarkably uniform pattern of church-state relations existed across Europe, thanks to the close union within states between the political and religious establishments, in which the former was usually able to exercise sufficient control over the latter for the purposes of stable government. This pattern suited both Protestant and, in an era of weak papal authority, Ro-

---

1 Cf. Van Eijnatten and Yates, *The Churches*; Viaene, *Belgium and the Holy See*; Heimann infra.
2 Blaschke, "Das 19. Jahrhundert".
3 For a criticism of the concept of material religion see Coleman, "Material Religion".
4 The choice of this set has been criticised in different reviews, for example by Peter van Dam on volume III, *Piety and Modernity*, in *Tijdschrift voor Geschiedenis*, 127 (2014), 155-157 (and also on volume II, *The Churches*, in 125 (2012), 598-599). The logic of the choice can, in hindsight, indeed be debated and it neglects the influence of and connections with other European regions: for example, the material culture of Christianity in the Netherlands, Belgium and Germany cannot be separated from the influences emanating from France as many references in this volume underline. Unlike earlier volumes in this series, we have designated the chosen geographical region as North-West Europe (rather than Northern Europe).
5 For the previous volumes, see: <https://lup.be/collections/series-dynamics-of-religious-reform>.

man Catholic states. However, this union was noticeably looser in places where the Protestant religious establishment was Calvinist. With the advent of modernity, this pattern of church-state relations began to break down and be transformed all over Europe. The monopoly of the state churches was gradually undermined by the Enlightenment, and according as dissident churches and Catholicism were allowed, the separation of church and state gradually became a reality. Because of secularisation, Christianity lost its hegemony, while society became emancipated from religion, which was turned into a personal matter.

The common pattern of church-state-society relations across the continent that could be identified in 1780 no longer existed in 1920 due to various 'reforms'. The differences in timescale between one part of North-West Europe and another are examined here, as is the impact on religious reform: were changes due to a changed church-state relation or to ecclesiastical reforms initiated by the churches? How much common ground was shared by the ideologies of ecclesiastical reform across Europe, how many common problems and how many common solutions?

The key word here is 'reform', a concept defined for the project as "the conscious pursuit of renewal with the aim of adapting organised religion to the changing relations between church, state and society". Reform could be induced or activated by a great variety of factors, such as the Enlightenment, rationalism, nationalism, colonialism, atheism, anti-clericalism, pietism, the growing moral power of the papacy and its ultramontanism,[6] theological and liturgical factors, industrialisation, urbanisation, demographic growth, and technical innovations.[7] More specifically, reform could be triggered by the relationship between the authorities of the church, state and municipalities regarding matters such as the imposition of rules for church buildings and the care of religious heritage. One of the major examples of common ground, across Europe, is to be found in the extensive programme of church building and restoration, whether state-aided or not. This common ground was also culturally determined by the growing interest after 1815 in picturesque, Romantic landscapes, the fascination with the ruins of medieval abbeys or of Gothic churches destroyed during the Revolution which became the foci of the cultural-historical tourism that gradually emerged among the nobility and upper bourgeoisie. However, interest in cultural history was equally spurred by the need of the new monarchies and emerging nation-states for historical legitimacy.[8]

In the context of material culture, modernity is to be interpreted not as a period in the history of art but as a post-traditional historical era, characterised by the philosopher Michel Foucault in various concepts: the prioritisation of individualism, freedom and formal equality; a belief in the inevitability of social, scientific and technological progress, rationalisation and professionalisation; a move away from feudalism (or agrarianism) towards capitalism and a market economy, industrialisation, urbanisation and secularisation; the development of the nation-state, representative democracy, and public education.[9] Based on his work on religious modernisation, Staf Hellemans redefined the concept of modernity as the privatisation of the spheres of life, the disappearance of an overarching religious canopy, a radical functional differentiation of society in which religion, science, the political and social order and education each acquired increasing autonomy and on the basis of this autonomy started to interact with each other. Church reform and material change were aspects of this.[10]

This fifth volume of the Reform series is a study of the ways in which Christian denominations and their members in North-West Europe gave material expression to their religious, political and sociocultural identity. It gives an overview of the performance and agency of the changing material expression of faith in interaction with modernity.

The new era forced churches to initiate change and to play a new and public role in

---

[6] Lamberts, *The Struggle with Leviathan*.
[7] Cf. Asad, *Formations of the Secular*.
[8] See Viaene, "Religieuze herlevers en religieuze hervormers".
[9] Cf. Foucault, *Discipline and Punish*, 170-177.
[10] Hellemans, *Religion and Modernity in Europe*; Id., *De grote transformatie van religie en van de katholieke kerk*; De Maeyer, "The Concept of Religious Modernisation".

the societies of the modern nation-states. This book, however, deals only with 'material Christianity', the material culture related to and influenced by the various denominations of Christianity, which was in theory the practiced belief of most of North-West Europe's population. However, within the region being studied there was no uniformity and none of the confessions was a closed community. New ideas of equality led to the emancipation of Catholics in various countries and schisms within the established Protestant churches, all of which had an enormous influence on the construction and renovation of church building and the production of art and artefacts. Reciprocally, this influenced and stimulated the Protestant denominations in their own material expressions.[11]

'Material' then in this collection of essays is to be taken broadly. On the public side, it includes parish infrastructures and land- and cityscapes with all the religious buildings: the architectural designs, the interior design and decoration of chapels, churches, monasteries, educational, charitable and health institutions, and cemeteries. It includes the fine arts of religious painting and sculpture, the applied arts (goldsmith, metal, furniture and textile work), as well as iconographic design. On the private side, it includes objects relating to the home and private devotions, with a great variety of popular devotional and everyday life objects, and booklets, cards, photographs, posters etc.[12]

Historiography, theory and methodology

Historiography

The interest in religious material culture started centuries ago with the collection and description of objects and monuments. In the nineteenth century religious objects came to be collected more systematically and professionally, initially mainly by art historians, classicists, ethnologists and folklorists, some of whom were affiliated with national or folklore museums. The latter two were more interested in the expressions of the people, often the seemingly not very valuable material culture of everyday life, while the art historians and classicists were oriented more towards the artistic expressions of an older age. Until the beginning of the twentieth century, the history of materiality with regard to religion or the churches was usually limited to traditional or classic descriptions of objects and styles as part of art history. However, since the beginning of the twentieth century the fear of worlds disappearing as a result of modernisation and being replaced by industrial forms has led to projects by (open-air) museums for collecting and inventorying objects.

In the 1970s research into material culture became somewhat diversified, although more traditional research based on drawing up inventories and taxonomies also continued. This was mostly done within art history, museum and cultural heritage environments. Then in the mid-1990s Colleen McDannell's study heralded a sea change in research on religious material culture. It took a step away from the overviews and inventories of material religion, although these remain popular often because of their attractive visuals.[13] While focusing on American culture, she foregrounded the overlooked aspects of material religion, especially the objects of popular religion in the private sphere and in the home. Within the context of the history of art this theme had never been given the value and attention it deserved. McDannell set the agenda for neglected types of Christian material culture – not merely the material culture but its functions, meanings, use and agency. Her research programme consisted of four categories: artefacts, art, architecture and landscapes, the latter including the idea of *Lieux de mémoire* or places of remembrance, which has become a genre in itself.[14] McDannell's book was a source of inspiration for scholars all over the world and led to national variants.[15]

11 See Van Eijnatten and Yates, *The Churches*, passim.
12 Cf. McDannell, *Material Christianity*.
13 Dühr and Groß-Morgen, *Zwischen Andacht und Andenken*; Perrin and Vasco Rocca, *Thesaurus des objets religieux*; Vandenbroeck, *Backlit Heaven*; Martini, *Medaglia devozionale*; Berthod and Hardouin-Fugier, *Dictionnaire des objets de dévotion*.
14 See <http://materialreligion.org>, with the results of the Material History of American Religion Project, which was carried out between 1995 and 2001. A publication was dedicated to Dutch Catholic places of remembrance: Jacobs, Winkeler and Van der Zeijden, *Aan plaatsen gehecht*.
15 Molendijk, *Materieel christendom*.

Criticism of contemporary material culture research came down to too much culture and too little material, that it focused too much on history from things and the history of things.[16] In 2005 a new step was taken with the launch of a new dedicated scholarly transdisciplinary journal. Its title *Material Religion. The Journal of Objects, Art and Belief* announced its mission to include histories, context and (belief) practices and its aim to explore "how religion happens in material culture – images, devotional and liturgical objects, architecture and sacred space, works of arts and mass-produced artefacts". This is done in combination with the various practices that put objects to work, or, in other words, study how religious material culture interacts with the worlds of belief.[17] This spirit also underpins this volume. To what extent the authors succeed is up to the judgement of the reader.

Theory and methodology

Research into religious material culture is a European tradition. Since the nineteenth century, this field of research and its concepts have been mainly dominated by the disciplines of ethnology, archaeology, anthropology, history, architectural and art history and by museum curators. In the twentieth century, thanks to scholars like Erwin Panofsky and Roland Barthes, fields such as iconography and semiotics – applied to reveal hidden layers of meaning within the object and the implicated references outside of the object – brought valuable new theoretical views relating to material culture.[18]

The term 'material culture' as a scholarly collective noun was first used in the second half of the nineteenth century, and stressed the relevance of materiality for "outward signs and symbols of particular ideas in the mind".[19] Under the wide umbrella of material culture, the specification 'material religion' appeared in the twentieth century and remains, despite some criticism about its seemingly contradictory wording[20], a broad concept to refer to those things or artefacts in the physical environment that are used or modified by culturally and religiously determined human behaviour. This implies clearly that a good understanding of the social world is not possible without knowing and researching its material realities.[21]

Historical research has undergone considerable changes in the last decades, particularly under the influence of the idea of the 'turn', starting with the first, the linguistic turn. Since the end of the twentieth century various new approaches and turns have been introduced in the humanities and the social sciences, heralding innovative views on interdisciplinary research. In the 1960s the 'cultural turn' broke open the history field by 'exchanging' the common positivist stance for an approach in which cultural processes are analysed for the meanings and ideas behind cultural practices. These meanings could also apply to what now is known, individually or collectively, as identity formation. Identity politics has become a major topic in modern history and particularly in relation to religious confessions and identities. The appropriation of culture, ideas or styles were building blocks in the formation of a social or cultural memory and identity through which imagined (religious) communities came into being during the long nineteenth century.

As part, or as a result, of the cultural turn, new turns like the material turn followed. The material turn asked for a new 'handling' of what was usually considered to be 'passive' materiality. Through this new lens, research into material culture has been able to come up with new insights. It involves a critical interpretation of practices or behaviour in relation to materiality, bringing matter more into an active relation with what people do. A key figure in this development was the sociologist Bruno Latour who developed the actor-network theory. According to this theory, materiality and objects – human and non-human – are parts of or actors in social networks that exercise power, or, put another way, have *agency*. This means that objects acquire meaning in relation to persons and

---

16 Hannan and Longair, *History Through Material Culture*, 32.
17 <https://www.tandfonline.com/action/journalInformation?show=aimsScope&journalCode=rfmr20>.
18 Panofsky, *Studies in Iconology*; Barthes, *Mythologies*.
19 Schlereth, *Material Culture*, 28.
20 Ibid., 4-5.
21 Ibid., 2-7; Hannan and Longair, *History Through Material Culture*, 7-9.

other objects in their social context, and act upon the other.[22]

Another new turn, the affective turn, pointed to the relation between materiality, emotion and sensory experience, and to the way in which aesthetics or the experience of the sublime exercises its influence.[23] It is therefore important to note that in the practice of religion sentiment and emotion play an important role, affording intimate and particular value to religious objects. In this way, religious objects, even in mass-produced forms, may gain power or agency.[24]

In addition, the anthropologist Igor Kopytoff pleaded for a cultural-biographical approach to objects, to include not only the production but the consumption and uses of objects.[25] Likewise, his colleague Appadurai stressed the importance of including in an ethnographic way the trajectories of objects in research.[26] Anthropologist Daniel Miller is one of the leading scholars on material culture, whose recent book *Stuff*, a state of the art study, discusses an integration of the various approaches, including "Object Oriented Ontology", the idea that organic and inorganic matter affects and shapes human behaviour and practices.

Many of the researchers in this volume are (art) historians and have applied (art) historical methodologies to their research, using material textual and visual sources from archives and publications, as well as taking account of the material culture itself, in many cases carrying out a personal scrutiny of objects and buildings. Additional sources include photographs, postcards, flyers, advertisements etc.[27] All are used to situate the objects and behaviours dealt with in people's cultural patterns and to formulate answers to the research questions. Methodological aspects relating to research on material culture have been discussed by Kingery.[28]

One of the problems encountered, especially in relation to smaller and mass-produced objects, is that of the random nature of what has been preserved. There is a gap between what was used and what has actually survived. Does what has survived represent what was made and how it was used? This reflects one of the paradoxes of mass-produced objects particularly: they are less well preserved, contrary to more precious, unique handmade objects which tend to survive better. It is their value then that keeps things safe and better known.

Finally, the surviving smaller examples of material culture are often displaced out of their original context and are dispersed over many museum collections. Consequently, mass-produced or cheaper objects are often not well described nor easily accessible in museum collections. Directly related to this is the fact that the presence, use or meaning of those 'obvious' everyday objects are seldom described. Likewise, archives of the producers of such material culture are also rare. This all make such objects and the related practices difficult to compare and analyse.

Another problem that has shown up is more of a theoretical kind and deals with questions about the secular or religious quality of objects.[29] Perspectives on this aspect of material religion differ between those of contemporaries and of later scholars. Religious objects that were not formally blessed or accepted by the Church may have been perceived as secular, while scholars sometimes assume that kitschy objects cannot be inherently 'religious' or acquire a religious quality. It is in this regard that pressure groups were influential in evaluating the quality of nineteenth- (and twentieth-) century material religion, and in advocating the fine arts as a requisite for fostering religious experience.

Threads in material reform and change

Religious identity and the emerging nation-states

Modernity could not be avoided in North-West Europe around 1780. It did not come like a tidal wave or involve radical social upheaval; rather, the establishment of modernity was a gradual process, as described

22 Latour, *Reassembling the Social*; cf. Morgan, *Religion and Material Culture*; Id., "The Sensory Web of Vision"; Hannan and Longair, *History Through Material Culture*, 19-20.
23 Meyer, "Aesthetics of Persuasion"; Viladesau, "Aesthetics and Religion".
24 Frykman and Povrzanović Frykman, *Sensitive Objects*; Downes, Holloway and Randles, *Feeling Things*.
25 For example: Brundin, Howard and Laven, *The Sacred Home in Renaissance Italy*.
26 Appadurai, *The Social Life of Things*.
27 See McDannell's view on the use of photographs and postcards: <http://materialreligion.org/journal/photographs.html> and <http://materialreligion.org/objects/june99obj.html>. On the interpretation of postcards see also Christian, *Divine Presence*.
28 Kingery, *Learning from Things*.
29 Cf. Morgan, *Visual Piety*.

above, a merging of mental political-ideological and socio-economic changes that profoundly changed European society in the transition from the eighteenth to the nineteenth century. Modernity also confronted the established churches (Lutheran, Calvinist, Anglican and Roman Catholic) with the challenge of how to position themselves against these changes. To what extent could they hold their own in a Europe where the French Revolution and the Napoleonic Wars (1789-1815) had put an end to the *Ancien Régime*, rendering obsolete the old adage "cuius regio, eius religio".[30]

The established churches realised that if they wanted to survive, 'reform' or 'change' was necessary. They realised that a convincing presence in a changing society was necessary and determined that their material representation should be on a mass, people-oriented scale. It was precisely this material space that became subject to change under the influence of modernity (urbanisation, development of industrial sites). The modern nation-states that were established in Europe after 1815 needed a new range of infrastructure in a changing urban context, such as parliament buildings, offices for the expanding administration, courthouses, barracks, prisons and houses of correction, buildings for the nascent medical care, schools for the provision of education provided by the civil authorities, etc.[31]

Perhaps the established churches were most challenged in the area of infrastructure by demographic developments. In the period 1780-1920, the population increased significantly in Europe and especially in North-West Europe. Between 1801 and 1921, the United Kingdom (England, Wales) recorded a population increase of 326% and Scotland of 201%; from 1787 to 1921, Denmark increased by 98%, Norway by 266% between 1769 and 1920, while Sweden recorded an increase of 192% between 1775 and 1920. Germany had an increase of 182% between 1816 and 1925 (a levelled-off increase due to World War I), although Ireland's population declined by as much as 35% between 1821 and 1911 due to the Famine and poverty-driven high emigration.[32] It is striking how the established churches affiliated with the nation-states in North-West Europe responded to these demographic increases with quite intensive and centrally-led church building programmes. Examples of such campaigns, which will be discussed later in this book, include Norway, where thanks to an Act of Parliament no fewer than 720 churches were built for the Protestant state church between 1850 and 1910; Prussia where, under the protection of Empress Augusta Viktoria (1858-1921), and the assistance of the Evangelischen Kirchen-Hilfsverein, hundreds of Protestant churches were erected after 1898 in the industrial regions of the Ruhr and in large cities such as Berlin; and the Netherlands where dozens of Calvinist 'Lodewijkkerkjes' were built during the reign of King Louis ('Lodewijk') Napoleon (1806-1815) as compensation for the return of medieval churches to Catholic worship. For its part, the Church of England, inspired by the Church Building Act of 1818, erected no fewer than 447 new church buildings between 1801 and 1830. These are just a few of the many examples that illustrate the great challenges facing the established churches and how they responded in interaction with the modernising states.[33]

The Enlightenment and modernity had yet another important effect in North-West Europe, namely in dismantling the monopoly of the established churches in favour of greater religious tolerance and religious freedom. Here again many examples can be cited. In the United Kingdom, the ban on the Roman Catholic Church was lifted in 1829 (the Roman Catholic Relief Act by the Parliament of the United Kingdom), making it easier for Catholic Irish immigrants to settle in the industrial centres or in port areas. In a later stage the Roman Catholic Church hierarchy was restored in England and Wales in 1850. As already noted, during the Napoleonic period, the Calvinist Netherlands again permitted all the non-Reformed denominations, leading to the construc-

---

30 Robbins, "Introduction", 7-25 and passim; Lamberts, *The Struggle with Leviathan*, 9-14 and passim; Van Molle, "Comparing Religious Perspectives on Social Reform", 24-32 and passim.
31 Bayly, *The Birth of the Modern World*, passim; Goodsell, *The Social Meaning of Civic Space*, passim; Minkenberg, *Power and Architecture*, passim; Van de Maele, *Architecture of Bureaucracy*, 6-12.
32 Mitchell, *European Historical Statistics*, 1-11.
33 Van Eijnatten and Yates, *The Churches*, 7-26 and passim.

tion of hundreds of Protestant churches. In addition, in 1853 the status of the Roman Catholic Church as a missionary church was abolished, and a church hierarchy was once again installed, resulting in the construction during the nineteenth century of about 600 Catholic churches.

In the United Kingdom as well as in the Scandinavian countries, free churches were permitted during the first half of the nineteenth century and quickly flourished. This led to a diverse range of denominations in North-West Europe, such as the Dissenters, Baptists, Methodists (in Denmark Grundtvigianism was close to this), Congregationalists, Doleants or Reformed. In the Anglican Church of England more and more differences emerged in the nineteenth century between the so-called Anglo-Catholics, the High Church and the Low Church, which was closer to Calvinism.[34] As Mary Heimann points out in her contribution here, North-West Europe was gradually transformed in the nineteenth century into an open religious market where each denomination endeavoured to gain as many members as possible. It seemed to be a period of unprecedented religious energy or zeal. Her observation is in line with the above-cited judgement of the German historian Blaschke, who labelled the nineteenth century a confessional era.[35] All those denominations that experienced considerable public success needed adequate infrastructure, especially in the cities where they competed among themselves to make their presence felt. This led to intensive building campaigns, certainly in the United Kingdom, the Netherlands and Scandinavia, with structures ranging from simple mission houses to majestic churches and prayer houses. An example of a private approach is to be found in Copenhagen where the *Kirkefondet* was able to erect the necessary infrastructure by raising capital from among the faithful.

Because of the interaction between the established churches and the modern states, the infrastructure of these churches was supported by the civil authorities and their design influenced by architects associated with the governments. Consequently, they had a certain supra-denominational uniformity. This was the case, for example, in the Netherlands with the aforementioned 'Lodewijkkerkjes', and later with the so-called 'Waterstaatkerken', which stood out because of their (neo-)classical design. In Prussia, many Evangelical 'Reichskirche' churches were given a neo-Romanesque, neo-Byzantine or early Christian design, reflecting the preference of King Frederick William IV. In Scandinavia, during the transition from the eighteenth to the nineteenth century, the popular Lutheran Baroque style was exchanged for the (neo)classicism associated with the Enlightenment. The Anglican state church in the United Kingdom initially espoused a classical style, but from the 1830s increasingly replaced this with Gothic Revival.

Around 1840-1850, a similar shift from neoclassicism to neo-Gothic took place in Belgium, where the Roman Catholic Church held a quasi-monopoly. In the Catholic Rhineland, in Westphalia and in the Netherlands, the neo-Gothic style was used for Roman Catholic buildings; this was an expression of the desire to integrate into the nation-state, a recognition of a shared Christian origin from before the Reformation as well as creating a symbolism of identity. It was at once a manifestation of historical legitimacy and of a historical identity. Because this 'neo-Gothicisation' of Catholic church buildings in North-West Europe took place on such a large scale, the neo-Gothic came gradually to be associated with a Rome-centred, militantly ultramontane, anti-Protestant Catholicism. As a result, the established Protestant churches in Scandinavia, Germany and the Netherlands opted for more local, pre-Reformation variants of the Gothic, or in the Netherlands for a 'Dutch Renaissance' style which referred to the 'Golden Age' of the Calvinist republic in the seventeenth century. The use of a historicising formal language was therefore dynamic, and not static in any way. The leitmotif was the effort of the established churches to express their loyalty

34 Ibid., 13-15 and passim.
35 Blaschke, *Konfessionen im Konflikt*, passim.

and commitment to the nation-state in a material way; they wanted nothing more than to be a part of it, without, however, identifying with it.[36]

The churches' stance in interacting with the nation-state calls up other processes, namely confessionalisation and aestheticisation, both of which were part of the process of raising awareness of the importance of the material culture of churches in modernity.

Confessionalisation and aestheticisation

Even more than the established churches, the free or dissident Protestant churches in North-West Europe were aware of their respective identities. They insisted on giving material expression to this themselves, with financial support coming not from the state but from their members and wealthy patrons. Foundations or associations dedicated to building churches were charged with doing what was necessary. The design and decoration of the interiors, which had to express identity, became a subject of debate and were determined within the churches themselves. In the dissident or free churches, the emphasis was on community building around the Bible. The preference therefore was for churches with an octagonal or fan-shaped floor plan or a longitudinal plan with open galleries, aimed to give churchgoers a good view of the pulpit, the baptismal font and the altar. The organ was also given a prominent place, as a way of encouraging the singing of psalms and hymns. Austerity in the decorations was intended to keep churchgoers focused on the Word.

The transnational circulation of ideas played a prominent role in the search for ways of materialising confessional identity. The free churches in Scandinavia were influenced by what happened in Methodist communities in the United Kingdom or the United States of America. Other churches resisted the influence of North German Lutheran brick Gothic architecture and adopted eclectic designs or incorporated local historical concepts. In fact, the interpretation of the Gothic could go in many directions, expressing a connection with the nation, or the region, or with the Middle Ages as a form of historical legitimacy. While the formal languages that circulated in Northern Europe did not stop at the borders of the nation-states, they lent themselves remarkably well to creating mental or cultural boundaries of identity.

Church reform went together with material change, as both the established as well as the dissident or free churches were well aware. Within each confession, this material change was the subject of important debates that took place, for example, during the *Kirchentagen* of the Roman Catholic Church in Germany, during the Catholic Congresses in Mechelen in Belgium or at the synods of the Protestant churches. Stipulations or guidelines were drawn up, such as the so-called 'Eisenach Regulativ' of the German Evangelical Churches, which was passed during their meeting in Eisenach in 1861. The 'Eisenach Regulativ' also had an impact in Scandinavia. The material expression of change clearly accompanied a process of confessionalisation, or in other words, material change was a process that the confessions wanted to control.

The so-called 'pressure groups' played a prominent role in these discussions. As will be discussed in the first section of this book, these included all kinds of organisations – archaeology circles, associations of connoisseurs or lovers of art, brotherhoods and sometimes also, as in the Netherlands, newspapers and magazines that campaigned both for and against certain forms of material expression of Christianity. They operated within their own confession but were not confined within the mental boundaries of their church communities. It is interesting to see how ideas and ways of working circulated across borders and this book reveals how a kind of family tree of circulating ideas developed. The role of pressure groups was multifaceted. They sparked discussion and sensitised church leaders and churchgoers to the importance of making informed choices

36 Viaene, "Religieuze herlevers en religieuze hervormers", 192-193.

about the material expression of their religious identity. They tried to guide this choice through tracts, handbooks, periodicals or guided visits to examples, both those to be emulated and those to be rejected. Especially in the established churches, the pressure groups put pressure on the church leadership and created mental support for 'material change'. They owed their success to their strong links with the confessions and their mixed composition of ministers and priests as well as prominent churchgoers and lay people, all with varied competences (for example theologians, liturgists, archaeologists or art experts, architects and engineers).

Perhaps the greatest importance of the pressure groups lay in the aestheticisation of the religion that these groups managed to launch and partly realise through material culture. This was a multifaceted process within which six perspectives can be distinguished.

First, aestheticisation acknowledged the fundamental function of religious art and architecture, namely the idea that authentic art and the images derived from it (for example, plates and prints) lead to God. Art and architecture were perceived as mediators between earth and heaven. They were supposed to be able to give the spectator, or rather the beholder, a glimpse of the divine, of the sublime. As the French art historian Isabelle Saint-Martin has shown, aestheticisation was a process that not only affected North-West Europe but was a cultural fact across Europe. The Frenchman François René de Chateaubriand (1768-1848) played a central role in this with his widely distributed book *Le Génie du Christianisme* (1802). According to Saint-Martin, he endeavoured to save Christianity in modernity by emphasising beauty and its aesthetic power: "ne pas prouver que le christianisme est excellent parce qu'il vient de Dieu; mais qu'il vient de Dieu parce qu'il est excellent."[37] Saint-Martin argues that the process of aestheticisation in itself involved a connection with modernity: "Justifier la religion par son utilité ou sa beauté et non par sa vérité intrinsèque ouvre une approche séculière du 'fait religieux' qui conduit à lire le Bible comme une œuvre littéraire et à visiter les églises comme des musées. Cette étape de la sécularisation des sociétés contemporaines s'accompagne d'une forme d'esthétisation du religieux du sens où l'entend Michel de Certeau."[38]

Second, this vision eventually generated a second paradigm, namely that religious art and architecture had a 'missionary' task, a didactic or catechetical function. They were supposed to introduce churchgoers to the truths of faith and bring them to share in the sacred perspective of religion. The church building and especially its interior had to form, as it were, a catechetical manual. This paradigm took hold in Protestant and Roman Catholic circles equally during the first decades of the nineteenth century.

Third, this paradigm was in line with the *Gesamtkunst* paradigm that was put forward during the same time period. In *Gesamtkunst*, exterior and interior enter into dialogue, and communicate the same substantive (read catechetical) narrative. The material expression of Christianity thus became a missionary vocation for the designer or architect of the church building. Architects also undertook to design the interior details (furniture, murals or other wall decorations, stained-glass windows, mosaics, etc.) and the liturgical objects (sacred vases, vestments, etc.) and to have the work carried out by art or craft ateliers.[39]

Fourth – and this is the paradigm presented here by William Whyte (see chapter 1.1) – was the view that the material expression of Christianity in religious art and architecture was a language in itself, a language of symbols and metaphors that, like any language, consisted of conventions or rules to convey messages intelligibly. This idea originated in what is perhaps the most important pressure group, the Cambridge Camden Society. Also the influential Augustus Welby Northmore Pugin (1812-1852) was a proponent of the idea architecture, iconography and symbolism constituted a sacred visual language. Pugin was able to

37 Saint-Martin, *Art chrétien/Art sacré*, 19-23, quotation p. 20.
38 Ibid., 21.
39 Ibid., 23-30 and passim; on 'Gesamtkunst' see Roberts, *The Total Work of Art in European Modernism*, 15-122; Id., "The Total Work of Art. Review Essay", 104-110.

valorise his insights better than anyone in his books. His main work, *The True Principles of Pointed or Christian Architecture* (1841) in particular, reached the continent through a French translation published in 1851. For Pugin, the Gothic was the only true Christian art because of its rationality and formal beauty. His ideas were well received in Anglican and Catholic circles in the United Kingdom. On the continent they were taken up by Catholic pressure groups such as the Guild of St Thomas and St Luke in Belgium, the circles around the Cologne Domverein and the *Orgän fur Christliche Kunst* and the St Bernulphus Guild in the Netherlands. These groups gave the neo-Gothic an exclusive character and connected it with the ultramontane vision of a thoroughly Christian society in Europe.[40]

The fifth paradigm circulating in North-West Europe was that of authenticity and truthfulness, which had to be communicated by the material expression of Christianity. Pressure groups emphasised that the materialising of the Christian faith had to be grounded in research. Knowledge-based iconography, symbols and architectural elements had to be the norm. Sacred places also required truthfulness. Material change demanded the use of honest materials such as natural stone or brick, wood, glass, cast iron or steel. Imitations based on composite materials were initially rejected as much as was possible. There was still a strong aversion to the use of concrete at the end of the nineteenth century; only in the twentieth century did concrete architecture make a breakthrough. This pursuit of truthfulness could also lead to purifying tendencies, although they were contained.

The sixth paradigm concerns the desire for 're-scaping', that is, through material Christianity, and especially through the construction and decoration of churches, to create a landscape suitable for building communities. Although there were certainly significant differences in emphasis between the many churches and denominations, community building was an important issue for all of them. This aspiration touches on the process of confessionalisation as well as that of aestheticisation. As will be later discussed, on the Protestant side – and pre-eminently on the side of the dissident or free churches – the focus was on the formation of authentic Christian faith communities that came together around the Bible, the Word and singing. In addition to church or prayer rooms, they also needed infrastructure for (Bible) schools or spaces for discussion groups and other sociocultural encounters that would promote the formation of religious communities.

On the Catholic side, and especially among the ultramontanes, the neo-Gothic style appealed as a formal language that referred to the ideal image of a harmonious society centred on the primacy of faith and the figurehead of the pope. The goal was to reconfigure or 're-scape' modern secularising society into a Christian community under the motto, "Omnia instaurare in Christo". The church and church buildings therefore had to become a point of reference around which gathered confessional education, neo-medieval professional guilds, parish halls and many other sociocultural organisations.

The whole had to be supported by a suitable subculture, about which more in the third thread "Devotionalisation, Popularisation and Industrialisation" of this introduction. In this process of community building, the churches and denominations also tried to push their boundaries into the public space: they erected statues of, for example, Luther or Melanchthon in town squares in Protestant states or of Mary in Catholic regions. Death and burial were also seen as the ultimate moment of the (material) expression of identity: no wonder that the use of religious symbols in secularised or denominational cemeteries in nineteenth-century North-West Europe became a point of contention.

The tendency to 're-scaping' and pushing the boundaries of the manifestations of identity in public spaces created tensions. At times these were very high in nineteenth-century North-West Europe, especially in

---

40 Lamberts, *The Struggle with Leviathan*, 177-181; De Maeyer, "The Neo-Gothic in Belgium".

combination with the 'Culture Wars' between the Roman Catholic Church and the modern liberal nation-states, of which the *Kulturkampf* (1871-1888) in the unified German empire was the prime example and even led to the emigration of religious institutions. The Culture Wars created an atmosphere of constriction and led to public protest and even violence that ebbed only around 1890-1900.[41] The very close relationship between the ultramontane church and social model and the Pugin-inspired neo-Gothic made it almost impossible for the Protestant side to adhere to the neo-Gothic formal language any longer. Protestant churches, for example the 'Grundtvigianism' in Denmark and other free churches in Scandinavia, turned therefore to contemporary designs such as Art Nouveau or later Art Deco. The influence of the Arts and Crafts Movement in the United Kingdom and its pursuit of authentic craftsmanship was felt in Scandinavia and the German Werkbund. As a result, the Protestant churches, contrary to the Catholic, adapted their material expression of identity more to modernity and to the new aesthetic culture of the turn of the century.[42]

Due to the confessionalisation of society, the Protestant and Roman Catholic churches were increasingly able to bind their congregations to themselves. It even made possible liturgical celebrations with thousands of churchgoers participating. On the Protestant side this led, for example, to Methodist auditorium-style temples in which up to 5000 people could participate, or on the Catholic side, in the context of the Liturgical Movement, to the basilical model with neo-Romanesque and neo-Byzantine influences (a central building, large dome spans, mosaics with religious aphorisms legible from a distance). Examples include Westminster Cathedral in London, the Basilica of Koekelberg (Brussels) in Belgium and the Saint Bavo Cathedral in Haarlem in the Netherlands.

On the eve of World War I, both the established churches and the dissident or free denominations were faced with new choices: continue with their traditional formal languages or adopt more contemporary expressions. The tensions in Germany between the Werkbund and the Heimatbewegung, which yearned for a historicising interpretation of German culture, heralded the disruptive choices of the interwar period.[43]

Devotionalisation, popularisation and industrialisation

The theme of aestheticisation and related pressure groups in the previous thread is clearly connected with the discussion in this third thread. Indeed, the desire to come to or return to true and 'authentic' Christian art, which was to be accomplished by truly religiously inspired artists with the help of their pressure groups, came increasingly into conflict during the long nineteenth century with the huge expansion of material Christianity on a scale that would broadly characterise material religion throughout the century. Three areas of enlargement that were connected to daily religious practice and its material culture are of interest here: devotionalisation, popularisation and industrialisation. They are also closely related to each other and to the modernity from which they emanated, which is the time frame of this book. These processes had initially more of an effect on Catholic culture, while Protestant culture would follow later, albeit to a lesser degree.

As already noted, various elements in Europe started to change at the beginning of the long nineteenth century: the growth of population, the beginning of nation-states, and the emancipation of Catholics in various countries. The Vatican reacted by aiming to create a stronger, overarching structure so as to be able to address and steer Catholics directly from the centre. Apart from reinforcing existing church provinces and creating new ones, the authority of the pope was stressed and the ties between the Vatican and the national churches tightened. This development was a move in the direction of ultramontanism and reflected the Church's

41 Clark and Kaiser, *Culture Wars*, passim; Bouwers, *Glaubenskämpfe*, passim.
42 Thiebaut, *1900*, passim; Rosenblum et al., *1900. Art at the Crossroads*, passim; Heynickx, *Meetzucht en mateloosheid*, 79-118; Heynickx and Avermaete, *Making a New World*, 9-23.
43 Bullen, *Byzantium Rediscovered*, passim.

attempt to bind the Catholic community to itself and thereby elicit broad support in the struggle to show the church's societal relevance in the struggle against modernity.[44]

This development also created a more effective means for Rome to steer or stimulate religious life in a more uniform way across Europe. By intensifying religious life, Catholics would also be better prepared to withstand new competing ideologies such as rationalism (secularism) and socialism. This devotional policy was also embraced in religiously mixed countries as a means of strengthening the Catholic community. Hence, top-down (Vatican) as well as grassroots (local) policies gave a boost to religious life, particularly by coming up with new universal or regional devotions and presenting older ones in a new way. This process of devotionalisation (or devotionalism) has been defined as the intensification and instrumentalisation of religious devotions and practices in everyday life by the clergy and lay communities as a tool for enhancing faith and piety, reinforcing cohesion and creating a Catholic identity.[45]

Rome increasingly espoused a double strategy of influencing, which was applied partly by the Vatican and partly by the headquarters of the various religious orders. These orders were, in an internal missionary way, eager to expand their influence and their specific spirituality to Catholics in various countries.[46] The Vatican was able to impose universal devotions on the world church and to homogenise existing or new devotions by creating archconfraternities with generic regulations. These devotions included the Holy Family (Liège 1845/47), the 'Perpetual Adoration and Work for Poor Churches' (Brussels, 1848), the Immaculate Conception, the Way of the Cross, Peter's Pence (1860), Saint Joseph (Rome, 1860/62), the Sacred Heart of Jesus (1899), all of which were usually organised at the base, again through local confraternities. The religious orders, independent as they were, had their own strategies. For example, by renewing its material culture, the Carmelite Order was able to popularise the devotion to the (brown) scapular, while the Redemptorist Order, with the help of the Vatican, conquered the world after 1865 with its devotion to Our Lady of Perpetual Succour and the mass reproduction of the accompanying icon. New apparitional devotions could, with Vatican blessing, gain more universal significance. For example, devotions to Our Lady of Rue du Bac (Paris) and her 'Miraculous Medal' (recognised 1832) and to Our Lady of Lourdes (recognised 1862) spread across the world.[47] The attractiveness and appeal of Marian shrines stimulated a general revival of pilgrimages throughout nineteenth-century Europe, affecting landscapes and regional infrastructure. The revival of pilgrimages and the revitalisation of former pilgrimage sites led to a great expansion of holy places, with buildings and facilities to host large numbers of pilgrims being constructed. As a result, infrastructures also had to be adapted to meet the demands of mass transportation (trains, trams) and to extend the landscape with specially arranged sacred roads and Ways of the Cross leading people to the shrines. At the same time those sites became centres for the production of devotional objects, which were sold in local shops as well as throughout the country and beyond. In general, urban and rural landscapes were increasingly furnished with mostly Catholic chapels, crosses, and statues, especially in Protestant territories where such public decorations had previously not been allowed.

The devotional policies introduced by the Vatican, religious orders and local clergy and laity were highly successful as they made devotional culture more popular than it had ever been during the *Ancien Régime*. As a means of reform, the churches were successful in reaching out to the mass of believers. Devotional culture, which was well received among Catholics, became mainstream, a sort of mass movement that brought Catholics together in a large variety of local religious organisations. Not only was this a strategy to bind people more closely to the churches, it also was intended to bring the 'church'

---

44 Lamberts, ed., *Een kantelend tijdperk*, passim.
45 Margry, "Dutch Devotionalisation", 127-128; cf. Taves, *The Household of Faith*, 21-45; Heiman, "Catholic Revivalism in Worship and Devotion".
46 Kselman, *Miracles and Prophecies*; Zimdars-Swartz, *Encountering Mary*, 25-67; Perry and Echeverría, *Under the Heel of Mary*, 71-160.
47 Kaufman, *Consuming Visions*; Harris, *Lourdes*.

into the family home, in an effort to connect individual and family lives by immersion in prayer and devotion. The introduction of images of the Sacred Heart of Jesus into homes at the beginning of the twentieth century was, for example, a way the church was successfully able to enter the home and influence the religious practices of families.[48]

Uniting Catholics in religious associations and confraternities was a form of socialisation that aligned with the opening up of nineteenth-century society. In religiously mixed countries particularly, the devotions and their confraternities proved effective vehicles for the creation of communities with a strong identity, providing a counterbalance in the denominational and political power struggles within the developing nation-states. This was especially important in those countries where Catholicism was freed from the constraints imposed by former Protestant domination.

As a consequence, the popularity of devotions and devotionalisation was an equally important factor in the exponential growth of religious material culture in that century. In connecting the believer to specific devotions and shrines, private prayer only was not enough. Catholicism thrived by emphasising the tactile and visual elements of the faith, developing strong media to communicate various qualities of the faith and capitalising on the spectacle, fascination and aesthetics connected to those beliefs.

The success of material Catholicism in that regard, from statues of saints to religious medals, encouraged Protestants to forego their rigid attitude towards visual and material religion, and to make use of religious plates, prints, cards and books as well.[49] This was facilitated by changing production forms and material innovations. Printing became cheaper, with possibilities for (coloured) images.[50] The centre of Protestant material culture was Scripture, the Bible. Various organisations came into being dedicated to the production and mass dissemination of bibles of every variety. Not only bibles but all kinds of handcrafted objects were increasingly industrially produced with materials that were easier to handle. Biblical texts or images of Christ could now be cheaply printed in colour and expensive Catholic woodcuts of saints were increasingly mass-produced through the technique of casting plaster in moulds. Cheap metals meant that medals, hitherto usually made of silver and copper, were available at a much lower price.

The reinstatement of religions, the popularity of devotional practices, in combination with the growth of population, likewise stimulated the building of new churches, chapels, cloisters and utility buildings. The speed and lower cost of new techniques and building materials (cast iron, steel) and the mechanisation of transport, building and decorating assuaged the hunger for new church-related buildings. Often those buildings were created to stand as religious landmarks in urban and rural landscapes. These were not just parish churches, but also buildings for new congregations or expanding existing religious orders. Growing populations spurred large-scale public housing, which in some countries become organised along denominational lines resulting in urban areas or districts of a specific Protestant or Catholic character, the latter sometimes being nicknamed 'Little Rome'. In this way the churches were able to exert an even stronger grip on the flock and stimulated the process of confessionalisation during the long nineteenth century.

Presentation of the volume

As is clear from the foregoing, Material Change is a versatile, complex and fascinating subject. For this reason, we decided on a basic structure for this volume other than the geographical (countries, regions) structure of the earlier volumes in the series, *The Dynamics of Religious Reform*. We chose to focus on four themes, each with a short introduction outlining the main features, followed by the research results of each geographical cluster. Though this is a new approach,

48 This paragraph on the Sacred Heart as well as earlier remarks on Marian devotion: Van Osselaer and Pasture, *Christian Homes*.
49 Morgan, *Visual Piety*.
50 Cf. De Maeyer et al., eds, *Religion, Children's Literature and Modernity in Western Europe*.

it yet remains in line with the underlying geographical approach of the other parts of the series. The four themes were determined after an exploratory workshop in Leuven on 10 December 2012. That workshop opened up a number of substantive perspectives that were crystallised during the concluding sessions into four themes: 'The Role of Pressure Groups', 'Space and the Fabric of Buildings and Constructions', 'The Building and Furnishing of Religious Architecture' and 'Material Reform in Everyday Religion'.

The book deliberately starts with the section on 'The Role of Pressure Groups'. As associations of church-affiliated intellectuals, archaeological or artistic circles, they provide a good insight into the substantive discussions or publications concerning Material Change in North-West Europe. All the actors and factors involved in the topic coalesced in the pressure groups. In their operation and approach, they were fully immersed in modernity, which makes the section a good eye opener on material reform.

The second section concentrates on 'Space and the Fabric of Buildings and Constructions'. It examines the growing need of the established, dissident and free churches for an adequate infrastructure necessary to express their identity. The section also discusses the churches' desire to manifest themselves in the public space with church buildings, statues or religious signs. Pilgrimage sites, Marian grottoes and cemeteries were symbolic landmarks and church towers symbolic watchmen in the battle with modernity.

'The Building and Furnishing of Religious Architecture' is the third section in this book. The construction and decoration of church buildings and, by extension, the religious infrastructure was an essential part in achieving Material Change. Through the symbolic design and orientation of church buildings, the choice of symbols and iconography and the materials used, certain accents could be placed in the expression of the desired or pursued identity. The section also highlights the great opportunities that Material Change gave to new or revived artisan workshops and to the paradigm of *Gesamtkunst* in which architects increasingly assumed a guiding role during the long nineteenth century. Architects saw themselves as the designers of consistent wholes that could be read as illustrated stories and viewed as a beautiful whole. This section reviews the leading architects, artists and atelier owners who were active in the field of material Christianity.

The fourth section deals with the various aspects of 'Material Reform in Everyday Religion'. In the material change that church communities wanted to achieve, both means of communication (for example wall plates, posters, prints, photographs, illustrated flyers) as well as all kinds of religious objects (busts, statues, devotions) played an important role. They brought the broad Catholic community to participate in material change, which was facilitated by the new and cheaper production or reproduction techniques. In this final section, we want to show how material change reached into all corners of nineteenth-century society, into the homes and bedrooms of families in North-West Europe. Material Change took hold of young and old through well-designed promotion and dissemination techniques. 'Material Reform in Everyday Religion' is therefore an appropriate conclusion for this book.

Words of gratitude

As editors, we are indebted to many for helping to bring this book to completion and would like to thank them wholeheartedly. Foremost, we thank all the authors for their contributions, their willingness to align their papers with the proposed structure or to place additional emphases on request. We are also grateful for their patience and understanding given the delay that this volume suffered due to various circumstances.

Much appreciation goes to colleague Timothy Brittain-Catlin, who undertook a great part of the text editing as an expert and as a native speaker. He did an excellent job for which we are very grateful.

Many thanks also to Maria Desmond-Kelly and Laura Bennett who took care of additional translating and the proofreading.

This book would not have been possible without the efforts of the KADOC collaborators Lieve Claes (technical editing), Alexis Vermeylen (lay-out) and Luc Vints (image editing and general supervision of the technical realisation). We are them very grateful and deeply appreciate their continued commitment. Finally, we would like to thank KADOC and Leuven University Press for their patience and continued trust.

Leuven-Amsterdam, 1 March 2021

BIBLIOGRAPHY

Appadurai, Arjun. *The Social Life of Things: Commodities in Cultural Perspective*. Cambridge, 1992.

Asad, Talal. *Formations of the Secular: Christianity, Islam, Modernity*. Stanford, 2003.

Barthes, Roland. *Mythologies*. Paris, 1985.

Bayly, Christopher Alan. *The Birth of the Modern World, 1780-1914: Global Connections and Comparisons*. Oxford, 2004.

Berthod, Bernard, and Elisabeth Hardouin-Fugier. *Dictionnaire des objets de dévotion dans l'Europe catholique*. Paris, 2006.

Blaschke, Olaf. "Das 19. Jahrhundert: Ein Zweites Konfessionelles Zeitalter?" *Geschichte und Gesellschaft*, 26 (2000) 1, 38-75.

Blaschke, Olaf, ed. *Konfessionen im Konflikt: Deutschland zwischen 1800 und 1970: ein zweites konfessionelles Zeitalter*. Göttingen, 2002.

Bouwers, Eveline G. *Glaubenskämpfe: Katholiken und Gewalt im 19. Jahrhundert*. Göttingen, 2019.

Brundin, Abigail, Deborah Howard, and Mary Laven. *The Sacred Home in Renaissance Italy*. Oxford, 2018.

Bullen, J.B. *Byzantium Rediscovered*. London, 2003.

Christian, William J., Jr. *Divine Presence in Spain and Western Europe 1500-1960: Visions, Religious Images and Photographs*. Budapest, 2012.

Clark, Christopher, and Wolfgang Kaiser, eds. *Culture Wars: Secular-Catholic Conflict in Nineteenth-Century Europe*. Cambridge, 2003.

Coleman, Simon. "Material Religion: A Fruitful Tautology?" *Material Religion: The Journal of Objects, Art and Belief*, 5 (2009) 3, 359-360.

De Maeyer, Jan. "The Neo-Gothic in Belgium: Architecture of a Catholic Society". In: Jan De Maeyer and Luc Verpoest, eds. *Gothic Revival: Religion, Architecture and Style in Western Europe, 1815-1914*. KADOC-Artes 5. Leuven, 2000, 19-34.

De Maeyer, Jan. "The Concept of Religious Modernisation". In: Jan De Maeyer, Hans-Heino Ewers, Rita Ghesquière, Michel Manson, Pat Pinsent and Patricia Quaghebeur, eds. *Religion, Children's Literature and Modernity in Western Europe, 1750-2000*. Leuven, 2005, 41-50.

De Maeyer, Jan, Hans-Heino Ewers, Rita Ghesquière, Michel Manson, Pat Pinsent and Patricia Quaghebeur, eds. *Religion, Children's Literature and Modernity in Western Europe, 1750-2000*. KADOC Studies on Religion, Culture and Society 3. Leuven, 2005.

De Maeyer, Jan, and Luc Verpoest, eds. *Gothic Revival: Religion, Architecture and Style in Western Europe, 1815-1914*. KADOC-Artes 5. Leuven, 2000.

Downes, Stephanie, Sally Holloway and Sarah Randles, eds. *Feeling Things. Objects and Emotions through History*. Oxford, 2018.

Dühr, Elisabeth, and Markus Groß-Morgen. *Zwischen Andacht und Andenken. Kleinödien religiöser Kunst und Wallfahrtsandenken aus Trierer Sammlungen*. Trier, 1992.

Foucault, Michel. *Discipline and Punish: The Birth of the Prison*. London, 1977.

Frykman, Jonas, and Maja Povrzanović Frykman, eds. *Sensitive Objects: Affect and Material Culture*. Lund, 2016.

Goodsell, Charles T. *The Social Meaning of Civic Space: Studying Political Authority Through Architecture*. Kansas, 1988.

Hannan, Leonie, and Sarah Longair. *History Through Material Culture*. Manchester, 2017.

Harris, Ruth. *Lourdes: Body and Spirit in the Secular Age*. New York, 1999.

Heiman, Mary. "Catholic Revivalism in Worship and Devotion". In: Sheridan Shelley and Brian Stanley, eds. *The Cambridge History of Christianity: World Christianities c. 1815 – c. 1914*, vol. 8. Cambridge, 2014.

Hellemans, Staf. *Religion and Modernity in Europe (1750-): New Stakes and Research Perspectives*. Leuven, not published paper. 2009.

Hellemans, Staf. *De grote transformatie van religie en van de katholieke kerk*. Tilburg, 2019.

Heynickx, Rajesh. *Meetzucht en mateloosheid. Kunst, religie en identiteit in Vlaanderen tijdens het interbellum*. Nijmegen, 2008.

Heynickx, Rajesh, and Tom Avermaete, eds. *Making a New World: Architecture & Communities in Interwar Europe*. KADOC Artes 13. Leuven, 2012.

Jacobs, Jan, Lodewijk Winkeler and Albert van der Zeijden, eds. *Aan plaatsen gehecht. Katholieke herinneringscultuur in Nederland*. Nijmegen, 2012.

Kaufmann, Suzanne. *Consuming Visions: Mass Culture and the Lourdes Shrine*. Ithaca-London, 2005.

Kingery, W. David. *Learning from Things: Method and Theory of Material Culture Studies*. Washington, 1996.

Kselman, Thomas. *Miracles and Prophecies in Nineteenth-Century France*. New Brunswick, NJ, 1983.

Lamberts, Emiel, ed. *Een kantelend tijdperk/ Une époque en mutation/Ein Zeitalter im Umbruch. De wending van de Kerk naar het volk in Noord-West-Europa/Le catholicisme social dans le Nord-Ouest de l'Europe/Die Wende der Kirche zum Volk im nordwestlichen Europa (1890-1910)*. KADOC Studies 13. Leuven, 1992.

Lamberts, Emiel. *The Struggle with Leviathan: Social Responses to the Omnipotence of the State, 1815-1965*. KADOC Studies on Religion, Culture and Society 18. Leuven, 2016.

Latour, Bruno. *Reassembling the Social: An introduction to Actor-Network-Theory*. Oxford, 2005.

Margry, Peter Jan. "Dutch Devotionalisation. Reforming Piety: Grassroots Initiative or Clerical Strategy?". In: Anders Jarlert, ed. *Piety and Modernity*. KADOC Studies on Religion, Culture and Society. The Dynamics of Religious Reform in Northern Europe, 1780-1920, vol. 3. Leuven, 2012, 125-156, 186-190.

Martini, Rodolfo. *Medaglia devozionale cattolica moderna e contemporanea in Italia ed Europa, 1846-1978*. Milan, 2009, 5 vols.

Material Religion. The Journal of Objects, Art and Belief, 2005 – present.

McDannell, Colleen. *Material Christianity: Religion and Popular Culture in America*. New Haven, CT, 1995.

Meyer, Birgit. "Aesthetics of Persuasion: Global Christianity and Pentecostalism's Sensational Forms". *South Atlantic Quarterly*, 109 (2010), 741-763.

Miller, Daniel. *Stuff*. Cambridge, 2019.

Miller, Daniel. *Home Possessions: Material Culture Behind Closed Doors*. Oxford, 2001.

Minkenberg, Michael. *Power and Architecture: The Construction of Capitals and the Politics of Space*. New York - Oxford, 2014.

Mitchell, Brian R. *European Historical Statistics, 1750-1970*. New York, 1978.

Molendijk, Arie L. *Materieel christendom. Religie en materiële cultuur in West-Europa*. Hilversum, 2003.

Morgan, David. *Visual Piety: A History and Theory of Popular Religious Images*. Berkeley, 1998.

Morgan, David, ed. *Religion and Material Culture: The Matter of Belief*. Abingdon, 2010.

Morgan, David. "Materiality". In: Michael Stausberg and Steven Engler, eds. *The Oxford Handbook of the Study of Religion*. Oxford, 2016, 271-289.

Morgan, David. "The Sensory Web of Vision: Enchantment and Agency in Religious Material Culture". In: Ivan Gaskell and Sarah Anne Carter, eds. *The Oxford Handbook of History and Material Culture*. May 2020 DOI: 10.1093/oxfordhb/9780199341764.013.6.

Panofsky, Erwin. *Studies in Iconology: Humanistic Themes in the Art of the Renaissance*. New York, 1939.

Perrin, Joël, and Sandra Vasco Rocca, eds. *Thesaurus des objets religieux. Meubles, objets, linges, vêtements et instruments de musique du culte catholique romain*. Paris, 1999.

Perry, Nicholas, and Loreto Echeverria. *Under the Heel of Mary*. London-New York, 1988.

Pounds, Norman J.G. *Hearth and Home: A History of Material Culture*. Bloomington, 1993.

Robbins, Keith. "Introduction". In: Keith Robbins, ed. *Political and Legal Perspectives*. KADOC-Studies on Religion, Culture and Society. The Dynamics of Religious Reform in Northern Europe, 1780-1920, vol. 1. Leuven, 2010, 7-33.

Roberts, David. "The Total Work of Art. Review Essay". *Thesis Eleven*, 83 (2005), 104-121.

Roberts, David. *The Total Work of Art in European Modernism*. Ithaca, NY, 2011.

Rosenblum, R. et al., eds. *1900. Art at the Crossroads*. London-New York, 2000.

Saint-Martin, Isabelle. *Art chrétien/Art sacré. Regards du catholicisme sur l'art. France, XIXe-XXe siècle*. Rennes, 2014.

Schlereth, Thomas J., ed. *Material Culture: A Research Guide*. Lawrence, KS, 1985.

Taves, Ann. *The Household of Faith: Roman Catholic Devotions in Mid-Nineteenth-Century America*. Notre Dame, 1986.

Thiebaut, Pierre. *1900*. Catalogue Galeries nationales du Grand Palais. Paris, 2000.

Tilley, Christopher, ed. *Handbook of Material Culture*. London, 2006.

Van de Maele, Jens. *Architecture of Bureaucracy: An Architectural and Political History of Ministerial Offices in Belgium, 1915-1940*. Ph. D. University of Ghent, 2019-2020.

Vandenbroeck, Paul, ed. *Backlit Heaven: Power and Devotion in the Archdiocese Mechelen*. Tielt, 2009.

Van Eijnatten Joris, and Paula Yates, eds. *The Churches*. KADOC Studies on Religion, Culture and Society. The Dynamics of Religious Reform in Northern Europe 1780-1920, vol. 2. Leuven, 2010.

Van Molle, Leen, ed. *Charity and Social Welfare*. KADOC Studies on Religion, Culture and Society. The Dynamics of Religious Reform in Northern Europe, 1780-1920, vol. 4. Leuven, 2017.

Van Molle, Leen. "Comparing Religious Perspectives on Social Reform". In: Leen Van Molle, ed. *Charity and Social Welfare*. KADOC Studies on Religion, Culture and Society. The Dynamics of Religious Reform in Northern Europe, 1780-1920, vol. 4. Leuven, 2017, 7-37.

Van Osselaer, Tine and Patrick Pasture, eds. *Christian Homes: Religion, Family and Domesticity in the 19th and 20th Centuries*. KADOC Studies on Religion, Culture and Society 14. Leuven, 2014.

Viaene, Vincent. "Religieuze herlevers en religieuze hervormers". In: Robert Houzee, Jo Tollebeek and Tom Verschaffel, eds. *Mise-en-scène. Keizer Karel en de verbeelding van de negentiende eeuw*. Antwerp-Ghent, 1999, 192-197.

Viaene, Vincent. *Belgium and the Holy See from Gregory XVI to Pius IX (1831-1859). Catholic Revival, Society and Politics in 19th-Century Europe*. KADOC Studies 26. Leuven, 2001.

Viladesau, Richard. "Aesthetics and Religion". In: Frank Burch Brown, ed. *The Oxford Handbook of Religion and the Arts*. Oxford, 2014, 25-43.

Zimdars-Swartz, Sandra L. *Encountering Mary: From La Salette to Medjugorje*. Princeton, 1991.

1.
THE ROLE OF 'PRESSURE GROUPS'

Introduction

Jan De Maeyer

'Pressure groups' played an important intermediary role in the interaction between material change, material Christianity and modernity in North-West Europe. They comprised organisations, societies, committees or other associations as well as press agencies involving interested church leaders, local pastors and clergy and, very significantly, dedicated churchgoers and lay people. They consisted of educated people, often intellectuals, and were thus empowered to make pronouncements about material Christianity according to the indicators of modernity. They included people who were competent in theology and liturgy, (church) history and archaeology, (engineer-)architects and atelier owners working on the infrastructure and decoration of churches. They knew what churches stood for both in terms of content and society, and what was at stake in the material expression of identity.

On the other hand, the pressure groups were also at the centre of the modern world, themselves part of modernity. Thanks to their expertise, they were aware of contemporary developments, as well as of the opportunities and threats that could arise. They felt called to show how churches could manifest their presence in the public space by actively materialising their identity. The pressure groups interacted with modernity through their actions and through the ways in which they disseminated knowledge about the material culture of Christianity. This section shows that the pressure groups functioned like the learned societies, clubs or salons of the Enlightenment period. The English Cambridge Camden Society (1839) can almost be seen as the model: ideas and visions were exchanged through regular meetings, debates, study trips and especially periodicals and magazines. Some groups also published textbooks or handbooks on the material culture or art of Christianity. Their way of exerting pressure in and on the churches was also modern in nature: through manifestos and personal interventions, in short, what today would be called lobbying. The impact of all this was significant, a fact that is indicated in several contributions below.

The pressure groups under review functioned within their own denominational community or culture, but also within the national context of the nation-states that developed in North-West Europe during the long nineteenth century. They sensed which arguments and material expressions would connect the established as well as the dissident and free churches with the cultural identity that the nation-states wanted to acquire or were developing in interaction with their monarchs. Thus, through their integrative or participatory action, they contributed to the positioning and legitimisation of the churches in the national context.

However, we should not limit the impact of the pressure groups to their role within the nation-state. Many of the ideas about the material culture of Christianity circulated transnationally, transcending borders and inspiring all of North-West Europe. The process of aestheticisation, the paradigms of which are described in the general introduction, was part of the transnational dissemination of ideas. Its aesthetic ideas became commonplace across churches and borders: art and architecture as symbolic mediators between Heaven and Earth, charged with a missionary or catechetical mission; *Gesamtkunst* as a way of meeting the challenge to give material expression to the sacred, including the obligation to strive for authenticity in the use of materials and to avoid artificial effects; and finally material Christianity as the instrument for reconfiguring the urban and rural landscapes into a Christian community. The changing perception of the Gothic with the Gothic Revival provides a good example of how the pressure groups contributed to the circulation of ideas. Thus, the conviction grew throughout North-West Europe that the Gothic should be the (only) material expression of Christianity. Still, despite transnational ideas about Christianity and the Gothic, the pressure groups studied here remained strictly within national boundaries in their organisational form and operation.

The idea that architecture, iconography and symbolism constituted a sacred visual language was perhaps the most important contribution of the pressure groups to the material culture of Christianity. Architecture, the plastic arts and crafts were called upon to speak the same symbolic language, one that would bring the churchgoer to the sacred and make the identity of the church or denomination visible and tangible. This was the case on both the Protestant and Roman Catholic sides. Realising the power of material expression was an insight with enormous potential: as William Whyte writes (cited by A.J.B. Beresford Hope), "Every stone, every window, was found to tell its own appropriate tale, to bear its own peculiar meaning". According to the pressure groups, if this symbolic language were to be used in a uniform manner, it could become a tool for transforming the modern world into a new, Christian community, visibly present in the public arena.

The latter insight made another important step possible. A uniform symbolic language, carried by a suitably tailored iconographic language, also enabled the churches to use industrial production methods (of reproduction and the mass manufacture of devotional objects) to reach the wider population. In the struggle to position religion in the modern world, turning to the people and retaining the masses for the churches were almost existential tasks. This section illustrates how various types of pressure groups such as tract, bible and finance societies not only sought to meet growing infrastructure needs (such as church buildings, parish halls, denominational schools) but also contributed to the dissemination of the faith through reproductions of prints, wall charts with instructional texts, books about the faith and devotional objects. The churches consciously used the power of symbolic language to convey their message not only convincingly but also on a mass scale.

The missionary zeal of the pressure groups contributed then to establishing and maintaining a religious subculture such as will be examined in the fourth section of this book. Through the symbolic language, an outsider could immediately see to which denomination a family or discussion partner belonged. Conversely, the legible and understandable symbolic language contributed to the integration of the wider population into the churches and so also into modern society. Thus, the pressure groups made it possible for the churches to effect both social reform and material change. That was no mean achievement.

THE QUEEN GIVING A TESTAMENT TO A HIGHLAND COTTAGER.

And it shall be, when he sitteth upon the throne of his kingdom, that he shall write him a copy of this law. . . . . . And it shall be with him, and he shall read therein all the days of his life; that he may learn to fear the Lord his God, to keep all the words of this law and these statutes to do them.—*Deut.* xvii. 18, 19.

Search the scriptures; for in them ye think ye have eternal life: and they are they which testify of me.—*John* v. 39.

1.1
Shaping Material Reform

'Pressure Groups' in Great Britain and Ireland

William Whyte

On 7 January 1912, the parishioners of Stockton in Warwickshire experienced a remarkable new addition to their normal Sunday service. Seeking to illustrate the saying that 'Death is the Gate of Life', the rector, the Venerable Thomas Colley, climbed into a glass-covered coffin and was carried round the church. He concluded by raising the cover and sitting up in the coffin to pronounce a blessing. It was a striking scene, one that was reported as far away as Sydney: "Some members of the congregation sobbed, while others, who were shocked at the proceeding, left the building."[1] Now, Colley – a leading spiritualist as well as an Anglican clergyman – was undoubtedly unusual.[2] Indeed, this bizarre behaviour led to his resignation. But the spectacle in Stockton is nonetheless indicative of a number of themes which run through this chapter. The church in which Colley confronted death, for example, was a product of this period: successively rebuilt in the nineteenth century, with the help of a significant pressure group, the Incorporated Church Building Society.[3] Colley himself was a man of the moment: a colonial archdeacon and antiquary whose researches on the parish church, published in a newspaper shortly after these events, are still the basis for our understanding of its material history.[4] Perhaps above all, the fact that his little local difficulty made the headlines throughout the world illustrates the ways in which new technologies and new modes of communication transformed life in the long nineteenth century.

This essay will have little to say about glass coffins. But it will seek to explore the new institutions, new ideas, and new forms of association which arose in this period. It will show the material and mental consequences of debates about church building: detailing some of the thousands of new edifices erected and old structures rebuilt or restored; arguing that the pressure groups of the period did not just affect how architecture was constructed but also how it was perceived. It will go on to show that debates about church buildings and furnishings were mirrored by other movements of material reform as new patterns of publishing provided opportunities for new pressure groups. The long nineteenth century thus witnessed the flourishing of a series of organisations devoted to the production of Bibles, prayer books, religious tracts, and Christian imagery. An unprecedented torrent of printing rained down on the British and Irish public. By 1884, the British and Foreign Bible Society, for example, had issued more than 100 million copies of the Bible – and it was just one of many organisations engaged in this work.[5] At the same time, other groups were responsible for the development of primary education in England, with thousands of rival schools – just like the rival churches they replicated – built across the country in a range of distinctive styles.[6] Denominational struggle likewise produced new secondary schools and new university colleges.[7] These developments helped create a distinctive culture of Christianity in which material expressions of faith were encountered at home and at school as much as at church.[8]

It has been suggested that the tremendous energy of these groups – and of the culture they sustained – simply dissipated in the years after 1870.[9] And there was certainly

1.1-1 'The Queen giving a Testament to a Highland Cottager'. Print published by the Religious Tract Society, c 1850. (See also col. ill. 1.)
[London, British Museum: 1870, 1210.562]

1. *Sydney Morning Herald*, 8 February 1912, 9.
2. Byrne, *Modern Spiritualism and the Church of England*, which first drew my attention to Colley.
3. Plans for the first phase can be found at <www.churchplansonline.org/> (accessed 1 June 2013). This is an invaluable source.
4. <http://archaeologydataservice.ac.uk/catalogue/adsdata/arch-841-1/dissemination/pdf/oxfordar1-72049_1.pdf> (accessed 1 June 2013).
5. Ledger-Lomas, "Mass Markets: religion", 329.
6. Seabourne, *The English School*, ch. 10.
7. See, Whyte, *Redbrick*; Howarth, "The Church of England and Women's Higher Education".
8. Williams, *Religious Belief and Popular Culture in Southwark*, 66-67.
9. See, for example, Cox, *The English Churches in a Secular Society*.

31

change: a decline in the number of churches built; a growing commercialisation of Christian publishing; the greater involvement of the state in public education.[10] As the title of one scholarly study has it, this can be seen as a period of "Religion and Voluntary Organisations in Crisis".[11] This essay, however, will conclude by arguing that the patterns of church building, religious publishing, and Christian education developed in the first half of this period were formative – and inescapable – in the second half. It was not just that the material deposits of a remarkably fertile era remained omnipresent, inescapable. More importantly, the ideas that were generated in the early nineteenth century continued to inform debates about the material expression of British and Irish religion. The new organisations and new modes of publishing, church-building, and education which developed in the years after 1870 all developed assumptions that had been first been articulated by pressure groups in the two generations before.

Church buildings

Almost a century before the events in Stockton, another Anglican clergyman and antiquary published a lengthy – a more than 200-page – letter to the prime minister. Entitled *The Church in Danger*, the Revd. Richard Yates' polemic of 1815 was just one of many contemporary pamphlets which proclaimed that established religion was under threat. Indeed, Yates himself acknowledged that what he called "the artifice of Faction and Bigotry" had frequently "endeavoured to conceal the real tendency of proceedings (…) by proclaiming that the Church is in Danger". Yates, however, maintained that this was a disinterested and rather different argument: "My endeavour", he wrote, "being to state the necessity of a legislative, – not to propose a Doctrinal, – Defence of the Church of England."[12] It was true, for the threat Yates sought to oppose was not strictly sectarian or purely constitutional: rather it was demographic. He pointed to the fact that the population had grown so much that, within London alone, there was now almost a million more people than the churches could actually accommodate. Across the country – from the rural south to the newly-industrialising north – the Church of England struggled to provide space for the ever-growing communities it was meant to serve. Yates therefore called on parliament to do what it had done a century before, when it had underwritten the cost of new churches for an expanding capital city.[13] But he demanded that this be done for the nation as a whole – and that it be done more successfully than it was in the eighteenth century, when a putative 50 new churches eventually resulted in only twelve being built. [Ill. 1.1-2]

The Church in Danger came at an opportune moment: just as the long and weary war against France was ending, and needed to be commemorated; just as the state turned its attention to state building, to creating a truly United Kingdom out of the newly-united Great Britain and Ireland – a union which had been effected only fourteen years previously. Yates' call to arms was taken up by the press, and by an increasingly vocal group of High Church Tories – the so-called Hackney Phalanx, who were concurrently seeking to reinvigorate the Church of England.[14] Little wonder, then, that Yate's lengthy letter, unlike so many other claims that the church was under threat, resulted in real change. Indeed, it provoked two significant and interlinked developments. In the first place, it eased the way for reformers to establish a new organisation: the Church Building – later the Incorporated Church Building – Society, which was founded in 1818. Over the next three decades, it would raise and spend more than half a million pounds, increasing the accommodation available in Anglican churches by almost one million seats.[15] Secondly, and perhaps more strikingly, Yates' words would be used to justify an act of parliament – an act which created a new church building commission and would eventually result in the erection of more than 600 new churches

---

10 For an excellent survey, see Cox, *The English Churches in a Secular Society*, ch. 6.
11 Yeo, *Religion and Voluntary Organisations in Crisis*.
12 Yates, *The Church in Danger*, 1-2.
13 Friedman, *The Eighteenth-Century Church in Britain*, ch. 19.
14 Webster, *Joshua Watson*, ch. 5.
15 Parry, *The Incorporated Church Building Society*.

1.1-2 *Portrait of Richard Yates (published in his* History and Antiquities of the Abbey of St. Edmund's Bury, *1843) and title page of his* The Church in Danger *(1815).*
[London, British Library]

at a cost of more than £3 million.[16] Moreover, this massive state-sponsored programme of church building was not just confined to England. It was accompanied by a similar effort in Ireland and followed by a smaller, but nonetheless significant addition of churches in the Highlands of Scotland too.[17]

This was however, a short-lived architectural experiment. Although the Incorporated Church Building Society continued to oversee projects well into the twentieth century; although the Ecclesiastical Commission, set up by the state in the 1830s, remained an architectural patron still longer: the truth is that the campaign initiated in the 1810s and intended to plant new churches across the newly-founded United Kingdom soon ran out of steam.[18] It was dependent on what the historian Stewart Brown has convincingly called the 'New Reformation' project: a campaign to define the state by defending the established Churches of England and Scotland and extending the influence of the established Church of Ireland. Yet the English constitutional crisis of the 1820s and 1830s; the Scottish Church schism – or Disruption – of the 1840s; and the growing realisation that Ireland was experiencing not a new Reformation but a belated Counter Reformation: all these brought the state's involvement in church building to an end.[19] Although Anglican clergy would repeat Richard Yates' cry throughout the nineteenth century, the time had passed when the state was able or willing to subsidise the architectural ambitions of the established churches.[20] Nor was the Incorporated Church Building Society able to initiate a replacement for this government support. For one thing, it was too closely associated with the New Reformation project, not least because most of its committee members also sat on the Church Building Commission. In that sense, they were two sides of the same coin; and as the importance of the Commission declined, so did the capacity of the Building Society to supplement or replace it.[21]

Church building, however, continued; indeed, it intensified across the nineteenth century. Thousands were built, and still more restored or rebuilt: throughout the 1860s, for example, a brand new Anglican church was consecrated in England every four or five days, whilst the number of Non-Conformist chapels increased exponentially.[22] This owed much to the fiercely competitive

16 Port, *600 New Churches*.
17 Sheehy, "Irish Church-Building"; Maciver, "Unfinished Business?".
18 Best, *Temporal Pillars*.
19 Brown, *The National Churches of England, Ireland, and Scotland*; Akenson, *The Church of Ireland*, 117-118.
20 See, for example, Hawkins, *A Sermon preached at the Cathedral Church of Rochester*.
21 Best, *Temporal Pillars*, ch. 21.
22 Brooks, "Introduction".

23 Yates, *Preaching, Word and Sacrament*, 63-64.
24 Wakeling, "The Nonconformist Traditions".
25 Saint, "Anglican Church Building in London"; Wiggins, *The History of the Salvation Army*, 233-234.
26 Friedman, *The Eighteenth-Century Church in Britain*.
27 Parry, *The Incorporated Church Building Society*.
28 Walker, "Religious Changes in Cheshire".
29 Smith, *Religion in Industrial Society*, 139.
30 For a recent exportation of the ambiguities of a single patron, see Uglow, *The Pinecone*.
31 London Free and Open Church Association, *Free and Open Churches*.

1.1-3 Sign of the Incorporated Church Building Society in the St Mary church in Lottisham, Somerset.
[London, The National Churches Trust; photo Martin Jones]

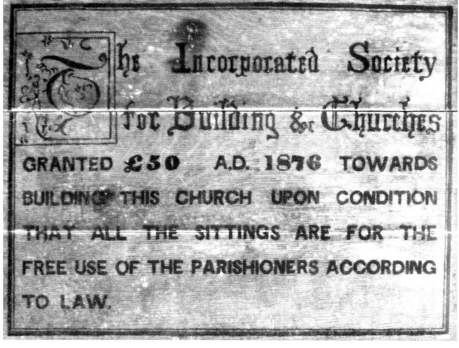

denominational rivalry of the period – in Scotland, for example, the Disruption of the 1840s produced virtually identical church buildings, often in the same street, for each of the contending denominations.[23] It was also the product of liberalising legislation from the 1790s onwards, which permitted Roman Catholics and Non-Conformists to erect distinctive church buildings of their own and which also increasingly freed the established churches from their dependence on parliamentary approval for the construction of new buildings or the creation of new parishes.[24] To some extent, too, novel forms of fund-raising facilitated expansion – with Anglican dioceses establishing their own local church building societies, and Non-Conformists pioneering systems of shareholding and cooperation.[25] Above all, however, this unprecedented programme of church building was the product – as it had been in the eighteenth century – of private patronage.[26] Overwhelmingly, therefore, it was still individuals who took advantage of the opportunity to build new churches, just as it always had been before.

All of which might make the impact of pressure groups on church building in this period seem nebulous at best, and irrelevant at worst. It is certainly true that perhaps the most obvious pressure group – the Incorporated Church Building Society – had only an indirect influence on the form that churches took. Although (as its name suggested) it assisted in church building, it was in reality only ever a contributor to funds raised by local benefactors. [Ill. 1.1-3] Aesthetically, too, it followed rather than led the fashion.[27] As a result, it can hardly be seen as the critical factor in a wider, longer-term process of material reform – though it was, indeed, one far from insubstantial factor. The same is also true of the Anglican diocesan church-building societies, which flourished briefly, but did little to determine the direction of national trends in church building for long.[28] It is important, too, not to overstate the success of Non-Conformists in finding new ways to pay for new chapels. As historians have shown, in the end, traditional forms of fund raising and recourse to chronic indebtedness were often more important still.[29] Moreover, given the sheer number of private patrons in this period, it is hard to conceive of them as amounting to anything like a pressure group; nor is it easy to see how one could say anything remotely useful about all of them in each of the four nations of the United Kingdom in the century and half that followed 1790.[30]

But this does not mean that it is impossible to reach conclusions about the impact of pressure groups on the material reform of churches in this period. Nor does it mean that pressure groups were unimportant. In fact, quite the reverse is true. For one thing, the work of these groups, not least in fundraising, profoundly changed the way in which churches were used. It was the Incorporated Church Building Society above all else, which moved Anglican parishes away from a system of renting out pews and towards the weekly collection of money which is now a central part of most churches' liturgy.[31] More dramatically, in the 1830s and 1840s, as the state's direct involvement in church building declined, a new breed of pressure group was created: one that did not seek to influence the government, and one that was not confined to the official structures and geographical limitations of individual parishes.[32] Taking advantage of technological developments like the advent of the railway and the growing cheapness of publication, these groups sought to influence individual patrons, parsons, and architects. In that sense, these were not pressure groups as the term is conventionally understood.[33] They were something more interesting than: spaces in which groups of individuals could negotiate the new church-state relations, new society, and new ideas about architecture together. They were also more important than the groups which had gone before, precisely because they did not just seek to agitate for church building but to transform the nature of church architecture more generally – and, in so-doing, to transform the nature of religious architecture across this period.

There were many such groups, ranging from the local archaeological and antiquarian societies which flourished in the late eighteenth and early nineteenth centuries, to more national – even international – associations.[34] Indeed, it is important to note the extent to which local groupings gained national prominence – and could even come to exert a global influence. The Oxford Architectural Society (founded 1839) provided the forum for some formative debates on the nature of ecclesiastical building and restoration.[35] The Exeter Diocesan Architectural Society (established in 1841) likewise served as a local focus for discussions of more general concern, both generating original ideas of its own and disseminating notions developed elsewhere.[36]

Chief amongst all these groups was the Cambridge Camden Society.[37] Founded in 1839 by a group of Cambridge undergraduates committed to the promotion of Gothic architecture, this group – which eventually became known as the Ecclesiological Society [Ill. 1.1-4] – took advantage of all the new technologies of the day: issuing a journal, travelling the country, printing proformas for its members and their allies to comment on new buildings – and then publishing the results for a wider public to see.[38] Intellectually, too, the Camdenians are significant, for their enthusiasm for Gothic grew out of more than just an antiquarian interest or a belief that it was typologically or psychologically appropriate for churches, all of which were arguments that had been made before.[39] No: the Ecclesiologists, as I have argued elsewhere, went well beyond all their predecessors – and even a little further than many of their contemporaries – in claiming that medieval architecture should inspire modern church building because it was more legible than any of the alternatives.[40] In the Gothic style, they declared, "Christian symbolism has found its most adequate exponent".[41] For them, architecture was text, and Gothic architecture the best language to convey Christian meaning.

This, then, was a new argument, an argument about the nature of architectural meaning – a similar argument at a similar time to the debates that Neil Levine has so brilliantly explored in his work on nineteenth-century French architecture.[42] It was an argument that radically changed church architecture and church furnishings, for it introduced a new dimension to them. They were to be judged not just by their beauty but by their

1.1-4 Seal of the Ecclesiological Society, designed by A.W. Pugin, 1844. [London, The Ecclesiological Society]

32 Though for an alternative view, which focuses on the state, see Thompson, *Bureaucracy and Church Reform*.
33 Though see Beyers, Eising and Maloney, "Researching Interest Group Politics", for the conceptual ambiguities of pressure groups more generally.
34 Sweet, *Antiquaries*; Bremner, *Imperial Gothic*.
35 Chitty, "John Ruskin, Oxford and the Architectural Society"; Bremner and Conlin, "History as Form"; Conlin, "Development or Destruction?".
36 Brooks, "Building the Rural Church".
37 Webster and Elliott, eds., '*A Church as It Should Be*'; White, *The Cambridge Movement*.
38 Webster, ed., '*Temples … Worthy of his Presence*'.
39 Aspin, "Our Ancient Architecture"; Bradley, *The Gothic Revival and the Church of England*; Whyte, "Restoration and Recrimination".
40 Whyte, "Sacred Space as Sacred Text".
41 *Ecclesiologist*, 4 (1845), 50.
42 Levine, "The Book and the Building"; Id., *Modern Architecture*, ch. 4.

capacity to bear meaning. Here was an epistemological revolution in architecture – and one conceived, articulated, and popularised above all by a pressure group. It was to transform Anglican architecture, as churches were turned as never before into vehicles for theology, with Gothic art and architecture becoming a universal language for the established church. As the Ecclesiologist, critic, and patron of the hugely influential London church of All Saints, Margaret Street, A. J. B. Beresford Hope put it, it was now the case that "Every stone, every window, was found to tell its own appropriate tale, to bear its own peculiar meaning".[43]

The impact of this new understanding of architecture as sacred text was not confined to the established church of England. Episcopalians in Scotland embraced it almost immediately too.[44] Roman Catholics in Ireland also increasingly inclined towards it.[45] Fascinatingly, from the 1860s onwards some within the established Presbyterian Church of Scotland also abandoned centuries of suspicion about such symbolical art and architecture.[46] A similar and equally unlikely change was experienced by many Protestant Non-Conformist groups, with Congregationalists like the architect James Cubitt and Methodists like the Wesleyan minister F. J. Jobson arguing in straightforwardly Ecclesiological terms that Gothic should be adopted by their denominations on the grounds of its legibility.[47] Gothic, Jobson claimed, was "the outward and visible representation of Christian worship".[48] It should thus become the basis of a new, national, Methodist style: a unified architecture symbolic of a unified church.

Thus it was that Gothic art and architecture became ubiquitous in nineteenth-century churches; ubiquitous, but never unchallenged in its supremacy. There were always those who sought other styles, with Roman Catholics sometimes preferring the Baroque and even Byzantine approaches more common on the continent, and some Protestants unwilling to adopt a mode of architecture that reminded them of papal practices. Ironically, indeed, both Roman Catholics and those who fiercely opposed Roman Catholicism each often favoured classical styles. Yet the epistemological revolution advanced by the Camdenians and their contemporaries even affected this debate. The Scots Presbyterian, Alexander 'Greek' Thomson had no place in his heart for medieval styles, but he completely accepted the idea that architecture – and especially church architecture – should be meaningful. Indeed, he simply reversed the Ecclesiologists' argument by maintaining that neoclassical, rather than Gothic, buildings conveyed a higher spiritual message.[49] The same was true of the Baptist preacher C. H. Spurgeon, who explicitly rejected the Gothic Revival and all its associations when he came to build his massive, 6,000-seater Metropolitan Tabernacle, but could not avoid the idea of buildings as text and architecture as language. The Tabernacle, Spurgeon affirmed, had to be "a Grecian place of worship". This was not because of the beauty or even practicality of Greek art, but because,

> It seemed to me, that there are two sacred languages in the world: there was the Hebrew of old; there is one other sacred language, the Greek, which is very dear to every Christian heart. Every Baptist place should be Grecian, never Gothic.[50]

Here the linguistic analogy with architecture that had been pioneered by the Ecclesiologists found its apotheosis – even if the neoclassical conclusion was rather different from theirs.

Tellingly, this broad consensus about church architecture owed much to the work pressure groups founded in imitation of the Ecclesiological Society. Sometimes the debt was self-conscious – as with the Roman Catholic Irish Ecclesiological Society, established in 1849.[51] Sometimes it was less apparent, with the rise of a neo-Gothic constituency in the Presbyterian Church of Scotland marked in 1865 by the foundation of the Church Service Society, which never firmly

---

43 Beresford Hope, "The Present State of Ecclesiological Art in England", 26.
44 Yates, *Preaching, Word and Sacrament*, 112.
45 Sheehy, *J. J. McCarthy and the Gothic Revival in Ireland*.
46 Brown, "Scotland and the Oxford Movement", 76-77.
47 Binfield, *The Contexting of a Chapel Architect: James Cubitt*.
48 Jobson, *Chapel and School Architecture*, 12, 14, 43.
49 Thomson, "On the Unsuitableness of Gothic Architecture to Modern Circumstances".
50 Carlile, *C. H. Spurgeon*, 155.
51 *Irish Monthly*, 24 (1896), 275-277.

identified itself with its Cambridge predecessor but nonetheless parroted Ecclesiological phrases.[52]

The pressure groups that emerged out of the early-nineteenth-century crisis of church and state were consequently of immense importance to the material reform of religion in this period. Initially concerned with the simple fact of church building, they came to articulate a powerful architectural philosophy – an epistemology – which reshaped the ecclesiastical landscape profoundly. Groups like the Ecclesiological Society provided a forum in which individuals could develop a common approach, a common language, a shared sense of purpose. The development of cheap printing and the demand of patrons and architects for advice completed the job, producing a paradox. On the one hand, this was an era of ever-increasing denominational competition, something manifested in aggressive church-building campaigns throughout the country. On the other hand, these churches grew increasingly like one another, as shared assumptions and (especially) a shared commitment to Gothic architecture affected all the churches of the United Kingdom.

Religious publishing

Similar reforming impulses helped to create a new world of religious publishing in this period – and, once again, we can trace a pattern of slow development from the 1790s followed by a sudden acceleration of pace around 1840. These changes were, of course, closely linked to wider transformations within publishing more generally: new modes of production and distribution; the removal of barriers to trade, not least the abolition of the advertisement tax in 1853, newspaper stamp duty in 1855, and paper duty in 1861. But, in truth, Christian publications were in their own right important drivers of change; as something like a fifth of all books and a third of all journals were devoted to religious themes, this could hardly be otherwise. Thus it was, as Simon Eliot observes, that amongst the key moments in Victorian publishing history was the battle which ensued on the re-establishment of the Roman Catholic hierarchy in 1850. This, claimed contemporaries, was the tipping point which finally created a truly mass-market press, as a slew of polemical books, tracts, pamphlets, and prints issued forth from a dizzying range of sources.[53] Although they were far from the only influences on this dynamic market, amongst the most important players within the field were what might be called religious pressure groups. It was they who pioneered the sorts of low-cost publications that would flood the market after the 1840s, and they who helped to transform the nature of publishing itself.[54] Again, these were not pressure groups as classically understood by political scientists. They did not seek to apply pressure to the state. But their impact was nonetheless considerable. For like the architectural reformers these religious pressure groups did not simply produce new material, they also helped to transform how this material was understood.

Naturally, this was not an isolated development. There was a whole world of religious material produced in this period – from maps of the Holy Land to ceramic figures of leading preachers and heroes of the past. Such icons were not confined to Roman Catholicism either, with John Wesley and John Bunyan proving popular for Non-Conformists, and even High Anglicans like Archbishop Laud being commemorated in similar ways. The religious reform movements of the nineteenth century capitalised on this to recruit and motivate the public. Missionary societies, for example, did not confine their efforts to printed texts. They encouraged children to contribute by producing attractive collecting boxes – often in the shape of elephants. They also sold cut-out dolls to be dressed in the clothes of exotic 'heathens'.[55]

Nor were these developments wholly new. The large-scale sale of religious ephemera dated back many decades. The canonical texts of British Protestantism like *Foxe's Book*

52 Sanders, "Ecclesiology in Scotland".
53 Eliot, "Some Trends in British Book Production".
54 Howsam, "The History of the Book in Britain", 182.
55 Cox, "Worlds of Victorian Religion", 444.

1.1-5 Frontispiece and title page of the 1806 edition of The Pilgrim's Progress. [Oxford, Bodleian Library]

of Martyrs, and – especially – *Pilgrim's Progress,* were already publishing sensations, with the latter reaching its fifty-seventh English impression by 1789 and spawning Welsh-language editions in 1688, 1699, 1713, 1722, 1744, 1770, and 1790.[56] The Bible itself was produced in huge quantities in the eighteenth century: by 1720, the printer John Baskett was making octavo and duodecimo editions in batches of 10,000 each. His duodecimo New Testament was described as "always printing".[57] Even the poorest families were likely to have access to religious literature; indeed, for some at the start of the nineteenth century, this was the only reading material they possessed. Recalling his impoverished Primitive Methodist mother, who learnt to read aged 48, the philologist Joseph Wright observed that she would only permit the *New Testament*, *Pilgrim's Progress*, and a translation of Klopstock's *Messiah* in the house. When he returned with the collected plays of Shakespeare, she threw the offending volume away.[58] [Ill. 1.1-5]

Nonetheless, there was undoubtedly a new intensity to religious publishing in this period. Not for nothing were the High Church radicals of the 1830s known as Tractarians, after their controversial series, *Tracts for the Times*. Likewise, the extreme Calvinist party within the Church of England were identified in the 1850s as 'Recordites', after their paper, *The Record*.[59] And it was not simply polemic that was thus politicised. In Ireland the Catholic Book Society (founded in 1827) actually produced a *Catholic Spelling Book*.[60] Less surprisingly, perhaps, rival theologies were reflected in competing histories, with the Tractarians' *Lives of the Saints* series challenged by the more Protestant texts produced by the Parker Society, established in 1840 precisely to offset the rise of High Church publishing. It soon had 7,000 members.[61] Even hymnody was affected, with more than 1200 hymn books published between 1837 and 1901: each one taking up a distinctive theological position. Used at home as well as in church; intended,

56 Colley, *Britons: Forging the Nation*, 28.
57 McKitterick, *A History of Cambridge University Press*, II, 180.
58 Rose, *The Intellectual Life of the British Working Class*, 31.
59 Conybeare, *Church Parties*.
60 Griffin, "The Catholic Book Society", 89.
61 McKitterick, *A History of Cambridge University Press*, II, 339.

as the editor of the High-Church Anglican *Hymns Ancient and Modern* put it in 1858, "for singing in mission rooms, at lectures in cottages or meetings of brotherhoods": these were great works of propaganda and all the more controversial for that, with arguments regularly traded over the orthodoxy of whole collections, particular verses, or even single words.[62]

Above all, religious publishing was radically changed by groups like the British and Foreign Bible Society (BFBS), founded in 1804.[63] It grew out of the Religious Tract Society (RTS), itself established only a few years earlier in 1799. Both were the products of the evangelical revival, and both sought to effect religious conversion through literature. Both were strikingly successful. By 1849, the Religious Tract Society had reached a circulation of more than 4 million children's books alone.[64] But even this success was dwarfed by the scale of the British and Foreign Bible Society's achievements. Although initially envisaged as a predominantly missionary enterprise, producing Bibles for use overseas and in those parts of Wales where English was still unused, it transmuted into a major publisher in its own right – transforming the market and incidentally reshaping old-established printing houses like Cambridge University Press, which struggled to keep up with the scale and the dynamism of the BFBS.[65] [Ill. 1.1-1]

The importance of the British and Foreign Bible Society was not confined to the scale of its enterprise – although it did claim to have distributed more than 2,500,000 Bibles and New Testaments in its first 15 years, and would of course go on the distribute still more.[66] Nor can its significance simply be measured by the rash of imitators that arose in its wake: organisations like the Prayer Book and Homily Society (founded in 1812) or the Society for Irish Church Missions (established in 1846). Rather, the BFBS was most intensely innovative – and important – in the way that it worked. Run in the most business-like manner, it did not seek to give Bibles away for free, but hoped to persuade

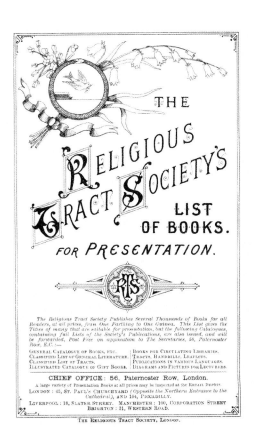

1.1-6 Cover of the Religious Tract Society publication catalogue, 1889. [www.gutenberg.org]

people to buy them. To that end, it worked hard to produce the most inexpensive publications possible at a time in which most other publishers put a premium on quality. Still more importantly, in 1809, the first of a series of local auxiliary societies was founded. These existed to sell Bibles by subscription, with potential purchasers to contribute as a little as a penny a week to acquire a volume of their own. These auxiliary societies were supplemented by Bible associations and local branches. By 1835, there were 269 auxiliaries, 347 branches, and 1,541 associations.[67] The Society had helped to create an associational culture based around the sale of Bibles. [Ill. 1.1-6]

These groups involved women and children as well as men. Moreover, even children were able to acquire their own copies of the Bible through subscription. The format of their books reflected this, with a small pica type proving particular popular, partly because it could compress the whole of the Bible into a single volume, and partly because

62 Bradley, *Abide with Me*, 61.
63 Howsam, *Cheap Bibles*.
64 Green, *The Story of the Religious Tract Society*, 49.
65 McKitterick, *A History of Cambridge University Press*, II, 269.
66 Mandelbrote, "The Publishing and Distribution of Religious Books by Voluntary Associations", 628.
67 Howsam, *Cheap Bibles*, 63.

it could be read in an ill-lit home by someone with poor eyesight.[68] The Religious Tract Society likewise issued a dizzying range of different publications intended for as wide a readership as possible, celebrating the effects of such sundry works of fiction as

> *The Swearer's Prayer*, in its warning influence on the profane; *Andrew Dunn*, in its exposure of Romanist practices and beliefs; *Sabbath Occupations*, in its vindication of the sanctity of the Lord's Day; *Tom Roberts, the Learned Cobbler*, in its popular refutation of Deistical cavils; *The Advantages of Drunkenness*, in its scathing satire against intemperance; and *Poor Joseph*, in its inimitable exhibition of the simplicity of the Gospel.[69]

The publications for children that it offered were equally wide-ranging, inexpensive – and attractive. "Oh, what beautiful books!" chorused a group of adolescent prisoners when introduced to the RTS's tracts in 1840.[70]

As this suggests, the groups that evolved in the early part of this period were able to reach people whose connection with organised religion was tenuous to say the least. Perhaps half of the population regularly attended Church in the 1850s. It is safe to assume that all of them nonetheless had access to some form of religious literature – even if it was used in unexpected and unorthodox ways, with the ubiquity of the Bible enabling it to become a lucky charm, carried by individuals to avert ill-fortunate or kept safely at home because "you won't have any luck if you don't have a Bible in the house".[71] The impact of this universal access to Scripture was often striking. "Though I was wholly unaware of it, the language of the Authorised Version [of the Bible] became somehow part of me", recalled one Norfolk farmer's son. "To me these stories were as real as if I had been a participant. Saul and the witch of Endor: David and Jonathan and the tragedy of Gilboa: Elijah and Elisha and Naboth's vineyard and Mount Carmel were more real to me than the history stories in our *Readers at school*."[72]

But the plethora of publications which these organisations produced also brought about a conceptual change. It helped to turn the religious book – even the Bible itself – into a commodity. By the 1850s the British and Foreign Bible Society began offering a whole range of highly differentiated impressions of the Bible, with wealthy subscribers able to commission their own expensive special editions. Revealingly, in 1853 the BFBS began to employ Bible-sellers to supplement the work of its volunteers. At about the same time, the Religious Tract Society found that the income generated by sales was beginning to outstrip the money raised by donations: it was now a profit-making company more than a charity.[73] *Hymns Ancient and Modern* achieved similar success, with its editors drawing in an annual dividend of over £1000 by 1891. In the words of Ian Bradley, "It was little wonder that their enthusiasm for bringing out new editions was regarded by critics as a money-spinning device which was not justified on other grounds."[74] Commodification, though, had another, more important consequence: it enabled individuals – even some of the very poorest individuals – to own their own Bible and a range of other theological works. Just like Joseph Wright's mother, they could learn to read them for themselves. Thus the ready availability of texts helped to turn reading from a public into a private act.

Christian education

These twin themes of buildings and books are brought together in the work of those who sought to provide a Christian education for the British and Irish people in this period. The Sunday School movement, which took off at the start of the nineteenth century, grew to become a massive undertaking. The number of children attending one in England and Wales was 425,000 in 1818; by 1911 it was more than six million.[75] Nor was it just plebeian education that experienced change. Elite institutions were also

---

68 Howsam, *Cheap Bibles*, 103.
69 Green, *The Story of the Religious Tract Society*, 43.
70 Rogers, "Oh, what beautiful books!".
71 Williams, *Religious Belief and Popular Culture*, 66.
72 Rose, *The Intellectual Life of the British Working Class*, 351.
73 Ledger-Lomas, "Mass Markets: religion", 330-336.
74 Bradley, *Abide with Me*, 57.
75 Snell and Ell, *Rival Jerusalems*, 277-278.

1.1-7 Reunion of the British and Foreign School Society in 1853.
[*The Illustrated London News*, 14 May 1853, 369]

reformed beyond recognition, with religious impulses underpinning much of what was done. Thomas Arnold's decision to combine his role as headmaster of Rugby with the post of chaplain was to prove formative to the mixture of 'Godliness and Good Learning' that came to shape the public schools.[76] So central would this ideal prove, indeed, that at newly-founded Radley College, the first headmaster felt able to declare that every aspect of the design of his school – including the carpets – was wholly dependent on the teachings of the Athanasian creed.[77] Higher education was likewise reshaped, with new institutions founded and old ones opened up to denominations which had previously been excluded. Indeed, religious dispute proved an important spur to university reform, with rival colleges for example founded in London in 1820s: the 'Godless institution on Gower Street' (the future UCL) counterpointed by the strictly Anglican King's College on the Strand. In Ireland, battles over the religious identity of higher education continued throughout the century.[78]

It was, however, in the provision of elementary day schools that the role of pressure groups in reforming the material conditions of religious life can most clearly be seen. This is especially true in England, Ireland, and Wales, which lagged far behind Scotland in the provision of basic teaching facilities. Indeed, it was not until 1870 that parliament acted to ensure that all English and Welsh children had access to elementary schools; not until 1880 that attendance became compulsory; and even as late as 1895 it remained the case that one in five of those eligible avoided attendance altogether.[79] In Ireland, too, attempts to provide universal elementary education foundered on sectarian disputes.

Into the vacuum that this produced came rival voluntary associations: the non-denominational (but actually Protestant) Kildare Place Society versus the (Roman Catholic) Irish National Society; the ecumenical (but broadly Non-Conformist) British and Foreign School Society [Ill. 1.1-7] opposed by the National Society for Promoting the Education of the Poor in the Principles of the Established Church. The contest between the latter two was especially keen – and notably public. "There was hardly a man, eminent as a statesman, politician, or writer, who did not take a side in the controversy between them", observed one contemporary historian.[80] The British and Foreign Society,

76 Newsome, *Godliness and Good Learning*.
77 Whyte, "Building a Public School Community", 618.
78 Whyte, *Redbrick*, ch. 1.
79 Sutherland, "Education", 145.
80 Adams, *The Elementary School Contest in England*, 63.

81 Seabourne, *The English School*, 188-189.
82 Ibid., 212.

although formally constituted in 1814, was initially set up in 1808 to give form to the existing work of nondenominational schooling pioneered by the Quaker educationist Joseph Lancaster. The National Society, founded in 1811, grew out of the same reforming Anglican impulse that later led to the establishment of the Church Building Society – and several of its leading members served in both.

From the first, the National Society and the British and Foreign Society operated in opposition. The superior resources of the former enabled it to establish more schools: some 5,000 by the end of the century. But the system established by the latter was nevertheless highly influential. Neither became predominant; and so each existed in a state of undeclared war against the other. This was something that found its expression in architecture, with the 'National' schools (as they were known) favouring the suitably ecclesiastical Gothic and 'British' schools tending towards the classical, rather as Dissenters did in their churches. It was a distinction made manifest at the opening of the Leicester Non-Conformist Proprietary School in 1837. This was a secondary school which had been established in direct competition with the recently-founded – Anglican, and hence Gothic – Leicester Collegiate School. The headmaster declared that

> He rejoiced greatly that they had adopted the Grecian style of Architecture in preference to the Gothic (…) To those whose associations fondly clung to the dark Monastic exploded institutions of our country, who love to dwell rather on the gloomy periods of our history, than to contemplate the blaze of light and knowledge which has since burst upon the world – to such persons he was aware the Gothic style of Architecture had great charms; but in an institution for the education of youth it was desirable that every association of the mind should be connected with a people who had carried literature to the highest point of perfection, whose love of liberty, of knowledge, of the fine arts, whose writings in History, in poetry had never been excelled, rather than with the superstitions of our Gothic ancestors who, with the exception of Architecture, were remarkable only for their ignorance and barbarism.[81]

With his condemnation of monasticism, 'superstition', 'ignorance and barbarism', he spoke for many of those who opposed the Church of England and the Gothic schools which it had fostered.

Even as he spoke, indeed, the National Society was becoming ever more committed to medieval modes of building. Under the influence of the Ecclesiologists, the 1840s saw it become almost exclusively Gothic in its architecture. This was especially clear in those schools which were also intended to serve as places of worship, like the building at Lounds, near Sheffield, which was opened in 1859-1860. As the *Sheffield Times* recorded, it was self-evidently "distinct from the mere secular or every-day architecture of modern times, and having sufficient character to inform the passer-by that it has been reared for the service of the God of Charity".[82] It was not just church buildings, therefore, that were intended to communicate a symbolic message: schools were similarly pressed into

1.1-8 National Society School of Aston, Oxfordshire, built in 1856.
[Wikimedia Commons; photo 2016]

service as vehicles for a particular – and a particularly religious – message. [Ill. 1.1-8]

And it was not merely in their outward appearance that these two types of schools differed from one another. 'British' and 'National' foundations relied on different schoolbooks, with each maintaining its own catalogue and (from 1812) producing its own publications.[83] The distinction between a 'British' education, which was intended to be as inoffensive to all Protestants as possible, and 'National' education, which was tightly circumscribed by adherence to strictly Anglican norms, was still more striking. Indeed, in 'National' schools religious knowledge – especially the catechism set out in the Book of Common Prayer – was at a premium, and attendance was conditional on participation in services at the local parish church. Here the school, both in form and function, had become an adjunct of – even a surrogate for – the church.

Material reform or religious decline?

From 1780 onwards, therefore, pressure groups – broadly conceived – did indeed help to effect the material reform of religion in the British Isles. Especially after the 1830s, they were central players in the process of church building, religious publishing, and educating a new generation of Christians. In so-doing, they did not just erect scores of new schools and hundreds of new churches, nor merely print thousands of Bibles, books, and tracts. It might also be suggested that they contributed to a wider change in the lives and beliefs of British and Irish people in this period. The epistemological revolution fostered by the Ecclesiologists helped to reshape attitudes to, and encounters with, church architecture. The commodification of the book – especially of the Bible – which was achieved with the assistance of various Christian publishing societies likewise helped to change individual's subjective experience of religion, not least by providing opportunities for private reading. So too, the elementary schools – with their stereotyped architecture and their distinctive patterns of teaching and worship – sought to impose a new sort of physical regime. Within them, pupils were taught how to worship as much as they were instructed in how to read or write: their hands at one point grasping an unfamiliar stylus and at another being clasped together for prayer; their heads looking up to their teacher and then bowing down in supplication to God. This was the most basic of material reforms: the reform of the body itself.

Yet many historians have suggested that little more than a generation later, this world was shattered and replaced by a newly secularising society. "All denominations, the Church of England especially, were on the back foot after about 1870", argues the architectural historian Andrew Saint in his own study of late-nineteenth-century church building.[84] The historian of the book, Michael Ledger-Lomas sees another problem, arguing that in this period organisations like the British and Foreign Bible Society and its parent body, the Religious Tract Society, encountered an uncomfortable truth, that "selling in the open market might verge on selling out to worldliness".[85] As for the elementary schools that religious denominations had set up: these too were challenged by the state's decision to become involved, legislating in 1870 to establish secular school boards. Little wonder that historians like Jonathan Rose have pointed to this as the moment when education started to move away from its religious origins.[86]

There is, of course, something in all these arguments. The Gothic Revival, which had been forged in the heat of Ecclesiological controversy, did indeed come under increasing attack. The new avant-garde – the Arts and Crafts movement – was, in the words of its most influential modern interpreter, "secular in spirit".[87] This was a tendency which found its expression in educational architecture, with most English school boards after 1870 abandoning Gothic, deliberately rejecting a style now seen as almost exclusively

83 Stray and Sutherland, "Mass Markets: education", 365.
84 Saint, "The late Victorian Church?", 22.
85 Ledger-Lomas, "Mass Markets: religion", 336.
86 Rose, *The Intellectual Life of the British Working Class*, 33.
87 Crawford, "Arts and Crafts Churches", 63.

88 Robson, *School Architecture*, 321.
89 Billington, "The Religious Periodicals and the Newspaper Press", 132.
90 Turner, *Boys Will Be Boys*, 88-89.
91 Harris, *Private Lives, Public Spirit*, 154.
92 Hunt, *Education in Evolution*, 224.
93 Ledger-Lomas, "Mass Markets: religion", 334-337.
94 Vance, *The Sinews of the Spirit*, 172.
95 Garnett, "The Nineteenth Century", 208-209.

1.1-9 Cover of the Juvenile Instructor, *a missionary periodical for children published by the Church Missionary Society, 1880.*
[New York, Columbia University Libraries]

associated with the Church – and especially with the Church of England. "It is clear", observed E. R. Robson, the pre-eminent board-school architect of the era,

> that a building in which the teaching of dogma is strictly forbidden, can have no pretence for using with any point or meaning that symbolism which is so interwoven with every feature of church architecture as to be naturally regarded as its very life and soul. In its aim and object it should strive to express civil rather than ecclesiastical character. A continuation of the semi-ecclesiastical style which has hitherto been almost exclusively followed in England for National schools would appear to be inappropriate and lacking in anything to mark the great change which is coming over the education of the country.[88]

At the same time, it is clear that contemporaries shared the sense that the "religious press was closer to its secular counterpart in tone and business methods than it had been at the beginning of the century".[89] Hence, for example, the satire which appeared in the comic magazine *Punch* in 1882, guying a typical story from the Religious Tract Society: "'Wet Bob, or the Adventures of a Little Eton Boy Amongst the Hotwhata Cannibals,' by the Author of 'the Three Young Benchers and How They All Got the Woolsack,' 'From Back Bench to Yard Arm' etc."[90]

It is important, however, not to confuse change with decay, nor to impose a master narrative of simple secularisation on a period which, in reality, showed signs of growth as well as problems for the Churches. After all – and *pace* Andrew Saint – by 1900, "a higher proportion of the British people were active members of religious denominations than at any earlier time during Queen Victoria's reign"; indeed, as Jose Harris goes on to observe, by 1910 the Church of England "was attracting a higher proportion of the population as Easter communicants than at any time in the previous century".[91] These more general trends are also borne out by the material remains of the era. Far from eradicating denominational education, the new board schools provoked the National Society into a renewed burst of building. Between 1870 and 1877, it erected enough new schools to cater for more than a million additional pupils.[92] The sheer scale of the publishing endeavour undertaken at the same time by groups like the Religious Tract Society was equally impressive. By the mid-1880s, the RTS was circulating more than 75 million items a year and its periodicals were reaching 1.5 million readers a week.[93] Moreover, this was not just an era of continued expansion, it was also one of innovation. New organisations were established like the Boys' Brigade (1883), founded on the 'twin pillars' of military drill and Bible classes and soon able to attract tens of thousands of members.[94] New technologies were also pressed into play, with the magic lantern in particular proving popular and even replacing evensong at churches like St Mary-at-Hill in the city of London. "That the right sort of people are attracted", observed one commentator, "is shown by the burglar's picklock and empty whisky bottle that were lately left in the pews."[95] It was, of course, in this specular

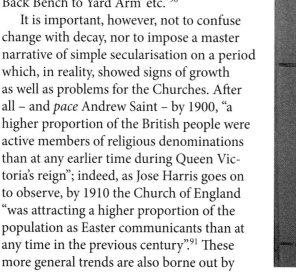

mode that Thomas Colley found himself carried round his church in a coffin. But other, less eccentric Christian propagandists were still more enterprising, with the English Church pageant of 1909, for example, involving no fewer than 3,000 performers and an audience of 24,000. "It is possible that the philosophic historian of the future", noted *The Times*, would see in this "one of the most significant instances of a great change in tastes and ideas."[96] Pressure groups played a key role in almost all these developments, with the Church Missionary Society alone calculating that it was reaching 200,000 people a year through its use of the magic lantern in 1891.[97] [Ill. 1.1-9 & 1.1-10]

The material reform of church buildings also continued after 1870. Indeed, in the words of one authority, it was then that England and Scotland each experienced the final "triumph" of Ecclesiology.[98] This was a development which once again drew on the activities of pressure groups and inspired the creation of new bodies, with the Roman Catholic Guild of St Gregory and St Luke established in 1879 ostensibly in imitation of the Belgian Guild of St Thomas and St Luke. In the same year, the Ecclesiological Society was itself re-founded by a group of Anglicans. Less polemical than its predecessor, its publications nonetheless perpetuated the assumptions set forth in the 1840s by the old Cambridge Camden Society. A series of ritualist organisations dedicated to the revival of medieval liturgical practices was also established towards the end of the nineteenth century: the Society of the Holy Cross, the English Church Union, the Confraternity of the Blessed Sacrament, the Guild of All Souls. Nor were these exclusively English. The Society of the Holy Cross, for example, infiltrated the Episcopalian Church in Scotland. The Church Service Society, too, played a major part in the rise of a more ritualist Presbyterianism after 1865, a movement exemplified by G. W. Sprott's call in 1882 for the denomination to replace churches which resembled "a circus, class-room, or music-hall" with structures built "in a churchly way".[99]

Increasingly, this effort was supported by serious scholarly research on the material culture of the medieval church. The Alcuin Club, founded in 1897 to publish liturgical texts, helped to bring about a fundamental re-orientation of Anglican worship. Its great goal was to establish an 'English Use': an authentic, national, non-Roman Catholic form of worship. To that end, it published scores of antiquarian pamphlets, with a special focus on the liturgy used at pre-Reformation Salisbury cathedral, the Sarum Rite. Not least because of its distinctive liturgical colours, the rediscovered Rite inspired much new design, with the vestments used by priests developing an entirely distinctive form. It also led members of the Alcuin Club to propose the re-erection of what became known as the 'English Altar', with a dossal instead of a reredos, framed by riddels (or curtains), and patterned after the model of late-medieval art. Not least because of its popularisation

1.1-10 Around 1900, the London Missionary Society produced a series of glass magic lantern slides depicting the missionary efforts of David Livingstone. [London Missionary Society]

96 *The Times*, 10 June 1909, 11.
97 Waller, *Writers, Readers, and Reputations*, 1017.
98 Yates, *Buildings, Faith, and Worship*, 151; Id., *Preaching, Word and Sacrament*, 122.
99 Sprott, *The Worship and Offices of the Church of England*, 233-235.

by the influential writer Percy Dearmer, this was soon seen throughout the worldwide Anglican Church. In 1912, members of the Alcuin Club founded the Warham Guild to market such goods and further agitate for the reform of vestments and church furnishings.

Pressure groups could also exercise a more direct control of the parish church, helped by the fact that the Church of England retained lay patronage. Advowsons – or livings – could be freely bought and sold; they could also be vested in trusts. From 1817 the avowedly evangelical Simeon Trust acquired a succession of advowsons with the express intention of appointing evangelicals to the livings. In 1865, they were joined in this attempt by the Church Society, which gradually acquired the patronage of more than 100 parishes: each of them to be filled by safely evangelical pastors. Anglo-Catholics were bound to respond – and in this period they certainly did, with Keble College, Oxford being endowed with 70 advowsons on its foundation as a bastion of the High Church in 1870. Four years later, the Society for the Maintenance of the Faith was established and quickly acquired 80 livings. By the beginning of the twentieth century more than 1,000 benefices were in the hands of expressly sectarian groups.[100] As they reformed the patterns of ecclesiastical patronage, so the beneficiaries of their work reshaped the churches under their care. The acquisition of an advowson by a High Church trust was consequently often followed by the acquisition of new vestments, the introduction of new rites, and the material reform of the parish as a whole.

The decades which followed 1870, therefore, cannot simply be written off as an era of decline, much less as a period in which the churches – and the pressure groups they spawned – simply gave up, unable to keep pace with social change. In reality, this was another moment of quite remarkable innovation and energy, in which often very new pressure groups played an important role. Whether moving swiftly to counter the non-sectarian educational ambitions of the state; seeking to flood the market with religious literature; researching past liturgical practice and intervening in current systems of clerical appointments: a variety of different organisations continued to mould the world of religion.

Conclusion

This necessarily impressionistic survey has, unfortunately, omitted much. There has been no room, for example, to explore the genuinely global reach of religious pressure groups. Many of these organisations were also involved in the production of materials for missionaries and new churches in the empire. Others had strong trans-Atlantic connections. Even Ecclesiology went worldwide, influencing the architecture of the empire and the Episcopal Church of the United States alike. Moreover, there is some evidence that the empire struck back, with attitudes and experiences forged in the mission field helping to shape those held at home. In a recent study, the architectural historian Alex Bremner declares that we would be mistaken to conceptualise Ecclesiology as "a purely 'English' invention, exported to other parts of the world by lesser mortals". Rather, he claims, it "was in every sense a global phenomenon".[101] What was true of Ecclesiology was surely also the case for many of the other developments that this essay has dealt with.

It would also be a mistake to attribute all change to the work of pressure groups within Britain and Ireland in this period. We cannot afford to discount the influence of powerful individuals; nor should we ignore the more general trends – the wider social, political, theological and economic issues – that are covered elsewhere in this series. In a highly localised, not to say particularist, religious landscape, there must also be room in our analysis for eccentrics like Thomas Colley; in some respects products of their time, in other ways entirely *sui generis*.

100 Evershed, *Party and Patronage in the Church of England*.
101 Bremner, *Imperial Gothic*, 267.

Nor should the historian be tempted to propose too concrete a definition of the groups with which we are dealing, for in reality they were a variegated lot. Some were founded to influence the state; others were created to supplement or even supplant government involvement in religion and education. Yet other groups evolved into successful businesses; while another category became the source of serious historical research and still another sort came to shape life within individual parishes in unprecedented ways. There is, in short, no satisfactory single model to account for their form, function, and development.

The significance of these pressure groups in reforming the material expression of religion between 1780 and 1920 is, however, undeniable. It was an influence which operated throughout this period, not diminishing substantially even in the last few decades. It can be traced throughout Britain and Ireland: from great Gothic churches to tiny village schoolrooms; from the vestments still used in parishes today to the antique family Bibles which now remain – generally unread – on the bookshelves in thousands of homes. More than anything, the legacy of these pressure groups was the attitudes to material culture which they fostered. It was they who popularised the idea of the church as a sort of text; they, too, which helped to commodify the book and thus to confirm private reading's role as a religious act for millions. In this, and especially in the schools that pressure groups helped to create, material reform also included physical reform. Pressure groups therefore did not merely effect material reform, they changed the ways that the material world was understood. As a consequence, the mental and the material, the discursive and the bodily experience of religion was reshaped for good – and, perhaps, for ever – by 'pressure groups'.

BIBLIOGRAPHY

Adams, Francis. *The Elementary School Contest in England*. London, 1882.

Akenson, Donald Harman. *The Church of Ireland: Ecclesiastical Reform and Revolution, 1800-1885*. New Haven-London, 1971.

Aspin, Philip. "'Our Ancient Architecture': Contesting Cathedrals in late-Georgian England". *Architectural History*, 54 (2011), 213-274.

Beresford Hope, A. J. B. "The Present State of Ecclesiological Art in England". *Proceedings of the Oxford Society for Promoting the Study of Gothic Architecture*, 23 June 1846, 26.

Best, G. F. A. *Temporal Pillars: Queen Anne's Bounty, the Ecclesiastical Commissioners, and the Church of England*. Cambridge, 1964.

Beyers, Jan, Rainer Eising and William Maloney. "Researching Interest Group Politics in Europe and Elsewhere: much we study, little we know?". *West European Politics*, 31 (2008), 1103-1128.

Billington, Louis. "The Religious Periodicals and the Newspaper Press, 1770-1870". In: Michael Harris and Alan Lee, eds. *The Press in English Society from the Seventeenth to the Nineteenth Century*. London-Toronto, 1986, 113-132.

Binfield, Clyde. *The Contexting of a Chapel Architect: James Cubitt, 1836-1912*. London, 2001.

Bradley, Ian. *Abide with Me: The World of Victorian Hymns*. London, 1997.

Bradley, Simon. *The Gothic Revival and the Church of England, 1790-1840*. PhD diss. London, 1996.

Bremner, G. A. *Imperial Gothic: Religious Architecture and High Anglican Culture in the British Empire, 1840-1870*. New Haven-London, 2013.

Bremner, G. A., and Jonathan Conlin. "History as Form: Architecture and Liberal Anglican Thought in the Writings of E. A. Freeman". *Modern Intellectual History*, 8 (2011), 299-326.

Brooks, Chris. "Introduction". In: Chris Brooks and Andrew Saint, eds. *The Victorian Church: Architecture and Society*. Manchester, 1995, 1-29.

Brooks, Chris. "Building the Rural Church: Money, Power, and the Country Parish". In: Chris Brooks and Andrew Saint, eds. *The Victorian Church: Architecture and Society*. Manchester, 1995, 51-81.

Brown, Stewart J. *The National Churches of England, Ireland, and Scotland, 1801-1846*. Oxford, 2001.

Brown, Stewart J. "Scotland and the Oxford Movement". In: Stewart J. Brown and Peter B. Nockles, eds. *The Oxford Movement: Europe and the Wider World 1830-1930*. Cambridge, 2012, 56-77.

Byrne, Georgina. *Modern Spiritualism and the Church of England, 1850-1939*. Woodbridge-Rochester, 2010.

Carlile, J. C. *C. H. Spurgeon: An Interpretative Biography*. London, 1933.

Chitty, Gill. "John Ruskin, Oxford and the Architectural Society, 1837 to 1840". *Oxoniensia*, 65 (2000), 111-113.

Colley, Linda. *Britons: Forging the Nation, 1707-1837*. London, 1992.

Conlin, Jonathan. "Development or Destruction? E. A. Freeman and the Debate on Church Restoration, 1839-1851". *Oxoniensia*, 77 (2012), 1-32.

Conybeare, William John. *Church Parties*. Edited by Arthur Burns. Woodbridge, 1999.

Cox, Jeffrey. *The English Churches in a Secular Society: Lambeth 1870-1930*. Oxford, 1982.

Cox, Jeffrey. "Worlds of Victorian Religion". In: Martin Hewitt, ed. *The Victorian World*. London-New York, 2012, 433-448.

Crawford, Alan. "Arts and Crafts Churches". In: Teresa Sladen and Andrew Saint, eds. *Churches 1870-1914*. London, 2011, 63-80.

Eliot, Simon. "Some Trends in British Book Production 1800-1919". In: John O. Jordan and Robert L. Patten, eds. *Literature in the Marketplace: Nineteenth-Century British Publishing and Reading Practices*. Cambridge, 1995, 19-43.

Evershed, William. *Party and Patronage in the Church of England, 1800-1945: A Study of Patronage Trusts and Patronage Reform*. PhD Oxford, 1985.

Friedman, Terry. *The Eighteenth-Century Church in Britain*. New Haven-London, 2011.

Garnett, Jane. "The Nineteenth Century". In: Richard Harries and Henry Mayr-Harting, eds. *Christianity: Two Thousand Years*. Oxford, 2001, 192-217.

Green, Samuel G. *The Story of the Religious Tract Society*. London, 1899.

Griffin, Sean. "The Catholic Book Society and its Role in the Emerging System of National Education, 1824-1834". *Irish Educational Studies*, 11 (1992), 82-98.

Harris, Jose. *Private Lives, Public Spirit: Britain, 1870-1914*. Oxford-New York, 1993.

Hawkins, Edward. *A Sermon preached at the Cathedral Church of Rochester*. London, 1839.

Howarth, Janet. "The Church of England and Women's Higher Education, c.1840-1914". In: Peter Ghosh and Lawrence Goldman, eds. *Politics and Culture in Victorian Britain: Essays in Memory of Colin Matthew*. Oxford, 2006, 153-170.

Howsam, Leslie. *Cheap Bibles: Nineteenth Century Publishing and the British and Foreign Bible Society*. Cambridge, 1991.

Howsam, Leslie. "The History of the Book in Britain, 1801-1914". In: Michael Suarez and H. R. Woudhuysen, eds. *The Oxford Companion to the Book*, 2 vols. Oxford, 2010, 180-187.

Hunt, John. *Education in Evolution*. London, 1970.

Jobson, F. J. *Chapel and School Architecture as Appropriate to the Buildings of Non-Conformists, Particularly to Those of the Wesleyan Methodists*. London, 1850.

Ledger-Lomas, Michael. "Mass Markets: religion". In: David McKitterick, ed. *The Cambridge History of the Book in Britain*. Vol. 6: *1830-1914*. Cambridge, 2009, 324-258.

Levine, Neil. "The Book and the Building: Hugo's Theory of Architecture and Labrouste's Bibliothèque Ste-Geneviève". In: Robin Middleton, ed. *The Beaux-Arts and Nineteenth-Century French Architecture*. London, 1982, 138-173.

Levine, Neil. *Modern Architecture: Representation and Reality*. New Haven-London, 2011.

London Free and Open Church Association. *Free and Open Churches: Facts and Opinions from Five Hundred Parishes in Town and Country*. 2nd ed. London, 1876.

Maciver, Iain F. "Unfinished Business? The Highland Churches' Scheme and the Government of Scotland, 1818-35". *Records of the Scottish Church History Society*, 25 (1995), 376-399.

Mandelbrote, Scott. "The Publishing and Distribution of Religious Books by Voluntary Associations: from the Society for Promoting Christian Knowledge to the British and Foreign Bible Society". In: Michael F. Suarez and Michael L. Turner, eds. *The Cambridge History of the Book in Britain*. Vol. V: *1695-1860*. Cambridge, 2010, 613-630.

McKitterick, David. *A History of Cambridge University Press*. Vol. 2: *1698-1872*. Cambridge, 1998.

Newsome, David. *Godliness and Good Learning*. London, 1961.

Parry, Timothy V. *The Incorporated Church Building Society, 1818-1851*. Oxford MLitt thesis, 1984.

Port, M. H. *600 New Churches: The Church Building Commission, 1818-1856*. 2nd ed. Reading, 2006.

Robson, Edward Robert. *School Architecture* (1874). Leicester, 1972.

Rogers, Helen. "'Oh, what beautiful books!' Captivated Reading in an Early Victorian Prison". *Victorian Studies*, 55 (2012), 57-84.

Rose, Jonathan. *The Intellectual Life of the British Working Class*. New Haven-London, 2001.

Saint, Andrew. "Anglican Church Building in London, 1790-1890: from state subsidy to the free market". In: Chris Brooks and Andrew Saint, eds. *The Victorian Church: Architecture and Society*. Manchester, 1995, 30-50.

Saint, Andrew. "The late Victorian Church?" In: Teresa Sladen and Andrew Saint, eds. *Churches 1870-1914*. London, 2011, 7-26.

Sanders, John. "Ecclesiology in Scotland". In: Christopher Webster and John Elliott, eds. *'A Church as It Should Be': The Cambridge Camden Society and its Influence*. Stamford, 2000, 295-316.

Seabourne, Malcolm. *The English School: Its Architecture and Organization, 1370-1870*. London, 1971.

Sheehy, Jeanne. *J. J. McCarthy and the Gothic Revival in Ireland*. Belfast, 1977.

Sheehy, Jeanne. "Irish Church-Building: Popery, Puginism, and the Protestant Ascendancy". In: Chris Brooks and Andrew Saint, eds. *The Victorian Church: Architecture and Society*. Manchester, 1995, 133-150.

Smith, Mark. *Religion in Industrial Society: Oldham and Saddleworth, 1740-1865*. Oxford, 1994.

Snell, K. D. M., and Paul S. Ell. *Rival Jerusalems: The Geography of Victorian Religion*. Cambridge, 2000.

Sprott, George Washington. *The Worship and Offices of the Church of England*. Edinburgh-London, 1882.

Stray, Christopher, and Gillian Sutherland. "Mass Markets: Education". In: David McKitterick, ed. *The Cambridge History of the Book in Britain*. Vol. 6: *1830-1914*. Cambridge, 2009, 359-381.

Sutherland, Gillian. "Education". In: F. M. L. Thompson, ed. *The Cambridge Social History of Britain 1750-1850*, vol. 3. Cambridge, 1990, 119-170.

Sweet, Rosemary. *Antiquaries: The Discovery of the Past in the Eighteenth Century*. London-New York, 2004.

Thompson, Kenneth A. *Bureaucracy and Church Reform: The Organizational Response of the Church of England to Social Change*. Oxford, 1970.

Thomson, Alexander. "On the Unsuitableness of Gothic Architecture to Modern Circumstances". In: Gavin Stamp, ed. *The Light of Truth and Beauty: The Lectures of Alexander "Greek" Thomson, 1817-75*. Glasgow, 1999, 58.

Turner, E. S. *Boys Will Be Boys*. 3rd ed. London, 1975.

Uglow, Jenny. *The Pinecone: The Story of Sarah Losh, Forgotten Romantic Heroine – Antiquarian, Architect, and Visionary*. London, 2012.

Vance, Norman. *The Sinews of the Spirit: The Ideal of Christian Manliness in Victorian Literature and Religious Thought*. Cambridge, 1985.

Wakeling, Christopher. "The Nonconformist Traditions: Chapels, Change, and Continuity". In: Chris Brooks and Andrew Saint, eds. *The Victorian Church: Architecture and Society*. Manchester, 1995, 82-97.

Walker, R. B. "Religious Changes in Cheshire, 1750-1850". *Journal of Ecclesiastical History*, 17 (1966), 77-94.

Waller, Philip. *Writers, Readers, and Reputations: Literary Life in Britain 1870-1918*. Oxford, 2006.

Webster, A. B. *Joshua Watson: The Story of a Layman, 1771-1855*. London, 1954.

Webster, Christopher, ed. *'Temples … Worthy of his Presence': The Early Publications of the Cambridge Camden Society*. Reading, 2003.

Webster, Christopher, and John Elliott, eds. *'A Church as It Should Be': The Cambridge Camden Society and its Influence*. Stamford, 2000.

White, James F. *The Cambridge Movement: The Ecclesiologists and the Gothic Revival*. Cambridge, 1962.

Whyte, William. "Building a Public School Community, 1860-1910". *History of Education*, 32 (2003), 601-626.

Whyte, William. "Restoration and Recrimination: The Temple Church in the Nineteenth Century". In: Robin Griffith-Jones and David Park, eds. *The Temple Church in London: History, Art and Architecture*. Woodbridge, 2010, 195-210.

Whyte, William. "Sacred Space as Sacred Text: Church and Chapel Building in Victorian Britain". In: Joe Sterrett and Peter Thomas. *Sacred Text-Sacred Space: Architectural, Literary, and Spiritual Convergences in England and Wales*. Leiden-Boston, 2011, 247-267.

Whyte, William. *Redbrick: A Social and Architectural History of Britain's Civic Universities*. Oxford, 2015.

Wiggins, Arch. R. *The History of the Salvation Army*. Vol. 4: *1886-1904*. London, 1964.

Williams, S. C. *Religious Belief and Popular Culture in Southwark, c. 1880-1939*. Oxford, 1999.

Yates, Nigel. *Buildings, Faith, and Worship: The Liturgical Arrangement of Anglican Churches, 1600-1900*. Oxford, 2000.

Yates, Nigel. *Preaching, Word and Sacrament: Scottish Church Interiors, 1560-1860*. London, 2009.

Yates, Richard. *The Church in Danger: A Statement of the Cause and of the Probable Means of Averting the Danger*. London, 1815.

Yeo, Stephen. *Religion and Voluntary Organisations in Crisis*. London, 1976.

1.2
A Varied and Remarkably Landscape of Pressure Groups
A Societal Debate as a Result in Belgium

Jan De Maeyer

That Belgium is something of an outsider in many a historical narrative is well-known. Within the time frame of this series on Church Reform 1780-1920, the territory belonged to the Austrian Netherlands until 1794, was then subsumed into the French revolutionary republic and the Napoleonic empire and in 1815 became part of the United Kingdom of the Netherlands. Eventually the country achieved independence in 1830. The new kingdom maintained a balance between tradition and modernity, grew into a modern liberal nation state endowed with the most progressive constitution in Europe at the time, poised between a constitutional, parliamentary monarchy and modern liberties.[1]

On the religious level also, the country was something of an exception, certainly in comparison with the situation in the rest of the north-western European region being discussed here. As the original home of the Spanish and later Austrian Habsburgs, the country was overwhelmingly Catholic. Other denominations such as Judaism or Protestantism were barely tolerated. Only after 1781, with the Edict of Tolerance of Emperor Joseph II (1741/1765-1790), was there any openness to non-Catholic beliefs. That the French revolutionary regimes attacked institutionalised religions is well-known; Napoleon, by contrast, concluded a marriage of convenience with the Catholic Church in the Concordat of 1801, allowing the Church to once again resume its operations, albeit under the control of the emperor. No significant developments took place during the period of the United Kingdom of the Netherlands. The situation changed radically with the liberal Belgian constitution of 1830: from now on all recognised religions could enjoy freedom of association, religion and education, to which was added freedom of the press in 1848. Because of its majority position, these new freedoms did not damage the Catholic Church, which now entered a period of religious revival and unprecedented flourishing. Given that there were few Protestants, not to mind Anglicans, in the country during the period under review, our contribution focuses mainly on the Roman Catholic Church.[2]

Why this overview of the relationship of the church(es) to the successive regimes in Belgian territory? The overview is important as it outlines the framework and limits within which the church(es) had to (re)position themselves. Pressure groups too had to take up positions and operate within this framework. What becomes immediately clear is that from 1830 on the churches especially got a new lease of life, could start to present themselves both substantively and materially, and pressure groups took shape.

The landscape of pressure groups in Belgium was remarkably heterogeneous and varied. From the viewpoint of the Material Reform of Culture, it is important to emphasise that these pressure groups were by no means confined to church organisations or church-affiliated organisations. The fact that organisations both within and outside the Church were concerned with the material expression of the Roman Catholic Church and religion in Belgium had much to do with the status of places of worship in the country. Since the time of the French regime and Napoleon's above-mentioned Concordat with the Holy See (1801, implemented from 1802), the confiscated Ancien Régime

1.2-1 The Guild of St Thomas and St Luke visiting the Netherlands in August 1891. Photo taken in Berg en Dal, near Nijmegen. All the leading figures were present, a.o. Bethune and Weale (standing, 14th and 13th from the right), Verhaegen (standing, 11th from the right), Helleputte (standing, 8th from the right) and Helbig (lying down in the grass).
[Leuven, KADOC-KU Leuven: KFD614]

1 For a general introduction to the context, see Blom and Lamberts, *History of the Low Countries*, 269-384; Lamberts, "Liberal State and Confessional Accommodation", 99-116.
2 Art et al., "Church Reform and Modernity in Belgium"; Viaene, "Religieuze herlevers en religieuze hervormers".

3   De Maeyer, "Kirchenfinanzierung seit Napoleon in Belgien"; Sägesser, "Le régime des cultes en Belgique"; Id., "De kerkfabriek als instelling in België".
4   De Maeyer, "Esprit de comparaison".

1.2-2 The Lion's Mound at Waterloo. Lithography by H. Gérard, 1842. [Amsterdam, Rijksmuseum: FMH 6036-8 Atlas van Stolk 6436-1/VIII]

churches and parish churches built since then had been given the status of 'public places of worship'.

The management of these churches or buildings was entrusted to a church council (*fabrique église / fabrica ecclesiae*), which legally was a 'public-interest institution with a special statute'. The composition and functioning of the church councils came under the supervision of both the civil authorities and the church; that is, both powers balanced each other out in the material management of the church (or, perhaps, held one another in a stranglehold). An interesting fact here is that in this Napoleonic system – which, uniquely in Europe, is still valid – the civil government or authorities committed to supplementing any financial deficits in the accounts of the church councils. In fact, from 1801-1802 the Roman Catholic Church only had usufruct of the church buildings at its disposal. In other words, it was responsible for renovations and refurbishment, for adapting to new liturgical and ecclesiological developments, and of course for re-opening negotiations, however protracted, with the civil authorities who also had to give their approval. The success of these negotiations was determined by the changing political majorities (see later tensions between anti-clericals and clericals, the so-called Culture Wars) in the country at both national and – very important – local levels.[3]

In fact, in matters of material expression or culture, the church in Belgium was not completely free and its ability to adapt or to modernise was somewhat hampered. The special legal configuration of the secular structure of the Roman Catholic Church (and of other recognised religions in Belgium) explains why religious institutes (orders and congregations) were able to assume a dynamic role in matters relating to material reform and material or cultural expression. In several respects, they formed a kind of advance guard and offered places for experimentation, both during the long nineteenth century and later in the twentieth century (which is beyond the scope of this series).[4]

The rediscovery of the past, c 1815 - c 1845

Paradoxically, the modern nation state of Belgium, with its belief in progress, modernisation (it had the first steam train on the European continent) and industrialisation, felt a strong need to legitimise itself historically. As a small country that existed by the grace of the contemporary European superpowers and considered by them to be a rather strange little bourgeois state, the new nation state, with its young dynasty and its unionist governments, endeavoured to show those at home and abroad that the country could boast of a grand (art) historical past. Leopold I – a German Coburg who, through his first marriage to Charlotte, the prematurely deceased only child and heir of King George IV, had good connections at the English court, including Queen Victoria, his niece-in-law – was deeply convinced of the importance of historical traditions and heritage. He set out to strengthen the cultural identity of the new nation by establishing museums (e.g. the Royal Museum of Fine Arts and Sculpture of Belgium), encouraging historical research (e.g. with the establish-

ment of the Royal Commission for History in 1834) and founding the Royal Commission for Monuments in 1835. By decontaminating and restoring – after decades of neglect – the country's many historic buildings, the new government also hoped to promote tourism, then gaining in popularity among the elites, to the historic towns and sites. English tourists, in particular, liked to come to Belgium for a visit to Bruges and the battlefield of Waterloo [Ill. 1.2-2], en route to the so-called 'Romantic Road/Romantische Strasse', the fortresses and castles along the banks of the Rhine. In this way, Belgium consciously responded to the Romanticism of the times. Another example is the regime's promotion of historical painting, as a way of immortalising the most important historical events and famous people. The design and placement of statues of historical figures at important intersections, in squares and parks is another example of this identity building.[5]

Providing a Belgian cultural identity was not only a government endeavour; the historically and archeologically minded urban elites also contributed by coming together in archaeological and historical societies. The oldest examples include the Société d'emulation pour l'histoire et les antiquités de la Flandre occidentale (Bruges, 1839), the Société royale des Beaux-Arts et de Littérature de Gand (Ghent, 1808) and the Académie d'archéologie de Belgique (Antwerp, 1842). All these societies formed, as it were, a kind of archaeological movement with local or regional accents, bringing together members of the aristocracy, prominent members of the bourgeoisie, wealthy lovers of antiquities and historically minded priests through their love of history, monuments and artefacts. Almost axiomatically, they became involved in the restoration of city halls and – the focus of this contribution – in the restoration of churches and (former) abbeys or monasteries.[6]

The impact of these study circles should not be overlooked, as prominent participants were also members of the aforementioned church councils. The believers among them were members of church communities or religious brotherhoods (which were very popular during the religious revival in the first half of the nineteenth century). Clerics who were more intellectually oriented also participated in these study circles during the core period of the nineteenth century, from 1830 to c 1875. The paths then diverged, under the influence of the Culture Wars. The most dynamic members devoted themselves to drawing up inventories of the art treasures and archaeological objects to be found in churches. They also paid attention to inscription stones, tombstones or devotional objects and thus fulfilled an important documentation role. In this way they grew into becoming experts in the archaeological or monumental past.[7]

Monument preservation of church buildings: a societal debate, c 1848 - c 1865

It is a remarkable fact that monument preservation became the subject of public cultural debate, albeit within the relative limits of such a discussion in nineteenth-century civil society. The debate centred on two topics: first, the position of church buildings in monument preservation and second, the expertise (or lack thereof) in this area. In a sense, monument preservation in Belgium lost its innocence or cultural idealism around 1848, largely because in the developing ideological debate about the orientation of the modern nation, church buildings had been given a symbolic value, and were even being viewed as trophies. In the second half of the nineteenth century, churches became reference points in the debate about the place of religion in society, symbolic crystallisation points in the debate as to whether the Roman Catholic Church could and should keep its regained dominant position in the revival period between 1830 and 1848. In particular, the Church's strong social presence in education and health care raised questions. Could such a position be reconciled with the con-

5 Tollebeek and Verschaffel, "Natie, geschiedenis en legitimatie"; Stynen, *De onvoltooid verleden tijd*, 13-71.
6 E.g. in Leuven, where they were involved in choosing and placing 300 images in the historic niches of the Town Hall, which became a kind of pantheon of the history of the ancient Duchy of Brabant; even the image of Victor Hugo (whose advice had been sought during a visit to the city) was added; Stynen, *De onvoltooid verleden tijd*, 76-96; Verpoest, "De architectuur van de Sint-Lucasscholen", 219-239.
7 Stynen, *De onvoltooid verleden tijd*, 76-96.

8   Viaene, "Religieuze herlevers en religieuze hervormers"; Lamberts, *The Struggle with Leviathan*, 9-309.
9   Original quotation in French, published in: Stynen, *De onvoltooid verleden tijd*, 66-67.
10 Original quotation in French, published in: Stynen, *De onvoltooid verleden tijd*, 66-68 and *La Renaissance*, 7 (1845-1846), 167.
11 Stynen, *De onvoltooid verleden tijd*, 66-67.

struction of a modern, liberal nation-state that itself wished to embody Enlightenment ideas? In short, would it be a modern nation-state incorporating a past that had developed organically, all under a heavenly canopy symbolised by church and pope, or would it be a modern society where citizens could autonomously determine the orientation of society and where church(es) and religion focused on their role as spiritual guides.[8]

In his in-depth study, Herman Stynen shows how the Royal Commission was already confronted in 1848 with the fact that a monument could also be understood ideologically and that therefore its care could become the subject of debate. This was expressed, *inter alia*, in the criticism of the Commission by *La Renaissance*, a magazine published by the Société belge pour la conservation des monuments historiques, which had been founded in 1846. [Ill. 1.2-3] What was the purpose of the Royal Commission? "So (...) what are the limits of the accomplishments of the said commission: it visits and draws up a report. (...) Is there a royal commission for historical monuments, or not?"[9] The magazine quickly denounced the unwillingness to incorporate the old chapel of St John's Hospital in Brussels into the new neighbourhood layout that accompanied the construction of the Pacheco hospice: "We dare to hope that the communal council will turn away from these Masonic prejudices against the churches, prejudices that certain members of the hospices council perhaps share, and will abandon the project to destroy the church of St Jean."[10] The magazine also repeatedly expressed its dissatisfaction with the dominant position of architects and engineers in the Royal Commission and the inadequate representation of archaeologists and (art) historians.[11]

No matter how much the Royal Commission challenged these accusations, criticism did not abate, quite the contrary. Its own provincial subcommittees especially called for a more adequate approach to the preservation of monuments and the construction of new churches (on which the Commission also had to advise). Not coincidentally, the criticism came from prominent members of what was sometimes referred to as the 'Catholic Monuments Commission', later to be called the Guild of St Thomas and St Luke,

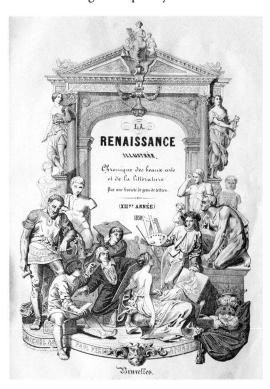

1.2-3 Title page of La Renaissance *and lithograph of the ruines of the abbey of Villers by T. Fourmois, published in the magazine in 1850.*
[Leuven, KU Leuven Libraries Artes University Library: Y10583]

namely the Liege painter and art historian Jules Helbig (1821-1906) and the English archaeologist and convert James Weale (1832-1917), who lived in Bruges. In 1861 Helbig stated bluntly: "Monuments are not built every day, but many small churches are and are very badly built; a publication that would publicise the interesting monuments in this category would be of great service."[12] In pleading for a publication with examples that might promote a more informed approach, he was joined by James Weale:

> At the moment we lack artists capable of making furnishings for our churches. The Monuments Commission must have repeatedly remarked that new altars, lecterns, and confessionals have been placed in churches that are in no way in accordance with the style of the building. I would therefore like this publication not only to make known our new monuments of architecture but to give a description of the furnishings.[13]

From 1861 on, James Weale openly expressed his hostility towards the Royal Commission. In a highly polemical manifesto issued in 1862, he accused it of "acts of vandalism", calling it "the Commission for the Denaturation of Monuments", and later the "Commission of Destruction". For Weale it was a fact that

> Much more damage has been done to our monuments in the last quarter of a century than in two centuries of contempt and neglect. (…) The word 'restore' means simply to 're-establish', 'put back in its original state' (…) from the moment that an architect's project does not have the sincere goal of returning a monument to its original state, it cannot any longer be called a restoration project.

In fact, Weale resolutely rejected the complete reconstructions advocated by a grand master such as Eugène Emmanuel Viollet-le-Duc (1814-1879), supporting rather the conservative approach of the art critic and writer John Ruskin (1819-1900), while yet not dismissing monument purification.[14]

In any case, the floodgates had been opened. The discussion about building and preserving churches and monuments segued into a public debate. The effect was that the Royal Commission pulled the brakes and from 1868 no longer allowed a general meeting of the committee with its provincial subcommittees to be held. Another consequence, highlighted by Herman Stynen, is the fact that frustration with the operation of the Royal Commission boosted the creation of more local, urban or regional study circles. Similar circles also emerged in smaller provincial towns such as Dendermonde (1862), Huy (1875) and Edingen/Enghien (1878). This development only made the debate more confusing. To remedy this, in 1884 all these archaeological, antiquities or (art) historical societies were united in the Fédération archéologique et historique de Belgique, which soon became the locus of struggles in the field of monument conservation.[15]

In the meantime, other contestants – perhaps even more professional – entered the cultural debate. A heavyweight such as the Société centrale d'architecture de Belgique (1872) with its leading and prominent magazine *L'Emulation* (1874-1939) devoted more and more space to notices about restorations and the accompanying discussions.[16] Another representative new player in the debate was the Société d'art et d'histoire du diocèse de Liège, which was founded in 1880 in Liège. The society wanted to stimulate scholarly research and to preserve the religious heritage by establishing a museum:

> it hopes above all to assemble a set of models for the study and intelligent imitation by all those who, with it, would like to reconnect the broken chain of the traditions of Christian art. (…) realising finally that religious art is the business to which we will devote ourselves, uniting our efforts to those of the schools of Saint Luke which, by the grace of God, are multiplying around us.[17]

12 Original quotation in French, published in: Stynen, *De onvoltooid verleden tijd*, 126-127.

13 Original quotation in French, published in: Stynen, *De onvoltooid verleden tijd*, 126-127. On Jules Helbig and the Royal Commission for Monuments, see also Bergmans, *Middeleeuwse muurschilderingen*, 17-55 and passim; on James Weale, see Van Biervliet, *Leven en werk van W.H. James Weale*, 25-90 and passim.

14 Original quotation in French, published in: Stynen, *De onvoltooid verleden tijd*, 127-145; Verpoest, "De architectuur van de Sint-Lucasscholen", 219-236 and passim; Van Biervliet, *Leven en werk van W.H. James Weale*, 73-82.

15 Stynen, *De onvoltooid verleden tijd*, 193-195.

16 Ibid., 195; Verpoest, "L'Emulation", 298.

17 Original quotation in French, published in: Stynen, *De onvoltooid verleden tijd*, 193-194; Van Biervliet, *Leven en werk van W.H. James Weale*, 81-87.

The above quotation highlights an important evolution. In addition to the discussion about the care of the religious patrimony, criticism had in the meantime also arisen about the injudicious, even careless attitude of the clergy towards the arts and the church's heritage. That criticism came partly from within and partly from the same critics who had levelled accusations against the Royal Commission for Monuments. The clergy were criticised for their negligence in this area, for the kitsch-like quality of the art works provided and for wanting to fill the churches during the religious revival with banal objects, and unfortunate or meaningless decorations. They were accused of lacking all knowledge of church and art history, not to mention iconology and iconography. Not surprisingly, around 1860 more and more people were calling for courses in church and art history (obviously with an emphasis on religious art) to be included in the curriculum of seminaries and in the Arts and Theology faculties at the Catholic University of Louvain (1834°). This development signalled the separation of spheres of influence discussed in the introduction to this contribution, as various Catholic initiatives were now emerging that wanted to assume sole, that is separate, responsibility for care.

Ultramontanism and the neo-Gothic: a powerful interaction, c 1865 – c 1894

That a separation of spheres began to emerge around 1865 may largely be attributed to deepening ideological tensions in Belgium. Fierce discussions arose around numerous themes and developed into an outright 'Culture War'. Within the liberal party, more and more voices were calling for an end to the dominance of the Roman Catholic Church and its occupation of the public sphere. The new liberal governments that emerged following the definitive end of Unionism in 1857 (the original governments of association between liberals and Catholics) wanted to establish a neutral public space, and to orient public life towards a secular perspective. So, in the period c 1865 - c 1884 heated debates erupted about foundations for church scholarships, the exemption of clerics and regulars from military service, the secularisation of cemeteries and above all the secularisation of primary education. The Roman Catholic Church and the Catholic elites were not silent either. They mobilised in various ways, including the great congresses of Mechelen (1863, 1864, 1867) which, in the style of the German Catholic Days, devoted several days to discussing a wide range of matters relating to the church and society at large (e.g. social themes, party formation). Among the subjects discussed were the preservation of religious heritage, the need for the development of a Christian art and the promotion of knowledge about it; also discussed, in the context of mobilising Catholics, was the possibility or desirability of establishing their own organisations where such matters would be actively debated.[18]

The fact that critical remarks were made within the Roman Catholic Church c 1860 - c 1865 was not entirely new. They had been made before, but the range now was wider. The remarks were also partly inspired by what had happened in other countries, as can be read elsewhere in this collection. We could point to France, for example (*Annales archéologiques*, with the restorations of the cathedrals), to Germany (with the Dombaühutte in Cologne and the *Organ für christliche Kunst*) and especially to England (with the Cambridge Camden Society/Ecclesiological Society and its journal *The Ecclesiologist*, and the Oxford Movement).[19] Critics of the Belgian situation were particularly interested in and partly fascinated by the discussions about the trend towards liturgical rediscovery (that is going back to the original meaning and sources of the liturgy, the historical explanation of symbols and their uses, as well as their material expression – for example, the origin of liturgical vessels, the evolution of the altar, choir and chancel screens, the placement and

18 Lamberts, *The Struggle with Leviathan*, 199-201 and passim; Id., "L'Internationale noire"; De Maeyer, "Les congrès catholiques en Belgique", 9-24; Id., "Belgium from 1831", 273-285; Id., "The Neo-Gothic in Belgium", 19-32.
19 Leniaud, *Les cathédrales au XIXe siècle*, 254-263; De Maeyer, "Pro Arte Christiana", 159-168; O'Donnell, "'An Apology for the Revival'", 35-43.
20 Strobbe, "De Gilde van Sint-Thomas en Sint-Lucas", 80-81; Verpoest, "De architectuur van de Sint-Lucasscholen", 232-233.

1.2-4 Portrait of Edmond Reusens. Lithograph by F. Van Loo. [Leuven, KADOC-KU Leuven: KPB225]

1.2-5 Title page of E. Reusens' Eléments d'archéologie chrétienne (vol. I; 1871). [Leuven, KADOC-KU Leuven: KB20747]

symbolism of the font, etc.). A central figure in this more substantive investigation was Fr. Edmond Reusens (1831-1904), who was appointed by the bishops in 1863 to be the first professor of Christian Archaeology and Antiquities at the Catholic University of Leuven. He achieved international renown with his *Eléments d'archéologie chrétienne* (1871-1875).[20] [Ill. 1.2-4 & 1.2-5]

Reusens' appointment to the chair of Christian Archaeology was part of a series of proposals to implement a more qualitative approach to heritage and Christian art within the Belgian Catholic Church. At the Mechelen congress of 1864, the vice-rector of Leuven university, Fr. Charles Cartuyvels (1835-1907) called for associations to be founded that

> by incorporating guilds imitative of those of the Middle Ages, would bring together Christian artists in a community of principles, action and mutual support, artists whose isolation condemns them to impotence, and whose abandonment delivers, defenceless, to the deleterious influences of the century.[21]

Another priest again explicitly suggested setting up a committee within each diocese that would shadow the disputed Royal Commission. The resolution proposed

> the creation of diocesan committees in every diocese in Belgium, with the responsibilities that have been specified. These committees would have a common link through the meeting of their presidents or their delegates, and would provide a central committee whose headquarters would be in Leuven, where there is an archaeological institution emanating from the Catholic Congress, or elsewhere if it were considered suitable for enabling its members to visit the monuments of various towns successively.[22]

21 Original quotation in French, published in: Strobbe, "De Gilde van Sint-Thomas en Sint-Lucas", 44-47; *Assemblée des catholiques*, 1864, 334.

22 Original quotation in French, published in: Strobbe, "De Gilde van Sint-Thomas en Sint-Lucas", 93; *Assemblée des catholiques*, 1864, 406.

23 Original quotation in French, published in: Strobbe, "De Gilde van Sint-Thomas en Sint-Lucas", 50-51 and 92-93.
24 De Maeyer, "Pro Arte Christiana", 162-166.
25 De Maeyer, "The neo-Gothic in Belgium", 31-32 and passim.

Strangely enough, these proposals could not count on much sympathy among the foremost critics of the Royal Commission, such as the aforementioned Jules Helbig, and especially James Weale. They distrusted the proposals because they had their own clearly defined programme. In fact, they were dogged followers of the ideas of Augustus Welby Northmore Pugin (1812-1852) and his paradigmatic argument that the (neo-) Gothic was the only true Christian material expression. As has often been noted, Pugin's ideas were introduced and implemented on the continent by the English architect and designer Thomas Harper King (1822-1892), a member of the British colony in Bruges (where he resided between 1849 and 1858) and by Jean-Baptiste Bethune, who, somewhat appropriately, was nicknamed Jan Gothic. James Weale was also living in Bruges at that time and, needless to mention, shared Pugin's ideas. They envisioned a completely different organisation, the aforementioned Guild of St Thomas and St Luke, which was somewhat hastily founded in 1863. Weale wrote the statutes, inspired by those of the Ecclesiastical Society. The mission was very clear: it would be "a society for the study of Christian Antiquities and for the propagation of the true principles of Christian Art". That the organisation was given the epithet 'Guild' was a deliberate reference to medieval guilds. A reference to the theologian Thomas Aquinas was intended to recall "the great church teacher who lived in the thirteenth century, the highpoint of Gothic art, and who also laid down the basic principles of aesthetics".[23]

The Guild then resolutely defended the concept of an archaeologically and liturgically based revival of the Gothic as the best style for the Roman Catholic Church and nascent organisational Catholicism (religious institutes – orders and congregations –, schools, parish halls, guild houses for emerging social organisations like workers' guilds or agricultural corporations). Perhaps nowhere else in Europe was this promoted on such a wide scale or with such enthusiasm. This was done on two levels: on the one hand, there was the Guild, which had roughly one hundred members, both clerical and lay. The organisation also had its own *Bulletin* to disseminate its ideas and in 1882 the Guild took over the famous French periodical *Revue de l'Art chrétien* (1857-1914). [Ill. 1.2-6] In annual excursions lasting several days, members visited sites at home and abroad that were considered of interest in the context of promoting true Christian art.[24] [Ill. 1.2-1]

As founders and/or teachers, the core members of the Guild were in contact with an entire network of neo-Gothic training institutes (for architects, arts and crafts practitioners), better known under the name of the St Luke Schools, which had been founded – not coincidentally – in the same period 1862/1867. The pedagogical leadership of these schools was entrusted by Jean-Baptiste Bethune and his associates such as Jules Helbig to the Brothers of the Christian Schools; however, lay people, especially architects, craftsmen and workshop owners, were also involved. All these groups enthusiastically promoted Puginian, Bethunian and St Luke neo-Gothic.[25] Thus, we see here a large, widespread pressure group at

1.2-6 *Cover of the* Revue de l'Art Chrétien, *a French magazine taken over in 1882 by the Belgian Guild of St Thomas and St Luke.*
[Leuven, KADOC-KU Leuven : KYC1092]

58

work. They introduced wherever they could the paradigm of the true Christian art, the neo-Gothic. They did this at the above-mentioned congresses of Mechelen, among the bishops and superiors of orders and congregations, in the circles of Catholic politicians or society leaders, and – not least – among the architectural engineering students at the University of Leuven. This training, spearheaded by Joris Helleputte (1852-1925), a neo-Gothic expert and engineer-architect from Ghent, started in 1867, again not by accident.[26]

However, before the Guild could take up its role fully, a sort of internal ideological or paradigmatic cleansing first took place in the 1863-1872 period. In fact, the first generation of more intellectually oriented members gradually disappeared from the guild and its international ambitions were shelved. The Tournai liturgist Mgr. Charles Joseph Voisin (1802-1872), the first chairman from 1863 until his death in 1872, espoused a more scholarly, nuanced view of the development of Christian material expression. However, his archaeological and liturgical research would not allow him to fully support a strict neo-Gothic paradigm. Another prominent member, the aforementioned Leuven professor Edmond Reusens, also had difficulty with this paradigm. He too disappeared from the Guild after 1872, even though according to Strobbe, he had acted as guide for the association. His disappearance was a loss:

> he knew better than anybody how to condense his own observations and those of these colleagues. Although he had not been endowed with the gift of eloquence, his clear presentation, which yielded nothing to the enthusiasms of the moment, instructed the most learned and effected a change in everybody's confused memories and accurate knowledge.[27]

Strobbe also confirmed that the Guild gradually gave up its international ambitions; whether this had anything to do with the increasingly paradigmatic approach is not entirely clear. It was a fact that the Aachen canon Franz Bock (1823-1899), the Catholic publisher and defender of Pierre J.H. Cuypers (the Dutch Viollet-le-Duc, 1827-1921), namely Jozef Alberdingk Thijm, and Jan Willem Brouwers had almost silently disappeared from the Guild before 1870. Bock proposed the co-option of six new honorary members in 1867, including people of such stature as August Reichensperger, Archbishop Paul Melchers of Cologne (1866-1885) and Auxiliary Bishop Johann Anton Baudri (1804-1893), but to no avail. From 1873 onwards, under Bethune, who became chairman after Voisin, the Guild retreated to its defensive Belgian position.[28]

As a pressure group, the Guild proved to be very effective. The St Luke neo-Gothic style was disseminated on different levels by different carriers or through different material expressions – such as architectural creations, interior furnishings, furniture and ironwork, stained glass, book designs, as well as magazines, neo-miniatures and devotional pictures, liturgical vestments, flags and banners, etc. Even though accomplishments such as Maredsous Abbey (1872) [Ill. 2.2-7] were major achievements, the importance of the guild lay rather in its promotion of smaller-scale projects, such as the construction of village churches or village schools of which the Vivenkapelle village site (1860-1877) at Damme-Bruges is an example. [Ill. 2.2-5] It is not surprising then that Catholic life in Flanders had a neo-Gothic tint. The zealousness of its network of patrons and the availability of St Luke pupils trained in true neo-Gothic principles enabled the paradigm to be turned into reality. Such a combination was missing elsewhere in Europe.

The promoters of St Luke Gothic were also actively involved because they saw in this design format a reflection of the ultramontane vision of church and society: the Church as the mirror of the *societas perfecta*, a well-structured whole with the position of pope and clergy clearly defined (cf. papal infallibility as a powerful symbol of this), the keepers of a medievally inspired, socially harmonious society, supported by corpo-

26 Ibid.
27 Original quotation in French, published in: Strobbe, "De Gilde van Sint-Thomas en Sint-Lucas", 81.
28 Strobbe, "De Gilde van Sint-Thomas en Sint-Lucas", 70-72.

29   De Maeyer, "The neo-Gothic in Belgium", 30-34.
30   Heynickx, *Meetzucht en mateloosheid*, 37-121; De Maeyer, "Towards a Modern Religious Art", 71-79; Id., "Esprit de comparaison", 228-236.

1.2-7 The Secret Heart House in Leuven, designed by J. F. Piscador, 1900-1903. [Leuven, KADOC-KU Leuven; postcard collection]

rate structures, and embodied in guilds of masters and craftsmen or workers with their own social solidarity projects. The promoters were so convinced of their case that they sought a single form, for everything and everyone. However, the pioneers of St Luke neo-Gothic were not supported in this by the Belgian bishops who preferred a more pragmatic approach that would leave room for variation or diversity. So in 1884-1885 the bishops did not respond to the repeated calls of the Guild of St Thomas and St Luke that the iconography of the hugely popular devotional pictures conform to the canons of St Luke neo-Gothic; the Guild had hoped in this way to combat the influence of pictures inspired by the Nazarenes – the so-called Düsseldorf pictures – as well as the Parisian Saint Sulpice pictures. Much to the displeasure of the Guild members, the bishops had no sympathy for their request, and were clearly reluctant to go so far as to put any kind of straitjacket on the tangible expression of popular devotion. The Guild therefore had to rely on its convictions, its unflagging promotion, and its distributive power through the growing network of the St Luke schools.[29]

A new time and a new Catholicism, c 1894 – c 1920

As the millennium approached, more and more criticism of the neo-Gothic paradigm began to emerge from Catholic circles of intellectuals, writers and visual artists. Increasingly, the Gothic Revival was accused of being bloodless, too inexpressive, too reliant on templates and rigid iconographic schemes. In the eyes of the critics, if ethics and aesthetics were to be separated, Catholicism could materially and artistically better express itself in contemporary materials and styles – for example, Art Nouveau and, in the 1920s, Art Deco.[30]

Strikingly, this criticism emerged in the circles of priest-intellectuals and artists connected with the Leuven Institute of Philosophy (1889), where a neo-Thomist approach to the study of aesthetics dominated. One cannot really speak here of a 'pressure group' as such, but it is interesting to see how the President – and from 1906 on, Cardinal – Désiré Mercier (1852/1906-1926) as well as professors such as Armand Thiéry (1868-1955) and priests belonging to their networks like Henry Moeller (1852-1918) or Fernand Crooÿ (1881-1949) were open to more contemporary forms of artistic expression. This was clearly evident in the professors' house in Mercier's Leo XIII Seminary – the somewhat Gaudiesque Sacred Heart House – where there was an Art Nouveau altar by the famous Liège artist Gustave Serrurier-Bovy (1858-1910). This choice was more than just a statement; it was

a sign of the more uninhibited association of this generation of neo-Thomists – and, from a societal point of view, supporters of Christian Democracy – with modernity, and with contemporary possibilities and aesthetic concepts.[31] [Ill. 1.2-7 & 1.2-8]

An important explanation for the interest of these intellectual priests in new or different developments in the world of design and art lies in their close contact, even interdependence with Brussels art circles. At the end of the nineteenth century Brussels became a hub of artistic modernism and of the contemporary avant-garde. Artistic circles such as the Cercles des Vingt or La Libre Esthétique attracted the European avant-garde to their activities, welcomed the French impressionists to their art exhibitions or maintained contact with the Wiener Secession. That a figure like Gustav Klimt (1862-1918) designed the interior of the urban mansion of the Stoclet family, built by architect Josef Hoffmann (1870-1956), speaks volumes. All these circles were receptive to and promoted the decorative arts, with the result that the ideas of William Morris and his Arts and Crafts movement became popular and caused an explosion of creativity. In 1923, the French Catholic painter – one of the co-founders in 1920 of the Ateliers de l'Art Sacré – Maurice Denis (1870-1943) looking back on his stay in Brussels, wrote:

> for us others, young French people, Belgium was therefore a privileged land, the promised land of art nouveau, where the most original forms of the visual arts, just like those of music and literature, could grow freely.[32]

Cracks developed subsequently in the neo-Gothic stronghold of the Guild of Saint Thomas and Saint Luke. Not only did dissident voices arise from among its own ranks, the Guild was also taken over by new and other forms of Catholic art or material expression. These new forms were supported by the new Catholic cultural and art circles where intellectual priests, writers, visual artists, owners of artisan workshops and wealthy patrons encountered one another. In fact, in many ways the Guild was overtaken by these new circles, partly because of the level and content of the discussions that took place there, and partly because of the quality of the creations exhibited. Perhaps even more important is that this new generation and these circles gave shape or witness to a 'new Catholicism', characterised by an authentic longing for and interest in the mystical. Converts often tended to assuage their hunger for mystical contemplation in Catholicism. Cathérine Verleysen describes this 'new Catholicism' based on the testimonies of Maurice Denis thus: "Their path to God is described in several publications that are imbued with a deep mystical inspiration. 'The intellectual activity of Catholicism had created a new spirit; religion was no longer disdained. The awakening of feeling was an undeniable fact', wrote Maurice Denis in 1939, discussing this period between the 1880s and the First World War."[33]

These new Catholic cultural circles, which were often intertwined with the emerging Christian Democracy movement and were therefore an expression of a new artistic, socio-cultural Catholicism, were quite diverse. One of the most remarkable circles consisted of the editors of the magazine, *Durendal. Revue catholique d'art et de littérature* (1894-1914/1919), itself the successor to the avant-garde *Le Drapeau* (1892-1893), which had as its subtitle *Catholiques et modernistes*. [Ill. 1.2-9] As a statement or programme announcement, this subtitle is very revealing. If *Durendal* was primarily a Brussels phenomenon, similar circles also sprang up around journals in Antwerp, journals that had more in common with the cultural Flemish Movement. These included *Le spectateur catholique. Mensuel de Science, Art et de Jugement religieux* (1897-1900) which was published simultaneously in Antwerp, Paris, Vienna, Madrid and Rome. However, this ambitious magazine was able to sustain this Europe-wide performance for only three years. The *Dietsche Warande en Belfort* periodical (1900 present) offered a

1.2-8 Design of an Art Nouveau altar by G. Serrurier-Bovy for the Secret Heart House in Leuven.
[Brussels, Royal Library of Belgium, Serrurier Archives]

31 Heynickx, *Meetzucht en mateloosheid*, 37-121; Smeyers, *Armand Thiéry*, 35-56 and 153-160; Bergmans, Coomans and De Maeyer, "Le style néogothique dans les arts décoratifs en Belgique", 53-59.
32 Original quotation in French, published in: Verleysen, *Maurice Denis et la Belgique*, 16 and passim; Brandstätter, Gregori and Metzger, *Wenen 1900*, 124-171; Thiébaut, *1900*, passim; Rosenblum et al., eds., *1900: Art at the Crossroads*, passim.
33 Original quotation in French, published in: Verleysen, *Maurice Denis et la Belgique*, 77, citing Maurice Denis, 1939, 293.

1.2-9 Cover of the catholic art magazine Durendal. *(See also col. ill. 2.)* *[Leuven, KADOC-KU Leuven: KYB1702]*

more lasting discussion forum. Of considerable significance also was the Kortrijk Arts Guild (c 1900), which had links with the highly religiously inspired impressionist, and above all expressionist art colony of Latem near Ghent. The leading figures in this colony were the sculptor and graphic artist, Georges Minne (1866-1941), the painters Gustave Van de Woestyne (1881-1947) and Albert Servaes (1883-1966).[34] Above all, the group behind *Durendal*, namely La Jeune Belgique catholique was very active and influential. They were responsible for a series of much-discussed religious art exhibitions in Brussels, the *Salons d'Art religieux* (1899-c 1920) in which foreign luminaries such as Maurice Denis participated. Another high-profile initiative along the same lines and supported by the same group was the 1912 *Exposition Internationale d'Art Religieux Moderne* in Brussels.[35]

Even if the supporters of these initiatives did not constitute any real pressure group, they still exercised a lot of influence for two reasons. First was the power of their ideas, promoted through their art magazines or exhibitions, but above all through the creative oeuvre that they presented. Second, they gained influence through their connection with the Benedictine-supported Liturgical Movement, which was reactivated after the great Catholic Congress of Mechelen in 1909, when it all but received official dispensation to insert itself in ecclesiastical and Catholic circles. This movement opted for radically new liturgical concepts (for example, removing the choir screen, placing the ambo to face the congregation, constructing a ciborium above the main altar, supplying missals in the vernacular and taking the first steps towards a dialogue celebration of the Eucharist) which had to find expression in a contemporary architecture and style. Faced with the substantive and artistic power of this movement, the old pressure guild of St Thomas and St Luke fell behind. The Liturgical Movement brought about a new material reform, although it did not make a breakthrough until the early 1920s because of World War 1.[36] However, some tensions with the neo-Gothic paradigm would continue until the 1950s, although churches were still being built in a somewhat modified neo-Gothic style well into the 1950s, and neo-Gothic devotional pictures were still being produced. In the meantime, old pressure groups, such as the Royal Commission for Monuments (and Landscapes) as well as the Centrale d'Architecture, remained active. The old Guild, weakened by the First World War, slowly faded away, its influence waning. After the war, Catholic circles also faced a new and major challenge: what design should be used to rebuild the country, and to repair or replace the many destroyed churches. In the post-war period, the St Luke Schools too gradually moved, albeit in an initially cautious and internally debated manner, towards a modernisation of religious architecture and art. It was the beginning of a new and fascinating discussion about the material design of Christianity in Belgium, a discussion and evolution that, however, falls outside the scope of this series on Church Reform.[37]

34 Heynickx, *Meetzucht en mateloosheid*, 37-121; De Maeyer, "Towards a Modern Religious Art", 71-79.
35 De Maeyer, "Towards a Modern Religious Art", 71-79; Verleysen, *Maurice Denis et la Belgique*, 81-154.
36 De Maeyer, "Esprit de comparaison", 228-236.
37 Heynickx, *Meetzucht en mateloosheid*, 33-121; Van de Perre, *Op de grens van twee* werelden, 29-99 and passim; Wouters, *Van tekenklas tot kunstacademie,* passim; Bullock and Verpoest, eds., *Living with History*, 9-28 and passim.

BIBLIOGRAPHY

Art, Jan, Jan De Maeyer, Ward De Pril and Leo Kenis. "Church Reform and Modernity in Belgium". In: Joris van Eijnatten and Paula Yates, eds. *The Churches. The Dynamics of Religious Reform in Northern Europe, 1780-1920*, 2. Leuven, 2010, 101-122.

Assemblée générale des catholiques en Belgique. Deuxième session à Malines, 29 août – 3 septembre 1864. Brussels, 1865.

Bergmans, Anna. *Middeleeuwse muurschilderingen in de 19de eeuw. Studie en inventaris van middeleeuwse muurschilderingen in Belgische kerken.* KADOC Artes, 2. Leuven, 1998.

Bergmans, Anna, Thomas Coomans and Jan De Maeyer. "Le style néogothique dans les arts décoratifs en Belgique". In: Claire Leblanc, ed. *Art Nouveau & Design. Les arts décoratifs de 1830 à l'Expo 58.* Brussels, 2005, 36-59.

Blom, J.C.H., and Emiel Lamberts, eds. *History of the Low Countries.* New York-Oxford, 1999.

Brandstätter, Christian, Daniela Gregori and Rainer Metzger, eds. *Wenen 1900.* Kerkdriel, 2018.

Bullock, Nicholas, and Luc Verpoest, eds. *Living with History. 1914-1964: Rebuilding Europe after the First and Second World Wars and the Role of Heritage Preservation / La reconstruction en Europe après la Première et la Seconde Guerre mondiale et le role de la conservation des monuments historiques.* KADOC Artes, 12. Leuven, 2011.

De Maeyer, Jan. "The Neo-Gothic in Belgium: Architecture of a Catholic Society". In: Jan De Maeyer and Luc Verpoest, eds. *Gothic Revival: Religion, Architecture and Style in Western-Europe 1815-1914.* KADOC Artes, 5. Leuven, 2000, 19-34.

De Maeyer, Jan. "Pro Arte Christiana. Catholic Art Guilds, Gothic Revival and the Cultural Identity of the Rhine-Meuse Region". In: Wolfgang Cortjaens, Jan De Maeyer and Tom Verschaffel, eds. *Historism and Cultural Identity in the Rhine-Meuse Region: Tensions between Nationalism and Regionalism in the Nineteenth Century / Historismus und kulturelle Identität im Raum Rhein-Maas. Das 19. Jahrhundert im Spannungsfeld von Regionalismus und Nationalismus.* KADOC Artes, 10. Leuven, 2008, 159-171.

De Maeyer, Jan. "Les congrès catholiques en Belgique: un signe de contradiction?". In: Claude Langlois and Christian Sorrel, eds. *Le catholicisme en congrès (XIXe-XXe siècles).* Chrétiens et Sociétés. Documents et Mémoires, 8. Lyon, 2009, 9-28.

De Maeyer, Jan. "Towards a Modern Religious Art: The Case of Albert Servaes". In: Rajesh Heynickx and Jan De Maeyer, eds. *The Maritain Factor: Taking Religion into Interwar Modernism.* Leuven, 2010, 70-83.

De Maeyer, Jan. "Kirchenfinanzierung seit Napoleon in Belgien – zwischen direkter staatlicher Finanzierung und Subventionspolitik. Ein historischer und aktueller Uberblick". In: Rudolf K. Höfer, ed. *Kirchenfinanzierung in Europa. Modelle und Trends.* Innsbruck-Vienna, 2014, 9-29.

De Maeyer, Jan. "Esprit de comparaison. Le mouvement liturgique et son interaction avec l'art sacré en Belgique dans une perspective internationale (1900-1980)". In: Claire Maingon and Nicolas Coutant, eds. *Modernité sacrée. Aspects du renouveau de l'art sacré en Normandie (1920-1960).* Mont-Saint-Agan, 2017, 219-242.

De Maeyer, Jan. "Belgium from 1831: A Model for the Ultramontane Movement in Europe or a Model Student of the Black International?" In: Olaf Blaschke and Francisco Javier Ramon Solans, eds. *Weltreligion im Umbruch. Transnationale Perspektiven auf das Christentum in der Globalisierung.* Frankfurt-New York, 2019, 273-294.

Heynickx, Rajesh. *Meetzucht en mateloosheid. Kunst, religie en identiteit in Vlaanderen tijdens het interbellum.* Nijmegen, 2008.

Lamberts, Emiel. "L'Internationale noire. Une organisation secrète au service du Saint-Siège". In: Emiel Lamberts, ed. *The Black International / L'Internationale noire. 1870-1878. The Holy See and Militant Catholicism in Europe / Le Saint-Siège et le Catholicisme militant en Europe.* KADOC Studies, 29. Leuven, 2002, 15-101.

Lamberts, Emiel. "Liberal State and Confessional Accommodation: The Southern Netherlands/Belgium". In: Keith Robbins, ed. *Political and Legal Perspectives.* The Dynamics of Religious Reform in Northern Europe, 1780-1920, 1, Leuven, 2010, 99-116.

Lamberts, Emiel. *The Struggle with Leviathan. Social Responses to the Omnipotence of the State, 1815-1965.* KADOC Studies on Religion, Culture and Society, 18. Leuven, 2016.

Leniaud, Jean-Michel. *Les cathédrales au XIXe siècle. Étude du service des édifices diocésains.* Paris, 1993.

O'Donnell, Roderick. "'An Apology for the Revival': the Architecture of the Catholic Revival in Britain and Ireland". In: Jan De Maeyer and Luc Verpoest, eds. *Gothic Revival: Religion, Architecture and Style in Western-Europe 1815-1914.* KADOC Artes, 5. Leuven, 2000, 35-48.

Rosenblum, Robert et al., eds. *1900: Art at the Crossroads.* London-New York, 2000.

Sägesser, Caroline. "Le régime des cultes en Belgique: origine et évolution". In: Caroline Sägesser and Jean-Philippe Schreiber, eds. *Le financement public des religions et de la laïcité en Belgique.* Louvain-la-Neuve, 2010, 11-41.

Sägesser, Caroline. "De kerkfabriek als instelling in België: een levensloop". In: Bart Van Dooren, ed. *Kerkfabrieken in Vlaanderen. Een erfenis van Napoleon voor de toekomst.* Bruges, 2015, 8-22.

Smeyers, Maurits. *Armand Thiéry (Gentbrugge, 1868 – Leuven, 1955). Apologie voor een geniaal zonderling.* De vrienden van de Leuvense Stedelijke Musea. Leuven, 1992.

Strobbe, Filip. "De Gilde van Sint-Thomas en Sint-Lucas (1863-1894). Een genootschap ter bevordering van de neogotiek". *Koninklijke Geschied- en Oudheidkundige Kring van Kortrijk. Handelingen. Nieuwe Reeks*, 55 (1989), 7-156.

Stynen, Herman. *De onvoltooid verleden tijd. Een geschiedenis van de monumenten- en landschapszorg in België, 1835-1940.* Brussels, 1998.

Thiébaut, Philippe, ed. *1900. Cata Galeries nationales du Grand Palais.* Paris, 2000.

Tollebeek, Jo, and Tom Verschaffel. "Natie, geschiedenis en legitimatie". In: Robert Houzee, Jo Tollebeek and Tom Verschaffel, eds. *Mise-en-scène. Keizer Karel en de verbeelding van de negentiende eeuw.* Antwerp-Ghent, 1999, 17-23.

Van Biervliet, Lori. *Leven en werk van W.H. James Weale. Een Engels kunsthistoricus in Vlaanderen in de 19de eeuw.* Verhandelingen van de Koninklijke Academie voor Wetenschappen, Letteren en Schone Kunsten van België, Klasse der Schone Kunsten, 55. Brussels, 1991.

Van de Perre, Dirk. *Op de grens van twee werelden. Beeld van het architectuuronderwijs aan het Sint-Lucasinstituut te Gent in de periode 1919-1965/1974.* Ghent, 2003.

Verleysen, Cathérine. *Maurice Denis et la Belgique. 1890-1930.* KADOC Artes, 11. Leuven, 2010.

Verpoest, Luc. "De architectuur van de Sint-Lucasscholen: het herstel van een traditie". In: Jan De Maeyer, ed. *De Sint-Lucasscholen en de neogotiek, 1862-1914.* KADOC Studies, 5. Leuven, 1988, 219-277.

Verpoest, Luc. "L'Émulation". In: *Dictionnaire de l'architecture en Belgique de 1830 à nos jours.* Antwerp, 2003, 298-299.

Viaene, Vincent. "Religieuze herlevers en religieuze hervormers". In: Robert Houzee, Jo Tollebeek and Tom Verschaffel, eds. *Mise-en-scène. Keizer Karel en de verbeelding van de negentiende eeuw.* Antwerp-Ghent, 1999, 192-197.

Wouters, Wilfried. *Van tekenklas tot kunstacademie: de Sint-Lucasscholen in België 1866-1966.* Kortrijk, 2013.

1.3
Pressure Groups and Networks in the Multi-Denominational Netherlands

Antoine Jacobs

The Netherlands has been a multi-denominational country since the sixteenth century, with freedom of conscience introduced during the period of the Republic (1588-1795). However, the Reformed Church was the only officially recognised church, and while the other Christian churches – the Roman Catholic and the various Protestant denominations – were tolerated, they were not allowed to practice their beliefs openly. Although the government became more tolerant in the course of the eighteenth century, this discrimination was ended only during the Batavian Republic (1795-1806). The Reformed Church lost its privileged status and the other denominations were given equal rights. Catholics recovered some of the churches that had been confiscated by Protestants at the time. In 1796, a Catholic church appeared once more in Amsterdam, for the first time in centuries.[1] During the period of the Kingdom of Holland (1806-1810), religious freedom was temporarily curtailed and a connection established between Church and State, which led to the state subsidising church building.[2]

During the era of the United Kingdom of the Netherlands (1815-1830), King William I (1814-1840), who reigned as an enlightened despot, also tried to gain control of the churches in his realm. Freedom of religion was not abolished, but it was restricted in various ways.[3] The king took control of the Dutch Reformed Church and tried to do the same with the Roman Catholic Church, which led to fierce resistance, especially in the Catholic South of the kingdom, in what today is Belgium. Although a concordat was concluded with the Holy See in 1827, it was never put into effect. Ministers, pastors and preachers received an annual salary and there were subsidies for and government supervision of church building.

With the accession of King William II (1840-1849), some liberalisation took place, particularly through the introduction of a liberal constitution in 1848 guaranteeing freedom of religion, assembly, association and the press. More and more voices called for the continuing ties between Church and State to be dissolved. The ministries of worship were finally disbanded in 1868.

Lobbying groups

In the course of the nineteenth century, various interest groups or networks of individuals and institutions emerged that exerted influence on ecclesiastical (building) art. These groups were most prominent among Catholics, who had freed themselves from a disadvantaged position. They included the clergy (albeit to a limited extent) and culturally important figures such as the publisher Joseph Alberdingk Thijm (1820-1889), the architect Pierre Cuypers (1827-1921), the diocesan priest Gerard van Heukelum (1834-1910) and the top civil servant Victor de Stuers (1843-1916). Institutions such as the St Bernulphus Guild, the Catholic press and certain confraternities can also be considered as having formed interest groups.

The Orthodox Reformed constituted another group that became emancipated towards the end of the nineteenth century. Their spokesperson, preacher, theologian, politician and publisher Abraham Kuyper

1.3-1 The St Bernulphus Guild, with Gerard van Heukelum (seated, 3rd from the left) en Alfred Tepe (standing at the right) during an arts tour c 1890. [Utrecht, Museum Catharijneconvent: ABM f146; photo Ruben de Heer]

1   Von der Dunk, "De katholieken en hun kerken", 152.
2   The Kingdom of Holland was ruled by Louis Napoleon Bonaparte, as a puppet state of France. Between 1810 and 1813, the Netherlands became part of the French empire. In 1813, the Northern Netherlands gained independence under the House of Orange-Nassau and became a kingdom in 1814. In 1815 the United Kingdom of the Netherlands came into existence, when the former Austrian Netherlands, the Principality of Liège and a series of small (semi-)independent principalities were added to Northern Netherlands.
3   Harinck and Winkeler, "De negentiende eeuw".

(1837-1920) developed ideas about church building and liturgy. The Gustaaf Adolf Association was active in financing Protestant church building.

In addition to the denominational interest groups, the architectural societies Maatschappij tot Bevordering der Bouwkunst (Society for the Promotion of Architecture) and Architectura et Amicitia played a modest role. Although they were neutral in terms of denomination, religious views began to play an increasingly important role in the style debate – neo-Gothic versus Classicism and Dutch Renaissance – which unfolded from around 1850. Gothic Revival was increasingly claimed and perceived as a Catholic style. Then around 1860, the ethics of restoration became a subject of discussion: was it necessary to exercise restraint, to respect and restore the existing structure as much as possible, or should the idealised 'original' condition be pursued?

Church building under state supervision

King Louis Napoleon had small houses of worship, known as Lodewijk (Louis) churches, built for the benefit of more than twenty Protestant congregations in the province of North Brabant which had been obliged to give up their churches to the Catholics.[4] In 1806, matters concerning Catholic and Protestant worship were transferred to the Ministry of the Interior. In 1815, when the United Kingdom was founded, two new ministries were established, one for the 'Affairs of Roman Catholic Worship' and one for the 'Affairs of the Reformed and other churches, except those of the Roman Catholic', both of which continued more or less until 1868.

In order to promote domestic peace in the sensitive area of religion, King William I pursued a benevolent policy with regard to church building. Priority was given to cleaning up those unseemly Catholic places of worship that recalled the barn and clandestine churches of earlier times. The director-general of the Ministry for Roman Catholic Worship soon had a full-time job planning and supervising church building. More than the Protestant communities, the impoverished Catholics had to rely on government subsidies and the number of applications grew steadily. In order to arrive at a National Church Plan, the Ministry for Roman Catholic Worship drew up an inventory of church buildings in 1818.[5] However, since the architectural quality of many newly-built churches left much to be desired, King William I decreed that no church should be built without his approval. The provincial governors had to implement this policy. They engaged engineers from the Department of Public Works (Waterstaat), who supervised the church building activities of both the Protestants and Catholics, but as the destitute Catholics needed more subsidies, government control over them was more intense.

Most churches, both Protestant and Roman Catholic, erected in the 1820s, 1830s and 1840s were built in a classicist style. Because of the involvement of the Waterstaat, these places of worship were also called *Waterstaatskerken*, although they were mostly designed by private architects and not by engineers.[6] The Waterstaat did not prescribe the style in which they should be built. In the 1830s, the first Catholic and Protestant churches in Gothic Revival style appeared.[7] The early Gothic Revival style was made *salonfähig* by the Crown Prince of Orange, later King William II, who had been introduced to it in England and had some palaces extended or built in the style.

The Protestant denominations

King William I saw religious communities as institutions of public benefit and tried to merge all Protestant denominations into one church. That attempt failed. Smaller churches, such as the Anabaptist societies, the Evangelical Lutheran Church and the Remonstrant Brotherhood maintained their independence. The majority of Protestants,

4 See the contribution by A.J.C. van Leeuwen elsewhere in this book.
5 Von der Dunk, "De katholieken en hun kerken", 142-143, 172-173.
6 Von der Dunk, "Wat er staat is zelden Waterstaat"; Id., "De katholieke kerken in Gelderland".
7 Krabbe, "Dageraad van de neogotiek". See also the contribution by A.J.C. van Leeuwen elsewhere in this collection.

about 90%, joined the Dutch Reformed Church after 1815. In 1835 the Netherlands had approximately 3000 church buildings, 57% of which belonged to the Reformed Church, 10% to the other Protestant denominations and 33% to the Catholics.

The Dutch Reformed Church adopted an enlightened, secular course, thereby alienating the Orthodox section of the faithful. In 1834, some of the these – about two to three percent – left the Reformed Church, creating a schism that has gone down in history as the Secession. The 130 municipalities involved in the secession received no state support and were initially persecuted by the government. However, under King William II, from 1840 onwards, the persecution, which had subsided, ceased altogether and a rapprochement became possible.

The secessionists renounced all claims to the Reformed Church. In exchange they were recognised by the government in 1841 and continued as the Christian Separated Congregations.[8] A number of congregations did not request government recognition and continued as Reformed Churches under the Cross. The Secession then brought about a series of further schisms within Dutch Protestantism.

In 1886 another major split occurred within the Reformed Church. Led by theologian, journalist, and politician Dr Abraham Kuyper [Ill. 1.3-2], a group of Orthodox reformed believers seceded out of dissatisfaction with what they considered to be too liberal a course of action. This second schism was called the *Doleantie* and its followers the *dolerenden* or 'doleful ones' (grieving the fate of the Reformed Church). They founded the Low German Reformed Churches.[9] In 1892 the *dolerenden* and the separated congregations merged, to become the Reformed Churches of the Netherlands.

By 1889, 49% of the population had been reformed. By 1909, membership of the Dutch Reformed Church, divided into a conservative and a liberal wing, had shrunk to 44%, while only 8% of the Dutch people belonged to the Low German Reformed Church. The Protestant part of the population was divided into a series of denominations, but together they still constituted the majority (approximately 40% were Catholic by now). Apart from the Orthodox Reformed who explicitly asserted their standing, there was no broad emancipation movement. Protestant circles had previously been concerned about the growing Catholic presence.

Between 1824 and 1868 the Dutch state financed the building of 284 Reformed churches, with construction supervised by the Waterstaat.[10] In the first half of the nineteenth century, Protestant church architecture, like the Catholic, was dominated by Classicism. However, as already noted, experiments in other architectural styles were carried out from the 1830s. In the second half of the nineteenth century the neo-Gothic could no longer be used by Protestants because of its increasing appropriation by the Catholic community, although there were sporadic exceptions, such as the Koepelkerk (1884) in the Leidsebosje in Amsterdam.[11]

1.3-2 Abraham Kuyper, c 1900. Photo. [Amsterdam, Rijksmuseum]

8   Since 1869 the Christian Reformed Churches.
9   We speak of 'churches' and not 'church' because the individual communities wanted the greatest autonomy possible.
10 Melchers, *Het nieuwe religieuze bouwen*, 40.
11 Hoogewoud, "De Koepelkerk".

Protestant church building

After the Secession, the small Reformed congregations needed their own places of worship. Generally poor, these congregations gathered in converted barns or houses. After some time they could afford austere, 'styleless' churches, although there were some church buildings in a mixture of Classicism with round and pointed arch elements.[12] Between 1848 and 1875, the Reformed congregations built 35 churches, partly with state subsidies.[13]

The *Doleantie* (1886) led to a new wave in church building as Kuyper and his followers also needed new churches. Kuyper saw church buildings primarily as meeting places and most of the Reformed places of worship belonged to the category of hall churches. In addition, gallery churches were erected on small and expensive building sites in the inner cities in order to create a maximum number of seats. As elsewhere in Europe, cross churches and central-plan churches were also built. The style was indeterminate, eclectic and occasionally neo-Gothic, and the buildings presented a subdued and austere appearance, both inside and out.[14] The Middle Ages were not the source of inspiration here; rather, the Protestant population identified with the Reformation, the freedom struggle against Spain and the establishment of the Republic. Their architects followed the church architecture of the sixteenth and seventeenth centuries, that of the Dutch Renaissance style. In short, Protestant circles lacked uniform regulations and an individual style.

Roman Catholic emancipation

After Belgium had become independent in 1830 the Netherlands shrank to its present borders. As in the former Republic, Dutch Roman Catholics again formed a minority of about 30% of the population.[15] In the first half of the nineteenth century, the convert, historian, and journalist Joachim George le Sage ten Broek (1775-1847) pioneered Catholic emancipation, directing his apologetic and polemical writings against Protestantism and liberalism.[16] He was not concerned about ecclesiastical (building) art.

About the middle of the nineteenth century Roman Catholic emancipation was given a boost when in 1840 King William II (1840-1849) rescinded the law abolishing convents. From then on, religious orders and congregations flourished, as in other European countries. New women's congregations were founded by local priests to work especially in the fields of education, health care and charitable work.[17] In the later nineteenth and early twentieth century, Dutch monastic life was given a new lease of life when German and French congregations, fleeing anticlerical legislation in their own countries, sought refuge in the Netherlands. They settled mainly in the Catholic south, in the dioceses of Roermond and 's-Hertogenbosch.[18]

Of even greater importance for Catholic emancipation was the introduction of the democratic constitution of 1848. This paved the way for the reintroduction of the episcopate in 1853, despite the massive protest of the Protestant majority — the so-called 'April Movement'. This more or less coincided with the sharp rise in popularity of the neo-Gothic (architectural) style.

Thijm and Cuypers

In the early 1850s, inspired by their thorough study of medieval monuments and history, Joseph Albert Alberdingk Thijm, a Roman Catholic merchant, editor, and writer from Amsterdam, and Pierre Cuypers, a Roman Catholic architect from Roermond, became the Dutch heralds of the 'true Gothic style'.[19] They met in 1854, quickly became friends, and, in 1859, even brothers-in-law. Thijm enthusiastically promoted Cuypers' true Gothic style, which was based on French examples of the thirteenth century. The two complemented one another, Thijm as the theoretician and Cuypers as the practical man. Their advocacy of Gothic art and archi-

---

12 Van Swigchem, "De kerkgebouwen van de christelijk gereformeerden".
13 Melchers, *Het nieuwe religieuze bouwen*, 49.
14 De Groot, "De kerkgebouwen van de Doleantie".
15 On denominational relations in the Netherlands, see: Knippenberg, *De religieuze kaart van Nederland*.
16 Gorris, *J.G. Le Sage ten Broek*.
17 See: Van Heijst, Derks and Monteiro, *Ex caritate*.
18 The bishops of Breda, Haarlem and Utrecht were very reluctant, not to say unwilling, to give foreign religious permission to settle in their dioceses. They wanted to avoid problems with the Protestants.
19 Geurts et al., eds., *J.A. Alberdingk Thijm*; Van der Plas, *Vader Thijm*.
20 Other historical styles like the neo-Romanesque are rather rare in the Netherlands of the nineteenth and early twentieth centuries.
21 De Jong, *Bijdrage tot de kennis der gothische bouwkunst*.
22 Pey, *Herstel in nieuwe luister*, 196.
23 Ibid., 96-108, 121-138; Geurts, *Pascal Schmeits*, 29.

tecture made this the Roman Catholic style par excellence.[20]

Thijm was not the only one to claim the Gothic as the typical Catholic architectural style; this had already been done in 1847 by the painter and art historian Servaas de Jong.[21] Thijm laid claim to the Gothic for Catholics in his own cultural journal, *De Dietsche Warande*, which appeared from 1855. He vehemently criticised the official classicist style as well as the picturesque Gothic style and their architects, which he described as 'pagan bathhouse architecture' or 'confectioner architecture'. Thijm had an aversion to the early Gothic Revival style because it was not based on art historical research and used inferior materials such as stucco. He also elaborated his ideas about iconography and the orientation of churches. His articles were brought together in a separate monograph *De Heilige Linie* (1858), which continued to influence church building for almost a century. Thijm based his ideas concerning the Gothic and church building partly on the European discourse on the subject, particularly the writings of Pugin, Reichensperger and Viollet-le-Duc, and corresponded with these forerunners of the neo-Gothic movement in Western Europe. [Ill. 1.3-3 & 1.3-4]

For Dutch Catholics, each Gothic spire became a landmark of their advancing emancipation and their ultramontanism. Between 1796 and 1840 approximately 150 new Catholic churches were built, and another 506 between 1853 and 1909, mostly in neo-Gothic style.[22]

The bishops and the clergy

The Dutch bishops – and in their wake most of the clergy – generally showed little interest in architecture and the visual arts. Nor was any attention paid to this in the training of priests.[23]

However, the bishops did not oppose the introduction of the Gothic Revival. The five churches that were elevated to the status of cathedral in 1853 became, some more than others, advertisements for the neo-Gothic style. In 's-Hertogenbosch, the medieval St John's Cathedral was restored and reconstructed from 1859 in neo-Gothic style. St Catherine's Church in Utrecht, which was also elevated to a cathedral, was decorated

1.3-3 J.A. Alberdingk Thijm in his study. Lithography by J.C. Braakensiek, published in De Amsterdammer, 24 March 1889.
[Amsterdam, Rijksmuseum]

1.3-4 Title page of Thijm's De Heilige Linie, *dedicated to the Gothic Revival publishers and architects Sulpiz Boisserée, Augustus W.N. Pugin and Jean-Baptiste-Antoine Lassus, 1858. [Leuven, KU Leuven Libraries Artes University Library: A9224]*

in the same style.[24] Local art studios were all involved in the interior furnishing of the austere cathedral of St Christopher in Roermond. Pierre Cuypers again drew up the designs for the neo-Gothic cathedrals of Breda (built in 1876) and Haarlem.[25] Haarlem however was built in neo-Romanesque style, because in the twentieth century Catholics too began to resist the ubiquity of the neo-Gothic style.

In 1865 the Dutch episcopate convened a provincial synod, in which it was laid down that the style of interior furnishings should match the style of the church building as closely as possible. However, not one style was preferred, though in practice the neo-Gothic was then by far the preferred Catholic style.

Not all priests were ignorant of ecclesiastical (building) art. In 1852, Fr. Theodore Ariëns encouraged Cuypers to set up an ecclesiastical art studio in Roermond, together with the vestments manufacturer Frans Stoltzenberg and the sculptor Edmond Georges.[26] In the second half of the nineteenth century Roermond became a centre of neo-Gothic art.[27] [Ill. 1.3-5]

Cuypers introduced Thijm to several priests of the diocese of Roermond, who were appointed as 'professors' (teachers) in the episcopal colleges of Roermond and Rolduc and the major seminary in Roermond.[28] The group included Jan Willem Brouwers (1831-1893) and the later deacon of Maastricht, François Xavier Rutten (1821-1893). The latter became a veritable font of information about ecclesiastical art and architecture for his colleagues, as well as being a promoter of the Gothic Revival.[29]

Jan Willem Brouwers was a priest teacher at the Diocesan College of Roermond and became a close friend of both Thijm and Cuypers. A skilled writer and orator, he frequently promoted Cuypers' work in speech and writing. He also acted as Cuypers' ghostwriter. Between 1863 and November 1870, Brouwers was editor of the Catholic daily newspaper *De Tijd*.[30] In all probability he owed the job to Thijm and moved to Amsterdam for this purpose. Because of their close cooperation, Alberdingk Thijm, Brouwers and Cuypers became known locally as the 'Catholic ABC'.[31]

Neither Cuypers nor Thijm ever launched the idea of founding a guild for ecclesiastical art and architecture. Perhaps they thought it unnecessary as the hierarchy and lower clergy were already advocating the Gothic style, studio assistants were loyal to their patrons and neither the government nor the Protestants were posing any challenges. Perhaps Thijm also feared for his intellectual freedom, while Cuypers, who had a large network thanks to his studio and his many young architect-apprentices, was afraid that a guild would impede his artistic and business freedom.[32]

---

24 De Blaauw, "De kathedralen van 1853", 243.
25 Ibid.
26 Schiphorst, *Een toevloed van werk*.
27 Jacobs and Van Leeuwen, "Roermond as Centre for Religious Art"; Van Ruyven-Zeman, "De firma Nicolas te Roermond".
28 Geurts, "Enkele minder bekende vrienden".
29 Jacobs, "Frans Xavier Rutten".
30 Schrama, *Dagblad De Tijd*, 65-68.
31 Van Leeuwen, *Pierre Cuypers*, 14, 28, 92, 103, 149, 168, 218, 266. Although an important role has been attributed to Brouwers, no biography has appeared to date.
32 Pey, *Herstel in nieuwe luister*, 212-213.

Catholic museums

In the second half of the nineteenth century, three museums for Catholic ecclesiastical art were opened in the Netherlands, following in the footsteps of other countries. The aim was to preserve the old religious art as well as glorify the country's own past. The museums thus acted as lobby groups. In the archdiocese of Utrecht, Fr. Gerard van Heukelum was an ardent advocate of neo-Gothic ecclesiastical art and architecture. In 1858 he had come into contact with the Cologne priest and antiquarian Franz Bock.[33] He had also attended the *Katholikentag* in Cologne that year where he became acquainted with August Reichensperger and became fascinated by Christian or Gothic art. Once home in Utrecht, Van Heukelum began to collect information about old ecclesiastical art and wrote some articles on the subject which he submitted to Alberdingk Thijm for publication in *De Dietsche Warande*. Thijm, however, did not publish the contributions as he considered them too superficial. Then in 1862 Van Heukelum opened the Archbishop's Museum in Utrecht, near the cathedral church of St Catherine.[34] The initiative did not go unchallenged in Protestant-dominated Utrecht. In founding the museum, Van Heukelum was inspired by examples in Germany where some episcopal museums already existed.[35] [Ill. 1.3-6]

Van Heukelum's initiative was widely imitated. In 1869, Fr. J.J. Graaf also founded an Episcopal Museum for Ecclesiastical Antiquity, Art and History in the diocese of Haarlem. In Amsterdam, the Amstelkring was started in 1884 to collect objects relating to Amsterdam's Catholic past. The clandestine church of O.L. Heer op Solder was purchased for the collection in 1887 and opened the following year as a Roman Catholic Museum.[36]

The treasury of the Saint Servatius Church in Maastricht can also be counted as one of the museums. The relics of this church had been kept in a reliquary for centuries. Between 1871 and 1873, Dean F.X. Rutten had the shrines and reliquaries restored or replaced with new ones. On 27 July 1873, the restored objects were presented to the people in a procession across the church square (the Vrijthof), and then placed in the relics chapel in the cloister of the St Servatius' church, decorated by Pierre Cuypers.[37] The holy objects and their partly centuries-old shrines

1.3-5 Pierre Cuypers at his desk. Photo. [Roermond, Cuypershuis]

1.3-6 The Archbishop's Museum in Utrecht, c 1905.
[Utrecht, Museum Catharijneconvent: ABMf140; photo Ruben de Heer]

33 Franz Bock (1823-1899) specialised particularly in historical ecclesiastical textile art.
34 The Archdiocesan Museum has since been merged into the St Catherine's Convent Museum.
35 The Diözesanmuseum of Cologne opened in 1855.
36 Pey, *Herstel in nieuwe luister*, 94.
37 Jacobs, "Frans Xavier Rutten", 122, 143-144.

could be admired by scholars, including the members of the St Bernulphus Guild in 1874, but also venerated by believers.[38] It should be noted that the less prestigious treasury of the Church of Our Lady in Maastricht was also open to the public.

The Guild of St Bernulphus

Along with a museum, Van Heukelum also established the St Bernulphus Guild in 1869.[39] By organising lectures and excursions, the guild aimed to educate the clergy in ecclesiastical art. Here Van Heukelum was inspired by the Belgian Guild of St Thomas and St Luke (1863) and by various German Kunstvereine that had emerged in the 1850s.[40] The guild's patron and promoter was Archbishop A.I. Schaepman (1868-1882). In principle, all Dutch priests could become members, but in practice the approximately 200 members were mainly secular priests from the archdiocese of Utrecht and the diocese of Haarlem. However, the guild was not restricted to the clergy of these dioceses.[41] From 1880 onwards, lay people who wanted to help the guild's cause either as performing artists or as friends of the arts could also become full members. [Ill. 1.3-1 & 1.3-7]

Van Heukelum gave his guild more cachet by, among other things, offering patron membership to the Dutch bishops and appointing as honorary members persons from home and abroad who had distinguished themselves in the field of Christian (neo-Gothic) art and architecture.[42] One would expect Alberdingk Thijm to have been an honorary member also, but he is missing from this list. The two men did not get along: Thijm did not regard Van Heukelum as an intellectual equal and must have chafed at Van Heukelum's influence on the above-mentioned Archbishop Schaepman.

As a true adherent of the Gothic Revival, Van Heukelum considered medieval art (in this case, Gothic) to be the only true art. In his view, the Reformation had started a decline that continued into the nineteenth century and could only be halted by returning to medieval examples. If ecclesiastical art improved, society would benefit. Gothic art was still blocked, however, and its advocates (Van Heukelum mentions Pugin, Didron, Reichensperger and Bock in this context) had to remain militant. Incidentally, his opinion was not shared by the influential and scholarly Haarlem priest, Mgr. Dr. Theodore Borret (1812-1890), also a patron of the guild, who argued in writing against the claim that Gothic was the only Christian art. In 1873 Van Heukelum began publishing *Het Gildeboek. Tijdschrift voor kerkelijke kunst en oudheidkunde*, in which he proclaimed his views and wrote articles on medieval ecclesiastical art. However, only three incomplete volumes appeared (1873, 1877, 1881), and by 1881, the *Gildebo*ek was already defunct due to a lack of copy. After that, between 1886 and 1900, annual reports were published in which articles and reports of study trips were also included. [Ill. 1.3-8]

Van Heukelum gathered a few young architects and artists around him with whom he worked out his ideas on the ideal church building. He was inspired by the later Gothic architecture of the fifteenth and sixteenth centuries in the Netherlands (especially Utrecht, Gelderland and Overijssel) and the German region of the Lower Rhine. He collaborated closely with the architect Alfred Tepe (1840-1920), the sculptor Friedrich Wilhelm Mengelberg (1837-1919) and the stained glass painter Heinrich Geuer (1840-1904), all three of German descent, and the gold- and silversmith Gerard Bartel Brom (1831-1882). They came known as the 'Utrecht Quartet', sharing Van Heukelum's ideals and decorating many churches in the archdiocese. Utrecht became another important centre of religious art and like Roermond had a variety of workshops.[43]

Van Heukelum regarded the guild as an instrument of ecclesiastical art policy and within the archdiocese of Utrecht nobody could ignore him or the guild. This led to tensions and conflicts with building pastors and architects. The latter group saw with

---

38 "Onze Kunstreis" in *De Maasbode*, 24 Sept. 1874.

39 See: Looijenga, *De Utrechtse School in de neogotiek* and "Die Utrechter neugotische Schule".

40 Paderborner Diözesan-Kunstverein (1852), Kunstverein der Diözese Rottenburg (1852) and the Verein für Christliche Kunst (1853, Cologne).

41 This can be deduced from the annual reports that appeared between 1886-1900. The membership fluctuated around 200 in these years.

42 "Statuten van het St. Bernulphus-Gilde".

43 See also the contribution by A.J.C. van Leeuwen elsewhere in this book.

44 Lankhorst, "Tussen commercie en apostolaat", 38-41.

45 Gijsen, *Joannes Augustinus Paredis*, 257.

46 Lankhorst, "Tussen commercie en apostolaat", 42-45.

47 From around 1870, more and more magazines were published by orders and congregations. However, these were mainly aimed at their own orders/congregations and were primarily devotional in nature.

regret that commissions for church buildings were almost always given to the architect Tepe. Anyone designing a church in the archdiocese had to comply with the regulations of the St Bernulphus Guild – even a great figure like Cuypers was not exempt. A weak point in the organisation of the guild was that architects and artists were excluded from full membership until 1880. Another weak point was Van Heukelum's autocratic leadership which accounted, at least partly, for the decline in the enthusiasm of the initial years. Until after Van Heukelum's death, the Guild continued to advocate the neo-Gothic style.

The press

Magazines and newspapers were also of great importance for the dissemination of the new ideas about ecclesiastical art. The *éminence grise* of the Catholic press was Le Sage ten Broek, who was the first to establish a Catholic newspaper in the years 1822 and 1823. A few years earlier, in 1818, he had started the much-read magazine, *Godsdienstvriend*. Alberdingk Thijm also played an important role in this area: in 1845 he was one of the founders of the newspaper *De Tijd* which was published in Amsterdam.

At the time of its inception, *De Tijd* was the only newspaper with an outspoken Catholic signature.[44] Most 'Catholic' newspapers followed a neutral line on religious matters until around 1870. Initially, the Dutch episcopate preferred not to see priests as editors: writing about political matters could harm their exercise of office, and an overly clerical editorial staff was not considered to be in the best interests of the newspaper itself. However, one of the editors of *De Tijd*, Judocus Smits, was a priest. Around 1850 *De Tijd* had only one hundred subscribers, but over the years it developed into the leading Catholic newspaper with a national reputation. The newspaper, *De Maas en Roerbode*, founded by Bishop Paredis in 1855, with Fr. H. Lom as editor, was also a purely Catholic newspaper, which was started as a counterbalance to the liberal newspaper, *De Volksvriend*.[45]

Catholic newspapers in the Netherlands flourished after the newspaper stamp tax was abolished in 1869.[46] At the same time, the increasing need for news among the Catholic population led to the creation of many regional and local daily and weekly newspapers that were explicitly Catholic, while already existing newspapers now openly declared themselves Roman Catholic. Priests mostly acted as (chief) editors.[47] Reports were often included on the completion of new churches, the restoration of old churches and the installation of stained-glass windows or altars. The articles were gener-

1.3-7 *Gerard van Heukelum (left) with Stuart Knill, president of the English Guild of St Gregory and St Luke, and Jean-Baptiste Bethune, founder and chairman of the Belgian Guild of St Thomas and St Luke, during the trip of the Belgian Guild to the Netherlands in 1891.*
[Leuven, KADOC-KU Leuven: KFA11665; photo J. Casier]

1.3-8 Cover of the first edition of Het Gildeboek, *the organ of the St Bernulphus Guild, 1873.*
[Leuven, KU Leuven Libraries Artes University Library: Y12073]

Financing

After government subsidies ended in 1868, the Catholic and Protestant church councils had to find ways to finance their new building plans themselves. Parishioners donated money or building materials and provided manual assistance. In addition, loans were taken out. In the diocese of Haarlem, the parishes took out loans which were then offered to investors through Catholic family businesses active on the Amsterdam Stock Exchange. These were mostly ecclesiastical institutions from within and outside the diocese. This method was so successful in raising money that it became possible to build a large number of churches. As the ecclesiastical infrastructure with schools and other social institutions became more and more extensive, the diocese of Haarlem established a 'Fund for Poor New Parishes' in 1916.[52]

The dioceses did not have the means to support the parishes, unless they had a special fund at their disposal as in 's-Hertogenbosch, where the wealthy Rotterdam stocks and shares dealer Jan Grewen (1839-1909) left the diocese some 1½ million guilders for the building of churches. This fortune was transferred to the diocesan 'Church Building Foundation' in 1911, which aimed to build churches and chapels in honour of Saint Anthony of Padua. Parish priests and church councils with building plans could turn to the fund for a financial contribution. From 1907 on, dozens of churches in the diocese of Den Bosch were fully or partially financed by Grewen and his fund.[53]

In the almost exclusively Roman Catholic provinces of North Brabant and Limburg, where there were close ties between the civil and ecclesiastical authorities, the provincial governments and/or municipalities endowed the building and furnishing of parish churches.[54]

In the province of Limburg and the region of Zeelandic Flanders (the southern part of the province of Zeeland), the local government was even obliged until 1 January 1877, under certain conditions, to provide

ally laudatory and far removed from evaluative art criticism. With the exception of the *Gildeboek* mentioned above, there were no journals devoted entirely to ecclesiastical art. The richly illustrated weekly *Katholieke Illustratie* (Catholic Illustration), which appeared from 1867 onwards, devoted its attention to old and contemporary ecclesiastical architecture and art among many other themes. The beautiful steel engravings of churches, chalices, reliquaries, and the like brought (neo-)Gothic architecture to the attention of a wide audience.[48]

On the Protestant side, the politician and historian Guillaume Groen van Prinsterer can be considered the first 'Christian' journalist of the Netherlands. Between 1850 and 1855 he brought out the Christian paper *De Nederlander*. However, circulation was low, with only about 350 subscriptions.[49] On 1 April 1872 the first issue of *De Standaard* ran off the press. This newspaper was an initiative of Abraham Kuyper, and until his death *De Standaard* was his mouthpiece on all matters including church building and liturgy.[50] Regional Protestant newspapers were also published in the last quarter of the nineteenth century.[51]

48 On *Katholieke Illustratie* see: Hottinga, *De Katholieke Illustratie*.
49 Puchinger, "Nederlandsche Gedachten"; Janse, "Krant en verzuiling", 78.
50 Van der Ros, "De Standaard".
51 Van de Ros, *Geschiedenis van de christelijke dagbladpers*.
52 Landheer, *Kerkbouw op krediet*.
53 Margry, "Bouwen onder Antonius", 26-29, 34.
54 Delheij and Jacobs, *Kerkenbouw in Limburg*. However, monasteries were excluded from these subsidies.

financial support to the church councils, if they ran into financial difficulties. In 1859 contributions amounted to more than 25%. This requirement resulted from the Imperial Decree of 30 December 1809, which was still valid in areas that were part of France between 1794 and 1814.[55] In Limburg, besides the provincial and local authorities, the state and private coal mines also provided building subsidies for the various denominations at the beginning of the twentieth century.[56]

In 1868 the Department of Public Affairs (Waterstaat) ceased to supervise building activities and henceforth became involved only in restorations that were subsidised by the government. From 1870 on large sums were distributed by the Ministry of Internal Affairs, in which the influential Roman Catholic legal secretary Victor de Stuers played a key role as head of the Department of Arts and Sciences.

In addition to taking out loans, Protestant church councils with building plans could also call on the Gustaaf Adolf Association. A Dutch branch of the German Gustav Adolf Verein (1832) was founded in Leiden in 1853 and became independent in 1854. The aim of the association was to give financial support to Protestant congregations in the diaspora – anywhere in the world – so that they would not be lost to Protestantism. In concrete terms this meant financial help for ministers and teachers, but also for the construction of churches and schools. The Gustaaf Adolf Association was internationally oriented and in principle helped all Protestant denominations, leading the Orthodox Protestants generally to keep their distance. The Association had several local branches in the Netherlands with 4115 members in 1899.[57] Among other things, it provided subsidies for the construction of churches in the Catholic south of the Netherlands, usually involving modest amounts for modest construction projects.[58]

Religious confraternities and associations

The nineteenth century was also the heyday of religious confraternities. Most, however, functioned purely on a parish level and were not focused on ecclesiastical art and architecture – except for the Vereniging tot Bevordering van het Allerheiligste Sacrament en tot versiering der behoeftige kerken (Association for the Promotion of the Most Blessed Sacrament and for the Adornment of Needy Churches).[59] From about 1859 onwards, branches of the association – in this case an (arch)confraternity – were established in thirteen Catholic parishes. It was started by the Belgian countess Anna de Meeûs d'Argenteuil (1823-1904), who had founded the Institute of Religious of Perpetual Adoration in 1857. In 1870 a convent of the Institute was opened in Rotterdam and the first Dutch branch was established in 1859 in Rotterdam's Church of Our Lady as a subsection of Brussels. Soon branches were founded in other places as well, including Roermond which was started in 1864 at the instigation of Bishop Paredis and consisted of ladies from well-to-do backgrounds, who mostly sewed vestments.[60] In 1895 the Confraternity of the Most Blessed Sacrament comprised a series of local branches with altogether about 40,000 members, which since 1859 had donated church furniture and vestments worth 860,054 guilders to poor churches. They combined piety with practical help in cash and kind, mostly in the form of mass vestments and altar linen.[61]

In order to raise the necessary funds for the restoration of the O.L. Vrouwe Munsterkerk in Roermond, the Association for the Restoration and Preservation of Our Lady of the Munster Church in Roermond, also known as the Maria Munster Association, was established in 1862, inspired by the Central Dombauverein of Cologne. Its board was drawn from the Catholic elite (clerical and lay) of the city. To achieve its goal, the association organised collections in the city and issued leaflets to raise funds. In addition,

55 De Coninck, *Een les uit Pruisen*, 268-272.
56 Jacobs and Wiekart, "De financiering van de katholieke kerkenbouw", 104-105; Korporaal, "De subsidies van de Staatsmijnen", 33-37.
57 There is no study as yet of the Gustaaf Adolf Association. See Kok, "Gustaaf Adolf Vereniging"; *Het Vaderland*, 14 January 1899.
58 Two definite projects were the Protestant churches in Valkenburg (1891) and Weert (1910). See: Compagner et al., *Twee heilige huisjes*, 58; "Kerknieuws", *Het nieuws van den dag: kleine courant*, 16 June 1891. These are just arbitrary examples.
59 Different names such as Vereniging van de Eeuwigdurende Aanbidding en tot steun aan arme kerken in Nederland (Association for Perpetual Adoration and in support of poor churches in the Netherlands) or in short, the Blessed Sacrament Association were also used.
60 Geelen, "Bewaard en opgeborgen", 61; *Maas en Roerbode*, 12 November 1864. As yet no study of this association has appeared.
61 Nolet, *Katholiek Nederland. Encyclopaedie*, 277-280; *Vereeniging tot bevordering der vereering*; Suenens, *Humble Women, Powerful Nuns*.

1.3-9 Memorial stones in the pilgrimage church of Our Lady of the Sacred Heart in Sittard given by among others the Dutch bishops, the bishop of Liège and the archbishop of Cologne. At the bottom the first stone of Pope Pius IX. [Photo J. Houben, 2007]

it endeavoured to hire experienced architects and to have building plans and specifications drawn up. The association continued until the 1880s.[62]

On one occasion only did a confraternity take charge of a construction project. In Sittard, the Ursuline archconfraternity of Our Lady of the Sacred Heart commissioned the eponymous pilgrimage church, which was elevated to the status of a basilica minor in 1883. The archconfraternity had hundreds of thousands of members at home and abroad. The neo-Romanesque-Gothic church was built between 1875 and 1878 and was financed by the faithful. Through its own monthly bulletin, the *Maandschrift van O.L. Vrouw van het H. Hart*, subscribers were informed about the progress and were called upon to finance the building by purchasing votive tiles. Pope Pius IX donated the foundation stone and the Dutch episcopate as well as the (arch)bishops of Cologne, Liège and Mechelen donated votive stones, while donations by archconfraternity members paid for the interior furnishings. [Ill. 1.3-9] Between 1891 and 1902 a covered Stations of the Cross was built in the same way across from the church.

The architectural societies

The lack of a distinctive architectural style, bad taste and inadequate architectural education were the motives that led to the foundation of the Society for the Promotion of Architecture in 1842.[63] In addition to architects, other professional groups were also represented. The neo-Gothic style was already being used sporadically and the Society was not a priori opposed to this new style. However, the unrelenting propaganda for the neo-Gothic style by Thijm, a member of the Society since 1851, led to fierce disputes. The Society was initially neutral on the subject, and its publication, *Bouwkundige Bijdragen* (Building Contributions) provided a forum for all opinions. From the late 1850s onwards, discussions were held about the question of what the national architectural style should be: Gothic Revival or Classicism. Most of the members respected the Gothic as a historical style but considered it unsuitable for their own time. The architecture of the Dutch Renaissance should be the national style, since it had originated during the Eighty Years' War (1568-1648), when the foundations for an independent Netherlands had been laid. The majority of the members of the architectural association Architectura et Amicitia (founded in 1855) were of the same opinion.[64] The style debate first focused on the competitions for the National Monument in The Hague and the 'Muzeum Koning Willem I' in 1863. Cuypers submitted neo-Gothic designs for both projects and was supported by Brouwers and Thijm. The architect Leliman, a prominent member of the Society, and the writer Carel Vosmaer were among the fiercest opponents. Leliman thought Gothic was unsuitable as a contemporary architectural style, while Vosmaer thought it was too Catholic. Another style discussion developed around the construction of the Rijksmuseum (from 1875). [Ill. 1.3-10] Meanwhile, the style debate had become more and more a matter of opinion.

This debate about style did not play a role in the construction and furnishing of new churches: after all, neo-Gothic had been the house style since 1850. However, dissension flared up again with the restoration of medieval monuments. The top civil servant De Stuers, considered to be the founder of Dutch monument conservation, criticised the absence of a national monument policy in his publication *Holland op zijn smalst* (Holland at its narrowest). In 1874, the Board of Government Advisers for Historic and Art Monuments was established to advise the Interior Minister and a year later De Stuers was appointed head of the Arts and Sciences Department of the Interior Ministry. He oversaw the granting of subsidies for historic preservation and was thus able to exert great influence.

The government advisers could have functioned as a pressure group, had it not

1.3-10 'Dedication of the Bishop's Palace, called the Rijksmuseum at Amsterdam.' Cartoon on the occasion of the opening of the Rijksmuseum in Amsterdam, with de Stuers, Thijm and Cuypers. Lithograph by J. Holswilder, 1885.
[Amsterdam, Rijksmuseum]

been for the fact that they were constantly at odds with each other. The two government advisers De Stuers and Cuypers formed a duo that effectively propagated Viollet-le-Duc's reconstructive ideas about restoration. They soon came into conflict with other members of the board who advocated greater respect for the existing building. Moreover, the government adviser Vosmaer thought that the restorations had an overly Gothic and therefore Catholic appearance. De Stuers and Cuypers were also blamed for the fact that too much subsidy money flowed into restoration projects in Catholic North Brabant and Limburg. The board was disbanded in 1879, after which De Stuers and Cuypers supervised every major restoration project, including Catholic and Protestant churches, for nearly thirty years.[65] However, De Stuers, although Catholic, was primarily motivated by the historical importance of buildings. Unlike Cuypers, he was not fixated on the Middle Ages and did not feel the compulsion to reclaim the Catholic past.[66]

62 Jacobs, "Frans Xavier Rutten", 100-101; Van Leeuwen, "Pierre Cuypers en het interieur van de Munsterkerk", 271-272.
63 On the inadequate architectural education, see: Pey, *Herstel in nieuwe luister*, 196ff.
64 Schilt and Van der Werf, *Genootschap Architectura et Amicitia*.
65 Pey, *Herstel in nieuwe luister*, 163-171.
66 Perry, *Ons fatsoen als natie*, 148-149.

67 Donkers, "Katholieke Kunstkring De Violier".
68 "Kunst en Wetenschap. St. Benedictusgilde", *De Tijd*, 21 December 1901.
69 In the beginning De Violier was called the St Benedict's Guild, but that name was soon replaced by De Violier, though Benedict remained its patron saint. Van Heukelum welcomed the foundation of De Violier, but regarded it not as a sister association, but as an association that operate in the same terrain. See: "Kunst en Wetenschap. St. Benedictusgilde", *De Tijd*, 21 December 1901.

Moving away from neo-Gothic dogma

In the 1890s the neo-Gothic (and neo-Romanesque) style became more rigid and came in for increasing criticism, not only from liberals and Protestants, but also (young) Catholic architects, artists, and intellectuals. This development may be noted in other European countries as well. In the Netherlands, the more progressive Roman Catholic intellectuals gathered around the magazine *Van Onzen Tijd* (From our time) and the Katholieke Kunstkring De Violier (The Lily Catholic Art Circle).[67]

At the general assembly of the St Bernulphus Guild in 1896, some members from Amsterdam proposed that membership of the guild should also be open to artists "who are not exactly of the same artistic persuasion, so that they can become better acquainted with the principles of Christian art". Van Heukelum was opposed to this, arguing that the guild had to retain its individuality and he advised the gentlemen from Amsterdam to found their own association, to which the St Bernulphus Guild could then lend its support.[68]

In the same year, the architect Joseph Cuypers – son of Pierre Cuypers – founded the Guild of Saint Thomas and Saint Luke, which was intended to become a society for Catholic art-workers. Unfortunately, the guild lacked vitality and was dissolved after five years.

The Saint Bernulphus Guild and the Guild of Saint Thomas and Saint Luke together gave rise to the Violier Art Circle, which was founded in Amsterdam on 7 December 1901.[69] In 1906 and 1907 local branches were established in The Hague and Rotterdam, but they lasted for only a few years. The initiative was taken by the architects Jan Stuyt (a close friend and associate of Pierre and Joseph Cuypers) and Antoon Joling, the journalist Jan Kalf and a priest, Fr A.H.W. Kaag. They had noticed that the younger generation of Catholic artists of various disciplines were especially in need of a forum where they could meet and exchange ideas. Everyone was welcome, provided they were Roman Catholic. The society included several clergymen amongst its members, but there was no clerical supervision. Neither was there an explicit vision on Catholic art, architecture, and literature. The members

1.3-11 Members of De Violier in Amsterdam on the occasion of a lecture by the Belgian priest Hugo Verriest, 1909. [Nijmegen, Katholiek Documentatie Centrum]

were seeking renewal, without explicitly condemning the neo-Gothic paradigm. They were cautious not to offend the feelings of the older members, who were still devoted to the Gothic style, or of the mainly conservative clergy, who were important players.

The vast majority of the Violier members (in 1907 the three branches together had 92 members[70]) lived in North and South Holland and Utrecht, with just a few living elsewhere in the Netherlands. The circle itself organised meetings, lectures, and excursions, but did not have its own magazine. However, it cooperated closely with the monthly magazine *Van Onzen Tijd*, which became the vehicle of the Violier Art Circle and offered the young generation the possibility of disseminating new ideas and opinions within the rather conservative Roman Catholic community. [Ill. 1.3-11]

In its early years, De Violier devoted much attention to the Beuron Art School as it offered a Christian art that was not beholden to the Gothic style and the Liturgical Movement. The Beuron Art School however had no great influence in the Netherlands, unlike the Liturgical Movement, which strove for more intense participation by the congregation in the liturgy by promoting frequent communion, children's communion at the age of six, folk singing and an unobstructed view of the altar. In 1902, Jan Stuyt and Jos Cuypers based their design of the parish church of St Antony in Utrecht on the new liturgical ideas, offering parishioners a view of the altar that was not obstructed by pillars. The church was a clarion call, but it proved too modern for the clergy. Cuypers and Stuyt also built the grand Haarlem cathedral of St Bavo in an eclectic neo-Romanesque style. Until 1914 the neo-Gothic style was predominant, although after that year the influence of the liturgical movement could no longer be ignored.

De Violier lasted until 1952, but after 1920 new organisations and magazines took over its role as a pioneer of modern ideas.

Conclusion

In the Netherlands of the nineteenth century, there were not any true lobbying groups, in the sense of broad movements for the building of churches. From 1806 onwards, the state provided subsidies and supervised construction, but did not impose any regulations concerning style. After 1868, state influence on church building virtually disappeared. From the beginning of the 1870s, state subsidies were granted for the restoration of ecclesiastical monuments.

Within Catholic circles the neo-Gothic style became the house style from the 1850s on, dominating Catholic art and architecture until 1914. The victory of the Gothic movement was an easy one. Outstanding individuals like Thijm, Cuypers, De Stuers and Van Heukelum and their network of like-minded lay people and clerics convinced their fellow Roman Catholics, including the bishops and clergy, that the Gothic style was the only true Roman Catholic style. There was not much discussion on this point, and there was no need for lobbying or struggle. The neo-Gothic style was a symbol of both emancipation and of loyalty to Rome. Van Heukelum's St Bernulphus Guild was something of an exception. It exercised extraordinary power in the archdiocese of Utrecht, obliging architects and artists to adapt to the Gothic style of the Lower Rhine and the Netherlands in the fourteenth and fifteenth centuries. However, the influence of the guild should not be overrated.

As the Gothic style was appropriated by Roman Catholics, it became almost impossible for Dutch Protestants, both the orthodox and more secular wings, to use this 'Catholic' style. They had to choose other styles for their houses of worship, either eclecticism or Dutch Renaissance. Since Protestants formed the majority within the Dutch population, they did not need a pressure group, except the orthodox Protestants around Abraham Kuyper to some extent.

70 In 1912 De Violier had 59 working members and 153 sympathisers.

BIBLIOGRAPHY

Asselt, Willem J. van, and Paul H.A.M. Abels. "De zeventiende eeuw". In: Herman J. Selderhuis, ed. *Handboek Nederlandse Kerkgeschiedenis*. Kampen, 2006, 359-496.

Blaauw, Silbe de. "De kathedralen van 1853". In: Jurjen Vis and Wim Janse, eds, *Staf en storm. Het herstel van de bisschoppelijke hiërarchie in Nederland in 1853: actie en reactie*. Bijdragen Vereniging Nederlandse Kerkgeschiedenis, 14. Hilversum, 2002, 233-259.

Bos, Emo. *Soevereiniteit en religie. Godsdienstvrijheid onder de eerste Oranjevorsten*. Hilversum, 2009.

Caspers, Charles, Wolfgang Cortjaens and Antoine Jacobs, eds. *De basiliek van O.L. Vrouw van het H. Hart te Sittard. Architectuur-devotie-iconografie*. Sittard, 2010.

Compagner, Jan, Kees Jansen, Bart Meinema and Nelleke Padmos-Jansen, eds. *Twee heilige huisjes. Protestanten in het Weerterland en Cranendonck*. Weert, 2012.

Coninck, Pieter de. *Een les uit Pruisen. Nederland en de Kulturkampf, 1870-1880*. Hilversum, 2005.

Defoer, Henri. "De katholieke kunstkring De Violier". *Cuypersbulletin*, 19 (2014) 3-4, 12-19.

Delheij, Volmar, and Antoine Jacobs. *Kerkenbouw in Limburg 1850-1914. Neogotische en neoromaanse parochiekerken en hun architecten*. Sittard, 2000.

Dominicus-Van Soest, Marleen. "Classicisten versus Gotiekers: de stijlstrijd binnen de Maatschappij tot Bevordering der Bouwkunst". In: Erik de Jong, Coert Peter Krabbe and Tiede J. Boersma, eds. *Maatschappij tot Bevordering der Bouwkunst. Schetsen uit de geschiedenis van het genootschap*, De Sluitsteen, 9 (1993) 3-4, 43-50.

Donkers, Geert. "De Katholieke Kunstkring De Violier, 1901-1920". *Trajecta. Tijdschrift voor de geschiedenis van het katholieke leven in de Nederlanden*, 10 (2001), 112-135.

Dunk, Thomas H. von der. "De katholieke kerken in Gelderland in en uit de Bataafse en Franse Tijd". *Bijdragen en mededelingen Gelre*, 79 (1988), 104-136.

Dunk, Thomas H. von der. "Wat er staat is zelden Waterstaat. Overheidsbemoeienis bij de vormgeving van katholieke kerkgebouwen in Gelderland in het tweede kwart van de negentiende eeuw". *Bulletin Koninklijke Nederlandse Oudheidkundige Bond*, 91 (1992), 1-14.

Dunk, Thomas H. von der. "De katholieken en hun kerken in Amsterdam tussen 1795 en 1853". In: J.D. Snel, P.H.A.M. Abels, G.N.M. Vis and J. Bakker, eds. *Een God bleef toch in Mokum. Amsterdamse kerkgeschiedenis in de negentiende en twintigste eeuw*. Bijdragen VNK 12. Delft, 2000, 141-212.

Erftemeijer, Antoon, Arjen Looyenga and Marike van Roon. *Getooid als een bruid. De nieuwe Sint-Bavokathedraal te Haarlem*. Haarlem, 1997.

Falize, J.J. "De kerkbouw voor en na 1900. Van neostijlen tot "berlagiaans". In: Regnerus Steensma and C.A. van Swigchem, eds. *Honderdvijftig jaar gereformeerde kerkbouw*. Kampen, 1986, 67-74.

Geelen, E.H.M. (Bets). "Bewaard en opgeborgen. De paramenten in de Munsterkerk en de Kathedraal te Roermond". *De Maasgouw. Tijdschrift voor Limburgse geschiedenis en archeologie*, 131 (2012), 56-62.

Geurts, P.A.M., ed. *Pascal Schmeits. Kladboek*. Memoreeks, 13. Nijmegen, 1984.

Geurts, P.A.M. "De Horstenaren Pieter Slits (1822-1883) en Gerard Slits (1829-1888), leraren te Rolduc". In: P.A.M. Geurts et al., eds. *Horster Historiën. 2: Van heren en gemeentenaren*. Horst, 1988, 227-246.

Geurts, P.A.M. "Enkele minder bekende vrienden van Jozef Albert Alberdingk Thijm". *Publications de la société historique et archéologique dans le Limbourg*, 126 (1990), 154-171.

Geurts, P.A.M.; A.E.M. Janssen, J.A.C. Peeters and Jan Roes, eds. *J.A. Alberdingk Thijm 1820-1889. Erflater van de negentiende eeuw. een bundel opstellen*. KDC Bronnen en Studies, 24. Baarn, 1992.

Gijsen, J.M. *Joannes Augustinus Paredis 1795-1886 bisschop van Roermond en het Limburg van zijn tijd*. Maaslandse Monografieën 8. Assen, 1968.

Gorris, Gerardus Carolus Wilhelmus. *J.G. Le Sage ten Broek*. Amsterdam, 1947-1948.

Groot, A. de. "De kerkgebouwen van de Doleantie 1886-1892". In: Regnerus Steensma and C.A. van Swigchem, eds. *Honderdvijftig jaar gereformeerde kerkbouw*. Kampen, 1986, 44-59.

Harinck, George, and Lodewijk Winkeler. "De negentiende eeuw". In: Herman J. Selderhuis, ed. *Handboek Nederlandse Kerkgeschiedenis*. Kampen, 2006, 601-721.

Heijst, Annelies van, Marjet Derks and Marit Monteiro. *Ex caritate. Kloosterleven, apostolaat en nieuwe spirit van actieve vrouwelijke religieuzen in Nederland in de 19e en 20e eeuw*. Hilversum, 2010.

Hoogewoud, Guido. "De Koepelkerk aan het Leidsebosje in Amsterdam. Een neogotische herdenkingskerk voor de Amsterdamse hervormden". In: Coert Peter Krabbe et al., eds. *Een huis voor de geest. Studies over kerkbouw in de negentiende en twintigste eeuw*. Jaarboek Cuypersgenootschap 2014. Amsterdam, 2015, 89-111.

Hottinga, Tijn. *De Katholieke Illustratie: de verkochte bruid. Honderd jaar tijdschriftgeschiedenis*. Baarn, 2000.

Jacobs, Antoine. "Deken Frans Xavier Rutten". *Publications de la société historique et archéologique dans le Limbourg*, 141 (2005), 89-186.

Jacobs, Antoine, and Wies van Leeuwen. "Roermond as Centre for Religious Art". In: Wolfgang Cortjaens, Jan De Maeyer and Tom Verschaffel, eds. *Historism and Cultural Identity in the Rhine-Meuse Region. Tensions between Nationalism and Regionalism in the Nineteenth Century*. KADOC Artes, 10. Leuven, 2008, 217-236.

Jacobs, Antoine, and Bart Wiekart. "De financiering van de katholieke kerkenbouw in Limburg na de Tweede Wereldoorlog". *De Maasgouw*, 130 (2011), 101-112.

Janse, C.S.L. "Krant en verzuiling". In: B. van der Ros, ed. *Het christelijk dagblad in de samenleving. Roeping en opdracht*. Leiden, 1991, 76-95.

Jong, Erik de, Coert Peter Krabbe and Tiede J. Boersma, eds. *Maatschappij tot Bevordering der Bouwkunst. Schetsen uit de geschiedenis van het genootschap*, De Sluitsteen, 9 (1993) 3-4.

Jong, Servaas de. *Bijdrage tot de kennis der gothische bouwkunst of spitsbogenstijl in Nederland*. Amsterdam, 1847.

Knippenberg, Hans. *De religieuze kaart van Nederland. Omvang en geografische spreiding van de godsdienstige gezindten vanaf de Reformatie tot heden*. Assen-Maastricht, 1992.

Kok, A.B.W.M. "Gustaaf Adolf Vereniging". In: *Christelijke Encyclopedie*, vol. 3. Kampen, 1958, 328.

Korporaal, T.L. "De subsidies van de Staatsmijnen aan de protestantse gemeenten in oostelijk Zuid-Limburg". *Historisch bulletin Het Land van Herle*, 48 (1998), 31-44.

Krabbe, Coert Peter. "Dageraad van de neogotiek. De Zuiderkerk in Rotterdam". In: Coert Peter Krabbe et al., eds. *Een huis voor de geest. Studies over kerkbouw in de negentiende en twintigste eeuw*. Jaarboek Cuypersgenootschap 2014. Amsterdam, 2015, 25-47.

"Kunst en Wetenschap. St. Benedictusgilde". *De Tijd*, 21 December 1901.

Landheer, Hugo. *Kerkbouw op krediet. De financiering van de kerkbouw in het aartspriesterschap Holland en Zeeland en de bisdommen Haarlem en Rotterdam gedurende de periode 1795-1965*. Amsterdam, 2004.

Lankhorst, Otto S. "Tussen commercie en apostolaat. De katholieke dag- en nieuwsbladen in Nederland tot 1940". In: Mechteld de Coo-Wijgerinck, Jan Roes and Otto S. Lankhorst. *De gezegende pers. Aspecten van de katholieke persgeschiedenis in Nederland tijdens de 19de en 20ste eeuw*. KDC Bronnen & Studies 20. Zeist, 1989, 37-83.

Lankhorst, Otto S. *Bibliografie van Katholieke Nederlandse periodieken*. 1: *Dag- en weekbladpers*. Nijmegen, 1999.

Leeuwen, A.J.C. (Wies) van. "De conflicterende restauratie-opvattingen van de Maatschappij tot Bevordering der Bouwkunst en P.J.H. Cuypers". In: Erik de Jong, Coert Peter Krabbe and Tiede J. Boersma, eds. *Maatschappij tot Bevordering der Bouwkunst. Schetsen uit de geschiedenis van het genootschap, De Sluitsteen*, 9 (1993) 3-4, 89-102.

Leeuwen, A.J.C. (Wies) van. *Pierre Cuypers architect 1827-1921*. Amersfoort-Zeist-Zwolle, 2007.

Leeuwen, A.J.C. (Wies) van. "Pierre Cuypers en het interieur van de Munsterkerk". In: Hein van der Bruggen, Erik Caris and Luc Wolters, eds. *De Munsterabdij van Roermond. Een ontdekkingstocht door achthonderd jaar geschiedenis van een vrouwenklooster*. Zwolle, 2020, 270-287.

Looijenga, Arjen J. *De Utrechtse School in de neogotiek. De voorgeschiedenis en het Sint-Bernulphusgilde*. Leiden, 1991.

Looijenga, Arjen J. "Die Utrechter neugotische Schule. Nationale Bestrebungen, grenzüberschreitende Wirkung". In: Wolfgang Cortjaens, Jan De Maeyer and Tom Verschaffel, eds. *Historicism and Cultural Identity in the Rhine-Meuse Region: Tensions between Nationalism and Regionalism in the Nineteenth Century*. KADOC Artes, 10. Leuven, 2008, 237-247.

Margry, Peter Jan. "Bouwen onder Antonius. Devotionalisering via de Bossche kerkbouwstichting". In: *Antonius 'De kleine en de grote'*. Uden, 1995, 25-35.

Melchers, Marisa. *Het nieuwe religieuze bouwen. Liturgie, kerken en stedenbouw*. Amsterdam, 2015.

Müllejans, Rita. *Klöster im Kulturkampf. Die Ansiedlung katholischer Orden und Kongregationen aus dem Rheinland und ihre Klosterneubauten im belgisch-niederländischen Grenzraum infolge des preußischen Kulturkampfes*. Veröffentlichungen des bischöflichen Diözesanarchivs Aachen, 44. Aachen, 1992.

Nolet, Willem, ed. *Katholiek Nederland. Encyclopaedie*. 2: *Broeder- en zusterorden en -congregaties*. The Hague, 1932.

Perry, Jos. *Ons fatsoen als natie. Victor de Stuers 1843-1916*. Amsterdam, 2004.

Peters, Elmer. *Naar de middeleeuwen. Het Aartsbisschoppelijk Museum in Utrecht vanaf het begin tot 1882*. Utrecht, 2012.

Pey, Ineke. *Herstel in nieuwe luister. Ideeën en praktijk van overheid, kerk en architecten bij de restauratie van het middeleeuwse katholieke kerkgebouw in Zuid-Nederland (1796-1940)*. Nijmeegse Kunsthistorische Studies, 1. Nijmegen, 1993.

Plas, Michel van der. *Vader Thijm. Biografie van een koopman-schrijver*. Baarn, 1995.

Puchinger, G. "Nederlandse Gedachten en De Nederlander". In: B. van der Ros, ed. *Geschiedenis van de christelijke dagbladpers in Nederland*. Kampen, 1993, 13-23.

Regels der Vereeniging tot bevordering der vereering van het Allerheiligste Sacrament en tot versiering der behoeftige kerken van Nederland. Sint-Michielsgestel, 1871.

Ros, B. van der, ed. *Geschiedenis van de christelijke dagbladpers in Nederland*. Kampen, 1993.

Ros, B. van der, ed. "De Standaard". In: B. van der Ros. *Geschiedenis van de christelijke dagbladpers in Nederland*. Kampen, 1993, 25-69.

Ruyven-Zeman, Zsuzsanna van. "De firma Nicolas te Roermond. Glasschilderkunst uit de negentiende en vroeg-twintigste eeuw". *Publications de la société historique et archéologique dans le Limbourg*, 132 (1996), 199-273.

Schilt, Jeroen, and Jouke van der Werf. *Genootschap Architectura et Amicitia 1855-1990*. Rotterdam, 1992.

Schiphorst, Lidwien. *'Een toevloed van werk, van wijd en zijd'. De beginjaren van het Atelier Cuypers-Stoltzenberg Roermond 1852 - ca. 1865*. Nijmeegse Kunsthistorische Studies, 13. Nijmegen, 2004.

Schmitz, Wolfgang. "Geschichte des Vereins für christliche Kunst". In: Dominik M. Meiering and Karl Schein. *Himmel auf Erden? Festschrift zum 150-jährigen Jubiläum des Vereins für christliche Kunst im Erzbistum Köln und Bistum Aachen e.V.* Cologne, 2003, 18-175.

Schrama, Nic. *Dagblad De Tijd 1845-1974*. Nijmegen, 1996.

Selderhuis, Herman J., and Peter Nissen. "De zestiende eeuw". In: Herman J. Selderhuis, ed. *Handboek Nederlandse Kerkgeschiedenis*. Kampen, 2006, 219-358.

"Statuten van het St. Bernulphus-Gilde te Utrecht". *St. Bernulphus-Gilde Utrecht Verslag 1886*. Utrecht, 1886, 32-34.

Suenens, Kristien. *Humble Women, Powerful Nuns: A Female Struggle for Autonomy in a Men's Church*. Leuven, 2020.

Swigchem, C.A. van. "De kerkgebouwen van de christelijk gereformeerden tot 1892". In: Regnerus Steensma and C.A. van Swigchem, eds. *Honderdvijftig jaar gereformeerde kerkbouw*. Kampen, 1986, 26-43.

Tillema, J.A.C. *Victor de Stuers. Ideeën van een individualist*. Assen, 1982.

Vrieze, J. "Abraham Kuyper en het gereformeerde kerkgebouw". In: Regnerus Steensma and C.A. van Swigchem, eds. *Honderdvijftig jaar gereformeerde kerkbouw*. Kampen, 1986, 60-66.

Wieten, Jan. "De Nederlander en de Nieuwe Nederlander". In: B. van der Ros, ed. *Geschiedenis van de christelijke dagbladpers in Nederland*. Kampen, 1993, 123-170.

1.4
The Institutionalisation of Christian Art and Architecture in Germany

Protagonists and 'Pressure Groups'

Wolfgang Cortjaens

The nineteenth century has often been labelled as the age of assembly culture. It is therefore no surprise that the development of religious art and architecture in Germany was part of the increasing institutionalisation of public life. As a result of the integration of the churches into the nascent nation state Prussia respectively the German Confederation (Deutscher Bund), religious art became the subject of political, clerical and artistic interest and soon was sustained and channelled by numerous public associations and interest groups. The process of institutionalisation benefited from the legal effects of the 1848 March Revolution and the constitution of the first freely elected Parliament. Some of the newly emerging associations were connected directly to the state organs, others attached themselves to or derived from clerical circles, some were primarily concerned about aesthetic questions as they rooted in the academic tradition, whereas others offered a platform for the bourgeoisie, with wealthy citizens acting as benefactors and promoters.

Despite their eclectic origins, all of these groups were unified by the idea that religious art needed guidance and promotion. The following article attempts to trace some of the 'pressure groups' and protagonists who shaped religious life and assembly culture in nineteenth-century Germany and as such contributed to the reformation and institutionalisation of religious art. Due to the variety of denominations and the complexity of the subject, some crucial points had to be excluded, in particular the Jewish Reform Movement which underwent a similar modernisation process as the Christian denominations. The article concentrates on the Christian churches which formed a dialectic pattern of either contrary or allied positions.

The 'Progressive Liturgical Movement' at the end of the eighteenth century

The first Catholic reform movement dealing programmatically with the conception of church interiors emerged in the last quarter of the eighteenth century. In retrospect entitled as 'Progressive Liturgical Movement' (*Aufklärerische Liturgie*) it was triggered by the ideas of the Enlightenment.[1] Its leading figure was the Constance vicar general and diocesan administrator Ignaz Heinrich Freiherr von Wessenberg (1774-1860).[2] [Ill. 1.4-2] He and his fellow reformers rejected the larger-than-life staging which had dominated architecture and liturgy since the Counter Reformation. In sharp contrast to the Baroque *theatrum sacrum*, which conceived ecclesiastical architecture as the shell of an overwhelming religious experience, the reformers demanded that the Catholic Church should abandon all signs of floridness and wealth: The mass would be celebrated in the local language instead of Latin, music was only allowed in exceptional cases. The interiors should be modest, sparse and assessable. Like Protestant churches, they should contain only one altar. A single yet important concession made by the reformers concerned the pulpit, which since the Counter Reformation had become more and more prominent as the place of Announcement also in Catholic churches.

1.4-1 "Hohenzollernzug" in the narthex of the Emperor Wilhelm Memorial Church (Gedächtniskirche) in Berlin-Charlottenburg: Mural depicting four generations of the Hohenzollern Dynasty, from left to right: Wilhelm I, Frederick III, Wilhelm II and his wife Augusta Viktoria. Behind them Crown Prince Wilhelm (1882–1951). Fritz Schaper, 1895.
[IAM / akg-images nr. AKG1078173]

1 Klueting, *Katholische Aufklärung*.
2 Hausberger, "Wessenberg, Ignaz Heinrich Freiherr von"; Bangert, *Bild und Glaube*. See also the research project by Christine Roll, Aachen University (RWTH, 2001-2005) and the EDP-assisted inventory of Wessenbergs' correspondence in the Municipal archive, Constance: <www.wessenberg.at\wessenbergiana\briefnachlass.htm> (accessed 4 January 2008).

1.4-2 Ignaz Heinrich Karl Freiherr von Wessenberg. Anonymous copper engraving, ca 1820. [akg-images nr. AKG826505]

The Progressive Liturgical Movement coincided with a financially troubled episode in the history of the Catholic Church which was menaced in its further existence subsequently first by secularisation and later by the territorial reshaping of Europe after 1815.[3] Thus, the calls for standardisation and simplification fell on fertile ground. Although the restrictions given by the financial situation, the influence of the state and the widely spread ignorance of the local clerics offered not much room for experimentation, the most able ones among the provincial architects in the German countries (respectively, after 1815, in Prussia) were able to create liturgical environments which were in accordance with the demands of the Progressive Liturgical Movement as well as with those of the Prussian Unionism.[4] Longitudinal schemes were the most widely applied scheme, however also central-planned churches are to be found here and there, as they guaranteed two central demands of the movement: 1) that the altar was visible from every angle of the church and 2) a satisfactory acoustic. The style itself was secondary and was dictated by Classicism up to the 1840s. [Ill. 1.4-3]

The role of the academies

Before religious art made its entry, cultural life and artistic taste in the German countries were mainly dictated by the academies, most notably those in Berlin, Dresden, Düsseldorf and Munich.[5] Only with the upcoming of the bourgeois artistic associations (i.e. 1817 in Hamburg, 1823 in Bremen, 1828 in Halberstadt), Christian art was indirectly propagated by new societies, which, by organising exhibitions and initiating contests, soon became platforms of artistic exchange as many of the contenders were students of the academies. For the development of religious art the probably most influential among these associations was the Düsseldorf-based Kunstverein für die Rheinlande und Westphalen founded in 1829 which was closely linked to the Academy of Fine Arts and its famous school of painting under the direction of Nazarene-influenced painter Wilhelm von Schadow (1788-1862).[6] Equally important was the Verein zur Verbreitung religiöser Bilder which made congenial use of the graphic media in order to establish a contemporary Christian iconography according to the Nazarene ideal propagated by the local Academy.[7] The canonisation was to remain a constant in the religious art until the avant-garde movements of the early twentieth century.

Catholic assembly culture and art associations

The phenomenon of nineteenth-century Catholic assembly culture has been appropriately described by Jürgen Herres as "Clericalisation as a sociopolitical programm" (*Klerikalisierung als gesellschaftspolitisches Programm*).[8]

The Cologne Cathedral Construction Society founded in 1841-1842 provided the casting mould for almost every local association of the following decades.[9] The involvement of the King of Prussia in the completion of Cologne Cathedral, surely the most

---

3   For the history of the Unified Church in Prussia see Goeters and Rogge, eds., *Die Geschichte der Evangelischen Kirche der Union*.
4   Cortjaens, 2.3 in this volume.
5   Mai, *Die deutschen Kunstakademien*.
6   Großmann, *Die Düsseldorfer Malerschule im Vormärz*; *175 Jahre Kunstverein für die Rheinlande und Westfalen*.
7   Gierse, "Das kleine Andachtsbild und der Verein zur Verbreitung religiöser Bilder".
8   Herres, *Städtische Gesellschaft und katholische Vereine*, 159.
9   Pilger, *Der Kölner Zentral-Dombauverein*.

1.4-3 Interior of St Pauls´ Church (Paulskirche) in Frankfurt/Main with the organ built by Eberhard Friedrich Walcker. Photo, c 1930.
[Photo: Bildarchiv Foto Marburg, nr. 1.255.460]

prolific restoration project of its time as well as the symbol of national unity,[10] not only secured the financial success of this undertake but also helped to strengthen the position of the Prussian Catholics within the still fragile domestic policy. Triggered by the enormously successful Trier pilgrimage in 1844, which generally is regarded the first massive demonstration of Catholic emancipation in Prussia,[11] the Church discovered the power of media attention. After the repressions put upon all kinds of political gatherings by the Prussian authorities in the pre-Revolutionary era, in 1848 the foundation of the Piusverein für religiöse Freiheit established a new kind of politically motivated, specifically Catholic assembly culture.[12] Events such as the *Katholikentage* (Catholic Congresses), the first of which took place in Mainz in 1848, were not only politically charged, but gradually became important platforms for the promotion of Christian art, where subjects on liturgical matters, on archaeology and recent restorations were discussed. As the local clergy was mostly unfamiliar with questions about art, style or taste, it soon became evident that there was need for artistic education and instruction, which offered the authorities multiple chances to interfere ideologically. Soon the gatherings were combined with exhibitions of recent artistic output (as was the case, for the first time, 1862 in Aachen)[13] or with limited competitions for, i.e., a new church building or a centre piece of the furnishing. Via leading figures such as the eloquent, multilingual politician August Reichensperger (1808-1895), the *Katholikentage* managed to gain international attention. In Belgium, they became the role model for the congresses of the Belgian Catholics held in Mechelen in 1863, 1864 and 1867 which successfully imported the distribution of religious art and craft via exhibitions and competitions.[14]

Another pillar of assembly culture and a regular participant of the Catholic General Assemblies were the *Gesellenvereine* which emerged in the late 1840s with the original purpose to stipulate and channel the educational activities of wayfarers.[15] Their cofounder, Priest August Kolping (1813-1865), was actively involved in the organisation of the assemblies of the German Catholics, i.e. as a member of the preparatory commission of the Tenth Annual Assembly in Cologne in 1858. [Ill. 1.4-4] As the purpose of the

10 Dann, *Religion – Kunst – Vaterland*.
11 Aretz et al., eds., *Der Heilige Rock zu Trier*; Schneider, "Wallfahrt, Ultramontanismus und Politik"; Id., "Entwicklungstendenzen rheinischer Frömmigkeits- und Kirchengeschichte"; Schieder, *Religion und Revolution*.
12 Schloßmacher, "Die Piusvereine in der preußischen Rheinprovinz 1848/49"; Herres, "Politischer Katholizismus im Rheinland 1848/49"; Id., *Städtische Gesellschaft und katholische Vereine*.
13 Bock, *Katalog der Ausstellung von neueren Meisterwerken mittelalterlicher Kunst zu Aachen*.
14 See the contributions in this volume as well as: Strobbe, "De Gilde van Sint-Thomas en Sint-Lucas" and the various contributions in De Maeyer and Verpoest, eds., *Gothic Revival*, and Cortjaens, De Maeyer and Verschaffel, eds., *Historism and Cultural Identity*.
15 Kracht, *Adolph Kolping*; Lüttgen, *Johann Gregor Breuer und Adolph Kolping*; Wietzorek, *Adolph Kolping*.

Gesellenvereine focused on social interaction, artistic education did not play an important role. However, after his denomination as cathedral vicar in 1849, Kolping was active in the restoration and completion of Cologne Cathedral.[16] Reportedly it was his close friend August Reichensperger who introduced him to the history and the principles of Christian art.[17]

Lays and local associations also played an important role in the organisation of the *Katholikentage*. In the wake of the Cathedral Construction Society, in most Catholic parts of Prussia, especially in the prospering Rhine Province, numerous bourgeois associations emerged.[18] Combining communal political interest with a sense of drawing public attention, those local players soon realised that visibility and public display were crucial to the success of their task and so the erection of monuments and the organisation of public events came into focus. That most members were part of the municipal elites and active in communal politics, secured the financing of the projects. However, only few of these undertakes were successful, in most cases due to a lack of financial backup. An early and memorable exception was the erection of the neo-Gothic Votive Church of Our Lady in Aachen (1859-1863) triggered by the local association Constantia (a gathering of local nobility) and financially backed by a wealthy private donor, the lawyer and politician Joseph Lingens (1819-1876).[19] Other projects failed, as was the case with the monument commemorating the late exiled bishop of Cologne, Clemens-August von Droste Vischering (1773-1845), planned by the Cologne-based Klemens-Verein which, after several years of unsuccessful fundraising, had to be abandoned.[20]

The emancipation process of the German Catholics was accompanied by the emergence of several diocesan artistic associations. The year 1852, for example, saw the foundation of the first German Diözesan-Kunstverein in Paderborn,[21] followed by the Kunstverein für die Erzdiözese Köln and the Rottenburger Diözesan-Kunstverein für Christliche Kunst in the diaspora diocese of Rottenburg (Kingdom Württemberg). Other associations soon followed, i.e. in Munich-Freising and Freiburg (both in 1857). Most of these associations were founded by priests, and the clergy was to dominate the ideological frame until the outbreak of World War I. The use of contemporary media by the diocesan associations was similar to that of their secular equivalents. The parishes benefited from the interactions between lays and clergymen, as they provided them with a large number of capable and educated men who acted out in favour of the clerical authorities and could serve as surveyors or consultants. However, the Christian art associations were not allowed to act freely, as the hierarchical nature of the church demanded that any decision concerning new buildings or furnishing was to be coordinated with the diocese. Some of them paralleled their activities with a museification of local collections of Christian art and archaeology (Paderborn 1853, Cologne 1853, Münster 1864). As many key figures were collectors of medieval art themselves, such as Bishop Johann Georg Müller (1798-1870) of Münster, Canon Franz Bock (1823-1899) of Aachen, city pastor Franz August Münzenberger (1833-1890) of Frankfurt and Canon Alexander Schnütgen (1843-1918) of Cologne, the activities of the associations were mainly archaeological.[22] At the same time, the collections were destined to serve as an additional means of artistic education for sculptors and silversmiths.

The local associations also founded their own periodicals, such as the Rottenburg *Kirchenschmuck* (1854) and the Freiburg *Christliche Kunstblätter* (1862).[23] They were all modelled on the Cologne-based *Organ für christliche Kunst*, which was established in 1851 as the official organ of the Cologne Christian Art Association and which was to become the most important bulletin for religious art and craft in Germany for the next decades,[24] initiated by auxiliary bishop Johann Anton Baudri of Cologne (1804-1893). Closely connected to the Cologne Cathedral Construction Movement

---

16 Lüttgen, "'Nur nicht nachlassen!' Adolph Kolping, der Kölner Dom und der Dombau".
17 Von Pastor, *August Reichensperger*, 333-334.
18 See, for example, the Klemens-Verein (Cologne 1842), the Borromäus-Verein (Bonn 1844) and the Aachen-based bourgeois association Constantia (1846). Herres, *Städtische Gesellschaft und katholische Vereine*, 153-159.
19 Holländer, "Katholische Avantgarden"; Cortjaens, 2.3 in this volume.
20 Herres, *Städtische Gesellschaft und katholische Vereine*, 153.
21 Tack, "Die Bestrebungen zur Hebung der kirchlichen Kunst im Erzbistum Paderborn seit 1800".
22 For Müller: Philippi, "Müller, Johann Georg"; Bock: Cortjaens, "Bock, Franz Johann Joseph"; Münzenberger: de Weerth, *Die Altarsammlung*; Schnütgen: Westermann-Angerhausen, ed., *Alexander Schnütgen*.
23 By this time, in the wake of the internal church reform and the Catholic Revival in the German Countries, a large number of ultramontane bulletins and reviews had already been established (i.e. *Der Katholik, Historisch-politische Blätter*). They dealt mainly with political opinions, whereas the propagation of Christian art was channelled not by these periodicals but by the organs of the various local art associations.
24 A study on the *Organ für christliche Kunst* within the context of German periodicals of Christian art is still missing.

1.4-4 *The inauguration of the Maria Column in Cologne on 8 September 1858. Engraving, 1858.*
[Kölnisches Stadtmuseum; © Rheinisches Bildarchiv, Cologne, nr. 149865]

(Dombaubewegung) and its periodical, the *Kölner Domblatt*,[25] the *Organ* contained historical treatises on Christian art and liturgy, reviews, artistic news from abroad and proceedings of congresses or excursions. Also more practical instructions concerning appropriate models for liturgical designs, including furnishing, textiles and vasa sacra, were included. The taste was dictated by the exponents of the ultramontane 'Kölner Richtung': priests, lays, theoreticians, artists and craftsmen. Unanimously, they favoured the thirteenth-century Gothic as the only appropriate style for new churches. Any deviation from the 'true principles' was regarded a betrayal of the neo-Gothic movement. The *Organ* managed to launch the careers of its favoured neo-Gothic architects like, for example, Vincenz Statz (1819-1898) and Heinrich Wiethase (1833-1893), as well as other craftsmen.[26] As a result of this protectionism, churches and monuments soon became visible manifestations of the ideas of the neo-Gothic doctrine.

Protestant associations

Throughout the nineteenth century, the king of Prussia, who, at the same time was head of the Protestant Church in Germany and *summus episcopus* of his Lutheran subjects, remained the central figure in church building practice. Whereas Frederick William III was mainly concerned with the unification of the Lutheran and the Reformed Church in Prussia, his successor to the throne, Frederick William IV, focused on the renewal of liturgy and architecture. As his ideal was the Apostolic Church of Early Christianism, the models he favoured rooted in Early Christian and Byzantine architecture, which is evident in the work of his foremost architects Friedrich August Stüler (1800-1865), Ludwig Persius (1803-1845) and August Soller (1805-1853), the former students and artistic inheritors of Karl Friedrich Schinkel.[27] Although the 'Rundbogenstil' remained the dominant building style for churches until the 1860s, the main concern was not so much a stylistic one but to implant the technical and artistic knowledge in all parts of Protestant Prus-

25 Germann, "Das Kölner Domblatt".
26 Regulars in the early editions of the *Organ für christliche Kunst* include the sculptors Wilhelm (1837-1919) and Otto Mengelberg (1841-1891), mason and sculptor Peter Fuchs (1829-1898) and the silversmith Gabriel Hermeling (1833-1904).
27 Börsch-Supan, *Berliner Baukunst nach Schinkel*; Krüger, *Rom und Jerusalem*. For monographs see Börsch-Supan and Müller Stüler, *Friedrich August Stüler*; *Ludwig Persius – Architekt des Königs*; Grundmann, *August Soller*.

sia.[28] An adequate media were the *Entwürfe für Kirchen, Pfarr- und Schulhäuser zum amtlichen Gebrauch* which were published by the Ober-Bau-Deputation (Central Building Deputation) from 1844 onwards.

After 1848, the Catholic assemblies became a role model for Protestant synods. Unlike the Catholic associations, where the clergy and the local nobility were dominant (especially in the Rhineland and in Westphalia), the Protestant associations recruited their protagonists also from the intelligentsia. The Verein für religiöse Kunst in der evangelischen Kirche (Association for Religious Art in the Protestant Church) triggered by the Innere Mission (Inner Mission) was founded in 1851/1852 in Berlin by members of the Berlin intelligentsia, most of whom were members of the Prussian Chamber or otherwise related to the ruling house, among them the famous art historian Karl Schnaase (1798-1875) and the eventual minister of cultural affairs, Moritz August von Bethmann-Hollweg (1795-1877).[29] Also, the senior court chaplain and other prominent churchmen were involved in the discussions and gatherings. The aim of the association, where also Catholics were admitted, was the "Stiftung von Werken der bildenden Kunst in evangelischen Kirchen und Schulen zu befördern, zu unterstützen, zu vermitteln und zu leiten" as well as "Kupferstiche, Lithographien oder Holzschnitte christlicher Darstellungen ins Leben zu rufen und zu verbreiten".[30] Any obscenity or vulgarity in the display of Bible history should be avoided and although the Catholic distribution pattern provided the role model for the use of visual media and illustrations, the gradual differences in the depiction of religious subjects are evident. Nazarene painter Julius Schnorr von Carolsfeld (1794-1872) and his *Bibel in Bildern* (first published in 1860) would play a crucial role in the propagation of a Protestant iconography and, via distribution of etchings and engravings based on his designs, found its way into mass production.[31] Schnorr's designs many of which were based on his earlier compositions, were equally successful with parts of the Catholic faction.

The graphic reproductions were spread in (school) bibles, illustrated books and pictorial broadsheets (*Bilderbogen*) with religious motives. Publishing companies specialised on religious motives, some of them, like Gustav Kühn in Neuruppin (Brandenburg), produced images for all denominations.[32] In addition, periodicals like the *Christliches Kunstblatt für Kirche, Schule und Haus* (Stuttgart, 1858-1904) and the *Mitteilungen des Vereins für religiöse Kunst in der evangelischen Kirche* (Berlin, 1904-1912) secured the use of appropriate images within the Protestant *milieu*.

After several synods on which the theoretical fundaments for a renewal of Protestant church building were laid (Dresden 1856, Eisenach 1861, Wiesbaden 1891),[33] the controversies between the two major confessions in Germany finally came to an end under the reign of Emperor Wilhelm II: In 1888, the Evangelisch-Kirchliche Hilfsverein and in 1890 the Evangelische Kirchenbauverein (Protestant Church Building Society) were erected under his protectorate, respectively under that of his wife, the Empress Augusta Viktoria (1858-1921).[34] The main motive was to erect a great number of new churches in the new agglomerations of the *Kaiserreich*, especially in the vast industry landscapes of the Ruhr and in the big cities such as Berlin where the lack of churches under the catchphrase *Kirchennot* had become evident. Both associations were explicitly not intended to rivalling the Inner Mission, as pastoral care and social welfare were to be integrated into the planning of the new city parishes.

The leading positions in both associations were held by members of the Imperial Court, among them Constable Ernst Freiherr von Mirbach (1844-1925), who had to take dismissal as chairman when during his appeal for donation for the interior decoration of the Emperor Wilhelm Memorial Church in Berlin [Ill. 1.4-1], his cash management proved to contain severe irregularities.[35]

---

28 Cortjaens, 2.3 in this volume.
29 Kaiser, *Evangelische Kirche und sozialer Staat*, 34-36.
30 *Mitteilungen des Vereins für religiöse Kunst in der evangelischen Kirche*, no 1, February 1912, 2.
31 Feldhaus, "Julius Schnorr von Carolsfeld".
32 Nieke, *Religiöse Bilderbogen aus Neuruppin*.
33 Weyres, "Der evangelische Kirchenbau", 270. See also Cortjaens, 3.4 in this volume.
34 Gundermann, *Kirchenbau und Diakonie*.
35 Gundermann, *Ernst Freiherr von Mirbach und die Kirchen der Kaiserin*.

Non-academic associations, guilds, brotherhoods and monastic workshops

Unlike other European countries, Germany knew no specific artists' colonies or brotherhoods specialised in religious art, let aside the Nazarenes, many of whom, after the dissolution of the brotherhood in 1821, returned to Germany and maintained some influence via the academies in Düsseldorf, Berlin, Dresden and Munich. Also, the Belgian and Dutch model of the 'guilds' (Gilde de St Thomas et de St Luc, Sint-Bernulphusgilde et al.) with their mingled constitution of artists, scholars, priests and lays was unknown.[36] Instead, their function was largely covered by the above-mentioned artistic associations who attached themselves to certain artistic 'schools'.

A rare and uncharacteristic exception in the field of monastic workshops is the textile manufacturing workshop of the order of the Sisters of the Poor Infant Jesus founded in 1844 by the local Aachen clergy and promoted by members of the municipal elite.[37]

It was not until the last quarter of the nineteenth century when with the Beuron School of Art there emerged a monastic movement, which soon would play a crucial role in the development of Christian art and craft, and then it was in close collaboration with contemporary and international artistic tendencies.[38] The demure, hieratic style of the Beuron School with its reworking of Egyptian and Byzantine art and its high level of abstraction, most notably evident in the monumental cycles executed for Monte Cassino (1876-1880) [Ill. 1.4-5] and St Emmaus Abbey in Prague (1880-1885), not only made impact on the Secessionist movement in South Germany and Austria, but also influenced the Nabis (the Hebrew name for the 'Illuminated') in France and the liturgical reform movement in Belgium, where Beuron provided the model for the Benedictine Abbeys Maredsous (1872) [Ill. 2.2-7] and Regina coeli in Louvain (1899).[39] Claiming a mathematically-based level of abstraction which would allow the recipient 'to think' instead of 'to feel', the writings of Peter Lenz (Pater Desiderius Lenz), the founder of the Beuron School, became manifests of the modern liturgical movement.

Officially, however, the first monograph on the movement did not appear until 1914, and whereas in France some of the Nabis and the Symbolists had some signs of interest to the Beuron artists[40], the official German periodicals on Christian art and liturgy largely ignored them, as their geometrical abstraction and anti-individualistic attitude was not in conformity with the ideals of the still predominant Historism and Late-Nazarenism.[41]

Progressive tendencies

Around 1900, the majority of the German episcopate, such as the bishop of Rottenburg, Paul Wilhelm von Keppler (1852-1926), still propagated a moderate Historism.[42] However, in the last quarter of the nineteenth century, the impact of new artistic movements such as Realism and Naturalism began to show their impact on religious art. Biblical subjects were abstracted, sometimes even eroticised, to an extent that, for example, a

1.4-5 Desiderius Lenz in Monte Cassino. Photo, 1878.
[akg-images nr. AKG174703]

36 De Maeyer, *De Sint-Lucasscholen en de neogotiek,* and the contributions of De Maeyer (1.2) and van Leeuwen (3.3) in this volume.
37 Cortjaens, 3.4 in this volume.
38 Siebenmorgen, "Kulturkampfkunst"; Lang, *Das Kunstschaffen des Benediktinerordens*; Standaert, *L'École de Beuron.*
39 Schuster, "München leuchtete!", 37.
40 Verleysen, *Maurice Denis et la Belgique.*
41 Smitmans, *Die christliche Malerei,* 189-201, sums up the participations of Beuron artists in recent exhibitions in Germany and Austria before Word War I. See also Siebenmorgen, "Kulturkampfkunst".
42 Keppler, *Aus Kunst und Leben*; Rivinius, "Keppler, Paul Wilhelm von".

Madonna could as well be interpreted as a *Mother and child* or a depiction of *Caritas*. The dichotomy between the prosaic of the present and the traditional pathos of Biblical and artistic canons triggered by the emergence of Realism soon affected religious painting. Biblical motives were now transformed into the present-day life of working class people (and thus referred to, with a certain disregard, as *Armeleutemalerei*). Prominent examples are the paintings of the Protestant painter Fritz von Uhde (1848-1911),[43] [Col. ill. 3] the Catholic Walter Firle (1859-1929), both active in Munich, or the Berlin-based Jew Max Liebermann (1847-1935), whose painting *The Twelve-year old Jesus in the Temple* (1879, Hamburger Kunsthalle) caused a storm of indignation by the traditionalists when it was first presented.[44] In spite of their flawless technique borrowed from the Dutch and Flemish Old Masters, von Uhde's blending of Biblical motives and contemporary settings were despised equally by the Protestant *and* the Catholic Church as they were regarded a profanation of the traditional principles of religious art.

Around 1900, the renewal of religious art in Germany was foreshadowed by the emergence of several pro-Modernist guilds, brotherhoods and artistic colonies all of which stressed upon artistic autonomy and subjectivity. The first and most influential of these organisations was the Munich-based Deutsche Gesellschaft für christliche Kunst, founded in 1893.[45] By integrating prominent artists into the organisation, the society managed to keep in touch with the contemporary artistic movements and with the Munich Academy. Among the founders of the Gesellschaft were not only the Bavarian *Hofstiftsvikar* (royal collegiate vicar) Sebastian Staudhammer, but also artistic leading figures such as the sculptor Georg Busch (1862-1943), long-time president of the artistic section (*Künstlerpräsident*), and the painter Gebhard Flugel (1863-1939).[46] Another reason for its relative success – in 1909 the society counted 5,500 members –[47] was that it encouraged individual artistic expression. For almost two decades the Gesellschaft remained independent of any interference by the Church – only the first president Dr. Georg Freiherr von Hertling (1843-1919, at the same time president of the Görres-Gesellschaft zur Pflege und Förderung der Wissenschaften) was given a right to veto. In 1912, however, the statutes were altered and the German episcopate was given the final vote to decide what would be published. This alteration was a reaction towards the restorative tendencies within the Catholic Church which in the same year had been expressed in the notorious decree by Archbishop Antonius Kardinal Fischer of Cologne (1840-1912), in which he clearly condemned Modernism in religious art in favour of the neo-Gothic and the neo-Romanesque, the only Historicist styles he regarded suitable for church buildings.[48] As a reaction towards the still conservative atmosphere within the German dioceses, the year 1913 saw the foundation of the Neue Münchener Secession, an artistic association of predominantly Expressionist-influenced artists, among them painter Karl Caspar (1879-1956), whose body of work includes important works for the Catholic Church, most notably such as the 'passion triptych' in the Church of Our Lady (Frauenkirche) in Munich which, in its toxic colours and vivid pencil gesture, seems to reflect the horrors of World War I.[49]

The increasing influence of Modernism on Christian art and architecture can be measured by the participation of the various artistic groups at the major exhibitions which took place after 1900: The major exhibitions flanking the emergence of the German Werkbund – 1906 in Dresden, 1907 and 1914 in Cologne, 1908 in Munich, 1909 in Düsseldorf, 1910 in Essen and 1912 in Vienna – all contained sections for modern church architecture, including the presentation of 1:1 scale interiors designed by prominent architects such as Eduard Endler (1860-1932), Heinrich Renard (1868-1923), Stephan Mattar (1875-1943) and Carl Moritz (1863-1944), who were all exponents of a moderate Modernism.[50]

43 Brand, *Fritz von Uhde*.
44 Faass, *Der Jesus-Skandal*.
45 Streicher, "das freie Schaffen der christlichen Künstler begünstigen!".
46 For Busch see: Busch-Hofer, *Bildhauer Georg Busch*; for Fugel see: Rothes, *Gebhard Fugel*; Streicher, *Gebhard Fugel. Apokalypse*.
47 Streicher, "das freie Schaffen der christlichen Künstler begünstigen!", 64.
48 Fischer, "Zum Bau und der Ausstattung von Kirchen".
49 Cf. the various contributions and the catalogue in: Schuster, *'München leuchtete!'*
50 "Religiöse kirchliche Kunst"; *Ausstellung für christliche Kunst Düsseldorf 1909*; *Ausstellung für moderne katholische Kirchenkunst*; *Ausstellung für kirchliche Kunst in Wien 1912*; *Officieller Katalog der Deutschen Werkbund-Ausstellung Cöln 1914*.

Ironically, next to Munich, it was another stronghold of Catholicism, Cologne that became the other important centre of the renewal of religious art in Germany.[51] Here, one of the most ambitious contenders of Modernism was Fritz Witte (1876-1937) who in 1918 followed Alexander Schnütgen as editor of the *Zeitschrift für christliche Kunst* as well as director of the Schnütgen Museum. Although passionate for medieval art, Witte's liberal attitude had already shocked the editorial team in 1912, when he published his pro-modernist essay "Stellung der Kirche zur Modernen", in which he claimed a rebirth of artistic originality by relying on the material itself: "Mit einigen aufgeklebten romanischen oder gotischen Elementen ist es nicht genug, die Form muß ganz und von innen heraus neu geboren werden aus dem Material".[52]

Witte was strongly influenced by the Werkbund and the Kunstgewerbeschule in Cologne, where the silversmith Ernst Riegel (1871-1939), the co-founder of the artists' colony Mathildenhöhe in Darmstadt, was named director of the section 'goldsmithery'. In the wake of the Cologne Werkbund-exhibition in 1914, which was forced to close down after only a few weeks due to the outbreak of World War I, Witte managed to gather around him a new generation of craftsmen, among them the painter Heinrich Brey (1872-1960)[53] and the Kevelaer-based silversmiths Heinrich and Johannes Vorfeld (1872-1960).[54] Witte's collaboration with Riegel and Brey resulted in a number of designs for liturgical objects which were executed by the members of Witte's own short-lived Cologne association Ars Sacra – Verein zur Förderung religiöser Kunst. Ars Sacra concentrated mainly on the applied arts. On a much more modest scale, it anticipated the activities of the Kölner Institut für religiöse Kunst which was founded by Witte in 1926 and which would revolutionise the liturgical movement of the *interbellum*.[55] The main tasks were identical with those of the earlier artistic associations of the mid-century, particularly the rejection of standardised, exchangeable mass production. Although Historicist elements were still present, the designs for *vasa sacra*, tapestries or murals were true to Witte's claims. [Ill. 1.4-6]

On the one hand, the emergence of these and other Secessionist movements before 1914 can in retrospect be regarded as an alternative draft to the doctrines of the diocesan artistic associations of the 1850s. At the same time, the nature of the task did not allow a radical break with the Church and the traditional Biblical iconography, as shows the example of the Deutsche Gesellschaft für christliche Kunst. It seems that the greatest dilemma of the pre-War Secessionist movements was the gasp between artistic autonomy and the socio-political reality of the German *Kaiserreich* respectively the position of the churches, which, despite new thought structures, artistically would still remain within the path of Historicism.

1.4-6 Fritz Witte and fellow members of the association Ars Sacra – Verein für religiöse Kunst in army uniform. Photo, ca 1915.
[© Rheinisches Bildarchiv, Cologne, nr. 64992]

51 Rapp, "Kirche und die Kunst der Zeit 1888-1920"; Streicher, "das freie Schaffen der christlichen Künstler begünstigen!".
52 Witte, "Die Stellung der Kirche zur Modernen", 7.
53 Lingens, *Kirchenmaler vom Niederrhein*.
54 Cortjaens, *Rheinische Altarbauten des Historismus*, 176.
55 Peters, *Kirchliche Wandmalerei*; Lingens, "Die feindliche Bewegung". An elaborate study on Witte and his activities is still very much in demand.

BIBLIOGRAPHY

175 Jahre Kunstverein für die Rheinlande und Westfalen. Düsseldorf, 2004.

Aretz, Erich, Michael Embach, Martin Persch and Franz Ronig, eds. *Der Heilige Rock zu Trier: Studien zur Geschichte und Verehrung der Tunika Christi*. Trier, 1995.

Ausstellung für christliche Kunst Düsseldorf 1909. Unter dem Protektorate Seiner Kaiserlichen und Königlichen Hoheit des Kronprinzen des Deutschen Reiches und von Preussen, vom 15. Mai bis 3. Okt. Düsseldorf, 1909.

Ausstellung für kirchliche Kunst in Wien 1912. Vienna, 1912.

Ausstellung für moderne katholische Kirchenkunst, Goldschmiedearbeiten, Paramente, Glasmalereien, etc. Exhibition Catalogue Museum der Stadt Essen, 11. August bis 9. September. [Essen, 1906].

Bangert, Michael. *Bild und Glaube. Ästhetik und Spiritualität bei Ignaz Heinrich von Wessenberg (1774-1860)*. Studien zur christlichen Religions- und Kulturgeschichte, 11. Fribourg- Stuttgart, 2009.

Bock, Franz. *Katalog der Ausstellung von neueren Meisterwerken mittelalterlicher Kunst zu Aachen, eröffnet bei Gelegenheit der XIV. General-Versammlung katholischer Vereine, nebst einer kunstgeschichtlichen Einleitung*. Aachen, 1862.

Börsch-Supan, Eva. *Berliner Baukunst nach Schinkel. 1840-1870*. Munich, 1977.

Börsch-Supan, Eva, and Dietrich Müller-Stüler. *Friedrich August Stüler 1800-1865*. Munich, 1997.

Brand, Bettina. *Fritz von Uhde. Das religiöse Werk zwischen künstlerischer Intention und Öffentlichkeit*. Diss. Heidelberg, 1983.

Busch-Hofer, Roswitha. *Bildhauer Georg Busch (1862-1943)*. Lindenberg, 2013.

Cortjaens, Wolfgang. *Rheinische Altarbauten des Historismus. Sakrale Goldschmiedekunst 1870-1918*. Rheinbach, 2002 (diss. RWTH Aachen University, 1999).

Cortjaens, Wolfgang. "Bock, Franz Johann Joseph". In: *Biographisch-Bibliographisches Kirchenlexikon*, vol. 33. Nordhausen, 2003, 128-135.

Cortjaens, Wolfgang, Jan De Maeyer and Tom Verschaffel, eds. *Historism and Cultural Identity in the Rhine-Meuse Region: Tensions between Nationalism and Regionalism in the Nineteenth Century*. KADOC Artes, 10. Leuven, 2008.

Dann, Otto, ed. *Religion – Kunst – Vaterland: Der Kölner Dom im 19. Jahrhundert*. Cologne, 1983.

De Maeyer, Jan, ed. *De Sint-Lucasscholen en de neogotiek, 1862-1914*. KADOC Studies, 5. Leuven, 1988.

De Maeyer, Jan, and Luc Verpoest, eds. *Gothic Revival: Religion, Architecture and Style in Western Europe, 1815-1914*. KADOC Artes, 5. Leuven, 2000.

de Weerth, Elsbeth. *Die Altarsammlung des Frankfurter Stadtpfarrers Ernst Franz August Münzenberger (1830-190). Ein Beitrag zur kirchlichen Kunst in der zweiten Hälfte des 19. Jahrhunderts*. Frankfurt et al., 1995.

Entwürfe zu Kirchen, Pfarr- und Schul-Häusern, zum amtlichen Gebrauch herausgegeben von der Königl. Preuss. Ober-Bau-Deputation. Berlin, 1844-1846 (2nd ed. Potsdam, 1852-1855).

Faass, Martin, ed. *Der Jesus-Skandal. Ein Liebermann-Bild im Kreuzfeuer der Kritik*. Exhibition catalogue Berlin, Villa Liebermann, 2009; Hamburg, Hamburger Kunsthalle, 2010. Berlin, 2009.

Feldhaus, Irmgard. "Julius Schnorr von Carolsfeld. Die Bibel in Bildern und andere biblische Bilderfolgen der Nazarener". In: *Die Bibel in Bildern und andere biblische Bilderfolgen der Nazarener*. Exhibition catalogue Neuss, Clemens-Sels-Museum. Neuss, 1983, 6-23.

Fischer, Antonius. "Zum Bau und der Ausstattung von Kirchen und anderen kirchlichen Gebäuden". *Kirchlicher Anzeiger für die Erzdiözese Köln*, 51 (1912), 29-33.

Germann, Georg. "Das Kölner Domblatt des 19. Jahrhunderts und die doktrinäre Neugotik". *Kölner Domblatt*, 35 (1972), 81-92.

Gierse, Ludwig. "Das kleine Andachtsbild und der Verein zur Verbreitung religiöser Bilder in Düsseldorf". In: *Religiöse Graphik aus der Zeit des Kölner Dombaus 1842-1880*. Exhibition catalogue Cologne, Erzbischöfliches Diözesanmuseum, 1980/81. Cologne, 1980, 21-28.

Goeters, J. F. Gerhard, and Joachim Rogge, eds. *Die Geschichte der Evangelischen Kirche der Union. Ein Handbuch*. Edited Evangelische Kirche der Union. 3 vols. Leipzig, 1992-1999.

Großmann, Joachim. *Die Düsseldorfer Malerschule im Vormärz und in der Revolution von 1848/49: eine Studie zum Verhältnis von Kunst, Gesellschaft und Politik*. Düsseldorf, 1985.

Grundmann, Günther. *August Soller (1805–1853). Ein Berliner Architekt im Geiste Schinkels*. Munich, 1973.

Gundermann, Iselin. *Kirchenbau und Diakonie: Kaiserin Auguste Victoria und der Evangelisch-Kirchliche Hilfsverein*. Hefte des Evangelischen Kirchenbauvereins, 7. Berlin, 1991.

Gundermann, Iselin. *Ernst Freiherr von Mirbach und die Kirchen der Kaiserin*. Hefte des Evangelischen Kirchenbauvereins, 9. Berlin, 1995.

Hausberger, Karl. "Wessenberg, Ignaz Heinrich Freiherr von". In: Manfred Heim, ed. *Theologen, Ketzer, Heilige. Kleines Personenlexikon zur Kirchengeschichte*. Munich, 2001, 398-399.

Herres, Jürgen. *Städtische Gesellschaft und katholische Vereine im Rheinland 1840–1870*. Essen, 1996. [Diss. phil. Trier, 1991].

Herres, Jürgen. "Politischer Katholizismus im Rheinland 1848/49". In: *Politische Strömungen und Gruppierungen am Rhein 1848/49. Vorträge gehalten auf dem Symposium anläßlich des 150. Jahrestages der Revolution von 1848/49 im Rheinland am 9. November 1998 im Landtag Nordrhein-Westfalen, veranstaltet von der Gesellschaft für Rheinische Geschichtskunde und vom Landschaftsverband Rheinland*. Publikation der Gesellschaft für Rheinische Geschichtskunde, Vorträge, 31. Düsseldorf, 1999, 39-70.

Holländer, Georg. "Katholische Avantgarden in der Reaktion auf 1848: Der Bau der Aachener Marienkirche". In: Guido Müller and Jürgen Herres, eds. *Aachen, die westlichen Rheinlande und die Revolution*. Aachen, 2000, 309-329.

Kaiser, Jochen-Christoph. *Evangelische Kirche und sozialer Staat. Diakonie im 19. und 20. Jahrhundert*. Stuttgart, 2008.

Keppler, Paul Wilhelm von. *Aus Kunst und Leben*. Freiburg im Breisgau, 1905.

Klüting, Harm, ed. *Katholische Aufklärung – Aufklärung im katholischen Deutschland*. Studien zum 18. Jahrhundert, 15. Hamburg, 1993.

Kracht, Hans-Joachim. *Adolph Kolping. Priester, Pädagoge, Publizist im Dienst christlicher Sozialreform. Leben und Werk aus den Quellen dargestellt*. Freiburg, 1993.

Krüger, Jürgen. *Rom und Jerusalem. Kirchenbauvorstellungen der Hohenzollern im 19. Jahrhundert*. Acta humaniora. Schriften zur Kunstwissenschaft und Philosophie. Berlin, 1995. [Habil. 1992].

Lang, Claudia. *Das Kunstschaffen des Benediktinerordens unter Rückgriff auf archaische Stilelemente und gleichzeitigem Aufbruch in die Moderne*. Regensburg, 2008.

Lingens, Peter. *Kirchenmaler vom Niederrhein. Der Gelderner Heinrich Brey (1872-1960) und seine Kevelaerer Berufskollegen*. Geldern, 1998.

Lingens, Peter. "Die feindliche Bewegung. Der Einfluß des Kölner Instituts für religiöse Kunst am Niederrhein". *Rheinische Heimatpflege*, 36 (1999) 4, 299-304.

Ludwig Persius – Architekt des Königs, Baukunst unter Friedrich Wilhelm IV. Edited by Stiftung Preußische Schlösser und Gärten Berlin-Brandenburg. Potsdam, 2003.

Lüttgen, Franz. *Johann Gregor Breuer und Adolph Kolping. Studien zur Frühgeschichte des Katholischen Gesellenvereins*. Paderborn, 1997.

Lüttgen, Franz. "'Nur nicht nachlassen!' Adolph Kolping, der Kölner Dom und der Dombau". *Kölner Domblatt*, 70 (2005), 237-258.

Mai, Ekkehard. *Die deutschen Kunstakademien im 19. Jahrhundert. Künstlerausbildung zwischen Tradition und Avantgarde*. Cologne, 2010.

Mitteilungen des Vereins für religiöse Kunst in der evangelischen Kirche, 1, 1912.

Nieke, Erdmute. *Religiose Bilderbogen aus Neuruppin: Eine Untersuchung zur Frömmigkeit im 19. Jahrhundert*. Europäische Hochschulschriften. Frankfurt am Main, 2008.

Nipperdey, Thomas. "Der Kölner Dom als Nationaldenkmal". *Historische Zeitschrift*, 233 (1981), 594-613.

Offizieller Katalog der Deutschen Werkbund-Ausstellung Cöln 1914. Cologne-Berlin, 1914 [reprint Cologne, 1981].

Pastor, Ludwig von. *August Reichensperger 1808-1895. Sein Leben und sein Wirken auf dem Gebiet der Politik, der Kunst und der Wissenschaft*. Freiburg im Breisgau, 1899.

Peters, Elisabeth. *Kirchliche Wandmalerei im Rheinland 1920-1940 – Zur Geschichte des Kölner Instituts für religiöse Kunst*. Rheinbach, 1996.

Philippi, Friedrich. "Müller, Johann Georg, Bischof von Münster". In: *Allgemeine Deutsche Biographie*, vol. 52. Leipzig, 1906, 513-514.

Pilger, Kathrin. *Der Kölner Zentral-Dombauverein im 19. Jahrhundert. Zur Konstituierung des Bürgertums durch formale Organisation*. Kölner Schriften zu Geschichte und Kultur, 26. Cologne, 2004.

Rapp, Urban. "Kirche und die Kunst der Zeit 1888-1920. Die 'Sektion Kunst' der Katholiken-Tagungen und ihr Urteil über die 'Deutsche Gesellschaft für christliche Kunst' in München". In: Peter-Klaus Schuster, ed. *"München leuchtete!" Die Erneuerung der christlichen Kunst in München um 1900*. Exhibition catalogue Munich, Haus der Kunst, 1984. Munich, 1984, 55-59.

"Religiöse kirchliche Kunst mit besonderer Berücksichtigung der Kunstgewerbeausstellung Dresden". *Der Baumeister*, 4 (1906), 2-10.

Rivinius, Karl Josef. "Keppler, Paul Wilhelm von". In: Traugott Bautz, ed. *Biographisch-Bibliographisches Kirchenlexikon*, vol. 3. Herzberg, 1992, 1379-1383.

Rothes, Walter. *Gebhard Fugel. Eine Einführung in des Meisters Werk und Leben*. Munich, 1925.

Schieder, Wolfgang. *Religion und Revolution. Die Trierer Wallfahrt von 1844*. Vierow, 1996.

Schloßmacher, Norbert. "Die Piusvereine in der preußischen Rheinprovinz 1848/49". In: Otfried Dacher and Ingeborg Schnelling-Reinecke, eds. *Petitionen und Barrikaden. Rheinische Revolutionen 1848/49*. Veröffentlichungen der Staatlichen Archive des Landes Nordrhein-Westfalen. Reihe D. Ausstellungskataloge staatlicher Archive, 29. Münster, 1998, 161-165.

Schneider, Bernhard. "Entwicklungstendenzen rheinischer Frömmigkeits- und Kirchengeschichte in der ersten Hälfte des 19. Jahrhunderts". *Archiv für mittelrheinische Kirchengeschichte*, 48 (1996), 157-195.

Schneider, Bernhard. "Wallfahrt, Ultramontanismus und Politik. Zur Vorgeschichte der Trierer Heilig-Rock-Wallfahrt". In: Martin Persch and Bernhard Schneider, eds. *Auf dem Weg in die Moderne: Das 19. Jahrhundert (1802-1880)*. Geschichte des Bistums Trier, 4, Trier, 2000, 275-369.

Schuster, Peter-Klaus, ed. *'München leuchtete!. Die Erneuerung der christlichen Kunst in München um 1900*. Exhibition catalogue Munich, Haus der Kunst. Munich, 1984.

Schuster, Peter-Klaus. "München leuchtete!" In: Peter-Klaus Schuster, ed. *'München leuchtete'. Die Erneuerung der christlichen Kunst in München um 1900*. Exhibition catalogue Munich, Haus der Kunst, 1984. Munich, 1984, 19-46.

Siebenmorgen, Harald. *Die Anfänge der 'Beuroner Kunstschule'. Peter Lenz und Jakob Wüger 1850-1875*. Sigmaringen, 1981.

Siebenmorgen, Harald. "'Kulturkampfkunst'. Das Verhältnis von Peter Lenz und der Beuroner Kunstschule zum Wilhelminischen Staat". In: Mai Ekkehard, Stephan Waetzold and Gerd Wolandt, eds. *Ideengeschichte und Kunstwissenschaft. Philosophie und bildende Kunst im Kaiserreich*. Kunst, Kultur und Politik im Deutschen Kaiserreich. Schriften eines Projektkreises der Fritz-Thyssen-Stiftung, 3. Berlin, 1983, 409-430.

Smitmans, Adolf. *Die christliche Malerei im Ausgang des 19. Jahrhunderts. Theorie und Kritik: Eine Untersuchung der deutschsprachigen Periodica für christliche Kunst, 1870-1914*. Tübingen, 1978.

Standaert, Felix. *L'École de Beuron. Un essai de renouveau de l'art chrétien à la fin du XIXe siècle*. Denée, 2011.

Streicher, Gebhard. "'... das freie Schaffen der christlichen Künstler begünstigen!' Zur Wirksamkeit der 'Deutschen Gesellschaft für christliche Kunst' zwischen 1893 und 1912/13". In: Peter-Klaus Schuster, ed. *'München leuchtete!' Die Erneuerung der christlichen Kunst in München um 1900*. Exhibition catalogue Munich, Haus der Kunst, 1984. Munich, 1984, 60-65.

Streicher, Gebhard, ed. *Gebhard Fugel. Apokalypse*. Exhibition catalogue Altötting, Stadtgalerie. Amberg, 2003.

Strobbe, Filip. "De Gilde van Sint-Thomas en Sint-Lucas (1863-1894): een genootschap ter bevordering van de neogotiek". *Handelingen van de Koninklijke Geschied- en Oudheidkundige Kring van Kortrijk*, nieuwe reeks, 55 (1989), 7-156.

Tack, Wilhelm. "Die Bestrebungen zur Hebung der kirchlichen Kunst im Erzbistum Paderborn seit 1800". *Alte und Neue Kunst im Erzbistum Paderborn*, 1 (1950), 5-22.

Verleysen, Cathérine. *Maurice Denis et la Belgique. 1890-1930*. KADOC Artes, 11. Leuven, 2010.

Westermann-Angerhausen, Hiltrud, ed. *Alexander Schnütgen. Colligite fragmenta ne pereant. Gedenkschrift des Kölner Schnütgen-Museums zum 150. Geburtstag seines Gründers*. Cologne, 1993.

Weyres, Willy. "Der evangelische Kirchenbau". In: Eduard Trier and Willy Weyres, eds. *Kunst des 19. Jahrhunderts im Rheinland*. Vol. 1. Düsseldorf, 1989, 269-337.

Wietzorek, Paul. *Adolph Kolping(1813-1865): Ein Leben im Dienst der Menschen*. Petersberg, 2013.

Witte, Fritz. "Die Stellung der Kirche zur Modernen". *Zeitschrift für christliche Kunst*, 25 (1912) 1, 3-11.

1.5 Church Building Societies in Scandinavia

Carsten Bach-Nielsen

The Grundtvig Church on the outskirts of Copenhagen was inaugurated five months after the German occupation of Denmark. It took place on Grundtvig's birthday, the 8th September 1940. The huge church on the Bispebjerg – Bishop's Hill – dominates the area and the new township that was built to enclose the cathedral-like building: a dream of the perfect interplay between the vast church and a human scale town. This medieval dream obviously was inspired by English urbanism and the German practice of *Siedlungen*, compounds.[1] [Ill. 1.5-1]

P.V. Jensen-Klint, the 'master builder' – not the 'architect' – made his first draft for the church in 1913. In 1927 the tower was finished and inaugurated in the presence of the king, the mayor, the magistrate, and representatives of the church and popular awakening movements – first and foremost the Grundtvigians. Due to the economic depression the completion of the church was delayed until 1940.

The bishop of Copenhagen, F. Fuglsang-Damgaard made a speech wearing his golden gown. It was transmitted by the wireless as to ensure that everyone even in the most remote parts of Denmark would be able to take part in the event: "The whole Denmark has been carrying stones for this church. Our People has been lifting collectively. The great task had been able to unite it. All strata of the populace has made its contribution."

So this church became a symbol of the cooperation between the church, state, civil society – and the social democracy. It was seen as a fortress against Nazi ideology and oppression. A huge Danish flag with its white cross on the red background made it up for the altarpiece until the end of the war. Although there was no international tourism during the war a poster was produced showing the characteristic skyline of the church and a Danish flag. The text sounded: "Denmark. Unconquered though captive" – expressing the firm but quiet resistance against the Germans. It is remarkable that a church commemorating once controversial N.F.S. Grundtvig (1783-1872) could become a unifying national symbol and bridge the gap between very different concepts of the Church.

The Grundtvig Church became the apex of Danish romantic brickwork architecture, an artistic and expressive line beginning with Architect Daniel Herholdt (1818-1902) in the mid-nineteenth century. The historicist Herholdt was able to build in impeccable Lombardian or Venetian style – and yet 'Danish'. Later the Nyrop-Kampmann national romantic school was a Nordic-Baltic school which Grundtvigian Jensen-Klint stubbornly developed into a specific Danish version.

The Grundtvig Church epitomises the material reform that took place between 1849 and 1922: a new way of organising church building by means of church building societies. It also represents a specific architectural and decorative strategy.[2] The Grundtvig Church however was not the result of a pressure group, but of a committee.[3] In 1922 the role of church building societies as pressure groups in their old form came to an end.

The material reform of Scandinavia has to do with response to industrialisation, urbanisation, and migration. The organisation

1.5-1 The Grundtvig Church in Copenhagen was planned as a memorial church of N.F. S. Grundtvig in 1911. Built by public and voluntary funds by master builder P.V. Jensen-Klint it became a national enterprise, a symbol of the modern social state based on Grundtvig's ideals of freedom and of citizenship. (See also col. ill. 4.) [Courtesy of the author]

1 Steen Petersen, *Som i ét stof*, 131-177.
2 Millech and Fisker, *Danske arkitekturstrømninger*, 207-306.
3 Marstrand, *Grundtvigs Mindekirke paa Bispebjerg*, 92-97.

of church building in Denmark is related to a period with political struggle for parliamentary rule and a tense relationship with neighbouring Germany. There are different concepts of the established churches in the three Scandinavian countries. Consequently there are differences and parallels in the products of material culture.

It is beyond doubt that Denmark was the country of Scandinavia in which powerful church building societies first developed; the reason being that the constitution of 1849 left an uncertainty as to what an established Lutheran church actually was to be. The Copenhagen type of church building societies inspired local movements in Norway, but they did not become acute in Sweden until building of the welfare state in the post-war period in the 1950s.[4]

The difference between Danish, Norwegian, and Swedish architecture is evident – especially concerning church architecture; partly as a result of differences in ecclesiastical organisation. The development in Norway and Sweden was that awakening movements organised as free and independent churches. As such they were free to build however they like. The state wasn't able to make any demands about the looks of such churches. Often the architecture of free churches was inspired by neo-Gothic trends – as the Gothic style on the Continent was considered an adequate expression of positive medieval and traditional Christian values. In Denmark inspiration from the international Gothic style is sparse. Some architects took their point of departure in traditional medieval Baltic brick architecture, but the neo-Gothic style proper with ribs and pointed arches was considered Catholic and even worse: German. The new romantic blend of Romanesque, Baroque and Baltic brickwork was embraced and developed by Danish and Swedish star architects. Building in that style and with the best of architects and materials was expensive. Only state institutions and the huge industries were able to afford building of that calibre. In Sweden imposing churches in the Art Nouveau inspired national Baltic style were built by the state or by industrial magnates. Standing firmly on solid rock and with their decoration they reflect the influence of the Swedish Young Church Movement with its vision of Sweden as a Christian country (Masthugget, Gothenburg; Uppenbarelsekyrkan, Saltsjöbaden; Engelbrektkyrkan and Högalidkyrkan, Stockholm).

The Copenhagen Church Building Society that was founded in 1896 however became determined to rival state and industry. In Copenhagen the beginnings were made with cheap churches in the dark backyards of the capital. At the end – 30 or 40 years later – a series of architectural gems had been erected by voluntary means; the Grundtvig Church being the final symbol of the adhesive power of culture, church and politics in Scandinavia; symbolic because it stylistically was looking backwards. Modern, rational concrete architecture was applied by the architect Frits Schlegel in the Mariehøj Crematory north of Copenhagen six years earlier.[5]

Background in Denmark

In 1848 the Schleswig-Holstein Rebellion broke out and Denmark was plunged into a fight against insurgents and their German allies at the root of the peninsula of Jutland. In the same year of rebellion in all Europe the Danish king granted a free constitution in the realm – not in the duchies Schleswig and Holstein that were defeated two years later and were held in a firm grip under absolutist Danish rule for the following years.

The constitution of 1849 granted religious freedom but the established Lutheran majority church remained under a new name. The established church of Denmark now was called the people's church (*Folkekirken*). The constitution demanded the king be a member of the official church. According to the constitution the actual rule of the church was to be regulated by law. Nobody knew what that meant. Was it a promise that the Danish church at some point would have a synod?

---

4   Gustafsson, *Småkyrkorörelsen*, 176-212.

5   Andersson Møller, *Arkitekten Frits Schlegel*, 99-113.

Or was it a statement that the church was to be governed by means of laws? As time went by laws and acts concerning the church were passed in Parliament. The Danish Church never had a synod but a Ministry of Cultural and Ecclesiastical Matters instead. The Church remained part of state rule and administration – and still it was considered a free and liberal church of the Danish people.

The intention of the constitution actually was that the people eventually take over power and administration of the church. Many questions were raised. Who had the right to choose the pastors; the congregations or the ministry? How wide were limits of freedom? Who were to provide the population with new churches?

The Grundtvigian movement traditionally had a considerable influence among members of the elder national liberal elites. The Grundtvigians succeeded in getting their demands fulfilled: freedom of choosing congregation and the right to establish free congregations within the framework of the official church. After the devastating defeat to Prussia in 1864 and the fall of national liberalism the Grundtvigians organised politically in the Left Party. Consequently this old awakening group and enlightenment movement ceased to act as a pressure group, as it was content pursuing its aims in Parliament through a political discourse and debate. The Grundtvigian movement acted by means of resolutions and addresses in order to generate certain general opinions to support their political claims.

After the cholera epidemic of 1853 the city walls of Copenhagen were abandoned. The city with its magistrate became independent in the 1850s. In the capital it was considered the obligation of the city magistrate to build new churches, to create new congregations and parishes, but hardly anything happened. In the 1850s the king still was active in donating areas in the old demarcation zones and supporting the building of at least one big church, St John's. In the 1860s the capital Copenhagen began to extend rapidly. Industrialisation brought about urbanisation and migration from the countryside to the capital. It meant alienation, rootlessness. A number of Grundtvigian pastors such as the church historian Ludvig Helveg (1818-1883) were among the first to launch the demand that new churches be built to the service of the rapidly growing population. Organisation of such a work was considered the task of the clergy – not of layman. Socialism offered itself as the new unifying power in the endless neighbourhoods where people were deprived of hope for the future and of pastoral service. In order to oppose socialism in the new densely inhabited areas of the city Pastor Rudolf Frimodt (1828-1879) succeeded in collecting funds for the building of St Stephen's Church in Nørrebro. Such a church was to serve as a bulwark against pagan socialism. Actually his initiative resulted in the building of three big new churches, but in 1877 this initiative came to a standstill. The mayor of Copenhagen took the initiative to yet another big church, but work proceeded very slowly. Meanwhile the size of the Copenhagen parishes steadily grew. St John's counted 70,000 inhabitants.

In 1853 the Inner Mission was established but it was not until 1862 that the movement was taken over by the dynamic leader Pastor Vilhelm Beck (1829-1901). Beck as a country parson was inclined to some of Grundtvig's ideas. Now the chief of a pretty conservative countrywide awakening organisation he became an adversary of the Grundtvigians and their participation in the world of politics. The true congregation, God's true community should not at all care for this world, but only for the world to come.

Inner Mission however remained loyal to the established church. The movement stayed within the framework of the established church. In the countryside the organisation began building numerous mission houses. These were only to be used for singing, reading, praying and preaching. The sacraments could not be ministered there. Their names such as Carmel, Bethesda, Sarepta, and Zion reveal the geography of the Inner Mission mind – contrary to the Grundtvigians and their poetical naming of buildings after flowers, nature, history, or pleasant mythological landscape.

The social needs of the migrant newcomers that had swapped the green meadows with the dark city jungle did not concern Inner Mission as such. Radical Protestant as they were their leaders only accepted mission by means of words – not in deeds. Their concern was the salvation of the souls, not of the bodies, as the movement ceased to be a laymen's movement only in order to be ruled by pastors.

In Copenhagen the huge Mission House, Bethesda, was built in 1881-1882. In Copenhagen Vilhelm Beck was challenged by the leader of the Deaconess Institution, Diakonissestiftelsen, Harald Stein (1840-1900) who was inspired by German Inner Mission activists such as Johan Heinrich Wichern and Friedrich von Bodelschwingh. The result was the split-up of the Copenhagen branch of the Inner Mission. It separated into two different branches: the countryside Mission under Beck's leadership and the Copenhagen Inner Mission under Stein. This meant that the city Mission lost much of its country wide support. The vast amount of problems of the church in the capital taken into consideration Copenhagen Inner Mission and the more conservative Copenhagen Grundtvigians joined in a remarkable co-operation. They gathered at the Bethesda Meetings. This new companionship resulted in a series of societies and initiatives that operated independently of the state and the magistrate of Copenhagen. In 1886 the first Bethesda Meeting took place. In a discussion about "the work among the pagan masses in Copenhagen" the Odense pastor Johannes Møller made the suggestion that instead of big churches Copenhagen be provided with a vast amount of – up till 60 or 70 – small churches.

Church building societies and other societies for the promotion of the church

In 1886 a group of upper-class ladies met with the Grundtvigian professor Fredrik Nielsen and the later bishop Skat Rørdam in order to establish a Society for Building of Small Churches in Copenhagen.

This was the beginning of the so-called *kirkesag*. The Danish word *kirkesag* is hard to explain as it has multiple connotations, and even lacks a German equivalent. It consists of 'church' followed by 'cause' or 'matter' or even 'favour'. A '-sag' in that respect is positive. Women's liberation was the 'kvindesag', the military defence of the country was the 'forsvarssag' – and so *kirkesag* emanated as an analogy to other urgent 'matters'. So the *Kirkesag* is a positive response to the needs of the church. *Kirkesag* is a general concept. Under it vague and loosely structured initiatives of promotion as well as organised and powerful church building societies or church funds may be subsumed.

The women's Society for Building of Small Churches in Copenhagen was inspired by the Berlin Chapel Society, Kapellverein, under the leadership of Court Chaplain Adolf Stöcker. In this – probably unmarried – young women paid a small fee of membership and made money by means of production and selling of art and crafts for the erection of chapels in districts of Berlin where people were living without any local church. The Danish society's aim was to build smaller churches in a more modest architecture than the ones in Berlin. Through the families Neergaard and Schiøler the society was able to network and gain support from families of the parsonages and manor houses all over the country. Local branches for young women were organised – although men also might become members at a double fee. After three years of activity the society was able to build its first small and humble church, the Bethlehem Church. [Ill. 1.5-2]

The women of the society wanted to pass their church to the proper church authorities as a gift, but the deans of Copenhagen did not want to receive such an ugly church. The ecclesiastical authorities held that women should not engage in church building. The bishop of Zealand, B.J. Fog (1819-1896) however did receive it and consecrate it. That was a sign of surrender of the old established church and of the state as such. Now the state was not necessarily in charge of church building. The church building initiative had shifted to laymen – and even laywomen.

The board for promotion of the kirkesag in Copenhagen

Only half a year after the inauguration of the Bethlehem Church a circle of five male academics met in order to boost the initiative for church building: one physician, an Egyptologist, the notorious Harald Westergaard (1853-1936), professor of national economy and a splendid organiser – and two pastors of the capital. One of them, Henry Ussing, was to become the dean of Copenhagen. They called themselves 'The Ring' or 'Friends of the Church'. They took their departure in economic and social theories and had been corresponding continuously since 1886. They published a pamphlet in 1890 with their seven points containing the program for small, active – or even activist – congregations. At the same time they send an address to the Ministry demanding establishment of a commission to take care of the needs of the church in Copenhagen. They constituted themselves as the Board of the Promotion of the *Kirkesag* in Copenhagen – or just the Copenhagen *Kirkesag*.

The 'Friends of the Church' were inspired by Thomas Chalmers' theory of pauperism, by John Malcolm Ludlow, Bishop A.C. Tait of London, and of Court Chaplain Adolf Stöcker in Berlin. The dynamic Harald Westergaard was educated in England and familiar with the British strategy of societies. He soon realised that it would take too long time to press the authorities to action. The lay people had to be involved actively in the work for the building of churches. It was however not only churches, Westergaard and Pastor Ussing wanted, they wanted living Christians, Christian personalities, responsible Christians who would organise and form a new church instead of the established Lutheran People's Church. Westergaard and Ussing were inspired by trends in England and the USA deeply rooted in Calvinist thoughts about Christian – self-governing and self-sustaining – communities.

The traditional Lutheran state church system of congregations had to be broken up by the Church Building Society that left it to the people in the new neighbourhoods to collect money for church building, as ordinary Christian people would never succeed in receiving any help from the state.

1.5-2 The Old Bethlehem Church in Blågårdsgade (Nørrebro, Copenhagen) built in 1889.
[Gennem 25 Aar. Udgivet af Foreningen til Opførelse af smaa Kirker i København (Copenhagen, 1911), 11]

It was the Egyptologist H.O. Lange who launched an audacious plan: it did not make sense to collect money in order to build churches for the state. The state authorities would still decide who being elected and appointed pastors – on basis of exams and seniority. He proposed a church fund with a board that would organise collections of money not only in the capital but in the whole nation. These funds would be used for the employment of young pastors. With the consent of the local pastor they were supposed to work in a certain, limited, area – organising new congregations that were to build their own new church in newly segregated parishes.

Part of the financing would come from the Church Building Society that was run by the economic genius Westergaard. People were told to take initiatives to establish congregational communities and they were offered help. As soon as a community was established it could begin to build. Often it started with just a crypt for the community; later a stately and costly building. The new communities would be taxed in order to support their own household. Self-taxation was the new buzz word. It was a matter of some importance that the Church Building Society provided more than half of the expenses for the building. Thereby it was able to maintain its power and influence – and decide who were to be appointed pastors of the new churches. The Copenhagen Church Building Society always chose conservative pastors of the Inner Mission type. One of its slogans was chosen from the gospel of Luke 14, 23: "Go out into the highways and hedges and compel them to come in, that my house may be filled". The society did not conceal using a certain degree of force or pressure. It was not aiming at costly building of 'empty' churches.

Pastor Ussing, the later dean of the Cathedral of Copenhagen compared the Christian community to the Temple of Salomon. Only the true believers were allowed into the holy. Others had to wait outside in the outer courtyards. Finally there was the courtyard of the pagans – the children of the world: members of the established church.[6] So the Copenhagen Church Building Society managed to establish a puritan membership church model within the Lutheran Established Church. All that was certainly not a Lutheran *folkekirke* model, not a people's church. Grundtvigian leftist Morten Pontoppidan fiercely attacked this elite ideology of 'God's living congregation'. He pointed to 'the living God's congregation': the congregation of sinners, the congregation of grace and equality.

Success

The board was successful and in 1891 the first chaplain was employed in a district in the parish of St John. The board of laymen appealed to the public for a moveable church at a price of 25,000 kroner. The iron church was bought in England and taken into use in 1892. Pastors offered their services to the board. They were willing to work under bad conditions at a salary lower than ordinary pastors.

The Society for Building of Small Churches in Copenhagen managed to build 16 small churches that were all handled over to the Board of the *Kirkesag*. The board realised that the small, ugly churched did not provide a real solution to the problems. One had to think differently. It had to transform its initiative for Copenhagen to a task and responsibility of the whole country; maybe even force this responsibility onto the public.

In 1896 the Copenhagen Church Building Society was created.[7] It was clearly inspired by English societies and thus, on the initiative of the bishop of Zealand, a general collection in all churches of the country was instigated – in favour of the Copenhagen Church Building Society. With this nationwide public support the time had come to build real and expensive churches on prominent spots in the capital.

6   Ussing, *Tanker til Overvejelse*, 88-117: the chapters "The Temple" and "The Walls of Jerusalem".
7   1890-1915. *Københavns Kirkesag*, 47-53.

Inspirations

The Grundtvigian congregation at the old hospital of Vartov in Copenhagen came in opposition to the conservative government as Grundtvig's successor, C.J. Brandt died in 1889. The Ministry refused to appoint Fredrik Jungersen as the new pastor of the congregation because of his anti-government utterings. So part of the congregation established itself as a free congregation. In the beginning the congregation held its services in the gym house of a folk high school in Copenhagen, but pretty soon the congregation was able to build a church that was to become an architectural icon of Copenhagen and of the Grundtvigian movement. It was the Immanuel Church designed by architect Andreas Clemmensen in 1890-1892 and decorated by the brothers Niels and Joakim Skovgaard and Thorvald Bindesbøll. [Ill. 1.5-3] With this building the Grundtvigians proved that they were able to raise money for a very expensive and modern church – designed in accordance with the liberal principles of Grundtvigianism. They did not rely on money from the state or the government. It was imperative to show that they did not intend to remain stored away in the gym shed; instead they set a visible mark on Copenhagen. The church was a free invention of a brick work Romanesque church. Danish and international at the same time – built in accordance with the dogma of the young and modern architects. Buildings were not to be pointed; they had to be modelled as a lump of clay. What was called the traditional Danish house actually was a baroque house: firm and heavy. That was to become the hallmark of the academic Scandinavian architecture since that time. Grundtvigians with their sense of art and crafts that was being taught at the Folk High Schools were modernists, they appealed to the modern taste, the Nordic and anti-German taste. Grundtvigians were conscious of the value of good craftsmanship. Architecture should be 'honest'.

That must have been an eye opener to Westergaard. His ecclesiology was contrary to Grundtigianism. But the two movements agreed in using the constitutional rights of establishing free congregations.

The constitution made it possible to the government to rule without assembling the Parliament – in times of emergency. In 1877 the law of the Finance was passed without the consent of Parliament. From 1885 to 1894 the government ruled entirely by means of provisory laws. The opposition thereby was brought to silence. No new laws could be passed, no initiatives could be taken. In that situation Westergaard and the Board of the Promotion of the *Kirkesag* – and later the

1.5-3 *The Grundtvigian Immanuel Church was listed among the efforts of the Copenhagen Kirkesag. The brothers Joakim and Niels Skovgaard made the decorations of the church. Here in the mosaic over the side entrance, the old dragon is conquered – a central Grundtvigian motiv.*
[København Kirkesag i Billeder. Udgivet af det københavnske Kirkefonds Forretningsudvalg *(Copenhagen, 1912), 58]*

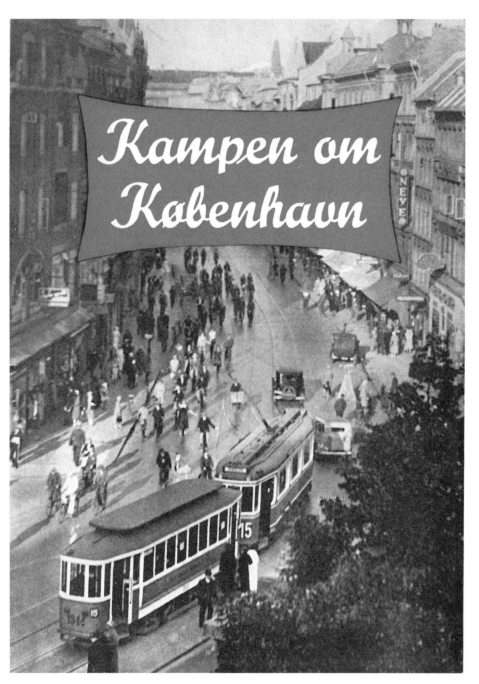

1.5-4 The title of Kampen om København – the Combat for Copenhagen, may refer to the lost battle against the overwhelming British enemy that left Copenhagen and its main church Our Lady's in ruins in 1807. That however was followed by the so-called Golden Age. The new battle has been a battle against an inner enemy, paganism, but Copenhagen and Christianity were rescued by the Church Building Society.

Copenhagen Church Building Society – developed the ambitious idea to turn the entire established church into a free church – or at least a network of free congregations. The Church Building Society would act as a general assembly and prepare the old established Lutheran majority church for a final break with the state. The protagonists of the new and more Calvinist church model now wanted to change its position as an underground church with poor buildings in humble positions to the position as the dominant church. That demanded quite a new type of church – modern churches in strategic positions – drawn by the best architects with rich materials and a design that did not leave anything to the national romantic Grundtvigians.

The leaders of the Copenhagen Church Building Society were eminent propagandists using all the modern strategies. Its accusations against state authorities were repeated for decades. Its leaders grossly exaggerated the needs of Copenhagen. Westergaard as an international renowned expert of national economy and statistics was able to prove the progress of the society beyond all doubt by means of endless columns of figures. The Society's financial politics could be – and was – discussed. But the organisation kept writing books and pamphlets about its deeds, achievements, and its success; about 'The battle for Copenhagen' that it had won. [Ill. 1.5-4] Still new projects came to life, and the churches built by the society became extremely expensive churches, build on the finest areas by the best architects. Westergaard's vision was the transformation of the capital's dark pagan townscape into a bright Christian skyline of towers, belfries, spires, domes, and crosses.

Once the concept of the *Kirkesag* had proven operational in relation to an established church, it might be applied to initiatives anywhere in the greater Denmark.

Arctics

Greenland originally was under the Norwegian crown and so it became Danish by the Kalmar Union of 1397. The Norse settlers seem to have died in the late Middle Ages and the land was sparsely populated by the Inuit. In 1721 a state mission was taken up among the Inuit but it was outmastered by the Moravians. As the Moravians claimed to have finished the mission and the Danish state declared the mission of Greenland complete in 1905 the question was who to sustain and support the Lutheran church in Greenland? There had to be a church that was independent of the Royal Greenland Company. In 1906 the *Kirkesag* of Greenland was founded as an intermediary organisation between the Greenland Church and Danish state authorities. It was a pressure group as well. Its existence contributed to the preservation of the church during British occupation 1940-1945 as there was no communication with Denmark. It worked vigorously for the building of new churches in the vast land. In 1982 Greenland acquired home rule and in 1993 the Diocese of Greenland became a new one among the Danish dioceses of 1922. The *Kirkesag* of Greenland survived until 2000.

Tropics

Much more complicated was the situation in the Danish West Indies. The Virgin Islands became a proper colony since 1755 as the Company was taken over by the crown. The islands had full religious freedom, as the settlers came from all nations. The majority was made up by Moravians, Catholics and Dutch Reformed. Only the members of the Danish civil servants were Lutheran. Even the Danish governor was a general dean and acted as minister of religious and cultural matters of the islands. In 1902 a referendum in Denmark decided to incorporate the colony into Denmark. How that would work was hard to imagine. Only 1,000 out of 37,000 inhabitants were Danish speaking. None the less it was decided to export the idea of an established Lutheran, European church to the islands – albeit it would be a minority church. The Lutheran church was considered the best agent to connect the people of the West Indies, Denmark – and the North Atlantic Islands, the Faeroe Islands and Iceland where a *Kirkesag* society also was founded. That was an ambitious plan supported by Grundtvigian bishop of Zealand Th. Skat Rørdam. The common Grundtvigians however did not see the relevance of this project – but the pastors of the Inner Mission and the leadership of the Copenhagen Church Building Fund did.

In 1904 the committee of the West Indian *Kirkesag* was founded. It was to consist of representatives of all denominations within the Danish Church. Some committee members were inspired by Booker Washington and his schools for the Black in Tuskegee, Alabama. They were considered to have a resemblance with the Danish Folk High Schools. The natives' skills should be developed in order to give them an increasing sense of autonomy. The agrarian Danish Grundtvigians knew that true liberation rested on the ownership of land, the responsibility for soil and family. Younger generations of the Grundtvigians of the Folk High School circles were influenced by the economic theories of Henry George. To them answer to all problems in the homeland and in the colonies was homesteading. The church however had the obligation to educate the Black people, teaching them to master the freedom.

The mid of the Island of St Croix was densely occupied by the workers that were left without proper work after abolition of slavery in 1848. Here the West Indian *Kirkesag* decided to build a church. Then problems began. The church was built by a rising star on the Danish architectural firmament, Povl Baumann. He was a member of the group of young architects that received their first education from P.V. Jensen-Klint. The majority of them went on to the workshop of State Railway architect Heinrich Wenck. Wenck like Hack Kampmann trained his many pupils in the national romantic style, but in 1911 something appalling to the young architects happened. Master Brewer Jacobsen of Carlsberg offered the main work of neo-classical architecture, C.F. Hansen's Church of Our Lady of Copenhagen a Baroque spire. The young architects immediately revolted by turning to neo-neoclassicism. Even their master and teacher Hack Kampmann did.

Baumann's family used to be civil servants in the West Indies. His family was intermingled with numerous families of Old

1.5-5 The inauguration of the Kings Hill Church at St. Croix, Danish West Indies, in 1913. It was built by the West India Kirkesag with only sparse contributions from the homeland.
[Courtesy of the author]

Danish West India. Baumann was given the task of building a new neoclassical West Indian church on Kings Hill in the St Croix Midlands. Due to the want of funds he could not build it out of traditional yellow bricks. Baumann engaged with a Danish engineer who proposed him to build it out of hurricane-proof concrete. The beautiful little church was inaugurated in 1913. [Ill. 1.5-5] The *Kirkesag* was not able to raise money for a parsonage. The committee hoped for the Danish state to build it if the church building was turned over to the state. The state however refused to receive the church and the expenses it would leave to the future. The state proved resistant to this pressure which was a severe disappointment to the committee and especially to the Lutheran pastor of Christian-sted, Povl Helweg-Larsen, the nephew of the governor and a member of the Copenhagen Church Building Society.[8] He was to be the first and only dean to the Islands – and later a mighty leader of the Copenhagen Church Building Society.

Denmark was the last country to sell a colony, namely to the USA in 1917. The *Kirkesag* of the Danish West Indies was transferred to the General Council, Philadelphia, USA, as the American constitution does not allow the state to own and support churches.

Schleswig

After the incorporation of Schleswig-Holstein into Prussia in 1867 the church had to come to terms with the new state authorities. In the former duchies the church remained a Lutheran church (*Landeskirche*) contrary to the Prussian united church. It was governed by the Ministry of Cultural Matters in Berlin and by the local consistory of Kiel. The Prussian king replaced the Danish king as the supreme head, the *summus episcopus* of the church. Since 1876 the church underwent a modernisation and democratisation that was even more liberal than in Denmark. The church had local and joint synods and thereby an extensive practical independence of the state.

The Danish speaking and Danish minded congregations however saw any German law and regulation as attempt to oppress Danish services. As a matter of fact Danish services remained in many parishes of Northern Schleswig; a society of pastors in Schleswig was established – half of them being the pastors of Northern Schleswig. The Danish congregations had their own Danish hymnals. The Grundtvigians even produced their own appendix to that. There was a visible difference between the Danish speaking

8   Bach-Nielsen, "En kirkesagsmand i Vestindien"; Id., "Povl Baumanns kirke på Sankt Croix".

church south of the border and north of it. Somehow nationalism was not able to accept such differences. Two responses were given. Inner Mission remained inside the framework of the established local German state church. The Grundtvigians however organised free congregations. In doing that they were breaking with the established, local, Lutheran state church. In 1914 there were nine free Danish congregations with six pastors. They existed in an atmosphere of constant conflict with German authorities that would not recognise them as ecclesiastical institutions. They were considered purely political inventions. The ecclesiological concepts and convictions of the Danish Grundtvigians were incomprehensible to the order of the German local church. The pastors were not to be called or addressed as pastors. They were called speakers, *Sprecher*. The church buildings could not be called churches; members of the established Lutheran church who wanted to join a free congregation were considered persons leaving not only the state church but the society of the universal church. Such individuals were considered next to pagans. The Danish pastors of the free congregations were forbidden to bury the members of their flocks. Ringing bells at funerals was forbidden just as any ceremony for members of free congregations at the cemeteries of the established church was against the law.[9]

In 1896 the first church building of a free congregation in Schleswig was inaugurated in Haderslev. All church buildings of the free congregations were delivered by Danish architects. They were to show off as Danish architecture, traditional and almost idyllic, contrary to the bold blood and iron mentality of Bismarck's and the Emperor's Germany. The hallmark of architect Magdahl Nielsen of Copenhagen actually was his romanticising of buildings according to the Danish concept of 'hygge', homeliness. He built the Free Church in Rødding in 1909. Even Grundtvigian Martin Nyrop procured the congregation of the peninsula of Sundeved with draw-

1.5-6 *Martin Nyrop's small, simple and 'honest' Free Church building at Sundeved dates from 1903.*
[Courtesy of the author]

ings for a cosy yellow brick church inspired by a hymn verse by Grundtvig. [Ill. 1.5-6]

The approximately 2000 members of the free congregations were not able to sustain themselves as such. The only way to gather strength as a pressure group was organising as a *Kirkesag* with heavy support form congregations and societies in Denmark. In 1907 the *Kirkesag* of Northern Schleswig was founded. It was not able to deliver any pressure on German authorities but it kept up spirits among the Danish Grundtvigians south of the border – and made it clear to the public in Denmark that the Danish cause had not been lost. As frontispiece of their Danish journal they used the apostle of the North, Scandinavia's first bishop, Ansgar – together with the motto "Hitherto the Lord has been helping". It was clear that the support was to come from the established congregations in Scandinavia.

A 1920 plebiscite under the control of the Allies divided old Schleswig. Northern Schleswig became Southern Jutland – and the Danish church in Germany chose full independence of the German Lutheran church. That undermined the existence of the free congregations; only two of them still exist within the framework of Danish free congregations. It is hard to say whether this

9 Petersen, *De sønderjyske Frimenigheders Historie*, 108-132.

kirkesag was a success. It did not succeed as a pressure group – only as a temporary protest organisation.

Provincial towns

Church building societies were not limited to the municipality of Copenhagen. Some of the smaller towns neighbouring the capital made use of church building societies.

The fastest growing town outside Copenhagen was Aarhus in Eastern Jutland. It was urgent to take up an initiative of work for the church without making the same mistakes here as in Copenhagen. The conservative government erected its one and only church during the years of provisory rule in Aarhus, St Pauls' Church. In 1907 a Church Building Society was formed. There was some uncertainty as to the role of the optional congregation councils. Should they necessarily be represented in a Church Building Society? They were finally established as permanent by law in 1912 and then they had to be represented. The bishop of Aarhus was the conservative, right-wing Grundtvigian, former professor of Church History at the University of Copenhagen, Fredrik Nielsen. He was the most internationally oriented and respected church historian of his time; a strong opponent to ultramontanism – and to modernism as well; as a type perhaps similar to Professor Ignaz von Döllinger of Munich. Being a specialist in Early Christianity he wanted to increase the power of the bishops. As to the constitution of the Aarhus Church Building Fund he specifically wanted to copy the Bishop of London's Fund. He succeeded as it was made part of its constitution that the bishop always be the chairman of it.

Nielsen's successor, Bishop H.S. Sørensen, made it clear that the Aarhus Fund – contrary to the Copenhagen Fund – would only exercise its work within the field and order of the established Danish church. The Aarhus Fund could not be used as an instrument of an ecclesiological view as Ussing's building on living congregational societies. The Aarhus Fund did not aim at founding a church within the church.[10]

The royal inspector of public buildings Hack Kampmann – the most respected architect of the country – was in charge of town planning of his home town Aarhus. He reserved squares for churches and gave propositions for the development of new parishes in his urbanistic visions for the town. Probably due to Kampmann's effort the churches of Aarhus were to be buildings of the highest aesthetic standards. It became a habit to arrange competitions between architects, which meant that Jensen-Klint was considered too old-fashioned and was disfavoured to modern neoclassicist Kai Gottlob in the competition for the Church of St Luke in 1918.

The Aarhus Church Fund contrary to the strategy of the Copenhagen Church Building Fund did not appeal to the widest public or to specific classes or strata of society. Money was raised by local collections and in collaboration with the local church authorities and the magistrate. New broad collaborations between church and town council came to function in Aarhus, one of the most thoroughly social democratic towns of Denmark. Churches were to be built by local, democratic committees.

Norway and Sweden

In Kristiania – now Oslo – the inspiration from the Copenhagen Church Building Society was obvious. Here the city authorities were less reluctant than the Copenhagen magistrate to build new churches. Therefore only a few churches were built by the Movement for Building of Small Churches especially in the limited workers' neighbourhoods of the Norwegian capital.

In Stockholm there was some interest in the Copenhagen movement during the 1890s, but the expansion of Stockholm was not as rapid as in Copenhagen. There was not a desperate need of churches. The somewhat pietistic Swedish clergy did not agree

10 Høirup, ed., *Århus Kirkefond*, 13-14.

with Henry Ussing's ecclesiological theories. The awakening movements did not cherish the idea of small independent communities. There were discussions of ecclesiology but very little action. The Society for ecclesiastical pastoral care only took part in building one church. In Stockholm it was expected that the proper state church authorities provided people with parishes and churches.[11]

Copenhagen strategies

The Copenhagen Church Building Society was not a real society; it remained a board or a trust. One could not apply for membership, although it was possible to become a friend of the Church Building Initiative – a supporter. The Copenhagen Church Building Society claimed to be representative of the entire Danish congregation – and its calls for help and support was directed to the congregations of the two thousand parishes in whole Denmark.

At the time of establishment of the Church Fund and the Copenhagen Church Building Society it had been a matter of discussion whether Christians could be addressed as a mass. Christians are neither a mass nor a mob and should not be subject to masters. Socialists conceived the workers as a mass. Christians are valuable individuals. It also was discussed if it was legitimate to propagate Christianity among Christians. The leaders of the initiative were uncertain to the role of propagation or propaganda. Could mass media be used in order to promulgate the good cause?

Westergaard was a master of propaganda. He succeeded in making the entire population feel responsible for the damages and disadvantages of industrialisation, urbanisation, proletarisation, and alienation. The Church Building Society addressed different strata and classes of society, and made them responsible for specific buildings. The people that remained in rural or provincial Denmark bought remission of their sins. One church was built by the nobility of Zealand,

one by the country pastors, others by house maids and so on. Jubilees and centenaries of reformers or hymn writers were used as pretexts for building new churches. So-called Anna committees were established all over the country in order to support the building of the Copenhagen Anna Church. A small amount was donated for every girl who was given the name Anna, even a schooner in Funen was named Anna and thereby contributed to the fund. [Ill. 1.5-7]

Another means of recognition was getting a lot of friends, well-known, respected people among artists, cultural debaters, politicians, and leaders of charitable organisations. They would recommend the initiative broadly. When getting a booklet with the recommendations of 50 people it would be strange not to know just a few of them. Westergaard created the impression that the Copenhagen Church Building Society received a general national support.

Professor at the Royal Academy of Fine Arts Joakim Skovgaard, 'the Grundtvig of

1.5-7 *The missionary Carl Hornbech issued a booklet of reports from the mission in India. In India the smallest coin is called an Anna. His booklet when sold was to be his Anna – his contribution to the building of the Anna Church at Nørrebro.*
[Courtesy of the author]

11 Gustafsson, *Småkyrkorörelsen*, 159-187.

1.5-8 Joakim Skovgaard's vignette "Rebuilding the Walls of Jerusalem" on the cover of a pamphlet by the Friends of the Copenhagen Kirkesag.
[Courtesy of the author]

1.5-9 At the entrance to the crypt of the Elijah Church, the main church of the Copenhagen Church Building Society, a tablet tells that this church was built and inaugurated in 1908 by means of voluntary gifts. It belongs to the Copenhagen Church Fund. "Elijah said to the people: Come near unto me. And all the people came near to him. And he repaired the altar of the Lord that was broken down. 1 Kings 18.30."
[Courtesy of the author]

painting', was the most respected artist in church and culture. He supported the Society letting it use a sketch from the Cathedral of Viborg as its emblem – namely "The rebuilding of the walls of Jerusalem", Nehemiah 4. 17-20.[12] Now it was made obvious that also the most prominent artist among the Grundtvigians supported the cause. [Ill. 1.5-8]

Only the best, most respected – and expensive – architects were employed for the building of the churches of the Society. Since 1864 there was a general nationalisation of culture. Any modern architect felt it was required to work in styles that could be called traditional.[13] Hardly any German architects were practising in Denmark; Joakim Skovgaard's aim to redesign material goods from the ground took its departure in the inspiration of British William Morris. So building and design in national, traditional style was necessary in order to be taken seriously.

It gave the Church Building Society prestige to employ Thorvald Jørgensen, architect of the Copenhagen Castle of Christiansborg, to build the lavish Isaiah Church in a neighbourhood of embassies and residences of industrial magnates and noblemen.[14] Most of the architects were adherents to or inclined to the Grundtvigian movement – as they were all more or less trained by Jensen-Klint or Martin Nyrop. There were close relations between architects, artists, the Left party, and the Grundtvigian movement. [Ill. 1.5-9]

It was easier to the Church Building Society to gain acceptance and respectability by building lavishly in traditional style than to invent a new expression. Incidentally most architects and artists belonged to a cultural elite whose concept of church and congregation did not reflect that of the Church Building Society.

Finally traditional architecture was well understood by the donators all over the country. The national romantic traditional

12 Kral, *Die Fresken Joakim Skovgaards im Dom zu Viborg*, 156.
13 Russell-Hitchcock, *Architecture*, 395-398.
14 Stidsen, "The Dynamics of Reform in Denmark", 279.

architecture somehow was a mirror of the history and architecture all Danes had in common. Even in the huge Grundtvig Church the traditional Danish country or small town church is recognisable.

The Church Building Society apparently appealed to the good taste. Not the bourgeois taste, but the ideals that were being propagated by the younger architects and designers. Industrialisation boosted building activity all over the land. Architects, builders, art historians, town planners and engineers were aware of the damages of low quality building and cheap materials. Inspired by the German reformist and architect Paul Schulze-Naumburg (1869-1949) they started the national Society for better Building. It was organised as a free professional help for builders and craftsmen who would like to have their drawings corrected and improved by professional, academic architects. Schulze-Naumburg was renowned for his method of 'example' and 'counter example' which he used in his nine volumes of *Kulturarbeiten* (Works of Culture) 1900-1917. The Copenhagen Church Building Society adapted this type of propaganda. It constantly proved and displayed how it contributed to the general embellishment of the capital – tearing down the first generation temporary, cheap material churches and replacing them with the best of architecture. [Ill. 1.5-10]

The Church Building Society was aware it could not win the battle against the established church if its buildings did not match or supersede the already existing ones. It became part of the story and of the propaganda that in the course of less than 25 years the Society had moved from dance halls and cheap iron or cocolith (a residue of coconuts) churches to lavish stone buildings. Iconographically new churches told stories about the church, the underground church, the Roman town church of the first Christian centuries, the elevated monasteries of the high Middle Ages – all dressed up with a modern Nordic architectural language. [Ill. 1.5-11]

In all these respects Westergaard and his men were ruthless. They did not care for the means they used – and they did not at all care for democracy. The aim of the Church Building Society always was to seize and cling to power, exercising their right of choosing conservative pastors. The Society clung to power even after new laws limited the influence of it in the congregations.

It was not hard to act as a pressure group under the rule of the undemocratic Right Party. There was no political debate and no

1.5-10 Clearly inspired by the Cultural Works of German architect P. Schulze-Naumburg this sheet of the Church Building Society addresses the Christian people of Copenhagen. It contrasts buildings erected in the poorest period of Danish history with buildings from the richest: example and counter example. The richest period suffers under small unworthy churches.
[Courtesy of the author]

1.5-11 The small Church of St Philip on the Island of Amager was build out of cocolith – with traditional Danish timber framing. In 1924 it was demolished and replaced by a boasting medley of Danish rural Gothic in an early church centre.
[Courtesy of the author]

democratic decisions. The Church Building Society was battling for the traditional values, for the Christianity, so the government made a lot of concessions to the Society. But in 1901 the old rule collapsed and the Left Party took over and instigated parliamentary order. The prime minister soon made an act about congregation councils in every parish – thus giving a certain amount of self-government to ordinary people – including women. That was a blow to the Church Building Society and its ideology. But it did not affect the Society that much as there was only little interest in these councils. They were established by law in 1912.

After the incorporation of Northern Schleswig a number of new acts were passed that secured democracy in the established church in 1922. The Church Building Society from the very beginning placed the churches at the disposal of the established church, but now claimed its half right to use the churches. The congregation councils took over the tasks of the boards of the churches. Until 1940 the Church Building Society paid part of the expenses of the churches. The normal way of building churches since 1922 became collaboration between a democratic elected committee and the state or municipal authorities.

At the 50 years anniversary in 1940 – the year of the inauguration of the Grundtvig Church – the Copenhagen Church Building Society regarded itself as a rescue initiative that not only had managed saving the established church, but also Christianity among the Danes. It saw its effort as a victory over modernism, paganism and godless socialism. At its beginnings the Copenhagen Church Building Society with its puritan or Calvinist ecclesiology was at odds with the establishment. 50 years later it was able to celebrate its universal and national victory. The royal family and other high ranking dignitaries of state and church were invited for the solemn celebration in the Elijah Church – built by the Copenhagen Church Building Society by Grundtvigian architect of the Copenhagen Town Hall, Martin Nyrop. 1940 therefore in more than one respect signifies the settlement between two formerly very different or even hostile models of maintaining and organising the church in the mind of the people and in public space.

The age of the Church Building initiatives and societies coincided with a golden age of Danish architecture. Church architecture due to the battle for the Church and the fight for Christianity – and plenty of funds – became one of the spearheads of developing what later was called Danish Design. It leaves state, church, and society with an enormous problem as a part of all too many brilliant churches in Copenhagen now face closing at the beginning of a new century.

BIBLIOGRAPHY

1890-1915. Københavns Kirkesag. Festskrift udgivet af Kirkefondets Forretningsudvalg. Copenhagen, 1915.

Aldenby, Claes, Jöran Lindwall and Wilfried Wang, eds. *20th Century Architecture. Sweden*. Munich-New York, 1998.

Andersson Møller, Vibeke. *Arkitekten Frits Schlegel*. Copenhagen, 2004.

Bach-Nielsen, Carsten. "En kirkesagsmand i Vestindien. 11 breve fra Povl Helweg-Larsen, 1910-1919". *Kirkehistoriske Samlinger*, 2001, 215-258.

Bach-Nielsen, Carsten. "Povl Baumanns kirke på Sankt Croix". *Architectura. Arkitekturhistorisk Årsskrift*, 23 (2001), 70-89.

Balslev-Clausen, Erik. "To 'kirkesager' – eller Hvad har Grønland og Dansk Vestindien med hinanden at gøre på det kirkelige område?". *Den grønlandske kirkesag. Meddelelser*, 135 (1999), 18-24.

Birkedal, Uffe. *William Morris og hans Betydning*. Copenhagen, 1908.

Clausen, Johannes. *Den sønderjyske Kirkesag*. Kolding, 1897.

Clausen, Johannes. *Hvad er Grunden? Og hvorom er Kampen? Betragtning angaaende den sønderjyske Sag*. Copenhagen, 1899.

Den københavnske Kirkesag. En Oversigt ved 20de Aarhundredes Begyndelse. Udgivet af "Det Københavnske Kirkefond". Copenhagen, 1900.

Dirckinck-Holmfeld, Kim, ed. *Dansk arkitektur 250 år. 250 Years of Danish Architecture*. Copenhagen, 2004.

Gennem 25 Aar. Udgivet af Foreningen til Opførelse af smaa Kirker i København. Copenhagen, 1911.

Gennem 60 Aar. 1886-1946. Udgivet af Foreningen til Opførelse af smaa Kirker i København. Copenhagen, 1946.

Gravgaard, Anne-Mette, ed. *Kirke og Kunst i 100 år. Historie – Arkitektur – Udsmykning – Sølv og Tekstil*. Copenhagen, 1990.

Gravgaard, Anne-Mette, ed. *Storbyens virkeliggjorte længsler. Kirkerne i København og på Frederiksberg 1860-1940*. Copenhagen, 2001.

Gustafsson, Berndt. *Småkyrkorörelsen - dess historiska bakgrund*. Stockholm, 1955.

Helweg-Larsen, P. *Københavns Kirkesag. Skal den gaa frem eller tilbage?* Copenhagen, 1923.

Helweg-Larsen, P. *Ved Skillevejen. Betragtninger over Københavns Kirkesag*. Copenhagen, 1926.

Helweg-Larsen, P. *Kirkesagens Venner. Det afgørende Punkt i Kirkesagen*. Copenhagen, 1931.

Helweg-Larsen, P., ed. *"Kirkens Venners" korrespondance*. Copenhagen, 1955.

Høirup, Henning, ed. *Århus Kirkefond 1907 - 29. Januar - 1967*. Aarhus, 1967.

Hornbech, Carl. *En Anna. Skildringer fra Indien*. Struer, undated.

Jelsbak, Jens, ed. *Grundtvigs Kirke*. Copenhagen, 1977.

Jensen, Thomas Bo. *P.V. Jensen-Klint*. Copenhagen, 2006.

Kampen om Kirkesagen. Copenhagen, 1925.

Kirkefondets første Tiaar. Udgivet af det københavnske Kirkefonds Forretningsudvalg. Copenhagen, 1907.

Kirkesagens Gennemførelse i København. Udgivet af Kirkefondets Hjælpeindsamling i København. Copenhagen, 1925.

Kjær, Ulla and Poul Grinder-Hansen. *Kirkerne i Danmark II. Den protestantiske tid efter 1536*. Copenhagen, 1989.

Københavns Kirkesag i Billeder. Udgivet af det københavnske Kirkefonds Forretningsudvalg. Copenhagen, 1912.

Kral, Martina. *Die Fresken Joakim Skovgaards im Dom zu Viborg. Religiöse Malerei für eine neue Zeit*. Bau+Kunst. Schleswig-Holsteinische Schriften zur Kunstgeschichte, 4. Kiel, 2001.

Lindahl, Göran. *Högkyrkligt, lågkyrkligt, frikyrkligt i svensk arkitektur 1800-1950*. Stockholm, 1955.

Lindhardt, Poul Georg. *Skandinavische Kirchengeschichte seit dem 16. Jahrhundert*. Die Kirche in ihrer Geschichte. Ein Handbuch. Göttingen, 1982.

Marstand, Jacob. *Grundtvigs Mindekirke paa Bispebjerg*. Copenhagen, 1932.

Millech, Knud, and Kay Fisker. *Danske arkitekturstrømninger 1850-1950*. Copenhagen, 1951.

Petersen, Thade. *De sønderjyske Frimenigheders Historie*. Copenhagen, 1921.

Rasmussen, Cai, ed. *Kirken og millionbyen. Det københavnske Kirkefond 1890-1965*. Copenhagen, 1965.

Rasmussen, Steen Eiler. *Nordische Baukunst*. Copenhagen, 1940.

Russell-Hitchcock, Henry. *Architecture: Nineteenth and Twentieth Centuries*. The Pelican History of Art. Harmondsworth, 1958.

Schädler Andersen, Lars. *Balancekunstneren. Harald Westergaard, kirkesagen og det sociale spørgsmål 1878-1907*. Copenhagen, 2012.

Sommer, Kr. *Kampen om København. 1812-1947*. Copenhagen, 1948.

Steen Petersen, Anne-Marie. *Som i ét stof – en fortælling om Grundtvigskirken og dens bygmester*. Copenhagen, 1997.

Stidsen, Enggard. "The Dynamics of Reform in Denmark, c 1780-1920". In: Anders Jarlert, ed. *Piety and Modernity*. KADOC Studies on Religion, Culture and Society. The Dynamics of Religious Reform in Northern Europe, 1780-1920, 3. Leuven, 2012, 265-285.

Stoklund, Bjarne, ed. *Kulturens nationalisering. Et etnologisk blik på det nationale*. Copenhagen, 1999.

Struwe, Kamma. *Kirkerevolution i 1890'erne. Biografisk-historisk kulturbillede*. Copenhagen, 1995.

Struwe, Kamma. "Kirkens venner". In: Henrik Wivel, ed. *Drømmetid. Fortællinger om Det sjælelige Gennembruds København*. Copenhagen, 2004, 192-203.

Ussing, Henry. *Tanker til Overvejelse om Menighedsliv og Kirkeliv*. Copenhagen, 1890.

Vellev, Jens, ed. *Joakim Skovgaards Fresco-malerier i Viborg Domkirke*. Viborg, 1997.

2.
SPACE AND THE FABRIC OF BUILDINGS AND CONSTRUCTIONS

Introduction

Jan De Maeyer

In the period 1780-1920, waves of church renovation and construction swept across Northwest Europe. This was remarkable for a century just following the Enlightenment, given the widespread perception that the nineteenth century heralded the beginning of a radical secularisation. The building activity might seem to have been a response to this impending development, but nothing could be further from the truth. From circa 1815 to 1820 the churches rebounded and gained favour among broad sections of the population. Unprecedented building campaigns were carried out, with hundreds of mostly smaller urban and rural churches erected or extended in each country. In addition, related community facilities were also built: parsonages (Protestant), rectories (Anglican) and presbyteries (Roman Catholic), parish halls, confessional schools, plots in public cemeteries as well as full confessional cemeteries. As the contributions in this section note, many of the same church buildings were demolished or radically repurposed about a hundred years later, as they no longer served a function in a time of far-reaching secularisation that marks the transition from the twentieth to the twenty-first century. The grand infrastructure of the period of Church Reform and the associated material changes no longer meet today's small-scale needs.

The various established churches felt challenged to undertake this intense construction activity, spurred primarily by the religious tolerance of the Enlightenment and by the fact that other religious communities were now allowed in addition to the state churches. Given infrastructure that had been confiscated during the Reformation, these other communities re-adapted it (restorations, renovations), or built new churches. In their turn, the state churches that had released confiscated property looked for new infrastructure for themselves. This may partly explain the boom in church building.

However, other factors also stimulated this activity. A second was that in the wake of the Enlightenment, several regions in Northwest Europe (the Netherlands, Belgium and parts of Germany) were affected by the anti-clerical politics of the French revolutionary occupiers and the destruction of churches and monasteries during the Napoleonic Wars. The revolutions and wars after Waterloo and the Congress of Vienna (1815) then sparked an unprecedented religious revival, a period of extraordinary religious activism. As mentioned above, the churches saw their congregations growing again, a development that was further stimulated by strong demographic growth and migration movements from the countryside to the cities and from impoverished Ireland to England.

Third, increasing religious tolerance also had an effect. Around 1840-1850, the established churches in Northwest Europe lost their monopoly and dissident Protestant churches and free churches were given free rein. These churches also needed infrastructure, from prayer houses and mission houses to large auditorium-style churches in the large cities.

This once again intensified the construction and renovation activity. The public space became a battleground, with every denomination wanting a visible architectural manifestation of its identity. Successive contributions in this section illustrate how churches tried to adapt their own material profiles and how church infrastructure, willy-nilly, became part of the urbanisation process and a reference point in rural areas. Churches that wanted to be visible also had to defend their own identities, and so used additional resources: on the Protestant side, memorials of Luther and Melanchthon, and on the Catholic side, Marian columns, columns with images of local saints or memorial plaques with references to historical religious events. The Catholic Church mobi-lised the faithful around Marian pilgrimage sites and built grand basilicas in honour of Mary. In the wake of the Marian apparitions in Lourdes, the second half of the nineteenth century saw the construction of Marian grottoes in girls' boarding schools, monastery gardens and in private parks, which were opened especially for this purpose. Contractors and suppliers of building materials went along with this new trend. In the Netherlands, the phenomenon of private Catholic procession parks emerged in the second half of the nineteenth century, as a way of circumventing the prohibition on processions in public spaces. Cemeteries and crematoria were also part of the often-grim battle for space, because nothing was as sensitive as death in the long nineteenth century.

The struggle for the public space was a struggle for the symbolism of recognition. Church towers became markers: the higher the tower, preferably the bell tower, the more visible the church in populated areas.[1] The symbols chosen referred to the particular confession: Catholic churches were crowned with a cross, although a statue of the Virgin Mary or an image of the Sacred Heart were also characteristic in the battle of symbols. A legendary example of this, partly due to its promotion via lithographs, was the Votive Church of Our Lady in Aachen (1859-1863).

Given the needs and demands of the churches, it is not surprising that the civil authorities interfered in church building. Contemporary agreements between church and state were a significant factor. As the contributions below indicate, various government agencies played a central role, financing and supervising construction projects: for example, the Oberbaudeputation in Prussia, the Waterstaat in the Netherlands and the Royal Commission of Monuments in Belgium.

Churches wanted to manifest themselves not only by occupying public spaces, but also by expressing their identity with their own formal language. Each church building was in a sense a public demonstration of faith. Still, it is difficult to find a fixed pattern in the use of the various formal languages by the established, dissident and free churches. Perhaps the Roman Catholic usage is the most obvious: after a transition phase between c 1780 and c 1820 in which neoclassicism and eclecticism dominated, neo-Gothic became the dominant formal language until the interwar period. The issue was much more complex on the Protestant and Anglican sides. In the Anglican Church, the influence of the Gothic Revival master, Augustus Welby Northmore Pugin was particularly strong. However, it also used a more eclectic or free Gothic formal language (for example the Scottish Episcopal Church). The Lutheran churches in Scandinavia preferred the Baroque style because it allowed galleries with additional seating. Dissident churches such as the Grundtvigians favoured (large) prayer halls, which also featured occasionally among the Doleants in the Netherlands. In Germany, neoclassicism with its single-nave churches was popular initially, but as neo-Gothic became more prominent on the Catholic side, German Protestants went back to the neo-Baroque or the Heimatstil, which also allowed the formula of galleries. Art Nouveau or Jugendstil was poorly represented. Around 1850, neo-Romanesque acquired a following among both Dutch and German Protestants, while Dutch Renaissance became popular in the Protestant churches in the Netherlands.

The formal languages used thus constituted a very varied palette, which made clear that the choice of design was not accidental but well thought out, aimed at expressing a singular identity. Church buildings, prayer

---

[1] On the symbol of towers, see Heyninckx, "A Law of Inertia: The Tower as Site and Symbol in Interwar Flanders". In: Rajesh Heyninckx and Tom Avermaete, eds., *Making a New World: Architecture & Communities in Interwar Europe*. KADOC Artes, 13. Leuven, 2012, 199-211.

houses, statues and images of saints, places of pilgrimage and cemeteries then became symbolic markers of the religious struggle in the rural and urban landscapes of Northwest Europe. That was their endeavour, as can be seen in the following pages.

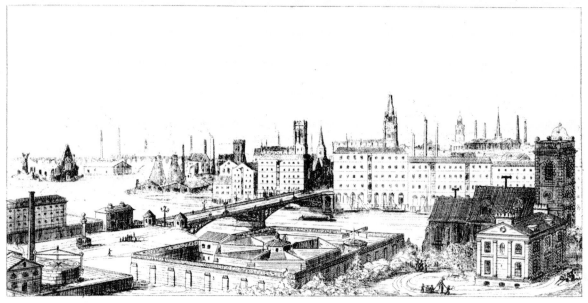

THE SAME TOWN IN 1840

1. St Michaels Tower, rebuilt in 1750. 2. New Parsonage House & Pleasure Grounds. 3. The New Jail. 4. Gas Works. 5. Lunatic Asylum. 6. Iron Works & Ruins of St Maries Abbey. 7. Mr Evans Chapel. 8. Baptist Chapel. 9. Unitarian Chapel. 10. New Church. 11. New Town Hall & Concert Room. 12. Wesleyan Centenary Chapel. 13. New Christian Society. 14. Quakers Meeting. 15. Socialist Hall of Science.

Catholic town in 1440.

1. St Michaels on the Hill. 2. Queens Cross. 3. St Thomas's Chapel. 4. St Maries Abbey. 5. All Saints. 6. St Johns. 7. St Peters. 8. St Alkmunds. 9. St Maries. 10. St Edmunds. 11. Grey Friars. 12. St Cuthberts. 13. Guild hall. 14. Trinity. 15. St Olaves. 16. St Botolphs.

2.1
Land Control and Development in the Politics of the Churches in the United Kingdom and Ireland

Timothy Brittain-Catlin & Roderick O'Donnell

The growing diversity and extent of religious practice in the United Kingdom and Ireland throughout the long nineteenth century ensured that there was evidence of material reform across the country in a myriad different ways. This is the era in which the established Church of England was reinvigorated, and to some extent reformed and restructured; other Christian denominations and Jews were enfranchised, and empowered by immigration and urbanisation; religious practices such as burial were reordered and resited; and the landscape of the nation as a whole was transformed by industrialisation and by new technologies. [Ill. 2.1-1] By all accounts, the Churches and church life were by the end of the century unrecognisable from the situation described in Peter Virgin's *The Church in an Age of Negligence*, a powerful indictment of the paralysed state of the late Georgian Church of England.[1]

It is important to recognise the overall differences between the nations of the United Kingdom – England, Scotland, Wales, and Ireland, and in particular the significant political, demographic and religious differences between Ireland and the mainland. In general, political and religious debate in Ireland was quite different from that of the rest of the country, not least because religious divisions carried specific political implications and consequently architectural and urban ones: the particular circumstances of the country are discussed separately below. As an example of the close relationship between Irish politics and the material reform of the Anglican Church in England, it was the decision by the United Kingdom parliament to make a realistic reduction in the number of Anglican dioceses in Ireland that triggered the launch of the Oxford Movement in England: that in turn was to have far-reaching and long-lasting implications for the reform of the Church of England.

At the beginning of our period the Church of England was the established church in England, and that meant it had an unbroken tradition of political and social privilege. The Church of Wales was likewise established, although it represented a minority of the population; in Scotland the 'national' (rather than 'established') church was the Presbyterian Church of Scotland, which underwent schism and reunion during the period. These positions of privilege and an ossified hierarchy within the Churches created opportunities for architecture in the form of official residences and of patronage over other church-related institutions: not just new or restored parish churches, but schools, halls, burial grounds and so on, and indeed the restoration or rebuilding of medieval cathedrals, which one by one underwent a reform process. In this way a cleric who was himself a reformer could stamp his image on his physical environment – and thus, often (but not always) simultaneously introduce ideas from architectural reform into his parish or diocese, a process much described in literature, especially around the middle of the century, for example in George Eliot's *Scenes of Clerical Life* (1857). For many, observing the changes in appearance of buildings in parish life at close hand, this was particularly evident in the case of the close alliance between the Oxford Movement and the ecclesiological movement which from bases in both Oxford and Cambridge called

2.1-1 'Contrasted Towns'; from the 1841 edition of A.W.N. Pugin's Contrasts.

1   Virgin, *The Church in an Age of Negligence.*

for architectural reform in the shape of the 'true' Puginite Gothic revival described in detail in section 3 in this book.

It is important to recall the essential elements of the Anglican Church establishment, because they have a direct bearing on the commissioning of the new buildings that came to represent a realisation of reform. Firstly, the bishops of the Church were appointed by the government, and had permanent places in the House of Lords, which then formed the primary executive chamber of the British parliament. The position of bishop was held for life, which meant (and this is significant at times) that the office holders were old, infirm, absent, and not motivated towards political or social change.[2] In fact it is useful to think of English bishops as having primarily a political rather than pastoral role. Within their diocese they dispensed considerable powers of patronage, which included for example appointments to well-paid, sinecure roles within cathedral chapters. The appointment of a priest to a parish with the title of vicar or rector was however the right mainly of a lay patron, and is properly referred to as an advowson; this right was inheritable or purchasable, like any other asset, and it was sometimes held by an institution, such as an Oxford or Cambridge college which had originally been a church foundation. The traditional general word used for any parish priest regardless of rank is parson; the holding by a parson of a parish was for life, and the term for the holding of this office was 'benefice'.

The status held by a parson was in nearly all cases either that of rector or vicar; briefly put, every parish had a rector, who received the tithes, a tax of ten per cent of agricultural produce, but in places where the rectorship was held by an institution or by an absentee, a vicar was appointed who received in effect an income drawn from that received by a rector. Either way, church services were in many cases held by curates, who were employed directly by the parson; the plight of the insecure and badly paid curate, who may well have been serving more than one parish, was a popular theme in early nineteenth-century literature. The division of parishes had been unchanged since medieval and even Saxon times; England was divided into approximately 10,000, each one responsible for a number of what are in effect civil duties such as poor relief and education, and in time lighting and drainage; this parish was run by the parson as the head of a committee called the vestry. These parsons received their income in part from the tithes, and also from pew rents, a tax on the occupation by a person or family of a place to sit in the church, which was levied on everyone and not just Anglicans, and fees from mandatory services such as weddings and funerals. Parish land, including the right to build on it, was invested in the parish itself but was controlled from the diocese; similarly, a parson might choose his own architect but required diocesan approval to restore or alter church fabric, or repair or rebuild a parsonage house.

Even without legislative or institutional reform, a number of changes were slowly taking place which were to change the material form of the church. The first of these is the demography of new parsons. From the late eighteenth century onwards the social status of the parish parson generally rose considerably, from being a person who, around 1700, had not necessarily been fully literate, to a university-educated person who may well have had family links to the gentry. Towards the end of the century a parson may well have been, for example, the younger son of the patron or another family of comparable social class, and may therefore have been appointed by them to the benefice. Alongside this the parson may well also have had a civic role, for example as a magistrate. Ancient parsonage houses had in nearly every case fallen into desuetude, and, as will be discussed below, the rebuilding or replacement of these houses constituted a widespread, prominent example of material change across, mainly, the middle of the nineteenth century.[3]

2 Ibid., 158-159.
3 Brittain-Catlin, *The English Parsonage*, chapter 1, describes this process in detail.

Religious movements both within and outside the Church of England began to make some impact on the role of the parson in parish life. In general, this was true of the Anglican evangelical movement, led for example by the politician William Wilberforce from the mid-1780s, which associated religious conviction with political activism. The principal evangelical movements outside the Church of England were those of the Methodists, founded as a distinct church in the 1790s, and the Baptists, who had a longer tradition in England. By and large, the Dissenters, or Nonconformists, as groups of Protestant non-Anglicans are generally referred to, were strongest in new urban areas where, in the nature of things, the influence of traditional landowners and patrons was weakest. These Dissenting organisations were non-hierarchical and some relied heavily on the charisma of a particular preacher.[4] There were in addition many splinter groups and sects who during the great increase in evangelical support in the early nineteenth century were able to build themselves churches, although often very cheap ones. [Ill. 2.1-2]

In contrast to the Anglican establishment, there was no Catholic hierarchy until 1850.[5] Catholic activity was considered as missionary, and the pope appointed at first four and then in 1840 eight vicars apostolic instead of bishops. They held titular sees, usually ones from towns in Asia Minor; sometimes chapels could be considered pro-cathedrals, as at St Mary Moorfields, London (1817-1820).[6] But St Chad's in Birmingham, the church of Thomas Walsh, vicar apostolic for the midland district from 1826 and Bishop of Cambysopolis, was considered to be a cathedral from the start, and the residence designed for Walsh by A.W.N. Pugin in 1839 was called from the outset 'the Bishop's House' – the first purpose-built Catholic bishop's palace built in England since the Reformation. [Ill. 2.1-3 & 2.1-4] From this position Walsh also commissioned what became Nottingham cathedral, a major landmark in the city. Walsh also presided over St Mary's College, Oscott, the first new foundation seminary in England.[7] There were to be five by 1920. These, with the relig-ious orders, produced the clergy.

The 'Restoration of the hierarchy' for England and Wales, as the Catholics termed it in 1850, established boundaries for thirteen new dioceses, though not yet parishes.

4   For a recent scholarly overview of the early history of the evangelical movement, see Hilton, *Mad, Bad and Dangerous*, 174-184.
5   See Norman, *The English Catholic Church*, for this period.
6   O'Donnell, "The Interior of St Mary Moorfields".
7   Champ, *Oscott College*.

2.1-2 Widcombe Baptist chapel, Bath, 1820-1821.
[London, Historic England Archive: DP166354]

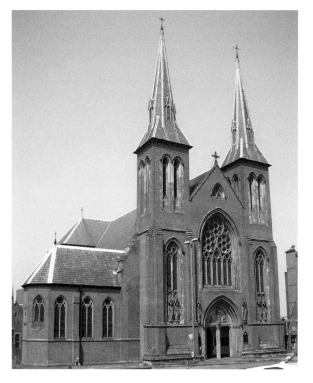 

2.1-3 St Chad's cathedral, Birmingham, by A.W.N. Pugin, 1839, with Sebastian Pugin Powell's chapel of 1933 projecting to the north-west.
[Wikimedia Commons; photo 2006]

2.1-4 A.W.N. Pugin's Bishop's House, Birmingham, 1839, photographed in 1958 shortly before demolition.
[National Buildings Record AA58/4257]

8   Quoted in Hulmes, "Faith in Crisis", 371.
9   Chadwick, *Oxford History of the Christian Church*, 117.
10 O'Donnell, "Catholic Architecture in England".

The process was notoriously mishandled politically by Nicholas Wiseman, up to that point Bishop of Melipotamus and appointed cardinal that year, who wrote in ultramontane language that 'England has been restored to orbit in the ecclesiastical firmament'.[8] The Prime Minster and the *Times* fulminated, Queen Victoria was not amused, and even Catholics such John H. Newman and Pugin were privately critical. In the words of Owen Chadwick, the leading twentieth-century Anglican church-historian, Wiseman became overnight "the most unpopular clergyman amongst the English people".[9] Political response came in the form of the Ecclesiastical Titles Act of 1851, which forbade the use by Catholic bishops of their new diocesan names; it threatened Catholics with legal penalties, but these were never enforced and the act was eventually abolished in 1871. The Scottish Hierarchy was restored in 1878.

Ireland

Overview

The use of Catholic territorial titles was never challenged in Ireland, and Catholics took the view that their hierarchy had never been broken. And in answer to popular jibes about the 'Irish occupation' of England, it should be noted that over the period 1801-1914 perhaps ten per cent of the Catholic clergy came from Ireland, and only one bishop.[10]

Ireland had both a tragic and, in Catholic terms, a 'triumphalist' long nineteenth century. From 1790 Ireland had an established Protestant church, the Anglican Church of Ireland, which provided for less than about a tenth of the population, although one which included the 'ascendancy', that is, the land-owning and titled classes. National politics in Ireland centred on the divide between the large majority of Catholics, with limited political and religious rights, and the minority of Protestants, whose church was established and thus supported by taxes drawn from the majority. This religious and political divide explains religious and church space in the

2.1-5 St Patrick's College, Maynooth, County Kildare, Ireland. St Patrick's Court by A.W.N. Pugin, 1845. Chapel by J.J. McCarthy 1875-1883; spire 1900 by J.L. Robinson.
[Wikimedia Commons; photo 2009]

country, and architectural developments in both churches were always related to political rivalry.

Ireland was ruled from London, but with a parliament in Dublin until 1800: the nationalist Repeal (1829-1843) and Home Rule movements (from the mid-nineteenth century to 1918) sought to re-establish it there: the union of the Irish parliament with the British one to create the United Kingdom, from 1 January 1801, had been an attempt to control Irish politics more closely from Westminster. Overwhelming numbers gave Catholics political weight: one million gathered on Clontarf hill outside Dublin in 1843 to demand Repeal. Rebellions broke out in 1798, 1848, 1916 and 1918-1921 – all of them except for 1848 very bloody and markedly sectarian. Traditionally, Britain had relied on the loyalist garrison represented by the landowning upper class and on the solidly Protestant and industrialising north-eastern province of Ulster; nationalists were, however, able to promote three hotly contested Home Rule bills (1886, 1894, 1912). Outside the north-east, 'secret-society' and agrarian unrest was endemic, culminating in the Land War of 1879-1882. The Land Purchase Act of 1903, one of a sequence aimed at a fairer distribution of land ownership, was to make twentieth-century Ireland a country of small peasant farmers. Its population peaked at around 8 million in the 1840s before the Great Famine (1846-1849) took place; as a result of this and other famines, it had halved by 1900. A million emigrated during the 1840s, to Britain and its empire, and to the United States, the Irish diaspora was thus of enormous political and religious importance, and, as a result, also extremely significant to the creation of Catholic space on the British mainland. At home, of course, there was some incentive to create a distinctly Irish (and Celtic) style of church architecture to distinguish it from that of the Anglican minority.

The Dublin parliament granted Irish Catholics relief in 1793, two years after that granted to Catholics in England, and finally in 1829 the Westminster parliament conceded 'Emancipation' – that is, the right to vote and sit in parliament – once again as a matter of political expediency.[11] A national seminary was set up with public funding in

11 For the political context of emancipation, see Hilton, *Mad, Bad and Dangerous*, 384-397.

1792 at Maynooth outside Dublin, in time a substantial building project viewed with suspicion by Anglicans in both Ireland and England, and by 1900 there were ten major seminaries for the 26 dioceses. [Ill. 2.1-5] The first national synod since 1642, called by the papal legate, was held in 1850, intended to establish full 'Tridentine' discipline for the Irish church and clergy. It was masterminded by Paul Cullen, appointed Ireland's first cardinal in 1866. Much legislation from the 1830s was concerned with education, intended to be non-denominational at elementary stage; but in practice it was almost immediately 'privat-ised', most notably by Catholics in the form of the 'national schools'. Secondary education was all 'private' in this way. The sixteenth-century university foundation of Trinity College, Dublin, was exclusively Anglican; the three new government-sponsored university colleges of 1845 were denounced as 'godless' by the Catholic bishops; their own attempts to set up a Catholic university, however, were frustrated by their own factionalism rather than by the government. The Protestant church was regulated in an act of 1833 – the event that led to John Keble's fulmination against 'National Apostasy', the key moment in the foundation of the Oxford Movement in England; it was disestablished but not disendowed in 1869. The other Protestant churches, especially the Presbyterian Church, strongest in the northeast, were 'voluntary': they were not state-funded, but enjoyed a much stronger, and middle-class, economic base.

Sites and boundaries in Ireland

Landholding and religious boundaries in Ireland were only settled in the wake of continuous religious and proprietorial conflict by the Protestant victory in the Jacobite-Williamite Wars (1689-1692). Thereafter all religious sites were in Anglican hands, and the 81% who constituted the Catholic population was unchurched. The 1800 Act of Union provided funds for yet more Protestant church-building, to be organised by a supervisory boards until 1833; £665,000 had been spent by 1834. In Cork, a medieval site with its eighteenth-century church was replaced by a new cathedral: this was a typical pattern of development, although in the case of Cork, the high architectural quality of the resulting St Finn Barre's cathedral, paid for by two brewers and erected from 1865, was not. [Ill. 2.1-6] Dublin's two medieval cathedrals, both in Protestant hands, were restored or rebuilt: St Patrick's (1860-1865), by the Guinness family of brewers, and Christchurch (1871-1878) by rivals.

The 1869 Disestablishment, which handed over some sites to the government as ancient monuments, ensured that they could not be transferred to Catholics. Many such sites had been thronged by Catholics on 'pattern days', or patron saint's days, socio-relig-

2.1-6 The Church of Ireland cathedral of St Fin Barre, Cork, designed by William Burges in 1863.
[Wikimedia Commons; photo Steven Lek, 2020]

ious gatherings which the Catholic bishops discouraged. Other pilgrimage sites were definitely penitential: these included the three-day 'St Patrick's Purgatory' at Lough Derg in remote County Donegal, which the railway reached in 1868. The large pilgrimage church was begun in 1921. In 1879, an apparition of the Virgin Mary took place against the more homely, not to say vernacular, setting of the gable of the Catholic chapel of Knock, County Mayo, during the disturbed days of the 'Land war'.

Despite the imbalance of population, no buildings or sites were returned to the Catholics. They received no state funding for church-building, but their cash base strengthened relatively as the population fell, and their per capita income rose after the Great Famine. Theirs was a 'voluntary' church, relying on the 'pennies of the poor' for its income. With land concentrated in Protestant hands, access by Catholics to building sites was severely restricted. There were a few enlightened landlords; an example is the Earl of Bective, who in the 1770s donated a prominent site at Kells in County Meath, although the famous local Celtic monastic site of St Columba, home of the eponymous *Book of Kells*, remained the Protestant church, its spire forming an eye-catcher from the Earl's house. Town sites were even more difficult to obtain, but earlier 'mass-houses' (or 'hidden churches', in the Dutch phrase) were given new frontages: the 'Adam & Eve' Franciscan church in Dublin is one of these.

By 1800, Catholic merchants in the towns were able to club together to build churches. For Protestants, Catholic church-building was in spite of the imbalance of power and money seen as 'triumphalist': the Catholic cathedral of Tuam (circa 1827-1837) "should overlook the land [and] like a 'tall bully' put Protestantism out of the province", and was accused of "driving the Protestants from [the province of] Connacht".[12] As Catholic and nationalist demands increased, so did the ascendancy and Protestant backlash. Catholics at the gates of the Powerscourt estate, who had worshipped in a barn since 1802, were refused a site by the landlord who was reported to say that one Catholic chapel in Ireland was one too many. But the next lord, on succession in 1857, did grant a site, and a church was built on it in 1858-1860. An even richer and prominent Protestant church was, however, also erected at the same time (1857-1859).[13] As with the cathedrals, this pattern of two rival churches, and two simultaneous rival building campaigns, was repeated all over Ireland. As a result of this largely unfriendly rivalry, the massive mid-century church and convent-building campaigns were intended by Catholics and nationalists to be 'triumphalist': in particular, the cathedral of Cobh (1859-1916) is internally laden with Catholic and historical-nationalist iconography, as well as being massive and prominently sited over Cork harbour, then still one of the main bases of British power, and imperial rule, the Royal Navy.

Churches and parsonages in England

The rebuilding or substantial remodelling of Anglican parish churches is one of the central events of British nineteenth-century history: almost every medieval building was altered or replaced. The church buildings themselves suffered from a number of problems which were profoundly embedded into English political history. From 1538 parliamentary acts, rather than popular iconoclasm, had stripped churches of rood and chancel screens, carved and painted images, stained glass, stone altars and reredoses, and other fixings had been removed or obscured.[14] Later legislation went on to control not only what went on in the buildings but to limit what could be displayed in them: this will be treated further in section 3 below. Thus the removal of galleries and eighteenth-century insertions and the introduction of new – but medieval-looking – extensions, fittings and ornamentation enabled reform in the Church of England to reach almost every parish, especially where a parson chose

12 Otway, *Tour in Connaught*, 184.
13 See Sheehy, "Irish Church-Building".
14 Duffy, *The Stripping of the Altars*, 478-503.

2.1-7 The west front of Canterbury cathedral in 1868: the north-west tower was completed in 1841.
[London, Historic England Archive: AL2400_116_1]

15 See Best, *Temporal Pillars*.
16 Brittain-Catlin, *The English Parsonage*, 33-34.
17 The process is described in Port, *600 New Churches*.

to patronise architects and designers, or even manufacturers, associated with the ecclesiological movement. Debates about style, historical reference and appropriate forms of religious symbolism were thus played out in the design and construction of churches in most towns and villages in England.

Income to support a church building was limited to what could be raised locally, and was usually drawn from pew rents. Most cathedral buildings and great churches were in a state of disrepair; Lichfield cathedral lost all of its figurative sculpture in the mid-seventeenth-century Civil War, and at Canterbury the north-west tower had never been erected in the first place. [Ill. 2.1-7] The general picture of the physical fabric of churches before the Victorian era can be seen in various sources, mostly engravings by topographic writers and antiquaries, although occasionally it can be understood from later correspondence dealing with attempts by the vestry (that is, the parish management committee headed by the parson) to improve their buildings. From these it is clear that the satirical illustrations of dilapidated and vandalised buildings by Pugin, in for example his book *Contrasts* (1836/1841), are not in fact exaggerations.

Legislation changed the picture from the beginning of the nineteenth century onwards. In the first place, there was an attempt to reorganise the finances of the Church of England in such a way as to distribute income away from its concentration in some cathedral chapters and their various sinecures and back towards the parishes.[15] This reform reached its peak in the establishment of the Ecclesiastical Commission mainly for that purpose in 1836, although in fact much of the Commissioners' time and money was taken up, in the early days, with funding new palaces for bishops.[16] In the meantime, the growing strength of the evangelical movement (and perhaps also the abolition of the Mortmain Act in 1803) enabled more private money to flow towards a church, which it then did in situations where a parish patron, or indeed its parson, may have had private resources; this also enabled the Church to fund a new parsonage house in certain circumstances. A further factor was the fact that the medieval parish structure was inadequate to cope with the rapid growth of industrial towns from the late eighteenth century onwards; because most local civil functions were exercised by the vestry, these small local committees were unable to cope with what was required of them. The purpose therefore of the Church Building Commissioners, established by the first Church Building Act in 1818, was as much to do with creating new parishes and thus local civic government, and the buildings for them, as it was to do with encouraging greater attendance at worship. The result of this act was an unprecedented flow of public money into the building of new churches for the first time for more than a century, and hundreds were built on the basis of this, and subsequent acts, up to mid-century.[17]

The most significant reform, however, was political and social unease regarding pluralism, that is, the holding of more than one benefice; what lay behind this was the growth of the evangelical belief that the parson's duty was primarily that of pastoral care rather than the holding of a political and social office. In the eyes of evangelicals within the Church of England and elsewhere, pluralism brought with it a number of ills. The principal of these was that a parson could accumulate a number of benefices, and live very well on the income from them; they could afford to live a life comparable to that of the county gentry and subcontract all the required execution of parish duties to a curate whose pay and position were insecure. The second point is that evangelical legislators wanted to build a much stronger relationship between the parson and the buildings in his parish.

A series of acts of parliament from the early years of the nineteenth century onwards addressed these problems – although they did so slowly because changes did not apply to parsons already in position, and of course the younger of these may well have retained their position for a further 50 years. Sir William Scott's Residency Act of 1803 in effect required a parson actually to live in their own parish, and the Pluralities Act of 1838 severely limited the holding of multiple benefices. Many parsonage houses, that is parish residences for parsons, were at the time in some cases medieval; they were not infrequently uninhabitable or let to lay tenants, and it was clear that for an educated, literate, perhaps socially elevated parson to live in their parish, some means needed to be found for an adequate parsonage to be built. Some generous parish patrons, and some well off parsons, had built new houses during the eighteenth century, but there are very few of these. For this purpose, a dormant act of parliament of 1777 usually called Gilbert's Act, was mobilised by the governors of the Queen Anne's Bounty, an underutilised fund established for supporting the upkeep of poor clergy and managed by a committee of bishops. This act established a process by which parsons could apply for a mortgage on favourable terms for the restoration or rebuilding of their parsonage.[18] This system was extremely effective and by the end of

the nineteenth century had resulted in the rebuilding or new building of almost every parsonage house, mostly through Gilbert's Act but also via other routes such as the Ecclesiastical Commissioners: this means that over time almost every parish in England was affected, and also that the design of the detached medium-sized house became, in particular from the mid-1840s, the subject of publicly subsidised experiment and development. [Ill. 2.1-8]

The Church of England was slow in the field of primary education, and only managed to stir itself into a school-building programme after witnessing the success of educational projects established by other denominations from the 1820s; up to that point, only a parson with considerable personal motivation would have funded or built a school building, although this of course did happen where a parson was particularly active in his parish. The arrival from the mid-1830s of the ecclesiological and Oxford Movements – for which see section 1 above – also brought with it new funds and new incentives to build within the Church of England; the impact of these is discussed in greater detail in section 3 below.

2.1-8 A.W.N. Pugin's rectory at Rampisham, Dorset, 1846.
[© Martin Charles, Rampisham]

18 Brittain-Catlin, *The English Parsonage*, 18-24.

2.1-9 West London Synagogue, Upper Berkeley Street, London, by David & Emmanuel, 1869-1870. [London, Marble Arch]

New spatial forms

A great deal of the language of the architectural reformers of the early-mid nineteenth century was taken up with the notion of Christian life taking the form of a distinct architectural community; the rediscovery of an medieval description of community life called the *Chronicle* of Jocelyn de Brakelond, the basis of a commentary by Thomas Carlyle in the form of a book called *Past and Present* in 1843, provided a lively picture for imitation. As a boy and young man Pugin drew both imaginary communities, and restored versions of real ones. As the architect of the first significant new convent buildings, for example at Handsworth near Birmingham (1840; second phase, 1844-1845), he was able to realise them. [Ill. 2.1-10] One of the outstanding architectural features of their plans was their long processional cloisters to create complete, internalised environments, which were also ones that felt safe to inhabitants worried about anti-Catholic demonstrations or acts of violence outside. Since these convents were located in urban or suburban areas, the architecture of the place could dominate the lives of the religious who resided there. The new Anglican convents and other residential institutions in turn drew on these characteristics for their own buildings.

This description provides the story for the Church of England, by far and away the dominant church-building organisation in Britain. The situation regarding the Protestant churches in Scotland is distinct and is discussed separately below. Likewise, non-Anglican English Protestant denominations, principally the Methodists and Baptists, built churches, manses and schools on the basis of local fundraising, operating as it were in a free market unconstrained by church hierarchies, and in the earlier part of the nineteenth century at least generally designed them in a way that made them architecturally distinct from their establishment counterparts. From then on, their outward appearance became increasingly similar. Jewish congregations, building substantial synagogues, for example those in London, Liverpool, Manchester and Brighton, from the 1860s onwards, created some prominent buildings but avoided Gothic Revival styles.[19] [Ill. 2.1-9]

This was to some extent possible even with non-institutional projects. Pugin had drawn, as a child, combinations of churches and ancillary buildings as if they were a single composition, and he realised this with, for example, the subtle orientation of his presbytery at Warwick Bridge, Cumberland (1840), towards the new church of Our Lady and St Wilfred, and with his positioning of the new Catholic church of St Peter, Marlow, in Buckinghamshire towards the medieval Anglican rectory, a building well known to antiquarians, in such a way as to suggest that the two were historically or functionally linked. Although he had, apparently, no interest in landscape design – and was thus quite distinct from previous designers in so-called Gothic styles – he was sensitive

19 See Kadish, *The Synagogues of Britain and Ireland*.

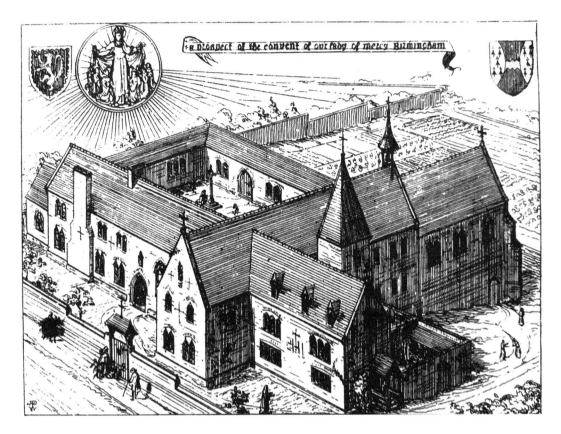

2.1-10 A.W.N. Pugin's design for the Convent of Mercy, Handsworth, Birmingham, 1840, published in his On the Present State of Ecclesiastical Architecture in England *(1843).*

to churchyard environments and designed medieval-type lychgates and stone crosses in order to mark out Christian territory. His bishop's house at St Chad's, Birmingham (1840) was large enough to be able to create a complex and prolonged interior processional space that featured a remarkably rich and modulated interior environment (see ill. 2.1-4). Finally, his own house at Ramsgate (1843-1844) was surrounded by other buildings which together form a distinct complex: a house; church; presbytery and, eventually, an abbey, architecturally distinct in style and forming a Catholic 'island' surrounded by a neoclassical late-Georgian townscape.

Other architects created architectural complexes of a similar type. George Edmund Street designed one at Boyn Hill, Maidenhead in Berkshire (1854-1865), for a congregation sympathetic to the Oxford Movement, comprising the church of All Saints, a vicarage, two clergy houses and a school. [Ill. 2.1-11] Street's impressive complex for Cuddesdon College, Oxfordshire (1852-1854), a High-Church theological college, was itself a new building type of the period. In many villages the restored or rebuilt church, designed, built or rebuilt in an ecclesiological acceptable style, was by far and away the largest and most significant building; the church of St Peter and St Paul, Cattistock in Dorset, mainly designed by George Gilbert Scott junior over more than fifteen years from the same year as Street's Boyn Hill onwards, and with a stupendous tower, is a particularly good example. [Ill. 2.1-12]

The Church of Scotland, although recognised as the 'national' church, was not as subject to parliament as the Church of England, and did not have a corresponding hierarchical structure with which to realise material reform. The General Assembly of the Church of Scotland launched a campaign for the financing and construction of new churches in 1834, with activities devolved in Presbyterian fashion to local committees: some 200 churches consequently date from the late 1830s, and their appearance is therefore, generally, somewhere between the weak Gothic of the English Commissioners'

129

2.1-11 Boyn Hill, Berkshire: an ideal complex of church, parsonage, school and almshouses, by G.E. Street, 1857. [London, Royal Institute of British Architects: RIBApix, RIBA93389]

2.1-12 St Peter & St Paul, Cattistock, Dorset, originally medieval but mostly by George Gilbert Scott (from 1857) and George Gilbert Scott junior (1874). [www.cattistockvillage.co.uk]

churches, and the 'true' Gothic of Pugin.[20] Reform and division within the church, for example the Disruption of 1843, and political pressure outside it, increased the number of churches, but in all the Presbyterian churches in Scotland distinctions between architectural arrangements were relatively insignificant. Architectural developments in the Episcopal – that is, Anglican – and Catholic Churches in Scotland followed more closely those in England, and Burial Acts in Scotland from the late 1850s likewise established suburban or rural cemeteries. By 1870, it is, however, already difficult to distinguish between one denomination and another, at least in terms of its public presence in a street or village.

Catholic space in town and country

England

Space was contested in most Victorian cities by more than one denomination, but only very occasionally could a Catholic David outstrip the Protestant Goliath. In the small towns of Cheadle in Staffordshire and Arundel in Sussex, the intervention of a great Catholic magnate was the key. As Pevsner noted in 1974, "Cheadle is *Pugin*-land (…) what haunts you for miles around is the raised forefinger of Pugin's steeple pointing heavenward".[21] John Talbot, 16th Earl of Shrewsbury, whose seat at Alton Towers was 12 kilometres away from Cheadle, bought up sites which placed the new Catholic church, its presbytery, a convent and a school, all building from the mid-late 1840s onwards, in the centre of this market-town – giving so much money in the process that even Pugin was overcome by his generosity. The latter wrote later that "Cheadle, (…) was origi-

20 Macaulay, *The Gothic Revival 1745-1845*, 253-274.
21 Pevsner, *The Buildings of England: Staffordshire*, 97.

nally designed for a plain parochial church, and it was quite an afterthought of its noble founder to cover it with coloured enrichment (…) all this is the result of a chain of circumstances over which I had no control"; the height of the tower and spire were raised to over 60 metres in the process.[22] [Ill. 2.1-13] The church with its steeple, the church-yard cross, and the adjacent school and convent gave a new Catholic heart to the town, whilst at the same time reclaiming its title St Giles for the Catholics, and overpowering the modest, recent, Anglican church. And all this was for a Catholic community used to worshipping in a converted military storehouse. It was, of course, far too ambitious, and the income supporting the Catholic project was found to be woefully inadequate once the Shrewsbury title and estates fell to a Protestant claimant in 1860.[23]

At Arundel, the new Catholic church was dedicated to Our Lady and St Philip Neri, underlining the links of the donor, Henry Fitzalan Howard, 15th Duke of Norfolk, with the Oratorians, particularly William Faber and Newman; it also anticipated the eventual canonisation of the duke's ancestor, the martyred Philip Howard, Earl of Arundel, more than a century later. The French High Gothic-style church (1870-1873), by the architects Joseph Aloysius Hansom and his son Joseph Stanislaus Hansom, dominates the town alongside the duke's principal seat, Arundel Castle, a defensive site since the Norman Conquest and itself rebuilt three times in the nineteenth century.[24]

The town also demonstrates a further aspect of Catholic use of space in the form of the control by the dukes of Norfolk of the chancel of the parish church for burials: in 1785 the 11th duke housed a Catholic mission nearby, and in 1873 the 15th duke bricked up its chancel arch to isolate it from the Protestants in the nave. This impasse went to law in 1879, with the architect William Butterfield using stylistic and standing-fabric analysis as evidence on behalf of the parish, and Herbert Gribble doing the same for the duke. The property was proved to be the duke's and

2.1-13 St Giles, Cheadle, by A.W.N. Pugin, 1839-1846.
[© Martin Charles]

the restoration of the chancel and its monuments continued; Mass was eventually being celebrated there on 1 April 1886 for the first time since the Reformation.[25] The 15th duke donated the prominent site for the Catholic church in Cambridge, and both this and the complete cathedral-scale church of St John the Baptist, Norwich (1882-1910), dominate the sky-line of otherwise notably Protestant cities.[26]

Seigneurial domination of a rural landscape was demonstrated by the building of Mount St Bernard's Abbey, Leicestershire. Here the convert squire, Ambrose Phillipps, was given the estate of Grace Dieu on his marriage in 1834: part of the attraction of the site was the fact that it included some surviving remains of a convent – "The ivied Ruins of forlorn GRACE DIEU: / Erst a religious House which day and night / With hymns resounded, and the chanted rite", as the poet William Wordsworth had put it in 1808.[27] Phillipps was fired by the romantic idea of atoning for the expropriation of the Cister-

22 Pugin, *Some Remarks*, 9; for the raising of the height of the tower, see Fisher, "*Gothic For Ever*", 170-174.
23 O'Donnell, *The Pugins and the Catholic Midlands*, 77-82.
24 Robinson, *The Dukes of Norfolk*.
25 Elvins, *Arundel Priory*. The court judgment of 1879 is given in Appendix III, 84-103. Our thanks to Dr J. M. Robinson for the reference to Gribble.
26 O'Donnell, "Dunn and Hansom's Church in Cambridge"; *A Great Gothic Fane*.
27 Wordsworth, *Inscriptions*.

cian abbey of Garendon, the site of his family's early eighteenth-century Palladian mansion. He invited Cistercians from Ireland and France to make a foundation, giving a site and paying for their buildings (1835-1837). But then the Earl of Shrewsbury advised that a much more picturesque and prominent site be considered, and offered to pay for a new monastery on condition that Pugin was involved; this duly happened. Pugin's monastic ranges and the nave of the projected church were built (1840-1844), the builder working at prime cost, and Pugin for nothing.[28] The Grace Dieu estate was the focus of the several Catholic centres begun by Phillipps, including three mission chapels and a school. In 1843 he built perhaps the first public Calvary since the Reformation, erecting a Way of the Cross with its fourteen stations culminating in a Pieta chapel, inspired by those seen in Bavaria.[29] Mount St Bernard's itself became a tourist attraction, queues of carriages attesting to the status of the visitors; these included the young Edward Burne-Jones, the painter, who kept a copy of the guide at his bedside for the rest his life. On inheriting Garendon, Phillipps changed his name to de Lisle, gothicised the interior of his house and converted classical garden buildings (such as a Temple of Vesta) into a shrine to the Immaculate Conception to mark the visit of Cardinal Manning in 1875.[30]

In some towns there were 'Catholic' areas that had their origins in the distant past: the southern end of Brook Green, Hammersmith, then a village to the west of London, had a reputation as 'Little Rome', beginning with the clandestine Benedictine convent established here during the reign of Charles II; the English Benedictine nuns of Dunkirk then settled in 1795. The diocesan seminary by John Francis Bentley (1875-1884) was built on its site. There was a Pugin-designed chapel, cloister and cells at the Good Shepherd convent to the south of the area in 1848-1849, and then came the large church of Holy Trinity and the adjoining St Joseph's almshouses by W.W. Wardell (1851-1853) facing the Green itself; Joseph Hansom added a prominent spire to Wardell's church tower in 1867. Nazareth House convent, and St Mary's teacher training college were also nearby.[31] But such characterisation was fluid: the Dunkirk nuns left for rural Devon in 1868, their site becoming the new diocesan seminary and from 1893 the Sacred Heart Convent, and Pugin's convent was demolished in 1921; finally, the training college moved out to Strawberry Hill in the 1930s. The Staffordshire town of Stone had a similar Catholic quarter, based on a very large Dominican convent site.

Catholic areas were however more usually within the poor residential districts of industrial cities or ports, inhabited by immigrants from Ireland. Much tighter lines were drawn round these, and the notorious 'rookeries' or slums to which they gravitated in London such as St Giles' on the north-eastern edges of Soho and, on the River Thames, at Bermondsey and Ratcliffe Highway. Soho had the first church in England dedicated to St Patrick (1802); it was contrived out of an existing assembly room on two floors, and was described in Dickens's *Barnaby Rudge* of 1842. A large Gothic Revival church was actually begun in the 1840s, but abandoned due to lack of funds. Bermondsey got its church in 1832-1834, the site cleared without payment by local Irishmen, and then its Pugin convent in 1838-1839. Ratcliffe Highway chapel was in time swallowed up by the docks, its congregation moving to Wardell's St Mary and St Michael, Commercial Rd (1851-1856), then the second largest Catholic church in London and sometimes nicknamed 'the cathedral of the East End'.[32] In Liverpool the Irish were confined to the low-lying riverside, beginning to the south with St Patrick's church (1821-1827), and then St Vincent de Paul by Edward Pugin (1856-1867).[33] As the city-centre English Catholics moved, they got their third mission with a large Gothic church, St Anthony, Scotland Road (1832-1833) but the ethnic and religious make-up changed so rapidly that the Scotland division of Liverpool returned, in 1885, the only Irish Nationalist Member of

---

28 O'Donnell, *The Pugins and the Catholic Midlands*, 99-101.
29 Ibid., 92-93.
30 Ibid., 87-88; Pawley, *Family and Faith*, 375.
31 See Evinson, *Pope's Corner*.
32 Maynard, *A History of St Mary and St Michael's Parish*.
33 O'Neill, *A Brief History and Guide to the Church of St Vincent de Paul Liverpool*.

Parliament outside Ireland, T.P. 'Tay-Pay' O'Connor.[34] Liverpool had over fifty Catholic parish churches by 1930.[35] Sectarian rivalry gradually attached itself to the two Liverpool football teams but Glasgow football was sectarian from the first, with the Glasgow Celtic Football Club being founded by a Christian Brother. In Ireland the Gaelic Athletic Association was founded in 1884 under the presidency of Thomas Croke, Archbishop of Cashel and Emly, an enthusiast for sports that were "racy of the soil" as opposed to the "effeminate follies" of English games.[36]

In Belfast, Catholics were concentrated in the unhealthy Falls Road on the west side – excluded, that is, from jobs in shipbuilding and the docks. Such settlement patterns and indeed ghettoisation were to be repeated for Irish immigrants, and others, in North America. Catholic migration to the towns was either internal (towards the industrial North, especially to Liverpool) or from Ireland. Where there was no pre-existing Catholic presence – as in South Wales – the lapsation rate was very high; the opposite was the case in Liverpool or London, both major port and manufacturing centres. The Irish were also associated with the military presence such as the army barracks at Woolwich, Sheerness in Kent, and the great naval ports of Plymouth or Portsmouth, where the Catholic cathedral (1882-1887) was built just outside the gates of the naval base. At Woolwich a site for a Catholic church was provided without charge by the Board of Ordnance, and the development of a church and ancillary buildings over the course of the century testifies to the growth and establishment of a significant Catholic presence: from 1842 the complex grew from a small brick church to accommodate a presbytery and sacristy (1845); a lady chapel (1850); a school (1858); a substantial clergy house (1870); an infant school (1871); and a chancel (1889). By contrast, the tower proposed for the original church by its architect never materialised.[37]

Ireland

Catholic Ireland was characterised by its vernacular T-plan or Latin cross-plan 'chapels', vernacular buildings of local stone, mud and thatch. These were known as chapels, rather than as churches, and they often housed the priest too. The *Catholic Directory* reported in 1842 that the small and poor Achonry diocese had thirty-four chapels of which "only six are thatched"; Bishop Durcan (1852-1875) is said to have replaced the last one. He chose the small market town of Ballaghaderreen, County Roscommon, as the site of his cathedral (1855-1861), by the Sheffield Catholic architects Hadfield & Weightman.[38] The diocesan seminary, initially housed in the former town chapel, took over in 1896 the barracks which for exactly one hundred years had embodied the militarised basis of British rule, before a further rebuilding by W.H. Byrne, architects, of Dublin, in 1916.[39] Such churches, presbyteries and schools clustered together, but convents preferred to be on fresh sites on the edges of towns, with two at Ballaghaderreen. Pilgrimage sites did not qualify for any buildings of note.

Religious houses multiplied, especially those of the 'active' rather than enclosed medieval orders, although Friars were prominent. The building most symbolic of the Catholic resurgence was the national seminary, St Patrick's College, at Maynooth, begun very quietly in 1795 as an 'R. Catholic college' by the Irish parliament, to replace the colleges lost to the Revolution in France and Belgium (see ill. 2.1-5). Denied a site in Dublin, it was instead granted one by the Protestant Duke of Leinster. Twelve miles west of Dublin, the main road out to the west passed through his planned town of Maynooth, with the gates of his Carton demesne at one end of it, and those of the seminary at the other. Its Georgian buildings (circa 1796-1799) were inadequate for its numbers by the 1840s.[40] Pugin was appointed, then resigned; he was then reappointed for the new buildings erected in 1846-1853, but without his chapel, which was eventually built to

34 O'Neill, *St Anthony's, Scotland Road, Liverpool*.
35 *The Catholic Directory 1930*, 215-220. The Catholic story of Liverpool can be followed in Doyle, *Mitres and Missions*; for a sampling of the wider church-building culture, see Brown and de Figueredo, *Religion and Place*.
36 Archbishop Croke, 18 December 1884: see <http://multitext.ucc.ie/d/Archbishop_Croke__the_GAA_November_1884>, accessed 6 June 2013.
37 Saint and Guillery, *Survey of London*, vol. 48: *Woolwich*, 400-406.
38 Swords, *Achonry and its Churches*; Id., *A Dominant Church*.
39 Kilduff, *St Nathy's College*.
40 Newman, *Maynooth and Georgian Ireland*; Id., *Maynooth and Victorian Ireland*.

2.1-14 Truro cathedral, by John Loughborough Pearson, from 1878.
[www.trurocathedral.org.uk]

2.1-15 St Colman, Cobh, County Cork, by E.W. Pugin and G.C. Ashlin, photographed before completion of the spire in 1900.
[Dublin, Irish Architectural Archive: 023_022_V014]

J.J. McCarthy's design in 1875-1880 and furnished c 1890-1900.[41] It became the nerve-centre of Catholic Ireland, producing the leading clergy and bishops of a definite ultramontane and nationalist stamp. By contrast Cullen, Archbishop of Dublin from 1852-1878, chose to build his rival diocesan seminary in the classical style, with a chapel (1873-1876) modelled on St Agata dei Goti, Rome (where O'Connell's heart was buried), and sent his architect to Rome to study it.[42]

Andrew Saint has indicated that Anglicans engaged in massive rebuilding and restoration campaigns in London eventually over-reached themselves.[43] Dioceses were subdivided, resulting in the building of new cathedrals – on a grand scale – at Truro for the new diocese of Cornwall (from 1878) and Liverpool (from 1903). [Ill. 2.1-14] In Ireland, however, the spires of the new Catholic churches began to dominate after 1850: the ecclesiastical capital Armagh gained a twin-towered Catholic cathedral, from 1840, that rivals the Anglican one from its hilltop site; and the harbour of Cobh was eventually completely dominated by the vast Catholic cathedral of St Colman (1867-1916).[44] [Ill. 2.1-15] Each of the Irish Catholic dioceses had a new cathedral, except for Cork and Dublin; the later had to make do with a pro-cathedral (1816-1840), a comment not only on the interim status of that building, but also on the Catholic aspiration for the return of one of the two medieval cathedrals in Protestant hands.

Other ways of claiming space

Even where the architectural style was not particularly remarkable or the building substantial or noteworthy, the nineteenth century saw many new ways in which the presence of a religious community could make its mark. Conventional speculative urban development, following the conventional type developed in London since Covent Garden in the early seventeenth century, was often centred around a new church or chapel which itself, in a new era of public piety, added appeal to potential buyers. This raised the attractiveness and thus sale value of surrounding houses: Pimlico and Belgravia, built by Thomas Cubitt for the Marquess of Westminster from the 1820s-1850s is like this; another prominent London example is the Ladbroke Estate, laid out by Thomas Allason in the 1820s and developed mainly by Thomas Allom up to and around mid-century, with both a large new Gothic church (St John the Evangelist, originally a chapel-of-ease) located axially and picturesquely,

and a stuccoed neoclassical parish church of St Peter on a tight urban site. [Ill. 2.1-16]

By the 1840s Anglican church-builders aimed wherever possible to orient their churches eastwards, with some implications for the urban scene. Industrial towns offered relatively cheap sites for Catholic and Nonconformist church builders, who saved money further by building in cheap brick and in styles that were scarcely ornamental at all. By contrast, the new resort towns that grew swiftly in the late Georgian era following the success of Brighton were heavily populated with churches to accommodate the different needs of their visitors. One clerical writer recalled in 1891 that in the Ramsgate of his youth there had been one Anglican church; by then, there were seven – and that of course excludes the many buildings erected in the centre of town by Nonconformists, not to mention Pugin's St Augustine's Catholic church, and his son Peter Paul's St Ethelbert's.[45] In Brighton itself over forty Anglican churches were erected, "one of the finest groups of churches outside London", a prominent testament to the range and scope of the Anglican Communion and its developing tradition.[46]

In England, as opposed to Scotland, the Continent, and Anglophone countries overseas, there was during the century very little centralised, publically controlled town planning, and thus equally little public debate around the siting of new urban churches. As noted above, the Church Building Acts funded new buildings with government money in areas that had no nearby church; the construction of many hundreds of these up to mid-century, usually in a cheap (and derided) neoclassical or nominally Gothic style, introduced a physical presence of that typically English combination of civic and religious government into new built-up areas.

The new suburban or rural cemeteries that followed the Burial Acts, from 1852 and revised regularly thereafter, were open to all religions, in segregated areas, and often had a pair of chapels: Anglican, and Nonconformist. The registration of births and deaths ceased to be an Anglican monopoly in 1837, but burials remained the responsibility of the Anglican parish. Private burial companies were established; the most important one in London was Kensal Green, established by act of parliament in 1832; part of it was consecrated for Anglican use, with separate chapels for different denominations.[47] [Ill. 2.1-17] But private companies did nothing to tackle the public health problem of over-burial in the towns, especially in London, and this was not solved before the 1850s when local burial boards took over the task; meanwhile intramural burials ceased and many church graveyards were closed. Nonconformists founded their own cemeteries.[48] Pugin lampooned non-denominational burial in plate IV of his book *An Apology for the Revival of Christian Architecture* (1843), clearly based on the Egyptian-style gateway to Nonconformist Abney Park cemetery, London.[49] On the other hand, Scott junior provided a good Gothic example in the form of a pair of linked chapels, at the public town cemetery in Ramsgate in Kent (1869).

At Kensal Green the Catholics built a parallel cemetery, St Mary's, (1859-1860) which,

2.1-16 St Peter's Church, Notting Hill, London, by Thomas Allom, 1855-1857: a rare classical church of its period designed to suit the style of the new residences on the estate.
[Wikimedia Commons; photo Andy Scott, 2019]

41 O'Donnell, "The Chapel of St Patrick's College, Maynooth".
42 *Holy Cross College Clonliffe*.
43 Saint, "Anglican Church-Building in London".
44 O'Donnell, "The Pugins in Ireland".
45 Oxenden, *The History of My Life*, 7.
46 Antram and Morrice, *Brighton and Hove*, 15.
47 Curl, *Kensal Green Cemetery*.
48 See Curl, *The Victorian Celebration of Death*.
49 Ibid.

2.1-17 Designs for Kensal Green cemetery, by H.E. Kendall, 1831.
[London, Royal Institute of British Architects: RIBApix, RIBA10338]

50 "Funeral Oration of Father Venturi on the Death of the Liberator…".
51 Atherstone, "The Martyrs' Memorial at Oxford".
52 Brittain-Catlin, "A.W.N. Pugin's English Convent Plans".
53 Clifton, *The Church of Our Lady of Consolation and St. Francis*.
54 For Anglicans and Walsingham, see Yelton, *Anglican Papalism*, 126-151.

with the graveyards surrounding the churches at Mortlake and Fulham, catered for the West End of London; the poor migrated to St Patrick's Cemetery, Leyton (1860-1861): here are buried the five Franciscan nuns exiled by the *Kulturkampf*, memorialised in Gerard Manley Hopkins' poem *The Wreck of the Deutschland* (1876). In the Irish countryside Catholics were buried in the church sites still in Anglican hands, but rival denominational cemeteries were provided for Dublin, Belfast and Cork. The Glasnevin cemetery for Dublin became a nationalist shrine following the burial of Daniel O'Connell who, characteristically, said "My body to Ireland, my heart to Rome, my soul to God"; one million people are said to have followed his cortege.[50]

Campaigns by ecclesiologists and others appealed to medieval traditions: an early example was the erection by subscription of the Martyrs' Memorial in 1838-1843 in Oxford to a design derived from the thirteenth-century Eleanor crosses, controversial to both camps because it used 'Catholic' forms to commemorate Protestant martyrs.[51] [Ill. 2.1-18] Public crucifixes were only to appear with some First World War memorials. Similarly, ecclesiologists aimed to broaden the appeal and scope of religious worship through vestment-wearing clerics and choirs, the revival of campanology, and so on. Many of these practices remained controversial.

Shrines and pilgrimages were little known in the Britain Isles outside Ireland; Pugin's own architecture reflected – indeed, encouraged – private processions through the use of plans in the form of attenuated cloisters.[52] The first claim of a new shrine to the Virgin in England is attached to the building of a church at West Grinstead, Surrey, in 1876-1879 by Jean-Marie Denis, a French priest, using money collected in France in honour of Our Lady of Consolation. This was at an historic recusant mission that had been supported by the Caryll family, sited in a chapel in the presbytery provided by them after the departure of the family from the estate in the mid-eighteenth century when the Franciscans took over.[53] The French connection was reflected in the burial of Hilaire Belloc and his family at the site; the tower was eventually completed in his memory (1964).

Most other Catholic processional traditions in England are twentieth-century. The Walsingham devotion restarted towards the end of the century; it was claimed by Anglican papalists from the early 1920s, but there was no permanent Catholic presence there until 1934.[54] The holding of the International Eucharistic Congress in London in 1908 did not deter the authorities from banning the procession carrying the sacrament through the streets round Westminster cathedral.

Processions were part of parish life until the 1960s, but they were held on church property; in general, these traditions were strongest in the Catholic areas of north and northwest England. The "most Catholic town in England", Preston in Lancashire, where the Catholic church of St Walburge has the tallest spire in the county (94 metres, construction from 1850), saw massive parish-based processions well into the 1970s, as did Manchester and Middlesbrough. Equally locally rooted were devotions to the relics of martyrs, such the hand of St Edmund Arrowsmith at Brindle, Lancashire; Nicholas Garlick and Robert Ludlam, the Padley Martyrs, at Padley Manor, Derbyshire; or St John Kemble at Welsh Newton. The most long-lived shrine in Britain was that of St Winefride at Holywell in North Wales, where Catholics maintained intermittent use of the holy well, aided by its proximity to Catholic Lancashire and routes to Ireland. The Jesuits built a classical church in 1832-1834 while the pilgrims bathed in the still standing medieval well-head chapel; the site was returned to Catholic management late in the nineteenth century.[55]

Bell ringing remained one of the few church-embellishment processes to survive the utilitarianism of the English Reformation. Catholics were forbidden to have towers or bells in the 1791 relief acts, and many churches (including at least two in Dublin) claim to have the first bell that rang out; the Jesuit church in Liverpool (1844-1848) was designed for bells, but these were installed only in the 1870s. Wardell's bell tower with a spire at St Mary, Clapham (1849) claims to be the first in London. Pugin stressed the symbolic role of towers and especially spires, building his greatest one at Cheadle, equipped with a set of bells.[56] The substantial and prominently sited Catholic church at Cambridge had bells and a very prominent clock which struck the quarters to the tune of the plainchant Easter Alleluia – even continuing to do so during the Second World War.[57]

Towards late century

The rebuilding or restoration of almost all England's medieval parish churches was however clearly the primary achievement of the nineteenth-century church, just as it was also the primary achievement of the Gothic Revival itself; in fact, given the more modest and often very run-down nature of these buildings before mid-century, it is fair to say that the modern and lasting image of the English village with a church at its centre was a creation of this period. It is possible too that writers and other artists interested in social reform, such as Charles Dickens, contributed to the change in the way that they deployed church imagery to signify a healthy and moral life – in the concluding illustration of *Nicholas Nickleby* (1838-1839), for example.

From the late 1820s onwards the nature of the Church of England had changed substantially from its Georgian forbearer. Distinct periods of political and legislative action on the one hand and architectural developments on the other led to a series of distinct waves

2.1-18 *The Martyrs' Memorial, Oxford, by George Gilbert Scott, 1840. (See also col. ill. 5.)*
[London, Royal Institute of British Architects: RIBApix, RIBA31344]

55 Pritchard, *St Winefride*.
56 Fisher, *"Gothic for Ever"*, 174.
57 Jackson, "There's a War on"; Brotchie, "The Clock Winders Tale".

of development. The early part of the period is marked by political moves to stem discontent – with new churches and parishes and reactions from theologians and scholars to political interference in religious matters – and in the latter part of the period by legislation towards cleaner, safer, and better coordinated towns. In both cases, there was some direct architectural response. A large amount of interest and activity mainly among young parsons had eradicated in all but the most old-fashioned parishes the idea of the village parson as being no more than a gentleman proprietor-manager. Legislation facilitated the widespread improvement of churches, and enabled the building of parsonage houses and schools; until 1870 the building of schools was also carried on by the church on the basis of local initiative. Every medieval English cathedral or major church was also substantially restored, in some cases more than once, although it took until 1880 until the foundations were laid for a completely new one, at Truro. It was probably the fact that it became possible to direct private finance towards church-building that resulted in some stupendous results, including vast new parish churches, for example that at Hoar Cross in Staffordshire, founded by Emily Meynell Ingraham and built from 1872. To some extent, church-building culture dominated architectural debate throughout the mid-century and beyond, and it certainly established the image of the church across the country and throughout the English-speaking world.

BIBLIOGRAPHY

A Great Gothic Fane: a Retrospect of Catholicity in Norwich. Norwich, no date, c. 1913.

Antram, Nicholas, and Richard Morrice. *Brighton and Hove*. Pevsner Architectural Guides. New Haven-London, 2004.

Atherstone, Andrew. "The Martyrs' Memorial at Oxford". *Journal of Ecclesiastical History*, 54 (2003) 2, 278-301.

Best, Geoffrey. *Temporal Pillars: Queen Anne's Bounty, the Ecclesiastical Commissioners, and the Church of England*. Cambridge, 1964.

Brittain-Catlin, Timothy. "A.W.N. Pugin's English Convent Plans". *Journal of the Society of Architectural History*, 65 (2006) 3, 356-377.

Brittain-Catlin, Timothy. *The English Parsonage in the Early Nineteenth Century*. Reading, 2008.

Brotchie, Tony. "The Clock Winder's Tale". In: Nicholas Rogers. *Catholics in Cambridge*. Leominster, 2003, 191-193.

Brown, Sarah, and Peter de Figueredo. *Religion and Place: Liverpool's Historic Places of Worship*. Swindon, 2008.

Chadwick, Owen. *Oxford History of the Christian Church: A History of the Popes 1830-1914*. Oxford, 1998.

Champ, Judith, ed. *Oscott College 1838-1988: A Volume of Commemorative Essays*. Birmingham, 1988.

Clifton, Margaret. *The Church of Our Lady of Consolation and St. Francis, West Grinstead: a Short History of the Church*. West Grinstead [?], not dated, c 1990.

Curl, James Stevens. *The Victorian Celebration of Death*. Stroud, 2000.

Curl, James Stevens. *Kensal Green Cemetery: The Origins and Development of the General Cemetery of All Souls, Kensal Green, London, 1824-2001*. Chichester, 2001.

Doyle, Peter. *Mitres and Missions: The Roman Catholic Diocese of Liverpool 1850-2000*. Liverpool, 2005.

Duffy, Eamon. *The Stripping of the Altars: Traditional Religion in England 1400-1580*. 2nd ed. New Haven-London, 2005.

Elvins, Mark Turnham. *Arundel Priory 1380-1980: The College of the Holy Trinity*. London, 1981.

Evinson, Denis. *Pope's Corner: An Historical Survey of the Roman Catholic Institutions in the London Borough of Hammersmith and Fulham*. London, 1980.

Fisher, Michael. *"Gothic for Ever": A.W.N. Pugin, Lord Shrewsbury, and the Rebuilding of Catholic England*. Reading, 2012.

"Funeral Oration of Father Venturi on the death of the Liberator…". Dublin, 1847.

Hilton, Boyd. *A Mad, Bad, Dangerous People: England 1783-1846*. The New Oxford History of England. Oxford, 2006.

Holy Cross College Clonliffe: College History and Centenary Record. Dublin, 1962.

Hulmes, Edward. "Faith in Crisis: From Holocaust to Hope 1943-2000". In: V. Alan McClelland and Michael Hodgetts, eds. *From Without the Flaminian Gate: 150 Years of Roman Catholicism in England and Wales 1850-2000*. London, 1999.

Jackson, Christopher. "There's a War on: Catholic Cambridge 1939-1945". In: Nicholas Rogers, ed. *Catholics in Cambridge*. Leominster, 2003, 176-191.

Kadish, Sharman. *The Synagogues of Britain and Ireland: An Architectural and Social History*. New Haven-London, 2011.

Kilduff, Xandra. *St Nathy's College Ballaghaderreen 1810-2020: Moments in Time*. St Nathy's College, 2010.

Macaulay, James. *The Gothic Revival 1745-1845*. Glasgow-London, 1975.

Maynard, Jean. *A History of St Mary and St Michael's Parish, London*. London, 2007.

Newman, Jeremiah. *Maynooth and Georgian Ireland*. Galway, 1979.

Newman, Jeremiah. *Maynooth and Victorian Ireland*. Galway, 1983.

Norman, Edward R. *The English Catholic Church in the Nineteenth Century*. Oxford, 1984.

O'Donnell, Roderick. "The Pugins in Ireland". In: Paul Atterbury, ed. *A.W.N. Pugin: Master of the Gothic Revival*. New Haven-London, 1995, 136-159.

O'Donnell, Roderick. "The Interior of St Mary Moorfields [London]". *The Georgian Group Journal*, 7 (1997), 71-74.

O'Donnell, Roderick. *The Pugins and the Catholic Midlands*. Leominster, 2002.

O'Donnell, Roderick. "Dunn and Hansom's church in Cambridge". In: Nicholas Rogers, ed. *Catholics in Cambridge*. Leominster, 2003, 246-256.

O'Donnell, Roderick. "Catholic Church Architecture in England: 'Irish Occupation' or 'the Italian Mission'?" In: David Crellin and Ian Dungavell, eds. *Architecture and Englishness, 1880-1914* [papers from the annual symposium of the Society of Architectural Historians of Great Britain, 2003]. London, 2006, 59-71.

O'Donnell, Roderick. "The Chapel of St Patrick's College, Maynooth". *Country Life*, 208 (2014) 16, 74-79.

O'Neill, Michael. *St Anthony's, Scotland Road, Liverpool*. Leominster, 2011.

O'Neill, Michael. *A Brief History and Guide to the Church of St Vincent de Paul Liverpool*. Gracewing, 2013.

Otway, Rev Caesar. *Tour in Connaught*. Dublin, 1831.

Oxenden, Ashton. *The History of My Life*. London-New York, 1891.

Pawley, Margaret. *Family and Faith*. Norwich, 1993.

Pevsner, Nikolaus. *The Buildings of England: Staffordshire*. Harmondsworth, 1974.

Port, M.H. *600 New Churches: The Church Building Commission 1818-1856*. Revised edition. Reading, 2006.

Pritchard, T.W. *St Winefride, Her Holy Well and the Jesuit Mission c650-1930*. Wrexham, 2009.

Pugin, A.W.N. *Contrasts; or a Parallel between the Noble Edifices of the Fourteenth and Fifteenth Centuries, and Similar Buildings of the Present Day; Showing the Present Decay of Taste* [2nd edition]. London, 1841.

Pugin, A.W.N. *The True Principles of Pointed or Christian Architecture*. London, 1841.

Pugin, A.W.N. *Some Remarks on the Articles which have Recently Appeared in the "Rambler" Relative to Ecclesiastical Architecture and Decoration*. London, 1850.

Robinson, John Martin. *The Dukes of Norfolk, a Quincentennial History*. Oxford, 1982.

Rogers, Nicholas, ed. *Catholics in Cambridge*. Leominster, 2003.

Saint, Andrew. "Anglican Church-building in London, 1790-1890: From State Subsidy to 'free market'". In: Andrew Saint and Chris Brooks, eds. *The Victorian Church: Architecture and Society*. Manchester, 1995, 330-350.

Saint, Andrew, and Peter Guillery, eds. *Survey of London*. Vol. 48: *Woolwich*. Swindon, 2012.

Sheehy, Jeanne. "Irish Church-Building: Popery, Puginism and the Protestant Ascendancy." In: Chris Brooks and Andrew Saint, eds. *The Victorian Church: Architecture and Society*. Manchester, 1995, 133-150.

Swords, Liam. *A Dominant Church: the Diocese of Achonry 1818-1960*. Dublin, 2004.

Swords, Liam. *Achonry and its Churches from the Sixth Century to the Third Millenium*. Eckbolsheim, 2007.

Virgin, Peter. *The Church in an Age of Negligence*. Cambridge, 1989.

Wordsworth, William. *Inscriptions for a Seat in the Groves of Coleorton* [1808]. In: Henry Reed, ed. *The Complete Poetical Works of William Wordsworth*. Philadelphia, 1839.

Yelton, Michael. *Anglican Papalism*. Norwich, 2005.

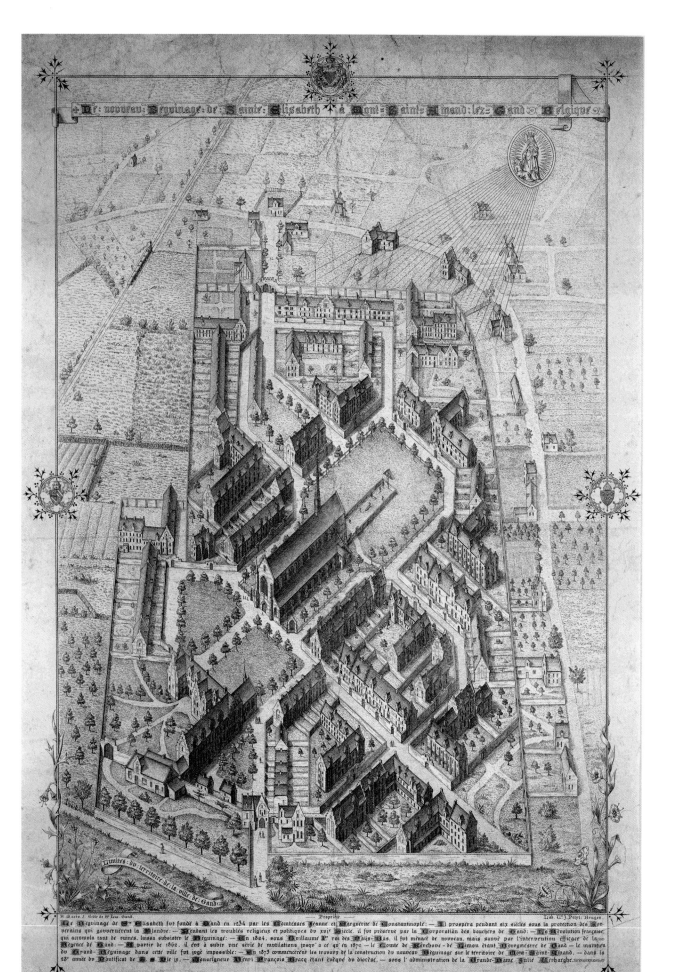

2.2
Reconquering a Lost Visibility
Catholic Revival in Early Industrial Belgium

Thomas Coomans

The religious reforms introduced by the Austrian regime in 1773 and subsequent secularisation in the wake of French annexation in 1792-1794 resulted in waves of demolition of religious buildings that was unprecedented in the southern Low Countries. The material presence of the Church in the public space through architecture underwent a profound change: urban skylines lost a great many steeples. With the religious revival of the nineteenth century, Belgian Catholics sought to regain their lost visibility in the public space. The Church was forced to rebuild and find a new place in a world that had changed forever.[1] The great debates between Liberals and Catholics, joined by the Socialists from 1885, between anti-clericals and ultramontans, left their mark on Belgian politics and society in the nineteenth century.[2] Beyond religious issues, Belgium – a new country born in 1830 and one in search of its own identity – discovered the social and urban planning consequences of a precocious and savage industrialisation.[3]

What follows centres on five themes: firstly, the consequences of secularisation on earlier religious architectural heritage; secondly, the churches used for public worship, both new constructions and historical monuments, in the light of the new relationship between Church and State; thirdly, the question of villages structured around their parish church, and the polarisation of society and areas between city and countryside in the nineteenth century; fourthly, the buildings of religious orders, often linked to educational and charitable institutions, as well as to pilgrimage sites; and fifthly, the specific issue of cemeteries.

Through its typological, topographical and stylistic diversity, nineteenth-century religious architecture in Belgium was the material expression of a multifaceted religious vitality, ranging from ultramontane conservatism to social progressivism, and of the Catholic Church's ability to adapt to the challenges of a changing society like never before.[4]

The secularisation of the public space

After the closure of Jesuit houses and schools in 1773, Emperor Joseph II suppressed all the contemplative religious communities, considered 'useless', in 1783.[5] In 1796, the French Directory pillaged and suppressed all other monasteries, convents and abbeys. A huge redistribution of ecclesiastical real estate and large-scale speculation were the immediate consequences, both in the cities and countryside.[6] The presence of religious architecture in the urban space changed completely in less than half a century: while the majority of parish churches survived,[7] nearly every convent was destroyed or recycled.

The massive freeing-up of the Church's real estate heritage, combined with the new production dynamic after the suppression of the corporations, was a veritable 'gift for the cities' at the dawning of the Industrial Revolution and the modern world.[8] Not only was public space redesigned with new straight streets and regular squares – in response to the new neoclassical canon – it was also se-

2.2-1 Gothic, rational and enclosed: the new Beguinage of Sint-Amandsberg and its gendered space, drawing by Brother Marès-Joseph, Ghent, 1875.
[Leuven, KADOC-KU Leuven: KPB303]

1 Art et al., "Church Reform and Modernity in Belgium".
2 Lamberts, "Liberal State and Confessional Accommodation".
3 De Meyer and Smets, "De recente stedebouwkundige geschiedschrijving in België".
4 See my contribution "Gothic Revival: Style, Construction and Ideology in Nineteenth-Century Belgium" in this volume (3.2). For details of the churches mentioned and their contexts, in Flanders: <https://inventaris.onroerenderfgoed.be/>; in Wallonia: Bertrand, Chenut and Genicot, Les églises paroissiales de Wallonie; in Brussels: <http://www.irismonument.be/>.
5 De Schepper, "Marie-Thérèse et Joseph II".
6 Antoine, La vente des biens nationaux dans le département de la Dyle.
7 Some parish churches were destroyed, however, in order to create public squares, for example: place Saint-Géry in Brussels and place du Marché aux Légumes in Namur.
8 Antoine, "La vente des biens nationaux à la fin du XVIIIe siècle".

2.2-2 The ruined St Lambert Cathedral in Liège. Aquarel by Jean Deneumoulin, 1802.
[Liège, Université de Liège; Art Collection 4/Alamy Stock Photo]

9   Loir, *Bruxelles néoclassique*; Van de Vijver, "La ville en chantier".
10 Klaarenbeek, *De herverkavelde stad*; Id., "The Secularisation of Urban Space".
11 Klaarenbeek and Coomans, "Reusing Urban Convents as State Schools in Belgian Towns"; Coomans and Klaarenbeek, "De ruimtelijke metamorfose van steden na de secularisatie van de kloosters"; Klaarenbeek and Coomans, "From Guessing to 'Gissing': HisGIS Analysis".
12 Dambruyne et al., *Een stad in opbouw*, 190-195.
13 Raxhon, "La démolition de la cathédrale Saint-Lambert à Liège".

cularised, expressing the vision of the Age of the Enlightenment.[9] Several scenarios were possible, ranging from conversion to demolition, with public or private allocations.[10] Almost everywhere, new public institutions of the state (courthouses, prisons, universities), municipalities (schools, libraries, museums, hospitals, other charitable institutions) and the army (barracks, arsenals) appropriated former urban religious houses.[11] Elsewhere, new streets and squares were laid out on the site of monasteries and the land developed in this way transformed into modern districts. Sometimes, only parts were destroyed entirely while others were instead reassigned. Many of the suppressed institutions were simply sold and privatised, becoming warehouses or factories. Ghent, the cradle of the modern textile industry, offers many examples.[12] Finally, in secularised towns and cities, street names with religious overtones or linked to the Ancien Régime were renamed. In addition, due to the disappearance of a great many bell towers and church bells, their sound no longer gave everyday life its rhythm.

This process of gradual metamorphosis would last for several generations. Properties were given to frequent changes of ownership and successive allocations accelerated transformations. For some time, the sight of ruined churches was not uncommon, offering the morbid spectacle of a world that was definitively over, while arousing the fascination of the Romantics. The ruins of the cathedral of St Lambert in Liège, symbol of the spiritual and temporal authority of the deposed prince-bishop, were painted by a generation of Romantics before disappearing from the memory of the Liégeois to make way for the creation of a public square.[13] [Ill. 2.2-2] Unlike urban areas that had little time for ghosts, the countryside was decorated with ruined abbeys. After serving as quarries for building materials, these ruins – particularly those of the Cistercian abbeys of Villers, Aulne and Orval – attracted tourists and eventually became historical monuments in the late nineteenth century.[14] Long known as 'black church goods', the land and buildings belonging to rural abbeys and monasteries passed into private hands and were converted into country estates, farms and factories.[15]

The renewed visibility of monuments and identity thanks to the Concordat

The Concordat agreed between Napoleon and Pius VII in 1801-1802 redefined the relationship between Church and State. The application of the Concordat was extended by the United Kingdom of the Netherlands, then in 1830 by the Kingdom of Belgium, a 'neutral' country from a religious perspective.[16] As early as 1802, the diocese map was redrawn to adapt its contours to those of the *départements* put in place by the French state in 1794. Three of the eight dioceses of the Ancien Régime were suppressed (Antwerp, Bruges, Ypres) and those of Mechelen, Tournai, Ghent, Liège and Namur were restored. While the *départements* became Belgian provinces, the dioceses remained unchanged, with the exception of the restoration of the diocese of Bruges in 1834, which corresponded to the province of West Flanders.[17] The upkeep of cathedrals and episcopal palaces fell to the provinces.[18]

In accordance with the Concordat, applicable until 2001-2004, Church Councils (*fabriques d'église / kerkfabrieken*) handled all questions related to the material organisation of public worship in Belgium.[19] The public authorities guaranteed the provision of locations suitable for the conduct of public worship, namely parish churches. While Catholic worship accounted for more than 95% of religious practice in Belgium in the nineteenth century and had been recognised since 1802, the state also recognised Protestant worship in 1802, Jewish worship in 1807 and Anglican worship in 1870.[20]

In the 1840s, the Royal Commission on Monuments contributed decisively to restoring the visibility of churches in the public

14 Coomans, "From Romanticism to New Age".
15 Coomans, *Life Inside the Cloister*, 127-151.
16 Sägesser, "Les rapports entre l'Église et l'État en Belgique au XIXe siècle".
17 The dioceses remained unchanged until 1962, when the archdiocese of Mechelen was divided into the dioceses of Antwerp and Mechelen-Brussels. The diocese of Hasselt, formerly part of the diocese of Liège, was created in 1967.
18 On the episcopal palace in Ghent, built in 1845 behind the apse of the cathedral: Collin, Robijns and Verpoest, *Het Gentse bisschopshuis*.
19 Coomans, "Les églises en Belgique", 50-58.
20 Islamic worship was not recognised until 1974; Orthodox worship in 1985 and organised secularism in 1993. The process of the official recognition of Buddhism has been ongoing since 2006.

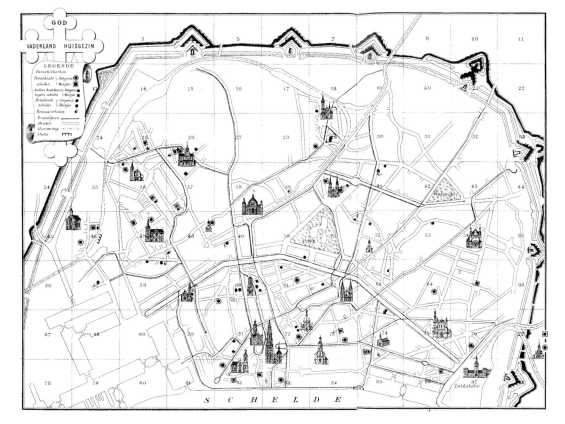

2.2-3 Map of Catholic Antwerp c1900: the facades of the cathedral and parish churches (as well as the two railway stations) are figured; the round dots indicate boys' schools and the square dots girls' schools; framed dots are parish schools. (The many catholic monasteries are not indicated.)
[Leuven, KADOC-KU Leuven]

space, not to support the Catholic Church, but to beautify towns and cities. The monumental churches punctuating new squares or new perspectives served to structure the urban landscape. This phenomenon was clearly not specific to Belgium and is found in the majority of large Western cities. As the capital, Brussels received the greatest attention.[21] The neoclassical church of St Joseph (1842-1849), on the main square of the Leopold Quarter, the 'Romano-Byzantine' church of St Mary (1845-1893), on the axis of rue Royale and rue des Palais, as well as the Gothic Revival church of Our Lady of Laeken (1854-1909), necropolis of the new Belgian royal family [Ill. 2.2-8], were the first in a series that would continue to expand following the successive phases of urban growth by which new bourgeois districts gradually replaced old peri-urban villages.[22] This movement continued after the First World War with markedly monumental modern churches in the new districts.[23]

Beyond Brussels, it was Antwerp that developed the most spectacular urban scenography in Belgium in the nineteenth century: a series of large churches with high Gothic spires punctuated the new districts of the metropolis.[24] Unlike the old, perfectly oriented churches, the new churches all turned their main façades towards the centre. [Ill. 2.2-3] The majority of Belgian cities – Ghent, Liège, Bruges, Spa, Verviers, Kortrijk, Charleroi, Ostend, Mechelen, Aalst, etc. – provided their new bourgeois districts with a monumental church built using local materials.[25] The other recognised religions – Protestant, Jewish and Anglican – enjoyed proportionally the same advantages as the Catholics and also built public places of worship.[26] This led to the construction of the Great Synagogue of Brussels in 1875-1878 next to the Conservatory and near the Palace of Justice on rue de la Régence, one of the most prestigious thoroughfares in the Belgian capital.[27]

Working-class parishes with churches financed by public money developed in the extensions of industrial towns and cities. The two scenarios merged in the large 'industrial basins' of Belgium. On the one hand, new districts developed from the centres of former outlying villages that became integrated into the cities of Liège, Charleroi and Mons, the three great coal and steel towns of nineteenth-century Belgium;[28] on the other, new districts were created *ex-nihilo,* with urban planning of variable quality,[29] forming in rare cases real 'working-class villages' of which the church was one component.[30] In the latter case, construction of the church was financed by the company in question and the dimension of identity and paternalism was explicit. The Gothic Revival church of St Joseph in Ghent (1880-1883), promoted by the Catholic textile magnate Joseph de Hemptinne, is a typical example of a periurban district developed as a dormitory district for the workers at a company, whose lives revolved around the church as if they lived in a village. Unlike Flemish cities and the rural world, the landscape of the industrial basins of Wallonia was not dominated by church towers but by the smoking chimneys of factories and headframes of mine shafts. Despite the efforts of the Church (*Rerum novarum*, 1891), the impact of Catholicism in working-class settings remained limited compared to that of the Workers' Party of Belgium (founded in 1885).

Many small towns rebuilt their main church during the nineteenth century. Often located on the edge of the main square, these churches were close to the town hall; their style and form express a ratio of power that was sometimes balanced, sometimes tense. The numerous examples include Our Lady in Sint-Niklaas (1841-1844) [Ill. 2.2-4], Our Lady and St Roch in Boom (1848-1850), St Gertrude in Wetteren (1861-1867), St Peter and Paul in Châtelet (1867-1881), St Peter in Antoing (1868-1870), St Amandus in Roeselare (1869-1872), Our Lady in Oudenburg (1870-1874) and St Vincent in Eeklo (1878-1883). With their high towers, these churches were more than just churches; they were monuments that gave local communities an identity and contrib-

21 Frisque, "Au fil de la Grande Ceinture".
22 In particular, the churches of St Josse in Saint-Josse-ten-Noode (1864-1891), St Gilles in Saint-Gilles (1866-1878), St Servais in Schaerbeek (1871-1876), Our Lady Immaculate in Cureghem (1856-1900), Holy Cross in Ixelles (1859-1865), Holy Family in Helmet (1898-1936), St Anthony in Etterbeek (1905-1935), St Remigius in Molenbeek (1907), St Anne in Koekelberg (1908), St Hubert in Boitsfort (1911-1939), and St Francis Xavier in Cureghem (1912-1915).
23 In particular, the remarkable concrete church of St Augustine in Forest (1932-1936), built on the highest point of the town, or the tower of the Jesuit church, the Gesù (1937-1939).
24 Parish churches of St Joris (1847-1853), St Joseph (1862-1867), St Amandus (1869-1874), St Willibrordus (1886-1891), St Michael (1893-1897), St Norbert (1901-1904) and St Anthony (1907-1910).
25 St Mary Magdalene in Bruges (1851-1853), St Anne in Ghent (1853-1869), St Joseph in Leuven (1854-1887), St Joseph in Eupen (1855-1869), Our Lady and St Remacle in Spa (1883-1886), St Juliana in Verviers (1900-1907), St John the Baptist in Kortrijk (1908-1911), St Pholien in Liège (1910-1914), Sacred Heart in Ostend (1914-1928), etc.
26 An interesting and unstudied phenomenon is the allocation of former convent churches to Protestant congregations when Belgium was under Dutch rule, for example the Augustines in Brussels 1818 and the Annunciates in Antwerp 1821.
27 Braeken, "Beth haknesset. Synagogen in België".

uted to making the area more attractive.[31] King Leopold II stimulated several projects for monumental Gothic Revival churches on sites with a symbolic identity. In Ostend, the 'queen of the beaches' and gateway to the continent for British tourists, the church of St Peter and Paul (1901-1907), with its two spires visible from the sea, was the only monument on the Belgian coast. [Ill. 3.2-1] At the other end of the country, the tall spire of the church of St Donatus in Arlon (1907-1914) stood close to the border with the Grand Duchy of Luxembourg. These two churches, the construction of which was costly, must be seen in the context of the country's economic prosperity, the absolute political domination of the Catholic Party from 1884 to 1914 and its desire to develop a national style, which was to be Gothic, Christian and rational.[32]

The same spirit prevailed in the restoration of historical monuments, particularly from the 1860s, when ultramontane Catholic architects successfully asserted themselves and obtained a monopoly on the restoration of religious buildings.[33] Without going into the details of these restorations, two points are worthy of note. On the one hand, the question of clearing monuments – in particular, the houses that often surrounded urban churches – was asked in Belgium as in France and other countries.[34] These clearances were intended to showcase the monument, as in the case of the church of St Nicolas in Ghent. On the other hand, the question of the completion of church towers arose relatively early on, notably with the cathedrals of St Paul in Liège (1810-1812) and St Saviour in Bruges (1843-1846). Elsewhere, collapsed towers were rebuilt, such as at the church of Our Lady in Sint-Truiden (1847-1852) and the collegiate church of St Gertrude in Nivelles (1859), or simply 'completed' according to Viollet-le-Duc's theory of the unity of style, as in St Hermes in Ronse (1868) and St Peter and Guido in Anderlecht (1898).

The rural world, between adaptation and resistance to modernity

In contrast with the growth of towns, cities and industrial basins, significant areas of Belgium remained deeply rural throughout the nineteenth century: the Campine, the Ardennes, the Hesbaye, the Condroz, the coastal polders, the Meetjesland, the Waasland, etc. The church retained a major influence in these areas of Catholic tradition that were fertile recruiting grounds for religious vocations. While the disappearance of the large abbey estates in 1796 had led to the redistribution of land and the emergence of a new elite of wealthy rural landowners, it is fair to say, in keeping with the proverb, that 'the church was the heart of the village'. However, despite this, it was inevitable that the rural world in Belgium would undergo the influence of societal transformations and adapt to these while at the same time resisting them. The old Catholic nobility and the new liberal elite had different views on the future of the countryside, which therefore became a political and ideological issue.

Given the relatively small size of the country, rural regions were never very far from an urban centre. The development of the railways and other modern means of

2.2-4 Aerial view of the centre of Sint-Niklaas, with town hall and church of Our Lady, 2008.
[Leuven, KADOC-KU Leuven; © Vier D bvba]

28 St Fiacre in Dison (1853-1867), St Martin in Jemappes (1863-1865), St Basil in Couillet (1865-1868), St Peter and Paul in Châtelet (1867-1881), St Martin in Ghlin (1877-1878), St Lambert in Grivegnée (1895-1897), Our Lady in Marchienne-au-Pont (1901-1904).

29 Smets, L'avènement de la cité-jardin en Belgique.

30 St Anthony in La Louvière (1898-1903), St Barbara in Houdeng-Aimeries / Bois-du-Luc (1904-1905).

31 On this phenomenon during the interwar period: Heynickx, "A Law of Inertia".

32 De Maeyer, "The Neo-Gothic in Belgium".

33 Particularly the architect Auguste Van Assche, Baron Bethune's right-hand man and one of the first teachers at the Saint Luke School in Ghent. Stynen, De onvoltooid verleden tijd, 149-219.

34 Buls, Esthétique des villes; Smets, Charles Buls.

35 De Block and Polasky, "Light railways and the rural-urban continuum"; De Block, "Planning Rural-Urban Landscapes".

36 Victoir and Vanderperren, *Henri Beyaert*, 140-143, 151-155; van Caloen, Van Cleven and Braet, *Het Kasteel van Loppem*, 153-158; Coomans, "L'intégration d'un passé séculaire dans une résidence aristocratique rénovée".

communication helped to reduce physical, social and psychological distances.[35] Rapid demographic growth caused a rural exodus that supplied manpower to the industrial basins of Belgium and Northern France, markedly limiting emigration to the New World. Industrialisation manifested itself in the rural world through the gradual mechanisation of agriculture, especially on the large estates of the Hesbaye, a cereal- and sugar beet-producing region. As a consequence, small sugar factories, industrial forges around former mills, breweries, sawmills, etc. sprang up in the countryside.

Nostalgic for the Ancien Régime, many conservative château owners re-established the material relationship between the château and the church in their village, an expression of a traditional and unchanging order in the countryside. The pairing of château-church could be found in hundreds of villages across the country. Among the châteaux and churches rebuilt by the same patron in the nineteenth century, Faux-les-Tombes near Namur by the architect Henri Beyaert for Chevalier de Sauvage-Vercour (1868-1874), Loppem near Bruges by architect Jean-Baptiste Bethune for Baron van Caloen (1858-1863 and 1870-1872), and Ham-sur-Heure near Charleroi by the architects Jozef Schadde and Pierre Langerock for the counts of Merode (1876-1880 and 1899-1908) are some of the most spectacular.[36] In general, château owners were satisfied with the building of a family funerary chapel in the cemetery and the provision of furnishings and stained glass to their church.

New rural parish churches were rebuilt on the same site as earlier churches that dated back to the Middle Ages and, for the most part, were still surrounded by their cemeteries. The new church retained the orientation of its predecessor because it structured the morphology of the village. This permanence was in keeping with the traditional spirit of the countryside and the Church. However, it was not unheard of for the arrival of a new road, regional tram or railway to shift the centre of gravity of a village and increase its population. In some villages, a new church was built near these new thoroughfares, while the old church was destroyed or fell

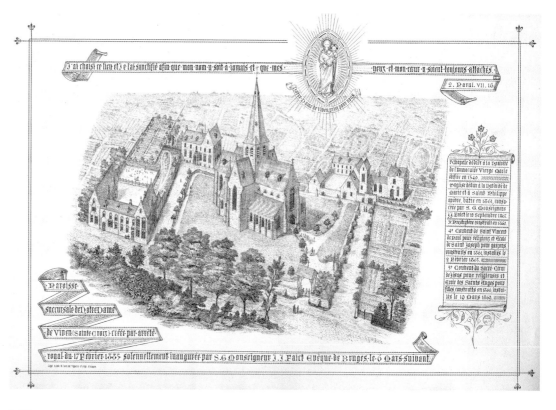

2.2-5 Bird's-eye view of the centre of the Gothic Revival village of Vivenkapelle, 1885. (See also col. ill. 6.)
[Marke, Bethune Foundation]

into ruin in the middle of the cemetery.[37] These parish churches could not be moved to new centres without the agreement of the civil and religious authorities. This involved the acquisition of land for the new church and the upkeep of the cemetery on the site of its predecessor. Such new churches were no longer bound to a strict east-west orientation and simply turned their main façade, preceded by a small square, towards the station or main road.

In the context of the First School War between official and free education that shook Belgium from 1879 to 1884, a law obliged all municipalities to have a secular primary school, funded by the state. In response, bishops stimulated the opening of Catholic primary schools run by religious teachers in every village.[38] Small schools, often Gothic Revival in style and flanked by a house for their teachers, were built in many villages thanks to the generosity of Catholics, in particular the ultramontans and château owners who thus ensured the identity of their villagers. For example, the village of Vivenkapelle near Bruges, an ideal Catholic village, has a Gothic Revival centre designed by Baron Bethune, comprising a presbytery and two separate schools for boys and girls around the church, each accompanied by a house for brothers and nuns. [Ill. 2.2-5]

The Catholic nature of the rural world was reinforced by new pilgrimages that were added to the Marian pilgrimages of the Middle Ages and Counter-Reformation[39] and were part of the reform of piety and the revival of Marian worship in nineteenth-century Belgium.[40] The construction in carefully chosen locations of sanctuaries around large basilicas clearly visible in the landscape responded to a concept of space founded on the polarisation between the liberal city and the Catholic countryside. Christian pilgrims were invited to visit and regenerate their faith in line with moral and traditional Marian values. Nineteenth-century Marian shrines included Our Lady of Dadizele (1857-1867) [Ill. 2.2-6] in the diocese of Bruges and Our Lady of Bon-Secours (1885-

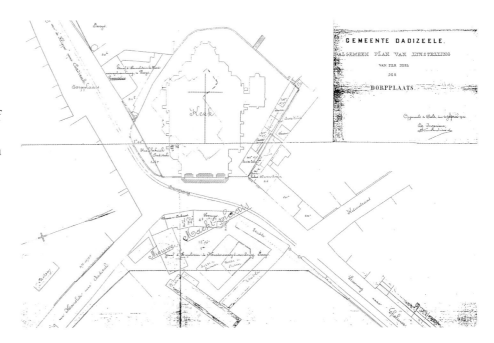

1892) in the diocese of Tournai. Small towns with shops and restaurants sprang up around these Marian shrines. From the 1860s, Belgium was also covered with replicas of the Grotto of Lourdes, usually set up near parish churches, calvaries or in convent gardens. Some resulted in 'miracles' and important pilgrimages such as in Oostakker (1875-1877), promoted by the Jesuits near the industrial city of Ghent, and in Jette (1915), on the outskirts of Brussels.

Convents, monasteries and abbeys

The four fundamental freedoms guaranteed by the Belgian constitution of 1831 – freedoms of religion, association, press and education – were not only favourable to the development of a great many religious communities in Belgium, but also made the country a land of asylum for communities expelled by the anticlerical governments of neighbouring countries.[41] In the context of the religious revival of the nineteenth century, many new religious institutions, male and female, active and contemplative, were added to the religious orders of the Ancien Régime that had survived the turmoil.[42] These communities all needed buildings in which to

2.2-6 In Dadizele, a large basilica was built on the site of the old parish church in 1857-1867, but with another orientation; a new square and a regional tramroad were arranged in front of the Marian shrine in 1900.
[Archives A. Samyn; © Ella Maes]

37 For example, the churches of St Amandus in Eke, St Eligius in Ettelgem, St Gertrude in Landen, St Eligius in Snellegem, etc.
38 Wynants, Dujardin, Byls & Van Ruyskensvelde, "Des conflits structurants et perturbateurs".
39 In particular in Tournai, Antwerp, Halle, Scherpenheuvel/Montaigu, Hanswijck in Mechelen, Virga-Jesse in Hasselt.
40 Van Osselaer, "Reform of Piety in the Southern Netherlands / Belgium".
41 Kulturkampf in the German Empire (1871-1887) and laws of separation of Church and State in France (1905).
42 Van Dijck, De Maeyer and Henneau, eds., "Historiographie et perspectives de recherche des ordres et congrégations sur le territoire des Pays-Bas méridionaux/Belgique"; Wynants, "Les instituts féminins en Belgique".

lead their communal lives and carry out their apostolate in the areas of education, healthcare, charitable institutions and missionary training. Unlike the parishes which, in accordance with the agreements of the Concordat, benefited from public funding for the material organisation of public worship, monasteries, convents and other religious establishments were private institutions that could not receive money from the state.[43] Their real estate investments and architectural projects were therefore essentially based on the generosity of benefactors and endowments from their members.

After 1830, some long-standing communities succeeded in recovering either all or part of the buildings they had owned before the secularisation of 1796. This scenario was quite exceptional because it required both the survival of the community and the recovery of the buildings, so-called 'black church goods', which were rarely intact and had to be rebuilt from ruins. The few communities that managed to ensure this continuity by recovering their property acquired considerable prestige.[44] Recovering monastic property, however, was nearly impossible in an urban context due to real estate speculation, except in towns with slow or no growth, such as Bruges.[45] Sometimes new communities settled in buildings that had belonged to other religious orders before the suppression.[46] In this case, there was a continuity of religious usage but a change of identity. It was also not unheard of for former monasteries and convents to be taken over by bishops and used for the installation of seminaries or diocesan colleges.[47]

The Catholic revival was reflected primarily in the development of new religious institutions whose apostolates responded to the specific needs of modern society: education, hospitals, orphanages, asylums, rest homes, missions, etc. These institutes were sometimes diocesan foundations, sometimes new international congregations. Their foundation was always modest and it was over time that these establishments developed, gradually acquiring neighbouring land to extend and build, in keeping with the classic pattern of progressive expansion. When critical mass was reached, they were able to erect large buildings and make their mark in the public space. The Jesuits, for example, who returned to Belgium in 1833 after half a century of suppression, recovered few of their former properties. They established their new colleges discreetly and it was not until a generation later that they built their first domed churches – the style of which expressed their Roman identity – in Brussels, Liège and Ghent.[48] When the political context was more favourable to them and the First School War had subsided, they began to build large school complexes along new urban boulevards, as in Antwerp and Brussels, with churches with highly visible Gothic and Romanesque façades and towers,[49] and developed training centres in the countryside.

This 'clericalisation' of the public space in the last decades of the nineteenth century benefited from extremely favourable political circumstances. The anticlerical tensions that marked Belgium in the 1860s-1880s – and reached their height with the First School War – began to subside in 1884 when the Catholic Party came to power in the country with an absolute majority until 1914. These thirty years of Catholic rule corresponded to Belgium's economic heyday. Religious institutions took advantage of this exceptional context to consolidate their properties and build large complexes in the St Luke Gothic Revival style.[50] These institutes played a part in the development of modern and Christian society by founding model schools and hospitals in accordance with standards of order and hygiene. Their visibility was therefore essential. In some medium-sized cities, such as Leuven, seat of the Catholic university, Mechelen, seat of the archbishopric, Bruges and Tournai – all Catholic and conservative cities –, there were at least as many new convents and religious institutes around 1900 as at the time of the suppression in 1796. The reconquest had therefore been a complete success. In larger cities, religious houses were sometimes grouped in certain districts,

---

43 Stevens, "Les associations religieuses en Belgique pendant le 19ᵉ siècle".

44 For example: the Premonstratensians at Park in Heverlee, Averbode, Grimbergen, Tongerlo and Postel managed to recover their old abbeys. This was also true of the Trappists of Rochefort and Westmalle, the Cistercians of Val-Dieu, the Benedictines of Affligem, the canonesses of the English Convent in Bruges, the Augustinians in Ghent, the Franciscans in Sint-Truiden, the Cistercians in Soleilmont and Marche-les-Dames, the Carmelites in Antwerp, etc.

45 Klaarenbeek, *De herverkavelde stad*.

46 For example: the Capuchin sisters in the former Charterhouse in Antwerp (1934), the Cistercians who took over the English Dominican convent in Bornem (1836), the Benedictines at a Capuchin convent in Dendermonde (1837), the Jesuits in the former Premonstratensian abbey in Drongen (1837), the brothers of the Christian Schools on the site of the abbey of the cannons of St Augustine in Malonne (1841), the Scheutist missionaries on the site of the Charterhouse in Anderlecht (1865), the brothers of the Christian Schools on the site of the Benedictine Abbey of St Wivina in Groot-Bijgaarden (1897), the sisters of the Sacred Heart on the site of the Cistercian abbey of La Ramée (1903), the Capuchins on the site of the Charterhouse in Louvain (1917).

2.2-7 Aerial view of the Benedictine abbeys of Maredret (nuns), in the foreground, and Maredsous (monks), in the background.
[© WBT - S. Wittenbol]

such as in Ghent around the Oude Houtlei, home to the Dominicans, Brothers of the Christian Schools, Poor Clares, Jesuits and a small beguinage. In these neighbourhoods, in addition to the buildings, the public space had also been taken over by the sound of bells and the presence of religious men and women in distinctive clothing.

A distinction must be made between monasteries for men and convents for women. Men, because they were priests, built larger monasteries with churches for preaching and stage certain sacraments. Convents were more introverted because they were subject to a stricter enclosure and content with a chapel that was barely accessible to the public. In their completed form, monasteries and convents were usually laid out around a cloister and those located in outlying districts had gardens, even large grounds.

It was not until the second half of the nineteenth century that the Catholic revival began to have a significant impact on contemplative monastic life.[51] Some large Trappist, Cistercian and Benedictine abbeys were built in locations far from cities and modernity, as if these communities of unshakeable tradition had to remain apart from the world. The Trappist abbey of Scourmont near Chimay and the Benedictine abbey of Maredsous, founded on the model of medieval abbeys in 1851 and 1872 respectively, dominated vast areas.[52] In 1897, the Benedictines began building the Abbey of Mount Caesar (Keizersberg) on top of the highest hill in Leuven, the site of the medieval castle of the Dukes of Brabant. In 1906, on a promontory, they erected a gigantic statue of the Virgin '*regina coeli*', protector of the university city in the valley. Benefiting from the same contemplative dynamic, abbeys were also built for communities of nuns. The Benedictine abbey of Maredret, founded in 1896 near the abbey of Maredsous, formed with its neighbour a remarkable Gothic Revival architectural complex on a splendid site, one of the most powerful statements of the ultramontane Belgian elite. [Ill. 2.2-7] Many more modest contemplative communities of Benedictines, Poor Clares, Dominican and Carmelite nuns were founded both in the countryside and in towns.

It remains to mention the beguinages, semi-religious female communities specific to Belgium.[53] Dating back to the thirteenth century, beguinages developed on the outskirts of cities until they were suppressed by the French rulers in the late eighteenth century. Unlike religious communities that were expelled from their convents, the Beguines were able to continue occupying their houses, but could no longer recruit novices. Some

47 For example: the seminary of Liège in the former Premonstratensian abbey of Beaurepart, the seminary of Bruges in the Cistercian abbey of the Dunes, the seminary of Tournai in the former Jesuit college, the diocesan college of Namur in the former abbey of Floreffe, the diocesan college of Tournai in the former Premonstratensian abbey of Bonne-Espérance.

48 Church of St John Berchmans College in Brussels (1852), church of the St Servais College in Liège (1852), church of St Barbara College in Ghent (1858).

49 Church of the Theology and Philosophy college in Leuven (1864-1866), Our Lady College in Antwerp (1878-1909), church of St Michael College in Brussels (1908-1912).

50 See my contribution "Gothic Revival: Style, Construction and Ideology in Nineteenth-Century Belgium" in this volume (3.2); Coomans, "Pugin Worldwide".

51 *La Belgique Monastique / Het Monnikenleven in België.*

52 Misonne, *En parcourant l'histoire de Maredsous*, 9-185.

53 Van Aerschot and Heirman, *Flemish Beguinages.*

149

54 Witte et al., *Nieuwe geschiedenis van België*, I, 303-307.
55 Sennesael, "Italiaanse inspiratie: het Campo Santo van Mariakerke".
56 Célis, Vandenbreeden and Van Santvoort, *Autour du parvis Notre-Dame à Laeken*.

beguinal communities died out while others regained momentum in Flemish towns after 1830. A new beguinage was even founded in Sint-Amandsberg near Ghent, forming a religious complex consisting of houses around the church, all surrounded by a wall to provide the enclosure. [Ill. 2.2-1] With this anachronistic foundation, the ultramontans of Ghent aimed to demonstrate their resistance to the city's liberal and anticlerical power. This foundation took place in 1874, against the backdrop of the anticlerical tensions of the First School War and the cemetery conflict.

Cemeteries, places of religious, political and social conflict

The issue of cemeteries, places with a religious, political and social identity, resulted in a clash over space between Catholics and Liberals in the 1850s-1880s.[54] In 1784, for reasons of hygiene and prophylaxis, Emperor Joseph II forbade the burial of the dead inside churches and required parishes to move their cemeteries out of towns. Following the secularisation of cemeteries under the French regime, the parishes lost their influence to civil powers. The freedom to worship guaranteed by the Belgian constitution of 1831 gave Church Councils a certain amount of control over their cemeteries. These would now be divided into separate areas according to the religious identity of the deceased: Catholic, free-thinker, Jew, Protestant, etc. The bishops consecrated the grounds of Catholic cemeteries and were opposed to the burial of laity on consecrated ground, considered an extension of the church.

In 1849, the Liberals appealed for the abolition of these exclusions and began a struggle for shared and unsegregated cemeteries. In 1857, they demanded that cemeteries be entirely dependent on the civil power of the communes and no longer on the Church Councils. Rejecting this secularisation, the Catholics orchestrated demonstrations at cemetery gates for several decades during civil burials. Mayors interpreted the law according to Catholic or liberal political affiliation. It was not until 1879 that the Court of Cassation decided to abolish the division of cemeteries, which then became shared by all citizens.

The conflict culminated when large liberal cities created new communal cemeteries and banned the bishops from performing any kind of consecration. The reaction of Catholics was to shun these 'cimetières de Gueux' or 'Geuzenkerkhof' (literally, 'beggars' cemeteries') in favour of burial in neighbouring Catholic villages. When the industrial and liberal city of Ghent built a new communal cemetery (Westerbegraafplaats) in 1866, the Catholics boycotted it and instead asked to be buried in several *campisanti* in the villages of Sint-Amandsberg and Mariakerke.[55] These Catholic necropolises were home to the graves of ultramontans and members of religious communities in particular.

Unlike in the villages, where the majority kept their dead around their church, the larger urban cemeteries of the nineteenth century lacked churches. The only notable exception is the Laeken cemetery in Brussels, which sprang up next to the large funerary church of the Belgian royal family.[56] The country's elite, Catholic and Liberal alike, thronged to what is tantamount to a 'Belgian Père Lachaise'. [Ill. 2.2-8]

2.2-8 The Laeken cemetery near the church of Our Lady, the funerary church of the Belgian royal family.
[Leuven, KADOC-KU Leuven: postcard collection]

2.2-9 Panoramic view of Brussels with in the centre, at the horizon, the National Basilica of the Sacred Heart of Koekelberg. Drawing by E. Hucq in Basilique nationale du Sacré Cœur de Jésus, à Koekelberg *(Brussels, 1904, 8-9)*.
[Leuven, KADOC-KU Leuven: KBRB 28519]

A reconquest with the support of the ultramontans and the goodwill of the Catholic Party

The metamorphosis of the industrial and urban landscape of nineteenth-century Belgium was not exclusively dominated by the belfries of town halls, factory chimneys and mine headframes. A great many church towers topped with spires and crosses of all sizes – sometimes even holy statues[57] – flourished in both towns and the countryside. They expressed the restoration and presence of the Catholic Church in the modern world. Despite the 'neutral' character of the Belgian state, the conflict between Catholics and Liberals was long at the heart of political debate. Depending on the colour of the ruling majority, the Catholic Church was either forced to stick strictly to the agreements of the Concordat of 1802 or was widely supported and favoured. The absolute domination of Catholics from 1884 to 1914 consecrated the triumph of the Church in modern society.

In this particular context, the project for a huge national basilica dedicated to the Sacred Heart came into existence in 1903.[58] Supported by King Leopold II, who dreamt of embellishing Brussels with a large religious building worthy of a capital, this national basilica was to include seven tall Gothic Revival spires to the west of Brussels, on the high ground of Koekelberg, and to form a counterpoint to the dome of the Palace of Justice, completed in 1883, on the urban landscape. The project was halted in 1911 and completed in another form after the First World War. [Ill. 2.2-9]

The restoration of the visibility of the Catholic Church in nineteenth-century Belgium was therefore largely funded by the public authorities through, on the one hand, Church Councils for the parishes, and, on the other, the policy of the Royal Commission on Monuments for historical buildings. The state gained from this insofar as it sought to promote its national heritage as a support for an identity still under construction. Many new churches were also designed as urban monuments intended to embellish the new districts of towns and cities undergoing transformation.

Only monasteries, convents and religious institutions were not financed by the state because they were not intended for public worship. It was precisely these religious communities that had lost all their assets in the late eighteenth century and whose interests had not been recognised by the Concordat.

We can therefore conclude that the reconquest of public space by the Catholic Church in nineteenth-century Belgium came about in strict application of agreements between Church and State, with the unconditional support of the ultramontans and the great benevolence of the Catholic Party when it was in power. In 1914, on the eve of the First World War, the Church had fully regained its visibility in Belgium. However, the massive destruction caused by the war would profoundly overwhelm Belgian society, its landscape and heritage.[59]

57 According to the French model (Marseille, Lyon, Avignon etc.): churches of Our Lady in Sint-Niklaas (1896) and the Sacred Heart in Tournai (c 1890), as well as the church of the college of the Redemptorists in Essen (1906).
58 Rion, *La basilique de Koekelberg*.
59 The subsequent waves of reconstruction transformed urban and rural spaces: Smets, *Resurgam*; Stynen, *De onvoltooid verleden tijd*, 249-271.

BIBLIOGRAPHY

Antoine, François. *La vente des biens nationaux dans le département de la Dyle*. PhD Université Libre de Bruxelles, 1997.

Antoine, François. "La vente des biens nationaux à la fin du XVIIIe siècle, nouvelle donne pour la ville". *Articulo. Journal of Urban Research*, 1 (2009) (online journal). <https://journals.openedition.org/articulo/1015>.

Art, Jan, Jan De Maeyer, Ward De Pril and Leo Kenis. "Church Reform and Modernity in Belgium". In: Joris van Eijnatten and Paula Yates, eds. *The Churches. The Dynamics of Religious Reform in Northern Europe 1780-1920*, 2. Leuven, 2010, 101-122.

Bertrand, Matthieu, Nicolas Chenut and Luc-Francis Genicot. *Les églises paroissiales de Wallonie (1830-1940)*. 3 vols. Namur, 2009-2010.

Braeken, Jo. "Beth haknesset. Synagogen in België 1865-1914". *M&L. Monumenten en landschappen*, 12 (1993) 1, 13-45.

Buls, Charles. *Esthétique des villes. L'isolement des vieilles églises*. Brussels, 1910.

Célis, Marcel M., Jos Vandenbreeden and Linda Van Santvoort. *Autour du parvis Notre-Dame à Laeken*. Les pierres pour le dire, 11. Brussels, 1994.

Collin, Ludo, Luc Robijns and Luc Verpoest. *Het Gentse bisschopshuis. Monument van vroege neogotiek*. Ghent, 1993.

Coomans, Thomas. "L'intégration d'un passé séculaire dans une résidence aristocratique rénovée: la métamorphose du château d'Ham-sur-Heure par l'architecte Pierre Langerock (1898-1910)". In: *Autour d'un château: Ham-sur-Heure*. Ham-sur-Heure, 2003, 25-46.

Coomans, Thomas. "From Romanticism to New Age: The Evolving Perception of a Church Ruin". *Téoros. Revue de recherche en tourisme*, 24 (2005) 2, 47-57.

Coomans, Thomas. "Les églises en Belgique. Aspects architecturaux, enjeux juridiques et approche patrimoniale". In: Lucie K. Morisset, Luc Noppen and Thomas Coomans, eds. *Quel avenir pour quelles églises? / What Future for Which Churches*. Patrimoine urbain, 3. Montreal, 2006, 41-72.

Coomans, Thomas. "Pugin Worldwide. From *Les Vrais Principes* and the Belgian St Luke Schools to Northern China and Inner Mongolia". In: Timothy Brittain-Catlin, Jan De Maeyer and Martin Bressani, eds. *Gothic Revival Worldwide: A.W.N. Pugin's Global Influence*. KADOC Artes, 16. Leuven, 2016, 156-171.

Coomans, Thomas. *Life Inside the Cloister. Understanding Monastic Architecture: Tradition, Reformation, Adaptive Reuse*. KADOC Studies on Religion, Culture and Society, 21. Leuven, 2018.

Coomans, Thomas, and Reinout Klaarenbeek. "De ruimtelijke metamorfose van steden na de secularisatie van de kloosters in België vanaf 1773 tot 1860". *Stadsgeschiedenis*, 9 (2014) 2, 149-165.

Dambruyne, Johan, Guido Jan Bral, Aletta Rambaut and Dirk Laporte. *Een stad in opbouw. Gent van 1540 tot de wereldtentoonstelling van 1913*. Tielt, 1992.

De Block, Greet. "Planning Rural-Urban Landscapes. Rails and Countryside Urbanization in South-West Flanders, Belgium (1830-1930)". *Landscape Research*, 2013. DOI: 10.1080/01426397.2012.759917.

De Block, Greet, and Janet Polasky. "Light railways and the rural-urban continuum: technology, space and society in late nineteenth-century Belgium". *Journal of Historical Geography*, 37 (2011), 312-328.

De Maeyer, Jan. "The Neo-Gothic in Belgium: Architecture of a Catholic Society". In: Jan De Maeyer and Luc Verpoest, eds. *Gothic Revival: Religion, Architecture and Style in Western Europe 1815-1914*. KADOC Artes, 5. Leuven, 2000, 19-34.

De Meyer, Ronny, and Marcel Smets. "De recente stedebouwkundige geschiedschrijving in België omtrent negentiende en begin twintigste eeuw". *Belgisch tijdschrift voor nieuwste geschiedenis*, 13 (1982), 467-517.

De Schepper, Gratianus. "Marie-Thérèse et Joseph II: leur politique à l'égard des maisons religieuses dans les Pays-Bas". *Revue d'histoire ecclésiastique*, 35 (1939), 509-529.

Frisque, Christian. "Au fil de la Grande Ceinture. Comment Victor Besme a structuré l'extension urbaine". *Bruxelles patrimoines*, 21 (2016), 26-45.

Heynickx, Rajesh. "A Law of Inertia: The Tower as Site and Symbol in Interwar Flanders". In: Rajesh Heynickx and Tom Avermaete, eds. *Making a New World: Architecture & Communities in Interwar Europe*. KADOC Artes, 13. Leuven, 2012, 199-211.

Klaarenbeek, Reinout. "The Secularisation of Urban Space: Mapping the Afterlife of Religious Houses in Brussels, Antwerp and Bruges". In: Thomas Coomans, Bieke Cattoor and Krista De Jonge, eds. *Mapping Landscapes in Transformation: Multidisciplinary Methods for Historical Analysis*. Leuven, 2019, 247-257.

Klaarenbeek, Reinout. *De herverkavelde stad. Kartografie van het naleven van de stadskloosters in de Belgische steden Brussel, Antwerpen en Brugge (1773/1796-1860)*. PhD KU Leuven, 2020, 2 vols.

Klaarenbeek, Reinout, and Thomas Coomans. "Reusing Urban Convents as State Schools in Belgian Towns (1773-1803)". *Revista História da Arte*, Série W, 5 (2016), 31-44.

Klaarenbeek, Reinout, and Thomas Coomans. "From Guessing to 'Gissing': HisGIS Analysis for Mapping Urban Transformation and Military Reuse of Suppressed Convents in Brussels, Antwerp and Bruges (1773-1860)". In: Ana Plosnić Škarić, ed. *Mapping Urban Changes / Mapiranje urbanih promjena*. Zagreb, 2017, 364-389.

La Belgique Monastique / Het Monnikenleven in België. Zottegem, 1954.

Lamberts, Emiel. "Liberal State and Confessional Accommodation: The Southern Netherlands / Belgium". In: Robbins Keith, ed. *Political and Legal Perspectives. The Dynamics of Religious Reform in Northern Europe 1780-1920*, 1. Leuven, 2010, 99-116.

Loir, Christophe. *Bruxelles néoclassique. Mutation d'un espace urbain 1775-1840*. Lieux de mémoire. Brussels, 2009.

Meul, Veerle. *Van waterstaatkerk tot mijncité. Een historiek van het bouwen in Limburg door drie generaties provinciale bouwmeesters Jaminé (1832-1921)*. Hasselt, 1999.

Misonne, Daniel. *En parcourant l'histoire de Maredsous*. Denée, 2005.

Raxhon, Philippe. "La démolition de la cathédrale Saint-Lambert à Liège". In: Benoît Van den Bossche, ed. *La cathédrale gothique Saint-Lambert à Liège: une église et son contexte. Actes du colloque international tenu du 16 au 18 avril 2002*. Études et recherches archéologiques de l'Université de Liège, 108. Liège, 2005, 59-69.

Rion, Pierre. *La basilique de Koekelberg. Architecture et mentalités religieuses*. Publications d'histoire de l'art et d'archéologie de l'Université catholique de Louvain, 47. Louvain-la-Neuve, 1986.

Sägesser, Caroline. "Les rapports entre l'Église et l'État en Belgique au XIXe siècle: l'application de la Constitution de 1831". In: Brigitte Basdevant-Gaudemet, François Jankowiak and Jean-Pierre Delannoy, eds. *Le droit ecclésiastique en Europe et à ses marges (XVIIIe-XXe siècles)*. Leuven-Paris-Walpole, 2009, 37-45.

Sennesael, Veronique. "Italiaanse inspiratie: het Campo Santo van Mariakerke". *M&L. Monumenten en landschappen*, 14 (1995) 6, 18-27.

Smets, Marcel. *L'avènement de la cité-jardin en Belgique. Histoire de l'habitat social en Belgique de 1830 à 1930*. Brussels, 1967.

Smets, Marcel. *Resurgam. La reconstruction de la Belgique après 1914*. Brussels, 1985.

Smets, Marcel. *Charles Buls: les principes de l'art urbain*. Liège, 1995.

Stevens, Fred. "Les associations religieuses en Belgique pendant le 19ᵉ siècle". In: Jan De Maeyer, Sofie Leplae and Joachim Schmiedl, eds. *Religious Institutes in Western Europe in the 19th and 20th Centuries: Historiography, Research and Legal Position.* KADOC Studies on Religion, Culture and Society, 2. Leuven, 2004, 185-202.

Stynen, Herman. *De onvoltooid verleden tijd. Een geschiedenis van de monumenten- en landschapszorg in België 1835-1940.* Brussels, 1998.

Van Aerschot, Suzanne, and Michiel Heirman. *Flemish Beguinages: World Heritage.* Leuven, 2001.

van Caloen, Véronique, Jean Van Cleven and Johan Braet. *Het Kasteel van Loppem.* Oostkamp, 2001.

Van de Vijver, Dirk. "La ville en chantier: l'espace urbain sécularisé et la nouvelle place". In: Laurence Baudoux-Rousseau and Youri Carbonnier, eds. *La place publique urbaine du Moyen Âge à nos jours.* Arras, 2007, 225-234.

Van Dijck, Maarten, Jan De Maeyer and Marie-Élisabeth Henneau, eds. "Historiographie et perspectives de recherche des ordres et congrégations sur le territoire des Pays-Bas méridionaux/Belgique / Historiografie en onderzoeksperspectieven van ordes en congregaties op het grondgebied van de Zuidelijke Nederlanden/Belgie". *Revue belge de philologie et d'histoire / Belgisch tijdschrift voor filologie en geschiedenis*, 86 (2008) 3-4.

Van Osselaer, Tine. "Reform of Piety in the Southern Netherlands / Belgium". In: Jarlert Anders, ed. *Piety and Modernity. The Dynamics of Religious Reform in Northern Europe 1780-1920*, 3. Leuven, 2012, 101-124.

Victoir, Jef, and Jos Vanderperren. *Henri Beyaert. Du Classicisme à l'Art Nouveau.* Sint-Martens-Latem, 1992.

Witte, Els, Jean-Pierre Nandrin, Éliane Gubin and Gita Deneckere. *Nieuwe geschiedenis van België.* 1: *1830-1905.* Tielt, 2005.

Wynants, Paul. "Les instituts féminins en Belgique. Bilan et perspectives de recherche". In: Jan De Maeyer, Sofie Leplae and Joachim Schmiedl, eds. *Religious Institutes in Western Europe in the 19th and 20th Centuries: Historiography, Research and Legal Position.* KADOC Studies on Religion, Culture and Society, 2. Leuven, 2004, 41-51.

Wynants, Paul, Vincent Dujardin, Henk Byls and Sarah Van Ruyskensvelde. "Des conflits structurants et perturbateurs. Les clivages idéologiques et les deux guerres mondiales". In : Jan De Maeyer and Paul Wynants, eds. *L'enseignement catholique en Belgique. Des identités en évolution 19ᵉ-21ᵉ siècles.* Brussel-Leuven, 2016, 79-85.

Websites

http://www.irismonument.be/
https://inventaris.onroerenderfgoed.be/

2.3
Spatial Concepts in Religious Architecture and the Politics of Building in the German Countries

Wolfgang Cortjaens

In the early nineteenth century, the German countries were marked by political disunity as well as by religious diversity.[1] The *Reichsdeputationshauptschluss*, a consequence of the Peace Treaty of Lunéville in 1801, had not only ended the war between Napoleon and the Holy Roman Empire, but had also weakened the power and wealth of the Catholic Church in the German territories, especially of the *Reichskirche* (Imperial Church) which hitherto had kept its special constitutional position within the former Empire. The prince bishops no longer held secular power, the property and territories of the church were confiscated, and the rights and entitlements which applied to their lands were transferred to their new territorial lords. The Wars of Liberation in 1813 and the Congress of Vienna in 1815 had reduced the former 300 states to a total of 39, including the four free cities of Bremen, Hamburg, Lübeck and Frankfurt, in the German Confederation (Deutscher Bund) that was established in 1815 under the leadership of Austrian statesman von Metternich. With Prussia on its way to becoming a superpower, the political landscape remained that of a still torn geographical 'patchwork state', making it especially difficult to refer to a German nation state in general terms. Until the Unification of 1870-1871, the German countries included not only the Prussian core region in the predominantly Protestant north and north east, but also the largely Catholic Rhine Province, then the most significant industrial region of Prussia. Apart from that, various smaller states existed, such as the kingdoms of Bavaria and Württemberg and the duchies of Baden, Hesse-Darmstadt, Saxony-Weimar-Eisenach, Anhalt-Dessau, Oldenburg, Mecklenburg-Strelitz and Mecklenburg-Schwerin.

Early Romanticism and the 'idea' of cultural heritage

As a result of the political changes between 1789 and 1815, the construction of new churches had come to an almost complete standstill. Building activity was exclusively confined to smaller feudal projects commissioned by local sovereigns. Although one can hardly speak of an architectural reform movement during this period, the ideas of Romanticism gradually amalgamated with various architectural theories. The nobility and the sovereigns were the only groups which had preserved an awareness of the cultural and architectural heritage of the past, but were also alone in being constantly in touch with the newest developments in architecture, style and materiality. Especially influential were the Gothic and the Picturesque which had swept over from England in the last quarter of the eighteenth century.[2] Before 1815, both movements had resulted in architectural follies which adapted neo-Gothic forms and set them into lavishly designed artificial landscapes.[3] Prominent examples of such feudal architectural phantasmagorias are the neo-Romanesque Lion's Castle (Löwenburg) in Cassel, commissioned by William IX, Landgrave of Hesse-Cassel (later Elector of Hesse), the chapel serving also as a burial church for the Landgrave and containing a cabinet of medieval paintings and stained-glass windows, and the buildings

2.3-1 Hanover, Christuskirche, by Conrad Wilhelm Hase, 1859. [© Burkhard Foltz, Hanover]

1 De Wall and Gestrich, "Constitutional and Confessional Diversity".
2 Frankl, *The Gothic*.
3 von Buttlar, *Der Landschaftsgarten*.

2.3-2 Dessau-Wörlitz, Gothic House (view from North), by Friedrich Wilhelm von Erdmannsdorff, 1795. [akg images / Bildarchiv Monheim, AKG1580222]

of the park area of Dessau-Wörlitz which the Principal of Anhalt-Dessau had commissioned from, among others, the architect Friedrich Wilhelm Freiherr von Erdmannsdorff (1736-1800), who was also responsible for the gardens. The so-called Gothic House built in several stages between 1773 and 1813 by Erdmannsdorff and Georg Christoph Hesekiel (1732-1818) was partly inspired by English Tudor Gothic, whereas its canal front was a reduced copy of the thirteenth-century church Santa Maria dell'Orto in Venice.[4] [Ill. 2.3-2] The other buildings, bridges and constructions which spread throughout the park conveyed their patrons' educational programme. In contrasting different materials of natural or artificial/industrial origin such as natural timber, cast iron and so on and by using models from different periods, the site became an open-air 'pattern book' of technology and styles. A similar approach can be found in the buildings commissioned by Frederick William II, King of Prussia, for his retreat on Peacock Island (Pfaueninsel) near Potsdam.[5] The exteriors of several buildings, such as the neo-Gothic dairy farm (Meierei, 1794), the Danziger Haus, a Gothic brick house which was moved from Danzig, or the Schweizerhaus (Swiss House) apparently resulted from the ruler's taste for the then-fashionable artificial ruins which, as in Dessau-Wörlitz, added up to a real-life pattern book of different styles and regions. Both functional and allegorical, they housed a dairy farm as well as a big neo-Gothic banquet hall. In Paretz, Brandenburg, Frederick William III had the former village with its twelfth-century church and old manor house completely reshaped when the site was chosen by him and his wife, Queen Louisa, as their regular summer residence.[6]

With the exception of Paretz, where the spatial organisation was based on pre-existing structures which provided the scenic setting for the feudal patronage of the paternalistic sovereign, all the above-mentioned projects were linked by their artificial, non-archaeological approach. Their dynastic context was literally inscribed into the topography of the sites and, although ideas of

4 Günther, "Anglo-Klassizismus".
5 Seiler, *Die Pfaueninsel*; Scharmann, *Königin Luise von Preußen*.
6 Schendel, *Studie zur Geschichte*; Scharmann, *Königin Luise von Preußen*.

2.3-3 Caspar David Friedrich, Eldena Abbey. Oil on canvas, 1825. [SMB, Nationalgalerie Berlin / Jörg P. Anders / bpk]

the Enlightenment were part of the concept behind them, they primarily confirmed the existing feudal order. It was only as a result of secularisation and the decline of the Holy Roman Empire that the cultural heritage of the past and, especially, the value of the artistic and historical religious architecture of the Middle Ages, came into focus. A new awareness of the preservation of monuments reflected the struggle for a restored German nation state, as echoed in the writings of Friedrich Schlegel (1772-1829).[7] Architecture, including church architecture, now was seen as part of a semiotic system.[8] Again, the first buildings were not churches but monuments: the memorial chapel that the Baron (Freiherr) Heinrich Karl Friedrich von Stein had commissioned from the building inspector Johann Claudius von Lassaulx (1781-1848) for himself and his family in Frücht near Nassau (Hesse); the neo-Gothic spire of his residence in Nassau designed by the same architect and destined to be a memorial of the Wars of Liberation; and the small mausoleum of the Counts of Wied-Runkel on the former castle grounds at Dierdorf (Rhineland-Palatine) are among the earliest examples of neo-Gothic architecture in post-Napoleonic Germany. They all resulted from a dynastic self-conception and a new approach to national history.[9] The use of neo-Gothic elements stressed that, despite the political changes, the old dynasties of the ancient regime had become part of the new order. As a religious building, the mausoleum at Dierdorf also reflected contemporary archaeological considerations, as it was intended by its patron, Prince Karl Ludwig Friedrich Alexander zu Wied-Runkel (1763-1824), to incorporate several ancient tombs of his ancestors which were threatened with demolition.[10] As in Nassau, the neo-Gothic forms were not dictated by structural needs but served as a mere symbolic shell for a small oblong roofed hall (Saalbau). The slender tracery above the entrance and in the windows was executed in cast iron, signalling the early use of this industrial material in a hitherto unknown, Picturesque context

7 Schlegel, *Kritische Schriften;* Hinderer, "Das Kollektivindividuum Nation".
8 Kocka, *Sozialgeschichte.*
9 Ronig, "Kirchenbau im Bistum Trier", 212-213, figs. 19-20.
10 The former Premonstratensian monastery of Rommersdorf (then used as a horse stable), the former pilgrimage chapel Hausenborn and the former Collegiate Church of St Florin's in Coblenz which had been misused as a slaughterhouse.

and foreshadowing Schinkel's Memorial on the Kreuzberg in Berlin (1818-1821).

In retrospect, it seems only logical that in Germany the Romanticists' fascination with 'the medieval' and with ancient ruins in general got only a faint response compared to that in France or England where the demolition of monasteries and churches was linked to significant events in national history: in England, the suppression of the monasteries under Henry VIII; in France, the secularisation. In the German countries, such a link did not exist, as the secularisation (even if it was welcomed by the Enlightenment ideas) had been imposed by the French occupation and thus could hardly be regarded as a genuinely national achievement. As a result, only a few monuments were preserved as ruins and as such they became the centre of attention and of tourism.[11] When early Romantic artists such as Caspar David Friedrich (1777-1841) or Carl Gustav Carus (1789-1869) depicted existing monuments in their paintings or sketches,[12] the ruinous churches and abbeys turned into symbols of the 'old' system such as the Ancien Régime, the Holy Roman Empire, or the Imperial Church, signalling disruption instead of historical continuity. [Ill. 2.3-3]

By contrast, the spatial organisation of historical church buildings in nineteenth-century Germany derived, at least partially, from the historical significance of a place. The chosen sites functioned as geo-spatial landmarks, as they were set apart by the exclusivity of their setting. The Romantic idea of the Picturesque came into play when remote locations such as Eldena Abbey near Greifswald, the thirteenth-century collegiate church in Altenberg near Cologne or Castle Malbork (Marienburg) in East Prussia, the former seat of the Teutonic Order of the German Knights, were singled out by regal patronage because as sites they gained historical momentum as a part of the national heritage and identity.[13] Numerous buildings like this, set in remote locations, were associated either with a traditional pilgrimage route or the ritual worship of a local saint (for example, the Hermitage near Kastel in the Rhine Province).[14] Their reclusiveness and spatial isolation became their trademark and heightened their aura. Many of these monuments were located in spectacular landscapes, near a river or a well, on the peak of a mountain or near an ancient cult place. The valley of the Middle Rhine with its countless medieval villages, castles and churches became the major attraction of early nineteenth-century tourism and the epitome of the Romantic landscape. Poets such as Heinrich von Kleist (1777-1811), Clemens von Brentano (1778-1842) and Achim von Arnim (1781-1831) defined the valley of the Middle Rhine as the epitome of Romantic landscape: "eine Gegend wie ein Dichtertraum",[15] Kleist wrote in 1801 about his voyage from Mainz to Coblenz, whereas Friedrich Schlegel accentuated the historical significance of the region as a place of national identity: "Nirgends warden die Erinnerungen an das, was die Deutschen einst waren, und was sie sein könnten, so wach als am Rheine."[16]

After 1815, the Rhine, now forming the natural frontier dividing France and Germany, became *the* symbol of Germany's struggle for unity and national identity. When in the 1820s and 1830s the crown prince and later king Frederick William IV and other members of the Hohenzollern monarchy came, by donation or by purchase, into possession of several medieval sites along the banks of the Rhine – Stolzenfels, Rheinfels, Sooneck – the fascination for the 'medieval' culminated in the so-called *Burgenromantik*. The myth of a glorious past triggered the imagination of thousands of tourists who travelled by steam boat or train along the banks of the Rhine in order to admire seemingly intact, authentic landscapes without realising that many of these sites were soon to be altered or to disappear forever because of industrialisation, traffic and technical progress.[17] At the same time, the sites, completely or partly rebuilt on medieval ruins, became symbols of the political presence of the Prussian monarchy in the Rhine Province: Stolzenfels Castle near Coblenz (1830-1842, under the direction of Karl Friedrich Schinkel and Friedrich August

---

11 Niehr, *Gotikbilder – Gotiktheorien*, 195-214.
12 For Friedrich, see Börsch-Supan and Jähnig, *Caspar David Friedrich*; for Carus, see Prause, *Carl Gustav Carus*.
13 For Altenberg, see Ritter-Eden, *Der Altenberger Dom*; for Malbork, see Woźniak, "Das Denkmal Friedrichs des Großen".
14 Verbeek, "Kunstwerke in der Landschaft", 17-19, fig. 6; Werquet, "Konstruktion historischer Kontinuität"; Id., *Historismus und Repräsentation*, 89-91, 98, 158-159.
15 Kleist, *Sämtliche Werke und Briefe*, II, 674.
16 Schlegel, *Europa*, 15.
17 Niehr, *Gotikbilder – Gotiktheorien*, 241-245.
18 Werquet, *Historismus und Repräsentation*, 100-106, 306-329.
19 Ibid., 322. For Malbork, Woźniak, "Das Denkmal Friedrichs des Großen".

Stüler)[18] and Sooneck Castle (1843-1861, Carl Schnitzler) were both commissioned by Frederick William IV. Under the hands of capable architects the castles rose from the ashes completely rebuilt and furnished according to the convenience and taste of their new proprietors: Stolzenfels, donated by the municipality of Coblenz, became the King's summer residence, whereas Sooneck was turned into a hunting lodge. For the surroundings of Stolzenfels, the Prussian landscape inspector Peter Joseph Lenné (1789-1866) conceived a 'natural' park in English manner with artificial grottos, waterfalls, ponds, ancient relics and a hippodrome. The most prominently placed part of the castle is the chapel designed by Carl Schnitzler (plans revised by Stüler) which is distinguished not only by its elaborate position on a projecting slab of rock at the centre of the front elevation, but also by the chosen material, dressed stone instead of rendered walls. The chapel has lately been interpreted as being inspired by the medieval *Ordensburgen* such as Malbork, which, by that time, also occupied the interest of the crown prince.[19] With this project, Frederick William established himself not only as an art-loving monarch, but also as a successor to the former electoral sovereigns, as ruler by the grace of God in the tradition of the Holy Roman Emperor and at the head of Catholic and Protestant subjects in all Prussia. After the castle was finished in 1842, the King´s festive entry to it was celebrated with a pageant in medieval costume.

A project which could be regarded as the Catholic counterpart of Stolzenfels and another landmark building of the early neo-Gothic *Rheinromantik* is St Apollinaire's Church in Remagen, a mere 40 kilometres up the Rhine. [Ill. 2.3-4] The position itself was at the location of an ancient Roman cult which in the fourteenth century had become the pilgrimage site of St Apollinaire, an early-Christian bishop and martyr. In 1839 the old church had been purchased by the wealthy Catholic landowner and politician Baron Franz Egon von Fürstenberg-Stammheim

2.3-4 Remagen, St Apollinaire Church, by Ernst Friedrich Zwirner, 1839. [Bednorz Images, Cologne, 200]

(1797-1859). When the remains of the medieval church proved so ruinous that restoration was impossible, the baron decided to have a new church erected on the very same spot to respect the historical nature of the site. Instead of taking an archaeological approach, the architect Ernst Friedrich Zwirner (1802-1861), who would soon become the first master builder of Cologne cathedral, conceived a unique, completely original building which was perfectly suited to the demands of the site as well as to the elaborate cycle of mural paintings which were to cover its interior.[20] In the case of Remagen, the new church re-established the site as a pilgrimage place; even pilgrimages by boat were organised, allowing the full appreciation of the architecture and its spectacular location.

To sum up, it can be said that early Romanticism and the idea of the Picturesque, together with a new scientific approach towards formerly neglected styles such as the Gothic, created a sensitivity towards the implantation of religious architecture into landscape and scenic settings in general. Before sacred architecture and liturgy developed their own theories, churches and chapels played an increasingly important role in the ideas behind the creation of spaces that held a specific symbolic value. The Romantic symbiosis of architecture and landscape provided accessible scenes of an imagined past and initiated a myth that was further nourished by technical progress. Many aspects of Romanticism would soon preoccupy movements for religious reform as much as those for urban planning.

Facing reality: urbanism and church architecture between 1800 and 1870

Apart from reflecting the recent struggle for national unity, the Romanticist vision of the medieval past was based on ideal spatial and architectural concepts. The many sketches and paintings Karl Friedrich Schinkel created roughly between the years 1810 and 1815 to compensate for his forced inactivity during the French occupation and the Wars of Liberation remind one of his theatrical designs: impressive Gothic churches rise, like Laugier's primitive hut,[21] from natural or geomorphologic formations such as an oak forest or a rock. Majestically they tower over cityscapes, as if they were anticipating the dismantling and subsequent reconstruction of the elevation of Cologne cathedral during the course of its completion (1842-1880).[22] The paintings also prefigure Schinkel's concept of urbanity, showing "an assortment of architectural elements and quotes from a variety of periods, including Gothic, and the classical period, the latter represented in antique temple buildings".[23] The churches, loosely recalling the cathedrals of Strasbourg, Reims or Cologne, seem to derive from an architect's pattern book. However artificial the settings may appear, they add up to a homogenous, apparently organic townscape. [Col. ill. 7]

In reality, classicism also dominated German building practice long after the Wars of Liberation. This is partly due to the fact that classicism was not just a style based on ancient classical Greek or Roman elements, but was interwoven with the rise of the industrial revolution and its new materials and technologies. From about 1750 onwards, the architect in the classical sense, as an inventor, made way for a new kind of species: the engineer-architect who was required to master the totality of the technical aspects of building practice and to be up to date with technical innovations. The architectural and urban historian Leonardo Benevolo has defined three different categories of classical architecture, two of which he summarised under the term "ideological classicism"; the third "empirist classicism" he described as "merely a convention to which not much importance is attached, yet which allows formal problems to be resolved once and for all, and, according to the requirements of the technical culture of the time, to master the distributive and constructional tasks through analytical methods".[24] This "empirist classicism" remained the most common practice

---

20 Pilger and Steiner, "Ernst Friedrich Zwirner".
21 Kuletin Ćulavić, "Marc Antoine Laugier's Aesthetic Postulates"; Herrmann, *Laugier and Eighteenth-Century French Theory*; Gaus, "Die Urhütte".
22 Dann, *Religion – Kunst – Vaterland*.
23 Maaz, ed., *A German Dream*, 106.
24 "lediglich eine Konvention, der keine besondere Bedeutung beigemessen wird, die es jedoch ermöglicht, die formalen Probleme als ein für allemal gelöst zu betrachten und den Anforderungen der technischen Kultur der Zeit entsprechend, die distributiven und konstruktiven praktischen Aufgaben mit analytischen Methoden zu bewältigen". Benevolo, *Geschichte der Architektur*, I, 66.

in the first two decades that followed the Wars of Liberation.

Even after the re-establishment of the Berlin Bauakademie in 1799, most Prussian architects had been trained at the École Polytechnique in Paris. Ledoux, Durand and Belanger provided the base for German classicism. Their traces can be found in the work of German architects such as Friedrich Gilly (1772-1800), Schinkel and many other local architects and urban planners. Prussia, the ascendant new great power, needing to control every single aspect of building practice, relied on an architect who could combine artistic and technical skills equally brilliantly: in 1804 the Oberbaudeputation, the central building agency in Prussia, was established, and in 1810 Schinkel became its supervisor. In this function, every single plan went across the desk of his Berlin office and, if necessary, was altered with his notoriously stern pen. The installation of the Oberbaudeputation reflected the reform tendencies of the Protestant church in Prussia after 1800. The separate consistory courts of the Protestant and Lutheran churches in Prussia were dissolved and their responsibilities transferred to the Ministry of Internal Affairs (Ministerium der geistlichen, Unterrichts- und Medicinalangelegenheiten), which supervised all religious matters including church building. In 1817, the Union (Unionismus) of the two Protestant churches under a third Protestant state church (Staatskirchentum) was declared. The new liturgical concepts would also considerably affect the theories of the 'ideal' church building, Protestant and Catholic. The ministry shared responsibility with parish councils, the general vicariates and the district administrations, whereas the Oberbaudeputation supervised execution and monument heritage.

In collaboration with *Gartenbauinspektor* Peter Joseph Lenné (1789-1866), Schinkel remodelled large parts of the Prussian capital according to the ideas of classicism.[25] From 1817, when Schinkel completed his master plan (*Idealplan*) for the reshaping of the inner city, a number of official buildings arose within its new centre. His first church buildings were characterised however by financial dictums: a royal commission, his first church design, the St Nicholas' Church in Magdeburg (1817, executed 1821-1824), established a model for the so-called 'standard' church (*Normalkirche*): single-naved, with sober classical exteriors, discreet references to neo-Romanesque arched windows, and a coffered barrel vault within. [Ill. 2.3-5] The moderate cost of only 4,000 thaler for this church and for another towerless church in Nakel (1819) in the Grand Duchy of Posen

2.3-5 Magdeburg, Normalkirche, by Karl Friedrich Schinkel, 1821-1824. [Sächsisches Universitäts- und Landesbibliothekzentrum, Dresden]

25 Ziolkowski, *Berlin*.

26 Rave, *Karl Friedrich Schinkel. Lebenswerk*, 301-342.
27 Schild, *Die Brüder Cremer und ihre Kirchenbauten*; Zimmermann, *Adolph von Vagedes*; Lutum and Vogelsang, "Die Wälle in Krefeld".
28 Mellinghoff and Watkin, *Deutscher Klassizismus*, 232-236; Schäfer, *Stadtspaziergänge in Karlsruhe*; Schumann, *Friedrich Weinbrenner*.
29 Watkin, *Deutscher Klassizismus*.

2.3-6 Karlsruhe, Market Place and Evangelische Stadtkirche, by Friedrich Weinbrenner. Lithography by J. Dyckerhoff, 1808. [Stadtarchiv Karlsruhe]

(today Poland) appealed to the thrifty and pragmatic King Frederick William III, and, in 1827, the King's standard church decree (*Normalkirchenerlass*) defined this design as the prototype not only for his capital[26] but for any Protestant parish church in the whole of Prussia. In rural areas, execution lay in the hands of local architects who were allowed to make only slight alterations. Sometimes a tower was added to underline a landmark function; sometimes the material differed. Where financial options were limited, Schinkel even designed a half-timbered structure. Whereas the exteriors left little freedom for alterations, the interiors could differ wildly as they were left to the parishes.

While in theory, in literature and in the fine arts the Middle Ages were rediscovered and incorporated into German national history, in reality, the big cities and the relics of their once glorious past were drastically altered. Curved streets were straightened and broadened, and old quarters which no longer reached standards of hygiene were torn down and replaced by new ones. With only few exceptions the medieval city walls and town gates were demolished so that the cities could be enlarged. Some medium-sized provincial cities, such as Krefeld and Düsseldorf, which were both transformed and enlarged under the direction of Adolph von Vagedes (1777-1842), benefitted from earlier urban planning. In Krefeld, for example, the town was subdivided into regular blocks surrounded by a square belt of broad streets, the so-called *Wälle* which based on already existing natural ramparts.[27]

Whereas in medieval times churches were supposed to have been implanted more or less organically into already existing urban structures, since the Renaissance and the early modern era the choice of a site was seen as an opportunity to create a scenic setting. When the architect and building director of the Grand Duchy of Baden, Friedrich Weinbrenner (1766-1826), who had been trained in Vienna, Dresden, Berlin and Rome, planned the Protestant City Church (Evangelische Stadtkirche) in Karlsruhe (1807-1816) as the episcopal church of the Grand Duchy as well as the principal church of the city, he situated it within his elaborate plan for the enlargement of the baroque residential city which had been started in 1797, the new synagogue being the first building executed.[28] The new church, together with the town hall, provided the main emphasis of the newly arranged market place, both buildings serving as landmark points on a new north-south axis, the *via triumphalis* of the city. The church itself adapted the Roman podium temple type. As a counterpart to the less grandiose town hall opposite, the spatial concept recalled the ancient forum and reflected civic self-representation within a feudal political system. [Ill. 2.3-6] Other important examples of classical urban planning are to be found in residential towns such as Kassel (under Simon Louis du Ry and Heinrich Christoph Jussow) and Darmstadt (under Georg Moller, architect to the court of Grand Duke Ludwig I).[29] The main accent in this period, which in most German states lasted until the 1840s, was placed on public buildings such as theatres, museums, prisons, mints and railway stations, and residential buildings for the wealthier citizens and the court.

In spite of the somewhat secondary role of religious architecture compared to other contemporary building activities, the in-

troduction of new churches remained an important task for urban planners, not only serving the needs of an increasing number of inhabitants and their different faiths but also creating spaces within rapidly changing urban patterns. In the expanding cities, the given morphological structure provided the setting for religious or sacred architecture such as parish churches, monasteries, cemeteries or religious monuments. Where they were directly linked to urbanisation projects, traffic or the planning of new city quarters, the churches could profit from a layout where they functioned as hinges between unconnected districts or as a visual axis that accentuated alignments across a spatial layout.

Sometimes the ideal clashed with reality. This was the case in the royal capital of Munich, where the plans of the sovereign, King Ludwig I of Bavaria, interfered with those of the city magistrate. Inspired by a journey to Italy and Sicily in 1822, Ludwig commissioned the two first new church buildings in Bavaria after the secularisation, both in the neo-Romanesque, neo-Byzantine style: the Ludwigkirche (Saint Ludwig's Church, by Friedrich von Gärtner) and the Allerheiligenhofkirche (All Saints, by Leo von Klenze). The latter was inspired by the twelfth-century Royal Chapel (Capella Palatina) in Palermo and destined to fulfil the same function in the Bavarian residence, whereas the former was elegantly integrated into the route of the new Maximilianstraße boulevard. The sovereign's plan for the location of St Ludwig's Church clashed with the interests of the highly indebted municipality which tried to pass the high costs of land acquisition and urban development on to the sovereign. Only when the king threatened to move the university and his residence out of the city did the magistrate concede to his plan.

In Aachen, where the town's expansion was hampered by its morphological structure and ring-shaped medieval centre, the first new church building after the Napoleonic occupation, Vincenz Statz' neo-Gothic Church of Our Lady (Marienvotivkirche, 1859-1863, demolished in 1978), was erected when the city's strategic importance as an industrial centre of the Prussian Rhine Province required the redevelopment of the area around the new main station.[30] [Ill. 2.3-7] The new church was topped by a large spire with an eight-metre-high column of the Virgin Mary which served several purposes: firstly, as a visible symbol of Catholic emancipation and Marian devotion; secondly, as the centre of a new quarter for wealthy citizens, among them the patrons of the church, the politician and lawyer Joseph Lingens (1818-1902) and his wife, who donated a large sum and set up a church building as-

30 Curdes, *Die Entwicklung des Aachener Stadtraumes*, 75-79.

2.3-7 The Votive Church of Our Lady (Marienkirche) in Aachen, by Vincenz Statz, 1859-1863, as envisioned by the architect himself surrounded by a 'ideal' neo-Gothic city quarter (a) and in a contemporary postcard (circa 1895) surrounded by the neo-Classicist architecture of the city enlargement (b). [Archive W. Cortjaens]

sociation; and thirdly, as a link to the main station at the southern end of the city and thus marking the entry into it.[31] Other examples of prominently sited neo-Gothic parish churches with comparable political implications are to be found in Munich (Mariahilfkirche in der Au, 1831-1839, Joseph Daniel Ohlmüller and Georg Friedrich Ziebland), and, on the Protestant side, in Hamburg (St Nicholas' Church, 1846-1857, Sir George Gilbert Scott), Wiesbaden (Marktkirche, 1853-1862, Carl Boos) and Hanover (Christuskirche, 1859-1864, Conrad Wilhelm Hase).[32] [Ill. 2.3-1] The archaeological interest in Gothic architecture coincided with the need to define new landmark points within rapidly changing urban settings, as the constant growth of urban architecture such as stores, banks and tenement buildings threatened to outgrow the function of the churches as landmark buildings within the urban cluster. Towers in particular received attention where it came to the extension of unfinished medieval churches, such as the Minster Church in Constance (1846-1860, Heinrich Hübsch); Cologne cathedral (1842-1880, Ernst Friedrich Zwirner, Richard Voigtel); and the Minster Church in Ulm (tower completed 1885-1890, August von Bayer).[33]

"Putz ist Lüge!" - architectural 'schools' and regionalism: concepts of materiality

Historicist church architecture followed a pattern of recognisable prototypes. For that reason, regionalism became an important criterion in the concepts behind new church buildings, as it singled out the local tradition in which the new building was rooted. However different the ideologies and theories of the different parties and interest groups such as clerics, laymen, freemasons, and engineers and so on may have been, they all agreed in one point: the strict rejection of render. "Putz ist Lüge!", as the Hanover architect Conrad Wilhelm Hase (1818-1902) – himself a freemason – proclaimed, and his credo would

influence architectural theories up to the twentieth century.[34] The use of native materials and the adaptation of traditional building schemes were strongly associated with the concept of regionalism. These also dealt with the question of how new churches (or any other kind of building) could be harmoniously introduced into an existing environment through, for example, an adjustment to a given structure.

The use of material was dictated by the geomorphic and topographic conditions of the respective regions.[35] The geological structure of the local stones, its toughness, granulation and graded bedding within its quarry became relevant criteria for their use in building practice, as shown in the theoretical writings of the geologist and mineralogist Johann Jacob Nöggerath (1788-1877) who in 1818 was appointed professor at the newly established University of Bonn.[36] In the south west of Germany, in the Middle Rhine and Moselle regions, deposits of trass and dark basalt were exploited for big building projects, whereas the Eifel provided greywacke. The *Landbauinspektor* Ferdinand Nebel (1782-1860) in Coblenz revolutionised the technique of lightweight construction by inventing a new process for the production of an artificial stone consisting of local pumice and limewash.[37] [Ill. 2.3-8] In the south and south-east of Germany, large deposits of red and yellow sandstone provided the building material for restoration projects and new churches. For the completion of Cologne cathedral, an unexploited quarry of trachyte in Berkum near Bonn on the left bank of the Rhine was exploited. Materials could be transported directly to the building sites by river. For regions with a lack of natural stone quarries, such as the northern Rhine Province, Lower-Saxony and the north-east of Germany, or ones that lacked suitable transportation routes, brick was used.

The variety of geological landscapes in the German countries provided ideal grounds for distinction without surrendering any general unifying concept. Churches differed in their use of material and colour, often

---

31 Holländer, "Katholische Avantgarden".
32 Schickel, *Neugotischer Kirchenbau*; Plagemann, *Kunstgeschichte der Stadt Hamburg*; Hirschfeld, *Geschichte des Mahnmals*; Kiesow, *Architekturführer Wiesbaden*; David-Sirocko, *Georg Gottlob Ungewitter*.
33 Reiners, *Das Münster Unserer Lieben Frau*; Brommer, Frey et al., *Das Konstanzer Münster*; Cologne: Wolff, "Die Baugeschichte der Domvollendung"; Wortmann, *Das Ulmer Münster*.
34 Mohrmann, "Conrad Wilhelm Hase"; Kokkelink and Lemke-Kokkelink, *Baukunst in Norddeutschland*; Id., *Conrad Wilhelm Hase*.
35 Cortjaens, "Sprache des Materials", 253-255.
36 Nöggerath, *Das Gebirge in Rheinland-Westfalen*; Id., "Zur architektonischen Mineralogie".
37 Dauber, *Ferdinand Jakob Nebel*.

2.3-8 Parish Church St John´s in Dieblich/Moselle, by Ferdinand Nebel, 1844-1848.
[© Creative Common License (Klaus Graf, 2005)]

recalling or revitalising formerly abandoned regional building traditions or modelled on historical prototypes. The building material used in Remagen was the same as that used several years later in Cologne. Furthermore, experiments with new materials – for example, in the case of balustrades and spires and sometimes choir stalls and other internal furnishings constructed in cast iron – were also adopted by Zwirner, much to the annoyance of traditionalist neo-gothicists. Ironically, Cologne cathedral was to prove that the mastery of the medieval builder's hut could not only be matched, but surpassed by nineteenth-century engineering and knowledge, although for the conservative, anti-modernist circles of Catholic emancipation the point of reference was still the master builders' skill which was identified with their moral integrity.

Schinkel's Friedrichswerdersche Kirche (1824-1831) in Berlin became the first post-medieval church building in Prussia entirely faced with brick. The architect designed four variants of the church: two were in the classical style and two were neo-medieval, which exploited the rather limited spatial volume and building elements to maximum effect.[38] The shining red brick shell of the church was way ahead of its time. Its effect was heightened further several years later with the completion of the neighbouring Bauakademie (1836) which was built in the same material. [Ill. 2.3-9] The two buildings complemented each other and demonstrated Schinkel's programmatic approach towards unusual materials and new techniques to create a genuinely 'Prussian' look in church architecture.

Other prominent Prussian architects who adopted Schinkel's ideas include Friedrich August Stüler (1800-1865), Johann Heinrich Strack (1805-1880) and Friedrich Adler (1827-1908). Until unification in 1871, most new places of worship in Prussia, Protestant, Catholic and synagogues alike, were designed in neo-Byzantine and neo-Romanesque styles. In contrast to the unifying spatial concept behind most churches, the materiality – whether render, exposed brick

38 Rave, *Karl Friedrich Schinkel. Lebenswerk,* 254-300; Abri, *Die Friedrichswerdersche Kirche;* Schultze-Altcappenberg, Johannsen and Lange, eds., *Karl Friedrich Schinkel,* 115.

165

2.3-9 Eduard Gärtner, Bauakademie and Friedrichswerdersche Kirche. Oil on canvas, 1836.
[SMB, Nationalgalerie Berlin / Andres Kilger / bpk]

or natural stone or applied terracotta tinted in various colours – became of especially importance.

The introduction of neo-Gothic forms by Schinkel was paralleled by the reorganisation of the applied arts and crafts and the establishment of new industrial branches, re-establishing long-forgotten antique or medieval techniques such as terracotta, mosaics or stained glass, as well as the introductions of new industrial materials such as cast iron or artificial stone.[39] England and, to a lesser extent, France provided the role models for these artistic and technical improvements. The foundation of the Technische Deputation für Handel und Gewerbe in 1821 (from 1827, the Gewerbeinstitut or industrial college) by Christian Peter Wilhelm Beuth (1781-1853), an intimate of Schinkel, aimed, on the one hand, to teach economic independence and entrepreneurial qualities in order to overcome any form of protectionism, and on the other, to introduce new techniques. Schinkel and Beuth's Gewerbe-institut, Prussia's first building with continuous storeys resting on iron columns, accommodated several workshops and laboratories, where machines, materials and models were gathered, and old and new techniques were further tested and developed. These included bronzes, cast iron, zinc, gildings, ceramics, terracotta and other techniques which were used for exteriors as well as for interior design and the furnishing of churches (see 3.4). The designs, mostly deriving from classical antiquity, were published in a pattern book, *Vorbilder für Fabrikanten und Handwerker*, which was displayed to manufacturers and other commercial and industrial organisations up to the 1890s and influenced building practice in Prussia for decades.[40]

The establishment of brick as a genuinely national building material also benefitted from the foundation of the royal brickworks (Königliche Ziegelei) in Joachimsthal, Brandenburg, in 1817.[41] [Ill. 2.3-10] The use of brick was claimed as a regional style by different parties and for differing reasons, both

39 Bender, "Karl Friedrich Schinkel"; Badde, "Coade stone".
40 Schinkel, *Vorbilder für Fabrikanten und Handwerker*.
41 Menzel, "Verfahren bei der Fabrication von Ziegeln".

2.3-10 Areal view of the Castle Church in Neustrelitz/Mecklenburg, by Friedrich Wilhelm Buttel, 1855-1859. [akg-images]

technical and ideological. After Schinkel's experiments with brick and terracotta, the Kölner Richtung in the late 1840s also discovered the advantages of brick construction, which was regarded as ideal for smaller projects with limited financial resources. For supporters of the Catholic neo-Gothic movement, among them the influential politician and theoretician August Reichensperger (1808-1895), brick construction with its solidity and long tradition were regarded as a way to overcome the errors of modernity.[42] The industrial aspects that were crucial for the establishment of brick by the Prussian authorities were toned down. Reichensperger's plea for a truly 'Christian' architecture was immediately borrowed and incorporated into official statutes by the general vicariate in Cologne, as was the use of surrogate materials such as cast iron, plaster, wooden vaults, and the like.[43] The same ideas were further developed, albeit under more theoretical and constructional aspects, by Georg Gottlob Ungewitter (1820-1864)[44] and Conrad Wilhelm Hase, the leading figures of the Hanover School of architecture, and by a circle of younger architects around Friedrich Adler, teacher at the Berlin Bauakademie and author of the voluminous publication *Mittelalterliche Backsteinbauwerke des Preussischen Staates* (1859).[45]

In addition to these practical aspects, as a native building material brick was of highly symbolic meaning. Size, colour and the method of laying bricks varied from region to region, and thus lent a regional component to the exteriors. Another advantage was that bricks could be fabricated by the parishes themselves, as was the case in Dortmund where, outside the city walls, the parish established its own brick factory on the site of the new Church of Our Lady (Liebfrauenkirche, 1881-1883, Friedrich von Schmidt), then Germany's biggest Catholic parish church.

42 Reichensperger, *Die christlich-germanische Baukunst*, 41-42.
43 Dumont, *Sammlung kirchlicher Erlasse*, 232.
44 David-Sirocko, *Georg Gottlob Ungewitter*.
45 Lemburg, *Leben und Werk des gelehrten Architekten Friedrich Adler;* Cortjaens, "Sprache des Materials", 263-264.

2.3-11 Wittenberg, Monuments of Martin Luther (Johann Gottfried Schadow and Karl Friedrich Schinkel, 1818-1821) (right) and Philipp Melanchthon (Friedrich Drake and Johann Heinrich Strack, 1858-1865) (left).
[Bildarchiv Foto Marburg, nr. C 452.284 / Gert von Bassewitz]

Religious monuments: the ornamentation of landscape

In the first half of the nineteenth century, the erection of religious monuments was of minor importance. However, in Protestant Prussia, sacred (that is, neo-Gothic) forms were applied to profane monuments in order to provide additional semi-religious overtones. One of the first examples is the cast iron Memorial Monument on the Kreuzberg in Berlin (1818-1821) designed by Schinkel and the sculptor Johann Gottfried Schadow (1764-1850) in commemoration of the Liberation Wars and modelled on the Gothic pinnacles of Cologne cathedral.[46]

The most important group of semi-religious monuments in this Protestant context are the numerous Luther monuments which were erected in the various 'Luther cities' (Lutherstädte), sites connected with the life and work of this crucial figure of the German Reformation. The first of these monuments is to be found in the market place in Wittenberg, Saxony-Anhalt (1817-1821, statue designed by Schadow).[47] [Ill. 2.3-11]

Not only was it the first free-standing, upright statue but also the first monument dedicated to someone who was not a member of the nobility, thus signalling the rise of the bourgeoisie. The neo-Gothic canopy was added by Schinkel at the demand of the Prussian crown prince Frederick William himself, free-standing statues then still being reserved for the nobility. The canopy was criticised for its use of Gothic forms which did not seem appropriate for the age of Reformation. In 1858, another monument (by Friedrich Drake and Johann Heinrich Strack) was inaugurated in the market place in commemoration of Philipp Melanchthon, the second leading figure of Reformation, formally adapting Schinkel's concept.[48] In the second half of the nineteenth century, the sculptor Ernst Rietschel's Luther Monument in Worms (1868), the largest monument of the Reformation worldwide, became the prototype for numerous imitations and replicas.[49] Important examples, all of which were designed by prominent sculptors, are to be found in Möhra (1861, Ferdinand Müller), Eisleben (1883, Rudolf Siemering), Magdeburg (1886, Emil Hundrieser), Berlin (1893, Robert Toberentz) and in the Protestant Memorial Church (Gedächtniskirche der Protestation) in Speyer (1903, Hermann Hahn).

Another key figure of great significance for the identity of the German Protestants was King Gustav Adolf of Sweden, commemorated for example by the monument in Lützen, Saxony-Anhalt, commemorating the Battle of Lützen, one of the crucial encounters of the Thirty Years War. This consists of a cast iron canopy (designed by Schinkel, 1837) over an irregular boulder, the so-called Schwedenstein, which had been placed in the seventeenth century on the exact site where the king's dead body had been found. Another important historical figure with a similar semi-sacred aura was the immensely popular Queen Louisa of Prussia (1776-1810). Early Louisa memorials such as Schinkel's monument in the market place in Gransee, Brandenburg (1810), adopted the form of a neo-

46 Nungesser, *Das Denkmal auf dem Kreuzberg*.
47 Maaz, *Skulptur in Deutschland*, I, 100-101, fig. 107.
48 Ibid., I, 146-147, fig. 173.
49 Ibid., I, 155-157, fig. 187.

Gothic canopy and thus sacralised her civic but noble grave (*bürgerliches Ehrengrab*).[50]

In contrast to these semi-religious monuments erected by the Prussian state in the first half of the nineteenth century, during the pre-March era (*Vormärz*) which was marked by rigid censorship and oppression of any deviant political manifestations, the Catholic minority was not allowed any public representation in the form of religious monuments. In the few cases where a public monument with semi-religious connotations was erected, such as the neo-Gothic fountain facing the Minster Church in Aachen (1847), its purpose had to be strictly functional. It was only three decades later, in 1877, that the fountain, formally inspired by the Hochkreuz in Bonn, a Gothic votive column, was transformed into a distinctly religious monument by adding four figures of saints, among them Charlemagne and the Virgin Mary, who were associated with the Minster and other neighbouring buildings. Away from the Prussian authorities, this originally secular fountain was thus turned into a memorial of the *Kulturkampf*.[51]

When after 1848 the oppression imposed on the Catholic minority in Prussia was relaxed, the erection of monuments for emancipated Catholicism became a symbolic, political act. In 1854, the Dogma of the Immaculate Conception triggered a series of Maria Columns which carried anti-Prussian, anti-Protestant and anti-materialist implications. The prototype of these columns was designed by Vincenz Statz, in collaboration with the painter Edward von Steinle (1810-1886) and the sculptors Peter Fuchs (1829-1898) and Gottfried Renn (1818-1900) for the city of Cologne.[52] Its inauguration in September 1858, on occasion of the tenth assembly of the Catholic Associations in Germany (*Katholische Vereine in Deutschland*) was seen as a symbol of Catholic unity. [Ill. 1.4-4] Numerous other columns followed, the majority of them in the Prussian Rhine Province (for example, in Trier, Eupen, Unkel, Linz, Düsseldorf, Aachen and Heinsberg) and in Bavaria, as the Holy Virgin is also the patron of the state.

2.3-12 Trier, Maria Column, by Vincenz Statz, 1858.
[Archive W. Cortjaens]

In Trier, after the Roman Basilica had been rebuilt and transformed by royal decree into a Protestant model church appropriate to the Prussian ideal of unionism, the Catholic population of the city raised the money for one of the first and largest Maria Columns in Germany. In 1859 the foundation stone for the 40-metre-high monument, designed by Christian Wilhelm Schmidt (1806-1893) and Renn, was laid at Markusberg on the left bank of the Moselle. [Ill. 2.3-12] Its orientation was dictated not by the needs of the pilgrims (for whom the Petersberg on the opposite bank of the river would have been more appropriate and more convenient) but by its relationship to the city and the fact that the peak on which it was located marked the highest point of its surroundings. By deliberately choosing the 'wrong' side, the column was placed axially in direct view of the basilica and could thus be seen as a symbol of Catholic emancipation as well as a counterpart to Protestant unionism as symbolised by the transformed Roman monument. The pedestal was built in ashlar sandstone taken partly from the ancient Roman city wall and thus also symbolised the antique (and Catholic) tradition of the city and the site.[53]

50 Werquet, *Historismus und Repräsentation*, 268, fig. 108.
51 Dünnwald, *Aachener Architektur im 19. Jahrhundert. Friedrich Ark*, 219-221, fig. 134; Cortjaens, "Die Mariensäule auf dem Rehmplatz", 151-152.
52 Maaz, *Skulptur in Deutschland*, 1, 348-351, fig. 452.
53 Fontaine, *Die Marienstätten am Trierer Markusberg*.

The locations of the Maria Columns differed; most of them were sited in the very heart of cities, such as in Linz, 1878, and Düsseldorf, 1872-1873, or formed the centres of new city districts (as Aachen, 1883).[54] Often, as was the case in Düsseldorf and Aachen, the design included a recreation area which provided a buffer from the surrounding secular city. Most Maria Columns adapted the model of a huge column with a towering statue of the Holy Virgin. Stylistically, the Rhenish columns are mostly in neo-Gothic or neo-Romanesque style, whereas in Bavaria the baroque Maria Column in Munich, erected in 1638 after Duke Maximilian of Bavaria had defeated his Protestant counterpart King Gustav Adolf of Sweden, provided the most frequently imitated prototype.

Other types of religious monuments included columns or statues in commemoration of a local saint or key figure of Catholicism, for example the Monument to Thomas à Kempis in Kempen, 1901, one of the few seated religious statues, and the Hermann Joseph fountain in Cologne, 1894, by the sculptor Wilhelm Albermann.[55] Another group was a variation on the late Romanesque type of triumphant cross, for example the calvary in front of St Jacob's Church, Aachen, 1893, by Wilhelm Pohl and Carl Esser, and the calvary on the Allerheiligenberg, Lahnstein, 1913.[56] Probably the most overlooked group of nineteenth-century religious monuments is that of the countless wayside crosses which not only marked places of contemplation but also served as points of orientation for travellers. In the Catholic parts of the still rural Münsterland, the Paderborn area and the neighbouring East Westphalia in particular a large number of piety columns and wayside shrines were set up during the nineteenth century by the landowners, as a sign of gratitude or to honour a vow, or simply as tokens of individual worship and faith. Their inscriptions often refer to the general idea of pilgrimage, stressing the motivation of those who built them and reflecting the personal aspects of devotion which were seen as an integral part of daily life – hence the increasing popularity of the image of the Holy Family – as well as part of an individual spiritual journey.

Aside from these manifestations of individual worship, religious monuments in cities and villages were erected by city councils or by local associations often linked to the parishes. Some of these placed their monuments within a green area, but most were erected on central public spaces which provided an historical background and setting. In most cases the monuments were placed in front of the church, and sometimes even at the centre of a new city quarter. The choice of site was left to the local authorities but in some cases was dictated by the sovereign. This was the case for example with the above-mentioned Luther Monument in Wittenberg, which had originally been destined for the neighbouring cities of Eisleben and Mansfeld which also had initiated and financed it. It was only by decree of the Prussian king that the monument was erected in Wittenberg, as this city provided more of an historical connection to the history of the Reformation. In Cologne, the Maria Column was originally destined for the Alter Markt, until the Prussian government, supported by burgomaster Hermann Josef Stupp, vetoed it, the market place being reserved for a monumental equestrian statue of the late King Frederick William III.[57] Only after harsh debates was the votive column erected in front of the Palace of the Archbishop.[58]

As a group, the religious monuments erected in nineteenth-century Germany are relatively small in number. The building culture in Prussia in the second half of the century was dominated by monuments of contemporary leading figures and founders of the *Kaiserreich*: Bismarck, the Hohenzollern family, war heroes and the like. In 1908 the Emperor William II himself donated, as a demonstration of imperial generosity towards his Protestant subjects, the Wiesbaden monument of William ('the Silent') of Orange (1533-1584) who in the German countries too was revered as a martyr of Protes-

54 Cortjaens, "Die Mariensäule auf dem Rehmplatz".
55 Maaz, *Skulptur in Deutschland*, 1, 391-393, fig. 408.
56 Ibid., 351, figs. 453-454.
57 Werquet, *Historismus und Repräsentation*, 205-208; Puls, *Gustav Hermann Blaeser*, 283-320; Id., "Ewig unzeitgemäß?", 73-76.
58 Trier, "Die Kölner Mariensäule".
59 Kiesow, *Architekturführer Wiesbaden*.
60 Molik, "Die Wacht an der Warthe. Das Bismarckdenkmal in Posen", 122.
61 Rodgera, *Vom Pesthof zum Allgemeinen Krankenhaus*.
62 *Berlin und seine Bauten*, vol. 2-3; Spode, "Das Krankenhaus der Diakonissen-Anstalt".
63 Murken, "Beispielhafte Krankenhäuser", 373-376. The convent was dissolved in 1908 and the buildings were demolished in 1912.

tant belief, and this was symbolically placed in front of the Marktkirche.[59] [Ill. 2.3-13] Whereas Prussian chauvinism fell on fertile ground in large parts of interwar Germany, it was rejected in the predominantly Catholic regions. For example, after the First World War the city magistrate of Posen (today Poznań in Poland) decided to replace the Bismarck Memorial which had been erected only 18 years earlier with a monument to the Sacred Heart of Jesus in order to express, ambiguously, the "Dankbarkeit des ganzen Landes für die Wiedererlangung der Freiheit".[60] For the replacement was, in fact, a statement of the strong anti-Prussian sentiments of the Catholic population.

Religious hospitals and convents

In the first half of the nineteenth century, the building of religious hospitals began to play a decisive role in urban planning. The negative consequences of industrialisation, such as pauperism, a lack of medical care, child labour, prostitution and a general decline of moral values, were harshly felt, especially in the big cities and the industrialised regions. This led to the foundation of several non- or ultra-confessional infirmaries in cities such as Hamburg (the Allgemeines Krankenhaus in the district St Georg, erected between 1821-1823 by Carl Ludwig Wimmel)[61] and Berlin (Diakonissenhaus Bethanien, 1845-1847, by Ludwig Persius and Theodor Stein), the latter of which was erected by order of the Prussian King as an educational institution for nursing.[62] [Ill. 2.3-14] After the German Revolution of 1848, the so-called *Ordensfrühling* (monastic spring) swept over from France to the Prussian Rhine Province (Aachen, Cologne) and spread throughout the German countries. A great number of charitable congregations arose, profiting from judicial relaxation in the wake of the revolution. The erection of religious hospitals and convents became a task of urban planning.

One of the earliest examples can be found in Aachen. Between 1848 and 1855 the town architect Friedrich Ark (1810-1877) erected the Maria-Hilf-Hospital, an elaborate three-winged complex with a wide, bright wards housing over 200 beds. Modelled on the Diakonissenhaus Bethanien, the Aachen version, nursed by the religious order of the Sisters of Mercy, was regarded by the time of its completion as the most modern hospital in the whole of Prussia.[63] The now vanished

2.3-13 Wiesbaden, Monument of William of Orange, 1908, in front of the Protestant Marktkirche.
[akg-images / Schütze / Rodemann]

2.3-14 Berlin-Kreuzberg, Diakonissenkrankenhaus Bethanien, by Ludwig Persius, 1845-1847. Lithography by Julius Umbach, 1855. [akg images nr. KG58889]

building – a broadly conceived neo-Byzantine architecture with receding wings and two flanking turrets – was situated in a surviving park area which had been designed by the Berlin landscape architect Peter Josef Lenné (1789-1866) and, before the enlargement of the city, lay outside the city walls (as was the case with most hospitals, for health reasons). The cupola and the Gothic tracery of the chapel window signalled the religious nature of the building, and its façade pointed towards the city centre. Soon after its completion, a new radial street with solid late-classical tenements for wealthy citizens was laid out axially in front of it and named Mariahilfstraße after the hospital. Together with the Baroque St Peter's Church, then the biggest parish of the city, at the other end of the street, the two religious buildings provided 'brackets' which connected the historical core of the city with its still virginal idyllic outskirts and promenades.

The erection of monasteries and convents within cities underwent, at least in Prussia, a similar development to that of hospitals. During the secularisation, the majority of the properties were confiscated, converted to new uses, sometimes as a parish church and, at worst, sold 'auf Abbruch' (for demolition). Whereas in Bavaria, thanks to the policy of King Ludwig I, a relatively pro-monastic policy stipulated the settlement of congregations, in Prussia it was only in the reign of Frederick William IV that the terms were improved. In 1872, the *Kulturkampf* put an abrupt end to this development. Under the repression of Bismarck's *Maigesetze* (Laws of May) many orders were exiled to neighbouring countries, Belgium, the Netherlands and France.[64] Only after 1888, when the Emperor William II attempted to pacify religious conflict, were congregations allowed to found new daughter houses. With only a few exceptions (such as Trier, where the seminary was reinstalled in surviving eighteenth-century buildings), congregations could not integrate themselves easily into the overall structure of the cities. The land costs were high and building plots became increasingly rare. The majority of convent buildings in the late nineteenth and early twentieth century were modest neo-Gothic or neo-Romanesque structures which adapted elements of monastery and convent-building traditions to the necessities of modern times. Often, they were laid out by members of the congregations themselves instead of by professional architects. The spatiality of these structures was extrapolated from the statutes of the order. An example is provided by the buildings

64 Müllejans-Dickmann, *Klöster im Kulturkampf*.

of the Order of the Good Shepherd, which was engaged in welfare for orphaned and neglected children as well as for girls and women in difficulty. The four-winged chapels characteristic of this order were modelled after the mother house in Angers, France, each wing expressing symbolically an aspect of the internal hierarchical structure of the order (sisters, alumni and Magdalens). From the outside, the order's buildings appeared less hermetic than did the reclusive complexes of other congregations, such as the daughter houses in Cologne-Melaten and Aachen. But overall, the newly built monasteries and convents were marked by their isolation. A common attribute was the completeness of most complexes. Sealed off, only the chapels were accessible to visitors from the outside world.

The size of the newly erected buildings depended largely on the financial capabilities of their congregations. The Dominicans for example chose for their Düsseldorf house a site in the centre of the city which, in size and execution, exceeded by far the order's financial means.[65] Trying to compensate for the failure of a former, much more modest daughter-house in Materborn which had collapsed, the order wanted self-consciously to construct a landmark. At about the same time, the Franciscan order chose a deliberately modest, irregular building plot in a much less prominent quarter of the city and adjusted their building to it.

After the Second World War, and following demographic change, many religious communities were forced to abandon their daughter houses. Since then, a large number of nineteenth-century monasteries and convents have either been destroyed or sold into the private sector. In most cases, no documentation exists and there is still no representative study for this rather underdeveloped field of research.

Reform of funerary culture: cemeteries and crematories

The prohibition of burials *intra muros* for health reasons was for the first time successfully asserted during the Enlightenment. France, through a series of reform movements since 1750, and Austria, by the *Josephinische Begräbnisreformen* named after its initiator, the Emperor Joseph II, set international standards for the renewal of a sepulchral culture. In 1788, the Alter Münchner Stadtfriedhof became by electoral decree one of the first central cemeteries located outside a city. During the French occupation, the gradual transition towards progressive burial rituals was introduced. By decree of 12 June 1804, the *Décret sur les sépultures*, Napoleon had prohibited the use of existing cemeteries inside the cities and villages for cremations for health reasons. Burial within churches and chapels was also officially forbidden. As a result, all cemeteries belonging to the parish churches were abandoned and flattened.

The nineteenth-century cemetery has been described as "domesticated cultural space" (*domestizierter Kulturraum*).[66] The division of cemeteries into areas divided by corridors, the planting, the integration of open spaces and, last but not least, the individual grave monuments themselves established a kind of *Gesamtkunstwerk*. In some cases, ideas deriving from English landscape architecture and the Picturesque, such as curving paths and dense and varied planting were adopted, for example in Brunswick (Domfriedhof) and during the enlargement of the Düsseldorf Golzheimer Friedhof under the direction of the landscape architect Maximilian Friedrich Weyhe (1775-1846). Many cemeteries were now conceived as recreation areas for the population and modelled on the ideas of landscape architecture, as was the case in Cologne, where Melaten (Gottesacker der Stadt Köln), the new cemetery, rose on the site of the medieval lepers' hospital in the western outskirts of the city. Its layout was modelled after Père Lachaise, the central cemetery of Paris. Melaten was

65 Schild, "Klöster", 352.
66 Fischer, *Vom Gottesacker zum Krematorium,* 35.

2.3-15 'Campo Santo' on the Western Cemetery in Aachen, by Joseph Laurent, 1899.
[Photo W. Cortjaens, 2009]

67 Abt and Vomm, *Der Kölner Friedhof Melaten*.
68 Leisner, Thormann and Schulze, *Der Hamburger Hauptfriedhof Ohlsdorf*.
69 Schiermeier and Scheungraber, *Alter Südlicher Friedhof in München*.
70 Maisel, *Gelehrte in Stein und Bronze*.
71 Cortjaens, "Frömmigkeit und Bürgertugenden".

planned by the botanist, mathematician, theologian, priest and art collector Ferdinand Franz Wallraf (1748-1824).[67] Similar approaches are to be found in the central cemetery of Hamburg, Ohlsdorf,[68] and on the aforementioned new Central Cemetery in Munich where in 1819 the architect Gustav Vorherr (1778-1848) devised burial crypts and graves in single rows laid out in a distinctly geometrical fashion after the model of the Campo Santo in Bologna. Friedrich von Gärtner (1791-1847) picked up this concept when in 1840 he took over the enlargement of the cemetery.[69] The Campo Santo model with its hermetically closed and hierarchically graduated structures allowed further social distinction and spatial separation. Illustrative examples of this model are the arcade court of Vienna University, destined to incorporate the tombs of the most famous professors and designed in neo-Renaissance style by Heinrich von Ferstel (1828-1883), the architect of the Ringstraße,[70] and the lesser known, stylistically unique neo-Gothic 'Campo Santo' on the Westfriedhof (Western Cemetery) in Aachen, commissioned in 1899 by the Catholic elite of the city.[71] [Ill. 2.3-15]

Although the reform of burial practice was originally based on Enlightenment thinking, social hierarchy was nevertheless reflected in the location of the burial grounds. Since Napoleon's *Décret*, all communal cemeteries were obliged to bury within the given area and in sequence of date of death (hence the German term *Reihengräber*, row graves), but there still existed privileged owners of so-called *Wahlgräber*, mostly family plots, prominently located along the paths, in contrast to the cheaper single-row graves which were allocated to less attractive plots at the back. The hierarchical structures and public awareness of the elites continued to exist in the afterlife, as reflected in the many monumental and lavish tombs that flank the paths of the cemeteries in Hamburg-Ohlsdorf or Cologne-Melaten.

Religious denominations were originally strictly separated: for example, Protestants were only permitted to be buried in Cologne-Melaten, from 1829 onwards, whereas Jews were buried in the ancient Jewish cemetery in Deutz on the right bank of the Rhine until 1918 when the Jewish community was given a new parcel of land in the district Bocklemünd. The population boom in the last quarter of the nineteenth century led to the installation of further burial grounds in the big cities. Apart from denominational distinctions, the design of cemeteries became more and more similar in the years before the First World War and during the interwar period.

The sepulchral culture of the nineteenth century displayed a wide range of styles which reflected the rapid changes that society itself underwent. In classical burial culture, the design of gravestones had been much more unified. Antique forms such as urns and obelisks were most common. Figurative representations of grief and of nobly restrained emotions included sculptures of guardian angels. Bertel Thorvaldsen's standing figure of the Resurrected Christ (1821), originally designed for the Church of Our Lady (cathedral) in Copenhagen, became the most frequently copied sculpture of the nineteenth century. Once the industrialisation of cast iron allowed standardisation, iron was widely accepted for grave crosses and iron railings, often with neo-Gothic ornamentation.[72] From the 1830s onwards, the design of tombs became more and more varied. During the *Gründerzeit*, when French reparations triggered a short-lived boom in German industry, lavish mausolea came into fashion. They were often enclosed by a natural hedge or an iron curb to seal them off from public paths. Wealthy families tended to build small chapels with crypts. From an aesthetic point of view, the tombs and their location reflected the social status of the deceased and his descendants.[73] Lockets and busts with the portrait of the deceased in marble, stone or bronze were especially favoured by bourgeois Protestants. Other variants include whole reclining figures, for example the tomb of the iron merchant Peter Louis Ravené in the French Cemetery in Berlin (1863-1867, sculptor: Gustav Blaeser) [Ill. 2.3-16], the earliest example of an originally feudal monument type used for a bourgeois grave,[74] or statues of seated figures, such as the grave monument of the Prussian geologist and mining officer Johann Jacob Nöggerath in the Alter Friedhof (Old Cemetery) in Bonn (1881, by Alfred Küppers). Protestant gravestones often show inscriptions citing popular psalms or quotes from the gospels, whereas representations of symbolic or allegoric figures such as angels or grieving guardian angels holding the cross as a symbol of the Resurrection were widely appreciated by Protestants and Catholics alike.

Towards the end of the century, new industrial methods of carving and polishing enabled the vast production of granite modular units.[75] Around 1900, electroplating again revolutionised sepulchral sculpture as the process enabled fabricators to produce endless replicas of the most popular designs. As a result, the seemingly individual became within reach of ordinary people.

Funeral chapels displayed a wide range of styles dictated by contemporary tastes and fashions, from Roman temples to neo-Baroque centrally-planned buildings. [Ill. 2.3-17] In some cases, ancient monuments threatened by demolition were moved into cemeteries and protected from destruc-

2.3-16 Grave monument of Peter Louis Ravené on the French Cemetery in Berlin-Mitte, by Gustav Hermann Blaeser, 1863-1867.
[Photo W. Cortjaens, 2012]

72 Fischer, *Vom Gottesacker zum Krematorium*, 68.
73 Zacher, "Friedhofsanlagen und Grabmäler"; Meyer-Woeller, *Grabmäler*.
74 Puls, *Gustav Hermann Blaeser*, 374-377; Maaz, *Skulptur in Deutschland*, I, 240-241, fig. 309.
75 Fischer, *Vom Gottesacker zum Krematorium*, 73.

2.3-17 Crematory in Dresden-Tolkwitz, by Fritz Schumacher, 1908-1913. [akg-images / Bildarchiv Monheim GmbH, nr. AKG404732]

Crematoria

Another important watershed in sepulchral culture was the establishment of crematoria.[78] In 1874, the first modern cremation in the world had taken place in the Siemens Glassworks in Dresden-Löbtau, followed four years later by the opening of the first German crematorium in Gotha and the first official cremation in December 1878. Once the practical and sanitary aspects had been established, several territorial churches, in Saxony-Coburg-Gotha, Baden, Württemberg and Hamburg, legalised cremations. In the north, east and south-east of Germany in particular, a number of crematoria were erected: in Mannheim (1901), Mainz (1903), Heilbronn (1905), Hagen (1907), Gera (1909-1910), Leipzig (1910), Dresden (1909-1911) and Freiburg (1913-1914).

This movement was supported by secular, reform-oriented elite organised through local friendly associations, the so-called *Feuerbestattungsvereine*, often supported by municipalities. In returning to the ancient rite of cremation, the movement made way for a more technical, pragmatic approach towards death and the cult of death. The Catholic Church strongly opposed cremations, as did, albeit to a somewhat lesser extent, the Protestants. In Prussia cremations became legal only in 1911 after the Prussian Union Church had allowed the involvement of the clergy at least in the obsequies, if still not in the interment itself. In 1886 the Catholic Church, struggling with its loss of influence, prohibited any participation of the clergy in cremations as incommensurate with the dogmas and traditions of the Church, which, from a liturgical point, required inhumation.

To heighten public acceptance, most crematoria were erected in rural, idyllic settings. Stylistically, the architecture ranged from traditional sacred forms (Gera, Mainz, Heilbronn) to an almost exaggerated, lavish neo-Renaissance (Leipzig). In Fritz Schumacher's daring design for Dresden-Tolkwitz, the first truly modern, non-historicist crematorium in Germany,[79] the central *Feierhalle* (celebra-

tion, as was the case with the Romanesque chapel of the Commandry Ramersdorf near Bonn, which had been saved by the Prussian building inspector von Lassaulx.[76] Other mausolea were rebuilt by using spolia from historical buildings, for example the neo-Romanesque chapel on the Ostfriedhof (Eastern Cemetery) in Aachen, a facsimile of the former St Quirinus Chapel at the abandoned medieval cemetery of Melaten.[77] Until the end of the *Kaiserreich*, hierarchical structures and historical references remained integral parts of bourgeois sepulchral culture. It was only after the First World War that the way was paved for the functional reform cemetery of the 1920s, when the funeral system became the function of communal or municipal administration.

76 Cremer, "Die Ramersdorfer Kapelle".
77 Schild and Janssen, *Aachener Ostfriedhof*, 45-47, figs. 17, 18.
78 Fischer, *Vom Gottesacker zum Krematorium*, 94-112.
79 Ibid., 123.

tion hall) was modelled after the early Christian monument of Theoderic at Ravenna, mixed with elements of Art Nouveau. [Ill. 2.3-17]

Due to the reservations still held by large parts of the population against cremation, which was regarded as irreligious and pagan, architects and patrons tended to 'hide' the true purpose of the buildings, especially the technical aspects of the process itself. In Tolkwitz, the two chimneys of the incinerator are elegantly integrated into the rear of the building. This is the more remarkable as crematoria were an essentially contemporary building task. Where modern construction materials were applied, they too were hidden, as was the case in Freiburg, Baden, where Rudolf Thoma's neoclassical architecture evoking a Roman temple, a nod to the ancient Roman rite of cremation, was clad with pre-cast concrete blocks hiding the ferroconcrete framework inside.

The planning of crematoria resulted in several clashes between the Church and the local supporters of cremation: in Gera (then a part of the Thuringian micro-state Reuß), the Protestant territorial church asserted that for non-Christian burials a separate immersion shaft (mocked as a 'Monistenloch') had to be applied in order to transport the coffin.[80] However, the German cremation movement did not derive from anti-clerical tendencies as it did in other European countries, for example in Italy, but from a rational approach to the funeral system in general, aptly referred to as the "Technisierung des Todes" (technologisation of death).[81]

The second phase of urbanisation (1870 to 1914): the fusion of traditionalism and modernism in the pre-war era

After the Franco-German War of 1870-1871, Germany experienced a short-lived economic boom known as the *Gründerzeit* ('Founders' Era'). For the first time, the country was a single economic entity, and old impediments to internal trade were lifted. The indemnities that France had to pay Germany after losing the war provided capital for railroad construction, large-scale building projects and intense financial speculation. This period of prosperity ended suddenly with the stock market crash of 1873. Despite the crash and several subsequent periods of depression, Germany's economy grew consistently. The development of coal mining and iron and steel production was followed by and interwoven with a Second Industrial Revolution, triggered by the development of chemical and electrical industries. The population also expanded rapidly, growing from 41 million in 1871 to 65.3 million in 1911. The rapidly expanding cities in the economically developed and industrialised parts of Germany, for example, the Rhine Province and the Ruhr, called for enlargement. In 1871, the capital Berlin comprised 826,000 residents; by 1895 the number had already doubled, and in 1905 the population reached 2,040,000.[82] As a result of the high population density in the German capital, the Evangelischer Kirchen-Hilfsverein (later renamed in Evangelischer Kirchbauverein) set up by the Emperor in 1890 and patronised by the Empress Augusta Victoria[83] inaugurated 35 new Protestant churches during this period (compared to nine Catholic churches). In the whole of Prussia, a new Protestant church was erected every four months between 1890 and 1914, in total about 75 churches.[84]

In cities with elaborate development plans, churches became important *points de vue* within the new city patterns and alignments, for example in Coblenz, where two Catholic churches and a Protestant one were erected in the course of the enlargement of the southern districts.[85] [Ill. 2.3-18] As part of his concept for the Neustadt in Cologne, the architect and urban planner Hermann Joseph Stübben (1845-1936) envisioned several sites for new churches which were later specified with their parishes and the municipal Stadterweiterungskommission (City

80 Ibid., 101.
81 Ibid., 129.
82 <https://de.wikipedia.org/wiki/einwohnerentwicklung_von_berlin#cite ref-16>.
83 Gundermann, "Kirchenbau und Diakonie".
84 Tacke, *Kirchen für die Diaspora*, 29.
85 Church of the Sacred Heart of Jesus, 1900-1903, by Ludwig Becker; Saint Joseph's Church, 1894-1897, by Joseph Kleesattel; Protestant church, 1901-1904, by Johannes Vollmer.

2.3-18 The Church of the Sacred Heart of Jesus in Coblenz, built in the wake of the city enlargement in the southern districts and designed by master builder Ludwig Becker of Mainz Cathedral, 1900-1903. Photo 1928.
[Sächsisches Universitäts- und Landesbibliothekzentrum, Dresden]

2.3-19 Railroad bridge across the Rhine (Johann Heinrich Strack, 1859) facing the choir of Cologne Cathedral. Photo, May 1877.
[© Rheinisches Bildarchiv, Cologne, no 208258]

86 Binding, "Der Dom in der Entwicklung des Kölner Stadtbildes".
87 Prisac, "Ein moralisches Bedenken sammt einer patriotischen Phantasie".
88 Groß, *St. Agnes in Köln*; Eickhoff, *St. Agnes in Köln*; Fraquelli, *Im Schatten des Domes*, 259-261. For the concept of the Neustadt, see Ibid, 247-269.
89 Tacke, *Kirchen für die Diaspora*, 29.
90 Sitte, *Der Städtebau*; Benevolo, *Geschichte der Architektur*, I, 410-412.
91 Petzold, *Cornelius Gurlitt*; Paul, *Cornelius Gurlitt*.
92 Fraquelli, *Im Schatten des Domes*, 230-234.

Enlargement Commission). Even Cologne cathedral became part of the urbanisation process, when the new railway and passenger bridge across the Rhine (1855-1859, replaced in 1907-1911 by the Hohenzollern Bridge, now restored) was situated in a visual axis pointing towards the choir of the still unfinished cathedral.[86] [Ill. 2.3-19] The proximity of modern traffic – the view being partly blocked by the new central railway station – and the unmistakeably modern iron construction aroused much lamentation among the traditionalist members of the *Dombau* movement who saw in it a symbol of sheer materialism: "(…) wenn ich das Ungeheuer betrachte, welches so verhängnisvoll dort lungert, so recht eine Signatur der Gegenwart mit ihren ordinären Ideen, der Engbrüstigkeit des materiellen Strebens."[87]

The location of building sites for new churches was mostly negotiated between the general vicariate, the municipality, and public and private investors. This was the case with Cologne's Neustadt, where a new church was donated by the ultramontane Zentrum party member and estate agent Peter Josef Röckerath who had inherited propriety in the district and who conceived the new church as a memorial for his deceased wife Agnes. Prominently sited on a star-shaped crossing, the Neusser Platz, Saint Agnes with its massive spireless tower became Cologne's second largest church after the cathedral.[88]

Minor city parishes and other churches and confessions, especially the Old Catholic Church and the Jewish communities, had to cope with more practical problems, land costs in the developing areas often being so high that the communities were forced to fall back on cheaper plots which did not allow freestanding buildings. As a result, symbolic decoration was limited to the façade and the interior. In north and east Germany it was mainly Catholics who were affected, but in big cities such as Berlin the smaller Protestant parishes were also forced to settle for less attractive sites.[89]

The foundation of new church buildings was sometimes derived from the ideas of a Picturesque cityscape, propagated half a century earlier by Ungewitter and Reichensperger. Around 1900, theoreticians and urban planners as Camillo Sitte (1843-1903), responsible for the enlargement of Vienna and author of the immensely successful handbook *Der Städtebau nach seinen künstlerischen Grundsätzen* (1889),[90] and Cornelius Gurlitt (1850-1938)[91] abandoned symmetry and orthogonal layouts in favour of quasi-natural cityscapes with irregularly shaped places and green spaces. Religious architecture was now seen in the spatial context of its surroundings.[92]

After 1900, industrialisation and the increasingly mixed religious nature of the population caused by mass immigration from distant provinces such as Silesia again required new spatial and architectural concepts. Many churches were erected on greenfield sites or had to be integrated into less attractive or poor suburbs and workers' colonies with a denominationally mixed population. As a result, building practice more and more became less a question of style than of social and religious integration. For the first time, the Churches were asked to take a stance. An important signal was given by the encyclical *Rerum novarum* (1891) of Pope Leo XIII which made clear that the churches could no longer withstand the challenges of a rapidly changing society and an unbridled capitalism resulting in social injustice and pauperism.[93] Working, living and pastoral care were being discussed in terms of the improvement of living conditions and social interaction. As a result, churches now became integral parts of larger architectural ensembles, with parsonage houses, schools and parish halls. Inventive spatial concepts can be found in industrial centres and their extended urban landscapes, especially along the Lower Rhine, the Ruhr district and the Saarland. [Ill. 2.3-20]

In 1896, architect Otto March (1845-1913), a descendant of the aforementioned Berlin company, had demanded a "gruppierte Bauweise" (grouped building) for Protestant parishes, arguing from a functional as well an aesthetic point of view.[94] At about the same time, the public had become sensitised to some degree to the consecutive symptoms of industrialisation. Traditional spatial structures and old townscapes were erased or overrun by the ever expanding industries. As landmark buildings within townscapes, churches occupied a prominent place within this discussion. Different lobbies emerged at different social levels, which can be summarised under the term of *Heimatschutz* – a reform movement which originated from the historical associations (Heimatvereine) for (urban)

93 Löhr, "Die Sozialenzyklika 'Rerum Novarum' und der rheinische Sozialkatholizismus".
94 March, "Gruppierter Bau bei Kirchen".

*2.3-20 Protestant Ascension Church in Düsseldorf-Oberkassel, by architects Verheyen & Stobbe, 1913/1914.
[Bildarchiv Foto Marburg, no fmd481726; Photo: Andreas Lechtape, 2013]*

2.3-21 St Aper Church in Wasserliesch/ Mosel, by Peter Marx, 1910. [Amt für kirchliche Denkmalpflege, Trier]

95 Klueting, *Antimodernismus und Reform*.
96 Roth, *Hermann Muthesius*.
97 Cortjaens, "Neubarock im rheinischen Kirchenbau".
98 Steinruck, "Die Auseinandersetzung um den Modernismus im Bistum Trier"; Embach, "Bischof Michael Felix Korum"; Cortjaens, "Neubarock im rheinischen Kirchenbau", 102-109, 122-123.
99 Fischer, "Zum Bau und der Ausstattung von Kirchen".

beautification. In contrast to the German Werkbund, the ideology of the *Heimatschutz* was ultraconservative, anti-progressive and anti-international, stressing the preservation of the traditional building practices.[95] It was primarily a reaction towards all international styles that were not rooted in local building traditions, although the British Garden City Movement via the Werkbund and the writings of its founder Hermann Muthesius (1861-1927) gained a certain influence on the *Heimatschutz*.[96] The prime of the *Heimatstil* was between 1900 and 1920. Stylistically, it borrowed its forms from Art Nouveau and neo-Baroque; it did not, however, possess its rich ornamental exuberance. From an ideological point of view, the neo-Baroque references were interpreted as a sign of a Catholic Counter Reformation and thus could be applied to the actual condition of the Church.[97] The spatial concept of *Heimatschutz* theories fitted perfectly into rural areas. Its organic forms and the use of local materials harmonised with the still intact landscapes of the Eifel and the hinterland of the Moselle. [Ill. 2.3-21] The diocese of Trier under the long episcopate (1881-1921) of the ultramontane and highly conservative bishop Felix Michael Korum became a refuge for moderate reform architects. Although Korum shared with the *Heimatschutz* movement its anti-modernist attitude,[98] the general vicariate in Trier allowed much more stylistic freedom in detail than for example the Archdiocese of Cologne, where the equally conservative Archbishop Antonius Fischer (1902-1912) continued to promote the neo-Gothic and the neo-Romanesque as the only appropriate styles for new church buildings.[99]

Because of their affinities with buildings and their emphasis on regionalism, the Deutsche Werkbund and the *Heimatschutz* became important links between traditionalist and progressive tendencies in German church architecture. As a consequence, historical reminiscences were gradually reduced and Catholic and Protestant churches became less and less distinctive. This artistic development foreshadowed the evolution of church building practice and the subsequent reform movements of the 1920s.

BIBLIOGRAPHY

Abri, Martina. *Die Friedrichswerdersche Kirche zu Berlin: Technik und Ästhetik in der Backstein-Architektur K. F. Schinkels*. Berlin, 1992.

Abt, Josef, and Wolfgang Vomm. *Der Kölner Friedhof Melaten. Begegnung mit Vergangenem und Vergessenem aus rheinischer Geschichte und Kunst*. Cologne, 1980.

Badde, Aurelia. "Coade stone – ein frühklassizistischer Kunststein aus England". In: *800 Jahre Kunststein - vom Imitat zum Kunstgut: Beiträge des 6. Konservierungswissenschaftlichen Kolloquiums in Berlin/Brandenburg am 8. November 2012 in Potsdam / Brandenburgisches Landesamt für Denkmalpflege und Archäologisches Landesmuseum*. Worms, 2012, 49-55.

Bender, Willi. "Karl Friedrich Schinkel und sein Einfluß auf die Technologie der Backstein- und Bauterrakottenherstellung". *Restaurator im Handwerk*, 2 (2010), 5-11.

Benevolo, Leonardo. *Geschichte der Architektur des 19. und 20. Jahrhunderts*. 3 vols. 4th ed. Munich, 1988.

Berlin und seine Bauten. Vol. 2-3. Edited by Architekten-Verein zu Berlin. Berlin, 1896.

Berlin und seine Bauten. Vol. 10, Band A: *Anlagen und Bauten für Versorgung. 3: Bestattungswesen*. Edited bij Architekten-Ingenieursverein Berlin. Berlin-Munich-Düsseldorf, 1979.

Binding, Günther. "Der Dom in der Entwicklung des Kölner Stadtbildes". In: Otto Dann. *Religion – Kunst – Vaterland. Der Kölner Dom im 19. Jahrhundert*. Cologne, 1983, 11-19.

Bormann, Alexander von, ed. *Ungleichzeitigkeiten der deutschen Romantik*. Würzburg, 2006.

Börsch-Supan, Helmut, and Karl Wilhelm Jähnig. *Caspar David Friedrich. Gemälde, Druckgraphik und bildmäßige Zeichnungen*. Munich, 1973.

Brommer, Hermann, Emanuel Frey et al. *Das Konstanzer Münster*. Regensburg, 2005.

Buttlar, Adrian von. *Der Landschaftsgarten. Gartenkunst des Klassizismus und der Romantik*. Cologne, 1989.

Cortjaens, Wolfgang. "Die Mariensäule auf dem Rehmplatz. Öffentlicher Raum und katholische Öffentlichkeit in Aachen (1882-1887)". In: Ulrike Schubert and Stephan Mann, eds. *Renaissance der Gotik – Widerstand gegen die Staatsgewalt? Kolloquium zur Kunst der Neugotik*. Goch, 2003, 133-161.

Cortjaens, Wolfgang. "Sprache des Materials, Politik der Form. Der katholische Kirchenbau in den linksrheinischen Gebieten der preußischen Rheinprovinz und im Rhein-Maas-Gebiet 1815-1914". In: Wolfgang Cortjaens, Jan De Maeyer and Tom Verschaffel, eds. *Historism and Cultural Identity in the Rhine-Meuse Region: Tensions between Nationalism and Regionalism in the Nineteenth Century*. KADOC Artes, 10. Leuven, 2008, 249-281.

Cortjaens, Wolfgang. "Neubarock im rheinischen Kirchenbau. Voraussetzungen und Genese eines Neo-Stils". In: *Die Anfänge des Neubarock im rheinischen Kirchenbau*. Geschichte im Bistum Aachen, Beiheft 6. Edited by Geschichtsverein für das Bistum Aachen e. V. Neustadt a. d. Aisch, 2009, 59-158.

Cortjaens, Wolfgang. "Frömmigkeit und Bürgertugenden: Die Selbstinszenierung der katholischen Aachener Oberschicht im 19. Jahrhundert". In: Stefan Lewejohann and Georg Mölich, eds. *Köln und Preussen. Studien zu einer Beziehungsgeschichte*. Geschichte in Köln - Beihefte, Beitrage zur Stadt- und Regionalgeschichte. Vol. 3. Cologne, 2019, 117-148.

Cremer, Sabine. "Die Ramersdorfer Kapelle – Ein Beispiel für rheinische Denkmalspflege in der ersten Hälfte des 19. Jahrhunderts". *Bonner Geschichtsblätter*, 47/48 (1998), 253-268.

Curdes, Gerhard. *Die Entwicklung des Aachener Stadtraumes. Der Einfluß von Leitbildern und Innovationen auf die Form der Stadt*. Stadt – Raum – Innovation, 3. Dortmund, 1999.

Dann, Otto. *Religion – Kunst – Vaterland. Der Kölner Dom im 19. Jahrhundert*. Cologne, 1983.

Dauber, Reinhard. *Ferdinand Jakob Nebel. Kgl. preußischer Landbauinspektor in Koblenz*. Aachen, 1975.

David-Sirocko, Karen. *Georg Gottlob Ungewitter und die malerische Neugotik in Hannover, Hamburg und Leipzig*. Petersberg, 1997.

de Wall, Heiner, and Andreas Gestrich. "Constitutional and Confessional Diversity". In: Keith Robbins, ed. *The Dynamics of Religious Reform in Northern Europe 1780-1920: Political Legal Perspectives*. Leuven, 2010, 149-202.

Dötsch, Anja. *Die Löwenburg im Schlosspark Kassel-Wilhelmshöhe*. Regensburg, 2006.

Dumont, Karl Theodor. *Sammlung kirchlicher Erlasse, Verordnungen und Bekanntmachungen für die Erzdiözese Köln*. Cologne, 1874 (2nd ed. 1891).

Dünnwald, Richard. *Aachener Architektur im 19. Jahrhundert. Friedrich Ark 1805-1877*. Aachen, 1974.

Eickhoff, Renate. *St. Agnes in Köln. Ein Viertel und seine Geschichte*. Cologne, 2001.

Embach, Michael. "Bischof Michael Felix Korum". In: Martin Persch and Bernhard Schneider, eds. *Geschichte des Bistums Trier. 5: Beharrung und Erneuerung*. Veröffentlichungen des Bistumsarchivs Trier 39/5. Trier, 2005, 37-47.

Fischer, Erzbischof Antonius. "Zum Bau und der Ausstattung von Kirchen und anderen kirchlichen Gebäuden". *Kirchlicher Anzeiger für die Erzdiözese Köln*, 51 (1912), 29-33.

Fischer, Norbert. *Vom Gottesacker zum Krematorium – Eine Sozialgeschichte der Friedhöfe in Deutschland seit dem 18. Jahrhundert*. Cologne, 1996 (Diss. Hamburg University, 1996).

Fontaine, Arthur. *Die Marienstätten am Trierer Markusberg. Das Ensemble von Mariensäule, Mariahilf-Kapelle und Stationsweg*. Geschichte und Kultur des Trierer Landes, 11. Trier, 2010.

Frankl, Paul. *The Gothic: Literary Sources and Inspirations through Eight Centuries*. Princeton, 1960.

Fraquelli, Sybille. *Im Schatten des Domes: Architektur der Neugotik in Köln (1815-1914)*. Cologne, 2008.

Gaus, Joachim. "Die Urhütte. Über ein Modell in der Baukunst und ein Motiv in der bildenden Kunst". *Wallraf-Richartz-Jahrbuch*, 33 (1971), 7-70.

Görres, Joseph (von). "Der Dom in Köln". *Rheinischer Merkur*, 1 (1814) 151, s.p. [683-684].

Groß, Linda. *St. Agnes in Köln*. Neuss, 1989.

Gundermann, Iselin. *Kirchenbau und Diakonie: Kaiserin Auguste Victoria und der Evangelisch-Kirchliche Hilfsverein*. Hefte des Evangelischen Kirchenbauvereins, 7. Berlin, 1992.

Günther, Hubertus. "Anglo-Klassizismus, Antikenrezeption, Neugotik in Wörlitz". In Frank Andreas Bechtold, ed. *Weltbild Wörlitz. Entwurf einer Kulturlandschaft*. Catalogue Deutsches Architekturmuseum Frankfurt am Main, 22. März bis 2. Juni 1996. Ostfildern-Ruit, 1996, 131-160.

Gurlitt, Cornelius. *Kirchen. Handbuch der Architektur*. 4. Teil, 8. Halbband, Heft 1. Stuttgart, 1906.

Herrmann, Wolfgang. *Laugier and Eighteenth-Century French Theory*. London, 1962.

Hinderer, Walter. "Das Kollektivindividuum Nation im deutschen Kontext. Zu seinem Bedeutungswandel im vor- und nachrevolutionären Diskurs". In: Alexander von Bormann, ed. *Volk – Nation – Europa. Zur Romantisierung und Entromantisierung politischer Begriffe*. Würzburg, 1998, 179-198.

Hirschfeld, Gerhard. *Geschichte des Mahnmals und der Kirchenbauten von St. Nikolai in Hamburg*. Edited by Förderkreis "Rettet die Nikolaikirche e.V.". Hamburg, 2010.

Holländer, Georg. "Katholische Avantgarden in der Reaktion auf 1848: Der Bau der Aachener Marienkirche". In: Guido Müller and Jürgen Herres, eds. *Aachen, die westlichen Rheinlande und die Revolution*. Aachen, 2000, 309-329.

Holthuis, Gabriele. *Gotik und Neugotik im 19. Jahrhundert. Die Elisabethkirche in Marburg und ihre Rezeption in der evangelischen Garnisonkirche in Straßburg*. Diss. Marburg, 1993.

Kiesow, Gottfried. *Architekturführer Wiesbaden - Durch die Stadt des Historismus*. Deutsche Stiftung Denkmalschutz. Monumente Publikationen. Bonn, 2006.

Kleist, Heinrich von. *Sämtliche Werke und Briefe*. Edited by Helmut Sembdner. 2 vols. Munich, 1993.

Klueting, Edeltraud. *Antimodernismus und Reform. Zur Geschichte der deutschen Heimatbewegung*. Darmstadt, 1991.

Kocka, Jürgen. *Sozialgeschichte. Begriff – Entwicklung – Probleme*. 2nd ed. Göttingen, 1986.

Kokkelink, Günter, and Monika Lemke-Kokkelink. *Baukunst in Norddeutschland. Architektur und Kunsthandwerk der Hannoverschen Schule 1850-1900*. Hannover, 1998.

Kokkelink, Günter, and Monika Lemke-Kokkelink. *Conrad Wilhelm Hase 1818–1902, Gründer der Hannoverschen Architekturschule*. Ausstellung zum 100. Todestag im Stadtarchiv Hannover. Hannover, 2002.

Krüger, Jürgen. *Rom und Jerusalem. Kirchenbauvorstellungen der Hohenzollern im 19. Jahrhundert*. Berlin, 1995.

Kuletin Ćulavić, Irena. "Marc Antoine Laugier's Aesthetic Postulats on Architectural Theory". *Spatium. International Review*, 23 (October 2010), 46-50.

Leisner, Barbara, Ellen Thormann and Heiko K. H. Schulze. *Der Hamburger Hauptfriedhof Ohlsdorf. Geschichte und Grabmäler*. Ed. by Andreas von Rauch. 2 vols. Hamburg, 1990.

Lemburg, Peter. *Leben und Werk des gelehrten Architekten Friedrich Adler (1827-1908)*. Diss. phil. FU Berlin, 1989 (microfiche).

Lennartz, Arno M. *Der Architekt Eduard Endler 1860-1932*. Diss. phil. Aachen, 1984.

Löhr, Wolfgang. "Die Sozialenzyklika 'Rerum novarum' und der rheinische Sozialkatholizismus". *Geschichte im Bistum Aachen*, Beiheft 3 (2003), 85-101.

Lutum, Reinhard, and Rosemarie Vogelsang. "Die Wälle in Krefeld. Ein Beitrag zur Erweiterung der Stadt". *Die Heimat*, 77 (2006), 62-66.

Maaz, Bernhard, ed. *A German Dream: Masterpieces of Romanticism from the Nationalgalerie Berlin*. Exhibition catalogue Staatliche Museen zu Berlin - National Gallery of Ireland, Dublin. Berlin, 2004.

Maaz, Bernhard. *Skulptur in Deutschland zwischen Französischer Revolution und Erstem Weltkrieg*. 2 vols. Berlin-Munich, 2010.

Maisel, Thomas. *Gelehrte in Stein und Bronze. Die Denkmäler im Arkadenhof der Universität Wien*. Vienna, 2007.

March, Otto. "Gruppierter Bau bei Kirchen". *Centralblatt der Bauverwaltung*, 16 (1896), 283-284, 298-299, 317-319.

Mellinghoff, Tilman, and David Watkin. *Deutscher Klassizismus. Architektur 1740-1840*. Stuttgart, 1989 (1st ed. London, 1987).

Menzel, Gottfried. "Verfahren bei der Fabrication der Ziegel und des Mörtels auf der königl. preuß. Ziegelei bei Joachimsthal". *Polytechnisches Journal*, 102 (1846) 37, 194-219.

Meyer-Woeller, Ulrike Evangelia. *Grabmäler des 19. Jahrhunderts im Rheinland zwischen Identität, Anpassung und Individualität*. Diss. Bonn, 1999. <http:hss.ulb.uni-bonn.de/diss-online/phil-fak/1999/meyer-woeller-ulrike/0215.pdf>.

Mohrmann, Klaus. "Conrad Wilhelm Hase". *Hannoversche Geschichtsblätter. Sonderdruck*. Hannover, 1902.

Molik, Witold. "Die Wacht an der Warthe. Das Bismarckdenkmal in Posen (1903-1919)". In: Rudolf Jaworski and Witold Molik, eds. *Denkmäler in Kiel und Posen. Parallelen und Kontraste*. Kiel, 2002, 107-125.

Müllejans-Dickmann, Rita. *Klöster im Kulturkampf. Die Ansiedlung katholischer Orden und Kongregationen aus dem Rheinland und ihre Klosterneubauten im belgisch-niederländischen Grenzraum infolge des preußischen Kulturkampfes*. Veröffentlichungen des Bischöflichen Diözesanarchivs Aachen, 44. Aachen, 1992 (Diss. Aachen University, 1992).

Murken, Axel Hinrich. "Beispielhafte Krankenhäuser". In: Eduard Trier and Willy Weyres. *Kunst des 19. Jahrhunderts im Rheinland*. 1: *Architektur I*. Düsseldorf, 1980, 363-390.

Niehr, Klaus. *Gotikbilder – Gotiktheorien. Studien zur Wahrnehmung und Erforschung mittelalterlicher Architektur in Deutschland zwischen ca. 1750 und 1850*. Berlin, 1999.

Nöggerath, Johann Jakob. *Das Gebirge in Rheinland-Westfalen, nach mineralogischem und chemischem Bezuge*. 4 vols. Bonn, 1822-1826.

Nöggerath, Johann Jakob. "Zur architektonischen Mineralogie der Preußischen Rheinprovinz". In: C. J. B. Karsten and H. von Dechen, eds. *Archiv für Mineralogie, Geognosie, Bergbau und Hüttenkunde*, 18. Berlin, 1844, 455-482.

Nungesser, Michael. *Das Denkmal auf dem Kreuzberg von Karl Friedrich Schinkel*. Berlin, 1987.

Paul, Jürgen. *Cornelius Gurlitt*. Dresden, 2003.

Petzold, Hans, ed. *Cornelius Gurlitt. Lehrer und Förderer der städtebaulichen Aus- und Weiterbildung an der Technischen Hochschule Dresden*. Institut für Ökologische Raumentwicklung e.V. Dresden, 1997.

Pilger, Andreas, and Kathrin Steiner. "Ernst Friedrich Zwirner – Sein Leben, sein Werk, seine Zeit". In: Nikolaus Gussone, ed. *Das Kölner Dombaufest von 1842. Ernst Friedrich Zwirner und die Vollendung des Kölner Doms*. Exhibition catalogue Ratingen 1992. Dülmen, 1992, 15-62.

Plagemann, Volker. *Kunstgeschichte der Stadt Hamburg*. Hamburg, 1995.

Prause, Marianne. *Carl Gustav Carus. Leben und Werk*. Berlin, 1968.

Prisac, Wilhelm. "Ein moralisches Bedenken sammt einer patriotischen Phantasie". *Kölner Domblatt*, (1859), 169.

Puls, Michael. *Gustav Hermann Blaeser. Zum Leben und Werk eines Berliner Bildhauers. Mit Werkverzeichnis der plastischen Arbeiten*. Cologne, 1996.

Puls, Michael. "Ewig unzeitgemäß? Begas' Denkmalkunst im Streif- und Zwielicht". In: Esther Sophia Sünderhauf, ed., in collaboration with Wolfgang Cortjaens. *Begas – Monumente für das Kaiserreich*. Catalogue exhibition Deutsches Historisches Museum, Berlin. Dresden, 2010, 73-87.

Rave, Paul Ortwin. *Karl Friedrich Schinkel. Lebenswerk. Berlin. 1: Bauten für die Kunst, Kirchen, Denkmalpflege*. Berlin, 1941.

Reichensperger, August. *Die christlich-germanische Baukunst und ihr Verhältniß zur Gegenwart. Nebst einem Berichte Schinkel's aus dem Jahre 1816 den Cölner Dombau betreffend, als Anhang*. Trier, 1845.

Reichensperger, August. "L'art et l'archéologie en France III (1845)". In: August Reichensperger. *Vermischte Schriften über christliche Kunst*. Leipzig, 1856, 570-586.

Reiners, Heribert. *Das Münster Unserer Lieben Frau zu Konstanz*. Konstanz, 1955.

Ritter-Eden, Heike. *Der Altenberger Dom zwischen romantischer Bewegung und moderner Denkmalpflege. Die Restaurierung von 1815 bis 1915*. Veröffentlichungen des Altenberger Dom-Vereins, 7. Bergisch Gladbach, 2002.

Rodgera, Heinz. *Vom Pesthof zum Allgemeinen Krankenhaus: Die Entwicklung des Krankenhauswesens in Hamburg zu Beginn des 19. Jahrhunderts*. Münster, 1977.

Roning, Franz. "Der Kirchenbau im Bistum Trier". In: Eduard Trier and Willy Weyres. *Kunst des 19. Jahrhunderts im Rheinland*. Vol. 1. Düsseldorf, 1980, 195-268.

Roth, Fedor. *Hermann Muthesius und die Idee der harmonischen Kultur. Kultur als Einheit des künstlerischen Stils in allen Lebensäußerungen eines Volkes*. Berlin, 2001.

Schäfer, Friedemann. *Stadtspaziergänge in Karlsruhe*. Karlsruhe, 2008.

Scharmann, Rudolf G. *Königin Luise von Preußen – ihre Schlösser und Gärten in Paretz, Charlottenburg und auf der Pfaueninsel*. Munich, 2010.

Schendel, Adelheid. *Studie zur Geschichte und Kunstgeschichte des Dorfes und des Schlosses Paretz*. Edited by Institut für Denkmalpflege, Arbeitsstelle Berlin. Potsdam, 1980.

Schickel, Gabriele. *Neugotischer Kirchenbau in München. Vergleichende Studien zu Architektur und Ausstattung der Kirchen Maria-Hilf in der Au und Heilig-Kreuz in Giesing*. Munich, 1987.

Schiermeier, Franz, and Florian Scheungraber. *Alter Südlicher Friedhof in München. Geschichte und Berühmtheiten. Übersichtsplan der Grabmäler. Herausgegeben zum 850. Stadtgeburtstag*. Munich, 2008.

Schild, Ingeborg. *Die Brüder Cremer und ihre Kirchenbauten*. Mönchengladbach, 1965.

Schild, Ingeborg. "Klöster". In: Eduard Trier and Willy Weyres. *Kunst des 19. Jahrhunderts im Rheinland. 1: Architektur*. Düsseldorf, 1980, 347-361.

Schild, Ingeborg, and Elisabeth Janssen. *Der Aachener Ostfriedhof*. Aachen, 1991.

Schinkel, Karl Friedrich. *Vorbilder für Fabrikanten und Handwerker*. Berlin, 1821-1837.

Schlegel, Friedrich. *Europa. Eine Zeitschrift*. Vol. 1. Frankfurt, 1803 (reprint Stuttgart, 1963).

Schlegel, Friedrich. *Kritische Schriften und Fragmente. Studienausgabe in 6 Bänden*. Edited by Ernst Behler and Hans Eichner. Paderborn-Munich-Vienna-Zürich, 1988.

Schultze-Altcappenberg, Hein-Th., Rolf H. Johannsen and Christiane Lange, eds. *Karl Friedrich Schinkel. Geschichte und Poesie*. Exhibition catalogue Staatliche Museen zu Berlin – Kupferstichkabinett / Hypo Kunsthalle, Munich, 2012/2013. Munich, 2012.

Schumann, Ulrich Maximilian. *Friedrich Weinbrenner, Klassizismus und "praktische Ästhetik"*. Berlin-Munich, 2010.

Schwieger, Frank. *Johann Claudius von Lassaulx 1781-1848. Architekt und Denkmalpfleger in Koblenz*. Neuss, 1968.

Seiler, Michael. *Die Pfaueninsel*. Berlin-Munich, 2012.

Sitte, Camillo. *Der Städtebau nach seinen künstlerischen Grundsätzen. Ein Beitrag zur Lösung moderner Fragen der Architektur und monumentalen Plastik unter besonderer Beziehung auf Wien*. Vierte Auflage, vermehrt um "Großstadtgrün". Vienna, 1909.

Spode, Hasso. "Das Krankenhaus der Diakonissen-Anstalt zu Berlin". In: *Geschichtslandschaft Berlin. Orte und Ereignisse. 5: Kreuzberg*. Berlin, 1994.

Steinruck, Josef. "Die Auseinandersetzung um den Modernismus im Bistum Trier". In: Martin Persch and Bernhard Schneider. *Geschichte des Bistums Trier. 5: Beharrung und Erneuerung*. Veröffentlichungen des Bistumsarchivs Trier 39/5. Trier, 2005, 611-626.

Tacke, Andreas. *Kirchen für die Diaspora. Christoph Hehls Berliner Bauten und Hochschultätigkeit 1894-1911*. Die Bauwerke und Kunstdenkmäler von Berlin, Beiheft 24. Berlin, 1993 (diss. Berlin, 1991).

Trier, Eduard. "Die Kölner Mariensäule. Studien zur Entstehung und Bedeutung eines neogotischen Denkmals". In: Werner Busch, Reiner Hausherr and Eduard Trier. *Kunst als Bedeutungsträger. Gedenkschrift für Günter Bandmann*. Berlin, 1978, 492-513.

Trier, Eduard, and Willy Weyres. *Kunst des 19. Jahrhunderts im Rheinland*. Vol. 1-5. Düsseldorf, 1979-1981.

Verbeek, Albert. "Kunstwerke in der Landschaft". In: Eduard Trier and Willy Weyres. *Kunst des 19. Jahrhunderts im Rheinland. 1: Architektur*. Düsseldorf, 1980, 11-33.

Werquet, Jan. "Konstruktion historischer Kontinuität. Der Ausbau der Klause bei Kastel unter Friedrich Wilhelm IV". In: Annette Dorgerloh, Michael Niedermeier and Horst Bredekamp, eds. *Klassizismus – Gotik. Karl Friedrich Schinkel und die patriotische Baukunst*. Munich-Berlin, 2007, 185-199.

Werquet, Jan. *Historismus und Repräsentation. Die Baupolitik Friedrich Wilhelms IV. in der preußischen Rheinprovinz*. Berlin-Munich, 2008.

Wolff, Arnold. "Die Baugeschichte der Domvollendung". In: Otto Dann, ed. *Religion – Kunst – Vaterland. Der Kölner Dom im 19. Jahrhundert*. Cologne, 1983, 47-77.

Wortmann, Reinhard. *Das Ulmer Münster*. 7th. ed. Munich-Berlin, 2000.

Woźniak, Michał. "Das Denkmal Friedrichs des Großen und die Wiederherstellung der Marienburg". In: *Visuelle Erinnerungskulturen und Geschichtskonstruktionen in Deutschland und Polen 1800-1939*. Munich, 2006, 233-244.

Zacher, Inge. "Friedhofsanlagen und Grabmäler der kommunalen Friedhöfe". In: Eduard Trier and Willy Weyres. *Kunst des 19. Jahrhunderts im Rheinland. 4: Plastik*. Düsseldorf, 1980, 385-442.

Zimmermann, Wolfgang. *Adolph von Vagedes und seine Kirchenbauten*. Cologne, 1964.

Ziolkowski, Theodore. *Berlin: Aufstieg einer Kulturmetropole um 1810*. Stuttgart, 2002.

2.4
Reforming Religious Material Landscapes in Nineteenth-Century Scandinavia

Arne Bugge Amundsen

Scandinavia – Norway, Denmark and Sweden – had much in common in the nineteenth century, including history, religion, politics and material culture. The three countries went through important political changes in this period, with Denmark-Norway's forced separation as an absolutist twin monarchy in 1814 and Sweden and Norway united as two separate states under one king between 1814 and 1905. The period saw political and cultural dreams of a united Scandinavia, but also the rise of national awakenings searching for cultural, historical and religious identities in the three countries.

From an eighteenth century with a rather monocultural situation nineteenth-century Scandinavia went through different phases of cultural and religious opposition, conflicts and liberalism. All three countries were dominated by national Lutheran churches controlled by the state. The Danish-Norwegian church had the king as its head, and with – in principle – equal bishops serving the king. Norway continued this structure with its 1814 constitution stating that the king was head of the church, but with a parliament with legislative power also in church affairs. In practice, church rule was exercised through the Norwegian government and the Ministry of Church Affairs. In Sweden, the Lutheran Church kept the office of an archbishop and was left with a more independent church rule than in Denmark and Norway. In the Swedish parliament the Lutheran clergy had its own representation until 1865, which gave the dominantly conservative clergy a substantial power over church politics. When it came to questions concerning religious freedom this had a huge impact in both a short term and a long term perspective. The conflicts on legislation were sharp and divisive, and free church members eventually became important political actors. In Denmark, the question of religious liberty found its solution with the democratic constitution of 1849, and in Norway, similar solutions were found during the 1840s.

These changes had deep influence on theology, culture and strategy both within the Lutheran majority churches and in the new religious groups and churches that established themselves in Scandinavia. Taking the historical background into consideration, these changes were expressed in conflicts over and competitions on the religious material landscape, the religious territory. The Lutheran churches had territorial monopoly with full control over the religious material landscapes through church buildings and church organisation based on territorial borders. Religion was practiced within a territory, the local congregation with its church and its minister. The new legislation on religious liberty established a new principle – civil and religious territories were different. That paved the way for new confessions and churches to regard the Scandinavian countries as missionary fields with possibilities for establishing their own territories, congregations and buildings.

As organisations, then, the Lutheran churches in Scandinavia were controlled by the Crown or 'the state'. In that way they were state churches. When it came to the church buildings, however, the Reformation meant that the local congregations stayed as owners with responsibility to contribute to or pay for maintenance, repairs or eventually the build-

2.4-1 The Borgund stave church, Norway, from ca 1200 and the Borgund church from 1868, drawn by Christian Christie.
[Oslo, Direktoratet for kulturminneforvaltning; photo Axel Lindahl, 1892]

2.4-2 The church of Kvinnherad, Norway, built c 1300, was one the many medieval stone churches that continued to be used after the Reformation. Until 1910 the church was privately owned by the Barony of Rosendal.
[Wikimedia Commons; photo Tomasz Halszka, 2006]

ing of a new church. With the local churches followed landed property and other sources of income that contributed to the maintenance. The legal question of the ownership of local church buildings has, however, been debated during the centuries. In the 1720s, the absolute monarch of Denmark-Norway, Fredrik IV, decided that he was entitled to sell the Norwegian rural churches in order to cover the Crown's debt. In some cases, the buyers were representatives of the local congregations, but also many private investors bought churches, not least in order to control the landed property and other sources of income. Especially in Denmark and Sweden, a number of churches were owned and maintained by manors, a system that has survived until now. Due to changes in the Norwegian legislation in 1837, the responsibility and for all practical reasons the ownership of churches that were not still on private hands was transferred to the new municipal councils (formannskap). That meant that all tax payers in the municipality – even members of other churches after 1845 – paid for the churches. Similar systems were found in Denmark and Sweden. [Ill. 2.4-2]

These overarching changes in the religious material landscapes of the Scandinavian countries constitute the focus of this contribution as an attempt to follow these changes through the diversification of religious and architectural practice during the nineteenth century. A main problem is that there are no comprehensive research or literature covering this field. Most overviews have national or regional perspectives, and comparative contributions have been few. It should be added that the nineteenth century has had low status among art historians and architects since the twentieth century, so there is not much research to be found. Especially when it comes to the material landscapes and buildings of the new denominations that found their way to Scandinavia, the problems of getting an overview are substantial. The article, therefore, has to be limited to some major developments and examples – with emphasis on ideology, architecture and cultural practice. An important question will be the relationship between these three phenomena.

The early Lutheran Scandinavia

With the introduction of the Christian religion in Scandinavia in the Middle Ages churches and monasteries were built, parishes were established and the Roman church organisation became decisive in the construction of landscape and society. After the introduction of the Lutheran religion to Denmark-Norway in 1536-1537 and the comparatively more slow Lutheran reformation of Sweden during the long sixteenth century, building of new churches was not of high priority. The main project of the Scandinavian kings was to consolidate the new religious and political situation. This consolidation had several elements: monasteries were torn down, monastery churches were in some cases changed into parish churches, and in general the number of churches was reduced, especially in the cities. Since very few new churches were built, the absolute majority of Scandinavian parishes were left with churches – both wooden churches and stone churches – that had been built, decorated and furnished in the Roman Catholic period. Of course, these churches were transformed into what was regarded as acceptable by the authorities of the new religion, but this transformation had different phases.[1] The changes of the Scandinavian churches in the decades after the Reformation had three important dimensions: ideology, economy and demography. [Ill. 2.4-3]

The ideology is seemingly the clearest dimension. It was an urgent issue to the reformers to remove anything that could prevent the smooth transition from one religion to another. In practice, however, the changes that the reformers regarded as urgent and necessary, were made during long processes. Side altars and sculptures of saints were removed, but much of the Roman Catholic interior that was not provoking or the object of superstition seems to have been kept. Examples of iconoclastic actions can be found in sixteenth-century Scandinavia, but they were few, local and organised by the authorities, not by the congregations.

Despite of this 'moderate' policy of change with regard to church buildings, an important part of the new ideology was to prohibit Roman Catholics to practice their religion within the borders of the realm. The subjects of the Lutheran kings were obliged to stay loyal to the Lutheran confession.

Economy was also substantial. The Lutheran reformation represented a dramatic economic change. In Denmark-Norway the Crown confiscated all property of monasteries and bishops. Left untouched was the economy of the local churches and the parishes. New laws regulated this part of the church economy, which partly was dependent on contributions from the congregations. This meant that negotiations between the authorities and the congregations were necessary when changes should take place.

Demography is the third, important dimension here. Most people lived in rural areas, and in most cases, the borders between the congregations were left unchanged. In the cites, however, there were not enough people to sustain the many churches. But this was to change in the following centuries, with urban expansion and general increased population in Scandinavia, not least in the nineteenth century:

2.4-3 *The Borgund stave church, Norway, built c. 1200 with original stone altar, but with added, post-Reformation furnishing: pulpit c. 1550-1570, altarpiece 1620/1654.*
[Wikimedia Commons; photo Micha L. Rieser, 2010]

Sweden's population was c. 900,000 in 1570, in 1800 2,347,000 and in 1900 5,136,000. C. 9% of the country's inhabitants were living in cities in 1800 and c. 21% in 1899.[2]

Denmark had a population of c. 600,000 in 1536, 929,000 in 1801 and 2,449,000 in 1901, of which 21% were living in cities in 1801 and 39% in 1901.[3]

Norway had c. 440,000 inhabitants in the 1660s, 883,000 in 1801 and 2,240,000 in 1900. In 1801 8% of the population was living in urban areas, in 1900 36%.[4]

In the seventeenth century a substantial number of new churches were built in Scandinavia, and important changes in the furnishing of the existing churches took place. This was the century when the Lutheran

1 Amundsen, "Reformed Church Interiors in Southern Norway".
2 Sundbärg, *Sveriges land och folk*, 90, 97.
3 <https://danmarkshistorien.dk/perioder/adelsvaelden-1536-1660/kongens-riger-og-lande/>; *Befolkningsforholdene i Danmark i det 19. Aarhundrede*, 10, 14. It must be taken into consideration that Denmark lost densely populated areas to Sweden in 1658.
4 <https://www.ssb.no/a/histstat/tabeller/3-1.html>.

2.4-4 The Church of Our Saviour (Vor Frelsers kirke), Christianshavn, Denmark, was built 1682-1696, with drawings by the Dutch architect Lambert van Haven (1630-1695). The spier was added in 1748 by the architect Laurids Thurah (1706-1759).
[Wikimedia Commons; photo. Ib Rasmussen, 2006]

5   Ekroll, "State Church and Church State"; Johannsen and Johannsen, "Re-forming the Confessional Space".

versions of the Baroque style – the main expression of the Roman Catholic Counter Reformation – were introduced to Scandinavian churches. Most of the churches received private donations making it possible to install new pulpits, altarpieces, pews, baptismal fonts and religious art according to the preferences of the day. This process has not been studied in detail for all Scandinavia, but the result is obvious: Scandinavian churches were during the seventeenth century furnished as Lutheran orthodox cultic centres with the Baroque style as its main expression.[5] [Ill. 2.4-4]

The religious ideologies of eighteenth-century Scandinavia were more complex. In the first half of the century the Danish-Norwegian kings – Fredrik IV (1671-1730) and Christian VI (1699-1746) – were deeply influenced by Pietism, and a number of state reforms took place within school and religious education systems. The expectations to the Lutheran clergy was also brought to a higher level, expecting deeper commitment to their mission, internalisation of religious ideals, performance of house inspections and other forms of religious control, everything under the auspices and control of the sovereign. In Sweden, on the other hand, Pietism was far more contested and lasting conflicts were created between Orthodox Lutherans and Pietists. In all Scandinavian countries, however, the organised assemblies of Pietists and other non-conformist groups were prohibited by new laws: Sweden in 1726 and Denmark-Norway in 1741. Technically, no other arenas than the churches were allowed for religious activities outside the household: the principle of the Lutheran territorial state church was kept and defended.

New Scandinavian churches were built also in this period. In the eighteenth century Pietism and Enlightenment ideologies had their imprint on the church architecture. In the beginning of the century, churches still were dominated by the Baroque style. Despite of its close connection with the Roman Catholic Counter Reformation, the Baroque style did not represent any Roman Catholic threat in countries totally dominated by Lutheran state churches.

Theology influenced by moderate enlightenment was the most influential ideology in the Lutheran churches in Scandinavia in the late eighteenth and early nineteenth century. Accordingly, less weight was put on the sacraments, and more attention paid to the effects of the word – in a wide sense. The clergy was expected to be and in most cases saw themselves as state propagators of enlightened religion, rationality, modern education and national economic growth. Accordingly, new built churches were intended as main local arenas for public instruction and improvement, and the Baroque style was regarded as old-fashioned and not fit for such arenas. The multi-faceted Baroque altarpieces were around the middle of the century replaced by more simple, meditative motives, often the Crucifixion, the Passion of Christ, or the Holy Supper.

A major accomplishment was the building of so-called central churches with 'pulpit altars', where altar, pulpit and eventually an organ were placed on top of each other at the eastern wall of the church. In most cases, churches with such constructions also had galleries – often in many floors – to house as many groups of churchgoers as possible. This architecture was favoured by the Pietist church regime in the middle of the eighteenth century, and used in places as different as the manor of Ledreborg in Zealand, the mining city Kongsberg in Norway, and a number of ordinary parish churches in Telemark and Hedmarken, also in Norway. The ideal was to construct churches as auditoriums where the congregation was able to hear, observe and respond to sermons and rituals. This ideal was shared by both Pietists and representatives of the Enlightenment.[6] [Ill. 2.4-5]

Moravianism

Despite the attempts to keep a religious monopoly for the Lutheran state churches, eighteenth-century Scandinavia was also marked by growing influence and challenges from Moravianism, that under its leader, Count Nicolas Ludwig von Zinzendorf (1700-1760), rapidly spread to Scandinavia in the 1730s. In Denmark-Norway Moravianism appealed to craftsmen, servants and theological students, even if the impulses are difficult to trace in detail. Attention from parts of the aristocracy can also be observed. Under any circumstance, the result was that in a number of cities small groups of Moravians met in private homes or in minor assembly halls, in most cases under the auspices of local clergy or a well-off tradesman. The Conventicle Act from 1741 forbade public meetings, but as long as the Moravians kept to themselves, they were 'tolerated'. In 1773, the Moravian settlement Christiansfeld was established in southern Jutland with permission and support from the Danish-Norwegian king, Christian VII (1749-1808).[7] For the very first time in Scandinavia, it was possible for a dissenting religious group to es-

2.4-5 Pulpit altar in Tynset church, Norway, built 1795.
[Wikimedia Commons; photo Hans A. Rosach, 2018]

6 Sørmoen, *1700-tallet*, 14, 26ff, 33ff.
7 Thyssen, *Herrnhuter-Samfundet i Christiansfeld*.

2.4-6 The Moravian church in Christansfeld, Denmark. [Ishøj, Lokalhistorische Forening]

tablish its own *public* arena and with support from the highest authorities. After a long period with meetings in private homes supported by ministers in the capital, the Moravians also established a church in Copenhagen in 1783.[8] [Ill. 2.4-6] In Sweden, similar royal permissions were granted to Moravians in Stockholm (1784)[9] and Gothenburg (1785).[10] The Moravian examples show that the monopoly of the Lutheran church buildings in the last part of the eighteenth century was challenged with support from the Scandinavian kings. The main reason for this support was that late-eighteenth-century Moravianism had developed moderate ideas and – not least – that state administrations found the Moravians to be industrious and loyal subjects that should be encouraged. The affluence of the state was prioritised higher than Lutheran confessionalism.

The Moravian churches, both in Christiansfeld and in other Scandinavian cities, were built with the church in Herrnhut as model: a central church with the pulpit as the main furnishing, a simple interior with benches and galleries separating the different 'choirs' of men and women, married and unmarried persons. These churches were lecture halls oriented towards preaching and singing. This was primarily an urban phenomenon. In rural districts, Scandinavian Moravians assembled more discretely in private homes, kept together by visiting Moravian missionaries and written information from Herrnhut.

Inner opposition and competition

In the last part of the eighteenth century, the Moravians had represented a silent but quite visible challenge to the monopoly of the Lutheran church buildings, primarily in some of the important cities, but also in rural districts. A further and even more influential challenge to this monopoly were the activities and strategies of different Pietist awakenings and lay movements in the nineteenth century.

These groups and movements developed a self-conscious political conviction when it came to religious liberty. A major object of their political strategies was to have the anti-conventicle acts abolished. The struggles about this part of the religious legislation followed different paths in the Scandinavian countries. In Norway, the Haugean and liberal representatives in the parliament were

8   Schrøder, *Om Brødremenighedens Betydning*, 25.
9   Lindahl, *Högkyrkligt, lågkyrkligt, frikyrkligt*, 28ff.
10 Lundin, *Nya Stockholm*, 223ff; Rehnberg, "En herrnhutisk plantskola i Göteborg".

successful in their campaign, and in 1842, the Conventicle Act was abolished. In Denmark, the last absolute king, Christian VIII (1786-1848) neutralised the act already in 1840 preceding the introduction of freedom of religion in the Constitution of 1849. In Sweden, the act from 1726 was moderated in 1858 and in practice abolished in 1868.

In most parts of Norway, the Pietist lay preacher Hans Nielsen Hauge (1771-1824) had sympathisers and followers opposing clergy and church authorities. His followers chose to stay as members of the state church, but they also confronted the 1741 act by arranging their own meetings and gatherings in private homes and by having migrant lay preachers competing with the Lutheran clergy. In his "Testament to his spiritual friends" from 1821, Hauge explicitly admonished his followers to stay loyal to the formal church organisation, but also to continue their independent religious activities. In practice, this meant that the Haugeans arranged their own meetings in private homes, thus establishing alternative religious arenas in local communities all over Norway.[11]

The first generations of Hauge followers stayed loyal to the 1821 admonitions of their founder – they did not oppose the formal authority of the clerics and they continued to gather in private homes. However, from the 1840s and onwards, local groups of Pietists started to build their own meeting-houses, in Norwegian called 'prayer houses' (bedehus).[12] These small timbered houses were built and paid for by the members, they were modest and discrete in expression and architecture. In some cases building of the prayer houses was initiated and paid for by a local consortium of stakeholders, in other cases a newly established organisation was responsible. Under any circumstance, the individual prayer house had a formal board independent of the municipal council and the Lutheran church organisation.

The very name – prayer houses – indicated that they did not compete openly with the local churches, but were extensions of the private homes where the 'believers' gathered to read religious texts, sing and pray according to their Pietist standards. At the same time, they challenged the territorial church organisation by building houses dedicated to religious practice open to anyone and visited by wandering preachers whom they appointed themselves.[13] The building of prayer houses expanded considerably from the 1870s, especially in urban areas,[14] where some of the houses were built with red bricks and with neo-Gothic, church inspired design.[15] The prayer houses were given Biblical place names, like Bethel, Bethesda, Bethlehem, Sion, Zoar, Ebenezer, Effata, Pella and Sarepta – a tradition that might have come from the Moravian culture.[16] [Ill. 2.4-7]

Eventually, these Pietist groups became more expanding and critical towards the Lutheran Church and the clergy. One example will show this development: the layman Erik Tønnesen (1816-1880), originally based in a radical, quite subversive religious group, established himself as a Pietist preacher in south-eastern Norway around 1850. He was critical towards local ministers, and argued – against Hans Nielsen Hauge – that 'inner mission' among the 'baptised heathens' of the Lutheran state church needed organisation and structure. He travelled from parish to parish and established a network of supporters who eventually took the initiative to establish a formal inner mission society for the region where Tønnesen was preaching. In the city of Sarpsborg, a formal prayer house for

11　Amundsen, "The devotion of the simple and pure"; Langhelle, "Haugianske møteplasser og samlingsformer".

12　The first houses of this kind seems to have been built in Rogaland, South-Eastern Norway, Swensen, *Moderne, men avleggs?*, 68f.

13　Cf. Swensen, *Moderne, men avleggs?*, 29, 126f, 200f.

14　Ibid., 68f. There have been discussions about the architectural impulses behind the prayer houses. Some have suggested inspiration from local school houses, others the Moravian assembly halls or the Bethlehem church in Stockholm (see below), Ibid., 152f; Sørby, "Religiøse forsamlingshus i Stavanger", 52ff.

15　E.g. the 'mission house' in Fredrikshald or the prayer house in Moss, both built in 1890, or Alvim prayer house outside Sarpsborg, built in 1900, Ørebech, *Bedehus i Østfold*, 146, 184, 231.

16　Ibid., 28; Larsen, "De 1073 danske missionshuse", 106f.

2.4-7 The prayer house in Sauda, Norway, called Bethel, under construction 1917.
[Sand, Ryfylkemuseet]

17 Ørebech, *Bedehus i Østfold*, 283; Amundsen, "'Naar Stormen kommer, tager Fuglen afsted'".
18 Dehli, *Fredrikstad bys historie*, II, 470f; Ørebech, *Bedehus i Østfold*, 88f.
19 Cf. Rønne, *Nyevangelismen*.
20 Ørebech, *Bedehus i Østfold*, 57ff.

his purpose was set up in 1855.[17] Outside the city of Fredrikstad, he used a house built in 1857 for the Teetotalists. This house – called 'Samfundshuset' (Community House) – also was an arena for other activities like charity and public lectures addressing the working-class population.[18]

The two wooden houses clearly signalled that they were meant for assemblies, but they were definitely not meant to be churches. Exterior and interior was very simple, with large windows, rostrum, pulpit and benches. In this way, they showed a clear distance to the churches. The buildings were made by local carpenters. An important dimension is the fact that these prayer houses had their own boards. That meant that they opened their building to Erik Tønnesen's activities, but they were not bound to him. That became very important when new preachers and impulses reached the Fredrikstad-Sarpsborg area in the 1870s. Tønnesen very much opposed this new interpretation of the Pietist message and tried to prevent it from spreading, but his campaign failed, and he left the local inner mission society. Some groups stayed loyal to Tønnesen and his conservative message, but since the two prayer houses in principle were independent of him, the boards permitted the 'new inner mission' to have meetings there. [Ill. 2.4-8]

The new trends of the 1870s created a new generation of migrant preachers, with much more expansive and ambitious strategies. In Scandinavia, these trends are often named as neo-Evangelicalism referring especially to the impulses from a reformed Swedish Pietism developing in the 1850s. Neo-Evangelism was openly opposing the older Pietist scheme of *ordo salutis* (the order of salvation) that had dominated eighteenth- and early-nineteenth-century Pietism in Scandinavia. In contrast to this old way of shaping religious experience, the neo-Evangelicals emphasised the more impulsive experience of conversion. Accordingly, they put weight on intensified inner mission, charity and publicity. By that, they intended to return to both Luther and the New Testament teaching.[19]

Again, the city of Fredrikstad might be used as an example. In 1874, when Erik Tønnesen's activities were marginalised, a new local society for inner mission was established – 'the new inner mission'. Their meetings started in 'Samfundshuset' as a contrast to Tønnesen's previous activities there, and they also started a school, an orphanage and charity. In 1887, this new inner mission society built its own prayer house, called Bethel. Their meetings and activities were also arranged in schools owned by the many industrial sawmills in the area. In the period between 1883 and 1908 the inner mission society built up an impressive consortium of new prayer houses, controlled by the board of the society and to which they could send their preachers. Only in the early twentieth century these prayer houses were made independent of the inner mission consortium.[20]

This development is quite typical for Norway in the late nineteenth century. There are local variations, of course, and an important factor has been the independence of the prayer house. Some of them stayed independent and local, others – mostly from the 1870s and onwards – were linked to regional

2.4-8 The prayer house in Sommerveiten, Norway, 1925.
[Sverresborg Trøndelag Folkemuseum]

or national organisations for inner mission, among which the Norwegian Luther Foundation – established in 1868 – was the most important.[21]

In Denmark there was also considerable opposition from disparate groups of Pietists criticising state church rituals and clergy in the early nineteenth century. In parts of Jutland, farmers in the 1790s reacted negatively on new catechisms, which they found not be according to Lutheran doctrine. In the 1820s, this opposition became more loud and organised, with the result that the authorities tried to revitalise the Conventicle Act from 1741 and bring the oppositional laymen and theologians to court. This strategy was not successful, but it created a very heated public debate, which eventually became the background for the more tolerant policy from 1840.[22]

An organisation for Pietistic inner mission was established in 1861. This organisation stayed within the Lutheran state church and sought cooperation with the clergy, but it was deeply sceptical towards 'the outwardness' of the state church. In the following years, other inner mission organisations were also founded, but the 1861 organisation was by far the most important.[23] Their first 'mission houses' (missionshuse) were built in the late 1860s, obviously inspired from the Swedish mission houses and the Norwegian prayer houses. Between 1870 and 1899 the 1861 society had built c. 435 such houses, many of them with names similar to and with the same ownership structure as the prayer houses in Norway.[24]

The other important organisation within the Danish Lutheran church was founded by Nikolai Frederik Severin Grundtvig (1783-1872), who became a leading theologian and minister from the 1820s. Grundtvig and his followers were more open towards culture in general, and they focussed on Christianity as formative force in Danish history and culture. In principle, they were oriented towards a free church ideal, theologically they were conservative confessionalists, but not Pietists. The Danish parliament in 1868 allowed members of the Lutheran state church to establish their own congregations with a pastor of their own choice (valgmenighed) and eventually their own churches. The intention was to create an alternative to leaving the church.[25] The Grundtvig followers to a large extent made use of this possibility, also building their own churches and assembly halls (forsamlingshuse). These halls and churches were owned and paid by the local 'valgmenighed'. The assembly halls differed from the mission houses when it came to activities and messages allowed to be presented there. The mission houses did only permit religious meetings with a Pietist message, while the assembly halls also were open to cultural and educational activities.[26] [Ill. 2.4-9]

In different parts of Sweden (and Finland, from 1809 a grand duchy in the Russian empire) a number of Pietist awakenings took place from the late eighteenth century and onwards. Some of these awakenings were separatist and ecstatic, while other stayed loyal to the Swedish church and to individual ministers. Of special importance in western and southern Sweden was the chaplain in Lund, Henric Schartau (1757-1825), who

21 Den norske Lutherstiftelse, in 1891 named Det norske lutherske Indremissionsselskab, the Norwegian Lutheran Society for Inner Mission.
22 Overgaard, "Vækkelse og kirke".
23 Ibid., 40, 44ff.
24 Larsen, "De 1073 danske missionshuse"; Overgaard, "Vækkelse og kirke", 45.
25 Overgaard, "Vækkelse og kirke", 32, 40ff.
26 Larsen, "De 1073 danske missionshuse", 108ff.

2.4-9 The church of the Grundtvigian 'valgmenighed' in Lemvig, Denmark, built in 1883.
[Wikimedia Commons; photo Leif Jørgensen, 2014]

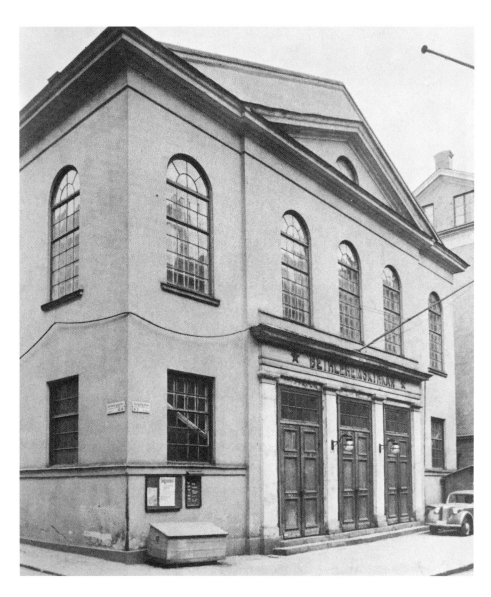

2.4-10 The entrance of the Bethlehem church in Stockholm, Sweden, built 1838-1840. The church was demolished in 1953.
[Stockholm, Stadsmuseet]

27 Gustavsson, "Väckelsernas mötesplatser", 157f.
28 Martling, "De inomkyrkliga väckelserörelserna".
29 Ibid., 172ff.
30 Lindahl, *Högkyrkligt, lågkyrkligt, frikyrkligt*, 33ff.

became the spiritual leader of wide-spread conservative groups of conservative Pietists. They were critical to liberal ministers, but showed deep respect for conservative Lutheran pastors. They did not oppose the Swedish conventicle act by arranging separate meetings, but crossed borders between congregations to seek advice and comfort from ministers they regarded as 'true teachers'. In this way, the Schartau followers challenged the territorial principle of the Swedish Lutheran church, but not as explicitly as the Haugeans.[27] Similar Pietist awakenings took place in eastern and western Götaland, in Småland and in Norrland in the first half of the nineteenth century. Neither these awakenings did organise in a formal way, they stayed loyal to Lutheran pastors in whom they trusted, and they did not openly oppose the Conventicle Act or build separate houses for religious activities.[28] One exception from this was some of the Pietist groups in Norrland, which eventually separated from the state church rituals.[29]

A new development started in the 1850s among those groups of Pietists that chose to stay as members of the Swedish Lutheran State Church, with more organised activities and formal buildings designed for religious meetings. The neo-Evangelical revival groups in Sweden were influenced from Anglo-American Methodism: from being an oppositional group within the Anglican Church rapidly also spreading in North America, the followers of John (1703-1791) and Charles (1707-1788) Wesley organised their own churches and chapels. Their doctrine was close to the Anglican Church, but with emphasis on immediate conversion, Puritan life style and individual holiness.

An important start was the mission started by the English Methodist George Scott (1804-1874), who arrived in Stockholm in 1830. He was supported by members of the Swedish aristocracy, and in 1838-1840 an assembly hall was erected (the 'English Chapel') modelled after English Methodist chapels. This building had room for 1,100 persons, and was meant for preaching, not for the distribution of sacraments. In 1842 Scott left Sweden and the hall was closed. In 1856 the newly established Evangelical Homeland Foundation (Evangeliska Fosterlandsstiftelsen) bought the building and renamed it the Bethlehem church.[30] Until his death in 1868, one of the founding fathers of this organisation, Carl Olof Rosenius (b. 1816), was minister of this church. [Ill. 2.4-10] In many other parts of Sweden the organisation built small assembly halls ('prayer houses/mission houses', 'bönhus/missionshus') to house local groups supporting the Christian mission initiated by the Evangelical Homeland Foundation. They show many parallels to the prayer houses in

194

Norway, in both exterior, interior and functions. The first 'mission houses' in Sweden were built in 1855.[31] With regard to their construction they seem to be inspired by Moravian assembly halls, and until the 1870s they consciously were constructed with no symbols making them similar to churches or chapels.[32]

Denominational competitions on the religious material landscape - Norway

In the last part of the nineteenth century the Scandinavian countries admitted their citizens to join non-Lutheran churches. In Norway that happened in 1845, and in Denmark legalisation took place through the constitution of 1849. Among the Scandinavian countries, Sweden was the last to grant religious and political rights to members both of Lutheran revival movements and of non-Lutheran churches, a fact that to a certain extent explains the very competitive and conflict oriented relationship between the Swedish Lutheran church, the revival movements and the dissenters in the nineteenth century. Laws passed by the parliament in 1860 and 1873 for the first time allowed Swedish citizens to leave the Lutheran state church and join other, recognised religious societies.

The Dissenter Act of 1845 paved the way for non-Lutheran churches to establish themselves in Norway. Their position was very different from the Pietist revival groups, since they actively sought to show their opposition and subversive attitude to the Lutheran state church. Already in 1843, two years before the Dissenter Act, Roman Catholics were allowed to perform rituals in a provisory chapel in the capital, Christiania, and in 1856 they built their own church in the city, St Olav's church. The church had as its main relic what was regarded as an arm of the most important medieval saint, St Olav, by which the Roman Catholics wanted to appropriate a legitimate historical connection to the historical period so important for the construction of a national identity in Norway. The first Roman Catholic church in Trondhjem (Trondheim),[33] consecrated in 1902, was also dedicated to St Olav.

Even in many other parts of Norway the Catholics established their activities and built churches. In Fredrikshald (Halden)[34] St Peter's church in neo-Gothic style, designed by the Dutch architect Pierre Cuypers (1827-1921), was built in 1877.[35] In Alta in Finnmark a mission was established in 1855, and in 1878 a church was consecrated, but replaced by a new one already in 1885. In Alta and elsewhere the Roman Catholic religious activities were closely accompanied by charity and medical care, often by nuns of the St Joseph order (CSJ). That was the case in Christiania (Oslo)[36] (Hospital of Our Lady, 1883) [Ill. 2.4-11], Kristiansand, Porsgrunn, Drammen, Bergen (St Paul's 1876), Fredrikshald and Fredrikstad, where the first church was built in 1882, replaced in 1899 by St Bridget's church designed in a national dragon style by the architect Ole Sverre (1865-1952).[37] Similar design and with drawings by the same architect was chosen for Catholic churches in Stavanger (St Svithun's) 1898[38] and Drammen 1899.[39] Ole Sverre in 1896 also designed the Hospital of Our Lady building in Christiania. With its Madonna sculpture on top of one of its spiers the Ro-

31 Ibid., 51f.
32 Ibid., 57f.
33 The name of the city was changed to Trondheim in 1930.
34 The name of this city was changed to Halden in 1928.
35 <http://www.artemisia.no/arc/historisk/halden/st.peter.kirke.html>.
36 The name of the capital was written Christiania until 1877, then the official spelling was changed to Kristiania, and in 1924 the name was changed into Oslo.
37 Klavestad, *Arkitekturen*, 135; <http://www.artemisia.no/arc/3/omraade/fredrikstad/ridehusgaten.26.html>.
38 *Hundre år i St. Svithuns*, 11ff.
39 *St. Laurentius*.

2.4-11 The Hospital of Our Lady, Christiania/Oslo, Norway, built close to St Olav's church 1896 after drawings by Ole Sverre.
[Oslo Museum]

2.4-12 The Methodist Church in Fredrikstad, Norway, built 1868, photographed in 1895. [Frederikstad Museum]

Norway was fervently anti-Catholic, so the actual number of conversions was small.

Another opposing Christian denomination was the Methodist church, introduced around 1850 by Norwegian sailors and rapidly expanding in urban and industrialised societies in southern Norway. The first congregations were established in the 1850s (Fredrikshald 1856, Sarpsborg 1856, Porsgrunn 1858, Mysen 1860), later followed Fredrikstad 1863 (1861),[41] Christiania 1865, Skien 1873, Kjølberg 1878, Bergen 1879, Trondheim 1881, Tromsø 1888, Lisleby and Hamar 1889. In all these places the Methodists started their activities in buildings not constructed for religious purposes, but formal churches were built few years after the establishment of congregations. [Ill. 2.4-12]

The Methodist churches were rather conservative in design, mostly with neo-Gothic windows and doors, eventually also church towers – but not belfries. Fredrikshald Methodist church was built in 1857. It even had a churchyard of its own until 1919,[42] but that was extraordinary. The Methodist church in Skien, inaugurated in 1887 after a devastating fire in the city, was designed by its own pastor, Johannes Arbo Wiel (1856-1942).[43] The first Methodist congregation in Christiania was organised in 1865, and their church – with no tower – was built 1874 in a neo-Roman style. The ambitions for the church were high, with room for 1,000 persons.[44]

There are many similarities between the Norwegian Methodist churches and the Lutheran Free Church, established in the 1870s as a protest against the legal and theological ties between the Lutheran Church of Norway and the Norwegian state. In the early churches built by theses dissenters, mostly neo-Gothic and in some cases neo-Roman style was preferred, often including symbolic church towers. One example was the Lutheran Free Church in eastern part of Christiania. The congregation was established in 1878 and its neo-Roman church built in 1885.[45] Similar in Kristiansand, where a Lutheran Free Church was established in 1877 and a church inaugurated the same year. The

man Catholic presence in the Norwegian capital was even more explicit. Absolutely striking was the Roman Catholic church in Porsgrunn (Church of Our Lady), replacing a chapel from 1890. The new church in Porsgrunn was consecrated in 1899, designed by the Norwegian architect Haldor Larsen Børve (1857-1933) in the style of a Norwegian stave church from the Middle Ages.[40]

An important factor behind the establishment of Roman Catholic congregations and churches in Norway was the royal benefactors, who had the power and the means to encourage this open opposition to the very idea behind the Lutheran reformation. The two first Bonaparte monarchs of Sweden and Norway (Carl III/XIV Johan, 1763-1844, and Oscar I, 1799-1859) had queens who stayed Roman Catholics for their whole life – Desideria (1777-1860) and Josephine (1807-1876), and they both used political networks and national and foreign economic resources in supporting this church. In the nineteenth century, most Norwegian Catholics were of foreign origin, and the dominant opinion in

---

40 Lund, *Porsgrund 1807-1907*, 36.
41 Dehli, *Fredrikstad bys historie*, II, 469 and III, 126; <http://www.artemisia.no/arc/3/omraade/fredrikstad/ridehusgaten.7.html>.
42 <https://www.norske-kirker.net/home/ostfold/halden-metodistkirke/>.
43 <https://www.norske-kirker.net/home/telemark/skien-metodistkirke/>; <http://www.artemisia.no/arc/historisk/skien/skien.metodistkirke.html>.
44 Hammelbo, ed., *Oslo første metodistmenighet*.
45 <http://www.artemisia.no/arc/historisk/oslo/bygninger/lakkegaten.47.html>.

churches indicated strong cultural links with the religious culture of the prayer houses.[46]

Similarly 'discrete' were the Norwegian Baptist churches, established in many parts of the country since the 1860s, as offspring of dissenting religious groups who left the Norwegian Lutheran Church one decade earlier, and whose leader was the former Lutheran minister Gustav Adolf Lammers (1802-1878). In most cases, these local congregations built or rented small houses or rooms and refurbished them for their own purposes, especially baptism of adult believers. When formal churches were built, they more resembled assembly halls than Protestant churches, for instance in Tromsø, where a Baptist church was built in 1872.[47]

Norway also saw the construction of more free and open buildings for 'Christian mission' in urban areas, often designed and planned by groups supporting one specific, charismatic preacher unbound by territorial state church organisation. One example is the impressive Calmeyergatens Missionshus (Mission House of the Calmeyer Street) in Christiania, built in neo-Gothic style in 1891 with drawings by the architect Henrik Nissen (1848-1915). The initiative was taken by the non-confessional preacher Otto Treider (1856-1928), and the house – partly paid by Treider himself – was very ambitious with room for 5,000 persons, which made it the largest religious building in Scandinavia at the time. [Ill. 2.4-13]

Denominational competitions on the religious material landscape - Sweden

In Sweden, a limited freedom of religion was granted to small groups of Roman Catholics immigrating in the 1720s. Their practice of religion was linked to the chapels established by foreign ambassadors to Sweden, and was expected to take place behind closed doors. This liberty was limited to non-Swedish citizens. The Roman Catholics were granted further liberties in 1781, but conversions from Lutheranism to Roman Catholicism were not allowed until 1873. Also Calvinists were given some privileges from 1741 to build churches and keep ministers.[48] Despite the support from the early queens of the Bernadotte dynasty, the strict rules seem to have put restrictions to Roman Catholic church building in Sweden until the last part of the nineteenth century. The churches were limited to a few larger cities, and closely linked to small groups of immigrants. In 1865, the first church was inaugurated in Gothenburg – the neo-Gothic St Joseph's church. The church was included in an ordinary building quarter in Gothenburg, the frontal facing the street, and with tower and church bells.[49] In Stockholm, St Eric's chapel was inaugurated in 1860. A formal church was built in the same area between 1890 and 1892, still dedicated to St Eric and designed in neo-Roman style by architect Axel Gillberg (1861-1915). [Ill. 2.4-14]

Considerably more visible and important all over Sweden in the nineteenth century were assembly halls and churches built by different Protestant denominations and or-

2.4-13 The mission house in Calmeyer street, Christiania/Oslo, Norway, built in 1891, photographed in 1957. The building was demolished in 1972. [Oslo Museum; photo Leif Ørnelund]

46 <http://agderkultur.no/pages/kirker/kristiansand-frikirke/kristiansand-frikirke.html>.
47 Stiansen, *Baptistkirkens historie*.
48 Bedoire, *Hugenotternas värld*, 268ff.
49 <https://web.archive.org/web/20150402121154/>; <http://www.kristuskonungen.se/historia.htm>.

2.4-14 St Eric's Cathedral, Stockholm, Sweden, designed by Axel Gillberg. [Wikimedia Commans; photo Allgau, 2008]

2.4-15 The Immanuel church, Stockholm, Sweden, built 1886 and demolished 1977. [Private Collection]

50 Some will have it that 1848 was the year of the first Baptist congregation.
51 <https://sv.wikipedia.org/wiki/Sveriges_baptistf%C3%B6rsamling>.
52 Lindahl, *Högkyrkligt, lågkyrkligt, frikyrkligt*, 159ff.
53 Walan, "De utomkyrkliga väckelserörelserna", 191.
54 Ibid., 195.
55 Ibid., 198-206.

ganisations. Due to the rather strict legislation the Baptists had difficulties in establishing themselves in Sweden. A main source of inspiration – and money – came from the United States. The first congregation was established in Stockholm 1854,[50] and in 1861 the Baptists formally established themselves in Gothenburg.[51] They furnished a number of halls and chapels according to their needs, but these buildings had no similarities with Lutheran churches. That was also the case with the more impressive Baptist churches from the later part of the nineteenth century. In 1884 they inaugurated the Tabernacle as their first formal church building in the city. The architect was Johan August Westerberg (1836-1900), himself being a prominent member of the congregation. In 1893, a Baptist Tabernacle was built in Stockholm, with Gustaf Lindgren (1863-1930) as architect.[52] The Baptist church saw a considerable expansion during the last part of the century. In 1857 representatives of c. 40 Baptist congregations met at a national conference in the capital,[53] and by 1897 the number of congregations had increased to 564 with c. 39,000 members.[54]

In 1878 a number of Evangelical Homeland Foundation members formally established an independent church, lead by Paul Peter Waldenström (1838-1917), thus competing both nationally and internationally with the state church loyal Foundation from 1856.[55] The Swedish Mission Society (Svenska Missionsförbundet), as the new, congregationalist church was called, built a number of churches where sacraments were administered by pastors. Also in this case, the church buildings in big Swedish cities became models for the church building elsewhere in the country. In Gothenburg the Swedish Mission Society built the Bethlehem church in 1881, and in Stockholm the Immanuel church was erected in 1886 based on drawings by the architect Gustaf Erik Sjöberg (1837-1897).[56] One important model seems to have been the world famous English Baptist preacher Charles Spurgeon (1834-1892) and his enormous Metropolitan Tabernacle from 1861 in London.[57] The Immanuel church was situated in one of the poorer parts of the Swedish capital. The first building in Stockholm to be included in the new Society was, however, Nya Missionshuset (the New Mission House), built in 1877 to house low-church preachers. From 1878 this building – designed by the brothers and architects Hjalmar (1837-1897) and Axel Kumlien (1833-1913) – was regarded as a church.[58] [Ill. 2.4-15]

As in Christiania, Stockholm saw the construction of religious assembly halls not specifically linked to a territorial church or one specific organisation, but built to house a charismatic, often non-confessional preacher. In Stockholm, the best example is the church at Blasieholmen, built with Spurgeon's Metropolitan Temple in London as inspiration, with Erik Gustaf Sjöberg (1837-1897) as architect and commissioned by the minister and preacher Gustaf Emanuel Beskow (1834-1899). The Blasieholmen church had room for 3,000 persons, and an important income was tickets sold to visitors at the different meetings. This church was primarily meant for preaching, it was not linked to a territorial congregation, but services including Holy Communion were practised. Its structure was that of a central church with everything centred on the altar, the pulpit and the organ, and with two galleries. The interior was very simple, which created some critical comments by contemporaries.[59] Beskow was also a leading figure in the Evangelical Homeland Foundation, and he was supported in his enterprise by members of the Swedish aristocracy, not least the Queen of King Oscar II (1829-1907), Sophia (1836-1913).

In Sweden the Methodist Church was officially recognised by the state authorities in 1876, but smaller local congregations had been organised in places along the Swedish coast already in the 1860s.[60] Their first formal church building was erected in Karlskrona in 1869-1870, the Emanuel church. Without formal recognition by the authorities the church was designed in a very discrete way, with no external signals of being a church. After the 1876 recognition the Methodist churches were more expressive, neo-Gothic with towers. In Stockholm, Methodists had organised in 1868 as the first Swedish congregation, which commissioned the building of St Paul's church in neo-Gothic style. This church from 1875 – also designed by Hjalmar and Axel Kumlien – became model for other Methodist churches in the country.[61]

Denominational competitions on the religious material landscape - Denmark

Different from the Norwegian capital Christiania, the Danish (and until 1814: Norwegian) capital Copenhagen already had a more differentiated religious material landscape. As early as 1689, a Reformed church was built due to an initiative from the Queen of Christian V (1646-1699), Charlotte Amalie (1650-1714), who never converted to Lutheranism.[62] The late medieval church St Petri was dedicated to the German speaking population in the city. And in 1764 the Jews in Copenhagen for the first time were allowed to build a synagogue. In the same period – in 1765 – the Austrian Empress Maria Theresa (1717-1780) paid for the building of a Roman Catholic chapel in the capital, and later several Catholics donated money or objects to a future formal church to be built.[63] These churches, however, were connected to small groups of immigrants and diplomats and not open to Danish citizens.

A new situation occurred, however, when the Roman Catholic Church was established in Denmark in the 1840s. In principle, this

56 Lindahl, *Högkyrkligt, lågkyrkligt, frikyrkligt*, 134ff.
57 Cf. Ibid., 41ff.
58 <https://www.andreaskyrkan.se/om-andreaskyrkan/historia>.
59 Lindahl, *Högkyrkligt, lågkyrkligt, frikyrkligt*, 40ff.
60 Walan, "De utomkyrkliga väckelserörelserna", 197.
61 Lindahl, *Högkyrkligt, lågkyrkligt, frikyrkligt*, 151ff.
62 Bedoire, *Hugenotternas värld*, 272f.
63 <https://sanktansgar.dk/om-kirken/historien/>.

2.4-16 *The interior of the Baptist church in Rønne, Denmark, built 1888.* [Rønne byarkiv]

64 <http://www.jesuhjertekirke.dk/kirkens-historie/>.
65 Larsen, "De 1073 danske missionshuse", 111; Overgaard, "Vækkelse og kirke", 35ff.
66 Larsen, "De 1073 danske missionshuse", 111, 113.
67 <http://danmarkskirker.natmus.dk/vejle/vejle-skt-pouls-kirke/>.

church was open to Danish citizens, even if the majority of members seems to have been immigrants to the capital. Their first church was the neo-Classic St Ansgar's, built in Copenhagen in 1842 and drawn by the German architect Gustav Friedrich Hetsch (1788-1864). The Church of the Sacred Heart of Jesus was built in Copenhagen in 1895 as the main church of the Jesuits in Denmark. The architectural style was neo-Gothic with tower and belfry.[64]

The Baptists started their activities in Denmark, not least in the city of Aalborg, where a congregation was organised as early as in 1840. The relative success of the Baptists in part of Denmark was closely linked to many of the dramatic conflicts around the conventicles during the first decades of the nineteenth century. The Baptists also were successful in Vejle, where they built a church in 1877, one year after the Methodists.[65] The first formal church building in Aalborg – the Bethel church in neo-Gothic style without tower – was built with grants from American Baptists as late as in 1888. That was also the case with the Baptist church in Rønne at Bornholm from 1888, with no tower. In Frederiksberg outside Copenhagen the Baptist church from 1896-1897 was designed in neo-Roman style with a tower. [Ill. 2.4-16]

Methodism came to Denmark in the 1850s, and it was recognised by the state authorities in 1865. St Paul's church in Vejle was built by the local Methodist congregation in 1876 in neo-Baroque style and with a 'church hall'.[66] In 1892 the building had an impressive tower added and a more formal church building was added. The architect in 1892 was Niels Peder Jensen (1853-1929).[67] In Copenhagen the Marcus Church (later called St John's church), designed in 1864-1865 by the architect Ferdinand Vilhelm Jensen (1837-1890), was the first Methodist church to be built in Denmark.

Responses from the national Lutheran churches

As can be understood from the previous overview, the Lutheran state churches in Scandinavia were confronted with a number of challenges during the nineteenth century: liberal politicians arguing the differentiation between civil rights and religious practice, new religious societies within the Lutheran churches challenging the ideological monopoly of the clergy, aggressive competition from new Christian denominations on the territorial monopoly of religion, and growing indifference on religion in general among all classes of society. The eighteenth-century solutions to these challenges had been Pietism and theological Enlightenment, the main nineteenth-century Lutheran solutions were confessionalisation, aestheticisation, and modernisation. The considerable growth of new Christian congregations and churches changed the religious material landscape of most Scandinavian cities. Roman Catholics, Methodists, Baptists, Lutheran free churches and Pietist groups within the Lutheran state churches built their own prayer/mission houses and churches. This development called for action and new strategies from the state churches, which tried to meet the new competition with arguments, control – and new and impressive churches placed in new demographic centres. And there are indications that justify naming these actions and strategies as reactions. The representatives of the Scandinavian state churches were not prepared or supportive of the changes, but as spokesmen of the majority culture they had to respond and react to make the changes as small as possible and to stay in control.

Confessionalisation had several elements: one was the new interest in the Lutheran confessional legacy; another was a new focus on the national dimensions of Lutheranism. Since the three Scandinavian countries during the nineteenth century developed a clearer distinction between citizenship and church membership, competition over the national religious material landscapes became of high importance. To claim historical and cultural legitimacy within the national and local borders and structures was a rational and emergent response from representatives of the Lutheran churches. In Norway, the new self-consciousness of the Lutheran state church as a separate institution with its history and identity, created the new concept of 'the Norwegian Church'. In Denmark, the 1849 constitution elaborated with the concept 'the Danish Folk Church', and in Sweden the expression 'the Swedish Church' was coined.[68]

Aestheticisation was also part of the Lutheran state church strategy. The question raised by many decision makers was how new aesthetic principles might contribute to secure the continuous success of the Lutheran church in a new, competitive situation. Another question raised was about confessionally specific elements of a Lutheran aesthetics. From the middle of the nineteenth century, it stood clear for many church leaders and architects that the architectural style of neo-Gothicism had the major qualities of modern religious aesthetics. It represented a timeless human longing for the Divine, it opened for simple and clean concentration on the necessity of salvation as the Lutherans conceived it, and it combined the impressive with the colourful and bright. A neo-Gothic church had an abstract reference to the timeless, non-confessionalised past, and it did not need more furnishing than benches, galleries, pulpit and an appealing painting as altarpiece.

Modernisation was the third part of the Lutheran state church strategy in Scandinavia. As in the century after the Reformation, demography, ideology and economy were important factors. The Scandinavian populations were growing, an increasing part of the populations settled in cities and urban areas, and it was in these areas that the new challenging religious movements and churches were most successful. A religious marked developed with competitions over the individual souls. In such a situation, the question of how the Lutheran church buildings could both house, convince and appeal to believers and non-believers became urgent.

These processes and ideas did, of course, not develop in an isolated Scandinavian church culture. Especially from Lutheran Germany new impulses and ways of thinking in the field of confessional re-orienting and church architecture found their way to the tree countries in the north. From the last part of the eighteenth century neo-Classicism with its references to ancient Greek and Roman aesthetics was dominating. The Baroque expressions were regarded as old-fashioned and unsuitable to express modern religious feelings and theological ideals. Simplicity, light colours, and motives with direct appeal to both Pietist and enlightened piety replaced old ideas. The model of the pulpit-altar-organ construction of church interiors was often preferred in new churches, symptomatically used in octagon churches with acoustics and visibility of optimal quality for the congregation.[69] The religious experience should not be disturbed by complex iconography – instead of the Baroque altarpieces a simple, golden cross or an easy-read meditative motif was recommended.

The nineteenth century opened with a continuous interest in neo-Classical churches. In Denmark and Norway the neo-Classical Church of Our Lady (Vor Frue kirke) in Copenhagen (consecrated 1829) became

68 Den norske kirke, Den danske folkekirke, Svenska kyrkan.
69 Sørmoen, *1700-tallet*, 33ff; Lindahl, *Högkyrkligt, lågkyrkligt, frikyrkligt*, 23ff.

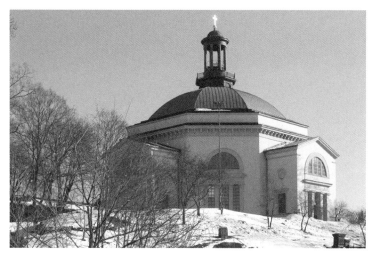

2.4-17 The church at Skeppsholmen, Stockholm, Sweden.
[Wikimedia Commons; photo 2013]

2.4-18 The cathedral of Gothenburg, Sweden, built 1815.
[Wikipedia Commons; photo Arild V, 2011]

70 Eldal, *Med historiske forbilder*, 33; Lysaker, *Høyalteret i Nidarosdomen*, 13.
71 Lindahl, *Högkyrkligt, lågkyrkligt, frikyrkligt*, 9ff, 13f, 19ff.
72 Amundsen, *Enighet og uenighet i 400 år*, 125ff; Eldal, *Med historiske forbilder*, 24.
73 Grydeland, *Hadsel kirke*.
74 Eldal, *Med historiske forbilder*, 12f.
75 Seip, ed., *Chr. H. Grosch*.
76 Linstow, *Udkast til Kirkebygninger*; cf. Eldal, *Med historiske forbilder*, 25ff.
77 Von Achen, "Fighting the disenchantment of the world"; Eldal, *Med historiske forbilder*, 36ff.
78 As mentioned, most Norwegian rural churches were sold to private owners by the Crown in the 1720s as a solution to cover the enormous state debt created by the long-time war with Sweden.
79 Eldal, *Med historiske forbilder*, 13f.
80 Ibid., 11f.

an important model: on the altar was placed the sculptor Bertel Thorvaldsen's (1770-1844) monumental figure of Christ, in white marble and with open, inviting arms and a warm and friendly gaze. [Col. ill. 8] In Norway, this model found a counterpart in the Immanuel church in Fredrikshald, designed by Christian Heinrich Grosch (1801-1865), built in the years 1828-1833, and with a copy of Thorvaldsen's sculpture on the altar. A similar copy was also placed on the altar in the cathedral of Trondhjem, as a personal gift from the sculptor himself.[70]

In Sweden, state control over church design had been quite strict also during the eighteenth century, favouring neo-Classical churches to be built. An important achievement was the cathedral of Gothenburg, built 1808 from drawings by Carl Wilhelm Carlberg (1746-1814), and the church at Skeppsholmen in Stockholm, designed by Fredrik Blom (1781-1853) 1823.[71] [Ill. 2.4-17 & 2.4-18]

However, aesthetic ideals were one thing; practical realities – for instance lack of money or local affinition to older furnishings – were others. An interesting example is Langestrand church in Norway, built in 1818 and designed by a local architect, Hans Christian Lind (1753-1820), who had studied at the Royal Art Academy in Copenhagen. The light-coloured church replaced an older, Baroque church, and had a simple and clear-cut pulpit-altar construction. However, some of the old furnishing was transferred to the new church – e.g. the baptismal font and a number of old-fashioned paintings. The original plans put a simple cross on top of the altar, but it is unclear if that part of the design plan was conducted.[72] [Ill. 2.4-19] Another example is Hadsel church in northern Norway, an octagon church built in 1824, replacing an older church. Hadsel church has many similarities with Langestrand church, but on the altar was put an altarpiece from c. 1520 and between the altar and the pulpit was placed a late fifteenth-century sculpture of St Olaf. In addition, a large number of seventeenth-century paintings, both portraits of pastors and their families and devotional paintings, were transferred to the new church.[73]

In post-1814 Norway, the new Ministry of Church and Education took an active part in church building and church architecture. Different from the situation in Sweden, this political control with church building plans was a novelty in Norway.[74] Norway's few architects had their education from Denmark. Of high importance were the already mentioned Christian Heinrich Grosch[75] and Hans Ditlev Frants von Linstow (1787-1851). Grosch designed around 80 churches, of which 10 had octagon shape. Linstow was hired to design the new Royal Palace in Christiania and he was also occupied with theatre architecture. In his writings, there are few theological reflections, but a concern about 'the effects' on people's minds and the economy of the local congregation. Linstow in 1829 published models for new rural church design in Norway, models that were widely used – around 80 churches, among them many octagon churches – and were built according to Linstow's neo-Classic models.[76]

As mentioned, neo-Classicism was, however, profoundly challenged around the mid-nineteenth century. From both Lutheran, Anglican and Roman Catholic leading theologians and architects the Christian Middle Ages and especially the Gothic aesthetics became to be regarded as the most genuine expression of Christian culture and piety. Confronted with modernism and secularism the neo-Gothic style was described as *the* Christian architectural style, while the ideals of neo-Classicism were regarded as secular, theatrical and heathen.[77]

Linstow did not follow up on this new development, but Grosch did. And so did Linstow's assistant from 1838, the German architect Heinrich Ernst Schirmer (1814-1887), and Wilhelm Hanno (1826-1882), another German architect who settled in Christiania. Grosch, Schirmer and von Hanno designed a large number of Norwegian churches in the neo-Gothic style, some of them with very simple interiors and just a golden cross as altar decoration – as was the case with Balsfjord church from 1856 designed by Grosch.

The last part of the nineteenth century saw an unprecedented number of new churches built in Norway. The formal condition was a law passed by the parliament in 1851 stating that all privately owned churches[78] were to be sold to the local congregations/municipalities and that all churches should have room for at least 30% of the members of the congregation. The law proposal had been through many political debates, mostly concerning the legal rights of the private church owners.[79]

The new law had, however, many other important elements: the ownership of the churches was linked to the territorial church structure, the congregation, the churches should be well kept in order to appeal to the new religious ideals, and they should be able to house a substantial number of congregation members. This was confessionalisation, aestheticisation and modernisation in one! And the result was astonishing. Between 1850 and 1910 no less than 720 new churches were built.[80] A large number of medieval stone churches and stave churches were torn down and replaced by modern neo-Gothic churches designed according to the new ideals. The new churches should be expressions

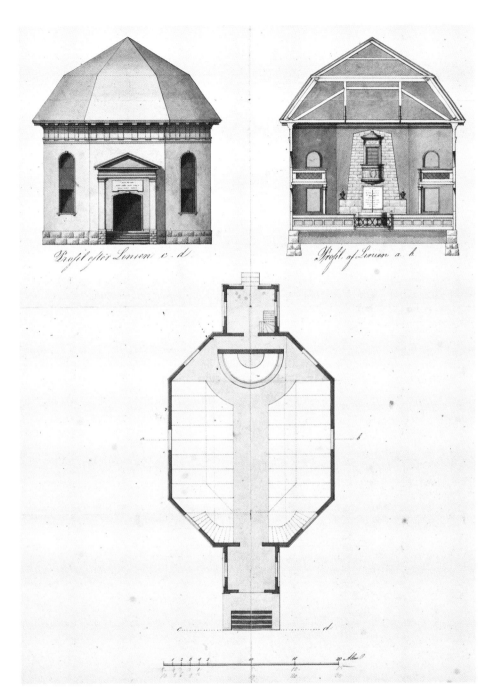

2.4-19 Langestrand church, Norway, the original drawings by architect Hans Christian Lind.
[Sandefjord, Vestfoldmuseene]

203

2.4-20 Trøgstad church, Norway, photographed before the radical changes took place in 1904.
[Oslo, Direktoratet for kulturminneforvaltning; photo C.C. Thomhav]

of Lutheranism with no references to other confessions, they should appeal to the religious sentiments of contemporary individuals, and they should be modern with regard to practical solutions and comfort without challenging the sacral and symbolic universe that a church should contain. [Ill. 2.4-1]

Accordingly, the contestation from the revivalist groups and the dissenting churches was met with new ideals of Lutheran church buildings and liturgical space. The old churches, with references to the old, static and paternalist society, with Baroque, Renaissance or pre-Reformation furnishing, were replaced by churches referring to the medieval Gothic aesthetics, but with no links to the immediate past. The solution in Hadsel was not followed in the new neo-Gothic churches. On the contrary, they were not filled with old interior details from older churches. At the same time, the musealisation of old churches and church furnishings commenced. The first Norwegian cultural history museums – Trondhjem (1767), Christiania (1811), Bergen (1825), Arendal (1832), and Tromsø (1872) – were filled with both pre- and post-Reformation items from the old churches all around the country.

The neo-Gothic churches were functional, with much light, easy to keep clean and heated, and with a furnishing that both referred to but also competed with the prayer houses or the mission halls. The altar pieces were simple, often with just a simple cross or with easy-read paintings depicting central Jesus motives – the resurrection or the meetings between Jesus and his disciples.

Not even the existing churches were left untouched by the new ideals. Trøgstad church in south-eastern Norway, a stone church from the middle ages, was the object of a local conflict over economy, religious ideals and 'legacy'. The 1851 law demanded changes, but the local wish to protect the result of past generations' investment and piety resulted in a compromise. The medieval church was extended with the aim of keeping its 'medieval' identity, while the interior was totally refurbished in a strange combination of neo-Gothic elements, historicism and 'prayer house' ideology.[81] [Ill. 2.4-20]

The combination of a new aesthetic orientation and the competition with a new, romantic and revivalist oriented piety, was striking. Again, Fredrikstad in south-eastern Norway will serve as an example: in the last part of the nineteenth century, the city was structurally changed by industrialisation and mass immigration, with immense conflicts as a consequence. The old social and cultural structures collapsed, and the inner mission activities and the dissenting religious opposition against tradition and authority was quite dominant. The city church was located in a marginalised part of the religious material landscape, the surrounding rural municipality tried to compensate this by building a new – neo-Gothic – church in 1853. However, contemporary commentators argued that this new church with room for 600 persons could not cover the needs of a population of 10,000! But state-church changes took time. [Ill. 2.4-21]

In the meanwhile, the Methodists had built their church in the new part of the city, and other dissenting churches were proudly and self-consciously expanding – Baptists, Roman Catholics and other 'free' groups

81 Amundsen, "En demokratisering av kirkerommet?".

opposing the historical territories of the Lutheran state church. Finally, in 1880, a new, impressive Lutheran church was built in the middle of the new city centre, with its own congregational borders and served by a minister and a chaplain. The architect was Waldemar Ferdinand Lühr (b. 1848) and the new church had room for 1,200 persons. The tower overshadowed any other building in the city.[82]

In other churches, the medieval or early post-Reformation wall paintings or other interior elements were covered with white paint, and the old order of church benches was replaced with open structures disconnected from the social order of the local society.[83]

In Sweden and Denmark, there are many parallels to the development in Norway. The neo-Classic churches were highly criticised during the first half of the nineteenth century and eventually replaced by neo-Gothic style preferences. Leading Swedish architects like Carl Georg Brunius (1792-1869), Adolf Wilhelm Edelsvärd (1824-1919), Lars Israel Wahlman and Helgo Zettervall (1831-1907) all supported the idea of 'the hitherto unmatched medieval art of building temples' (Brunius).[84] The result was a large number of impressive neo-Gothic Lutheran state churches all over Sweden.

What about 'the old'?

With the Scandinavian Lutheran state churches sticking to the strategies of confessionalisation, aestheticisation, and modernisation – what about the problem of 'the old', the old churches with references to church history and older aesthetic preferences? In the national awakenings of the nineteenth century the material heritage was addressed, not least the medieval parts of it, while post-Reformation churches were not left much honour or attention. The investigation and revitalisation of the medieval past, on the other hand, was left with private organisations, museums, architects, politicians and academic research. The revival movements did not address questions of material cultural heritage, and there was – with a few exceptions – little room for such questions in the debates within the state churches.[85]

In Norway, the mortal blow on many of the old churches was the law of 1851, starting an broad scale modernisation process of local churches. This process called, however, for action from concerned citizens on a national level. In 1844, the National Trust of Norway (Foreningen for norske Fortidsmindesmærker Bevaring) was established, supported by artists, civil servants and academics. This organisation took part in public debates arguing the cultural value of preserving the nation's material culture, not least the stave churches. The Trust ended up with buying some significant medieval churches, thus preserving them for the future. This strategy was not rooted in a concern for the future of the Lutheran church of Norway, but in a strategy focusing on the medieval heritage of the young Norwegian nation. The most important Norwegian example of this process is the cathedral of Trondhjem. For centuries, this church had been regarded by historians as the most important symbol of the heroic national past of a country that only in 1814 had regained its cultural and in-

2.4-21 *The Western Fredrikstad church, Norway, built 1880, photograph from 1905.*
[Østfoldmuseene, Østfold fylkes billedarkiv]

82 Dehli, *Fredrikstad bys historie*, III, 127ff; Klavestad, *Arkitekturen i Fredrikstad*, 125ff.
83 Sørmoen, *1700-tallet*, 42ff.
84 Lindahl, *Högkyrkligt, lågkyrkligt, frikyrkligt*, 63-130.
85 Amundsen, "Pastoralt kulturminnevern".

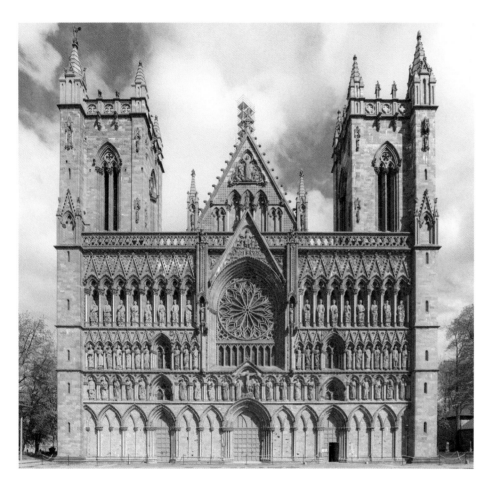

2.4-22 *The cathedral in Trondhjem after the extensive restoration, photograph of the western part of the church, unknown date.*
[Wikimedia Commons; photo 2015]

tellectual independence. In the constitution of 1814, the Trondhjem cathedral was appointed the future venue for royal crowning ceremonies. Accordingly, the political debate ended in 1869 by declaring the cathedral a national monument that was in urgent need of reconstruction. In the following decades the cathedral was rebuilt and reconstructed, all elements of post-Reformation church furnishing were removed, and the search for the tombs of St Olav and other medieval Norwegian kings started.[86] [Ill. 2.4-22]

With Norway and the Trondhjem cathedral project as the perhaps most striking Scandinavian example, a last development of the religious material culture can be identified. The Middle Ages and the material symbols of the glorious religious past were nationalised and made part of new national narratives of self-conscious Scandinavian nations. This strategy was not part of the Pietist or confessional debates over piety, church or-

ganisation or religious territorial control. On the contrary, the debate over national heritage presupposed a de-confessionalisation of history and of medieval churches: they were not focused as remnants of a Roman Catholic past, but of a past national glory.

Urban and rural religious material landscapes – some concluding remarks

Nineteenth-century Scandinavia was a vibrant laboratory for new religious expressions, uses of history, and competitions over territorial landscapes. The Lutheran state churches attempted to sustain their social and cultural control based on the old territorial system for religious belonging and devotion. To demonstrate their historical and aesthetical superiority, the state churches of Scandinavia developed strategies for building dominant, impressive churches according to new aesthetic preferences. This strategy was, however, not convincingly successful in the new religious market. The religious Pietist awakenings and the intrusion of new, dissenting religious groups and churches nurtured new ideals of religious community, social interaction, and non-territorial belonging. The religious material landscapes in Scandinavia that developed were shaped by believers following a preacher, searching for their equals. Their material culture was linked to houses built at their own cost and furbished according to their aesthetic preferences. Their main occupation was the success of the Divine Word preached and interpreted by authorities appointed by them and supported by a local group. Especially in rural districts the new religious material landscape framed close communities different from the territorial communality of the pre-modern society.

In the new urban religious material landscapes the competition between the different churches and groups was more explicit and the boundaries between the close communities of believers more fluent. Free preachers, non-Lutheran denominations and inner mis-

86 Ekroll, ed., *Katedralbyggerne*.

sion societies formally loyal to the Lutheran state churches built new buildings and symbolic territories. This competition had different levels and dimensions. To some of the most radical groups, like the Baptists or the more successful free preachers, the references to traditional Lutheran churches was of no relevance.[87] Instead, their models were taken from Anglo-American 'tabernacles' and assembly halls with the charismatic religious leader as the main person. That demonstrated the otherness and the radical critique of the existing religious material culture. Others, e.g. the Methodists, were more discretely copying the neo-Gothic style, thus referring both to the new churches of the Lutherans and to English Methodist chapels – with one, important difference: the Methodist churches did not have belfries. Even the Roman Catholic churches came to influence some of the larger Scandinavian cities. These churches had belfries, thus also competing over the urban 'soundscapes', and they dedicated their churches to old national saints, and especially in Norway they actively connected their churches to medieval church architecture. Among the nineteenth-century dissenters, the Roman Catholics were the most conscious of tradition and history, so their attempts at appropriating the national medieval legacies can be interpreted as a territorial re-claiming of Scandinavia.

To conclude: during the nineteenth century the physical and symbolic structure of the religious material landscapes in Scandinavia was profoundly changed. The church geography of Scandinavia in 1900 was radically different from the church geography of the year 1800.[88] Many dimensions have been important here. Demography changed radically, with an increasing part of the population living in cities. The urban population had important groups of immigrants and of people bringing with them religious impulses from other parts of the world. With new impulses, also in the Lutheran state churches, ideology changed, and the quest both for confessional identities and new aesthetic expressions of these identities was raised.

Economically, the building of new Lutheran churches represented a new willingness to spend money on modernisation of the state churches – not by the state itself, but by the local authorities who were in charge of the church buildings. That demonstrates a fact that can easily be overlooked; namely that the absolute majority of Scandinavians stayed loyal to their state churches during the nineteenth century. The new ideologies, however, both among leading representatives of the Lutheran state churches, national politicians, architects and artists, were responding to overarching changes in demography and social structures. Urbanisation and industrialisation created a rapidly growing working class, and it was especially over these groups the religious battles were fought. The winners were the dissenters and the Pietist inner mission groups, who had a broader appeal to the workers and perhaps also a simpler access to them. The Lutheran state churches had one complication compared with the newcomers in the religious market places, i.e. to find the balance between historical legacy and urgent change, a question that always is connected to a historically embedded religion like Christianity.

Given all these processes of change, it is difficult to decide which were the driving forces in the field of religion and in the religious markets of the nineteenth century. Especially when it came to representatives of the state churches and of the national political level, leading forces were united in their defence of the Lutheran legacy and the state church structures. In the actual choices of aesthetical expressions and of strategies for 'winning souls', however, the interaction between the competing Lutheran state churches and the dissenters and Pietist organisations seems to have been quite close.

In nineteenth-century Scandinavia the differences between urban and rural religious material landscapes became more explicit, but in general the century was dominated by an increasing competition on religious modernisation, aesthetics, visibility and cultural capital.

87 Hellspong, *Korset, fanan och fotbollen*, 86.
88 Nordbäck, "Trons mötesplatser".

BIBLIOGRAPHY

Literature

Achen, Henrik von. "Fighting the disenchantment of the world: the instrument of medieval revivalism in nineteenth-century art and architecture". In: Henning Laugerud and Salvador Ryan, eds. *Devotional Cultures of European Christianity, 1790-1960*. Dublin, 2012, 131-154.

Amundsen, Arne Bugge. "'Naar Stormen kommer, tager Fuglen afsted'. Erik Tønnesen og indremisjonen i Fredrikstad-distriktet 1850-1880". *MindreAlv*, 5 (1992-1993), 51-74.

Amundsen, Arne Bugge. "The devotion of the simple and pure: devotional culture in the Haugean movement in Norway, 1796-1840". In: Henning Laugerud and Salvador Ryan, eds. *Devotional Cultures of European Christianity, 1790-1960*. Dublin, 2012, 13-33.

Amundsen, Arne Bugge. "En demokratisering av kirkerommet? Norske kirker på 1800-tallet". *Fortidsminneforeningen*. Årbok, 2013, 91-110.

Amundsen, Arne Bugge. "Reformed Church Interiors in Southern Norway, 1537-1700". In: Lars Ivar Hansen et al., ed. *The Protracted Reformation in Northern Norway: Introductory Studies*. Stamsund, 2014, 73-93.

Amundsen, Arne Bugge. *Enighet og uenighet i 400 år. Kirkene på Langestrand*. Instituttet for sammenlignende kulturforskning. Serie B. Skrifter CLXXI. Oslo, 2018.

Amundsen, Arne Bugge. "Pastoralt kulturminnevern: Gerhard Schøning, Jacob Neumann og Magnus Brostrup Landstad". *Årbok - Foreningen til norske fortidsminnesmerkers bevaring*, 173 (2019), 9-26.

Bedoire, Fredric. *Hugenotternas värld. Från religionskrigens Frankrike till Skeppsbroadelns Stockholm*. Stockholm, 2009.

Befolkningsforholdene i Danmark i det 19. Aarhundrede. Copenhagen, 1905.

Dehli, Martin. *Fredrikstad bys historie*. Vol. 2. Fredrikstad, 1964.

Dehli, Martin. *Fredrikstad bys historie*. Vol. 3. Fredrikstad, 1973.

Ekroll, Øystein. "State Church and Church State: Churches and their Interiors in Post-Reformation Norway, 1537-1705". In: Andrew Spicer, ed. *Lutheran Churches in Early Modern Europe*. Farnham-Burlington, 2012, 277-309.

Ekroll, Øystein, ed. *Katedralbyggerne. Nidarosdomens gjenreisning 1869-2019*. Trondheim, 2019.

Eldal, Jens Christian. *Med historiske forbilder. 1800-tallet*. Kirker i Norge III. Oslo, 2002.

Grydeland, Ane Solvik. *Hadsel kirke 1824-1999*. Stokmarknes, 1999.

Gustavsson, Anders. "Väckelsernas mötesplatser i ett norskt-svenskt perspektiv". In: Arne Bugge Amundsen, ed. *Vekkelsens møtesteder*. Bibliotheca historico-ecclesiastica lundensis, 57. Lund, 2014, 157-169.

Hammelbo, Trygve, ed. *Oslo første metodistmenighet 1865-1945*. Oslo, 1945.

Hellspong, Mats. *Korset, fanan och fotbollen. Folkrörelsernas kulturmiljö i ett jämförande perspektiv*. Stockholm, 1991.

Hundre år i St. Svithuns by 1898-1998. Jubileumsskrift for den katolske menighet i Stavanger. Stavanger, 1999.

Johannsen, Birgitte Bøggild, and Hugo Johannsen. "Re-forming the Confessional Space: Early Lutheran Churches in Denmark, c. 1536-1660". In: Andrew Spicer, ed. *Lutheran Churches in Early Modern Europe*. Farnham-Burlington, 2012, 241-276.

Klavestad, Lars Ole. *Arkitekturen i Fredrikstad. Arkitektur- og byplanhistorien 1567-2017*. Fredrikstad, 2014.

Langhelle, Svein Ivar. "Haugianske møteplasser og samlingsformer med eksempel fra det sørvestre Norge". In: Arne Bugge Amundsen, ed. *Vekkelsens møtesteder*. Bibliotheca historico-ecclesiastica lundensis, 57. Lund, 2014, 77-88.

Larsen, Kurt E. "De 1073 danske missionshuse, deres internationale baggrund og særpreg". In: Arne Bugge Amundsen, ed. *Vekkelsens møtesteder*. Bibliotheca historico-ecclesiastica lundensis, 57. Lund, 2014, 103-116.

Lindahl, Göran. *Högkyrkligt, lågkyrkligt, frikyrkligt i svensk arkitektur 1800-1950*. Stockholm, 1955.

Linstow, Hans Ditlev Frants. *Udkast til Kirkebygninger paa Landet i Norge*. Christiania, 1829.

Lund, Carl. *Porsgrund 1807-1907. Et Hundreaars Minde*. Porsgrunn, 1907.

Lundin, Claës. *Nya Stockholm*. Stockholm, 1887-1890.

Lysaker, Trygve. *Høyalteret i Nidarosdomen*. Småskrifter 11. Trondheim, 1996.

Martling, C. H. "De inomkyrkliga väckelserörelserna under förra hälften av 1800-talet". In: Anders Pontoppidan Thyssen, ed. *Väckelse och kyrka i nordiskt perspektiv*. Skrifter utgivna av Nordiskt Institut för kyrkohistorisk forskning, 1. Copenhagen-Lund-Helsingfors-Oslo, s.a., 155-183.

Nordbäck, Carola. "Trons mötesplatser. Ett kyrko- och väckelsehistoriskt perspektivt". In: Arne Bugge Amundsen, ed. *Vekkelsens møtesteder*. Bibliotheca historico-ecclesiastica lundensis, 57. Lund, 2014, 9-52.

Ørebech, Kai. *Bedehus i Østfold*. Oslo, 2006.

Overgaard, Frands Ole. "Vækkelse og kirke i det egentlige Danmark i det 19. århundrede". In: Anders Pontoppidan Thyssen, ed. *Väckelse och kyrka i nordiskt perspektiv*. Skrifter utgivna av Nordiskt Institut för kyrkohistorisk forskning, 1. Copenhagen-Lund-Helsingfors-Oslo, s.a., 27-52.

Rehnberg, Bertil. "En herrnhutisk plantskola i Göteborg". In: Anders Jarlert, ed. *Arkiv, fakultet, kyrka. Festskrift till Ingmar Brohed*. Bibliotheca historico-ecclesiastica lundensis, 48. Lund, 2004, 149-168.

Rønne, Finn Aa. "Nyevangelismen set med danske øjne". *Dansk Teologisk Tidsskrift*, 81 (2013), 300-319.

Schrøder, Ludvig. *Om Brødremenighedens Betydning for Kirkelivet i Danmark*. Copenhagen, 1902.

Seip, Elisabeth, ed. *Chr. H. Grosch – arkitekten som ga form til det nye Norge*. Oslo, 2001.

Sørby, Hild. "Religiøse forsamlingshus i Stavanger – arkitektur og utsmykning". In: Pål Repstad et al. *Kunst og pietisme. Noen trekk ved den religiøse kulturen i Rogaland*. Stavanger, 1977, 41-87.

Sørmoen, Oddbjørn. *1700-tallet. Skjønnhetens århundre*. Kirker i Norge, 2. Oslo, 2001.

Stiansen, P. *Baptistkirkens historie i Norge. Første del inntil 1880*. Oslo, 1935.

St. Laurentius. Drammen katolske menighet 1899-1999. Drammen, 2000.

Sundbärg, Gustaf. *Sveriges land och folk*. Stockholm, 1901.

Swensen, Grete. *Moderne, men avleggs? Foreningers byggevirksomhet 1870-1940 i formativt perspektiv*. Oslo, 1997.

Thyssen, Anders Pontoppidan. *Herrnhuter-Samfundet i Christiansfeld*, 1-2. Aabenraa, 1964.

Walan, Bror. "De utomkyrkliga väckelserörelserna under senare hälften av 1800-talet". In: Anders Pontoppidan Thyssen, ed. *Väckelse och kyrka i nordiskt perspektiv*. Skrifter utgivna av Nordiskt Institut för kyrkohistorisk forskning, 1. Copenhagen-Lund-Helsingfors-Oslo, s.a., 184-214.

Digital resources (accessed September 2019)

http://agderkultur.no/pages/kirker/kristiansand-frikirke/kristiansand-frikirke.html

http://danmarkskirker.natmus.dk/vejle/vejle-skt-pouls-kirke/

http://www.artemisia.no/arc/3/omraade/fredrikstad/ridehusgaten.26.html

http://www.artemisia.no/arc/3/omraade/fredrikstad/ridehusgaten.7.html

http://www.artemisia.no/arc/historisk/halden/st.peter.kirke.html

http://www.artemisia.no/arc/historisk/oslo/bygninger/lakkegaten.47.html

http://www.artemisia.no/arc/historisk/skien/skien.metodistkirke.html

http://www.jesuhjertekirke.dk/kirkens-historie/

https://danmarkshistorien.dk/perioder/adelsvaelden-1536-1660/kongens-riger-og-lande/

https://sanktansgar.dk/om-kirken/historien/

https://sv.wikipedia.org/wiki/Sveriges_baptistf%C3%B6rsamling

https://web.archive.org/web/20150402121154/

http://www.kristuskonungen.se/historia.htm

https://www.andreaskyrkan.se/om-andreaskyrkan/historia

https://www.norske-kirker.net/home/ostfold/halden-metodistkirke/

https://www.norske-kirker.net/home/telemark/skien-metodistkirke/

https://www.ssb.no/a/histstat/tabeller/3-1.html

3.
BUILDING AND FURNISHING OF RELIGIOUS ARCHITECTURE

Introduction

Timothy Brittain-Catlin

The most striking characteristic of the design and furnishing of religious buildings across Northern Europe during the nineteenth century was the strong correlation between liturgical and theological reform and the increasingly precise architectural prescription that went with it. This is a process that appears to have started in the United Kingdom of Great Britain and Ireland, a single country from 1801, and it was here that this parallel development was so pronounced that Church and architectural reform became in practice the same thing. The result by the end of the century was that nearly all of the approximately 10,000 parish churches across England alone had been restored, remodelled, or rebuilt and, with countless new buildings constructed for non-Anglican congregations, provide an easily accessible record of the changing political strengths of opposing factions. If the predominant style of new church architecture at the beginning of the century was in Britain overwhelmingly classical, with by the 1820s only a few idiosyncratic Gothic constructions, the precise opposite situation had been reached by 1914 – and the pattern was repeated across the north of the continent.

The fact that this process was at its most pronounced in Britain may be related to the fact that the early decades of the nineteenth century saw a great deal of interest there in positivistic thinking across the sciences, culture and politics in general. Theologians from the rival Christian factions to the established Anglican Church, which were increasingly politically liberated from the late 1820s onwards, took the opportunity of their relatively stable and growing position to investigate the details of religious practice and life. In the case of the Catholic Church, this phenomenon was encouraged by the establishment of new religious institutions – the first since the sixteenth-century Reformation – to prescribe precise ways of living and praying, following the tradition of the Rules of medieval orders. At the same time, architectural writing in Britain likewise encouraged a greatly increased level of precision in design and construction.

In Britain there was also a figurehead for architectural reform who combined a propagandist's zeal with a designer's brilliance, and managed also to be astonishingly prolific during the course of a short working life. A.W.N. Pugin (1812-1852) was a Catholic, or to be more precise a revivalist of the late fifteenth-century English church. As such, he was a member of a small minority in England. The authors in the chapters that follow demonstrate in different ways how the rivalry within and between the factions of the predominant religious denominations threw up distinctive developments in style, layout, furnishing and decoration which, broadly, reached their peak in the third quarter of the nineteenth century; from that point on, influences from other fields of cultural history – specifically, from nationalism, romanticism, symbolism, and other late nineteenth-century movements – began to make an impact on what had previously been arguments primarily between theologians of various types. This was perhaps a reflection of the high prestige and quality of the new churches of this period which in all the countries under consideration here were by now amongst the most sophisticated and expensive buildings in existence, worked on by the finest class of workmen and by designers who may well have been academicians or otherwise leaders in their fields, not to mention mystics, agnostics or perhaps even atheists.

Jens Christian Eldal's chapter explains how Lutherans in Norway, Denmark and Sweden followed different paths across the century: Norwegians remained largely within a national church that was intended to accommodate different factions within a single stream, whereas in Denmark the Lutheran Church took on a different colour depending on the local congregation, and in Sweden there was a marked tendency to split from the mother church altogether. The survival of centralised church plans across the century in all three nations indicated, however, a strong common religious culture; this in time was influenced, sometimes directly, by pastors who joined or rejoined local congregations from evangelical communities overseas, in particular from English Methodism or the United States. But the greatest international impact on the Scandinavian church came arguably from Germany – from the Moravians, and then more specifically from the outcome of a series of conferences held in Germany – the Eisenach Regulativ of 1861. Eldal writes that the Regulativ can be understood as "an Evangelical version of the Ecclesiological programme in England", in that it prescribed the arrangement of spaces and fittings, but by the end of the century that was seen as too Catholic, and was replaced in some circles by another German import, the Wiesbaden Programme of 1891. All nations had their own distinct religious factions – in Denmark, this was the theology of N.F.S. Grundtvig (1783-1872), a feature of which was the social programme and its concomitant building projects around a church.

The German countries constituted a much larger and more diverse religious situation. The picture described by Wolfgang Cortjaens at the beginning of the period is one where romanticism and the picturesque are emerging in buildings of all kinds where a patron wished to instil a feeling of shared past or nationhood; this meant that architects were later prepared to adopt the Gothic style for churches too. As in all the other countries discussed here, the predominant style at the start of the period was classical, or, as Cortjaens explains, the empiricist version of it that admitted adaptation to modern technical methods.

A distinctive element in the development of German church architecture was the degree of centralisation and of secular state control. The establishment in Prussia, the dominant power, of an *Oberbaudeputation*, under Karl Friedrich Schinkel (1781-1841) from 1810, and the transfer of building powers from church consistory courts to a single Prussian ministry meant that an individual person could not only decide church building applications but also design them himself for royal or state commissions. In Bavaria, King Ludwig II could in practice also instigate large new church buildings. The Romanesque or Gothic style was preferred by political patrons for central urban sites where it was important to emphasise the national story: the Englishman George Gilbert Scott did this for the city of Hamburg in 1846. This was a theme that repeatedly emerged, with the newly completed cathedral in Cologne forming the centrepiece of a major complex of infrastructure projects by the end of the century. All this implies a rationalist and national approach to the Gothic style, but Pugin's moral message – that Gothic architecture was inherently Christian – was introduced to the German countries by August Reichensperger (1808-1895) towards the middle of the century.

Schinkel, drawing from Pugin's work in England, placed importance on the relationship of building styles to local stone and brick, and revived craft practices including medieval techniques in Prussia as part of the process of developing and establishing the Gothic style; these sometimes operated on an industrial scale, and by the end of the century German stained-glass windows were common across Northern Europe from

Ireland to Sweden. The German countries built ambitious Romanesque or Gothic religious institutions such as monasteries and convents in some towns; Gothic monuments with religious messages or references were a feature, and crematorium architecture began early in Germany, in 1878.

In the Netherlands too, the predominant style in church building across the century also moved from austere, barn-like interiors, in the case of the Dutch Reformed Church, or Baroque and Rococo, with Dutch Catholics, to 'national' styles. Wies van Leeuwen's chapter illustrates the process, and a case can be made for saying that the transition here was at its most extreme, as the substantial oeuvre of large, ornate Gothic churches designed by Pierre Cuypers towards the end of the century suggests. Cuypers built almost exclusively for Catholic congregations and the centralisation of the national Catholic Church in 1853 had decreed that buildings should be in this style; as elsewhere, Gothic architecture was also intended as a reference to the pre-Reformation Catholic past and as a public statement of loyalty to the nation. New Protestant churches at the start of the century followed familiar models: they were essentially centralised preaching houses with galleries, sometimes octagonal in plan. Once the Gothic style had become associated with new Catholic churches, Protestants began to favour picturesque and Dutch Renaissance styles which were well suited to concentric planning.

As Thomas Coomans explains, the situation in Belgium during the period was fundamentally different because of the near monopoly of the Catholic Church in new church building. This meant that there was no need for a building to take a distinct form in style or layout in order to make a statement about a particular denomination. It was also the country in which Puginism had the most direct impact, thanks to the activities of the English community in Bruges – which published a version of his *True Principles* as *Les vrais principes* – and in particular to the prolific career of Baron Jean-Baptiste Bethune (1821-1894). At the same time, Pugin's emphasis on the revival of medieval arts and crafts struck a chord with adherents of a way of building first proclaimed in 1849 as being the Belgian national style, and the foundation of the Saint Luke Schools in 1863 by Bethune and others resulted in a network that spread across Belgium and in time had an international impact.

If at home Pugin's 'true' Gothic had emphatically been an English style, in Belgium it was the ultramontanes who developed, promoted and enriched it. The great variety of different types of work promoted by the Schools, which included furniture, metalwork and the graphic arts, also meant that the impact of church art was more comprehensive than elsewhere, and the Catholic Party, in power for three decades from 1884, ensured its continuing life and influence. Bethune's Benedictine Abbey of Maredsous, completed in 1890, is the masterpiece of the movement. A further feature of Gothic Belgium was the marriage of archaeology with architectural study. Archaeologists had been involved with the founding of the St Luke Schools; the relationship was cemented by the important role played in the Royal Commission on Monuments by Joris Helleputte (1852-1925), a Gothic architect with a more progressive attitude to modern materials and processes after the example of E.E. Viollet-le-Duc. Overall, the story from Belgium provides a vivid illustration of the ways in which groups of the most industrious and hardworking of men, from many backgrounds, used their vision and commitment to transform the history of architecture across half a continent, or more.

Inside View of the Altar End.

Outside View of St. Peter's Chapel, Winton.

NORMAN DOORWAY LEADING TO THE CHAPEL, FROM ST. PETER'S STREET.

3.1
The Pugin Revolution and its Aftermath
The United Kingdom and Ireland

Timothy Brittain-Catlin & Roderick O'Donnell
with a section on stained glass in Ireland by Caroline M. McGee

The story of reform in British nineteenth-century architecture as a whole – far-reaching, richly varied and heterogeneous as it was – is indistinguishable from the story of the material reform of religious architecture. For some thirty years from the launch of the 'true' Gothic Revival in the mid-1840s, the most prestigious and best-endowed new or substantially restored buildings were religious ones. Their architects saw themselves as being part of a movement of religious reform and identified themselves with factions within it. To a remarkable extent, religious reform is part of the overall history of British architecture – possibly evidence not only of the Erastian nature of the Church of England, but also of the assimilation of Catholics into English culture and of the deep local roots of many Nonconformist denominations. In the words of Andrew Saint, "Churches were the most important buildings the Victorians built".[1]

Furthermore, the integral design of furnishing and fittings, down to the smallest detail, was inherent in the architectural reform movement of mid-century: this was a central part of the pervasive message of Augustus Welby Northmore Pugin (1812-1852), the dominant figure, even beyond his death, for most of the century. Consequently, new, restored or rebuilt churches and other religious buildings were often fitted out with objects that in prestigious cases had been especially designed for them, or were otherwise designed by architects and artists, as part of a coherent design scheme. Members of the ecclesiological movement, described in section 1 above, believed that the revival of medieval architecture and craftsmanship was an essential part of liturgical and spiritual rebirth. In their most popular text, which immediately ran to new and ever longer editions, they exhorted church builders and restorers to "LET EVERY MATERIAL BE REAL": the implication of this, in the light of Pugin's writings, was not only that every individual construction material should be what it appeared to be, but also that it should blatantly *express* that authenticity, and indeed the practical purpose to which it was deployed.[2] Certainly by mid-century it seemed inconceivable to the architects of churches that internal fittings or even other aspects of liturgical life such as vestments or music should be inconsistent with their idea of the building as a whole, or, for that matter, with their entire concept of what any building should be like. For the most part, there was little correlation between a specific medieval style and a religious denomination: what began, for example, as the 'Catholic' Gothic style was propagated at first by Pugin for his Catholic commissions and thereafter by High-Church Anglicans, but critical developments and fashions in the style were the result of architectural debate rather than liturgical or religious ones. It was the increasing commitment of large sums of money to church-building during the course of the nineteenth century that in turn contributed to the arts and crafts movement in architecture, often seen as the most internationally influential aspect of British design up to recent times.[3]

3.1-1 St Peter's Catholic chapel, Winchester (1792), by James Cave (1798). [Hampshire Record Office]

1. Saint, "The Late Victorian Church", 7.
2. [Neale], *A Few Words to Church Builders*, 5. See Brittain-Catlin, "Realism in Nineteenth-Century British Architecture".
3. The most recent comprehensive textbook of the course of the Gothic Revival in British culture is Brooks, *The Gothic Revival*. The best description of the role of church building and its significance to Victorian life and architecture as a whole remains Girouard, "All That Money Can Buy".

4 For a comprehensive description of eighteenth-century church building see Friedman, *The Eighteenth-Century Church in Britain*. An early scholarly overview of Anglican church planning was Addleshaw and Etchells' *The Architectural Setting of Anglican Worship*.
5 For the Commissioners' churches, see Port, *600 New Churches*.
6 See McParland, "Who was 'P'?".
7 *Dublin Penny Journal*, 29 December 1832, 213.

3.1-2 A contemporary model of the design for the pro-cathedral, Dublin, 1814, by 'P'.
[Dublin, Irish Architectural Archive: 010_073_Rossmore_Contacts_3_010]

Religious architecture and the design of buildings

Protestant architecture in Britain of all denominations, from the established Church of England and 'national' Church of Scotland to the various Nonconformist groups, was at the start of the period very plain in style; they functioned as preaching houses with little regular ritual activity beyond very occasional communion services. Such churches placed pulpit, reading desk and lectern close together, usually centrally, and the altar in a lesser place, often in a shallow apse, as it was not used every Sunday. Private or family pews, or those of town officials, were usually fixed, with lesser benching and finally moveable forms brought out for lesser worshippers such as children. Most of England's approximately 10,000 parish church buildings were medieval in origin, and dilapidated; they had lost their original decorative features, and had been extended or altered unsympathetically, for example to accommodate galleries. After the church-building programme to replace those lost in the Great Fire of London of 1666, and the passing of the 50 Churches Act of 1711 (of which very few were actually built), only a handful of new parish churches, and a small number of private and college chapels had been erected: and although these college chapels were generally fitted out in a grandiose way, and some had altarpieces and heraldic coloured glass, the interiors were whitewashed and sometimes decorated with paintings in frames, if at all.[4] There were few church schools beyond those built in villages following local initiatives, and no church seminaries, monasteries or convents of any kind. Parsons were ordained usually following studies at Oxford and Cambridge colleges, and although these, in common with the 'public' schools (that is, residential private schools run as educational charities) originated in religious institutions, and maintained religious discipline and traditions, they were not diocesan institutions. Legal restrictions controlled the display or religious art and artefacts, which were limited in Anglican churches to the royal arms, and painted texts such as the Ten Commandments; a parson wore academic dress comprising a plain black robe and hood. Funerary sculpture provided the only significant opportunity for the creative arts within most parish churches in England.

Although there was serious study of the Gothic and there were restorations of medieval churches before the 1840s, the classical styles predominated, for example in the many churches erected soon after the passing of the Church Building Act of 1818.[5] James Gibbs's evolution of the porticoed temple cella with tower and spire over the pediment (in the manner of his St Martin in the Fields) was universally applied: Francis Bedford's St John's, Waterloo Road, London (1822-1824), set the tone for many. But neoclassical architects began to experiment with more primitive forms and geometry. One of the most radical was the Catholic pro-cathedral, Dublin, in Ireland, won in competition in 1814 by the otherwise anonymous 'P', with a primitive Greek Doric trabeated, apsed basilica.[6] Irish Catholics gravitated towards classical styles because they reminded them of Rome, a point made by the *Dublin Penny Journal* in 1832, while in England larger classical Catholic church projects at Clifton, Bristol, and Prior Park, Bath, were both left unfinished in the 1840s.[7] [Ill. 3.1-2]

Church reform itself preceded significant material reform by some decades, but when the latter arrived, its impact was sensational. It did not, however, come entirely out of the blue. In 1792, almost immediately after the Catholic Relief Act of 1791 had permitted freedom of worship to Catholics, an antiquary, draftsman and architectural writer called John Carter (1748-1817) designed a chapel in a naive Gothic style in Winchester for John Milner, the Catholic missioner (who later, as a vicar apostolic, founded the Oscott College seminary) [Ill. 3.1-1]; Carter had championed the Gothic as both authentically English and better suited for churches.[8] Although Gothic had made some reappearance mainly in domestic and collegiate architecture and was certainly associated with religious architecture, Carter's view that it was a national style was a relatively new one. For his part, Milner intended his building to be self-evidently different from contemporary Catholic chapels – one that instead spoke of England's pre-Reformation past as his minute description of it in his *History of Winchester* (1798) made clear. Thus this little chapel at Winchester heralded the realisation that Gothic architecture could be talked about in the symbolic and moral terms which suited reformers of all kinds. Over the next fifty years this innovation created an extraordinarily powerful alliance between a more sophisticated and authentic version of Gothic on the one hand, and church reformers on the other. Milner himself used the study of the Gothic to make controversial historical-religious points in much the way Pugin was to do.

Other aspects were at work, too. Both Carter and Milner may have been somewhat ahead of their time, but the outrage they felt at the gratuitous, fashion-oriented despoliation of medieval buildings, for example of the cathedrals at Salisbury, Lichfield, Hereford and Durham by the architect James Wyatt, nicknamed 'the Destroyer', was increasingly shared by many.[9] Furthermore, in the era of the French Revolution, and of a widespread interest in antiquarianism, discussions about the Englishness of medieval architecture cropped up naturally in the many journal articles about the Englishness of everything else, from literature and art to political settlement and history. Perhaps the most significant name to precede the revolution in architecture itself is that of John Britton (1771-1857), the topographical writer and publisher, who has some claim to be considered the father of British architectural history.[10] Through his many richly illustrated serial publications, such as the five-volume *Architectural Antiquities of Great Britain* (1807-1826), Britton strove to circulate among a wide and informed readership unprecedentedly accurate illustrations of medieval, mainly church, buildings in an ordered way, alongside what he called 'scientific' explanatory texts and chronological categorisations.[11] [Ill. 3.1-3] In fact, the impact of Britton's illustrations was considerably enhanced by the contributions made by his occasional collaborator, the French émigré designer Auguste Charles Pugin (1768/9-1832): the latter drew views or measured drawings of damaged or mutilated churches as if they had

3.1-3 Thaon church, Normandy, as if restored, by A.C. Pugin, from John Britton's Architectural Antiquities of Normandy *(1828).*
[Cambridge University Library]

8 Sweet, *Antiquaries*, 59-60, 260-264, 289-299. For Milner's chapel, see Milner, *The History Civil and Ecclesiastical, & Survey of Antiquities of Winchester*, 240-259; O' Donnell, 'From Whitehall Palace to Wigan Pier', 191-194.
9 Sweet, *Antiquaries*, 104-106.
10 For Britton see Ibid, 266-267, 325-330; Brittain-Catlin, *The English Parsonage*, 71-76.
11 'Scientific': Britton, *The Architectural Antiquities of Great Britain*, V, preface, i.

219

been accurately restored. Towards the end of Britton's career, and before the ecclesiological movement, the Oxford Movement, and the Catholic revival had begun to affect the appearance of buildings, it had thus become possible for artists and designers to see how medieval precedents had actually appeared before vandalism or destruction had damaged them. This was a novelty which cannot be overstated, and it opened the way to the full-blown 'true' Gothic revival that followed.

'True' Gothic

'True' Gothic is understood to mean authentically constructed, historically correct Gothic. The use of the word, and of a moral vocabulary in general when describing the design of buildings, are undoubtedly the legacy of Pugin's architect son, A.W.N. Pugin, a figure who loomed so large in the imagination of architects that his influence was inescapable all the way through to the end of our period: to a great extent the story of nineteenth-century church building and furnishing is the story of Pugin, his innovations and his legacy, and even to some extent of opposition to him. The fact that Pugin *fils* knew and understood the historical form and logic of medieval church architecture from his earliest training in his father's drawing school is clearly significant; he understood for example the logic behind the construction of a pointed arch, something not grasped by architects at least until his father, with Britton, had worked it out and illustrated it accurately. He thus grew up at the centre of a circle of antiquaries who were beginning to tell the difference between inherent ornament and applied decoration, and who realised therefore that medieval design was essentially different from that of the various recent attempts at imitating it: real Gothic churches provided a powerful contrast to the superficial 'Gothic' of the Commissioners' churches, with their applied ornamentation, perhaps modelled in cement. But perhaps most significantly of all, Pugin lived and worked at a time when architects were under professional pressure because of the sheer illogicality of much of what they had traditionally been doing. The Georgian architect, used to composing elevations and plans (sometimes in that sequence) on the basis of neoclassical convention knew little about construction, or the structural properties of materials, and in the first decades of the nineteenth century there were several high-profile cases of large new buildings that had failed: the construction of the ambitious new penitentiary at Millbank on a marshy site by the Thames (1812-1821) was constantly impeded by constructional failure, and the career of the Victorian builder Thomas Cubitt was effectively launched when he came to the rescue after architects of London institutions had failed to detail or supervise their buildings properly.[12] Furthermore, the architect now had difficulties both with the incorporation into his structures of many technical novelties that were now rapidly appearing – water closets, and sophisticated heating, kitchen and plumbing installations, for example – let alone working on appropriate designs for new building types altogether such as railways.

All these problems had one point in common: they were based on the lack of rationality and coherence in attempting to solve a design problem. Pugin described this lack of rationality as if it were a kind of moral failure: what he sought above all else was consistency – or in his words, "1st, that there should be no features about a building which are not necessary for convenience, construction, or propriety; 2nd, that all ornament should consist of the enrichment of the essential construction of the building".[13] Churches, fittings or even decorations which evaded a logical correspondence between their physical form and construction on the one hand, and their liturgical and symbolic purpose on the other, were unnatural and thus somehow morally deficient. This point, which was perfectly consistent in a newly positivist age where scientists and writers in all fields were trying to define and describe

12 Russell Institution, c. 1812; London Institution, 1815-1819: Hobhouse, *Thomas Cubitt*, 15-19.
13 Pugin, *The True Principles of Pointed or Christian Architecture*, 1.

specific links and phenomena, is important if one is to grasp the close relationship between architectural reform, and the material reform of church buildings, because of the way in which it provided a common language for both sides. Church reformers, who were paying for buildings, could use the same words as their architects: buildings, in common with belief which allows no dissonance or illogicality, could be 'true'. On both sides this meant that their design and purpose was coherent and consistent in all their aspects. For church-builders the coherence was to be with liturgical needs; for architects, the coherence extended further still to include all the components of the building, in all its aspects, and with no embarrassment about the incorporation of every constructional device that made the building function better: tall roofs and deep eaves for a rainy climate, for example. Following medieval architecture appeared to provide a solution for all these challenges at once. In fact Pugin gave some thought to apparently sacramental aspects of medieval architecture, such as tall church spires and east-facing plans, and tried to find pragmatic as well as symbolic explanations for them.[14] It is consistent with his approach that although he came to prefer a 'decorated' style of Gothic, from fourteenth-century precedents, he was not particularly wedded to the decorative style of any one historic period and moved from one to another without any obvious reason, as did most of his followers; although there were periods in the mid-late nineteenth century when one specific style or another (French, 'decorated', 'perpendicular') was favoured, the result was that the churches of the Gothic Revival between Pugin's lifetime and the rest of the century are full of change and surprise.

Pugin's manifesto was published first in his book *Contrasts*, of 1836 and then again in an enlarged edition in 1841; his more practical books *The True Principles* of 1841 and *An Apology* of 1843 were directed at architects and provided illustrations and simple explanatory texts. These publications were easy to understand, and the language in them pragmatic, and sometimes personal. Pugin also introduced to church architects the architectural vocabulary of medieval worship: sepulchre; sedilia; sacrarium; dossell; and so on. Two articles originally written for the *Dublin Review*, and published in 1843 in a book under the title *The Present State*, describe and illustrate in detail his own church designs, and his convent and other religious buildings: he thus continued Britton's work in the sense of providing modern examples to supplement the old ones, and an argument might thus be made that the process of modernisation in printing and illustration reproduction, and in journalism and readership habits, also contributed to the material reform of religious buildings.

Some broad and easily graspable concepts quickly emerged from Pugin's writings and his own buildings: that materials should be what they appear to be, and that details should function as they appear to function. Similarly, elements such as roofs and towers should explicitly express their construction and purpose: this is the 'realism' that came in time to characterise progressive Victorian architecture;[15] also, "Strange as it might appear at first sight" (in Pugin's own words), medieval architecture could provide a precedent for all new buildings, especially if principles derived from medieval design could be reinterpreted to create unprecedented plans for modern life and labour.[16] Of these basic strictures, the first was influential to the extent that cement renders imitating stone rapidly disappeared from church buildings, and early-mid-century 'true' Gothic churches are built of brick or stone. Thanks in a large part to the propagandising publications of the ecclesiologists, buildings were increasingly becoming 'real'. Pugin experimented with the applied arts in churches, playing an active, first-hand role in the recreation of medieval methods for creating stained-glass windows (the result of a series of disappointments with contemporary craftsmen), encaustic tiles for flooring, and timber and brass fittings. In time he developed strong relationships with manufacturers: his close

14 For example in Pugin, *The Present State of Ecclesiastical Architecture in England*, 14.
15 For 'realism', or 'reality', see Brittain-Catlin, "Realism in Nineteenth-Century British Architecture"; Brooks, *The Gothic Revival*, 305.
16 Pugin, *True Principles*, 1; Id., *An Apology for the Revival of Christian Architecture*, 39.

17 See Fisher, *Hardman of Birmingham*.
18 The range of Pugin's output is described and illustrated by contributors to Atterbury and Wainwright, *Pugin: A Gothic Passion*. Pugin's stained glass has recently been described in detail, with a gazetteer, in Shepherd, *The Stained Glass of A.W.N. Pugin*; his metalwork in Fisher, *Hardman of Birmingham*; and his memorial brasses in Meara, *A.W.N. Pugin and the Revival of Memorial Brasses*. Pugin's own compendium of ecclesiastical design was his *Glossary of Ecclesiastical Ornament and Costume*, first published 1844; see edition of 2013 with introduction by Michael Fisher.
19 Fisher, *"Gothic for Ever"*, 163-218.
20 St Chad's: Foster, *Pevsner Architectural Guides: Birmingham*, 47-52; St Barnabas: Harwood, *Pevsner Architectural Guides: Nottingham*, 50-54. For Pugin's work in the Midlands, see O'Donnell, *The Pugins and the Catholic Midlands*.
21 Pugin, *Present State*, 91-96, plates 7 and 8.

friend John Hardman Junior, whose family firm in Birmingham originally sold brass buttons, made ironmongery and eventually stained glass to Pugin's designs and thus provided much of the catalogue of 'real' items that enabled the Gothic Revival to spread.[17] More expensive or one-off items of church design – memorial brasses, windows, fonts, vestments and so on – were often funded by private donation: for all of these Pugin had himself provided usable models, as indeed he had also for other churchyard structures: memorial crosses and lych-gates, for example.[18] Ecclesiologists, meanwhile, continued to visit and comment upon new buildings and their fittings, providing a continuous commentary that some architects must have lived in dread of. Much of Pugin's work was necessarily cheaply built, since it consisted of providing simple churches for the poor in industrial areas; however, his church of St Giles, in the small market town of Cheadle in Staffordshire, built from 1841-1846 for the Earl of Shrewsbury, provided a model church complete in every detail, including the revival of the Easter Sepulchre and other features of the medieval Sarum rite, which the clergy would never otherwise have seen.[19] [Col. ill. 9]

Pugin also added a number of other factors to the appeal of his version of Gothic beyond its theoretical coherence and practical appeal. He was adopted as architect by Shrewsbury, the political leader of English Catholics, who went on to require that Pugin was chosen as architect for any of the large number of building projects he was associated with as fundraiser, including the cathedrals of St Chad, Birmingham (1839-1841) and St Barnabas, Nottingham (1841-1844), and new houses for the Order of Mercy; some key connections with members of the Oxford Movement also ensured that Pugin was indirectly involved with alterations and furnishing at a handful Anglican parish churches.[20] He designed the first new monastery building in England since the reformation at Mount St Bernard's Abbey in Leicestershire, and this, or at any rate his illustrations of it as he envisaged it complete, must surely too have had lasting impact.[21] [Ill. 3.1-4] Thus, firstly, he established the iconography of English Catholicism and

3.1-4 A.W.N. Pugin's scheme for Downside Abbey, from his *Present State*, 1843. [Cambridge University Library]

High Church Anglicanism for a very long period, at least until the First World War. Secondly, he acquired great knowledge of the historic forms of church liturgy, designs, and artefacts, aided by a photographic memory; it is a significant part of Pugin's contribution that he himself made designs for every aspect of Catholic worship and thus provided models that could be imitated or copied. Thirdly, his deep involvement with the Palace of Westminster project gave considerable impetus to his revival of medieval crafts, such as the recreation of encaustic tiles, metalwork and stained-glass windows, making manufacture of these items on a large scale viable and increasing their availability and prestige.[22] Finally, the most distinct characteristics of his own house – the practical plan, the central staircase hall, the distinctive detailing for different rooms and their expression externally, brought to perfection at the rectory at Rampisham in Dorset (1846-1847) [Ill. 2.1-8], appeared very fast in other parsonage houses of similar scale right across the country.[23] Far less well known are Pugin's innovative plans for other religious buildings: the elongated corridors and cloisters that he designed even for cheap buildings, such as the Convents of Mercy in Handsworth outside Birmingham (1840/1844-1845), Liverpool (1841/1847 onwards), Nottingham (1844 onwards) and, especially, at Cheadle (1848), with their theatrical axiality and strong differentiations in the detailing and form of rooms and routes, suggest an attempt to interpret in an exaggeratedly positivistic way the Mercy Order's recent Rule and its programme for living.[24] Although published as bird's eye views in *Present State*, the idiosyncratic internal arrangements of these institutions must have remained unknown even to Pugin's architect admirers and their plans were not published; unlike many other features of his work they were apparently never imitated by other architects.

Beyond Pugin

Just as the success of the 'true' Gothic Revival endangered or ended the church-building careers of some pre-Gothic church designers, it also turned its back on experimentation with new materials that had, for example, created some memorable results in cast iron in some of the Commissioners' churches.[25] Pugin, a convert, exercised great personal influence over some of the most prolific Victorian architects, including Anglican imitators as his message was transposed through the Cambridge Camden Society.[26]

The result of all this was that by mid-century, it was already unusual for a new Anglican or Catholic church not to follow medieval Gothic precedent as far as the budget allowed; that included, for example, the revival of the east-west orientation for new churches wherever possible, and the reintroduction of rood screens and medieval layouts and furnishing for chancel areas. The restoration of nearly all of England's parish churches, often with new towers and restored tracery, established the image of the rural church at the heart of its village in precisely the way romantic and political writers at the start of the century had wanted to happen; and inside, parsons sympathetic to ecclesiology dismantled private, rented pew enclosures and replaced them with public open benches, which were now available to good quality standard designs. Thus material reform served not only church reform, but to some extent social reform, and changes in popular piety too. In cities, even the cheapest Gothic church would stand out from the flat-fronted terraces that invariably surrounded it. George Gilbert Scott (1811-1878) (who worked on the restoration of over thirty cathedrals and major churches), his former pupils, especially George Edmund Street (1824-1881), and the many others who followed them, built, altered or restored thousands of churches which often attracted professional attention through publications such as the *Builder*. Of Scott himself it has been said that his mature churches and restorations

22 Wedgwood, "The New Palace of Westminster".
23 Brittain-Catlin, *The English Parsonage*, 153-157, 255-261.
24 Brittain-Catlin, "A.W.N. Pugin's English Convent Plans".
25 For cast-iron churches, see Saint, *Architect and Engineer*, 71-75. A fine example is St George's Everton, by the iron founder John Cragg, 1813-1814, for which see Ibid., 73-74, and Sharples, *Pevsner Architectural Guides: Liverpool*, 264-267.
26 For a series of contributions by scholars on the subject of the influence of the Cambridge Camden Society, see Webster and Elliott, "The Church As It Should Be".

3.1-5 All Saints', Margaret Street, London, an ideal town church, by William Butterfield, 1849-1859.
[© Keith Diplock]

3.1-6 St James the Less, Pimlico, London, by G.E. Street, 1859-1861.
[© Jim Linwood]

27 Stamp, "George Gilbert Scott and the Cambridge Camden Society", 173-174.
28 Cook and Wedderburn, *The Works of John Ruskin*, XI, 229, quoted in the course of a description of the church in Brooks, *John Ruskin and Victorian Architecture*, 110.

"more fully exemplify the principles of the Cambridge Camden Society, perhaps, than the work of any other architect".[27] William Butterfield (1814-1900) was the favoured architect of the Cambridge Camden Society and the Anglican High-Church movement in general. His All Saints', Margaret Street (1849-1859), in central London, with its characteristic expressive coloured brickwork was created as a *Gesamtkunstwerk* of the applied arts; it moved Ruskin to say "Having done this, we may do anything".[28] [Ill. 3.1-5] This was an urban church designed for a cramped site, and Street likewise provided models for town or suburban churches in different settings, notably St James the Less in Pimlico (1859-1861), a building which exemplifies Pugin's 'realist' constructional principles in an expressive way that seems to exaggerate the weight of the brick or stonework carried by their piers and arches.[29] [Ill. 3.1-6] The 'town church' type was also explored by A.W.N. Pugin at St Mary's Liverpool (1844-1848/9) and by E.W. Pugin at Our Lady of La Salette (1859-1860) Liverpool.

In common with ecclesiological principles, new churches generally included all distinct medieval features – a chancel, porches, side-chapels, and so on – even where space was limited. They avoided post-medieval interventions such as galleries, which ecclesiologists had described as "UNDER ANY

CIRCUMSTANCES… TOTALLY INADMISSABLE": organs were now being placed wherever possible in a north chancel aisle rather than symmetrically on the west side as had been the case in late Georgian churches.[30] Pugin's own style was closely imitated by the two Hansom brothers, Joseph (1803-1882) and Charles (1817-1888), who built many Catholic churches and institutions over a career of some thirty years; by William Wilkinson Wardell (1823-1899); and, initially, by his oldest son and successor E.W. Pugin (1834-1875).

The Episcopal Church in Scotland adopted the same 'true' Gothic style for new churches and institutions from mid-century onwards: the masterpiece of the style in Scotland is the three-spired St Mary's Cathedral in Edinburgh (1874-1917), won in competition by Scott and completed by his son John Oldrid Scott (1841-1913) long after the father's death to his design; it dominates the late neoclassical streetscape of the 'Third' Edinburgh new town of the 1820s. It is worth noting also that substantial parts of some major medieval Gothic buildings – for example the chapter house and north transept of Westminster Abbey in London – owe their currently form entirely to nineteenth-century restoration works, in those specific cases by two consecutive surveyors to the fabric, Scott (from 1849-1878) and John Loughborough Pearson (1817-1897; surveyor, 1878-1897) respectively.

Anglican 'Anglo-Catholics' also created some extravagantly rich interiors in poor areas, often with an Early French Gothic feel to them both inside and out; the red-brick churches of James Brooks to the north-east of the city of London were originally like this, with a continuous volume to nave and chancel topped by a fleche. The church of St Bartholomew, Brighton (1872-1874), designed by Edmund E. Scott and one of a series of High-Church missions in the town established at his own cost by Rev. Arthur Wagner, provided an extreme example of this phenomenon even in its unfinished state: this is a tall, narrow, massive building over

41 metres high, with a lush, mystical interior, dominating the urban scene by the railway station. Interior fittings were by the arts-and-crafts architect Henry Wilson, and in a glittering, swirling, Art Nouveau style.[31] [Ill. 3.1-7] In Scotland the Episcopalian church of St Salvador (1865-1875) of George Frederick Bodley (1827-1907), although a small building, would once have had a similar effect. Bells hung in the many bell towers, sometimes the gift of private donors, extended the presence of the new church building further. Even in the evangelical wing of the Church of England, Gothic could be uncoupled from any connotation of 'popery' by certain architects such Bassett Keeling, and E.B. Lamb whose unorthodox plans, under great, beetling roofs, still centred on the pulpit. Buildings by these architects are composed, mainly, of Gothic elements, but the results were unconventional, sometimes with a frenzied appearance; the architectural historian H.S. Goodhart Rendel, writing in the mid-twentieth century, named them 'rogue architects', and the name has stuck.[32] The common nomenclature in describing these styles and phases originates in fact largely in the mid or late twentieth century: Nikolaus Pevsner's term 'High Victorian' architecture was defined and developed by Stefan Muthesius (1972).[33]

3.1-7 *The interior of St Bartholomew, Brighton, by Edmund E. Scott, furnished by Henry Wilson and others, from 1899. [Wikimedia Commons; photo 2019]*

29 See Crook, *The Architect's Secret*.
30 In [The] Cambridge Camden Society, *Church Enlargement and Church Arrangement*, 7; quoted in Webster, "Absolutely Wretched"', 7.
31 Antram and Morrice, *Pevsner Architectural Guides: Brighton and Hove*, 52-54.
32 Goodhart-Rendel, "Some Rogue Architects of the Victorian Era".
33 Muthesius, *The High Victorian Movement in Architecture*.

34　de l'Hopital, *Westminster Cathedral and its Architect*, II, 453-455, 523, 538.
35　Ibid., I, 129-130; II, 564-565.
36　See Hall, *George Frederick Bodley*.
37　Allingham and Radford, *William Allingham*, quoted in *Country Life*, 2 November 1907, 639.

3.1-8 *The Catholic church of Holy Rood, Watford, by J.F Bentley, 1889-1900, drawn by Raffles Davison in 1890. [London, Royal Institute of British Architects: RIBApix, RIBA22429]*

Beyond Pugin: the revival of medieval artefacts

High-Church Anglican patrons were more sympathetic than Catholics to some medieval customs – for example the reintroduction of chancel screens, which Pugin had supported but for which he found little sympathy among Catholic clergy. In fact notwithstanding his early death at the age of 40 in 1852, the influence of Pugin's personal style and strictures continued as far as, or even beyond, the end of the century in the work of, for example, Pearson; and Bodley, whose church of All Saints', Jesus Lane, Cambridge (1863-1870) is frankly Puginian. This extended to the vision of a church interior fitted to the last detail in accordance with the architect's concept of the church building as a whole. One of the finest examples of a late *Gesamtkunstwerk* in a Catholic church can still be found at Holy Rood, Watford (1883-1890), by John Francis Bentley (1839-1902), the most meticulous of Pugin's Catholic heirs. [Ill. 3.1-8] Bentley designed widely in the applied arts, notably metalwork, organ-cases and stained glass, passing through various artists and stained glass manufacturers such as N.H.J. Westlake for painting, in conjunction with Lavers and Barraud for stained-glass, but at the chapel of Our Lady of Perpetual Succour (1885) of W.W. Wardell's church at St Mary's, Clapham, he kept in his own hands not only the design but the cartoon-making, the glass cutting and colouring of the glass.[34] He was also a notable designer of electric lights pendants at Watford; those in Westminster Cathedral (always intended for electric lighting) are by the successor firm Bentley, Sons and Marshall.[35]

Bodley has, retrospectively, been reinstated as the figure who spanned between the early 'true' revival and the final developments of it.[36] He had been Scott's first pupil in the late 1840s; later, he was connected with William Morris and the Pre-Raphaelite circle of artists whose work – for example windows by Edward Burne-Jones and Dante Gabriel Rossetti – featured in his churches, and on occasion, for example in Cambridge, and at St Michael and All Angels, Brighton, the work of these designers added an unexpected degree of modern piquancy to the medievalism of the overall design: of Rossetti a contemporary remarked that "he must have strong savours, in art, in literature, in life. Colours, forms, sensations are required to be pungent, mordant".[37] Bodley himself lived long enough to act as supervisor after the competition to design a new Anglican cathedral for Liverpool was won by the very young Giles Gilbert Scott (1880-1960) in 1903, the largest cathedral in England and a

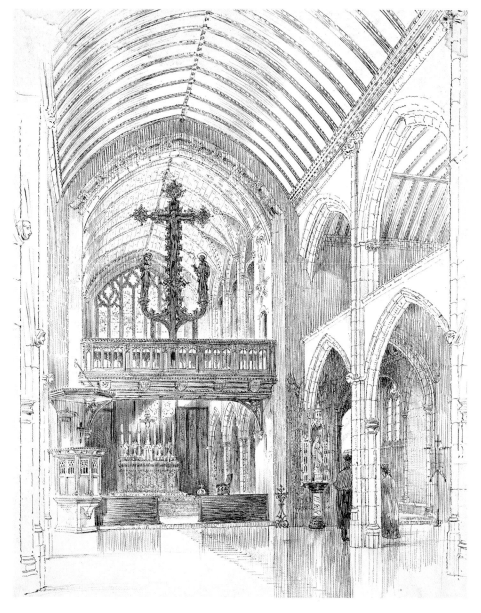

massive project which continued the Gothic Revival through to the last quarter of the twentieth century; that in turn meant that the life of the Gothic crafts was extended yet further too.

The effect of all this on church architecture and artefacts was comprehensive over the course of the nineteenth century as a whole, but it was not immediate. In some areas there was active, or even violent, opposition to the revival of medieval ritual and the associated artefacts, for example the use of the surplice, and at least in one Cornish parish a procession outside a church was attacked. A specific medieval feature that remerged in the Victorian church was that of the iconographic cycle: for the first time since the Middle Ages, churchgoers would now encounter sets of images in glass or stone across the church fabric. An unusually potent example of this can be found at the Anglican cathedral of St Fin Barre at Cork in Ireland, the only building designed and won in competition by the Gothic designer William Burges that was actually executed as he intended.[38] Here a series of statues of the apostles decorates the north portal, and of the wise and foolish virgins, and their bridegroom, the western one. Burges' earthy interpretation of medieval traditions can also be seen in the fine series of misericords in the church of St Michael and All Angels in Brighton, a building he greatly extended.[39] Several craftsmen established names for themselves as suppliers of iconographic ornament to churches; Bodley himself was instrumental in the establishment of the firm of Burlison and Grylls in 1868, and of that of his former pupil Charles Kempe (1837-1907), who designed glass for some eight cathedrals. Clayton and Bell, active from 1853, were a further significant name in this craft: they provided windows for Pearson's Truro Cathedral, as well as for Gothic Revival churches abroad.[40] [Ill. 3.1-9] Clayton and Bell made painted cycles at St Michael, Garton-on-the-Wolds, Yorkshire (1865); so did Hardman and Co, at St Peter, Hascombe, Surrey (1890). Hardman's painter was Alphege Pippett, who also decorated E.W. Pugin's Catholic church of All Saints, Barton-on-Irwell, Lancashire, depicting the architect holding the plan of the church together with his noble patrons; compared to similar work of the Continent, however, the lack of an academic or atelier-based teaching was telling.

As we have seen with Bentley, dissatisfaction with all such firms led architects to reproduce their designs themselves. Bodley, together with his partner Thomas Garner and George Gilbert Scott junior, set up the furnishing firm Watts and Co in 1874. By the end of our period, the Gothic style, and the English idea of the medieval fitting out of it, were almost unchallenged in Anglican architecture, and were seen as models by American and other Anglophone churches – indeed, in the case of the British Empire, architects and their designs were exported directly: a recent study has tracked the eventual spread and development of the imagery of Puginian Gothic across the British Empire, especially in Tractarian hands, reaching for example the city of Christchurch in New Zealand where George Gilbert Scott senior

38 Lawrence and Wilson, *The Cathedral of St Fin Barre at Cork*; Crook, *William Burges*, 160-178.
39 Antram and Morrice, *Pevsner Architectural Guides: Brighton and Hove*, 48-51; Crook, *William Burges*, 181-186.
40 Harrison, *Victorian Stained Glass*.

3.1-9 Stained glass (Clayton & Bell, 1880s) in the church of St Remigius, Water Newton, Huntingdonshire. [© Steve Day]

41 Bremner, *Imperial Gothic*.
42 Sladen, "Embellishment and Decoration, 1696-1900".
43 See Ward-Jackson, "Accommodating Ritual Display".
44 O'Donnell, "The Chapel of St Patrick's College, Maynooth".
45 O'Donnell, "The Pugins in Ireland". For Cobh, see Wilson, "Material and Visual Culture".
46 Elliot, *Art and Ireland*, 307.

himself designed the Anglican cathedral in 1858.[41] A lengthy debate about how to decorate St Paul's Cathedral in London involved architects such C.R. Cockerell, F.C. Penrose, Burges, Bodley and Garner, and painters and sculptors; and there was considerable discussion about the role of stained glass, fresco and mosaic in church architecture. Where decoration was carried out in an Italianate style, much artistic and church-party posturing followed; and the actual results, as in the earlier debate about the decoration of the Houses of Parliament, were widely considered to be unsatisfactory.[42] By contrast, the English tradition of commemorative statuary in churches, one of the many medieval arts reconverted to the Gothic style by Pugin, flourished during the same period.[43]

Beyond Pugin in Ireland

Catholic Ireland followed the Pugin revolution but before 1850 often without the resources to finish yet alone decorate churches. His Killarney Cathedral (1842) was completed by J.J. McCarthy, E.W. Pugin, and Ashlin and Coleman to 1912. McCarthy also built the chapel at Maynooth (1875-1880) which had been omitted from Pugin's scheme. Furnishings often came a generation later (at Maynooth in 1890-1891).[44] Much furniture and stained glass was imported, from Belgium, France and Italy, as well as ordered from English firms such as Hardman and Company, who set up a Dublin branch in 1853. English architects received important commissions, even cathedrals – such George Goldie's Cathedral of the Immaculate Conception at Sligo (1867-1874); E.W. Pugin set up an Irish partnership with his brother-in-law George Ashlin, of which the Cathedral of St Colman at Cobh (1859-1916) is the outstanding result.[45] [Ill. 3.1-10]

By 1900 there was a reaction against this culture as something foreign and its decoration mass-produced; recourse to early Irish models and Irish manufacture was recommended. The Gothic Revival was dismissed as littering the countryside with "the angular spires of Puginism".[46] Daniel O'Connell was reburied in 1869 and was commemorated under a massive Irish round tower at Glasnevin cemetery, but so direct a quotation of Irish forms would not serve for the large scale required for Catholic churches. They were, however, suitable for some Protestant ones: an early example is W.H. Lynn's St Patrick, Jordanstown, County Antrim (1865-1868). Artistically, this 'Irish Revival' was more successful in the applied arts, for example the fittings and decoration of the Honan Hostel chapel in Cork (1915-1916) – a contested space, as the chapel, designed for the use of Catholic students only, had to

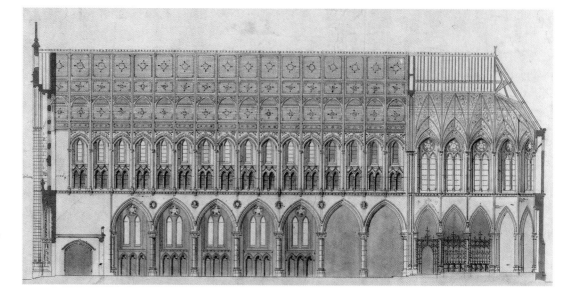

3.1-10 A section through St Colman's cathedral, Cobh (then Queenstown), by Pugin & Ashlin, 1869.
[Dublin, Irish Architectural Archive: 0076_001_B_06]

be just beyond the boundary of the non-denominational government-funded university college.[47] But the standards of the Honan hostel were too expensive to translate into practice elsewhere, except in metalwork, textiles and stained glass (notably by Harry Clarke); this work looks symbolist in European terms.[48]

Stained glass in Ireland
By Caroline M. McGee

Religious reform in Ireland at the midpoint of the nineteenth century drove the expansion of the religious art industry.[49] With increased demand for stained glass in Ireland's 3,000 churches and a paucity of Irish producers, the (Catholic) Irish Ecclesiological Society advised "judicious encouragement" of suppliers from other countries.[50] Thus, some ninety British studios, including the aforementioned Hardman, Burlison and Grylls and Clayton and Bell, went on to make windows Ireland-wide. By the end of the century continental producers, among them Capronnier of Brussels and Lobin of Tours, were active in Ireland; of these, the Munich firm Mayer and Co was the most patronised.[51] In time new Irish firms were founded in Cork, Belfast, and in Dublin and their work gradually eclipsed that of overseas studios.

Some of the earliest church windows were made by English studios, among them William Wailes, William Warrington, and Ward and Nixon.[52] Hardman's commissions followed Pugin's architectural activity in Ireland and led to the establishment of the firm's Dublin branch office. Windows for the Anglican church of St Nicholas at Adare, Limerick, (1850) show the characteristic medievalist figural depictions and vivid, harmonious colours that reflect the success of Pugin's 'true' Gothic style in stained glass design. Taking their lead from Pugin, the Irish architects J.J. McCarthy and George Ashlin employed Hardman for Catholic projects large and small, for example Killarney cathedral (1854); the parish church of St Patrick at Celbridge, Kildare (1858); and multiple orders for St Colman's cathedral, Cobh (1877-1916). From 1895 the studio moved more towards an arts and crafts style as illustrated by the chancel window in the parish church of Charleville, Co. Cork (1902) [Ill. 3.1-11] and nave aisle windows for St Patrick's cathedral, Armagh (1904).

The enamel-like quality of Mayer glass, along with finely drawn figures and towering architectural canopies, appealed greatly to Irish patrons. The firm's work is found in almost four hundred churches throughout Ireland. Early commissions include windows for the Anglican church of St John the Baptist, Eyrecourt, Galway (1867) and a rose window for the Catholic cathedral at Thurles, Tipperary (1869). Some of the studio's finest work however, dates from the final decades of the century when it employed the former Clayton and Bell-trained artists William Francis Dixon (1848-1928) and George Daniels (1854-1940) as studio designers (the former in Munich, the latter based in London). Their work is characterised by delicate facial and figural depictions, animated poses and undulating draperies. Examples include iconographical cycles for the nave of St Colman's cathedral, Cobh (1896-1899) and transept windows for St Patrick's parish church at Trim in Meath (1910). [Ill. 3.1-12]

Cobh cathedral is also home to work by Earley and Co, the studio founded in 1869 by former Hardman employee Thomas Earley (1819-1893). Along with the firm founded by Joshua Clarke, father of the aforementioned Harry, these commercial stained glass studios developed a strong portfolio of Irish clients producing work in a medievalist idiom.[53] Both firms traded well until cultural and religious nationalists began calling for patrons to choose Irish artist-designed stained glass in lieu of windows "from the crude paw of the tradesman".[54] This critique also saw the establishment of An Túr Gloine (The Tower of Glass), Ireland's first studio working in an arts and crafts idiom.[55]

This cooperative group, founded by Sarah Purser (1848-1943) and managed by English

47 O'Connell, *The Honan Hostel Chapel*; Teehan and Heckett, *The Honan Chapel*.
48 Sheehy, *The Rediscovery of Ireland's Past*.
49 Larkin, "Economic Growth".
50 Quoted in Sheehy, *J.J. McCarthy and the Gothic Revival in Ireland*, 12.
51 McGee, "Power, Patronage and the Production of Catholic Material Culture".
52 A digital archive of stained glass in churches of the Anglican communion in Ireland is available at <www.gloine.ie>, last accessed 7 October 2019.
53 Bowe, Caron and Wynne, *Gazetteer of Irish Stained Glass*. Stained glass works in Irish churches are also listed in the Dictionary of Irish Architects <www.dia.ie>, last accessed 7 October 2019.
54 Elliott, *Art and Ireland*, vii.
55 Bowe and Cumming, *The Arts and Crafts Movements in Dublin & Edinburgh*; Bowe, *Wilhelmina Geddes*.

3.1-11 East end chancel window, church of the Holy Cross, Charleville, Co. Cork, by Hardman and Co. (1902).
[© Caroline M. McGee]

3.1-12 South transept window, St Patrick's Catholic church, Trim, Co. Meath, by Mayer and Co., (1902).
[© Caroline M. McGee]

56 Bowe, *The Life and Work of Harry Clarke*.

arts and crafts artist A.E. Child (1875-1939), drew its inspiration from early Christian Irish insular art. The result was a dramatic shift in stained glass aesthetics away from the broadly painterly towards stylised figures and designs verging on abstraction. The group's work includes windows by Child and Evie Hone (1894-1955) in St Brendan's cathedral, Loughrea, Galway (1903-1934) and by Michael Healy (1873-1941) for Ashlin's Clongowes Wood College chapel, Kildare (1916) and SS Augustine and John, Dublin (1934). Windows by Child and Ethel Rhind (1878-1952) in the Honan Hostel chapel, Cork (1914-1916) contrast strongly those of Harry Clarke (1889-1931) whose work is now synonymous with Irish stained glass design. Trained in Dublin and London, Clarke's early precocious talent developed into a signature style of glittering, exotic Symbolist compositions that are found in churches and cathedrals across Ireland.[56] The hot-house aesthetic of his religious stained glass art is very much at odds with the conservative design preferences hitherto demonstrated by Irish patrons.

Nineteenth and early twentieth-century stained glass commissions for Irish churches represent the country's most significant episode of modern religious arts patronage. By the early 1920s the work of Harry Clarke and An Túr Gloine artists had surpassed the achievements of their overseas counterparts whose Irish activity was greatly affected by war in Europe and revolution in Ireland. Mayer was the exception to this pattern and the Bavarian firm received Irish commissions, albeit sporadically, until 1949; the firm continues to work on new and conservation stained glass projects in Ireland to the present day.

230

Liturgical change among English Catholics

From the descriptions above it is possible to see that Anglican worship developed side-by-side with its architecture. The situation regarding Catholics was more closely constrained. At first, both poverty and the habits of worship in secret ensured that Catholic liturgy was performed in the most minimalist fashion – habits Pugin successfully challenged. His antiquarian approach was, however, resented by many, and challenged in the 'Rood Screen Controversy' that followed his design of a double-jube screen for St George's Cathedral, Southwark (1848).[57] Pugin resisted post-medieval developments in the liturgy and popular devotions such that to the Sacred Heart, an iconography which he countered with that of a Risen Christ with his victorious banner. He disliked Benediction, but he did evolve a spired tower reliquary-like monstrance for it. He also evolved the 'Benediction altar', that is, an altar with a tabernacle fixed into a reredos topped with an open niche under a spire, known as a 'throne', but of four-square and modest proportions.

Even this was inadequate for clerical taste, as demonstrated by Wardell's much grander tabernacle-throne-spire at St Mary, Clapham (1849). Wardell provided sedilia at Clapham but not at Holy Trinity, Brook Green, his Hammersmith church (1853-1854), because by then they had been banned by Cardinal Nicholas Wiseman's first provincial synod. An acknowledgment of the thrust of the Counter-Reformation liturgy for basilican plans and generous sanctuaries was in fact first achieved by E.W. Pugin at Our Lady of Salette, Liverpool (1859-1860), hailed as a "complete revolution in church-building".[58] A more scholarly approach was attempted by the Guild of St Gregory and St Luke, associated with the liturgist Edmund Bishop. Its most remarkable expression was in the decoration of Downside Abbey and of Bentley's Westminster Cathedral (see below). Catholics were excluded from the restoration of medieval churches in Anglican hands, but Guild members were involved with the restoration (1874-1878) of the one medieval church passing back to the Catholics, St Etheldreda, Holborn, London where Bentley designed the screen and organ-cases. Such exclusion from restoration activity perhaps explains a certain coarseness in the style of the second generation of Catholic High Victorian architects such Pugin and Pugin (under this title 1875-1928), exemplified by the massive 'Benediction altar' of c. 1885 against the windowless east end of St Francis, Gorton.[59] Peter Paul Pugin (1851-1904), the firm's designer, was A.W.N.'s younger son, and designed in a similar style up to the end of the century.

Other denominations and non-Gothic styles

As section 2 above has made clear, the nineteenth century was an era of continuous church building by Nonconformists as much as by Anglicans and Catholics. In the early days of the 'true' revival, authentic Gothic was considered to be expensive; Pugin dedicated some efforts to disproving this, pointing out for example that a simple brick church could subsequently be extended or decorated just as medieval buildings had been. It seems likely from empirical evidence that in some staunchly Protestant parts of England, the style was also seen as Catholic. For these reasons most Nonconformist buildings, schools and manses, as much as churches, continued at first to be built in simple and cheap neoclassical styles, but in time the logical consistencies of Gothic, and no doubt changing fashion, meant that the use of the Gothic style became acceptable. Probably the only religious groups that almost never built in Gothic were Jews. An early synagogue, that at Canterbury of 1847-1848 by Hezekiah Marshall, is an unusual cement-rendered structure that resembles an Egyptian temple; once the Gothic Revival

57 O'Donnell, "A.W.N. Pugin's Rood Screen".
58 *Tablet*, 1859, 629.
59 O'Donnell, "The Church of St Francis of Assisi".

60 See Kadish, *The Synagogues of Britain and Ireland*.
61 Wakeling, *Chapels of England*; Stell, *An Inventory of Nonconformist Chapels and Meeting-Houses*.
62 Wakeling, "The Nonconformist Traditions", 96.
63 Stell, *An Inventory of Nonconformist Chapels and Meeting-Houses: Eastern England*, 123-124.
64 Sharples, *Pevsner Architectural Guides: Liverpool*, 284-288.
65 Newman, *North East and East Kent*, 441.
66 Stell, *An Inventory of Nonconformist Chapels and Meeting-Houses in Eastern England*, 86.
67 Hall, *Farm Street*.
68 O'Donnell, "Brompton Oratory Revisited".

3.1-13 The octagonal hall of the Congregationalist Union Chapel, Islington, by James Cubitt, 1876-1877.
[© Julian Osley]

was established, however, the largest synagogues are usually in mixed eclectic, vaguely Moorish or byzantine styles; the West London Synagogue (by Davis and Emmanuel, 1869-1870) and the splendid Princes Road Synagogue, Liverpool (W. and G. Audsley, 1872-1874) are both like this, as are the two major places of worship for Sephardi Jews, the Lauderdale Road Synagogue in London (Davis and Emmanuel, 1896), and the Manchester Spanish and Portuguese Synagogue in Cheetham (Edward Solomons, 1873-1874).[60]

Studies of Nonconformist architecture – churches and chapels built for Congregationalists, Unitarians, and the various denominations associated with Methodists and Baptists amongst others – have shown that these organisations built in many different styles over the period, probably in direct reflection of the skills of architect-members and the funds available.[61] Any one town might have at least as many Nonconformist places of worship as it did Anglican churches (or more). In fact the argument has been made that "the chapels of Victorian nonconformity come closer to exemplifying the social variety of the nineteenth century than do the churches of the Anglican establishment" in the styles of their architecture, and neoclassical or simple late-Georgian styles continued for longer than in the case of the Church of England.[62] In general, Congregationalist churches were more middle class in their membership than other Nonconformist denominations, and their architecture more expensive, and more likely to reflect national movements in design. A good example is the centrally planned Congregationalist Union Chapel, Islington, by James Cubitt of 1876-1877 – Gothic in its west front and detailing, but with a large octagonal hall at its centre [Ill. 3.1-13]; Cubitt designed the large Welsh Presbyterian Chapel in Charing Cross Road in Soho, London, in 1888, in a similar fashion but with 'Norman' detailing. The larger Congregationalist churches generally had interiors that resembled auditoria, with horseshoe or elliptical plans and galleries on iron columns, and with organs at the east end; architecturally, they might be seen more as the minor offspring of the Royal Albert Hall (1865). Alfred Waterhouse (1830-1905), a Quaker and perhaps the best-known and most commercially successful Nonconformist architect of the Victorian period, designed one in this form in Mayfair, in an ornamental Romanesque style and expensively clad in red brick and terracotta in 1888-1891.[63] It could be argued that the fact that Nonconformist congregations, in common with evangelical Anglicans, had no objections to galleries around at least three sides of their churches meant that the historical authenticity of the 'true' Gothic architecture was less important to them. A rare example of a Nonconformist church that closely resembled an Anglican one, however, is the Sefton Park Unitarian church, Ullet Road, Liverpool (1896-1899) by Thomas and Percy Worthington, with glass by Burne-Jones, but figurative iconography was confined to ancillary spaces, such as for example the murals by Gerald Moira in the vestry and library of 1902. [Ill. 3.1-14] In this location it vied for architectural prominence with Pearson's St Agnes (Anglican, 1883-1885) a moment away to its west, and Leonard Stokes' free

Gothic St Clare (Catholic, 1889-1890), one block to the north east.[64]

By the end of the nineteenth century some Methodist churches also rivalled Anglican ones, especially in middle-class seaside resort towns where there was some element of competition between denominations: one example of many is the early French Gothic-style Methodist church in Margate, Kent (Drewe and Bower, 1876-1878), described by one historian as "without a doubt the finest Victorian building" in the town.[65] The Catholic Apostolic (or 'Irvingite') church, which had well-heeled supporters, built splendid Gothic churches in Bloomsbury (by Raphael Brandon, 1853), in Edinburgh (Robert Rowand Anderson, 1885) and on a smaller scale in Albury, Surrey (William McIntosh Brookes, 1840), where the funder was Henry Drummond, a patron of Pugin with aristocratic connections. Likewise, the small Agapemonite sect founded and led by H.J. Prince built a richly decorated Gothic church at Clapton in east London, designed by Joseph Morris in 1895.[66] The Greek Orthodox church, now cathedral, of St Sophia, Moscow Road (1877-1882), in a Byzantine style but executed externally in yellow and red brick, is considered by some to be the masterpiece of John Oldrid Scott; similarly, the Lutheran Gustav Adolfs Kyrka in Liverpool, the Swedish seamen's church of 1883-1884, by the English architect W.D. Caröe, is Baltic in style.

The Gothic style was universal for Anglicans and Catholics for the forty years following the publication of *Contrasts* (1836). However, some Catholic architects whose careers had begun before Pugin's, such as J.J. Scoles, built both Gothic and occasional neoclassical churches. Scoles's Gothic-style Jesuit church in Mayfair London, 1844-1849 sidestepped Pugin's liturgical strictures, while his completion from 1844 of Prior College chapel, Bath, completed after his death by his son A.J.C. Scoles in 1871-1882, was achieved as a trabeated and coffer-vaulted neoclassical basilica.[67] Other Catholics favoured Italianate and ultramontane modes of worship, as epitomised by the Oratory founded by Frederick William Faber and John Newman. The chief architectural outcome of this was the Brompton Oratory in South Kensington, won in a competition which specified "the style of the Italian Renaissance" in 1876 by Herbert Gribble but executed in a more blatantly Roman classical style.[68] [Ill. 3.1-15] An earlier

3.1-14 "Time and Truth" by Gerald Moira, Unitarian church library, Sefton Park, Liverpool, completed 1902.
[© Anna Jane Neilsson]

3.1-15 Brompton Oratory, London, by Herbert Gribble: competition design of 1879.
[London, Royal Institute of British Architects: RIBApix, RIBA111528]

3.1-16 Westminster Roman Catholic Cathedral, London, by J.F. Bentley, 1895-1903: exterior and interior view looking towards the liturgical east end. [© Lawrence Lew OP]

69 For a recent overview of Catholic church architecture of the later part of the period, see Howell, "Between Medievalism and the Counter-Reformation". A general illustrated description of nineteenth-century Catholic church-building can be found in Martin, *A Glimpse of Heaven*. St Charles Borromeo: Neave and Neave, *Hull*, 46-48.

70 O'Donnell, "The Interior of St Mary Moorfields [London]".

example is St Charles Borromeo, Kingston upon Hull (1828-1829 by John Earle; 1834-1835 by Scoles; 1894-1896 by Smith and Brodrick), its eclecticism and multi-phasing more typical of Irish developments.[69] The Baroque character of the interiors of both churches comes largely from later decorative schemes.

In all cases, the associations of a given style seem to have been the dominant factor when erecting a new building, for example where Catholics and Nonconformists were rebuilding earlier chapels or reusing certain fittings or monuments. At St Mary Moorfields, London, Wiseman's pro-cathedral, the Corinthian screen, altar and altar piece were retained in the rebuilding (1899-1902) by George Sherrin.[70] These dated from the church (1817-1822) which was sold by Archbishop Herbert Vaughan to raise funds for a cathedral on a site which had been carefully assembled at Westminster. Here he actively avoided the Gothic style of the medieval Westminster Abbey; the resulting Italo-Byzantine Westminster Cathedral (1895-1903), designed by Bentley, itself established a new image for English Catholicism over the following period, and was echoed later on in the many much simpler and cheaper, nominally Byzantine, Catholic suburban churches of the interwar period.[71] [Ill. 3.1-16] Bentley's providential appointment as architect for Westminster Cathedral was due to Vaughan, who by-passed Bentley's clamorous *confrères* and, setting aside previous Gothic schemes, forced Bentley to evolve from Early Christian, Lombardic and Byzantine models into a style that was novel in England. The architect also had to investigate unfamiliar decorative techniques: instead of stained glass and wall stencils he deployed marble revetment, *opus sectile*, and mosaic applied in the 'direct' method, as in the Holy Souls chapel (1902-1904). These decorative techniques were to clothe the interior of the brick and concrete domed structure over time.[72] A further aspect of the pre-Gothic style was that it also made the claim for the Catholic cathedral of Westminster as primitive, and thus historically anterior to the abbey nearby. The Goths were disappointed: Edwin de Lisle, the son of Pugin's close friend and patron Ambrose Phillipps de Lisle, saw the cathedral as "a sort of pre-Heptarchical evolution – Byzantine-Babylonian, bizarre … a megalo-maniac hulk"; and the maverick writer 'Baron Corvo' (Frederick Rolfe) memorably described it as a "pea-soup and streaky-bacon-coloured caricature of an electric light station".[73] But Richard Norman Shaw found it to be "Beyond all doubt the finest church that has been built for centuries", and his former pupil William Lethaby that it "goes altogether beyond stylism … a building serious, serene and really modern".[74] The principal building of the Methodist Church, Central Hall, also in Westminster, was founded to mark the centenary of Wesley's death in 1891. It is located directly opposite the abbey and was therefore, perhaps, for a similar reason to Westminster Cathedral designed in a contrasting style – this time Baroque, by Lanchester and Rickards, mainly commercial and institutional architects. Its ground floor housed a bank.

Scotland and Wales

The wave of church-building in Scotland from the late 1830s was referred to in section 2: the timing of these buildings meant that they were invariably in the pre-'true' Gothic of their period, using Georgian plans, and thus resemble the thin style of the Commissioners' churches in England: the architect James Gillespie Graham, who later worked with the young A.W.N. Pugin, designed over 27 of these, as well as Catholic chapels (later cathedrals) in both Edinburgh and Glasgow.[75] The parish church in Dollar, Clackmannanshire, of 1841 is a representative example of this style, even though it was designed by an English architect, the eclectic William Tite. The 1843 disruption in the Church of Scotland and subsequent further divisions increased the number of church-building bodies: Thomas Chalmers's Free Church of Scotland had established 730 new churches by 1847, designed in increasingly authentic Gothic styles that were representative of their period.

The larger Scottish parish churches – some of them former cathedrals – were in most cases in an advanced state of decay by mid-century: that at Glasgow was in so bad a state that, uniquely, it was taken over by the state, but others underwent a process of restoration comparable to that in England. A fine example of a late Victorian interior within a restored medieval church is that of Dunblane Cathedral, restored by Robert Rowand

71 O'Donnell, "Catholic Church Architecture in England".
72 Rogers, *The Beauty of Stone*; Id., *Reflections on Westminster Cathedral Mosaics*.
73 Purcell and de Lisle, *Life and Letters of Ambrose Phillipps de Lisle*, II, 212-213; Rolfe, *Hadrian*, 36.
74 Saint, *Richard Norman Shaw*, 391; de l'Hopital, *Westminster Cathedral*, I, vii; Howell, *Bentley*.
75 The authoritative study of the early Gothic Revival in Scotland is Macaulay, *The Gothic Revival 1745-1845*, especially 236-239 and 253-274. The book also includes a section on the revival in northern England: 275-294.

3.1-17 St Peter's RC Church, Falcon Avenue, Edinburgh, by Robert Lorimer, 1906-1907, nave completed 1928-1909. [Edinburgh, St Peter's RC Chruch]

3.1-18 Caledonia Road United Presbyterian Church, by Alexander 'Greek' Thomson, 1855-1857.
[London, Royal Institute of British Architects: RIBApix, RIBA6324]

76 Nicholson and Spooner, *Recent English Ecclesiastical Architecture*, 217-220.
77 Sewell, *Two Friends*.
78 For an overview of the Victorian church in Scotland see Stamp, "The Victorian Kirk". For Hillhead, see Ibid, 104.
79 Ibid, 106-107.

Anderson (1834-1921) in 1889-1893, and furnished with fine joinery by Robert Lorimer (1864-1929) in 1912. Lorimer also worked at St Giles' Cathedral, Edinburgh, where he designed and fitted out the Thistle Chapel (1909). Lorimer, like Anderson, had begun his training in Bodley's office, and his sensitivity to Gothic detail drew Pugin's tradition into its final pre-First-World-War form, the free-style arts-and-crafts architecture of the new century; his Catholic church of St Peter, Falcon Avenue, in Edinburgh (1905-1906) is already 'free-style', with its sheer white interior walls and round arches setting off neo-Baroque fittings and altar-pieces by Frank Brangwyn and Glynn Philpot (all since destroyed).[76] [Ill. 3.1-17] This exotic taste was that of two Catholic converts who had been acolytes of Oscar Wilde: John Gray, the founding priest, and Andre Raffalovich, his companion, both of whom paid for the church.[77] The Catholic architect Reginald Fairlie, who briefly trained with Lorimer and who lived until 1952, continued the arts and crafts tradition well into the interwar period.

Within the Presbyterian Church of Scotland an increasingly evident desire to build in the 'true' Gothic was sometimes resolved with the requirement for single auditory space without a chancel or chapels through the skilful reinterpretation of suitable historic models: Belmont and Hillhead parish church in Glasgow, by James Sellars of Campbell, Douglas and Sellars (1875-1876) was based on the Sainte-Chapelle in Paris, with the addition of a west gallery.[78] Only towards the end of the century did it become possible to erect a new Presbyterian church that (but for the gallery) more closely resembled a contemporary English Anglican one: an example is Govan Old Church, in Glasgow (1883-1888), by Anderson, built for a minister who consciously looked to Anglo-Catholicism for inspiration.[79]

The architecture of the Episcopal Church in Scotland is generally seen as being derivative of that of the Anglican Church in England, and in architectural terms closely related to the English story: in fact about a quarter of the Episcopal churches built between 1840-1860 were designed by English architects.[80] A recent study has identified some of the reasons behind the differences between the development of Scottish and English Anglican churches; in the case of the former, there were far fewer surviving medieval precedents to go by; campaigning ecclesiological movements were more diverse, at least until an Aberdeen Ecclesiological Society was founded in 1886; and the building of churches along ecclesiological lines was subject to campaigns by individual ministers rather than by architectural movements.[81]

236

On the other hand, the buildings designed from mid-century onwards increasingly resemble English ones, in their 'true' Gothic style and their ecclesiologically 'correct' fittings; and the first true ecclesiological church restoration came in 1871, with the work of Anderson at St Vigeans, Arbroath.[82] It is a measure of the eventual impact of ecclesiology that a chancel screen was eventually installed in Dunblane Cathedral, during the course of Lorimer's work there from 1912, even though a screen has no role in Presbyterian worship.[83]

A handful of Scottish churches outside the mainstream denominations produced some remarkable architecture, however. Of these, the three monumental buildings designed for the United Presbyterian Church in Glasgow by Alexander Thomson (1817-1875) are the most unusual: all three were based around the idea of a Greek temple on a tall plinth, but their detailing was idiosyncratic and in places somewhat Egyptian. That at Queen's Park (1868-1869) had a tall narrow dome shaped in the form of a pinecone; the other two, at Caledonia Road (1855-1857) [Ill. 3.1-18] and St Vincent Street (1857-1859 – the only survivor) had tall towers. Henry-Russell Hitchcock, coining another stylistic designation, described them as "three of the finest Romantic Classical churches in the world".[84] By contrast, the other maverick designer was a Goth: the English-born Frederick Pilkington, whose work was on occasion Gothic at its wildest, marked by florid, organic and almost grotesque and Gothic detailing, possibly Venetian in influence. All three of the major buildings designed for the Free Church – Trinity Church in Irvine, Ayrshire (1861); Barclay Church, Edinburgh (1862); and St John's, Kelso, Roxburghshire (1863) have tall, crocketed spires; there is little about their exterior to suggest that they are designed around auditorium plans. Catholic High Victorianism fits in here, in the work of Pugin and Pugin, ubiquitous in the Glasgow archdiocese and the central industrial belt. These churches were largely for the immigrant Irish, and were called for by the restored Scots hierarchy (1878).[85]

Wales was also a Presbyterian country, and the great majority of its population were members of Nonconformist churches: in some towns these denominations might have two institutions, one for English speakers and one for Welsh.[86] In common with English Nonconformist churches, these varied greatly in size and were often designed by local members; the styles employed were for the same reasons the cheaper ones, and less progressive architecturally. In the towns, massive Bethel, Siloh and Tabernacle chapels were built by rival ministers and congregations. Almost all Nonconformist chapels had rectangular plans with centrally positioned pulpits at the east end; the larger and more expensive of these buildings had galleries, and placed an organ on the eastern side. In general, the architectural value of these buildings lies in the quality of the joinery and other fittings rather than in their style or coherence.

Musical aspects of Catholic worship

The great reform of the mid-nineteenth-century Anglican Church was the removal of singers and musicians from galleries to a choir in the stalls in conjunction with an organ, with all-male choirs treated as if clerics chanting the services: this was a tradition borrowed from the cathedrals. Congregational singing and hymnody were successfully reformed, beginning with the publication of *Hymns Ancient and Modern* (1861) and the *English Hymnal* (1906). Amongst the Nonconformists, hymn-singing was a tradition only with the Methodists. The Catholic scene was much more contested. Devotional practices at low mass excluded congregational participation, such as music. But the splendours of ritual and music had been found in eighteenth-century Catholic London at least in the Embassy chapels, where professional musicians and singers led the operatic or 'Viennese' tradition of four-part masses.[87] Such music was adver-

80 Sanders, "Ecclesiology in Scotland", 300.
81 Sanders, "Ecclesiology in Scotland".
82 Ibid, 315.
83 Ibid, 316.
84 Hitchcock, *Architecture: Nineteenth and Twentieth Centuries*, 63.
85 Sanders, "Pugin & Pugin in the diocese of Glasgow".
86 For Welsh churches and chapels see Howell, "Church and Chapel in Wales"; Orbach, "Welsh Chapels 1859-1914". According to Howell, "Church and Chapel in Wales", 119, 85% of the population were identified as Nonconformists in the 1851 census.
87 Muir, *Roman Catholic Church Music in England*, 46, 75-77, 168-171.

88 *Tablet*, 1840, 72.
89 In a letter to Shrewsbury, probably 13 May 1849, reproduced in Belcher, *The Collected Letters of A.W.N. Pugin*, IV, 132. Pugin presumably meant 'benediction'.

3.1-19 *The closing page of A.W.N. Pugin's* Glossary of Ecclesiastical Ornament, *1849.*
[Cambridge University Library]

tised, as for example at the Royal Sardinian Chapel on Whitsunday 1840: "Grand High Mass… with full orchestral accomplishment [and] eminent vocalists… Mme Persiani, Sig. Rubini, Tamburini and Lablanche".[88] This type of performance was decried by Pugin as the "Shilling Opera-house": "one night a *masqued ball*, next *Benedictus*".[89] Something of this standard was also achieved in the leading London churches and private chapels on the big estates, but not on the missions.[90]

The staple in Catholic churches was a *sotto voce* Latin Low mass responded to by "*one urchin*", as Pugin put it.[91] The historian John Lingard (1771-1851), providing for the vernacular, wrote *A Manual of Common Prayers* for his Lancashire congregation.[92] But his much better known hymn version of the Ave Maris Stella – "Hail Queen of Heaven, the ocean star" – was written not for the congregation but for the Gillow family of Leighton Hall.[93] Pugin was a propagandist for plainchant, and stormed out of the opening of his church at Derby after a figured sung mass was substituted, taking the Earl of Shrewsbury and their Gothic vestments with him.[94] The consecration and opening of St Chad's Cathedral, Birmingham, was much better orchestrated. Here a choir dedicated to Gregorian chant was paid for and maintained by John Hardman Junior, who appears in a cantor's cope as the donor of the 1867 Immaculate Conception window in the cathedral. By 1856, this choir had banned non-plainchant.[95] At Ramsgate, Pugin and his pupil John Hardman Powell also acted as cantors, E.W. Pugin later claiming to be the mainstay of singing in the church even when it was staffed by Benedictines – an example of how the true Gothic concept of completeness could also require the involvement of its designers as operatives. Pugin's friend and patron Phillipps de Lisle had each Sunday at his house Grace Dieu in Leicestershire not only the ordinary but the proper of the mass in plainchant, often with many medieval sequences from the suppressed Sarum rite.[96] [Ill. 3.1-19]

Pugin designed organs and had them made, in collaboration with Sir John Sutton. Lingard dismissed one of them as "so like one of my fowls flapping his wings".[97] Henry Formby, another Lancashire priest, was a plainchant researcher and publisher, along with John Lambert, a publisher and musical reformer who had been patron of Pugin's church of St Osmond's, Salisbury (1847-1848).[98] Little of this music can have been congregational, and as late as the 1880s a few as twelve churches across the land were noted as able to chant the ordinary of the mass and the creed. The Gothic revivalists opposed vernacular singing or hymns, but

these were championed by F.W. Faber and the Oratorians. Faber's hymn book was one of the most ubiquitous; in this he recommended "modern Catholicism… services in the vernacular … hymn-singing and prayer meetings".[99] Perhaps inevitably, Pugin characterised these in his *Earnest Appeal for the Revival of the Ancient Plainsong* of 1850 as "the doggerel rhymes and poetic effusions of a few individuals [which] should have led them down to Geneva, but who appear to have mistaken their road and found their way into the Catholic Church [using] the ancient liturgy as a mere vehicle for the display of their Methodism".[100] But hymnody was one of the few situations in which the vernacular was used in Catholic churches, and was very popular.[101]

During the latter half of the century, vespers was everywhere being ousted by popular services and by the Benediction.[102] Around 1900 a commentator found vespers in only five London churches and in all the cathedrals, except for Bishop Herbert Vaughan's at Salford.[103] The study and reform of plainchant on Solemnes Abbey lines, begun at Belmont Abbey, was first achieved by nuns at Stanbrook Abbey.[104] This restoration of the full divine office chanted in choir was also the intention of the 'Downside Movement' and at Westminster Cathedral, where Cardinal Vaughan originally had monks in mind, but subsequently priests and a choir school. Here Richard Terry, first master of music (1902-1924), was crucial in the publication and performance of both continental and English Tudor polyphony.[105] In 1903 Edward Martyn founded the Palestrina choir at the pro-cathedral, Dublin. Music at Downside Abbey and Westminster Cathedral therefore immediately anticipated the rulings of Pius X in *Tra le Sollecitudini* (1903).

Directions at the end of the long nineteenth century

Changes in the design of churches and their furnishings towards the end of the nineteenth century reflect trends elsewhere among architects: most notably, the arts-and-crafts interest in vernacular architecture and simple forms resulted in some remarkable new designs for churches that resembled craft-made barns. The pioneer here was Philip Webb (1831-1915), the architect

90 Muir, *Roman Catholic Church Music*, 77-80. Muir analyses the liturgy, musical books and the liturgical practice of the period but his use of architectural evidence is limited: 31-36, 36-40, 40-48.
91 Belcher, *Collected Letters of A.W.N. Pugin*, I, 127.
92 Muir, *Roman Catholic Church Music*, 51-52.
93 John Lingard's *Manual of Prayers for Sundays and Holidays* (1844) included the hymn.
94 Belcher, *Collected Letters of A.W.N. Pugin*, I, 125-126.
95 Cathedral Clergy, *A History of St Chad's Cathedral*, 123-129.
96 Purcell and de Lisle, *Life and Letters of Ambrose Phillipps de Lisle*, II, 291-293.
97 Lingard to Robert Tate, 23 April 1844, quoted in Phillips, *John Lingard*, 400-401.
98 For Lambert's musical career, see Muir, *Roman Catholic Church Music*, 100-101.
99 Faber, *Jesus and Mary*, xiv (first published 1849).
100 Pugin, *An Earnest Address*, 4.
101 Muir, *Roman Catholic Church Music*, 137-163.
102 Heimann, *Catholic Devotion in Victorian England*, appendix 1, 174-182.
103 Little, "The Conversion of England".
104 Muir, *Roman Catholic Church Music*, 104-105, 208-210.
105 Ibid., 223-235.

3.1-20 All Saints', Brockhampton, Herefordshire, by William Lethaby, 1901-1902.
[London, Royal Institute of British Architects: RIBApix, RIBA105407]

of St Martin's, Brampton, in Cumberland (1874-1878): this was a Gothic structure, but the bold vernacular of its timber ceilings over the nave and aisle pointed towards a different direction from the refined contemporary Gothic of Bodley and others.[106] Among its progeny are the domestic style St Michael's Bedford Park (1878-1887), by Shaw (1831-1912); and the tiny thatched All Saints', Brockhampton (1901-1902), by William Lethaby (1857-1931), who had worked for ten years in Shaw's office but who saw himself as a disciple of Webb.[107] [Ill. 3.1-20] Lethaby's writing on the origins of architecture – such as his *Architecture, Mysticism and Myth* of 1891 – and the intimate, finely worked, primitive, almost pagan detailing of All Saints' already indicate that Gothic church architecture was moving away from its medieval, ecclesiastical roots. Lethaby's church was constructed of concrete, exposed internally in the ceiling; this essentially Ruskinian combination of roughness and delicacy found expression on a grand scale in arts-and-crafts architecture with the influential church of St Andrew's, Roker, in County Durham (now Tyne and Wear), by Edward Prior (1905-1907).[108]

If the richly exotic interior of St Bartholomew, Brighton, referred to above, has any overall style, it is surely 'byzantine' as interpreted by fin-de-siècle designers. An increasing interest in mosaic, glass tiles and much gold leaf from the 1870s resulted in some remarkable church interiors, both on a large scale – including the new decoration by William Blake Richmond applied to the ceilings of St Paul's Cathedral in London in the 1890s – and on a small one, sometimes in rural locations: the effect must surely have been remarkable when first encountered, for example in the case of the Church of the Wisdom of God at Lower Kingswood in Surrey (1891-1899), by the arts and crafts architect Sidney Barnsley, designed following a long trip to Greece. In contrast to these, at Christ Church, Brixton, A. Beresford Pite designed a large and austerely decorated and fitted-out Byzantine church for an evangelical congregation in 1899-1902. It was perhaps the first time since the Regency period that architects who saw themselves as being progressive high-art designers were working in exotic styles.[109]

Nevertheless, the emphasis on Pugin throughout this chapter would not have surprised older architects still in practice before the First World War: in the words of John Dando Sedding (1838-1891), a former pupil of Street's and a prolific church architect, "We should have had no Morris, no Street, no Burges, no Shaw, no Webb, no Bodley, no Rossetti, no Burne-Jones, no Crane, but for Pugin".[110] A recent study has looked again at the ways in which the style of Puginism was developed over the second half of the century, and in particular at how established Gothic architects reacted as the dogmatic influences of the ecclesiologists had waned by the 1870s, allowing experimentation with styles which had earlier been disapproved of.[111] Sedding himself, for example, has been described as "one of the first to defend the merits of English Perpendicular Gothic from blinkered prejudice".[112] Some architects, such as Butterfield, stuck rigidly to High Victorian norms; others, like Pearson and Bodley, changed their style from time to time as Pugin himself had done, but nevertheless remained 'true' Goths.[113] Bodley's large and richly furnished parish Church of the Holy Angels, Hoar Cross, Staffordshire (1872), a project funded by a single benefactor, is unmistakably a Gothic church, but one with tall square-headed windows, as if it were an unusual development of the medieval 'decorated' style. An important conclusion of the study was that church building and decorating programmes were lengthy affairs, and so the architectural ideas of mid-century might easily have stretched out for another couple of decades within a single building.[114] In any case, the longevity of some designers, holding to earlier architectural principles, resulted in much continuity of Gothic design, especially where existing churches were being remodelled, rebuilt or completed.

---

106 Kirk, *Philip Webb*, 261-269.
107 St Michaels: Saint, *Richard Norman Shaw*, 230-232; Blundell Jones, "Masters of building. Design from first principles: All Saints, Brockhampton".
108 See Crawford, "Arts and Crafts Churches".
109 See Sladen, "Byzantium in the Chancel".
110 Sedding, *Art and handicraft*, 144.
111 Saint, "The Late Victorian Church".
112 Stamp, "The Architecture of Good Taste", 152.
113 Saint, "The Late Victorian Church", 16-18.
114 Ibid., 9-10.
115 O'Donnell, "The Abbey Church as First Imagined and as First Built".
116 Hall, "Thomas Garner and the Choir of Downside Abbey Church"; Stamp, "Downside Abbey and Sir Giles Gilbert Scott".
117 Bellenger, "The Work of Sir Ninian Comper and Frederick Walters".
118 O'Donnell, "F.A. Walters, Archaeologist and Architect".
119 Symondson and Bucknall, *Sir Ninian Comper*: St Cyprian's, 87-97; St Mary's, 190-205.
120 For an overview of Anglican design at 1914 see Stamp, "The Architecture of Good Taste".

The story of the design and construction of Downside Abbey, the premier Benedictine abbey in England, provides a case in point. The original Regency Gothic church by H. E. Goodridge, was to have been replaced by Pugin's great scheme of 1842 [Ill. 3.1-4]; but the scheme eventually executed, from 1874, was by Dunn and Hansom, its transepts and chevet of chapels following from 1876-1894.[115] Bodley's former partner Thomas Garner, by now a Catholic, built the aisled choir (completed in 1906); and the aisled nave, a war memorial built from 1922-1928, was by Giles Gilbert Scott.[116] In the meantime, Dunn and Hansom's Lady Chapel of 1885-1888, one of the best works of the practice, was eventually furnished, from 1898-1924, by Ninian Comper (1864-1960).[117] [Ill. 3.1-21] Thus all the important elements of the 'true' Gothic reform movement, from architectural concept to style and furnishing, were continuously redeveloped and re-expressed at Downside over a period of about 80 years. Another example is the monastery, begun 1886, and the church (1907-1932) at Buckfast, Devon, both by the architect Frederick Arthur Walters (1849-1932). A medieval site bought by exiled French Benedictine monks, and its excavation in part by Walters, provided the architect with the plan of both. And Walters's devout Puginism and a maecenas in Abbot Vonier saw the completion and furnishing of the church, down to the Vonier's jubilee vestments, Walters' last work.[118]

Comper was a former pupil of Bodley's active in the most 'extreme' High-Church Anglican circles. His ornamental design and liturgical planning at St Cyprian's, Clarence Gate, in London (1902-1903) and St Mary's Wellingborough (1904-1931), were, he claimed, inspired by that of the earliest Christian churches, heralding what was to become an important theme in twentieth-century church architecture.[119] Unlike Morris, Webb and Lethaby – loquaciously post-Christian – Comper continued Pugin's and Butterfield's belief that only the devout architect should be chosen to design churches; and he was still engaged in the design of dec-

3.1-21 The Lady Chapel of Downside Abbey, furnished by Ninian Comper, 1898-1924.
[By courtesy of Downside Abbey]

orative work for churches after the Second World War as he reached his ninth decade; some prolific, but not especially remarkable, Gothic church designers, for example Sir Charles Nicholson, who had trained before the First World War found themselves in demand at least until 1939.[120] The twentieth century indeed was to see one of the greatest Gothic cathedrals – and the largest – brought to completion: Giles Gilbert Scott's at Liverpool, won in competition when the architect was 22 years old and finally accomplished in 1978, 18 years after the architect's death.

241

BIBLIOGRAPHY

Addleshaw, George, and Frederick Etchells. *The Architectural Setting of Anglican Worship: an Inquiry into the Arrangements for Public Worship in the Church of England from the Reformation to the Present Day*. London, 1948.

Allingham, H., and D. Radford, eds. *William Allingham. A Diary*. London, 1907.

Antram, Nicholas, and Richard Morrice. *Pevsner Architectural Guides: Brighton and Hove*. New Haven-London, 2004.

Atterbury, Paul, and Clive Wainwright, eds, *Pugin: A Gothic Passion*. New Haven-London, 1994.

Belcher, Margaret. *The Collected Letters of A.W.N. Pugin*. Vol 1: *1830 to 1842*; Vol. 4: *1849 to 1850*. Oxford, 2001; 2012.

Bellenger, Aidan. "The Work of Sir Ninian Comper and Frederick Walters". In: Aidan Bellenger, ed. *Downside Abbey Church: An Architectural History*. London-New York, 2011, 151-175.

Blundell Jones, Peter. "Masters of Building. Design from First Principles: 'All Saints, Brockhampton; Architect (1901): W. R. Lethaby'". *Architects' Journal*, 192 (15 August 1990) 7, 24-43.

Bowe, Nicola Gordon. *The Life and Work of Harry Clarke*. Revised edition. Dublin, 2012.

Bowe, Nicola Gordon. *Wilhelmina Geddes: Life and Work*. Dublin, 2015.

Bowe, Nicola Gordon, David Caron and Michael Wynne. *Gazetteer of Irish Stained Glass: The Works of Harry Clarke, the Artists of an Túr Gloine (The Tower of Glass) and artists of succeeding generations to the present day*. Revised new edition by David Garon. Dublin, 2021.

Bowe, Nicola Gordon, and Elizabeth Cumming. *The Arts and Crafts Movements in Dublin & Edinburgh 1885-1925*. Dublin, 1998.

Bremner, G.A. *Imperial Gothic: Religious Architecture and High Anglican Culture in the British Empire c. 1840-1870*. New Haven-London, 2013.

Brittain-Catlin, Timothy. "A.W.N. Pugin's English Convent Plans". *Journal of the Society of Architectural Historians*, 65 (2006) 3, 356-377.

Brittain-Catlin, Timothy. *The English Parsonage in the Early Nineteenth Century*. Reading, 2008.

Brittain-Catlin, Timothy. "Realism in Nineteenth-Century British Architecture". In: Harry Mallgrave, Martin Bressani and Christina Contandiopoulos, eds. *The Companions to the History of Architecture*, vol. 3. Hoboken, 2017, 174-191.

Britton, John. *The Architectural Antiquities of Great Britain*. Vol. 5. London, 1826.

Brooks, Chris. *The Gothic Revival*. London, 1999.

Brooks, Michael W. *John Ruskin and Victorian Architecture*. London, 1989.

Cambridge Camden Society. *Church Enlargement and Church Arrangement*. Cambridge, 1843.

Cathedral Clergy. *A History of St Chad's Cathedral, Birmingham, 1841-1904*. Birmingham, 1904.

Cook, E.T., and Alexander Wedderburn. *The Works of John Ruskin*. London, 1903-1912.

Crook, John Mordaunt. *The Architect's Secret: Victorian Critics and the Image of Gravity*. London, 2003.

Crook, John Mordaunt. *William Burges and the High Victorian Dream*. Revised edition. London, 2013.

de l'Hopital, Winefride. *Westminster Cathedral and its Architect*. 2 vols. London, 1919.

Elliot, Robert. *Art and Ireland*. Dublin, 1902.

Faber, William. *Jesus and Mary: or, Catholic Hymns*. London, 1862 (first published 1849).

Fisher, Michael. *Hardman of Birmingham*. Ashbourne, 2008.

Fisher, Michael. *'Gothic for Ever': A.W.N. Pugin, Lord Shrewsbury, and the Rebuilding of Catholic England*. Reading, 2012.

Foster, Andy. *Pevsner Architectural Guides: Birmingham*. New Haven-London, 2004.

Friedman, Terry. *The Eighteenth-Century Church in Britain*. New Haven-London, 2011.

Girouard, Mark. "All That Money Can Buy". In: Alec Clifton-Taylor et al. *Spirit of the Age*. London, 151-187.

Goodhart-Rendel, H.S. "Some Rogue Architects of the Victorian Era". *RIBA Journal*, 4 (1949), 251-259.

Hall, Michael. *George Frederick Bodley and the Later Gothic Revival in Britain and America*. New Haven-London, 2015.

Hall, Michael, ed. *Farm Street: the Story of the Jesuits' Church in London*. London, 2017.

Harrison, Martin. *Victorian Stained Glass*. London, 1980.

Harwood, Elain. *Pevsner Architectural Guides: Nottingham*. New Haven-London, 2008.

Heimann, Mary. *Catholic Devotion in Victorian England*. Oxford, 1995.

Hitchcock, Henry-Russell. *Architecture: Nineteenth and Twentieth Centuries*. 2nd ed. Baltimore, 1963.

Hobhouse, Hermione. *Thomas Cubitt: Master Builder*. Revised edition. Didcot, 2000.

Howell, Peter. "Church and Chapel in Wales". In: Chris Brooks and Andrew Saint, eds. *The Victorian Church: Architecture and Society*. Manchester, 1995, 118-132.

Howell, Peter. "Between Medievalism and the Counter-Reformation: Catholic Church Building after Pugin". In: Teresa Sladen and Andrew Saint, eds. *Churches 1870-1914*. Studies in Victorian Architecture and Design, 3. London, 2011, 26-43.

Howell, Peter. *John Francis Bentley: Architect of Westminster Cathedral*. London, 2020.

Kadish, Sharman. *The Synagogues of Britain and Ireland: an Architectural and Social History*. New Haven-London, 2011.

Kirk, Sheila. *Philip Webb: Pioneer of Arts and Crafts Architecture*. Chichester, 2005.

Larkin, Emmet. "Economic Growth, Capital Investment and the Roman Catholic Church in Nineteenth-Century Ireland". *The American Historical Review*, 72 (April 1967) 2, 852-884.

Lawrence, David, and Ann Wilson. *The Cathedral of St Fin Barre at Cork: William Burges in Ireland*. Dublin, 2006.

Little, Sydney H. "The Conversion of England: a Reply". *Dublin Review*, 3rd series, 12 (1884) 95, 358-387.

Macaulay, James. *The Gothic Revival 1745-1845*. Glasgow-London, 1975.

Martin, Christopher. *A Glimpse of Heaven: Catholic Churches of England and Wales*. Reprinted and corrected edition. Swindon, 2007.

McGee, Caroline M. "Power, Patronage and the Production of Catholic Material Culture in Nineteenth-Century Ireland". In: Raphaël Ingelbein and Susan Galavan, eds. *Figures of Authority in Nineteenth-Century Ireland*. Liverpool, 2020, 139-160.

McParland, Edward. "Who was 'P'?" *Architectural Review*, 157 (February 1975) 936, 71-73.

Meara, David. *A.W.N. Pugin and the Revival of Memorial Brasses*. London, 1991.

Milner, John. *The History Civil and Ecclesiastical, & Survey of Antiquities, of Winchester*. 2 vols. 2nd ed. Winchester, 1809.

Muir, Thomas E. *Roman Catholic Church Music in England, 1791-1914: A Handmaid of the Liturgy?* Aldershot, 2008.

Muthesius, Stefan. *The High Victorian Movement in Architecture 1850-1870*. London, 1972.

[Neale, John Mason]. *A Few Words to Church Builders*. 3rd ed. Cambridge, 1844.

Neave, David, and Sarah Neave. *Pevsner Architectural Guides: Hull*. New Haven-London, 2010.

Newman, John. *North East and East Kent*. The Buildings of England. Revised edition. New Haven-London, 2013.

Nicholson, Charles, and Charles Spooner. *Recent English Ecclesiastical Architecture*. London, no date, c. 1910.

O'Connell, John R. *The Honan Hostel Chapel: Some Notes on the Building and the Ideals which Inspired it*. Cork, 1916.

O'Donnell, Roderick. "The Pugins in Ireland". In: Paul Atterbury, ed. *A.W.N. Pugin: Master of the Gothic Revival*. New Haven-London, 1995, 136-159.

O'Donnell, Roderick. "The Interior of St Mary Moorfields [London]". *The Georgian Group Journal*, 7 (1997), 71-74.

O'Donnell, Roderick. *The Pugins and the Catholic Midlands*. Leominster, 2002.

O'Donnell, Roderick. "Catholic Church Architecture in England: 'Irish Occupation' or 'the Italian Mission'?" In: David Crellin and Ian Dungavell, eds. *Architecture and Englishness, 1880-1914*. (Papers from the annual symposium of the Society of Architectural Historians of Great Britain, 2003). London, 2006, 59-71.

O'Donnell, Roderick. "The Church of St Francis of Assisi, (1865-1885) Gorton, Manchester". *True Principles, the Journal of the Pugin Society*, 3 (2006) 3, 36-38.

O'Donnell, Roderick. "Brompton Oratory Revisited". *Ecclesiology Today*, 40 (July 2008), 30-35.

O'Donnell, Roderick. "The Chapel of St Patrick's College, Maynooth". *Country Life*, 208 (16 April 2014) 16, 74-79.

O'Donnell, Roderick. "A.W.N. Pugin's Rood Screen at St George's Cathedral, Southwark, London, an Unpublished Pugin Drawing for the Jube, 1848". In: Charlene Vella, ed. *At Home in Art: Essays in Honour of Mario Buhagiar*. Valetta, 2016, 317-325, 351.

O'Donnell, Roderick. "From Whitehall Palace to Wigan Pier, English Catholic Places of Worship 1685 to 1829". In: Paul Barnwell, P.S. Barnwell and Mark Smith, eds. *Places of Worship in Great Britain, 1689-1829*. Rewley House Studies in the Historic Environment. Donington, 2021, 184-199.

Orbach, Julian. "Welsh Chapels 1859-1914". In: Teresa Sladen and Andrew Saint, eds. *Churches 1870-1914. Studies in Victorian Architecture and Design*, 3. London, 2011, 44-61.

Phillips, Peter. *John Lingard, Priest and Historian*. Leominster, 2008.

Port, M.H. *600 New Churches: the Church Building Commission 1818-1856*. Revised edition. Reading, 2006.

Pugin, A.W.N. *The True Principles of Pointed or Christian Architecture*. London, 1841.

Pugin, A.W.N. *An Apology for the Revival of Christian Architecture*. London, 1843.

Pugin, A.W.N. *The Present State of Ecclesiastical Architecture in England*. London, 1843.

Pugin, A.W.N. *Glossary of Ecclesiastical Ornament and Costume*. First published 1844; new edition with an introduction by Michael Fisher. Reading, 2013.

Pugin, A.W.N. *An Earnest Address, on the Establishment of the Hierarchy*. London, 1851.

Purcell, Edward Sheridan and E.J. De Lisle, eds. *Life and Letters of Ambrose Phillipps de Lisle*. 2 vols. London-New York, 1900.

Rogers, Patrick. *The Beauty of Stone: Westminster Cathedral Marbles*. London, 2008.

Rogers, Patrick. *Reflections on Westminster Cathedral Mosaics*. London, 2010.

Rolfe, F.R. ["Baron Corvo"]. *Hadrian VII: a Romance*. London, 1904.

Saint, Andrew. *Architect and Engineer: a Study in Sibling Rivalry*. New Haven-London, 2007.

Saint, Andrew. *Richard Norman Shaw*. Revised edition. New Haven-London, 2010.

Saint, Andrew. "The Late Victorian Church". In: Teresa Sladen and Andrew Saint, eds. *Churches 1870-1914. Studies in Victorian Architecture and Design*, 3. London, 2011, 6-25.

Sanders, John. "Pugin & Pugin in the diocese of Glasgow". In: Gavin Stamp, ed. *Caledonia Gothica: Pugin and the Gothic Revival in Scotland*. Architectural Heritage, 8/1. Edinburgh, 1997, 89-107.

Sanders, John. "Ecclesiology in Scotland". In: Christopher Webster and John Elliott, eds. *'The Church as It Should Be': the Cambridge Camden Society and Its Influence*. Stamford, 2000, 295-316.

Sewell, Brocard. *Two Friends: John Gray and André Raffalovich*. Aylesford, 1963.

Sharples, Joseph. *Pevsner Architectural Guides: Liverpool*. New Haven-London, 2004.

Sheehy, Jeanne. *J.J. McCarthy and the Gothic Revival in Ireland*. Belfast, 1977.

Sheehy, Jeanne. *The Rediscovery of Ireland's Past: the Celtic Revival 1830-1930*. London, 1980.

Shepherd, Stanley. *The Stained Glass of A.W.N. Pugin*. Reading, 2009.

Sladen, Teresa. "Embellishment and Decoration, 1696-1900". In: Derek Keene and Andrew Saint, eds. *St Paul's: the Cathedral Church of London 604-2004*. New Haven-London, 2004, 233-257.

Stamp, Gavin. "The Victorian Kirk: Presbyterian Architecture in Nineteenth-Century Scotland". In: Chris Brooks and Andrew Saint, eds. *The Victorian Church: Architecture and Society*. Manchester, 1995, 98-117.

Stamp, Gavin. "George Gilbert Scott and the Cambridge Camden Society". In: Christopher Webster and John Elliott. *'The Church as It Should Be': the Cambridge Camden Society and its Influence*. Stamford, 2000, 173-189.

Stell, Christopher. *An Inventory of Nonconformist Chapels and Meeting-Houses in Central England*. London, 1986.

Stell, Christopher. *An Inventory of Nonconformist Chapels and Meeting-Houses in South West England*. London, 1991.

Stell, Christopher. *An Inventory of Nonconformist Chapels and Meeting-Houses in North of England*. London, 1994.

Stell, Christopher. *An Inventory of Nonconformist Chapels and Meeting-Houses in Eastern England*. Swindon, 2002.

Sweet, Rosemary. *Antiquaries: The Discovery of the Past in Eighteenth-Century Britain*. London-New York, 2004.

Symondson, Anthony, and Stephen Bucknall. *Sir Ninian Comper*. Reading, 2006.

Teehan, Virginia, and Elizabeth Wincott Heckett. *The Honan Chapel: a Golden Vision*. Cork, 2004.

Wakeling, Christopher. "The Nonconformist Traditions: Chapels, Change and Continuity". In: Chris Brooks and Andrew Saint, eds. *The Victorian Church: Architecture and Society*. Manchester, 1995, 82-97.

Wakeling, Christopher. *Chapels of England: Buildings of Protestant Nonconformity*. Swindon, 2017.

Ward-Jackson, Philip. "Accommodating Ritual Display: Episcopal Monuments 1896-1915". In: Teresa Sladen and Andrew Saint, eds. *Churches 1870-1914. Studies in Victorian Architecture and Design*, 3. London, 2011, 100-119.

Webster, Christopher. "'Absolutely Wretched': Camdenian Attitudes to the Late Georgian Church". In: Christopher Webster and John Elliott, eds. *'The Church as It Should Be': the Cambridge Camden Society and Its Influence*. Stamford, 2000, 1-21.

Webster, Christopher, and John Elliott, eds. *'The Church as it Should Be': the Cambridge Camden Society and its Influence*. Stamford, 2000.

Wedgwood, Alexandra. "The New Palace of Westminster". In: Christine Riding and Jacqueline Riding, eds. *The Houses of Parliament: History, Art, Architecture*. London, 2000, 113-135.

Wilson, Ann. "The Material and Visual Culture of the Construction of Irish Catholic Identity: Saint Colman's Cathedral, Queenstown, County Cork". In: Timothy Jones and Lucinda Matthews-Jones, eds. *Material Religion in Modern Britain: the Spirit of Things*. New York, 2015, 37-55.

3.2
Gothic Revival

Style, Construction and Ideology in Nineteenth-Century Belgium

Thomas Coomans

Unlike most northern European countries in which several religious denominations coexisted, the Catholics occupied almost the entire religious landscape in Belgium during the long nineteenth century. Consequently, there was no need for them to identify with a particular architectural style; nearly all churches, whether Romanesque, Gothic, Renaissance, Baroque, classical, or neoclassical, were Catholic. However, by the middle of the century, the question of the architectural style of churches emerged as crucial. A specific form of 'Belgian Gothic', the St Luke Gothic Revival style, became a benchmark, carrying with it a precise national and ideological meaning. [Ill. 3.2-1]

What were the conditions and reasons behind the emergence of the St Luke Gothic style in the architectural landscape of nineteenth-century Belgium? How did it evolve and what caused its decline? Were other styles used for churches? We will be dealing only with the churches themselves in this chapter; the place held by churches in the public space is dealt with in another chapter.[1] Surprisingly, nineteenth-century churches in Belgium have yet to be subject to a full synthesis, and their place in syntheses of the history of architecture is limited to the few most monumental buildings or the biographical records of architects.[2] Gothic Revival art and architecture has been the subject of several syntheses,[3] inventories,[4] and heritage approaches from which it is clear that the subject has received greater study in Flanders than Wallonia and even Brussels. As a result, most Gothic Revival churches are considered historical monuments in Flanders, while in other regions the process of their heritagisation is much more recent.[5]

Neoclassicism: from the Enlightenment to the Concordat

Marking the end of the Baroque brought about by the Counter-Reformation, the neoclassical style gradually imposed itself in the southern Low Countries and the Principality of Liège from the mid-eighteenth century. In 1751-1767, St Aubain in Namur, the only cathedral in Belgium that is not medieval in style, was built according to plans by the Italian architect Gaetano Matteo Pisoni. The reforms fostered by the spirit of the Enlightenment aimed at making the Austrian Netherlands a modern state. They were initiated by the ministers of Empress Maria Theresa, supported by Charles Alexander of Lorraine, whose governor's court was in Brussels (1744-1780), and radicalised by Emperor Joseph II (1780-1790). The Church, religious orders in particular, were subject to reform. The Jesuits and many contemplative communities considered 'useless' were suppressed in 1773 and 1783 respectively.[6] Abbeys, meanwhile, were obliged to sell off part of their landed properties and invest their capital in large construction programmes. The state wanted to kill two birds with one stone: not only did this release land from mortmain, it also revitalised the construction sector and injected fresh money into the economy. Equally, it promoted the neoclassical style as an expression of a new order by requiring abbeys to use the court architect Laurent-

3.2-1 Church of St Peter and Paul in Ostend (1901-1907), a national monument at the gate of a sea harbour. [Wikimedia Commons; photo Marc Ryckaert, 2014]

1. See my contribution "Reconquering a Lost Visibility: Catholic Revival in Early Industrial Belgium" (2.2) in this volume.
2. Dierkens-Aubry and Vandenbreeden, *Le XIXe siècle en Belgique*; Van Loo, ed., *Dictionnaire de l'architecture en Belgique*.
3. De Maeyer, "The Neo-Gothic in Belgium", 32-34; Van Cleven, "Neogotiek en neogotismen"; Van Cleven et al., eds., *Neogotiek in België*; De Maeyer, Coomans and Weyns, "Le néogothique à Bruxelles".
4. Inventories also mention churches, in Flanders: <https://inventaris.onroerenderfgoed.be/>; in Wallonia: Bertrand, Chenut and Genicot, *Les églises paroissiales de Wallonie*; in Brussels: <http://www.irismonument.be/>.
5. Coomans, "Veel zorgen, weinig zorg"; Id., "Op weg naar bescherming van 19de-eeuwse kerkgebouwen in Vlaanderen"; Id., "Quelle protection pour les églises à Bruxelles?"; Id., "Églises, couvents et chapelles".
6. De Schepper, "Marie-Thérèse et Joseph II".

3.2-2 Church of St Saviour in Ghent, with its neoclassical façade (1810-1812). [Brussels, Agentschap Onroerend Erfgoed: beeldbank 18455; photo 1978]

7   Van de Vijver, "L'architecture dans les Pays-Bas autrichiens et la Principauté de Liège".
8   For example, the churches of Our Lady in Dendermonde (1830), St Amandus in Oudenaarde (1830), St Remacle in Verviers (1834-1838), St Joseph in Brussels (1842-1849), St Albanus in Riemst (1845-1846) and St Gertrudis in Herzele (1846-1848).
9   Toman, ed., *Neoclassicism and Romanticism*, 14-229.

Benoît Dewez.[7] Trained in Naples alongside Luigi Vanvitelli and in England with Robert Adam, Dewez obtained the majority of large monastic commissions between 1760 and 1780. Designed in accordance with symmetrical plans consisting of large forecourts and a succession of cloisters around churches and abbots' palaces, Dewez's abbeys were sumptuous and contrasted completely with the medieval and baroque traditions of the southern Low Countries. Due to the French invasion in 1792-1794 and the suppression of all abbeys in 1796, few of these large monastic complexes were completed. The Benedictine abbey of Gembloux and the Norbertine abbey of Heylissem, as well as the abbey churches of Vlierbeek near Leuven, Bonne-Espérance and Andenne, are the best-preserved examples. Dewez also converted medieval churches, including the Norbertine abbey of Floreffe, to suit neoclassical tastes. The most spectacular complex of the Austrian new order is the Quartier de la Cour in Brussels, whose Place Royale is dominated by the church of St James (1776-1787). Designed by the French architect Louis Montoyer, the Greek temple façade of this large neoclassical church is integrated into the regular, white order of the square.

No more churches were built during the decades that followed, but plenty were demolished. After 1801-1802, some churches displayed their concordatory identity, sometimes highly explicitly. While the Gothic church of St Saviour in Ghent was provided with a neoclassical facade in 1810-1812 – completing the contrast of colours, shapes and proportions – it expressed a break with the past and the Church's adaptation to the new society. [Ill. 3.2-2] Few churches were built during the Dutch period (1815-1830), but the churches of the first generation after 1830 were still neoclassical.[8] In Belgium, as in most European countries, neoclassical architecture survived the succession of political regimes and the profound reforms of society, the Church and the construction sector.[9] It owed this astonishing continuity to its universal character and was applied equally to all building types, including churches.[10]

Romantic and eclectic historicism

After the Concordat of 1801-1802, the majority of the old urban and rural parish churches returned to their usage. From around 1830, however, the need for new construction was felt quickly due to population growth and initial urban development linked to industrialisation. The religious freedom guaranteed by the Belgian constitution was conducive to a religious revival. Between 1830 and 1857, no fewer than 1,200 churches were built, restored or enlarged.[11] At the parish level, Church Councils (*fabriques d'église / kerkfabriek*) were responsible for the material organisation of public worship. It was therefore the responsibility of these public institutions to initiate projects by acting as the client in agreement with the public authorities. These constructions were financed with public money; the plans were drawn up by municipal or provincial architects and countersigned by the civil authorities (local mayor and minister for religious affairs). These plans also had to be ratified by the Royal Commission on Monuments, a body created in 1835 with a mission to ensure the aesthetic quality of new public buildings, including churches.[12] In cities, the commission favoured large-scale projects and the construction of monumental buildings that would beautify the public space.[13] Also required to rule on the restoration of historical monuments, the commission effectively controlled all public religious building projects in Belgium.

Through the restoration of the large urban monuments of the Middle Ages, the first generation of Belgian restoration architects – all from classical academies – discovered Gothic architecture and were, from the 1840s onwards, the precursors of its renewal in Belgium during the prevailing artistic climate of Romanticism.[14] It was in 1841 that Antoine Schayes published the first history of "ogival architecture in Belgium" in response to a question asked by the Royal Academy of Belgium.[15] This study, followed in 1849 by the first "history of architecture in Belgium", aimed first and foremost to define the features of a national style: Belgian Gothic.[16] It served as an undisputed reference until the 1890s, when the theory of regional schools was developed. Municipal architects also taught at the fine arts academies in their cities. Believers in the 'Beaux-Arts system', they practised several styles indifferently, were not specialised in building churches, and were open to technical innovations, metallic structures in particular. The most brilliant of these 'eclectics' was undoubtedly Joseph Poelaert, the city architect of Brussels from 1847 to 1859, who designed the church of St Catherine (1851-1887) in the 'ogival-renaissant' style and the Gothic Revival church of Our Lady of Laeken (1852-1907), the necropolis of the new Belgian royal family.[17] [Ill. 3.2-3] Henri Van Overstraeten, architect of the 'Romano-Byzantine' church of St Mary in Schaerbeek (1848-1894), published a book in 1850 on how to design new churches by combining references to historical styles with modern construction techniques.[18] The churches of Our Lady in Sint-Niklaas (1841-1844) and St Anne in Ghent (1853-1869) are among the most remarkable churches of this eclectic generation.

While the Royal Commission on Monuments encouraged prestige projects in the

3.2-3 *Our Lady of Laeken, Brussels (1852-1907), the uncompleted royal funerary church.*
[© THOC, 2009]

10 Loir, *Bruxelles néoclassique*.
11 Schayes, *Coup d'œil sur les travaux de construction ou de restauration en style du moyen âge*, 24.
12 Stynen, *De onvoltooid verleden tijd*, 13-71.
13 See my contribution "Reconquering a Lost Visibility: Catholic Revival in Early Industrial Belgium" (2.2) in this volume.
14 The generation of Joseph-Jonas Dumont, Louis Roelandt, Tilman-François Suys, Bruno Renard, etc. all trained at the École des Beaux-Arts in Paris.
15 Schayes, *Mémoire sur l'architecture ogivale en Belgique*.
16 Schayes, *Histoire de l'architecture en Belgique*.
17 *Poelaert et son temps*, 174-184.
18 Van Overstraeten, *Architectonographie des temples chrétiens*.

new outlying urban districts, it was nevertheless budget-conscious and favoured standard plans for the construction of new rural churches. Population growth led to the enlargement or reconstruction of hundreds of rural churches in Belgium. As in cities, under agreements between the Church and State, work on rural parish churches as well as the construction of presbyteries was funded with public money. Conversely, these new churches were often built from standard plans designed by provincial architects.[19] This standardisation of churches without a precise style designed by architects-cum-civil servants, not all of whom were even Catholic, began to receive criticism in the 1850s from supporters of the archaeological movement who saw it as a loss of local identity and the trivialisation of architecture, in keeping with the adage "seen one, seen them all".

However, Gothic Revival did not impose itself as the preferred church style until the 1860s.[20] As in the teaching of architecture and other styles, France remained the model for the first Gothic Revival architects. For example, a blend of romantic historicism and the early influence of Viollet-le-Duc can be seen in the churches of St Georges in Antwerp (1847-1853), St Mary Magdalene in Bruges (1851-1853) and Our Lady in Laeken (from 1852).

Church construction and technical innovation from the industrial age

The Royal Academy of Belgium attached great importance to the use of new technologies from the industrial age. In 1846, the Class of Fine Arts raised a question on the construction of churches taking into account Belgium's climate, resources and technological progress, in particular the capabilities of the country's flourishing iron industry.[21] The first accepted dissertation on the architecture of churches, published in 1847, was written by the engineer Charles-Armand Demanet.[22] He argued for the greater use of innovative materials: cast-iron columns, walls in concrete instead of stone (as seen in England), wrought-iron sheets for roofing (as in Russia), and chemically fireproofed timber. He recommended the use of wrought iron for roof trusses due to its increased fire resistance and relatively low cost. When writing about vaulting, he advocated for iron ribs to be used in the construction of lightweight brick vaults.

Wrought and cast iron – materials abundantly produced in industrial Belgium and increasingly used in construction – thus appeared on church building sites, although without becoming widespread: window frames, columns, metal structures, spires, etc. The earliest known use of full-iron trusses in a Belgian church dates from 1842-1849 and forms the roof of the church of St Joseph, a neoclassical church designed by the architect Tilman-François Suys and erected in Brussels as the main monument of the capital's first urban extension.[23] The trusses of the main nave have a span of 10 m, with wrought iron used for all bars and nodes of the trusses, as well as for the purlins. The same architect designed the Gothic Revival church of St George in Antwerp (1847-1853). Its iron trusses were made by the Atelier de Construction belonging to Charles Marcellis, a prominent iron industrialist in the Liège area. Other early iron roof structures in the churches of St Anne in Ghent (1853-1862) and St Catherine in Brussels (1851-1866) use 'Polonceau trusses', a type developed by the French railway engineer Camille Polonceau in 1840. This type of truss would be widely used in the roofs of large urban churches from the 1860s onwards.[24]

At the church of Our Lady in Lize (1851-1855), in the industrial municipality of Seraing, the vaults of three naves are supported by thin and slender cast-iron columns. The collegiate church of St Gertrude in Nivelles had a remarkable tall cast-iron spire (1859, destroyed in 1940), while the structure of the dome of St Mary in Schaerbeek (1848-1894) is made from iron. A Gothic Revival church made entirely of wrought and cast iron was designed by the

---

19 Meul, *Van waterstaatkerk tot mijncité*; Cornilly, *Architect en ambtenaar*.
20 The churches of Our Lady in Borgerhout (1841-1846, demolished) and St Bonifacius in Ixelles (1847-1849) were the oldest Gothic Revival churches in Belgium.
21 *Bulletin de l'Academie royale des sciences, des lettres et des beaux-arts de Belgique,* XIII, 2, 1846, 231-232.
22 Demanet, *Mémoire sur l'architecture des églises*, 70.
23 Wibaut, Coomans and Wouters, *Un patrimoine insoupçonné,* 60-64, 169-170.
24 Wibaut, *Hidden Innovation*; Wibaut, Wouters and Coomans, "Hidden Above Church Vaults".

architect Raymond Carlier and built in Argenteuil (1855-1862, destroyed in 1941).[25] This experience remained a unique case, with the exception of the iron octagonal domed 'glass church' designed by architect Alphonse Balat as a part of the glass houses complex in the park of the Royal Palace in Laeken (1895, converted in 1936).[26]

Belgian construction firms designed, produced and exported iron buildings, such as railway stations and bridges, all over the world. A number of iron churches made in Belgium are still in existence, notably the Gothic Revival minor basilica of San Sebastian in Manila, the only all-steel church in Asia (1888-1891), manufactured in Binche according to plans by the Spanish architect Genaro Palacios, who designed a fire- and earthquake-proof steel structure.[27] In Boma, then the capital of the Congo Free State, the iron church that was built by the Ateliers d'Aiseau for Belgian missionaries (1899), still partially remains.

Rational and archaeological Gothic

In the 1850s, two theoretical works by Viollet-le-Duc and Pugin exerted a major influence on architects in general and on church builders in particular. On the one hand, the *Dictionnaire raisonné de l'architecture française du XIe au XVe siècle* by Eugène Viollet-le-Duc, published in ten volumes from 1854 to 1868, provided a genuine initiation to the problems of medieval architecture and construction. This was no longer approached in a romantic or formal way, but rationally, in search of the logic of the art of building, in accordance with new scientific discourse based on the positive knowledge of things. Viollet-le-Duc's scientific or 'archaeological' method of analysing buildings from the Middle Ages influenced several generations of architects and restorers.

On the other hand, *Les vrais principes de l'architecture ogivale ou chrétienne par A.W. Pugin*, printed in Bruges in 1850, was a compilation and translation into French of

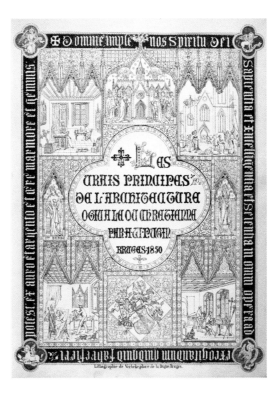

texts with plates from several publications by Augustus N.W. Pugin between 1836 and 1844.[28] [Ill. 3.2-4] This transmission of the aesthetic and moral theory of Pugin was to exert a considerable influence among Belgian ultramontane Catholics and their leader in artistic matters, Baron Jean-Baptiste Bethune.[29] He used Pugin's True Principles to legitimise his criticism of romantic historicism, which he considered ridiculous and superficial. Christian art had to be true, to use authentic materials, forms and ornaments, and be inspired by models from the Middle Ages, the knowledge of which was based on archaeological study. For Pugin and Bethune, architecture played a central role and determined all the other decorative arts.

Viollet-le-Duc influenced several generations of rationalist and historicist architects in Belgium,[30] but he was long excluded from Catholic circles because of his secularism. Conversely, Pugin barely infiltrated the academies, but would determine the method and identity of the Catholic movement of the St Luke schools.[31] This polarisation was part of the changes that had been affecting Belgian society since 1848 and the radicalisation

3.2-4 *Cover of Thomas Harper King's* Les vrais principes de l'architecture ogivale ou chrétienne, avec des remarques sur leur renaissance au temps actuel, remanié et développé d'après le texte anglais de A.W. Pugin *(Bruges, 1850).* [Leuven, KADOC-KU Leuven: KC2996]

25 Cordier and Pirard-Schoutteten, "Au fil des trouvailles: la construction de l'église de fer d'Argenteuil".
26 Wibaut, Coomans and Wouters, *Un patrimoine insoupçonné*, 121-139.
27 Submitted in 2006 to the World Heritage tentative list: <https://web.archive.org/web/20150323202626/https://whc.unesco.org/en/tentativelists/518/>.
28 King, *Les vrais principes de l'architecture ogivale ou chrétienne*. This book is an anthology of Pugin's theories from *Contrasts* (1836), *The True Principles* (1841) and the *Glossary of Ecclesiastical Ornament and Costume* (1844), augmented with personal considerations from King and some additional illustrations.
29 Helbig, *Le Baron Bethune*; Van Cleven et al., eds., *Neogotiek in België*, 167-211.
30 Loyer, *Paul Hankar*, 28-41.
31 Coomans, "Pugin Worldwide".

of political life between Catholics and Liberals during the 1850s. The Unionism that had marked the first two decades of Belgian political life had passed: the two rival parties no longer held back and offered different worldviews. The dogmatic character of 'Pugianisme' was perfectly suited to the most conservative Catholics, the ultramontans, who adopted it wholeheartedly, but remained isolated within the Catholic world.[32]

The early 1860s were marked by reforms that allowed the archaeological movement to make progress and the ultramontans to infiltrate a number of institutions. Thus, in 1860, with the aim of decentralisation and expansion to archaeologists, the government gave the Royal Commission on Monuments nine provincial chambers.[33] As early as 1861, James Weale, one of the new members and someone close to Bethune, vehemently denounced the incompetence of the restoration architects and pleaded for archaeological and historical studies to be carried out prior to any restoration. At the Mechelen congresses of 1863, 1864 and 1867, the union of Belgian Catholics was strengthened and the social organisation of Catholic works redefined.[34] The 1863 congress took three important decisions in favour of Christian art: it created a chair of Christian archaeology at the Catholic University of Leuven; it laid the foundations for the Guild of St Thomas and St Luke to promote and propagate Christian art; and it encouraged the foundation of a school of Christian art that would become the St Luke school. These three complementary institutions promoted the archaeological approach to a national medieval art as a way of creating authentic Christian art.

Baron Bethune and St Luke Gothic

The first school of the St Luke movement began modestly in Ghent in 1862-1864 thanks to the coming together of three ultramontans: Jean-Baptiste Bethune, the ideologist and guarantor of the aesthetic orthodoxy, Joseph de Hemptinne, an industrialist who backed the project financially, and Brother Marès-Joseph of the Brothers of the Christian Schools, the school's educationalist and director.[35] Classes were given in the evening and aimed at working-class men who wanted to acquire skills and become artisans. After ten years, St Luke was an established school with a firm plan, proven teaching method and network of influence. Other St Luke schools were founded in Tournai in 1877, Lille in 1878, Liège in 1880, Schaerbeek (Brussels) and Kortrijk in 1882, and Saint-Gilles (Brussels) in 1898, all run by Brothers of the Christian Schools.[36]

Bethune had made Pugin's guiding principle his own: "Christian or Gothic art is not one of several styles that are equally beautiful and suitable, but the only one that, as Catholic Christians, we can use in a rational way to build our churches".[37] The ultramontans viewed the medieval community and the art of the thirteenth century as a period of harmonious interaction between religion and society, Church and Country, and between Thomism, art and science. "This selective and ideological interpretation of the Middle Ages is reflected in a rigid paradigm – the triad 'true, beautiful and good' as a reflection of the Divine –, in the choice of a sober architecture made with regional materials (brick, oak and fir), but rich in symbolic and liturgical expression, expressed through the rather opulent interior fittings in response to a rigorous iconography that constituted a direct challenge to the artistic professions."[38]

The aesthetic reference of St Luke therefore depended entirely on 'Maître Jean Bethune', who was capable of creating anything – architecture, sculpture, stained glass, painting, furniture, goldsmithery, etc. – as he had brilliantly demonstrated at the château in Loppem near Bruges (1858-1863), which re-expressed the spirit of Pugin in the Bruges Gothic style of the fifteenth century.[39] The church built by Bethune in Vivenkapelle (1859-1867), also near Bruges, became an archetype for rural churches in the fourteenth-century Flemish style, with complete Gothic Revival furnishings in the service of

32 De Maeyer, "Kunst en politiek", 63-91.
33 Stynen, *De onvoltooid verleden tijd*, 119-147.
34 Verpoest, "De architectuur van de Sint-Lucasscholen", 229-233.
35 Wouters, "Broeders en Baronnen".
36 Wouters, *Van tekenklas tot kunstacademie*.
37 King, *Les vrais principes de l'architecture ogivale ou chrétienne*, XIV.
38 Bergmans, Coomans and De Maeyer, "Arts décoratifs néo-gothiques en Belgique", 49.
39 van Caloen, Van Cleven and Braet, *Het kasteel van Loppem*.
40 Goossens, "De Onze-Lieve-Vrouw-Geboorte en Heilige Philippuskerk te Vivenkapelle".
41 De Maeyer, "The Neo-Gothic in Belgium", 27-31; Id., "Kunst en politiek", 68-71.
42 The models were analysed, measured, drawn and reproduced, according to the method of Brother Marès-Joseph, *Modèles gradués pour servir d'exercices préparatoires à l'étude du dessin à main levée*.

an authentic Catholic liturgy.[40] [Ill. 3.2-5] Surrounded by two schools, a presbytery and a convent also designed by Bethune, the church in Vivenkapelle formed the nucleus of a traditional rural village that looked to have escaped the modernity of the industrial world, its social tensions and the First School War between Liberals and Catholics. Bethune's total art rested on a unity of flawless style and design, promoted the model of craftsmanship and asserted itself as the antithesis of eclecticism and modernity.

As architecture was the mother of all arts, architects had to be able to imagine everything while craftsmen had to be ready to implement superior ideas. The St Luke schools became the instrument through which the Gothic of Bethune and Pugin, the style of the ultramontans, was taught and disseminated throughout society. The architects and craftsmen who graduated from the St Luke schools became 'crusaders' in the battle that opposed the Catholic tradition against liberalism.[41] Teaching at the St Luke schools was based on the drawing and study of the models of the Middle Ages, from sculptural moulding and architectural fragments.[42] In order to make 'good models' of Gothic art and craftmanship available to pupils, St Luke published albums of plates of tracings of religious and civil architecture, medieval structures, profiles and Gothic capitals, as well as technical drawings of furnishings, metalworking, etc. St Luke also published monographs of restored medieval churches, as well as the influential *Revue de l'Art Chrétien* (1857-1914). All these publications adopted the Gothic Revival graphic style taught at the school and thus helped spread the spirit of St Luke.[43]

Founded in Mechelen in 1863, the Guild of St Thomas and St Luke formed a network of Catholic artists, clergyman and archaeologists involved in the promotion, study and conservation of medieval art. This network numbered a hundred or so members, not all of whom were ultramontans. They went on excursions in Belgium and further afield, publishing a bulletin from 1863 to 1913.[44] This first-hand source offers an insight into architectural debates about restoration, aesthetic interpretations and political priorities. The 'guild' was part of the associative model that Belgian Catholics developed during the second half of the nineteenth century for their socio-professional corporations.[45] These guilds of craftsmen and workers were a Catholic reaction to the unions and other socialist worker associations. Organised Catholicism had its own premises, just as socialists had their '*maisons du peuple*'. The Catholic model rejected modern industry, made reference to the arts and craftsmanship of the Middle Ages and to an idealised

3.2-5 Interior of the church of Vivenkapelle by Jean-Baptiste Bethune and his team of craftsmen (1859-1867). [© Oswald Pauwels, 2007]

43 Dujardin, "The Saint Luke School Movement and the Revival of Medieval Illumination in Belgium".
44 *Bulletin des séances de la Gilde de Saint-Thomas et de Saint-Luc*, Ghent, 1863-1913.
45 Deferme and De Maeyer, "Ultramontaans corporatisme en Sint-Lucasneogotiek".

social solidarity; it was conservative and anti-modern.

The Benedictine abbey of Maredsous (1872-1890), the most ambitious monastic revival project in Belgium, is also one of Bethune's most remarkable buildings. The project was supported by conservative ultramontans and inspired by the ideal abbeys designed by Pugin.[46] Bethune adopted the style of the thirteenth century – with lancet windows – and used local construction materials, including a dark grey limestone. Situated at the top of the hill and dominating a vast landscape of forests, Maredsous resembles a timeless medieval abbey. [Ill. 2.2-7]

The example of Bethune was soon emulated by those who were also the first teachers at the St Luke school in Ghent. The prominent architect of this first generation was Auguste Van Assche, who had been trained at the Academy in Ghent but converted to Puginism in the early 1860s. Unlike Bethune, who was self-taught, Van Assche was an architect, builder and restorer. He taught architecture at St Luke and his students were also interns in his studio. Van Assche built and restored over a hundred churches in Belgium, built religious houses and châteaux and published monographs on his major restorations. His restoration method was archaeological and based on precise studies.[47] Not fond of painting or wall coatings, he would strip interiors to show the ashlar and the colours of the materials.[48]

A turning point in the history of St Luke came in 1875, when Pierre Van Kerkhove, the first architect to graduate from St Luke, was commissioned to build the new town hall in Sint-Niklaas. This was an official recognition of the school's ability to train talented architects capable of constructing public buildings. Similar to a model by Pugin, the town hall in Sint-Niklaas was a victory for the St Luke style in its fight for Catholic, Gothic and national architecture.

Saint Luke Gothic: a national, Catholic and rational style

After the long political domination of the Liberals, the Catholic Party governed Belgium with an absolute majority from 1884 to 1914. These three decades corresponded to Belgium's industrial and economic heyday, but were also marked by social movements, the birth of modern arts and the rejection of historicism. Once in power, the Catholics promoted St Luke Gothic, which went from its combat position to that of official 'national style'.[49] From then on, public commissions for post offices, town halls, railway stations and other official buildings were added to churches, schools, convents, private houses and châteaux. More and more architects and craftsmen trained at the St Luke schools were able to flood the country with buildings, arts, prints, furnishings, objects, etc.[50] The movement became a system producing a stereotyped total art in the service of an ideology and gradually lost its originality and original spirit.

Joris Helleputte was a key figure in the Gothic Revival generation after 1884.[51] This ultramontane engineer from Ghent became a professor at the Catholic University of Leuven in 1874 and laid the foundations for independent training in architectural civil engineering. Although much younger than Bethune, Helleputte faithfully adopted Pugin's canon,[52] but did not reject the use of metallic structures and sometimes even left them visible, as at the church of St Francis de Sales in Liège (1888-1894, destroyed in 1988). [Ill. 3.2-7] This understanding of a historicist and rational architecture, open to the modern techniques produced in industrial Belgium, was not unlike the teaching of Viollet-le-Duc. Helleputte showed that his point of view was not incompatible with the heritage of Pugin, provided that it retained its Catholic identity. Historians have called this approach the 'ingenious Gothic Revival'.[53] Helleputte, however, was a well-connected man of the system, working in the service of a society project and a Catholic worldview.

46 Misonne, *En parcourant l'histoire de Maredsous*, 10-21 and 77-130.
47 Coomans, "Saint-Christophe à Liège".
48 Bergmans, *Middeleeuwse muurschilderingen in de 19de eeuw*, 114-183.
49 De Maeyer, "The Neo-Gothic in Belgium", 32-34; Id., "Kunst en politiek", 91-123.
50 Bergmans, Coomans and De Maeyer, "Arts décoratifs néo-gothiques en Belgique".
51 De Maeyer and Van Molle, eds., *Joris Helleputte*.
52 Maes, *Joris Helleputte*.
53 De Keyser, De Maeyer and Verpoest, *De ingenieuze neogotiek*.

At the Royal Commission on Monuments – of which he became a member in 1885, then vice-president from 1895 to 1925 – he promoted the projects of St Luke architects, both for the restoration of historical monuments and the construction of new public buildings. In 1889, he was elected to Parliament, becoming a minister from 1907 to 1918, notably of Public Works, Railways, Post and Agriculture. In this capacity, he awarded numerous public commissions to St Luke architects, also promoting them to architectural posts in the administration. Certain projects, amongst others the large churches of St Donatus in Arlon (1907-1914) and St Peter and Paul in Ostend (1901-1907), were designed as national, Gothic, rational and Catholic monuments. [Ill. 3.2-1] The megaproject for a national basilica of the Holy Heart on the Koekelberg plateau in Brussels was promoted by King Leopold II for the embellishment of the capital. This large Gothic cathedral with seven spires, designed by the architect Pierre Langerock, would have marked the triumph of St Luke Gothic as the national style. [Ill. 2.2-9] Work began in 1903 with the laying of reinforced concrete foundations, but was halted soon after the death of Leopold II (1909).[54]

From 1884, hundreds of parish churches were built, enlarged or restored in the St Luke style, with public money through the intermediary of Church Councils. Forming the centre of villages or urban neighbourhoods, these new churches were accompanied by a presbytery, a parish hall

3.2-6 *The church of St Anthony in Pepinster (1893-1899), a total work of art. (See also col. ill. 10.)*
[© SPW-AWaP; photo Guy Focant]

3.2-7 *Interior of the church of St Francis de Sales in Liège by Joris Helleputte (1888-1894).*
[Brussels, IRPA-KIK: KN000243; photo Jacques Declercq]

54 Rion, *La basilique de Koekelberg*.

253

and often a Catholic school or sometimes a small convent. Moreover, congregations and religious orders, the number of which had increased even further in Belgium following the *Kulturkampf* in Germany and the laws of secularisation in France, systematically used St Luke architects and craftsmen. This resulted in projects that integrated architecture and other decorative arts produced by specialised and experienced workshops.[55] The chapel of St Juliana in Saint-Josse-ten-Node (1884-1886) and the church of St Anthony in Pepinster (1893-1899) are among the best preserved of this total art. [Ill. 3.2-6]

Until the First World War, the St Luke Gothic style thus retained a monopoly on the construction of churches.[56] The architects who had been trained by Bethune, Van Assche and Helleputte remained loyal to the aesthetic canon of their teachers, in the service of the ultramontane ideology.[57] One of them, Alphonse De Moerloose, became a missionary in northern China and built St Luke churches there until the 1920s.[58]

Disputed Gothic

Paradoxically, it was as the St Luke style reached its peak that a dispute emerged, both inside and outside the movement. The death of Bethune in 1894 marked the end of the strict application of his dogmatic ideology. The younger generation was finally allowed to refer to Viollet-le-Duc, to use modern structures and industrial techniques. However, by now, Viollet-le-Duc was already a thing of the past. In 1894, the year of Bethune's death, Henry van de Velde published his famous essay *Déblaiement d'art* in Brussels, one of the founding texts of modernity.[59] Art Nouveau and the various forms of avant-garde that developed in the 1890s among the progressive elites spurned St Luke Gothic as one of the old systems from which liberation was needed. Around 1900, progressive Christian Democrats promoted a contemporary Christian art and invited supporters of the St Luke style to follow them on the path of modernity.[60]

Of the architects who tried to open up the St Luke schools to other influences, forms and structures, Louis Cloquet is the most interesting.[61] When he taught at the St Luke school in Tournai (1880-1891), his first buildings and restorations were in line with Bethune and Van Assche. Appointed professor at the University of Ghent, his projects became increasingly eclectic and free, while remaining under the influence of Gothic architecture. His most creative work can be seen in his few university buildings, the central post office and the station in Ghent completed for the Universal Exhibition of 1913. Cloquet published many articles, was the driving force behind the *Revue de l'Art Chrétien,* and published a masterful treatise on architecture in five volumes (1898-1901), based on his university teaching and influenced by Viollet-le-Duc's rational architectural theories.[62] Furthermore, his archaeological studies were the starting point for Belgium's regional art schools and a new artistic landscape.[63] From the 1890s, reference was no longer made to Belgian Gothic architecture, but to Scaldian Gothic, Mosan Gothic, Brabant Gothic, etc, designating the regions of Scheldt, Meuse, Brabant etc. respectively. Cloquet thus contributed to laying the scientific foundations for the regionalism that was to have consequences both in architecture and architectural history, as well as playing a leading role in reconstruction after the First World War.

In 1901, the St Luke movement began publishing a new journal, the *Bulletin des métiers d'art,* that promoted regional identities and was part of the Arts and Crafts movement.[64] It was a long way from the Gothic canon, the dogmatic character of which was becoming more and more anachronistic when compared to the freedom advocated by Art Nouveau. For civil architecture, domestic architecture in particular, regionalism drew its inspiration primarily from vernacular architecture with St Luke architects such as Jos Viérin and Valentin Vaerwyck. For religious architecture, regional influences were based on historical foundations, with reference to the regional vari-

---

55 Van Cleven, "Sint-Lucasateliers".
56 Van Cleven, "Neogotiek en neogotismen", 50-55.
57 Including the architects Pierre Langerock, Jules Coomans, Stéphane Mortier, Alfons De Pauw and Modeste de Noyette.
58 Coomans, "Pugin Worldwide"; Id. and Luo, "Exporting Flemish Gothic Architecture to China".
59 Coomans, "The St Luke Schools and Henry van de Velde".
60 De Maeyer, "Kunst en politiek", 107-123.
61 De Maeyer, "Regionalism, Secularisation and the Emancipation of St Luke Architecture", 125-128.
62 Cloquet, *Traité d'architecture*.
63 Coomans, "L'historiographie de l'architecture romane en Belgique"; Id., "Vom Nationalismus zum Regionalismus".
64 *Bulletin des metiers d'art*, 1901-1913; Van Impe, "Regionalism, Rationalism and Modernity".
65 Lemaire, *Les origines du style gothique en Brabant*.
66 *L'art et ses applications / De kunst en hare toepassingen*.
67 Stynen, *De onvoltooid verleden tijd*, 249-271.

ants of the Gothic and Romanesque styles in Belgium. Gothic lost its monopoly to Romanesque architecture, the study of which was promoted by Canon Raymond Lemaire, a professor of Christian art at the Catholic University of Leuven.[65] Another influence of regionalism on religious architecture was the abandonment of painted interiors for raw materials (brick, local stones, exposed wooden vaults and timber roof structures), the natural colours of which displayed the authentic accents of regional identities.

Epilogue

The First World War marked the end of St Luke Gothic. The question that arose in the aftermath of the conflict was that of reconstruction. The St Luke style, of course, had the support of conservators and laid claim to official commissions for the reconstruction of churches and the restoration of monuments and historical centres,[66] but the world had changed profoundly. The Catholics had lost the absolute majority they had held since 1884, the Socialists had entered Parliament following the introduction of universal suffrage, and modern architecture rejected the Gothic paradigm once and for all, including for its churches.

The St Luke architects played an active part in the restoration of historical monuments.[67] The historicist reconstruction of the martyred towns of Ypres – by the municipal architect Jules Coomans, a former student of Helleputte –, Diksmuide, Nieuwpoort and Dinant was stimulated by the Royal Commission on Monuments and Sites.[68] However, regional styles and modern architecture definitively replaced the 'national style'.[69] The national basilica of the Sacred Heart in Koekelberg is the supreme symbolic example of this paradigm shift. With building halted in 1911, the Gothic project was replaced in 1922 by a large domed building with Art Deco accents, designed by the architect Albert Van huffel, trained at the academy in Ghent.[70] Having lost its monopoly, support-

ers of the St Luke movement understood that the Gothic page had to be turned and the school had to evolve towards modernity.[71] This was not without difficulty, as conservatives remained influential in a certain number of organisations, in particular the Guild of St Luke and St Joseph, which brought together former students of the St Luke schools.

Finally, the use of reinforced concrete in architecture also impacted the debate around churches.[72] Despite the pioneering role of Belgian engineers in reinforced concrete,[73] and the use of this material for churches in France from 1899,[74] a single school chapel was built from reinforced concrete in Belgium before the First World War, for the Ursulines in Overpelt (1909-1911, converted in 1912).[75] [Ill. 3.2-8] This chapel translates Gothic forms into concrete. After the war, the St Luke architects could no longer continue to promote their artisanal model or to oppose reinforced concrete, which offered larger spaces for significantly lower budgets.[76] By now Gothic had lost its ideological dimension. Its forms survived only by becoming geometrical and adapting to the possibilities offered by reinforced concrete, thus becoming 'modern Gothic'.[77]

3.2-8 The school chapel of the Ursulines in Overpelt (1909-1911), a concrete box. [© Oswald Pauwels, 2007]

68 Smets, Resurgam.
69 Meganck, "Domi or Dom-Ino?".
70 Vandenbreeden and De Puydt, Koekelberg basiliek.
71 Wouters, Van tekenklas tot kunstacademie; Van de Perre, Op de grens van twee werelden, 31-55.
72 Van de Voorde, Bouwen in beton in België.
73 The Frenchman François Hennebique spent the first 25 years of his career in Belgium, where he founded his famous design office in 1892. The Belgian firm Blaton-Aubert was founded in 1897, and the Belgian Concrete Company in 1909.
74 The church of St John in Montmartre, by Anatole de Baudot (1899-1905).
75 Pauwels, "Het ursulinenklooster met lager school van Overpelt".
76 Jaspers, "Huib Hoste and the Reconstruction of Zonnebeke".
77 As with the churches of Paul Bellot: Culot, Dom Bellot: moine-architecte.

BIBLIOGRAPHY

Bergmans, Anna. *Middeleeuwse muurschilderingen in de 19de eeuw. Studie en inventaris van middeleeuwse muurschilderingen in Belgische kerken.* KADOC Artes, 2. Leuven, 1998.

Bergmans, Anna, Thomas Coomans and Jan De Maeyer. "Arts décoratifs néo-gothiques en Belgique". In: Claire Leblanc, ed. *Art Nouveau et Design: 175 ans d'arts décoratifs en Belgique.* Brussels, 2005, 36-59.

Bertrand, Matthieu, Nicolas Chenut and Luc-Francis Genicot. *Les églises paroissiales de Wallonie (1830-1940).* 3 vols. Namur, 2009-2010.

Bulletin des metiers d'art, 1901-1913.

Bulletin des séances de la Gilde de Saint-Thomas et de Saint-Luc. Ghent, 1863-1913.

Cloquet Louis. *Traité d'architecture. Éléments de l'architecture. Hygiène. Types d'édifices. Esthétique et composition.* 5 vols. Paris-Lille, 1898-1901.

Coomans, Thomas. "Op weg naar bescherming van 19de-eeuwse kerkgebouwen in Vlaanderen. Een status-quaestionis". *M&L. Monumenten en Landschappen*, 21 (2002) 4, 38-61.

Coomans, Thomas. "Veel zorgen, weinig zorg. De lotgevallen van negentiende-eeuwse kerkgebouwen in de twintigste eeuw in België". In: Anna Bergmans, Jan De Maeyer, Wim Denslagen and Wies van Leeuwen, eds. *Neostijlen in de negentiende eeuw: zorg geboden?* KADOC Artes, 7. Leuven, 2002, 130-159.

Coomans Thomas. "Saint-Christophe à Liège: la plus ancienne église médiévale du mouvement béguinal". *Bulletin monumental*, 164 (2006) 4, 359-376.

Coomans, Thomas. "Vom Nationalismus zum Regionalismus. Die Geschichtsschreibung zur romanischen Architektur in Belgien". In: Leonhard Helten and Wolfgang Schenkluhn, eds. *Romanik in Europa: Kommunikation - Tradition - Rezeption.* More Romano. Schriftenrheie des Europäischen Romanik Zentrums, 1. Leipzig, 2009, 143-166.

Coomans, Thomas. "L'historiographie de l'architecture romane en Belgique: entre nationalisme, régionalisme et internationalisme". In: Jacques Toussaint, ed. *Pierres-Papiers-Ciseaux. Architecture et sculpture romanes (Meuse-Escaut).* Monographies du Musée provincial des Arts anciens du Namurois, 53. Namur, 2012, 25-41.

Coomans, Thomas. "Quelle protection pour les églises à Bruxelles? Vers une approche patrimoniale concertée". *Bruxelles Patrimoines*, 2 (2012), 52-77.

Coomans, Thomas. "Églises, couvents et chapelles: évolution et signification d'un patrimoine multiple dans le paysage culturel de Bruxelles". *Bruxelles patrimoines*, 13 (2014), 6-34.

Coomans, Thomas. "Pugin Worldwide. From *Les Vrais Principes* and the Belgian St Luke Schools to Northern China and Inner Mongolia". In Timothy Brittain-Catlin, Jan De Maeyer and Martin Bressani, eds. *Gothic Revival Worldwide: A.W.N. Pugin's Global Influence.* KADOC Artes, 16. Leuven, 2016, 156-171.

Coomans, Thomas. "The St Luke Schools and Henry van de Velde: Two Concomitant Theories on the Decorative Arts in Late Nineteenth-Century Belgium." *Revue Belge d'Archéologie et d'Histoire de l'Art / Belgisch Tijdschrift voor Oudheidkunde en Kunstgeschiedenis*, 85 (2016), 123-148.

Coomans, Thomas, and Wei Luo. "Exporting Flemish Gothic Architecture to China: Meaning and Context of the Churches of Shebiya (Inner Mongolia) and Xuanhua (Hebei) built by Missionary-Architect Alphonse De Moerloose in 1903-1906". *Relicta. Heritage Research in Flanders*, 9 (2012), 219-262.

Cordier, Willy, and Josette Pirard-Schoutteten. "Au fil des trouvailles: la construction de l'église de fer d'Argenteuil". *Revue d'histoire religieuse du Brabant wallon*, 6 (1992), 128-144.

Cornilly, Jeroen. *Architect en ambtenaar. De West-Vlaamse provincial architecten en de 19de-eeuwse architectuurpraktijk.* Leuven, 2016.

Culot, Maurice. *Dom Bellot: moine-architecte 1876-1944.* Paris: Norma Éditions, 1996.

Deferme, Jo, and Jan De Maeyer. "Ultramontaans corporatisme en Sint-Lucasneogotiek. Ideologie en praktijk in de ateliers rond Bethune en Helleputte". *Trajecta*, 17 (2008) 2, 108-128.

De Keyser, Bart, Jan De Maeyer and Luc Verpoest. *De ingenieuze neogotiek: techniek en kunst 1852-1925.* Leuven, 1997.

De Maeyer, Jan. "Kunst en politiek. De Sint-Lucasscholen tussen ultramontaanse orthodoxie en drang naar maatschappelijk-culturele vernieuwing". In: Jan De Maeyer, ed. *De Sint-Lucasscholen en de neogotiek 1862-1914.* KADOC studies, 5. Leuven, 1988, 58-123.

De Maeyer, Jan. "The Neo-Gothic in Belgium: Architecture of a Catholic Society". In: Jan De Maeyer and Luc Verpoest, eds. *Gothic Revival: Religion, Architecture and Style in Western Europe 1815-1914.* KADOC Artes, 5. Leuven, 2000, 18-34.

De Maeyer, Jan. "Regionalism, Secularisation and the Emancipation of St Luke Architecture". In: Linda Van Santvoort, Jan De Maeyer and Tom Verschaffel, eds. *Sources of Regionalism in the Nineteenth Century.* KADOC Artes, 9. Leuven, 2009, 122-137.

De Maeyer, Jan, Thomas Coomans and Eva Weyns. "Le néogothique à Bruxelles: un foisonnement de concepts et de pratiques". *Bruxelles patrimoines*, 19-20 (2016), 52-65.

De Maeyer, Jan, and Leen Van Molle, eds. *Joris Helleputte (1852-1925). Architect en politicus. Biografie.* KADOC Artes, 1. Leuven, 1998.

Demanet, Armand. *Mémoire sur l'architecture des églises.* Brussels, 1847.

De Schepper, Gratianus. "Marie-Thérèse et Joseph II: leur politique à l'égard des maisons religieuses dans les Pays-Bas". *Revue d'Histoire ecclésiastique*, 35 (1939), 509-529.

Dierkens-Aubry, Françoise, and Jos Vandenbreeden. *Le XIXe siècle en Belgique. Architecture et intérieurs.* Brussels, 1994.

Dujardin, Carine. "The Saint Luke School Movement and the Revival of Medieval Illumination in Belgium (1866-1923)". In: Thomas Coomans and Jan De Maeyer, eds. *The Revival of Medieval Illumination: Nineteenth-Century Belgium Manuscript and Illuminations from a European Perspective.* KADOC Artes, 8. Leuven, 2007, 269-293.

Goossens, Miek. "De Onze-Lieve-Vrouw-Geboorte en Heilige Philippuskerk te Vivenkapelle: de volmaakte neogotische dorpskerk". *M&L. Monumenten en Landschappen*, 9 (1990) 5, 38-56.

Helbig, Jules. *Le Baron Bethune, fondateur des Écoles Saint-Luc. Étude biographique.* Lille-Bruges, 1906.

Jaspers, Patrik. "Huib Hoste and the Reconstruction of Zonnebeke, 1919-1924". In: Nicholas Bullock and Luc Verpoest, eds. *Living with History, 1914-1964. Rebuilding Europe after the First and Second World Wars and the Role of Heritage Preservation / La reconstruction en Europe après la Première et la Seconde Guerre mondiale et le rôle de la conservation des monuments historiques.* KADOC Artes, 12. Leuven, 2011, 218-229.

King, Thomas Harper. *Les vrais principes de l'architecture ogivale ou chrétienne, avec des remarques sur leur renaissance au temps actuel, remanié et développé d'après le texte anglais de A.W. Pugin.* Bruges, 1850.

L'art et ses applications / De kunst en hare toepassingen. Verzameling van platen der werken uitgevoerd door leden van de Gilde der oud-leerlingen, Sint-Lucasschool Gent. 2 vols. Ghent, 1922-1923.

Lemaire, Raymond. *Les origines du style gothique en Brabant. Première partie: l'architecture romane.* Brussels-Paris, 1906.

Loir, Christophe. *Bruxelles néoclassique. Mutation d'un espace urbain 1775-1840.* Lieux de mémoire. Brussels, 2009.

Loyer, François. *Paul Hankar. La naissance de l'Art Nouveau*. Brussels, 1986.

Maes, Krista. *Joris Helleputte (1852-1925). Architect en politicus. Oeuvrecatalogus*. KADOC Artes, 1. Leuven, 1998.

Marès-Joseph [brother]. *Modèles gradués pour servir d'exercices préparatoires à l'étude du dessin à main levée*. Bruges-Lille, 1870.

Meganck, Leen. "Domi or Dom-Ino? The Role of the Genius loci in post-war Reconstruction and Interwar urbanism". In: Nicholas Bullock and Luc Verpoest, eds. *Living with History, 1914-1964: Rebuilding Europe after the First and Second World Wars and the Role of Heritage Preservation*. KADOC Artes, 12. Leuven, 2011, 231-243.

Meul, Veerle. *Van waterstaatkerk tot mijncité. Een historiek van het bouwen in Limburg door drie generaties provinciale bouwmeesters Jaminé (1832-1921)*. Hasselt, 1999.

Misonne, Daniel. *En parcourant l'histoire de Maredsous*. Denée, 2005.

Pauwels, Dirk. "Het ursulinenklooster met lager school van Overpelt, een creatie van Hyacinth Martens, met kapel van kanunnik Joannes Broux". *M&L. Monumenten en landschappen*, 26 (2007) 4, 41-69.

Poelaert et son temps. Brussels, 1980, 174-184.

Rion, Pierre. *La basilique de Koekelberg. Architecture et mentalités religieuses*. Publications d'histoire de l'art et d'archéologie de l'Université catholique de Louvain, 47. Louvain-la-Neuve, 1986.

Schayes, Antoine Guillaume Bernard. *Mémoire sur l'architecture ogivale en Belgique*. Brussels, 1841.

Schayes, Antoine Guillaume Bernard. *Histoire de l'architecture en Belgique, depuis les temps les plus reculés jusqu'à l'époque actuelle*. Brussels, 1849.

Schayes, Antonin Guillaume Bernard. *Coup d'œil sur les travaux de construction ou de restauration en style du moyen âge, exécutés en Belgique depuis 1830*. Paris, 1857.

Smets, Marcel. *Resurgam. La reconstruction en Belgique après 1914*. Brussels, 1985.

Stynen, Herman. *De onvoltooid verleden tijd. Een geschiedenis van de monumenten- en landschapszorg in België 1835-1940*. Brussels, 1998.

Toman, Rolf, ed. *Neoclassicism and Romanticism: Architecture, Sculpture, Painting, Drawings: 1750-1848*. Cologne, 2000.

van Caloen, Véronique, Jean Van Cleven and Johan Braet. *Het kasteel van Loppem*. Oostkamp, 2001.

Van Cleven, Jean. "Neogotiek en neogotismen. De neogotiek als component van de 19de-eeuwse stijl in België". In: Jan De Maeyer, ed. *De Sint-Lucasscholen en de neogotiek, 1862-1914*. KADOC-studies, 5. Leuven, 1988, 17-55.

Van Cleven, Jean. "Sint-Lucasateliers in de plastische kunsten en de toegepaste kunst". In: Jan De Maeyer, ed. *De Sint-Lucasscholen en de neogotiek 1862-1914*. KADOC studies, 5. Leuven, 1988, 279-380.

Van Cleven, Jean, Frieda Van Tyghem, Ignace De Wilde and Robert Hozee, eds. *Neogotiek in België*. Tielt, 1994.

Vandenbreeden, Jos, and Raoul Maria De Puydt. *Koekelberg basiliek, art-decomonument / Basilique de Koekelberg, monument art déco*. Tielt-Brussels, 2005.

Van de Perre, Dirk. *Op de grens van twee werelden. Beeld van het Sint-Lucasonderwijs aan het Sint-Lucasinstituut te Gent in de periode 1919-1965/1974*. Ghent, 2003, 31-55.

Van de Vijver, Dirk. "L'architecture dans les Pays-Bas autrichiens et la Principauté de Liège". In: Luc Dhondt, Jean-Christophe Hubert, Christophe Vachaudez, Jean Van Cleven and Dirk Van de Vijver. *Architecture du XVIIIe siècle en Belgique. Baroque tardif, rococo, néo-classicisme*. Brussels, 1998, 127-168.

Van de Voorde, Stephanie. *Bouwen in beton in België (1890-1975). Samenspel van kennis, experiment en innovatie*. PhD dissertation, UGent. Ghent, 2011.

Van Impe, Ellen. "Regionalism, Rationalism and Modernity in the Early Twentieth-Century St Luke Movement. Bulletin des metiers d'art, the Arts and Crafts Movement and 'Les leçons de l'art local', 1901-1914". In: Linda Van Santvoort, Jan De Maeyer and Tom Verschaffel, eds. *Sources of Regionalism in the Nineteenth Century*. KADOC Artes, 9. Leuven, 2009, 138-159.

Van Loo, Anne, ed. *Dictionnaire de l'architecture en Belgique de 1830 à nos jours*. Antwerp, 2003.

Van Overstraeten, Henri. *Architectonographie des temples chrétiens, ou étude comparative et pratique des différents systèmes d'architecture applicables à la construction des églises, spécialement en Belgique, précédée d'une introduction sur l'architecture religieuse de l'Antiquité*. Mechelen, 1850.

Verpoest, Luc. "De architectuur van de Sint-Lucasscholen: het herstel van een traditie". In: Jan De Maeyer, ed. *De Sint-Lucasscholen en de neogotiek 1862-1914*. KADOC studies, 5. Leuven, 1988, 219-277.

Viollet-le-Duc, Eugène-Edouard. *Dictionnaire raisonné de l'architecture française du XIe au XVe siècle*. 10 vols. Paris, 1854-1868.

Wibaut, Romain. *Hidden Innovation. Roof Frame Design and Construction in Parish Churches in Brussels and Charleroi, 1830-1940*. PhD dissertation KU Leuven and VUB. Leuven-Brussels, 2021.

Wibaut, Romain, Thomas Coomans and Ine Wouters. *Un patrimoine insoupçonné. Les charpentes en bois, metal et béton armé dans les églises de la Région de Bruxelles-Capitale 1830-1940*. Urban Research / Architectural Heritage, 1. Brussels, 2021.

Wibaut, Romain, Ine Wouters and Thomas Coomans. "Hidden Above Church Vaults: The Design Evolution of Early Iron Roof Trusses in Mid-Nineteenth-Century Belgium". *International Journal of Architectural Heritage. Conservation, Analysis, and Restoration*, 13 (2019) 7, 963-978.

Wouters, Wilfried. "Broeders en Baronnen: het ontstaan van de Sint-Lucasscholen". In: Jan De Maeyer, ed. *De Sint-Lucasscholen en de neogotiek 1862-1914*. KADOC studies, 5. Leuven, 1988, 157-217.

Wouters, Wilfried. *Van tekenklas tot kunstacademie: de Sint-Lucasscholen in België 1866-1966*. Kortrijk, 2013.

http://www.irismonument.be/
https://inventaris.onroerenderfgoed.be/

3.3
To Induce a Beneficial Impression in Their Souls

Church Architecture and Interior Décor in the Netherlands

Wies van Leeuwen

Church building and the visual arts have been intimately connected over many centuries. In the Netherlands, the period 1780-1920 reflected important changes in the design and building of churches, religious buildings and convents. They were a reflection of important religious reform movements. After the restoration of the episcopal hierarchy in 1853, hundreds of new Roman Catholic buildings rose up in cities and villages, mostly in the Gothic Revival style. A powerful, centralised authority replaced the missionary church of the secular and regular clerics. Meanwhile the Dutch Reformed Church occupied the medieval city and town churches, but became splintered. In this period it saw several splits away from official doctrine. Each group of course needed new churches or chapels. Religious architecture reflected denominational independence: the so-called *verzuiling*. Each denomination had its own architects and artists, and its own doctrine of style. Buildings and their interiors reflected religious reform, that is, the way in which religion wanted to manifest itself in a changing society. Not only was the skyline of cities and villages altered: changes were reflected in the design and arrangements of interior spaces and decoration.

Catholic style, from Baroque to Gothic Revival

A theatrical liturgy, orchestral music and incense characterised the Baroque house and barn-churches of Catholics in the eighteenth century. Catholics and Old Catholics – a group that separated itself from the Roman Catholics in 1723 – were tolerated as minorities in relation to the official Dutch Reformed Church. Protestants confiscated the medieval churches after the Reformation, and the churches of the minorities were hidden in cities and villages. The *schuilkerken* or house-churches had austere brick façades, and were almost invisible; richness and decoration were confined to the interior. White walls and stuccoed barrel vaults directed the attention of the pious to a liturgy that was celebrated at wooden altars in a Baroque or Rococo style. These altars were mostly marbled or painted in bright colours, and the altar pieces depicted religious stories from the Bible. The paintings could sometimes be changed or rotated, to theatrical effect. A good seventeenth-century example is the Amsterdam *schuilkerk* of Ons Lieve Heer op Solder, now a museum. Almost all the other house churches disappeared in the nineteenth-century building boom; only the neoclassical church of Moses and Aaron at the Amsterdam Nieuwmarkt (T.F. Suys, 1839-1841) still houses the high altar of the previous church, an impressive Baroque work, made around 1700.[1]

Of course there were a few larger and more typical city churches. A good example was the Rotterdam Rosaliakerk, built between 1777 and 1779 by the Italian architect Jan Giudici and destroyed by bombing in 1940. [Ill. 3.3-2] The somewhat earlier Gouda church of St Joseph (1767; demolished 1903) was designed by Pieter de Swart.[2] Outwardly they showed no recognisable religious elements; the interiors, however, were richly decorated, and they had galleries after the example of the famous Versailles palace

3.3-1 Jutphaas (Nieuwegein), St Nicholas church (1874-1875). The priest G. van Heukelum decorated his small village church by A. Tepe in a typically Dutch late Gothic style, representative of the 'Utrecht movement' in Gothic Revival. The magnificent medieval organ case was bought from the later demolished Amsterdam Nieuwezijds Kapel. [Amersfoort, Rijksdienst Cultureel Erfgoed: 343.391; photo G.J. Drukker, 2002]

1 Barends, *Geloven in de schaduw*; Van Eck, *Clandestine Splendor*.
2 Schmidt, *Pieter de Swart*, 238-240.

3.3-2 Rotterdam, Rosalia church (1777 and 1779). A large galleried city church, built by the Italian architect Jan Giudici, destroyed by bombing in 1940. Engraving 1781.
[Amsterdam, Rijksmuseum]

3   *Modeste Barok.*
4   *Naar gothieken kunstzin.*
5   Brom, *Herleving van de kerkelike kunst in katholiek Nederland*; Van der Meer, "De kunst in de negentiende en twintigste eeuw". Rosenberg, *De 19de-eeuwse kerkelijke bouwkunst in Nederland*, gives an analysis of Dutch church building in the nineteenth century.

chapel. Their Baroque fittings were rather exuberant. The barn-churches in the province of Noord-Brabant, the so-called *schuurkerken*, had more modest fittings.[3]

New churches after 1800

The repression of Roman Catholics and other religious minorities ended in 1795 and all denominations received equal rights. In the southern provinces, several medieval churches that had been used by the Protestants since 1648 were returned to Catholics and rebuilt in neoclassical and Baroque styles. Baroque furniture was ordered from Belgium, for example at the workshop of H. Peeters-Divoort at Turnhout or J.J. Peeters at Antwerp.[4] The incumbents of Zundert and Grave bought impressive altars at the sale of dissolved abbeys in the Southern Netherlands to add decorum and richness to the restored spaces. After 1815 many new Catholic churches were built, either subsidised by the state or paid for with money received in return for the upkeep of churches that had fallen in state hands after 1648.

The state remained in control of church building from 1824 until 1868. New churches were built by local architects under supervision of the department of Rijkswaterstaat, the department for the maintenance of bridges and canals.[5] They had to be as cheap as possible; there even seem to have been standards for the number of square metres per communicant. When many authors characterise these buildings as 'Waterstaatsstijl', they appear to be saying that those churches were built in a more or less neoclassical style: they were sometimes richly decorated with neoclassical elements, but sometimes just a development of the three-aisled house and barn-churches. They had simple brick walls and round-headed or ogival windows, an echo from the period of repression. Sometimes the church and priest's house were built under one roof. Neoclassical elements were confined to a tower, dome or cupola, entrance, cornice or pediment, for example at Nistelrode (L. Rijsterborgh, 1842) and St Bonifacius, Dordrecht (P. Plukhooy, 1823-1826). More richly decorated were the classical temple fronts of St Augustine, Utrecht (K.G. Zocher, 1839-1840) and St Joseph, Haarlem (H.H. Dansdorp, 1841-1843). Interiors were neoclassical in style with classical orders and entablatures, although the windows were sometimes ogival, a traditional element to show the religious character of the building. Other examples are the previously mentioned Amsterdam church of Moses and Aaron, with its temple façade and impressive twin towers, and the more austere village church of Erp (A. van Veggel, 1843-1844). Very typical is the Breda church of St Anthony (P. Huijsers 1836-1838), a hall church with an impressive façade crowned by a tower and cupola. Apart from the altars in the apse, this building was almost identical to Huijsers' somewhat earlier Reformed church of Steenbergen (1832-1834).

The attractive three-aisled church of Udenhout (1839-1841) has survived as a good example of a village church. It was threatened with demolition around 1900, when Roman Catholics had apparently turned against their once beloved Baroque or classical styles. The exterior is mostly brick with an attractive tower and small cupola. J.H. Laffertée designed the interior with its Doric pillars and a barrel vault above round arches. In the apses we see richly decorated altars with sculptures and statues of Mary and the church patron, St Lambert. The high altar has playful and attractive reliefs of the Adoration of the Shepherds and the Holy Trinity, made by the southern master J.J. Peeters. These altars, the pulpit and the Stations of the Cross are the focal points of the interior. A comparable church is St Bartholomew at Waspik by J. Brands, with a rich interior also by the Flemish sculptor J.J. Peeters. [Ill. 3.3-3] More unusual are the churches of Goirke (Tilburg) (1835-1839) and Schijndel (1839), both by H. Essens and relatively early examples of gothicising Catholic churches. At Goirke, Prince William, later King William II, made a generous donation under condition that the church would be built in his beloved Gothic style, from windows to arcades and even the vaulting. Most neoclassical churches however followed the stylistic traditions of the early nineteenth century. Their interior focus was on the altars, as a theatrical background to the Tridentine liturgy.

The Gothic Revival after 1853

After the introduction of the new episcopal hierarchy in 1853, Dutch Catholics lost their missionary status and the organisation of the church was entirely reformed. A new, centralised diocesan organisation of bishoprics and parishes was established, through which the Church intended to gain control of Catholics in the struggle against the anti-Catholic movements. The Gothic Revival was increasingly adopted as the dominant Roman Catholic style, as an instrument of reform, and to represent the Catholic view of society. Neoclassicism and Baroque gave way to a new, neo-medieval Roman Catholic corporate design. Up to 1910 some 600 new churches were built. Impressive books such as *Neerlandia Catholica* (1888) and *De katholieke kerken in Nederland* (1906-1914) by J. Kalf and the architect P.J.H. Cuypers provide a well-documented survey of this enormous building boom, which must have cost millions.[6] Fundraising became an important business. Financed by loans, shares and gifts, the debts must sometimes have seemed everlasting.[7]

The Catholic businessman, scholar and art critic J.A. Alberdingk Thijm was the foremost theorist of this Gothic movement. He looked back to the Middle Ages, when all stages of life and society seemed filled with Catholic doctrine and faith.[8] His view of a golden age of Catholicism was of course a fantasy, but it inspired him to promote the Gothic Revival, following the path of England, Belgium and Germany. Alberdingk Thijm befriended A.W.N. Pugin, Adolphe Napoléon Didron and August Reichensperger; he remarked: "there is no distance any

3.3-3 Waspik, St Bartholomew (1837-1841). This church by J. Brands has a rich interior by the Flemish sculptor J.J. Peeters.
[Amersfoort, Rijksdienst Cultureel Erfgoed: 318.596; photo J.P. de Koning, 1996]

6 <www.reliwiki.nl> gives information about all existing church buildings in the Netherlands.
7 Landheer, *Kerkbouw op krediet*, gives a representative overview of the way in which church buildings were financed.
8 Van Leeuwen, "J.A. Alberdingk Thijm, Bouwkunst en symboliek"; Van Kesteren, *Het verlangen naar de Middeleeuwen*; Raedts, *De ontdekking van de Middeleeuwen*.

261

3.3-4 Amsterdam, Mary Magdalene church (1889-1891). The spire of this Gothic Revival church by Pierre Cuypers amplifies the historic city silhouette of Amsterdam. It was demolished in 1968. [Amsterdam, Stadsarchief; photo Jacob Olie]

9   Van der Woud, *Waarheid en karakter*, 114.

more between London, Vienna and Paris". The works of Pugin were translated into French in 1850, edited in Bruges and Brussels under the title *Les Vrais Principes de L'Architecture*. In his own magazine, *De Dietsche Warande*, Alberdingk Thijm promoted Gothic church art, especially the work of his architect friend Cuypers. He harshly criticised neoclassical churches built by architects like Th. Molkenboer, who is best known for designing them in different styles, from neoclassical to Gothic Revival, almost all with stuccoed details. In Alberdingk Thijm's view, such versatile architects were "heathens through and through", the "slaves of the colossal orders". The revival of medieval Gothic must run parallel with the return of the people to Catholicism. Most priests, however, hardly appeared to be interested in the correct style of their new churches. They preferred practical, cheap buildings in a more or less correct Gothic style, an approach that was also promoted by the pragmatic Utrecht archbishop Joannes Zwijsen. The erudite Alberdingk Thijm stood almost alone in his idealism against the pragmatism of the many bishops and parish priests who preferred a correct liturgical arrangement within an efficiently designed church, with stuccoed decoration and vaulting executed as romantic Gothic décor, the so-called *stucadoorsgotiek*. Good examples include the church of the Papegaai in Amsterdam (G. Moele, 1848) and Saint Lambert's, Helmond (Th. Molkenboer, 1856-1862), a large Gothic Revival church with a very rich interior.

After 1853 Roman Catholics tried vehemently to give their own history a legitimate place within the national context of a Protestant nation. In their eyes, the current Protestant history of the Reformation and Eighty Years War was in need of correction and completion through a re-evaluation of the Catholic Middle Ages as a way of strengthening their own reform movement and emancipation. The building of Gothic Revival church spires had spurred Protestants and liberals into vehement protest, even in parliament. Before 1853, Protestant and Catholic churches alike could be built in medieval styles; after 1853 this was no longer possible. The Netherlands stood alone in Western Europe in the use of Gothic motifs as a Catholic corporate style, *een katholieke huisstijl*, and the adoption of them can be seen as representing the reform of church organisation.

Discussions about the Gothic Revival as a new national style focused on secular buildings such as the famous Amsterdam Rijksmuseum by Cuypers. For Catholic churches, however, Gothic was universally accepted; it was perfectly in line with current theories on architectural decorum and the character of buildings. After 1853, therefore, Catholic churches had to be Gothic.[9] The illustrations in *De katholieke kerken in Nederland* show brand-new churches with their proud silhou-

3.3-5 Vierakker, St Willibrord church (1869-1870). A picturesque village church by H. Wennekers with a complete interior of the so-called 'Utrecht movement'.
[Amersfoort, Rijksdienst Cultureel Erfgoed: 14424-64914; photo W. van der Sar, 2017]

ettes and tall spires. Factory chimneys and towers rose alongside each other at Eindhoven and Tilburg; the new church at Woerden had to be representative because it is situated near the railway line. Parish buildings, churches, schools and convents formed Catholic islands in cities and villages, almost like strongholds in a sea of infidelity. Some streets became dominated by Catholic buildings: the seventeenth-century spires in the skyline of Amsterdam were now seen against a backdrop of new Catholic towers. St Mary Magdalene, by Cuypers (1889-1891) is typical. [Ill. 3.3-4] At Eindhoven, the 1898 tower of the Augustine friars was crowned by a gilded sculpture of the Sacred Heart of Jesus; with its outstretched arms, it seems to protect the growing industrial city. In Amsterdam, Cuypers' new Willibrord church (1864-1923) was designed with nine towers, a French cathedral to dominate the river Amstel, but was demolished in 1969-1970. The Nijmegen Canisius College of the Jesuits, by N. Molenaar (1898-1900), is an enormous building, its Renaissance detail an echo of Cuypers' Rijksmuseum.

Most churches were not the focal point of new city developments; they were inserted in existing street patterns. The brick façades of the Willibrord church, Utrecht, by Alfred Tepe, for example, just formed part of a housing block. The interior is a real surprise, a high rising cage of glass and light, well-proportioned with rich colouring and beautiful fittings in late Gothic style. The Amsterdam Jesuit church of the Krijtberg has an impressive façade onto the canal; the interior is also richly painted and detailed. The Cuypers' churches of The Hague (Jacobuskerk, 1875-1878) and Groningen (St Joseph, 1885-1887) have impressive Gothic spires, the Groningen tower providing a real landmark on a street corner. Smaller village churches had lively silhouettes that dominate houses and farms. Good examples are the churches at Vierakker by H. Wennekers (1869-1870) [Ill. 3.3-5] and at Stiphout by H. van Tulder (1883-1884), with a high spire surrounded by four spirelets. Sometimes the new church was an echo of its predecessor, for example the churches at Mierlo and Oss, where Van Tulder drew regional Gothic elements from the Middle Ages. The neo-Romanesque style was seldom used; some impressive examples are the churches of C. Weber at Lierop (1890-1892) and Geldrop (1889-1891) with dominant domes and towers. Neoclassicism and Baroque were no longer in vogue. Only W. Hellemons, the parish priest of Oudenbosch, succeeded in forcing Cuypers to design his new church in the neo-Baroque style. For the realisation of this impressive copy of St Peter's basilica combined with the façade of St John Lateran (1867-1880), he sent the architect on a study trip to Rome. In this building the ultramontane Catholics did their best to combine the best of Roman architecture.

Catholic architects

The development of the architectural profession in the second half of the century led to intricate designs by professional architects such as Cuypers and Tepe. Cuypers was a highly individual and creative architect who developed new forms from a study of French thirteenth-century architecture. He was a student of the Antwerp Academy, inspired by Pugin and E.E. Viollet-le-Duc; he founded a workshop for church art at Roermond in 1852.[10] Cuypers and his colleagues greatly favoured a doctrinaire Gothic Revival that used honest materials and abhorred stucco. It preferred brick vaulting and combined brick with stone. Their architecture was developed from that of the French cathedrals and of English High Victorian churches.[11] Tepe had German parents; after studying at the Berlin Bauakademie, he worked at the Cologne Dombauhütte and then started his independent practice in Utrecht. The local diocese promoted his work thanks to his use of motifs from the Dutch and German brick architecture of the fifteenth century.[12] This so-called 'Utrecht movement' began when in 1869 the priest J. van Heukelum founded the Sint Bernulphusgilde, a clerical association for the promotion of Gothic church art. Around this society there gathered a group of architects and artists who designed churches, altars, stained-glass windows and painted decoration in late Gothic style. This energetic priest was the founding father of the Utrecht episcopal museum of church art, now the national museum of religious culture, the Catharijneconvent.[13] Its collection was intended to inspire artists in the decoration of new churches.

Cuypers and Tepe were very prolific; they each built some 60 churches. Joseph Cuypers, the son of P.J.H. Cuypers, and his companion Jan Stuyt were also relatively productive. Most churches however were built by less well known, and sometimes minor masters. The most active were H.J. van den Brink, C. Franssen, C. Weber, the brothers Margry, N. Molenaar, J. Kayser, Th. Molkenboer, H. Wennekers, A.C. Bleys, P. Soffers and H. van Tulder. Their work was mostly confined to one or two dioceses. Medieval churches were adapted to Gothic and sometimes Romanesque taste through intensive restoration. Interior fittings from the Renaissance or Baroque period were removed. Good examples are the St Servaaskerk and Lievevrouwekerk at Maastricht, both restored by Cuypers to their former Romanesque glory. They were purged of Baroque and neoclassical altars and stucco decoration: one of these altars now adorns the neo-Baroque Brompton Oratory in London. It was the dean of St Servaas, F.X. Rutten, who stated that a newly decorated interior is indispensable to induce a beneficial impression in the souls of the faithful.[14] Rutten also reinstated the historic and traditional procession of relics, the so-called *Heiligdomsvaart*. The late-Gothic cathedral of the diocese of 's-Hertogenbosch was now completed with exterior sculpture in Gothic style, while the interior was stripped, losing its Baroque high altar and Renaissance rood loft. This latter famous work of art is now in the London Victoria and Albert Museum; its sale inspired Victor de Stuers to institute the state care of historic monuments. In its place, Gothic Revival altars and more than 100 sculptures adorn the chapels and pillars of the cathedral.

10 Van Leeuwen, *Pierre Cuypers architect 1827-1921*; Jacobs and van Leeuwen, "Roermond as Centre for Religious Art".
11 Van Leeuwen, "Pierre Cuypers the architect: 'a sort of Dutch Viollet-le-Duc'".
12 Looyenga, *De Utrechtse school in de neogotiek*.
13 Peters, *Naar de middeleeuwen*.
14 Jacobs, *Deken Franciscus Xaverius Rutte*, 77.

Interior design, liturgy and iconography

Around 1840 the Tridentine liturgy was celebrated in Baroque and neoclassical interiors, sometimes in an exuberant 'theatre' style accompanied by choir and orchestra. The old *Missale Romanum* was still used in the traditional way. Churches such as St Catherine at 's-Hertogenbosch were renowned for their orchestral high masses. After 1845, church orchestras and women singers were mostly banned; from then on, mass could only be accompanied by an organ, male choir, and Gregorian and polyphonic chant. Singers stood on a high organ loft, usually situated above the entrance of the church. The chancel was the focal point of the building, not deep, and dominated by a high, sculpted or painted reredos. Mass was celebrated in Latin and the priest faced the altar. Altars and pulpits were rather exuberant, for example at the Goirke church (Tilburg, 1853), where Alberdingk Thijm criticised the designer because the preacher stood above the crowned head of the Saviour. The pulpit of the former St Pieterskerk at 's-Hertogenbosch (1843; now at Oirschot) was adorned with expressive, life-size sculptures of the liberation of St Peter from prison. Pews dominated the aisles: the most expensive places were at the front, whereas the poor had to stand or sit behind pillars, far away from the altar.

The church and its decoration were almost part of religious doctrine: one of the few places where the illiterate public could receive religious and moral messages, delivered by paintings, stained-glass windows and sculpture. Gothic revival interiors were designed in accordance with the style of the building; all parts harmonised in a so-called 'Gesamtkunstwerk'. Artists used medieval elements, but the multiple altars and the heterogeneous use of the medieval church by guilds were of course wholly absent. The traditional Baroque unity of the seventeenth and eighteenth-century interiors was translated into a Gothic style; its iconography was based on medieval examples, sometimes very intricate and refined ones.

3.3-6 Sittard, Basilica of Our Lady of the Sacred Heart (1875-1876). A richly decorated 'miniature cathedral' in thirteenth-century style by J. Kayser. [Amersfoort, Rijksdienst Cultureel Erfgoed: 149-893; photo G.J. Dukker, 1971]

In 1858 Alberdingk Thijm published *De Heilige Linie*, an elaborate book about the eastward layout of churches which gave a symbolic meaning to even the smallest parts of the church building. He tried to establish the higher order of creation in number, measure and weight. A church building represented this higher order and was an allegory of the body of Christ. In Alberdingk Thijm's eyes, Gothic forms conveyed a morally laden message; the stones and the superposition of columns, capitals and vaults represented the place of every man in the ideal, corporate Catholic society. The build-

15 Caspers, Cortjaens and Jacobs, *De basiliek van Onze Lieve Vrouw van het Heilig Hart te Sittard*, 44.
16 Verstijnen and Hoogbergen, *Huis vol symboliek*.

ing had to be orientated correctly, of course; its plan was governed by geometry, rectangles and triangles with symbolic meanings. Cuypers and Alberdingk Thijm, for example, gave a symbolic meaning to each part of the three stages of the Gothic tower of Veghel parish church: its three niches illustrated the Holy Trinity, and the four spires and gables represented the Evangelists and the points of the compass. There are numerous High Church examples of intricate iconographical plans, mostly designed in dialogue between architect and patron. At Veghel, Cuypers designed an expensive altar in the French Gothic style (1862-1863), with a multitude of Dutch saints from Lidwina of Schiedam to Pepijn van Landen. [Col. ill. 11] At the Sittard basilica of Our Lady of the Sacred Heart, a magnificent miniature cathedral by J. Kayser (1875-1876), a crown of rose windows reminds us of the Virgin Mary as 'rosa mystica'. [Ill. 3.3-6] The consecration sermon of this basilica compared the sanctuary with the Eucharist and the martyrdom of Christ, with the central aisle as the road of truth and the side aisles the roads of sin from which only the humility of the faithful could delivered them.[15]

For Alberdingk Thijm church buildings were a metaphor for the community of the faithful: the revival of medieval Gothic must inevitably lead to the restoration of the ideal Catholic corporate society. Delicate, high church symbolism can also be found at the Cuypers churches of The Hague (St Jacobus) and Groningen (St Joseph). In his own newly-built parish church at Jutphaas (Nieuwegein), the Utrecht founder of the Sint Bernulphusgilde, J. van Heukelum, introduced a great many iconographic elements. The late Gothic style of the rich interior was derived from a magnificent medieval organ case which he had bought from the subsequently demolished Amsterdam Nieuwezijds Kapel, a good example of the ideals of the 'Utrecht movement'. [Ill. 3.3-1] In 1887 the Helvoirt priest H. Everts published a popular version of Thijm's *Heilige Linie* for parish priests, *Onze Kerken*. Later on, the new church of St Nicholas at Helvoirt (1901-1903), was richly decorated and painted as a small Catholic universe, designed by chaplain A. van Dijck. Even the foliage in the spandrels of the arches has its own symbolic meaning.[16] [Ill. 3.3-7]

3.3-7 Helvoirt, St Nicholas church (1901-1903). The church is built by J.H.H. van Groenendael in a late Gothic style. The rich furniture is by H. van der Geld and Van Bokhoven en Jonkers. [Amersfoort, Rijksdienst Cultureel Erfgoed: 541.044; photo S. Technau, 2008]

Church decoration was carried out by a growing number of workshops at The Hague, Utrecht, 's-Hertogenbosch and Roermond. Of these, the most famous were the workshops of Cuypers and Stoltzenberg (Roermond), Hendrik van der Geld ('s-Hertogenbosch) and Friedrich Wilhelm Mengelberg (Utrecht). Mengelberg even designed a highly picturesque village church at Olburgen in 1869. [Ill. 3.3-8] His design was executed by the architect G. te Riele. Most of the paintings and sculptures of these workshops mixed medieval Gothic and Romantic Nazarene elements. Later altars were interpretations of late Gothic Dutch and Flemish examples.[17]

For most believers, the detailed symbolism of altars, wall paintings and stained glass would have been difficult to understand. Most clerics were not very interested in Alberdingk Thijm's message. Many churches offered a more down-to-earth, almost Low Church, devotional space. The high altar was dedicated to the Eucharist and the windows in the apse usually depicted the seven sacraments. A triumphal cross over a triumphal arch would have reminded the congregation of the suffering of Christ. Side altars were dedicated to the church patron, the Virgin Mary, St Joseph or the Holy Family. There was a subtle hierarchy in the height of the steps to the sanctuary and the altar steps. Sometimes there were sacred symbols in the foliage of the capitals or in the decorative painting. The baptistery was situated near the entrance to symbolise the entrance of the newly baptised into the religious community. In the side aisles there would have been several confessionals. Good examples include the recently restored church of St Joseph at Groningen and the Sacred Heart church of the Augustine friars at Eindhoven.[18] Atmosphere, colour and material expression prevailed in the pious luxury of the nineteenth century.

Pope Pius IX in his encyclical *Quanta Cura* (1864) and the annex *Syllabus Errorum* fought against the erroneous ideologies of Darwinism, liberalism and socialism. The

3.3-8 Olburgen, St Willibrord church (1869). The Utrecht sculptor Friedrich Wilhelm Mengelberg designed this picturesque village church.
[Amersfoort, Rijksdienst Cultureel Erfgoed: 145-184; photo A.J. van der Wal, 1971]

Roman Catholic Church maintained a view of an ideal corporate society and tried to maintain and strengthen its position through a process of the clericalisation of daily life. It was integral to the Catholic reform movement in Dutch society to found Catholic schools, hospitals and guest houses for the old and poor. The faithful were organised into devotional associations and brotherhoods of the Holy Family or the Virgin Mary, and schooled by *volksmissies*, church missions. New religious congregations of sisters and brothers were founded. Apart from strengthening the position of the pope, reform was also introduced through new devotions, intended to fortify the believers and to make them part of Catholic society. In 1854 the dogma of the Immaculate Conception of Mary was introduced; the veneration of the Sacred Heart of Jesus followed in 1856. In 1870 St Joseph was elevated to become patron of the Church. As a result, the Catholic elite felt responsible for the care of churches. Gifts and donations made it possible to enrich the interiors over the years. Altars were dedicated to these new devotions and used by the brotherhoods.

Real liturgical innovations were scarce until around 1900. Then an important movement emerged towards liturgical and archi-

17 Jansen, van Leeuwen and Vrins, "Arbeyd sere voert tot eere".
18 Van der Werf and Hilhorst, *Van volkskerk tot kathedraal*; Van Leeuwen, *De 100 mooiste kerken van Noord-Brabant*, 2012, 191-193.

19 Mulder, *Hendrik Andriessen*, 1993.
20 Looyenga, "Voorbereidingen tot de bouw – de architect Joseph Cuypers", Van Hellenberg Hubar, *De nieuwe Bavo te Haarlem*.
21 Van Swigchem, Brouwer and van Os, *Een huis voor het Woord*.

tectural innovation, according to the *Motu Proprio* of Pope Pius X. This liturgical movement had originated years beforehand in the French convent of the Benedictines at Solesmes. In the same year, the artist Th. Molkenboer pleaded for *volkskerken*, churches for the people, with broad spaces that gave a good view of the liturgy. Eucharist, daily communion and children's communion were promoted. While mass was said or sung in Latin, participation was stimulated by mass books in the Dutch language and by community singing.[19] This was another way in which the Catholic Church tried to intensify its influence on the faithful.

Architects and artists came together to form a new society for the promotion of art: *De Violier* was founded in Amsterdam in 1901, and the art historian Jan Kalf was one of their spokesmen. New centrally-planned churches were designed and decorated by more original and independent artists, for example Onze Lieve Vrouw van Goeden Raad at Tilburg (J. van der Valk, 1913) and St Jacobus, 's-Hertogenbosch (Joseph Cuypers and Jan Stuyt, 1906-1907). A very important building is the eclectic St Bavo's Cathedral in Haarlem by Joseph Cuypers and Jan Stuyt (1895-1930) in a mixed Gothic Revival and neo-Romanesque style.[20] It was decorated by artists including J. Toorop, J.P. Maas and J. and L. Brom. Prominent domes were an integral part of these buildings inspired by Romanesque and Early Christian buildings. Later examples are the central-plan churches of St Catharina, 's-Hertogenbosch (1916-1917) and Heilig Landstichting near Nijmegen (1913-1915), both by Jan Stuyt. These buildings were dominated by concrete domes, decorated internally with impressive paintings in the Beuron Style by Jan Oosterman and Piet Gerrits respectively. These heralded the beginning of a new period in which Christocentric theories of church building gained importance. The Gothic Revival was more freely interpreted, and gradually lost its predominance over new brick churches that used basilica

expressionist forms – broad spaces designed to unify the religious community.

Protestant churches, neoclassical, Gothic and Dutch Renaissance

Around 1800 the official Dutch Reformed Church had a great number of churches at its disposal. Following the Reformation, medieval Catholic churches were taken over by the followers of the new religion. Most of these were much too spacious, and so the former sanctuaries and aisles were often used as a *wandelkerk*, a walking space used for commercial and social purposes. Sometimes parts of the churches were partitioned off and used as school rooms, municipal halls or store rooms for wood. The interiors were mostly whitewashed and dominated by pews, an organ, a pulpit and a baptistery-screen. The Dutch Reformed Church did not approve of ostentatious interiors; a love for the arts was originally considered rather suspicious in its circles.[21] Seventeenth-century paintings show spacious churches, furnished with groups of pews. There was some figurative art, in the form of stained glass, painted

3.3-9 Boxtel, Protestant church (1812). The small, so-called Lodewijkskerk by Hendrik Verhees stands literally in the shadow of the medieval church. [Amersfoort, Rijksdienst Cultureel Erfgoed: 110289; photo G.J. Dukker, 1967]

3.3-10 Veenhuizen, Protestant church (1825-1826). This octagonal galleried church is built by the local builder H. Wind.
[Amersfoort, Rijksdienst Cultureel Erfgoed: 64.615; photo G.T. Delemarre, 1962]

text boards with the Ten Commandments and the confession of faith, and there were colourful funeral monuments and achievements. In some places, older Catholic elements, such as screens, choir stalls, stained glass and monuments, had been retained. In the eighteenth century many interiors demonstrated sobriety and distinction. The colourful funeral achievements of important families were mostly destroyed in 1795 and the nineteenth century was characterised by modest whitewashed interiors. Very simple and barn-like are the so-called *vermaningen*, the meeting-houses of the Mennonites. The churches of the Lutherans were very dignified and refined.

New buildings became necessary when after 1795 medieval buildings in the southern provinces were returned to the Roman Catholics. In small villages, the Protestants built so-called *Lodewijkskerkjes*, financed by a grant from King Louis Napoleon. These were small single-spaced buildings, mostly in the form of elongated octagons. The king's intention had been to prevent religious conflicts by providing for buildings like this.

Good examples are found at Bergeijk (1812) and Boxtel (Hendrik Verhees, 1812). [Ill. 3.3-9] The church at Oosterhout (H. Huijsers, 1811) is a good example of a larger Protestant church on a Greek cross plan. All these buildings were traditionally built with brick walls, round-headed or ogival windows, and with a high roof above a cornice. A central, octagonal, plan was used for the church at Arkel (1855). At Arnhem (Koepelkerk; A. Aytink van Falkenstein, 1837-1838) and Veenhuizen (H. Wind, 1825-1826) an octagon on a central plan included galleries to provide more seating. [Ill. 3.3-10] These buildings follow early examples, such as the octagonal Renaissance church of Willemstad (1599), the classical Leiden Marekerk (A. van 's-Gravezande, 1639-1649) or the magnificent Middelburg Oostkerk (B.F. Drijfhout, 1647-1667). Centrally planned spaces were designed for an austere liturgy, dominated by the preaching of the word of God and the singing of psalms. Ostentatious elements were shunned as "Eenvoudige netheid en doelmatigheid", plainness, tidiness and propriety, were pursued by clerics.[22]

22 Ibid., 165.

269

3.3-11 Apeldoorn, Protestant church (1892). The church, an impressive design in Dutch Renaissance by J. Verheul Dzn, was often visited by the Royal family. [Amersfoort, Rijksdienst Cultureel Erfgoed: 325.032; photo J.P. de Koning, 1999]

Protestant styles

New Protestant churches were mostly designed in traditional or neoclassical styles, also under the control of public servants from the department of Rijkswaterstaat. Neoclassical elements such as columns, cupolas and pediments are found at the Grote Kerk of 's-Hertogenbosch (J. de Greef, 1820-1821) and the stately churches of St. Jacobiparochie (Th. Romein, 1843-1844), Zierikzee (G.H. Grauss, 1848) and Steenbergen (P. Huijsers, 1832-1834). The three-aisled church of Steenbergen was built with an impressive tower and cupola above a pediment. 's-Hertogenbosch has a plain interior with high windows and stucco rosettes. The interior was originally filled with pews, and the pulpit had a sounding board dominated by a magnificent Bätz organ. Sometimes the Gothic Revival style was used, in accordance with French theories on the decorum and character of buildings: ogival arches and windows had been traditional elements of church design since the eighteenth century, and the style was taught at the Utrecht drawing school by C. Kramm in 1843.

The Gothic Revival was deployed for several Protestant churches, even where it was a more expensive way of building. An interesting example is the Rotterdam Zuiderkerk, a centrally planned Gothic Revival building (A.W. van Dam, 1846-1849) that was sadly destroyed in the 1940 bombing. A. van Veggel used this style in churches at Helmond (1847-1848) and 's-Hertogenbosch (former Waalse kerk, 1847). This last building was an echo of the late Gothic style of the Catholic cathedral, with stucco vaulting. The original design even included two towers on a very small scale. The Zeist Reformed church was an intricate Gothic Revival basilica, with a tower and stucco vaulting characteristic of the English perpendicular style (N. Kamperdijk, 1841-1843). In 1863 J.H. Leliman designed a more or less Gothic church, a design in which minor changes made it fitting for Protestants or Catholics alike. A later example is the Amsterdam Koepelkerk at the Leidsebosje (A.J. van Beek, 1879-1884), demolished in 1972, which demonstrated a rather limited use of eclectic and Gothic Revival elements but composed into a striking form that dominated its surroundings.[23] More eclectic are the centrally planned church of Purmerend, with its cupola, and the basilica church of Gorinchem (I. Warnsinck and A.N. Godefroy, 1849-1851). Both show a decorative use of brick, eclectic Romanesque forms with round-headed arcades and windows. Gorinchem has a whitewashed stucco interior with a magnificent organ.

The Gothic Revival was not however much used for Protestant churches after 1853. We have already seen that church designs were almost exclusively made by architects who worked for their own denomination: Catholics worked for Catholics; Protestants designed for Protestants. Only once did P.J.H. Cuypers, a Catholic architect, make an unexecuted design for a Protestant church in Amsterdam (1876-1877), but this remained an exception. It had an interesting plan, a semicircle in the form of a Roman theatre. Later on, the Gothic Revival was only used at Schagen (A.G. van der Steur, 1895-1897) because the style had to be a reminiscence of its late Gothic predecessor that had been destroyed by fire. New Protestant churches were mostly designed in a Dutch Renaissance revival or *Oudhollandse Stijl*, an interpretation of the seventeenth-century Protestant churches by the famous architect Hendrick de Keyser. In using this style, the Dutch Reformed Church sought to revive its heyday during the Dutch Golden Age. De Keyser's Amsterdam Zuider- and Westerkerk were reinterpreted many times, for example at Hoorn by C. Muysken (1881-1883) and at Katwijk aan Zee by H.J. Jesse (1887). They comprised picturesque brick forms with classical stone details and trac-

eried round-headed windows. Towers or turrets provided a lively silhouette. The Katwijk church is one of the best examples of this typical picturesque style, which provided an authentic church-like character for Protestants. Essential were good acoustics, the absence of columns and a centrally planned space focused on the pulpit. A famous example of this Protestant 'corporate style' is the new church at Apeldoorn, where an 1890 competition led to a vehement discussion about the character of the building. An impressive Dutch Renaissance design by J. Verheul Dzn was eventually realised in 1892.[24] [Ill. 3.3-11] For acoustic reasons, architects were by now preferring a roof construction with flat panelling to wooden barrel vaulting.

Romanesque and Jugendstil tendencies can be seen around 1900, for example at the new central plan Nieuwezijds Kapel in Amsterdam by C.B. Posthumus Meyjes

3.3-12 Rotterdam, Koninginnekerk (1907). This brick building by B. Hooykaas Jr. and M. Brinkman had an impressive, almost cathedral front with two towers. It was demolished in 1972. [Amersfoort, Rijksdienst Cultureel Erfgoed: 149.866; photo G.J. Dukker, 1971]

23 Hoogewoud, "De koepelkerk aan het Leidsebosje in Amsterdam".
24 Van Neck, "Een Apeldoorns 'onderonsje'".

(1908). Other motifs were borrowed from the architectural renewal movement centred on H.P. Berlage, whose Amsterdam exchange became well known. Good examples are the Rotterdam Remonstrantse or Arminiuskerk, in a variation of Romanesque and Byzantine styles with interior galleries (H. Evers, 1895-1897). It has a brick interior with wooden vaulting and several annexes and meeting rooms. The Rotterdam Koninginnekerk (B. Hooykaas Jr. and M. Brinkman 1907; unfortunately demolished in 1972) was a brick building with interesting Jugendstil elements and an impressive, almost cathedral front with two towers. With its galleries and organ it was one of the most impressive Protestant churches in the Netherlands. [Ill. 3.3-12]

Most interiors were devised around central plans so that there would be a good view of the pulpit, organ and baptistery screen from all directions.[25] In older churches, believers also gathered around the pulpit. After 1829, when burial in churches was forbidden, chairs were replaced by pews, sometimes in a concentric style as in a theatre auditorium, to show the unity of the community, listening to the preaching of the word of God. Examples are still to be found in the medieval churches of Vorden, Gouda (I. Warnsinck, 1853) and Sneek (A. Breunissen Troost, 1871). At Gouda the floor was inclined so that all attention was directed towards the liturgy which traditionally consisted of prayer, psalm singing and of course the sermon. These 'theatres' sometimes give the impression of a church within a church. A good example is the galleried theatre that was constructed by T.F. Suys (1826) in the medieval Utrecht Domkerk. It was destroyed in 1925, during the restoration of the church.

Increasingly after 1875, the rebuilding and redecoration by Protestants of medieval churches in plaster and whitewash led to vehement criticism by lovers of historic monuments, such as the Catholic public servant De Stuers. As a result, from around 1880, Protestant churches were restored with state funds. At Stedum (1877-1878) and Zutphen (1889-1918) Catholic elements such as medieval wall paintings were reconstructed. At Zutphen the historic St Mary's Portal was restored. Protestants strongly resisted the reconstruction of these Catholic elements, no longer feeling themselves at home in the changed atmosphere of the restored churches. They had become accustomed to austere whitewashed interiors, almost without figurative decoration, colour or stained glass. Strangely enough, the reconstruction of Catholic elements looked forward to much later liturgical innovations: G. van der Leeuw, for example, who in 1921 restored the original arrangements of medieval churches. Sanctuaries were again used for the evening meal service, for example at Ginneken (1934-1938). Quite a lot of typical nineteenth-century Protestant interiors within medieval churches were destroyed after the Second World War during the reconstruction of medieval interiors. Whitewashed interiors with wooden screens and partitions, oak painted pews and light blue vaulting are extremely rare nowadays. A good example can still be found in the medieval church of Heesbeen.

Churches of dissenting Calvinist groups

Just as Roman Catholics were strengthening their organisation during the nineteenth century, the dominant Protestant State Church was weakened by several *afscheidingen*, Calvinist dissenting groups who wanted to strengthen their true religion and to differ about the interpretation of the Holy Bible. These groups consisted mainly of working-class people, the so-called *kleine luyden*. They of course needed new churches, but their love of the arts was almost non-existent. The first dissenting group was the 1834 *Afscheiding* which led to the formation of several new Calvinist groups. In 1886 Abraham Kuyper's so-called Doleantie movement – the movement of complainants – created another important dissenting group which saw itself as a purification movement of Protestant doctrine and practice.

25 Steensma, *Protestantse kerken hun pracht en kracht*, 45-49.
26 Steensma and van Swigchem, *Honderdvijftig jaar gereformeerde kerkbouw*.

There was a real building boom of *Doleantiekerken* and dissenting chapels.[26] The oldest examples are small brick single-space churches, sometimes with round-headed windows and very austere neo-classical or traditional decoration. Mostly *timmermanskerken*, they were designed and built by local building firms or carpenters (Heerde, c. 1840; Middelstum, 1869-1870). They were rather modest and plain, not unlike the Catholic barn-churches. The dissenters sometimes made use of the services of official architects, for example at the eclectic brick Zwolle Plantagekerk (J.W. Bosboom, 1874), with its round-headed arches, windows and gables. The interiors were not very different from those in the Dutch Reformed churches, often with wooden or stuccoed barrel vaults and galleries to hold large numbers of believers.

Kuyper, the leader of the Doleantie, held an important position in Protestant church reform. He pleaded for centrally planned preaching houses, real auditoria. In his eyes, a religious service was a gathering of believers who meet God and pray to Him. The emphasis lay on the combination of pulpit and organ. Kuyper was also an art lover; he believed that true religion did not require the sensuality of Catholic church art, which he abhorred. In his view beauty was connected with biblical magnificence.[27] A very rich example of his influence on church building is the Amsterdam Keizersgrachtkerk (G.

3.3-13 Amsterdam, Keizersgrachtkerk (1888). G. and A. Salm gave the so-called 'cathedral of the Doleantie' a Venetian inspired Gothic façade. The interior has galleries and wooden vaults. The liturgical centre consists of a pulpit, crowned by the organ.
[Amersfoort, Rijksdienst Cultureel Erfgoed: 511.723; photo S. Technau, 2005 / Photo of the interior by Job van Nes]

27 Schoon & Vroom, *Kunst in de kerk aan het eind van de vorige eeuw bij gereformeerden en katholieken*, 3-4.

and A. Salm, 1888) [Ill. 3.3-13], which has a Venetian inspired Gothic façade. This so-called 'cathedral of the Doleantie' was built with galleries and wooden vaults. The liturgical centre consisted of a pulpit, crowned by the organ.

Most architects at this time made use of the very popular Renaissance revival or Oudhollandse Stijl. Good examples are the Amsterdam Funenkerk with its galleries (1888-1889) by the very popular architect T.E. Kuipers, and the Amsterdam Raamkerk, with its two small towers (E.G. Wentink, 1888-1889), both demolished. The characteristically Dutch Renaissance church of Heeg by Kuipers (1889) still exists. These buildings combine elements from the churches of De Keyser with typical nineteenth-century revival details. Almost all have galleries on classical columns, to hold as many believers as possible. Later on, around 1900, somewhat eclectic, Berlagian motifs were used by Kuipers in churches for Dordrecht (Wilhelminakerk, 1898-1899) and Groningen (Zuiderkerk, 1901). The Wilhelminakerk in particular is an important building, with a centralised, circular plan that drew the believers around the pulpit. The central planning preferred by Kuyper was a harbinger of important architectural innovations during the period between the two World Wars. Good examples of this renewal are the magnificent, almost tent-like expressionist Reformed church by B.T. Boeyinga for Bergen op Zoom (1928) and the expressionist Reformed 'cathedral' at Andijk by Egbert Reitsma (1930).

Conclusion

The building boom of Catholics, Protestants and dissenting groups consisted of many important buildings. It thus changed the countryside and the skyline of many cities, and these stately piles also reflect the way in which religion was reformed over the course of the nineteenth century. We can see how religion expressed itself, and tried to cope with enormous changes in industrial society. Church interiors provide an insight into contemporary ideas about liturgy; new devotions represented moral thoughts about society. In all their sobriety, Protestant churches also represented the way the *'kleine luyden'* expressed their unity and love for the word of God. Church buildings are an expression of the nineteenth-century moral plea for religion and the way it wanted to transform and reform society.

BIBLIOGRAPHY

Bakhuizen van den Brink, J.N., ed. *Protestantsche kerkbouw. Een bundel studies*. Arnhem, 1946.

Barends, Frederik F. *Geloven in de schaduw. Schuilkerken in Amsterdam*. Ghent, 1996.

Beyer, Marc de, Pia Verhoeven and Albert Reinstra, eds. *Kerkinterieurs in Nederland*. Zwolle, 2016.

Bierenbroodspot, J., et al., eds. *Een huis voor de geest. Studies over kerkbouw in de negentiende en twintigste eeuw*. Jaarboek Cuypersgenootschap 30 (2014). Amsterdam, 2015.

Blaauw, S. de. "De kathedralen van 1853". In: J. Vis and W. Janse, eds. *Staf en storm. Het herstel van de bisschoppelijke hiërarchie in Nederland in 1853. Actie en reactie*. Leiden, 2002, 233-259.

Brom, Gerard. *Herleving van de kerkelike kunst in katholiek Nederland*. Leiden, 1933.

Caspers, Charles, Wolfgang Cortjaens and Antoine Jacobs, eds. *De basiliek van Onze Lieve Vrouw van het Heilig Hart te Sittard. Architectuur – devotie – iconografie*. Sittard, 2010.

Cuypers, P.J.H., ed. *De katholieke kerken in Nederland, dat is de tegenwoordige staat dier kerken met hunne bemeubeling en versiering beschreven en afgebeeld*. Amsterdam, 1906-1914.

De Maeyer, Jan and Luc Verpoest. *Gothic Revival. Religion, Architecture and Style in Western Europe 1815-1914*. Leuven, 2000.

Dunk, Th. H. von der. "Hoe katholiek is de neogotiek? De Hervormden en de herwaardering van het middeleeuwse verleden rond het midden van de negentiende eeuw". *Tijdschrift voor Geschiedenis*, 105 (1992), 565-584.

Eck, Xander van. *Clandestine Splendor. Paintings for the Catholic Church in the Protestant Dutch Republic*. Zwolle, 2008.

Everts, H.J.M. *Onze kerken, over kerkgebouw, kerkgemeubelte, kerkgereide, kerkversiering, etc.* 's-Hertogenbosch-Zwolle, 1887.

Gaal, F. van, W. van Leeuwen and Th. van Oeffelt. *Jan Stuyt. Architect en netwerker tijdens het rijke roomse leven*. 's-Hertogenbosch, 2017.

Hellenberg Hubar, Bernadette van. *De nieuwe Bavo te Haarlem. Ad orientem. Gericht op het oosten*. Zwolle, 2016.

Hoogewoud, Guido. "De koepelkerk aan het Leidsebosje in Amsterdam. Een neogotische herdenkingskerk voor de Amsterdamse hervormden". In: Jenny Bierenbroodspot et al., eds. *Een huis voor de geest. Studies over kerkbouw in de negentiende en twintigste eeuw*. Jaarboek Cuypersgenootschap 30 (2014). Amsterdam, 2015, 89-113.

Jacobs, Antoine. *Deken Franciscus Xaverius Rutte (1822-1893) en zijn plaats binnen de neogotiek in Limburg* [typescript]. Utrecht, 1994.

Jacobs, A. "Frans Xavier Rutten, deken van Maastricht (1822-1893)". *Publications de la Société Historique et Archéologique dans le Limbourg*, 141 (2005), 89-166.

Jacobs, Antoine and A.J.C. (Wies) van Leeuwen. "Roermond as Centre for Religious Art". In: Wolfgang Cortjaens, Jan De Maeyer and Tom Verschaffel, eds. *Historism and Cultural Identity in the Rhine-Meuse Region / Historismus und kulturelle Identität im Raum Rhein-Maas*. KADOC Artes, 10. Leuven, 2008, 217-237.

Jansen, A.H.E.M., A.J.C. van Leeuwen and G. Vrins. *"Arbeyd sere voert tot eere". Hendrik van der Geld, de neogotiek en de Brabantse beeldhouwkunst*. Tilburg, 1989.

Kesteren, Ronald van. *Het verlangen naar de Middeleeuwen. De verbeelding van een historische passie*. Amsterdam, 2004.

King, T.H. *Les Vrais Principes de L'Architecture Ogivale ou Chrétienne avec des Remarques sur leur Renaissance au Temps Actuel. Remanié et developpé d'après le texte Anglais de A.W. Pugin et traduit en francais par P. Lebrocquy*. Brussels-Leipzig-Aachen, 1850.

Landheer, Hugo. *Kerkbouw op krediet. De financiering van de kerkbouw in het aartspriesterschap Holland en Zeeland en de bisdommen Haarlem en Rotterdam gedurende de periode 1795-1965*. Diss. Utrecht, 2004.

Leeuwen, Wies van. "J.A. Alberdingk Thijm, Bouwkunst en symboliek". *De Sluitsteen. Bulletin van het Cuypers Genootschap*, 5 (1989), 1-44.

Leeuwen, A.J.C. (Wies) van. *De maakbaarheid van het verleden. P.J.H. Cuypers als restauratiearchitect*. Zeist-Zwolle, 1995.

Leeuwen, A.J.C. (Wies) van. *Pierre Cuypers architect 1827-1921*. Zwolle-Zeist, 2007.

Leeuwen, A.J.C. (Wies) van. "Pierre Cuypers the architect: 'a sort of Dutch Viollet-le-Duc'". *True Principles. The journal of the Pugin Society*, 4 (2009) 1, 56-70.

Leeuwen, A.J.C. (Wies) van. *De 100 mooiste kerken van Noord-Brabant*. Zwolle, 2012, 2017.

Looyenga, Arjen J. *De Utrechtse school in de neogotiek. De voorgeschiedenis en het Sint Bernulphusgilde*. Diss. Leiden, 1991.

Looyenga, Arjen J. "Voorbereidingen tot de bouw – de architect Joseph Cuypers". In: Antoon Erftemeijer, Arjen J. Looyenga en Marike van Roon. *Getooid als een bruid. De nieuwe Sint-Bavokathedraal te Haarlem*. Haarlem, 1997, 39-52.

Meer, F.G.L. van der. "De kunst in de negentiende en twintigste eeuw". In: *Cultuurgeschiedenis van het christendom*, vol. 2. Amsterdam-Brussels, 1951.

Melchers, M. *Het nieuwe religieuze bouwen. Liturgie, kerken en stedenbouw*. Amsterdam, 2015.

Modeste Barok. Beeldwerk in Brabant in de zeventiende en achttiende eeuw. Uden, 1994.

Mulder, Etty et al. *Hendrik Andriessen en het tijdperk der ontluiking*. Conference proceedings. Utrecht, 1993.

Naar gothieken kunstzin. Kerkelijke kunst en cultuur in Noord-Brabant in de negentiende eeuw. Catalogue. 's-Hertogenbosch, 1979.

Neck, Niels van. "Een Apeldoorns 'onderonsje'. De veelbesproken prijsvraag voor de protestantse kerk te Apeldoorn (1890-1891)". *Bulletin KNOB*, 111 (2012), 170-180.

Nelissen, N. *Geloof in de toekomst! Strategisch plan voor het religieus erfgoed*. Heeswijk, 2008.

Peeters, C.J.A.C. "De neogotiek tussen nijverheid en kunst". *Tijdschrift voor Geschiedenis*, 104 (1991), 356-380.

Peeters, C.J.A.C. "Het schemerlicht van de neogotiek. Wisselend oordeel over een stroming in de negentiende-eeuwse kunst". In *J.A. Alberdingk Thijm. Erflater van de negentiende eeuw*. Baarn, 1992, 103-123.

Peters, Elmer. *Naar de middeleeuwen. Het Aartsbisschoppelijk Museum in Utrecht vanaf het begin tot 1882*. Utrecht, 2012.

Raedts, Peter. *De ontdekking van de Middeleeuwen. Geschiedenis van een illusie*. Amsterdam, 2011.

Rosenberg, H.P.R. "De neogotiek van Cuypers en Tepe". *Bulletin KNOB*, 70 (1971), 1-14.

Rosenberg, H.P.R. *De 19de-eeuwse kerkelijke bouwkunst in Nederland*. The Hague, 1972.

Schmidt, Freek. *Pieter de Swart. Architect van de achttiende eeuw*. Zwolle, 1999.

Schoon & Vroom. Kunst in de kerk aan het eind van de vorige eeuw bij gereformeerden en katholieken. Catalogue. Amsterdam, 1980.

Steensma, Regnerus. *Protestantse kerken: hun pracht en kracht*. Gorredijk, 2013.

Steensma, Regnerus, and C.A. van Swigchem. *Honderdvijftig jaar gereformeerde kerkbouw*. Kampen, 1986.

Swigchem, C.A. van, T. Brouwer and W. van Os. *Een huis voor het Woord. Het protestantse kerkinterieur in Nederland tot 1900*. The Hague-Zeist, 1984.

Thijm, J.A. Alberdingk. *De Heilige Linie. Proeve over de oostwaardsche richting van kerk en autaar als hoofdbeginsel der kerkelijke bouwkunst*. Amsterdam, 1858.

Verstijnen, Jan, and Theo Hoogbergen. *Huis vol symboliek. Nicolaaskerk Helvoirt*. Helvoirt, 2008.

Werf, Egbert van der, and Anton Hilhorst, eds. *Van volkskerk tot kathedraal. De St.-Jozefkerk in Groningen*. Groningen, 2012.

Wesselink, Herman. *Een sterke toren in het midden der stad. Verleden, heden en toekomst van bedreigde Nederlandse kerkgebouwen*. Amsterdam, 2018.

Woud, Auke van der. *Waarheid en karakter. Het debat over de bouwkunst 1840-1900*. Rotterdam, 1997.

<http://geoplaza.vu.nl/projects/kerken/> All Dutch church buildings 1800-1970.

<www.reliwiki.nl> A website with information about all churches in the Netherlands.

3.4
The Dialectics of Religious Architecture and Liturgy in the German Countries

Wolfgang Cortjaens

During the nineteenth century, the German-speaking countries generated many artistic theories, which, from an aesthetical or a technical standpoint, have inspired the various reform movements in religious art and architecture. In all denominations, religious practice and liturgical worship were now seen in a broader context of spatial conception and style, of building, engineering and constructing. Ideologically, this process was marked by a dialectic of traditionalist/orthodox and progressive/reformative elements, although the borders are often not clearly separated. Around 1900, these delicate proportions were outbalanced by the upcoming modernity which led to what has lately been described as the 'crisis' of historicist church architecture.[1]

The static and dynamic elements of churches not only include the basic furnishing (*Prinzipalstücke*) like altar and pulpit, mobile fittings such as pews and statues of the Saints and mural paintings, but also objects which are only temporarily displayed in liturgy: portable altars, procession canopies, liturgical vestments and *vasa sacra* and new technical achievements such as heating systems and electrification.

Nazarene influences: the Gothic Revival and the *Gesamtkunstwerk*

The Romantic Movement in Germany, prepared and supported by literature and philosophy – one of the earliest manifestos of Romanticism being Wilhelm Heinrich Wackenroder's and Ludwig Tieck's *Herzensergießungen eines kunstliebenden Klosterbruders* (1796)[2] – regarded religious art and architecture as constitutional elements of the national heritage, as Friedrich Schlegel pointed out in his *Grundzüge der gotischen Baukunst* (1805). The Romantic Movement embraced all domains of artistic expression, such as poetry, music, philosophy, religion and the natural sciences. In spite of the fragile position of the Churches and the political turmoil of the post-Revolutionary period, religious architecture was the domain where the concept of national heritage articulated itself most prominently (cf. the various plans for the completion of Cologne Cathedral which was begun only in 1842 but which hark back to the first decade of the nineteenth century)[3] and where theories of religious and liturgical reform movements found strong resonance.

Artistically, it was in the field of painting that the ideas of Romanticism materialised for the first time in the visual arts. In 1810, a group of German and Austrian painters, led by Friedrich Overbeck and Franz Pforr, went to Rome and, in the abandoned Monastery of Sant'Isodoro, gathered a growing community of pupils and fellow painters, known as the Brotherhood of Saint Luke. Schlegel's central thesis that the original and most noble destination of art was to serve religious worship and public purpose was adopted by the Brotherhood. The 'Nazarenes' as they were nicknamed, because of their unusual appearance, their long hair and beards reminiscent of the Apostles,[4] not only became the first independent artistic community of the nineteenth century but also the first reform movement in the field of religious art. Although most members of the community

3.4-1 Interior of the Court Church of All Saints (Allerheiligenhofkirche) in Munich, paintings by Heinrich Maria von Hess and Joseph Schwarzmann, 1829-1837. Watercolour by Franz Xaver Nachtmann, 1839.
[Munich, Münchner Stadtmuseum, Sammlung Grafik/Plakat/Gemälde]

1. Heinig, *Die Krise des Historismus in der deutschen Sakraldekoration*.
2. Wackenroder and Tieck, *Herzensergießungen eines kunstliebenden Klosterbruders*; Hellerich, *Religionizing, Romanizing Romantics*; Bisky, *Poesie der Baukunst*.
3. Dann, *Religion – Kunst – Vaterland*; Fraquelli, *Im Schatten des Doms*.
4. *Die Nazarener*; *Religion Macht Kunst*; *Die Nazarener – Vom Tiber an den Rhein*.

3.4-2 Peter von Cornelius, The Recognition of Joseph by his brothers. *Fresco with tempera from the Casa Bartholdy in Rome, 1816-1817.*
[Staatliche Museen zu Berlin, Nationalgalerie; photo Andres Kilger / bpk]

were Catholics (following Schlegel's example, Overbeck converted to Catholicism in 1813, as did Philipp Veit), the circle also included a number of Protestants, among them Julius Schnorr von Carolsfeld, so that one can justly speak of a supra-confessional movement. Their concept of Christianity treated art itself as a religion. Friendship was an integral part of the Nazarene ideal, as was expressed in collaborative projects such as the frescoes in the Palazzo Zuccari, also named Casa Bartholdy after its then proprietor, the Prussian consul Jakob Salomon Bartholdy, an important promoter of several Nazarene artists himself. The Brotherhood revived the art of fresco painting from a technical as well as from a stylistic point of view. [Ill. 3.4-2] The Late-Renaissance masters, in particular Raphael, but also long forgotten painters of the Early Renaissance such as Fra Angelico and Sano di Pietro were rediscovered and imitated. The *Italianità* of their works was congenially combined with reminiscences of the North-Alpine Old Masters such as Dürer and Holbein. It has often been overlooked that Nazarene aestheticism was not strictly retrogressive but that its hybrid style and the revitalisation of neglected techniques contained some essentially modern aspects: not the painting *al fresco*, but also medieval oil painting, which hitherto had been regarded as ugly, distorted and primitive, had only recently come to the attention of the art-loving public, i.e. via the famous collection of the brothers Boisserée in Cologne.[5]

When the Brotherhood of Saint Luke broke up in 1820, Nazarene ideology was re-imported to Germany by Overbeck's fellow painters and pupils. Among them were Schnorr, Wilhelm Schadow, Peter von Cornelius and Phillip Veit, each of whom became the head of influential artistic 'schools' at the newly founded or re-established local academies: Cornelius in Düsseldorf and

5   Goldberg, "Die Sammlung Boisserée". Among the admirers of their collection was Schlegel, who published several articles in his (short-lived) magazine *Europa*.

later in Munich, Schadow in Düsseldorf, Veit in Frankfurt.[6] Their synthesis of Italian Renaissance and German Late-Gothic was adopted for various prestigious decoration concepts in official buildings as well as in churches. For example, in 1826, Cornelius was lured from Düsseldorf to Munich by King Ludwig I of Bavaria, on whose commission he not only designed and surveyed the historical *Nibelungen* frescoes in the royal Residenz, but also the altar fresco in the St Ludwig Church, the largest altar piece ever executed.[7] Projects like this or the even more lavish interior decoration of the neo-Byzantine Court Church of All Saints (Allerheiligenhofkirche) were realised between 1826 and 1837 by Leo von Klenze.[8] For the interior, painters Heinrich Maria von Hess and Joseph Schwarzmann developed figurative and ornamental frescoes on a gold ground which originally decorated the vaulting and the apses was inspired by the Palatine Chapel in Palermo.[9] [Ill. 3.4-1] Painting was no longer regarded a mere decorative addition but a complement to the unity of architecture, fittings and liturgy.

Germany in the 1820s and 1830s became the first European country to develop national schools of monumental mural painting, with Munich, Düsseldorf and Frankfurt as the artistic centres. The projects realised by the second generation of Nazarene painters, in particular the frescoes in the Pilgrimage Church of St Apollinaire in Remagen and in the Chapel of Stolzenfels Castle,[10] established fresco painting as a means to create a *biblia pauperum*, a monumental visualisation of Christian iconography. Remagen was, according to the intentions of its patron, a wealthy Catholic maecenas, conceived from the beginning as a 'shrine' for the monumental paintings inside which should convey the ideas of Christian faith and should equally be accessible to a lesser educated public. The four young pupils of Schadow who were finally commissioned for the project – Ernst Deger, Franz Ittenbach and the brothers Andreas and Carl Müller, generally referred to as the *Apollinariskünstler* – were first trained by Overbeck in Rome for several years before they started their work. The result was criticised by contemporary critics because of the missing interrelation between the murals and Ernst Friedrich Zwirner's architecture (a fact that partly is due to the paintings being conceived elsewhere, far away from the building activities). It is only in the circular windows of the transepts that the paintings take up the structure of the architecture.

Despite some criticism, German activities in the field of fresco painting in the above mentioned projects, as well as in Munich, Speyer and Aachen, were attentively noticed in the neighbouring countries.[11] Foreign painters who visited the building sites were mostly more interested in the technical innovations than in iconography, as the German artists' approach towards the ancient technique was far more 'modern' than was generally assumed. In fact, the murals realised in Remagen, Stolzenfels and Rheineck Castle (Edward von Steinle) combined oil painting, encaustic and marouflage painting.[12] Ancient methods of reproduction were combined with new techniques. In Remagen, for example, repetitive decorative elements such as the nimbi of the saints were not painted, but a plaster layer was applied, ornamented and gilded in order to achieve a three-dimensional impression. In Stolzenfels, the King had commissioned backgrounds of paintings executed in the manner of Quattrocento frescoes, so the walls were pre-treated with a mixture of oil and chalk into which ornaments were scratched in order to achieve the impression of gold mosaics.[13] [Ill. 3.4-3]

The neo-Gothic *Gesamtkunstwerk* incorporated all aspects of interior design. For Schlegel, it symbolised "der ganze Inbegriff der gesammten christlichen Bildlichkeit (…), Ausdruck, Hülle und Spiegel der unsichtbaren Welt nach christlicher Erkenntnis derselben".[14] Ideologically and aesthetically it adopted a medieval concept of liturgy and space. In this sense, it was extremely restorative, as it propagated a one-sided understanding of archaeology and medieval techniques which excluded all non-medieval pe-

6   Cornelius: see Büttner, *Peter von Cornelius*; Schadow: Grewe, "Nazarenisch oder nicht?"; Veit: Suhr, *Philipp Veit*.
7   Büttner, *Peter von Cornelius*.
8   Nerdinger et al., *Leo von Klenze*, 383.
9   Schrödter, *Die Frescomalereien der Allerheiligen-Capelle in München*.
10 Remagen: see Rösler-Schinke, *Die Apollinariskirche in Remagen*; Verbeek, "Gesamtkunstwerke im sakralen Bereich", 37-47; Baumgärtel, "National, regional und transnational. Die Monumentalmalerei der Düsseldorfer Malerschule", 117-120; Stolzenfels: see Schiffer, *Die malerische Ausstattung der Schloßkapelle von Stolzenfels*.
11 The technical innovations of the monumental painting in Germany were especially appreciated in the young nation state Belgium, where the successful struggle for national unity had created the need for appropriate media to propagate national identity, and were adopted for the decoration of public buildings and churches. Ogonovszky, *La peinture monumentale*; Ogonovszky-Steffens, "Godefroid Guffens et Jean Swerts"; Bergmans, *Middeleeuwse muurschilderingen in de 19de eeuw*. The Pre-Raphaelites in Great Britain were also influenced by the German Nazarenes and the Düsseldorf School of Painting from which they borrowed the compositional schemes and the sentimental affection.
12 Elenz, "Die monumentale Wandmalerei", 75.
13 Ibid., 81.
14 Schlegel, "Fragmente. Zur Poesie und Literatur, Fragment 199", in: Id., *Kritische Schriften und Fragmente*, VI, 51.

3.4-3 Stolzenfels Castle near Coblenz, Chapel. Detail from the fresco Adoration of the Magi, *by Ernst Deger, 1849–1859.*
[Bildarchiv Foto Marburg / Rudolf Schulze-Marburg, nr. LAC 9.062/9]

Purification and preservation

Never would the idea of the *Gesamtkunstwerk* have had such enormous impact on religious architecture, were not for the numerous purifications the medieval churches underwent in the first half of the nineteenth century – a development we can also see in the Netherlands, Belgium and France.[15] Led by still lingering Classicist aesthetical principles, many medieval churches which had retained their original painting and furnishing were deprived, in most cases irreversibly, of all decoration. The monochrome of the constructional material itself was regarded the peak of purity and simplicity. When in 1828 King Ludwig I of Bavaria commissioned architect Friedrich von Gärtner to remove the post-medieval decoration and furnishing in Bamberg Cathedral, many contemporaries, among them Sulpiz Boisserée, were alienated by the monotony and coolness of the plain stone and brick walls: "Klagen über die Restauration des Doms. Roheiten bei Entfernung der Grabmäler der Fürst-Bischöfe und Domherren etc. Vandalismus gegen den Perücken-Stil und Ignoranz in Betreff auf Cultus und kirchliche Altertümer."[16] Only a decade later, in an attempt to compensate for the heavily attacked clearing out at Bamberg, the King commanded that the interior of Speyer Cathedral, another landmark monument of Romanesque architecture in Bavaria, should be entirely decorated. Together with the bishop of the Diocese of Speyer, Nikolaus Weis, the Nazarene painter Johann von Schraudolph developed an ambitious elaborate iconographic programme which combined *Heilsgeschichte* and real historical events linked with the patrons of the church, the Virgin Mary and the Saints Stephen and Bernard of Clairvaux. This resulted in one of the most ambitious decoration projects of Romantic Historicism, which blended ultramontane Catholicism and, at the same time, the restorative tendencies of the Monarchy.[17] Ironically, most of Schraudolph's work was destroyed in the 1960s in the wake of an-

riods. The German neo-Gothicists, especially the ultramontane *Kölner Richtung*, regularly clashed with either the local authorities or the official institutions of monument preservation.

other purification wave, this time led by the aesthetics of Post-War Modernity…

Bamberg and Speyer represent two extreme positions of nineteenth-century monument preservation. However, both are marked by an unawareness of the artistic value of the previous interior decoration. It was not until the 1840s that in the German Countries the need for preservation of the interiors came into focus. From the most prestigious of all restoration projects, Cologne Cathedral, to the smallest parish church almost every restoration project was overshadowed by methodical debates. The completion of Cologne Cathedral was hampered from the very beginning by different approaches towards preservation. When in 1842 master builder Zwirner and the King of Prussia commissioned Nazarene painter Edward von Steinle to substitute the fragmentary remains of medieval mural painting in the pendentives of the arcades "im Geiste der Alten gehaltenen Compositionen",[18] the unsatisfying results provoked a debate about whether the patron or the ecclesiastical authorities were authorised to judge in terms of artistic topics. The ultramontane circle around August Reichensperger, who was also secretary of the Central Cathedral Construction Society (Zentral-Dombau-Verein) opted for an ecclesiastical superintendence, which the other party around Zwirner and Sulpiz Boisserée heavily rejected.

A similar debate took place during the interior restoration of the Early-Gothic Church of Our Lady in Trier, which provoked the so-called *Methodenstreit* between the agency of monument preservation in Prussia represented by the architects Friedrich August Stüler and Ferdinand von Quast and the local authorities represented by the Diocese of Trier, the two parish councils involved and several protagonists of the *Kölner Richtung* including restoration architect Vincenz Statz, politician August Reichensperger and the painters Edward von Steinle and Peter von Cornelius.[19] [Ill. 3.4-4] The two opposing parties were not so much occupied with the preservation of the underlying historical dec-

3.4-4 Trier, Church of Our Lady, Gothic choir with neo-Gothic furnishing by Vincenz Statz, ca 1900. [Trier, Bistumsarchiv]

oration itself, whose true nature and quality, partly due to a lack of knowledge, and partly due to purposeful disguise, had been obscured by the local authorities (the priest, for example, described the Gothic decoration as "abscheuliche Schmutzkruste" / disgusting dirt crust),[20] but with the manner in which it should be removed without harming the structure of the underlying walls. Interestingly, the interior restoration aroused much more further controversy and was more expensive than the exterior restoration which was seen more as a practical, technical challenge.[21]

Several years later, the so-called *Lettnerfrage* (Rood Screen Controversy) repeated a similar debate that had been led two decades earlier in the United Kingdom by A.W.N. Pugin's design of a double-jube screen for Southwark (1848).[22] Pugin's abhorrence of post-medieval developments and his conception of a spatially enclosed performance of the mass was anathema to many Catholics. It was exactly this archaeological approach which triggered off the debate in Germany, when in Münster and Xanten two

15 Bergmans, *Middeleeuwse muurschilderingen in de 19de eeuw*.
16 Diary of Sulpiz Boisserée (1839), cit. Dümler, *Der Bamberger Kaiserdom*.
17 Schönenberg, *Die Ausmalung des Speyerer Domes*.
18 Lauer, "'Der Traum meiner Jugend'. August Reichensperger und der Kölner Dom", 15-16 (cit. 15).
19 Borger-Keweloh, *Die Liebfrauenkirche in Trier*, 160-165; Buch, *Studien zur preußischen Denkmalpflege*, 182-198.
20 Buch, *Studien zur preußischen Denkmalpflege*, 184.
21 Borger-Keweloh, *Die Liebfrauenkirche in Trier*, 163.
22 Pugin, *A Treatise on Chancel Screens and Rood Lofts*.

Early-Renaissance rood screens were threatened by purification concepts. Again, the Cologne neo-Gothicists were pro-conservation, whereas the majority of the local clergy – with the exception of Bishop Müller – was against. In Münster, the screen which had separated the nave from the transept, the crossing and the choir was demolished,[23] whereas in Xanten it was saved, largely due to Reichensperger and his fellow members of the Belgian Guild of St Thomas and St Luke who had visited the Collegiate Church St Victor´s in 1868 on one of their annual journeys abroad. In a petition the Guild opted for the artistic unity of medieval sacred architecture and its liturgically fitting equipment.[24] Apart from stylistic considerations, the German Rood Screen Controversy touched liturgical aspects such as the spatial organisation of the interior and the question whether laymen were to be involved in the celebration of the mass or excluded.

One of the first restoration projects which respected the original decoration was the Cathedral of Limburg (St Georgs-Dom). The restoration was initiated by King William I of Prussia after the annexation of the Kingdom of Hesse in 1868. Here, the Late-Romanesque mural paintings which had been covered in later times, were carefully brought to light again in a then-unprecedented manner.[25]

New techniques and industries

In the history of nineteenth-century architecture, stylistic questions have widely overshadowed the aspect of materiality. In fact, the question which material should be applied to a new building was essential for almost any reformative or ideological movement in religious architecture, including church furnishings. In most historicist art theories, materiality not only provided historical reminiscences but was an integrative part of an overall 'organic' concept.

Several lines of argument should be distinguished: For the ultramontane *Kölner Richtung* around the lawyer, politician and theoretician August Reichensperger, the architect and the artist embodied the virtues of the medieval builders' hut, their work being the result of a quasi-religious act of creation. The use of modern materials and means of industrial reproduction was strictly proscribed. In his early writing *Die christliche Kunst und ihr Verhältniß zur Gegenwart* (1844), Reichensperger articulated his lifelong credo most emphatically:

> Mitten in dem Gepolter, dem Rasseln und Zischen der Maschinen steht die Kunst als dienende Magd, der vom Frohnvogte ihr bestimmtes, einförmiges Tagewerk zugewiesen ist, wie den übrigen Fabrikarbeitern. Alles, was sie schafft, trägt daher auch den Charakter der Chablone an sich und verräth die unbedingt zwingende mechanische Gewalt. Das "Zeitalter der Intelligenz" weiß nur todte Automate zu schaffen, während die Jahrhunderte, die man so oft "die finstern" zu nennen beliebt, Allem und Jedem ein individuelles Leben einhauchten und damals jedweder Stoff, den die Menschenhand berührte, die Herrschaft des Menschengeistes bekundete. Wo ist die Kunst des Schmiedens, des Treibens, Ciselirens, Durchbrechens hingerathen? Wo finden sich die Filigranarbeiter, die Holz- und Elfenbein-Schnitzer, wo die Gold- und Seidenwirker, wo die Emailleurs, deren Prachtwerke wir kaum noch zu enträtseln wissen?[26]

According to Reichensperger and his fellow campaigners of the Cologne Movement the structure of the building should be reflected in every single part of the exterior as well as the interior and should be developed out of the constructive conditions of the architecture.[27] Reichensperger's praise of the medieval master builders and craftsmen was an attack on the increasing industrialisation and standardisation of sacral art. As there existed no guidelines for the proper design of liturgical fittings, the number of unsuccessful designs in inferior quality and cheap materials had increased immensely. Many furnishings and liturgical objects hardly paid any atten-

23 Schrörs, *Der Lettner im Dom zu Münster*.
24 Liessem, "August Reichensperger", 374; Cortjaens, *Amis gothiques*, 96-97, ill. 29.
25 Zensen, *Der Dom St. Georg zu Limburg*.
26 Reichensperger, *Die christlich-germanische Kunst und ihr Verhältniß zur Gegenwart*.
27 Ibid.
28 Ibid., 1.
29 Kokkelink and Lemke-Kokkelink, *Conrad Wilhelm Hase*.
30 Kühne, "Über die Beziehung Sempers zum Baumaterial".
31 Holzamer, *August Essenwein*, 44-51; Cortjaens, *Rheinische Altarbauten*, 86-89 and Dok. 3.1–3.2, 4.
32 Zietz, *Franz Heinrich Schwechten*; Streich, *Franz Heinrich Schwechten*.
33 Giersbeck, *Christoph Hehl*.
34 Holzäpfel, *Der Architekt Max Meckel*.
35 Vogts, *Vincenz Statz*.

tion to the structure or the liturgical function of the object. To distinguish themselves from these "soulless manufactured goods" (*seelenlose Fabrikkunst*),[28] which were offered in printed catalogues, the 'authenticity' of the material and the production process itself became a central postulation not only of the traditionalists. As a central postulation it permeates also many progressive artistic theories of the nineteenth century, from Conrad Wilhelm Hase's famous credo "Putz ist Lüge!" (Rendering is lying)[29] to the writings of architect Gottfried Semper who would dissolve the distinction between structure and ornament, suppressing the "Präsenz des Stoffes" (presence of the material) in order to subordinate it under his ideal of a "kunstvollen Monumentalität" (ornate monumentality) of the architecture itself. Without differentiating between materials, Semper's colour schemes amalgamated with the shell and the use of materials was subordinated to the general dimensions and the destination of the building (cf. the main lecture hall of the Swiss Federal Polytechnic in Zurich, 1858-1864).[30]

In opposite to the building practice of Romanticist Historicism, which differentiated between patron, architect and the executive artists, the reform movements of the second half of the nineteenth century strengthened the position of the architect who now became responsible for every single detail of the interior design, from the murals to the heating elements, from the *vasa sacra* to electrification. The German countries had at their command an extremely well equipped and organised body of private architects, who, in the last decades of the nineteenth century, advanced the domain of public building which previously had been confided to government orders. A similar infiltration can be traced for religious architecture, although here the clerical authorities represented by the dioceses and the state kept a watchful eye on the commissioning. Among those who managed to get a foot into building activities and, at the same time, to maintain their independence were prominent

architects like museum's director August von Essenwein in Nuremberg, who in the 1860s was involved in some prestigious restoration projects in Cologne,[31] Franz Schwechten in Berlin,[32] Christoph Hehl in Hanover [Ill. 3.4-5], Hildesheim and Berlin,[33] Max Meckel in the Diocese of Limburg and in Freiburg,[34] August Rincklake in Münster, Braunschweig, Düsseldorf and Berlin, Heinrich Wiethase and Heinrich Renard in Cologne and, of course, Vincenz Statz, who was named architect of the Archdiocese of Cologne although he had not passed the required academic training.[35] Many of them, like Essenwein, Hehl and Statz, managed to

3.4-5 Interior of the Protestant Garrison Church in Hanover by Christoph Hehl, taken from: Christoph Hehl, Die Garnison-Kirche zu Hannover, (Hannover, 1896).
[Archive W. Cortjaens]

publish their designs and theories in own publications or in periodicals.[36]

Altars, interior fittings and religious sculpture

Among all elements of the Christian church interior, the altar was the centre of liturgical worship and as such has always attracted the most attention. Its function, position and relationship to other principal fittings – especially the pulpit, which traditionally has a more dominant function in the Protestant liturgy – vary in the Reformed Church, the Lutheran Church and the Catholic Church.

Throughout the nineteenth century, the altar was the foremost challenge when it came to reflecting the changing styles and tastes. Three main types of altars can be identified: the retable, the winged altarpiece and the altar canopy. The need to comply with the regulations of the Church and the requirements of the liturgy offered only limited artistic freedom. In coordination with the ecclesiastical authorities and the parishes, competitions were tendered by the parish councils which scheduled the dimensions, material, costs and delivery conditions. In most cases, the design was delivered by the architect who later commissioned subcontractors (i.e. building contractors, sculptors and painters) for the various works. The Cologne Cathedral Construction Movement and the Catholic revival after 1848 not only triggered a boom of building activity of neo-Gothic churches, especially in the Catholic Rhine Province,[37] but also had enormous impact on the furnishing of churches. Altars became the ideal spot for transmitting Christian ideals and ideologies. They offered ideal possibilities for the application of elaborate narrative cycles which, from a theological point of view, satisfied the authorities, while at the same time fulfilling the needs of the worshippers and making use of increasing popular devotion. Sculpted and painted altarpieces recalled the lives of Christ (cf. the high altar in Hüls near Kempen, St Cyriacus Church, circa 1870, by Josef Anton Reiss), the Virgin Mary (cf. the high altar in Trier [Ill. 3.4-4] or the Maria altar in Krefeld, Church of Our Lady, by the brothers Bong)[38] and other Saints.

From the 1830s, several treatises dealt with the history of the Christian altar. Some of them, like Carl Alexander Heideloff's *Der christliche Altar* (1838), served as artistic model books, containing the authors' own designs (Heideloff was named royal conservator in Bavaria in 1837).[39] The two most influential writings on the Christian altar, however, were written by clergymen: the *Studien zur Geschichte des christlichen Altars* (1857) by the Swabian priests Friedrich Laib and Franz-Joseph Schwarz presented a liturgically rooted history of the Christian altar, seen from a Catholic and ontological point of view.[40] Three decades later, the Frankfurt city pastor (*Stadtpfarrer*) Ernst Franz August Münzenberger published the first volume of *Zur Kenntniß und Würdigung der Mittelalterlichen Altäre Deutschlands*, which was edited partly posthumously in several volumes between 1885 and 1910.[41] Münzenberger, like his intimate Alexander Schnütgen in Cologne, was also a famous art collector and saved many late-medieval altarpieces from destruction. Many fragments saved by him were used for new altarpieces, as was the case with the Maria altar he donated in 1890 to the St Leonard Church in Frankfurt. [Ill. 3.4-6] It consists of fragments of an Antwerp altar-shrine (circa 1480) which was combined with a medieval predella, a neo-Gothic mensa and painted wings with copies after Flemish and Old-Frankish masters, executed in the workshop of the Kevelaer-based painter and designer Friedrich Stummel.[42] The Frankfurt altarpiece is a perfect example for the blending of different periods and regions, of neo-Gothic ingredients and original substance. In this sense, it shows an essentially Historicist approach where an overall impression of the seemingly 'true' triumphs over archaeological 'truth'. Thus, it may not surprise that Münzenbergers' *Altarwerk* circulated around the workshops

---

36 Essenwein, *Die innere Ausschmückung der Kirche Gross-St. Martin in Köln*.
37 Fraquelli, *Im Schatten des Domes*.
38 Maaz, *Skulptur in Deutschland*, I, ill. 466, 467.
39 Cortjaens, *Rheinische Altarbauten*, 61-64.
40 Ibid., 64-69.
41 de Weerth, *Die Altarsammlung*; Cortjaens, *Rheinische Altarbauten*, 71-75.
42 *Ad majoram Dei gloriam*, 53, Cat. D 25, 26; de Weerth, *Die Altarsammlung*, 65, Cat. 27.
43 Vogts, *Vincenz Statz*, 6.
44 Cortjaens, *Rheinische Altarbauten*, 74.
45 Ibid., 48-58 and 58-59.

of contemporary sculptors and painters who found inspiration in historical prototypes. Another reason for its success was the use of heliotype, which allowed a far more detailed reproduction than older publications which, before the invention of photography, contained mostly etchings or simple outlines.

The most common material for altarpieces was wood; only the mensa and the antependium had to consist of stone or marble. The substructure of the altar was to consist of stone, as wood was regarded as inappropriate and contrary to the dignity of Christian worship.[43] A fireproof tabernacle and an expository niche for the temporal display of the Blessed Sacrament were constitutional elements of the Catholic altar. Where stone or marble could be afforded, they were sometimes given a polychromatic finish. The majority of the carved wood altarpieces were gilded (respectively painted with gilt-like colour) and sometimes even painted enamel was applied to imitate the appearance of precious metal.[44]

A relatively small sub-species that can be identified are altars in precious metals which appear after 1870. Consisting of either gilded brass and copper, silver, bronze or electroplating (see below) and richly decorated with stones and enamel, niello, statues and embossments, they offered the possibility of combining ancient techniques which had been neglected for several centuries and were now rediscovered and industrialised by the nineteenth-century craftsmen. As historical models were scarce, the gold- and silversmiths relied on the few originals which had survived, the two most prominent being the altarpiece of Klosterneuburg in Austria (ca 1180, by Mosan artist Nicolas of Verdun), the former retable of the St Castor Church in Coblence (ca 1160/70, today Musée Cluny, Paris) and the former antependium of Basle Cathedral (ca 1020, today Historisches Museum, Basle).[45] All three of them were widely imitated and many neo-Romanesque retables show similar segmental arches and covered with relief. Neo-Gothic altars in precious metal were less common. They adapted the form of winged altarpieces or of the late-Romanesque and Gothic shrines and, in the central axis, added a tabernacle and an expository for the cross.

New inventive techniques such as electroplating were used for whole ensembles, cf. the high altars of the Rosary Basilica (Rosenkranzbasilika) in Berlin-Steglitz (1900), the Church of the Sacred Heart of Jesus in

3.4-6 Frankfurt, Church St Leonhard, Altarpiece, 16th and late 19th Century, with painted wings by Friedrich Stummel, Kevelaer, 1890.
[Wikimedia Commons; photo 2008]

46 Ibid., 251-268. For Herz-Jesu also: Heinig, *Die Krise des Historismus*, 33.
47 Rave, *Karl Friedrich Schinkel*, 224.
48 Hoffmann, *Die Serapions-Brüder*, II, 416-471.
49 Maaz, *Skulptur in Deutschland*, I, ill. 465.
50 Gravgaard and Henschen, *On the Statue of Christ by Thorvaldsen*.

Berlin-Prenzlauer Berg (1900) or the Church of Saint Apostles in Cologne (ca 1905), all of which were fabricated in the Galvanoplastische Kunstanstalt in Geislingen-Steige, a subsidiary of the WMF (Württembergische Metallwarenfabriken).[46]

Less common was the use of terracotta, which was predominant in the North and North-East of Germany. It was mainly used for larger sized sculptures within and outside churches as well as for replicas of ancient works of art, such as Peter Vischer's apostle figures from the Monument of Saint Sebaldus (1519) in Nuremberg. They were reproduced for the first time for the new choir screen Karl Friedrich Schinkel designed for the (old) Cathedral Church in Berlin.[47] Throughout the nineteenth century, partly due to the rediscovery of Vischer as one of the leading craftsmen of the late-medieval period (immortalised in E.T.A. Hoffmann's novella *Meister Martin der Küfner und seine Gesellen*, 1818),[48] the statues became so popular that they were reproduced in various materials for several smaller churches.[49]

Another example is the monumental standing statue of Christ by Danish sculptor Bertel Thorvaldsen (1821), originally designed for the Church of Our Lady in Copenhagen, which was reproduced several times in Germany, mainly for Protestant churches (cf. the bronze reproduction in the narthex of the Friedenskirche in Potsdam, 1851, and copy in French limestone by Leipzig sculptor Arthur Trebst for the Christuskirche in Kassel, 1903),[50] but also for cemeteries (see 2.3). In total, the practice of placing numerous altars and sculptures was much less common in the Protestant regions of Germany, as the Reformed Church and, to a somewhat lesser extent, the Lutheran Church concentrated on the principal elements of liturgical fittings: the altar, the cross and the pulpit.

Towards the end of the nineteenth century, the increasing taste for lavish interiors was supraconfessional. When in 1913 the synagogue in Essen, then the largest and most expensive synagogue to date in Germany, was inaugurated, the choice of precious materials (mosaics, marble) stressed the similarities to contemporary Christian church buildings and can be seen as a sign of the increasing assimilation of Jews into

3.4-7 Interior of the Synagogue in Essen, Edmund Körner, 1911-1913. Photo, 1914.
[Alte Synagoge Essen]

the *Kaiserreich*, who on the Eve of World War I, regarded themselves equal to the other denominations.[51] In the now vanished interiors of the synagogues of Berlin and Essen this attitude was evident in the design of the former Torah shrine, which in both cases adopted the form of the Christian canopy. [Ill. 3.4-7]

Iconographically, liturgical fittings of the Late-Historicist period were much more varied than their stylistically purist predecessors. In their designs, architects and sculptors now included scenes from every-day life, depicting the living and working conditions of the worshippers, or containing German-language inscriptions instead of Latin.

The renaissance of medieval techniques: stained glass, mosaics and textiles

The archaeological approach towards medieval techniques triggered a renaissance of long forgotten artistic traditions and methods. Medieval theoretical writings such as the *Diversa schedularum artium* (circa 1125) by the Benedictine monk Theophilus Presbyter containing formulas for the different kinds of applied arts including book illumination, stained glass and enamelling, or the book on Gothic architecture and ornamentation written by Regensburg master builder Matthias Roritzer (1486) were re-edited and became basic sources of knowledge of ancient techniques and their ideological implications.[52]

Chronologically, the first technique that was revived in the nineteenth century was the production of stained-glass windows.[53] King Ludwig I of Bavaria and King Frederick William IV of Prussia each became patrons of stained-glass manufactures and established the first institutes in their respective residences: the Königliche Glasmalereianstalt in Munich which was erected in 1827 and its Berlin equivalent in 1843. [Col.ill. 12] In addition, there existed a number of local workshops, the most prominent being that of Cologne painter Friedrich Baudri, a brother of the later auxiliary bishop Johann Anton Baudri.[54]

Stained glass and mosaics share many similarities, from a technical point of view as a well as from an aesthetic one. Both techniques are based on the use of paste, both have a basically planar character, both are species of mural painting and as such are often mentioned in the same breath in the artistic literature of the nineteenth century. As in both techniques the overall image consists of numerous fragments which only add up to a whole, stained-glass window piece by piece: these were often referred to as *Mosaikfenster* (mosaic windows). Another similarity lies in the history of their reception, as both techniques had been somewhat neglected since the late Middle Ages. Their archaeological and scientific 'rediscovery' and their technological adaptation by the various reform movements were often seen as depending on another during the second half of the nineteenth century.[55]

Knowledge of the proper manufacturing process of stained-glass windows and the composition of the paste and the procedure of the firing were still underreported. The craftsmen responsible for this task, most of them painters, relied on the study of historical models and experimented with new recipes and processes to achieve similar effects and colourfulness. Often, the results were unsatisfactory or unsuitable for serial production. The different methods – painting on glass or firing – and the styles which inevitably derived from the applied technique soon aroused a public debate. Whereas the workshops in Munich and Berlin favoured a naturalist, picturesque style similar to oil painting,[56] the ultramontane Gothicists of the Cologne movement favoured an archaic style which separated the fields by lead cames and where the colours were built up out of the primary colours. Due to the often poor results of the domestic enterprises, foreign firms were commissioned.[57] In the late 1850s, August Reichensperger lured the Flemish architect and designer Jean-Baptiste Bethune, who in

51 Alte Synagoge Essen, ed., *Stationen jüdischen Lebens*, 41.
52 The first German translation of Theophilus Presbyter was published in 1874; Roritzer was re-edited in 1845, cf. Reichensperger, *Das Büchlein von der Fialen Gerechtigkeit*.
53 Rode, "Zur Wiedergewinnung der Glasmalerei"; *Glasmalerei des 19. Jahrhunderts in Deutschland*.
54 Baudri, *Tagebücher*.
55 Blümel, "Zur Idee des Wandmosaiks in deutschen Kirchen um die Jahrhundertwende"; Müller, *Bunte Würfel der Macht*; Cortjaens, "Das Mosaik als Technik und Kunstform".
56 Dahmen, "Die Bayernfenster im Kölner Dom".
57 For the newly erected chapel of Wissen Castle near Kevelaer, Hardman & Co. in Birmingham delivered a cycle of figurative stained-glass windows; cf. Cortjaens, "Kulturkampf im Gewand der Gotik", 219.

3.4-8 Installation of the canvases for the Bethunian Cupola mosaic in the Carolingian octagon of Aachen Cathedral in 1880.
[© Domkapitel Aachen]

58 Van Cleven, "Meester Jean-Baptiste Bethune"; Cortjaens, *Amis gothiques.*
59 *Glasmalerei des 19. Jahrhunderts in Deutschland*, 192-193, Cat. 70. For the correspondence relative to Mönchengladbach see Cortjaens, *Amis gothiques*, passim, ill. 15.
60 Wehling, *Die Mosaiken im Aachener Münster und ihre Vorstufen.*
61 Springer, *Das Kölner Dom-Mosaik.*
62 Geisert and Moortgat, *Wände aus farbigem Glas.*
63 Frowein-Ziroff, *Die Kaiser-Wilhelm-Gedächtniskirche.*

his Ghent workshop had successfully experimented with stained glass,[58] to Germany and provided him with several prestigious projects, among them the restoration of the thirteenth-century choir window in the Minster Church of Mönchengladbach which still today is regarded an outstanding example of an archaeological approach towards the original material.[59] A decade later, Bethune was commissioned to reconstruct the lost Carolingian cupola mosaic in the Minster Church of Aachen which had been stripped of its late-Baroque stucco. When, against the expectations of the artistic commission, the walls underneath did not reveal enough authentic material for a reconstruction, the church which, through the figure of Charlemagne, was crucial for the legitimisation of the German *Kaiserreich*, was decorated with mosaic and marble incrustation evoking an almost neo-Byzantine atmosphere.

Mosaics had been neglected for centuries before they were rediscovered in the 1830s first by Italian, French and Russian makers. As there were no firms in Germany experienced enough to deliver mosaics of the required quality, the cupola of Aachen Cathedral was commissioned from the Italian mosaicist Antonio Salviati. Bethune, together with fellow painter Jules Helbig, had travelled Italy and Sicily in order to find inspiration for the central representation of the Twenty-Four Elders and the *Majestas*.[60] After the completion of the cupola in 1880, the rest of the octagon was decorated in a more decorative ornamental style, a neo-Byzantine phantasmagory quite different from Bethune's antiquarian approach. [Ill. 3.4-8]

The Cathedrals of Aachen and Cologne (with mosaics designed by August von Essenwein and executed by mosaicist Fritz Geiges and Villeroy & Boch in Mettlach/Saarland)[61] [Ill. 3.4-9] became landmark projects in the application of large-scale mosaics in Germany. In general the high costs and tdifficult techniques limited the use of mosaics. After Unification in 1871, the Berlin-based fabrics of Puhl & Wagner became the leading mosaic makers in Germany and completed a number of interior decorations.[62] Emperor William II himself commissioned several prestigious mosaics, the most programmatic being the *Hohenzollernzug* in the narthex of the Emperor Wilhelm Memorial Church in Berlin, a monumental depiction of the members and ancestors of the House of Hohenzollern.[63] [Ill. 1.4-1] The Imperial family was also present, in effigy or indirectly by making prominent donations, in several other projects which had special meaning to the Hohenzollern because of their genealogical relations, a special symbolic meaning of the site, or out of political interest: the Protestant Saint Saviour Churches in Bad Homburg vor der Höhe/Hesse (1908) and Gerolstein/Eifel (1913) [Ill. 3.4-10], the Protestant military church (Garnisonkirche) in Hanover/Lower-Saxony [Ill. 3.4-5], the

Catholic Chapel of Saint Saviour in Mirbach/ Eifel (1900) and the Benedictine Abbey in Maria Laach, where the Emperor donated a costly (and somewhat oversized) high altar and interfered in the concept behind the apsidal mosaic.[64]

With only few exceptions, such as the former Anglican St George's Church in Berlin decorated with mosaics by Puhl & Wagner (1897), the mosaics were mainly reserved for neo-Romanesque or neo-Byzantine church buildings. Many church interiors of the period around 1900 display a heterogenic use of various precious materials: marble, mosaic, gold background painting etc.

After 1900, mosaic technique was further developed by the upcoming art institutes, such as the Kunstgewerbeschulen in Munich, Düsseldorf and Cologne, which had an enormous impact on the establishment of Modernism in sacred art (i.e. Jan Thorn Prikker's stained-glass windows for the Church of the Three Holy Kings in Neuss, 1913, or his mosaics and murals in the Old-Catholic Friedenskirche in Essen, 1914-1916)[65] and soon was integrated into the beginnings of the modern ecclesiastical movement. With an increasing number of workshops, mosaics became more commonplace. They were especially popular in lay buildings such as public baths, theatres, office buildings and private dwellings. Together with stained glass production, mosaics belonged to the few techniques that were originally developed or rediscovered in a sacral context and were only afterwards industrialised and applied to non-religious building practice.[66]

The exact opposite development can be traced in the revitalisation of the textile industry. Here, it was the industrialisation and

3.4-9 *The figure of Opifex in the choir of Cologne Cathedral, designed by August von Essenwein, with a selfportrait of the mosaicist Fritz Geiges, 1887-1889.*
[Cologne, Dombauarchiv / Dombauverwaltung Köln]

3.4-10 *Interior of the Church of Saint Saviour in Gerolstein, Franz Schwechten, 1913.*
[Bildarchiv Foto Marburg, nr. C437.612 / Michael Jaiter]

64 Cortjaens, "Das Mosaik als Technik und Kunstform", 37-49, ill. 12-19; Krüger, *Die Erlöserkirche in Bad Homburg v.d.H.*; Id., *Die Erlöserkirche in Gerolstein.*
65 Heiser-Schmid, *Kunst – Religion – Gesellschaft. Das Werk Johan Thorn Prikkers.*
66 Oidtmann, *Die Glasmalerei in ihrer Anwendung auf den Profanbau.*

mechanisation of textile fabrication which led to a counter-movement in clerical circles. Until the middle of the nineteenth century, printed fabrics used for ecclesiastical ornaments and vestments consisted of luxury garments produced by French companies (mostly in Lyon) comprising designs that were not originally destined for a specific liturgical or clerical purpose.

In the wake of religious renewal and the establishment of several new congregations in the late 1840s, several monastic workshops such as the Congregation of the Sisters of the Poor Infant Jesus in Aachen (exiled in 1877 to Simpelveld/the Netherlands) specialised in the fabrication of ecclesiastical vestments in neo-medieval style. Their practical training was effected according to medieval standards. Still current Baroque paraments, such as chasubles in the form of the violoncello (*Bassgeigenform*), were now regarded as inappropriate for the Roman liturgy which demanded bigger fashions.[67] Instead, neo-Gothic motifs and broader patterns became popular. Ornamental and figurative embroidery with Christian motifs from the twelfth to the sixteenth centuries provided models for the new designs. Where a particular iconography was demanded, the Sisters also consulted model books from other artistic branches (golds- and silversmiths, painting etc.). The inscriptions mostly consisted of Gothic majuscules.

The workshop of the Sisters was strongly promoted by the Aachen clergymen Andreas Fey and Franz Bock and Bishop Georg Müller of Münster/Westphalia. Not only would Bock write the first fundamental publications on liturgical textiles which offered hundreds of models suited for reproduction [Ill. 3.4-11],[68] he also became an internationally acknowledged collector of antique and medieval textiles.[69] So successful was the Aachen enterprise that the Sisters were soon able to expand their business and founded subsidiaries in Cologne and Vienna.[70] Fed by the growing demand of the parishes, a new industry emerged in the core regions of the textile industry. In the Lower-Rhine area (Krefeld, Kevelaer, Mönchengladbach) in particular, several firms seized on the designs of the Sisters' workshop. Whereas the practical training of the nuns was exercised according to medieval standards and techniques, industrial manufacturers such as Casaretto and Gotzes in Krefeld or van den Wyenbergh in Kevelaer optimised the process by using mechanical weaving looms.

The common practice was to buy industrially fabricated garments, mostly silks with structures based on medieval motives, which were processed further by the local parament associations, which applied embroidery relating to the individual needs of the parish or the patron. The parament associations were also important for the feminisation of communal life, as they enabled women, who were still widely excluded from active participation in parish life, to contribute their share. Pieces of special importance, such as banners, procession canopies or tapestries, however, were still being trusted to the more qualified monastic workshops.

Musica sacra

Although somewhat overlooked due to its auditive character, *musica sacra* played an important role in the history of liturgical reform movements. Regarded as equal to the other arts *ad majoram Dei gloriam*, musical art should express the everlasting truths of religion and promote meditation. The movement was triggered by several important theological and philosophical writings of the later bishop of Regensburg, Johann Michael Sailer, the writer-composer E. T. A. Hoffmann and the Heidelberg lawyer Anton Friedrich Thibaut, author of the pamphlet *Über Reinheit der Tonkunst* (1824).[71] Romantic literature also glorified the spiritual power of music and its effect on the individual: in Wilhelm Heinrich Wackenroder's novella *Das merkwürdige musikalische Leben des Tonkünstlers Joseph Berglinger* (1796) it is dealt with on a philosophical level,[72] whereas Heinrich von Kleist in his novella *Die heilige*

---

67 *Kirchenschmuck*, II, 1859, 49-51.
68 Bock, *Die liturgischen Gewänder des Mittelalters*; Id., *Die Musterzeichner des Mittelalters*.
69 Cortjaens, "Bock, Franz Johann Joseph"; Borkopp-Restle, *Der Aachener Kanonikus Franz Bock und seine Textilsammlungen*.
70 Borkopp, "An die verlorenen Fäden wieder anknüpfen"; Hesse, *Kunstreich und stylgerecht*.
71 Geck, "E.T.A. Hoffmanns Anschauungen über die Kirchenmusik"; Schuh, *Johann Michael Sailer*; Harnoncourt, "Der Liturgiebegriff bei den Früh-Cäcilianern".
72 Wackenroder and Tieck, *Herzensergießungen eines kunstliebenden Klosterbruders*.
73 Kleist, *Sämtliche Erzählungen*, 288-302.
74 Brecher, *Musik im Aachener Dom in 12 Jahrhunderten*, 90-104.
75 Blume, *Geschichte der evangelischen Kirchenmusik*.

Cäcilie oder die Gewalt der Musik (Eine Legende) (1810) satirises and exposes the mechanisms and stereotypes of the creation of Christian myths. In the sixteenth century, a convent is threatened by Dutch iconoclasts; after they hear a nun playing the organ they are so overcome by her performance that they reconvert. In the end, the nun turns out to be none other than Saint Cecilia herself.[73]

In the second half of the nineteenth century, Cecilianism (*Cäcilianismus*) would become the most influential reform movement of musica sacra in the Catholic parts of the German countries. Aachen, due to the merits of the two head conductors of the Cathedral (*Stiftskapellmeister*), Heinrich Böckeler and Franz Nekes, became a centre of the Cecilian movement. Its restoration character, for which the term *Aachener Einseitigkeit* became common,[74] was evident, for example, in the rejection of orchestral or operatic works and mixed choirs and its preference of the Gregorian harmonies or the classical sixteenth-century vocal polyphony of Palestrina. The Catholic dioceses made an effort to suppress any reform tendency, including forbidding mixed choirs, the use of instruments during the advent season and the fasting period, and even the recital of compositions of the 'Viennese' classical school (for example Joseph Haydn) and four-part masses which, by including operatic elements, had become extremely popular during the eighteenth century. These restoration tendencies were propagated in periodicals such as the *Organ für christliche Kunst* (Cologne, 1851-1873) and *Musica sacra. Halbmonatsschrift für Hebung und Förderung der katholischen Kirchenmusik* (Regensburg, 1868-1910). A similar stagnation can be detected within the Protestant and Reformed Church where, after the decline of musical tradition during the Enlightenment, no innovative concept had emerged. Instead, development during this period is marked by numerous reworkings of older compositions from the Reformation period.[75]

On the Catholic side, after the foundation of the Allgemeine Cäcilien-Verein in 1868 numerous musical associations and choirs emerged within parishes, often choosing Saint Cecilia as their patron. Although the possibilities of permanent visual presence within the church buildings were limited, the movement did have some influence on the spatial organisation of church interiors when it came to the positioning of the choir and the organ. The most visible element of musical worship within churches was the organ. Challenged by the development of Romantic

3.4-11 Neo-Gothic banner of the choir of the parish of St Peter's in Aachen, made in the workshop of the Sisters of the Poor Infant Jesus, Simpelveld, 1880. The presentation of Saint Cecilia is based on an early-sixteenth-century altarpiece of the so-called Master of Saint Bartholomew.
[© Kath. Kirchengemeinde St. Peter Aachen / Anne Gold, Aachen]

harmonies, the organ builders were forced to adjust the technique of the instruments. The technically groundbreaking organ Eberhard Friedrich Walcker created for St Paul's Church in Frankfurt (1833) [Ill. 1.4-3] was a turning point and Walcker became the leading organ builder in the German countries and abroad.[76] The interior of St Paul's, dominated by an acoustically problematic central cupola, demanded a novel balancing of the different elements of the organ (pedals, manuals, registers) in order to achieve a satisfactory sound. Walcker's family enterprise in Ludwigsburg would create organs for every type of church building, from the sober Classicism of St Paul's to the lavish neo-Gothic of Ulm Cathedral (1857) which was inspired by its tower, Vienna (Votive Church, 1878) and Strasbourg (Military Church, 1887), to neo-Renaissance in Riga/Latvia (1884). In the second half of the nineteenth century, technical innovations and new mechanical tools affected the process of organisation. Organ builders experimented with new kinds of membranes, pneumatic regulation/steering (*Steuerung*) and electric *Traktur*.

When during the last quarter of the nineteenth century new spatial concepts came into focus (see below), their wide spaces and the prominent location of the organ were rejected and ridiculed by traditionalists, not coincidentally, as 'opera houses'.

Among the other denominations, the musical reform movement affected especially the Jewish liturgy. Whereas the traditional orthodox liturgy allowed only chanting as an adequate expression of musical worship, for the first time it was possible to perform compositions accompanied by instruments. Berlin composer Louis Lewandowski, often referred to as the 'Mendelssohn of synagogal music' became the key figure and the most important theoretician of the renewal of Jewish liturgy.[77] In the strongholds of the Jewish reform movement, organs became part of the furnishing in newly erected synagogues, as was the case in Frankfurt am Main (Hauptsynagoge, 1855-1860, by Johann Georg Kayser) and in Berlin (Neue Synagoge, 1859-1866, by Friedrich August Stüler and Eduard Knoblauch).[78]

Church interiors within the liturgical reform movements around 1900

The evolution of religious architecture in Germany can be traced back to both a Protestant and a Catholic line, which, at times, were in strong opposition towards each other.[79] After a first synod held in Dresden in 1856, in 1861, sixteen statutes for the building of Protestant churches were formulated in the so-called Eisenach Regulative (*Eisenacher Regulativ*).[80] Among the most influential points were the adaptation of Germanic (!) medieval styles, and the combination of a cross-shaped layout and a long nave which still allowed orientation. The latter statute had some impact on the orientation of the interior. Although the layout according to the Eisenach Regulative still included elements of east-west orientation and the plan of the Roman Catholic longitudinal *Prozessionskirche* (procession church), with the organ placed in the west and the pulpit at one side of the nave, the statutes clashed with the Catholics' plea for clearly oriented longitudinal layouts.

After the *Kulturkampf* (Cultural Struggle), from 1884 onward, the confessional borders dissolved. The changing attitude of the Catholic Church, resulting partly from a diversification of pastoral practice and pastoral care, with more and more working-class members becoming priests and laymen taking over the function of the pastor or priest, affected liturgical worship as well as manifested itself in the design of church interiors. Especially in the Catholic milieu, where local associations formed important instruments of organisation and representation, the focus shifted toward socially oriented forms of worship. A symptom of this pacification was the increasing similarity between Catholic and Protestant church building programmes. This development was to a great extent

---

76 Fischer, *Das Orgelbauergeschlecht Walcker*; Moosmann and Schäfer, *Eberhard Friedrich Walcker*.
77 Joseph and Seligman, "Orgelstreit". Lewandowski: Goldberg, "Neglected Sources for the Historical Study of Synagogue Music"; Nemtsov and Simon, *Louis Lewandowski*.
78 Frankfurt: Künzl, *Islamische Stilelemente im Synagogenbau*, 260; Berlin; Gauding and Simon, *Die Neue Synagoge Berlin*.
79 Blaschke, *Konfessionen im Konflikt*.
80 Seng, *Der evangelische Kirchenbau*; Mertin, "Kirchenbau Regulativ"; Ellwarth, *Evangelischer Kirchenbau in Deutschland*, 136-167 and 168-171.

triggered by the Wiesbaden Programme (*Wiesbadener Programm*), a Protestant reform movement initiated in 1890/91 by the Wiesbaden priest Emil Veesenmeyer, Berlin-based art historian K. E. O. Fritsch and architect Johannes Otzen. The Ringkirche in Wiesbaden (Hesse)[81] designed by Otzen and erected between 1892 and 1894 was the first church building in Germany to realise these theories in practice. Outwardly not recognisable, its approach towards the interior was regarded revolutionary. [Ill. 3.4-12-13]

By abandoning the choir and the naves in favour of a unity of pulpit, organ and altar which were all placed in the central axis, the pulpit as the locus of preaching was accentuated and became equal to the altar. Elements that had hitherto been crucial to Catholic and Protestant church building, such as the orientation of the exterior, were neglected and subordinated to the conditions of the site and practical liturgical needs: as a result, in the Ringkirche the altar is to be found under the twin-tower façade in the west where a pseudo-porch in fact contains an assembly room for the confirmands, whereas the main entrance is located under the apse in the east. The layout plan of the interior is accentuated by the furnishing: the seating is arranged in ring-shaped segments which drop towards the altar. The altar is surmounted by the pulpit and the organ. The reticulated vaulting which spans above the centre of the church was realised without underpinning. It could only be built by using new lightweight construction materials instead of natural stone. All the walls are roughcast and painted in warm yellow and gold, simulating gilding.

3.4-12-13 *The Protestant Ringkirche in Wiesbaden, Johannes Otzen, 1892-1894: exterior and interior.*
[Bildarchiv Foto Marburg]

81 Kiesow, *Architekturführer Wiesbaden*, 165-167.

The Ringkirche was soon followed by other examples especially in the Protestant parts of Germany and in Switzerland (i. e. Wuppertal-Elberfeld, Hamburg, Hanover and Basle).

The anti-hierarchical, theologically grounded Wiesbaden Programme found strong resonance in other liturgical reform movements of the early twentieth century, with which it had in common the tendency to incorporate practitioners into the liturgy. In almost all denominations a dialectic of reformative and orthodox movements can be traced, often split into various sub-movements (for example, *Trierer* versus *Kölner Richtung*).[82]

For example, what today is generally known as the Liturgical Movement (*Liturgische Bewegung*) in fact consisted of several sub-currents.[83] It was, in first degree, a mass-liturgical movement, which means that the central ingredients of the mass should guide and govern the practitioners, for example by introducing the so-called *Betsingmesse* (with the text spoken in Latin and the songs sung in German) and the administration of the Communion after mass. All these measures which were meant to strengthen the active participation of the worshippers demanded an adjustment of the spatial organisation of the church interiors: the altar should be visible for all worshippers; the other liturgical stations (pulpit, tabernacle, confessional, baptismal fonts, organ and singer tribune) should be accentuated in a similar way. The Benedictines of Maria Lach Abbey under Abbot Ilfons Herdewegen became the first station of the movement in the German-speaking countries. At the turn of the century, the Beuron School of Art with its contemporary reworking of Early Christian, Byzantine and medieval art became another important player within the artistic reform movement. Although monastic, it managed nevertheless to keep in touch with contemporary secular developments such as the Secessionists in Southern Germany and Austria and had a major influence on other neighbouring countries and even overseas.[84] The artistic schools of Beuron and Maria Laach both strongly influenced the liturgical reform movement in Belgium and provided the model for the Benedictine Abbeys at Maredsous (1872) [Ill.2.2-7] and Regina coeli in Louvain (1899).

At the turn of the century, the Deutsche Werkbund and the Heimatschutz movement became important links between traditionalist and progressive tendencies in German church architecture, although both movements originally derived from profane building practice. They picked up several ideas of the Wiesbaden Programme, especially the orientation of the church interior, and mingled them with a Historicist approach. Neo-Baroque and neo-Renaissance layouts were preferred for the interiors, as the wide spaces of these periods were regarded as a compromise towards the internal liturgical reform movements without giving up historical references.[85] As a consequence, Catholic and Protestant churches became less and less distinctive in their appearance. However, this could not obscure the lingering conflicts between and inside the different denominations. The gradual reduction of ornament in the years before First World War (also apparent in neo-Classical architecture of the pre-war era) reflected the changing demands of liturgy. The lurking 'crisis' of Historicism in ecclesiastical architecture and art and the unchurching (*Entkirchlichung*) of parochial life, for which a decrease in the number of church attendees was a clear sign, formed a point of departure towards modernity.

82 Rönz, *Der Trierer Diözesanklerus*.
83 Trapp, *Vorgeschichte und Ursprung der liturgischen Bewegung*.
84 Siebenmorgen, "Kulturkampfkunst"; Lang, *Das Kunstschaffen des Benediktinerordens*; Standaert, *L'École de Beuron*.
85 Cortjaens, "Neubarock im rheinischen Kirchenbau", 157.

BIBLIOGRAPHY

Ad majoram Dei gloriam. Der Kirchenmaler Friedrich Stummel und sein Atelier. Kevelaer, 1979.

Alte Synagoge Essen, ed. *Stationen jüdischen Lebens: von der Emanzipation bis zur Gegenwart.* Exhibition catalogue Essen. Bonn, 1990.

Baudri, Friedrich. *Tagebücher. Bd. 1: 1854-1857.* Edited by Ludwig Gierse and Ernst Heinen. Publikationen der Gesellschaft für Rheinische Geschichtskunde LXXIII. Düsseldorf, 2006.

Baumgärtel, Bettina. "National, regional, transnational. Die Monumentalmalerei der Düsseldorfer Malerschule – Apollinariskirche und Schloss Heltorf". In: *Weltklasse. Die Düsseldorfer Malerschule und ihre internationale Ausstrahlung 1819-1918.* Exhibition catalogue Düsseldorf, Museum Kunstpalast. Vol. 1. Petersberg, 2011, 114-139.

Bergmans, Anna. *Middeleeuwse muurschilderingen in de 19de eeuw. Studie en inventaris van middeleeuwse muurschilderingen in Belgische kerken.* KADOC Artes, 2. Leuven, 1999.

Bisky, Jens. *Poesie der Baukunst. Architekturästhetik von Winckelmann bis Boisserée.* Weimar, 2000 (Diss. Humboldt Universität Berlin, 1999).

Blaschke, Olaf, ed. *Konfessionen im Konflikt. Deutschland zwischen 1800 und 1970 – ein zweites konfessionelles Zeitalter.* Göttingen, 2002.

Blume, Friedrich. *Geschichte der evangelischen Kirchenmusik.* Kassel, 1965.

Blümel, Anne. "Zur Idee des Wandmosaiks in deutschen Kirchen um die Jahrhundertwende". In: Helmut Geisert and Elisabeth Moortgat, eds. *Wände aus farbigem Glas. Das Archiv der Vereinigten Werkstätten für Mosaik und Glasmalerei Puhl & Wagner, Gottfried Heinersdorff.* Berlinische Galerie – Museumspädagogischer Dienst, Begleitpublikation zur Ausstellung im Martin-Gropius-Bau, 8.12.1989-21.1.1990. Berlin, 1989, 175-190.

Bock, Franz. *Die liturgischen Gewänder des Mittelalters.* Bonn, 1859-1870.

Bock, Franz. *Die Musterzeichner des Mittelalters. Anleitende Studienblätter für Gewerb- und Werkschulen, für Ornamentzeichner, Paramenten-, Teppich- und Tapetenfabriken nach alten Originalstoffen eigener Sammlung.* Leipzig, 1860.

Borger-Kewelloh, Nicola. *Die Liebfrauenkirche in Trier. Studien zur Baugeschichte.* Trier, 1986.

Borkopp, Birgitt. "An die verlorenen Fäden wieder anknüpfen… Zur Reform der Paramentenkunst im 19. Jahrhundert". In: Hiltrud Westermann-Angerhausen, ed. *Alexander Schnütgen. Colligite fragmenta ne pereant. Gedenkschrift des Schnütgen-Museums zum 100. Geburtstag seines Gründers.* Cologne, 1993, 207–222.

Borkopp-Restle, Birgitt. *Der Aachener Kanonikus Franz Bock und seine Textilsammlungen.* Riggisberg, 2008.

Brecher, August. *Musik im Aachener Dom in 12 Jahrhunderten.* Aachen, 1998.

Brepohl, Erhard. *Theophilus Presbyter und das mittelalterliche Kunsthandwerk.* 2 vols. Vienna, 1999.

Buch, Felicitas. *Studien zur preussischen Denkmalpflege am Beispiel konservatorischer Arbeiten Ferdinands von Quast.* Worms, 1990 (Diss. TU Darmstadt, 1989).

Büttner, Frank. *Peter von Cornelius. Fresken und Freskenprojekte.* Vol. 1. Wiesbaden, 1980.

Cortjaens, Wolfgang. "Kulturkampf im Gewand der Gotik. Die Schlosskapelle Wissen". In: *Geldrischer Heimatkalender 2002.* Edited by Historischer Verein für Geldern und Umgegend. Geldern, 2001, 214-222.

Cortjaens, Wolfgang. *Rheinische Altarbauten des Historismus. Sakrale Goldschmiedekunst 1870-1918.* Rheinbach, 2002 (Diss. Aachen, 1999).

Cortjaens, Wolfgang. "Bock, Franz Johann Joseph". In: *Biographisch-Bibliographisches Kirchenlexikon,* vol. 33. Nordhausen, 2003, 128-135.

Cortjaens, Wolfgang. "Neubarock im rheinischen Kirchenbau. Voraussetzung und Genese eines Neo-Stils". In: Geschichtsverein für das Bistum Aachen e. V., ed. *Die Anfänge des Neubarock im rheinischen Kirchenbau,* Beiheft 6. Neustadt a. d. Aisch, 2009, 59-158.

Cortjaens, Wolfgang, ed. *Amis gothiques. Der Briefwechsel von August Reichensperger und Jean-Baptiste Bethune.* Commission royale d'Histoire/Koninklijke Commissie voor Geschiedenis, coll-in-8°. Brussels, 2011.

Cortjaens, Wolfgang. "Das Mosaik als Technik und Kunstform im Kirchenbau der Kaiserzeit". In: Geschichtsverein für das Bistum Aachen e. V., ed. *"Malereien für die Ewigkeit". Mosaiken im sakralen Raum. Geschichte im Bistum Aachen,* Beiheft 7. Neustadt a. d. Aisch, 2013, 17-65.

Cortjaens, Wolfgang, Jan De Maeyer and Tom Verschaffel, eds. *Historism and Cultural Identity in the Rhine-Meuse Region. Tensions between Regionalism and Nationalism in the Nineteenth Century / Historismus und kulturelle Identität im Raum Rhein-Maas. Das 19. Jahrhundert im Spannungsfeld von Regionalismus und Nationalismus.* KADOC Artes, 10. Leuven, 2008.

Dahmen, Stephan. "Die Bayernfenster im Kölner Dom und die Entwicklung des Architekturfensters in der königlichen Glasmalereianstalt München". *Kölner Domblatt,* 65 (2000), 201-214.

Dann, Otto. *Religion – Kunst – Vaterland. Der Kölner Dom im Jahrhundert seiner Vollendung.* Cologne, 1983.

de Weerth, Elsbeth. *Die Altarsammlung des Frankfurter Stadtpfarrers Ernst Franz August Münzenberger (1830-1890). Ein Beitrag zur kirchlichen Kunst in der zweiten Hälfte des 19. Jahrhunderts.* Frankfurt-Vienna-Basel-New York, 1995.

Dümler. Christian. *Der Bamberger Kaiserdom. 1000 Jahre Kunst und Geschichte.* Bamberg, 2005.

Elenz, Reinhold. "Die monumentale Wandmalerei des 19. Jahrhunderts in Rheinland-Pfalz. Technologische Untersuchungen zur Maltechnik an ausgewählten Objekten". In: *Die Nazarener – Vom Tiber an den Rhein. Drei Malerschulen des 19. Jahrhunderts.* Exhibition catalogue Landesmuseum Mainz. Regensburg, 2012, 75-93.

Ellwarth, Kathrin. *Evangelischer Kirchenbau in Deutschland.* Petersberg, 2008.

Essenwein, August Von. *Die innere Ausschmückung der Kirche Gross-St.-Martin in Köln.* Nuremberg, 1866.

Fischer, Johannes. *Das Orgelbauergeschlecht Walcker in Ludwigsburg.* Kassel, 1966.

Fraquelli, Sybille. *Im Schatten des Domes: Architektur der Neugotik in Köln (1815-1914).* Cologne, 2008.

Frowein-Ziroff, Vera. *Die Kaiser Wilhelm-Gedächtniskirche. Entstehung und Bedeutung.* Die Bauwerke und Kunstdenkmäler von Berlin, Beiheft 9. Berlin, 1982.

Gauding, Daniela, and Hermann Simon. *Die Neue Synagoge Berlin. "… zum Ruhme Gottes und zur Zierde der Stadt".* Berlin, 2011.

Geck, Martin. "E.T.A. Hoffmanns Anschauungen über die Kirchenmusik". In: Walter Salmen, ed. *Beiträge zur Musikanschauung im 19. Jahrhundert.* Regensburg, 1965, 61-71.

Geisert, Helmut, and Elisabeth Moortgat, eds. *Wände aus farbigem Glas. Das Archiv der Vereinigten Werkstätten für Mosaik und Glasmalerei Puhl & Wagner, Gottfried Heinersdorff.* Berlinische Galerie – Museumspädagogischer Dienst, Begleitpublikation zur Ausstellung im Martin-Gropius-Bau, 8.12.1989-21.1.1990. Berlin, 1989.

Giersbeck, Andrea Elisabeth. *Christoph Hehl (1847-1911). Ein Kirchenbaumeister zwischen Dogmatismus und Emanzipation.* Quellen und Studien zu Geschichte und Kunst im Bistum Hildesheim, 7. Regensburg, 2014.

Glasmalerei des 19. Jahrhunderts in Deutschland. Exhibition catalogue Angermuseum Erfurt 1993/1994. Leipzig, 1993.

Goldberg, Geoffrey. "Neglected Sources for the Historical Study of Synagogue Music: The prefaces to Louis Lewandowski's 'Kol Rinnah u'T'fillah' and 'Todah w'Simrah'; annotated translations." *Musica Judaica,* 11 (1989-1990), 28-57.

Goldberg, Gisela. "Die Sammlung Boisserée 1827 und 1998 (Konkordanz)". In: Hiltrud Kier and Frank Günter Zehnder, eds. *Lust und Verlust II. Corpus-Band zu Kölner Gemäldesammlungen 1800-1860.* Cologne, 1998, 354-403.

Gravgaard, Anne Mette, and Eva Henschen. *On the Statue of Christ by Thorvaldsen.* Thorvaldsen Museum & The Church of Our Lady. Copenhagen, 1997.

Grewe, Cordula. "Nazarenisch oder nicht? Überlegungen zum Religiösen der Düsseldorfer Malerschule". In: *Weltklasse. Die Düsseldorfer Malerschule und ihre internationale Ausstrahlung 1819-1918.* Exhibition catalogue Düsseldorf, Museum Kunstpalast. Petersberg, 2011, 76-87.

Gundermann, Iselin. *Ernst Freiherr von Mirbach und die Kirchen der Kaiserin.* Hefte des evangelischen Kirchenbauvereins, 9. Berlin, 1995.

Harnoncourt, Philipp. "Der Liturgiebegriff bei den Früh-Cäcilianern und seine Anwendung auf die Kirchenmusik". In: Hubert Unverricht, ed. *Der Cäcilianismus. Anfänge – Grundlagen – Wirkungen.* Tutzing, 1988, 75-108.

Heinig, Anne. *Die Krise des Historismus in der deutschen Sakraldekoration im späten 19. Jahrhundert.* Regensburg, 2004 (Diss. Kiel, 2002).

Heiser-Schmid, Christiane. *Kunst – Religion – Gesellschaft. Das Werk Johan Thorn Prikkers zwischen 1890 und 1912. Vom niederländischen Symbolismus zum Deutschen Werkbund.* Diss. Rijksuniversiteit Groningen, 2008.

Hellerich, Sigmar Von. *Religionizing, Romanizing Romantics. The Catholico-Christian Camouflage of the Early German Romantics: Wackenroder, Tieck, Novalis, Friedrich and August Wilhelm Schlegel.* Frankfurt am Main et al., 1995.

Hesse, Petra. *Kunstreich und stylgerecht. Die Paramentenstickereien der Schwestern vom Armen Kinde Jesus aus Aachen und Simpelveld (1848-1914). Ein Beitrag zum sakralen Kunsthandwerk des Historismus im Rheinland.* Munich, 2001.

Hoffmann, E. T. A. [Ernst Theodor August Wilhelm]. *Die Serapions-Brüder. Gesammelte Erzählungen und Märchen.* Darmstadt, 1995.

Holzamer, Karin. *August Essenwein 1831-1892. Architekt und Museumsmann. Seine Zeichnungen und Entwürfe in Nürnberg.* Darmstadt, 1985 (Diss. University Regensburg, 1985).

Holzäpfel, Wolf-Werner. *Der Architekt Max Meckel 1847-1910. Studien zur Architektur und zum Kirchenbau des Historismus in Deutschland.* Lindenberg, 2000.

Joseph, Max, and Cäsar Seligman. "Orgelstreit". In: *Jüdisches Lexikon*, vol. 4. Berlin, 1930, 601-604.

Kiesow, Gottfried. *Architekturführer Wiesbaden – Durch die Stadt des Historismus.* Deutsche Stiftung Denkmalschutz. Monumente Publikationen. Bonn, 2006.

Kirchenschmuck, Der. Ein Archiv für christliche Kunstschöpfungen und christliche Alterthumskunde. Edited by Leitung des christlichen Kunstvereins für die Diözese Rottenburg. Stuttgart, 1857-1870. Neue Folge, 1-12, Amberg, 1873-1880.

Kleist, Heinrich von. *Sämtliche Erzählungen.* Stuttgart, 1986.

Kokkelink, Günter, and Monika Lemke-Kokkelink. *Conrad Wilhelm Hase 1818-1902, Gründer der Hannoverschen Architekturschule.* Ausstellung zum 100. Todestag im Stadtarchiv Hannover. Hannover, 2002.

Krüger, Jürgen. *Rom und Jerusalem. Kirchenbauvorstellungen der Hohenzollern im 19. Jahrhundert.* Berlin, 1995.

Krüger, Jürgen. *Die Erlöserkirche in Bad Homburg v. d. H. – Schlüssel zum Kirchenbauprogramm Kaiser Wilhelms II.* Königstein im Taunus, 2008.

Krüger, Jürgen. *Die Erlöserkirche in Gerolstein. Ein Beispiel für das Kirchenbauprogramm Kaiser Wilhelms II.* Königstein im Taunus, 2013.

Kühne, Hellmut R. W. "Über die Beziehung Sempers zum Baumaterial". In: *Gottfried Semper und die Mitte des 19. Jahrhunderts.* Symposium vom 2.-6. Dezember 1974, Institut für Geschichte und Theorie der Architektur an der Eidgenössischen Technischen Hochschule Zürich. Basel-Stuttgart, 1976, 109-119.

Künzl, Hannelore. *Islamische Stilelemente im Synagogenbau des 19. und frühen 20. Jahrhunderts.* Frankfurt am Main et al., 1984.

Lang, Claudia. *Das Kunstschaffen des Benediktinerordens unter Rückgriff auf archaische Stilelemente und gleichzeitigem Aufbruch in die Moderne.* Regensburg, 2008.

Lauer, Rolf. "'Der Traum meiner Jugend'. August Reichensperger und der Kölner Dom". In: Mario Kramp, ed. *August Reichensperger. Koblenz – Köln – Europa.* Coblenz, 2005, 11-19.

Liessem, Udo. "August Reichensperger (1808-1895), the Journeys abroad of an Art Theorist and Politician". In: Wolfgang Cortjaens, Jan De Maeyer and Tom Verschaffel, eds. *Historism and Cultural Identity in the Rhine-Meuse Region. Tensions between Regionalism and Nationalism in the Nineteenth Century / Historismus und kulturelle Identität im Raum Rhein-Maas. Das 19. Jahrhundert im Spannungsfeld von Regionalismus und Nationalismus.* KADOC Artes, 10. Leuven, 2008, 367-379.

Maaz, Bernhard. *Skulptur in Deutschland zwischen Französischer Revolution und Erstem Weltkrieg.* 2 vols. Berlin-Munich, 2010.

Mertin, Andreas. "Kirchenbau Regulativ. Evangelische Kirchenbauprogramme von 1856 bis 2008". *Ta katoptrizizómena. Das Magazin für Kunst Kultur Theologie Ästhetik*, 58 (2009).

Moosmann, Ferdinand, and Rudi Schäfer. *Eberhard Friedrich Walcker, 1794-1872.* Kleinblittersdorf, 1994.

Müller, Dorothea. *Bunte Würfel der Macht. Ein Überblick über Geschichte und Bedeutung des Mosaiks in Deutschland zur Zeit des Historismus.* Europäische Hochschulschriften, Reihe 28. Frankfurt am Main et al., 1995 (Diss. Saarbrücken 1994).

Die Nazarener. Exhibition catalogue Städelsches Kunstinstitut. Frankfurt, 1977.

Die Nazarener – Vom Tiber an den Rhein. Drei Malerschulen des 19. Jahrhunderts. Exhibition catalogue Landesmuseum Mainz. Regensburg, 2012.

Nemtsov, Jascha, and Hermann Simon. *Louis Lewandowski. "Liebe macht das Lied unsterblich!".* Berlin, 2011.

Nerdinger, Wilfried, Sonja Hildebrandt, Ulrike Steiner and Thomas Weidner, eds. *Leo von Klenze. Architekt zwischen Kunst und Hof 1784-1864.* Munich, 2000.

Ogonovszky-Steffens, Judith. *La peinture monumentale d'histoire dans les édifices civils en Belgique (1830-1914).* Mémoires de l'Académie royale de Belgique, Classe des Beaux-Arts. Série 3, T. 16. Brussels, 1999.

Ogonovszky, Judith. "Godefroid Guffens et Jean Swerts: la peinture monumentale belge sous l'influence des Nazaréens." In: Hubert Roland and Sabine Schmitz, eds. *Pour une iconographie des identités culturelles et nationales. La construction des images collectives à travers le texte et l'image. / Ikonographie kultureller und nationaler Identität. Zur Konstruktion kollektiver Images in Text und Bild.* Studien und Dokumente zur Geschichte der romanischen Literaturen, 51. Frankfurt a. M. et al., 2004, 87-116.

Oidtmann, Heinrich. *Die Glasmalerei in ihrer Anwendung auf den Profanbau.* Berlin, 1873.

Pugin, Augustus Welby Northmore. *A Treatise on Chancel Screens and Rood Lofts.* First published London, 1851; facsimile edition Leonminster, 2005.

Rave, Paul Ortwin. *Karl Friedrich Schinkel. Lebenswerk. Berlin 1 - Bauten für die Kunst, Kirchen, Denkmalpflege.* Berlin, 1941.

Reichensperger, August. *Das Büchlein von der Fialen Gerechtigkeit von Mathias Roriczer weyland Dombaumeister in Regensburg. Nach einem alten Drucke aus dem Jahre 1486 in die heutige Mundart übertragen und durch Anmerkungen erläutert.* Trier, 1845.

Reichensperger, August. *Die christlich-germanische Baukunst und ihr Verhältniß zur Gegenwart.* Trier, 1845.

Religion Macht Kunst. Exhibition catalogue Schirn Kunsthalle. Frankfurt, 2005.

Rode, Herbert. "Die Wiedergewinnung der Glasmalerei. Mit einem Exkurs zu den Mosaiken". In: Eduard Trier and Willy Weyres, eds. *Kunst des 19. Jahrhunderts im Rheinland. Bd. 3: Malerei*. Düsseldorf, 1979, 275-312.

Rönz, Helmut. *Der Trierer Diözesanklerus im 19. Jahrhundert. Herkunft, Ausbildung, Identität*. 2 vols. Cologne-Weimar-Vienna, 2006.

Rösler-Schinke, Stephanie. *Die Apollinariskirche in Remagen – ein Gesamtkunstwerk des 19. Jahrhunderts*. Diss. Munich, 1994.

Schiffer, Anne. *Die malerische Ausstattung der Schloßkapelle von Stolzenfels durch Ernst Deger. Ein Beitrag zur Kunstgeschichte des 19. Jahrhunderts*. Frankfurt a. M., 1992.

Schlegel, Friedrich. *Grundzüge der gotischen Baukunst*. Berlin, 1805.

Schlegel, Friedrich. "Fragmente. Zur Poesie und Literatur". In: Friedrich Schlegel. *Kritische Schriften und Fragmente. Studienausgabe in 6 Bänden*. Edited by Ernst Behler and Hans Eichner. Paderborn-Munich-Vienna-Zürich, 1988.

Schönenberg, Marianne. *Die Ausmalung des Speyerer Domes (1846-1853/54) durch Johann Schraudolph und seine Gehilfen*. Diss. Berlin, FU, 1989.

Schrödter, Gottlieb Heinrich von. *Die Frescomalereien der Allerheiligen-Capelle in München*. Munich, 1836.

Schrörs, Tobias. *Der Lettner im Dom zu Münster – Geschichte und liturgische Funktion*. Forschungen zur Volkskunde, 50. Norderstedt, 2005.

Schuh, Josef. *Johann Michael Sailer und die Erneuerung der Kirchenmusik – Zur Vorgeschichte der Cäcilianischen Reformbewegung in der ersten Hälfte des 19. Jahrhunderts*. Cologne, 1972.

Seng, Eva-Maria. *Der evangelische Kirchenbau in Deutschland im 19. Jahrhundert. Die Eisenacher Bewegung und der Architekt Christian Friedrich von Leins*. Tübinger Studien zur Archäologie und Kunstgeschichte, 1. Tübingen, 1995.

Siebenmorgen, Harald. "Kulturkampfkunst. Das Verhältnis von Peter Lenz und der Beuroner Kunstschule zum Wilhelminischen Staat". In: Ekkehard Mai, Stephan Waetzold and Gerd Wolandt, eds. *Ideengeschichte und Kunstwissenschaft. Philosophie und bildende Kunst im Kaiserreich*. Berlin, 1983, 409-430.

Springer, Peter. *Das Kölner Dom-Mosaik. Ein Ausstattungsprojekt des Historismus zwischen Mittelalter und Moderne*. Studien zum Kölner Dom. Cologne, 1991.

Standaert, Felix. *L'École de Beuron. Un essai de renouveau de l'art chrétien à la fin du XIXᵉ siècle*. Denée, 2011.

Streich, Wolfgang Jürgen. *Franz Heinrich Schwechten (1841-1924). Bauten für Berlin*. Petersberg, 2005 (Diss. RWTH Aachen, 2003).

Stummel, Friedrich. "Ueber alte und neue Mosaiktechnik". *Zeitschrift für christliche Kunst*, 8 (1895), 209-222.

Suhr, Norbert. *Philipp Veit (1793-1877). Leben und Werk eines Nazareners*. Weinheim, 1991.

Trapp, Waldemar. *Vorgeschichte und Ursprung der liturgischen Bewegung vorwiegend in Hinsicht auf das deutsche Sprachgebiet*. Diss. Würzburg, 1939.

Van Cleven, Jean. "Meester Jean-Baptiste Bethune (1821-1894), een kunstenaarsloopbaan". In: Jean Van Cleven, Frieda Van Tyghem, Ignace De Wilde and Robert Hozee, eds. *Neogotiek in België*. Tielt, 1994, 158-199.

Verbeek, Albert. "Gesamtkunstwerke im sakralen Bereich". In: Eduard Trier and Willy Weyres, eds. *Kunst des 19. Jahrhunderts im Rheinland, vol. 1: Architektur I: Kulturbauten*. Düsseldorf, 1979, 35-54.

Vogts, Hans. *Vincenz Statz (1819-1898). Lebensbild und Lebenswerk eines Kölner Baumeisters*. Mönchengladbach, 1960.

Wackenroder, Wilhelm Heinrich, and Ludwig Tieck. *Herzensergießungen eines kunstliebenden Klosterbruders*. Edited by Martin Bollacher. Stuttgart, 1955.

Wehling, Ulrike. *Die Mosaiken des Aachener Münsters und ihre Vorstufen*. Arbeitshefte der rheinischen Denkmalpflege, 46. Cologne, 1995.

Zensen, R.-J. *Der Dom St. Georg zu Limburg an der Lahn*. Nassauische Annalen, 110. Wiesbaden, 1999.

Zietz, Peer. *Franz Heinrich Schwechten. Ein Architekt zwischen Historismus und Moderne*. Stuttgart-London, 1999.

3.5
The Lutheran State Churches of Denmark, Norway and Sweden and Emerging Minorities

Jens Christian Eldal

Seen from the outside, the three Scandinavian countries, Denmark, Norway and Sweden, may look very similar. They still have political distinctions and historical traditions which make them different, not least in the fields of religion, even if all three had a Lutheran national or state church. With close relations and many similarities, they may also be interpreted as siblings in a larger European context, but they are far from being identical triplets.

There is a popular way of expressing the principal differences in the development in Scandinavian church life when speaking of the Church of Sweden, the congregations of Denmark, and the Christians of Norway.[1] Many Swedes left the national church to join free churches, whereas in Denmark there was an established freedom to found new Evangelical congregations within the unity of the national church. In Norway the tendency among the awakened was to stay within the congregation of the state church – as their influential leader, Hans Nielsen Hauge (1771-1824) had insisted on in his last will.[2]

Material culture in the light of religious reform has not been much researched in these three countries. The material presented here will therefore be more like a collection of examples and some trends than a thorough study of the topic. The important elements of it will include reform within the Lutheran churches that represented the big majority, but also popular revivals within or outside the national churches, including several of the new denominations which emerged during the period.

Around 1800

Centralised church plans, octagonal or more or less square, had been introduced at the beginning of the eighteenth century in all three countries and were still being built throughout Scandinavia into the nineteenth century. These plans favoured the spoken word and can be seen as the church design of Evangelical Pietism continuing into the period of Rationalism. However, the rectangular ground plan was still the most common, usually with a chancel of the same width as the nave resulting in one single and wide space. This created a close connection between officiator and congregation, favourable to both acoustics and visibility. This preference for such rectangular plans was expressed clearly in 1829 by the architect of the Royal Palace in Oslo in his pattern book for rural church designs.[3]

The interior furnishing of these churches demonstrated clearly that they were Lutheran. Parts of the furnishing could be organised and combined in different ways, but three important elements were always there. There was a centrally placed altar for the preparation of Holy Communion, a sacrament in the Lutheran Church. And there was always just a single altar, as the Lutherans had no cult of saints which needed more. An altar rail fenced the altar on one or more sides and supported a kneeling bench for groups of the congregation to receive communion together. This kneeling bench could also be used for the collective confession before communion, as was still the practice well into the nineteenth century. Less obliga-

3.5-1 Karlstad Cathedral, Sweden. Altar designed by Erik Palmstedt, 1790. [Wikimedia Commons; photo Håkan Svensson, 2006]

1. Jarlert, "Political Reform in Sweden", 234.
2. Breistein, "Reform of Piety in Norway", 315.
3. Linstow, *Udkast til Kirkebygninger*; see also Eldal, *Med historiske forbilder. 1800-tallet*, 19.

3.5-2 *Christiansborg Royal Palace Church, Copenhagen, Denmark, by C.F. Hansen, 1813–1826. Photo montage showing the sculpture of Christ by Bertel Thorvaldsen from 1824 in its original place on the altar.*
[By courtesy after Danmarks Kirker, København, vol. 1.5. (Copenhagen 1983)]

tory, but still common was some kind of work of art to emphasise the altar.

The second element was the baptismal font shaped as a small stand on the floor and often placed to the side of the chancel. The sacrament of baptism was performed here to receive a new member, usually in its very early childhood, into the congregation as a symbolic purification with three handfuls of water.

The third obligatory element was the pulpit for the pastor's sermon. It had traditionally been placed to the side of the altar, often at the junction of the nave with the chancel, but even further down the nave if necessary to enhance acoustics. A uniquely Lutheran solution occurred first in German palace chapels about 1620 where the pulpit was placed on the central axis of the church, above the altar.[4] This vertical combination of altar and pulpit was developed and widespread in German churches, and brought to Scandinavia where it became popular, after a start in Copenhagen in the 1730s, far into the nineteenth century in Norway.[5] It also became widespread in Sweden, but it never became the most common solution anywhere in Scandinavia.

In a few churches the pulpit was even placed axially in front of the altar, as in the Christiansborg Royal Palace Church in Copenhagen. [Ill. 3.5-2] This was a solution that had been designed 100 years earlier for the important Lutheran Church of Our Lady (Frauenkirche, 1722-1743) in Dresden, Saxony. This Copenhagen variety was practised by the same architect in another Danish church, and also spread to Norway where the Royal Palace architect promoted the solution without much success during the 1820s.[6]

These different Lutheran combinations of pulpit and altar are illustrative of the specific Lutheran situation in Scandinavia about 1800 which was now soon to be challenged. Both these axial solutions have of course to do with a desire for symmetry in Baroque and classicistic aesthetics, but also with the importance of the need to demonstrate the balance in Lutheran theology. It is often said in a very simplified way that the vertical solution placed the word above the sacrament, but it is not as easy as that. In Denmark-Norway the pulpit above the altar was always part of a large altarpiece and as such both emphasised the altar and explained the meaning and importance of the sacrament. Even in the period of rationalism when the mystery of the sacrament was less focused and its importance was reduced, it was still practised and represented through a visually striking emphasis on the altar. Furthermore, when the pulpit was placed in front of the altar, it was important to place the latter at a high enough level so that it, and its decoration, were still clearly visible behind and above the pulpit and officiator.[7]

Church, barn or meeting house?

The early nineteenth century saw an enormous growth of population, and many churches became too small. This was a common problem in rural Sweden and Norway, but less so in Denmark which had been much more densely built with churches during the Middle Ages. Both in Sweden and Norway this increase in population resulted in many churches being enlarged, as well as enormous activity in the erecting of new church buildings.

These new churches were classical in detailing and proportions, with a typical low roof and a modest tower more often surmounted by a low pyramid or a small cupola than a steeple. Inside there was usually just one big open room, often with an apse or a niche accentuating the central axis and the altar. Nave and chancel were gathered under the same ceiling, usually designed as a low segmental barrel-vault. The furnishing was traditional, with the pulpit usually placed to the side or sometimes above the altar. In Sweden, skilled architects were commissioned for the design process, but the mass production of these churches, characterised by a rather plain and basic version of classicism, made them uniform and simple. When the new ideas of Romanticism and Historicism emerged, critics soon started to compare them with barns possessing nothing of what was now considered necessary to strengthen the Christian mind and belief.[8]

Development in Norway was similar, but reflected the fact that it was a society with far fewer economic and artistic resources. The young nation had only a few architects, and therefore the government published a pattern book for rural church architecture. The originally quite simple designs became simpler still when transformed into buildings by local builders not trained in academic architecture. The economic capabilities of the congregations were also not well suited for creating much more than the basics. The results were churches with some character, but simple and heavily shaped by local vernacular architecture. Here too the critics soon described these relatively new churches as barns.[9]

To enforce all the required building activity, and not least deal with private church owners resisting their payment of costs, the Norwegian parliament passed a church building act. This act secured privately owned churches for the congregations and required the building of new churches where the old ones were not large enough for the congregation. When this act was finally passed in 1851, after many years of political struggle with the king and other defenders of private property, it initiated church building activity unseen in Norway since the age of conversion during the eleventh century. The costs were normally paid by every farmer and based on the size of the farm, the traditional method of taxation in rural Norway where the farm constituted the economic and social entity. The proper size for a church in the Norwegian countryside was defined as sufficient space to accommodate 3/10 of the population.[10]

New religious movements also started to challenge the form of the Scandinavian national churches. Early examples on a larger scale could be seen in Stockholm where the Moravians (Herrnhut Brethren) had been established and worshipping in their own halls or meeting houses since 1779.[11] The group also had a whole colony in the town of Christiansfeld in Denmark and had some influence in other parts of Denmark and in Norway. The simple and rectangular interiors of their meeting halls were oriented towards a modest table or lectern on the short axis of the room. With a distinct orientation along the short axis, the 'breadth plan' was a typical feature of this group which also influenced some Lutheran churches in Scandinavia during the second half of the eighteenth century.

A token of what was to come was a religious revival organised by English Methodists in Stockholm. With support of an English industrialist and Swedish aristocracy they built a meeting house under English influence and, from 1840, held meetings appar-

4 Schlosskapelle Schmalkalden, see: Mai, *Der evangelische Kanzelaltar*.
5 Frederiksberg Church, Copenhagen, see: "Frederiksberg kirke", 412-465.
6 In Denmark: Hørsholm Church, Seeland (architect C.F. Hansen), 1820-1823; in Norway Grue Church (architect H.D.F. Linstow), 1823-1828 and Hornnes Church, 1826-1828.
7 Linstow, *Udkast til Kirkebygninger*, 8-9.
8 Lindahl, *Högkyrkligt, lågkyrkligt, frikyrkligt*, 23-26, 63-64; Alm, "Arkitekturen och inredningskonsten", 95. See also Lindblom, *Sveriges konsthistoria*, 708-710.
9 Aubert, *Professor Dahl*, 224.
10 Eldal, *Med historiske forbilder. 1800-tallet*, 13-14.
11 Lindahl, *Högkyrkligt, lågkyrkligt, frikyrkligt*, 30-32.

ently to promote a revival within the Swedish state Church. The Church authorities were suspicious about the hidden aims behind this new activity in what was misleadingly called the English Church, and after some disturbances outside the building, it was closed after only two years.

Revival movements within the Swedish Church continued growing, and in 1854 a new society was organised and bought the former Methodist building, now named the Bethlehem Church. This original meeting house, following English models, welcomed people in from the street through three wide doors instead of the standard Scandinavian layout which had only one. The new building had a rectangular ground plan and galleries around the hall supported by slim columns. There was originally no altar as the building was intended for meetings with changing groups of people rather than a regular congregation of members receiving the sacraments together.[12] This building type and the activity introduced into it were to pose a great challenge to the form of traditional churches and religious life in Scandinavia. But before that became more visible and widespread, the Lutheran state church architecture took a contrary direction.

Demand for 'churchly' churches

A wish for a new and traditionally Christian style in church architecture had been clearly expressed by A.W.N. Pugin and the Ecclesiologists in England about 1840. They also argued for a much more historically correct Gothic Revival architecture than the freer and more Romantic versions which had been typical of its early period. These new ideas also reached Scandinavia via Germany, which gained immense influence on Scandinavian culture after the Napoleonic wars and throughout the rest of the nineteenth century. This applied not least to architecture. Given also the Lutheran connection between Germany and the Scandinavian national churches, the German impact on matters of the church was massive.[13]

The new and more historically correct Gothic Revival style had reached Germany during the early 1840s and found its first main expression in Norway when the German architect Alexis de Chateauneuf (1799-1853) from Hamburg presented his plans for a new church in Oslo in 1847. His design for this Trinity Church was further developed in an architectural competition two years later, and the church was completed in 1858.[14] The building material was red brick, typical of Northern Germany, and the detailing representative of the German Gothic Revival style of this time. [Ill. 3.5-3]

The main building concept was less common as the plan was a combination of an octagon and cross with an addition of a relatively deep chancel. The nave was surrounded by a wide ambulatory which carried galleries above. The central structure was crowned by a dome surrounded with gables and pinnacles on eight sides. Two smaller turrets and a slender lantern on top of the cupola added verticality to the building. Chateauneuf intended his concept to be an ideal one for a Protestant church. It seems his project was more influenced by the chapel built by Charlemagne in Aachen around the year 800 than by the solidly Lutheran tradition of octagon churches in both Germany and Scandinavia.

In Norway and in Sweden numerous octagonal churches were also built over the following decades.[15] Soon, however, Evangelical influences based in Germany developed other preferred models, also to have great impact in Scandinavia.

The Evangelical state churches in many of the German states met through different connections to discuss mutual issues and problems, and the results of these meetings in the Lutheran homeland also influenced the Lutheran sister churches in Scandinavia. During the 1840s and 1850s the question of the design of churches arose. Already by 1852 it had been specified that church buildings should express both their historic and

12 Ibid., 33-39.
13 There are also examples of direct influences from England in Sweden, for example the Haga Church from 1852-1859 in Gothenburg: see Lindahl, *Högkyrkligt, lågkyrkligt, frikyrkligt*, 78-84.
14 Bjerkek, "Alexis de Chateauneuf".
15 Chr. H. Grosch (1801-1865) designed many octagonal churches in Norway in 1847-c1860: see Eldal, "Et mangfold av kirker", 232-256. In Sweden E.V. Langlet (1824-1898) advocated the central church 1865-1896 and designed many varieties of the octagonal and similar plans: see Malmström, *Centralkyrkor inom svenska kyrkan*, 116-262.

3.5-3 *Plan for the Trinity Church in Oslo, Norway, by Alexis de Chateauneuf, 1849.*
[Oslo, Nasjonalmuseet; photo Børre Høstland]

liturgical significance. That meant in practice that a distinct chancel for the altar and holy communion was needed and should be identifiable as an exterior element of the building. At a liturgical conference in Dresden in 1856 this was taken further by specifying medieval building styles such as the Gothic and Romanesque to be the right choice for Lutheran churches. The theologian Theodor Kliefoth (1810-1895) of Mecklenburg-Schwerin now also became deeply involved and secured a close relationship with his influential Lutheran orthodoxy.[16]

After thorough deliberations by architects and theologians at the meeting of German Evangelical Churches in Eisenach in 1861, it was finally agreed on the so-called Eisenach Regulativ, a full set of rules defining the appropriate design of an Evangelical church. In short, this was an interpretation of the 'High Gothic' cathedral, but with some important modifications: the conditions for the congregation to see every part of the service and hear the whole sermon should be as good as possible within a building. 'Unevangelical' (that is to say, Catholic) elements, such as deep chancels and narrow openings between chancel and nave, should be avoided. The longitudinal ground plan was preferred, but the total length was restricted for acoustic reasons, while the octagon plan was tolerated, but not really recommended. A cross plan could be significant if the transepts were placed close to the altar to optimise visibility from most seats.[17]

The 'Regulativ' appears to be more like an expression of what was already common in church architecture than the creation of a new direction. It was also important for these Protestants to define boundaries between appropriate Evangelical architecture and elements considered to be merely Catholic. Leading theologians took part in these deliberations and secured its theological foundation. The result may still easily be understood as an Evangelical version of the

16 Seng, *Der evangelische Kirchenbau im 19. Jahrhundert*, 212-220.
17 Fritsch, *Der Kirchenbau des Protestantismus,* 237-243; Seng, *Der evangelische Kirchenbau im 19. Jahrhundert*, 262-315.

303

3.5-4 Sagene Church, Oslo, Norway, by Christian Fürst, 1887-1891.
[Oslo, Riksantikvaren, Directorate for Culture Heritage]

Ecclesiological programme in England. It may also be judged as a success, as the rules were immediately practised by most Evangelical state churches. They do not seem to have been strictly formalised by law or by other means,[18] but they had an immense influence on Evangelical church architecture until the end of the century, not least in the Lutheran churches in Scandinavia.

In Norway the Eisenach Rules were soon put into practice by the board of the Royal Art School which examined church designs before they were approved by the State Ministry of Church and Education and the government. This board even made a draft for a Norwegian version of the Eisenach rules in 1865, but the State Ministry refused to formalise them as an official norm. The board commented that they would continue to practise these rules anyway in their evaluations of church designs, and they obviously did.[19] The initiative was evidently taken by architects on this Norwegian board, as it seems the case had changed to an architectural issue only; theologians have not been identified in the discussions and the state church bureaucracy was not interested.

The strong influence of Lutheran orthodoxy on Swedish Lutheran theology after the middle of the century can be clearly identified through a study of Swedish church architecture of this period. This theology is interpreted as a substantial strengthening of church organisation at the cost of the individualism represented in popular revivalism.[20] This Swedish study also presents theories for Gothic Revival church design both from theologians and from the architect Helgo Zettervall (1831-1907), the superintendent of state architectural works in Sweden. He collected and finally published his theories in his handbook on church design in 1887.[21] These theories and design rules were late transmissions of the rules from Eisenach. And the theology upon which the architecture was founded was obviously the teachings of Theodor Kliefoth in Mecklenburg, who had been influential at the

German Lutheran conference on liturgy in Dresden 1856.[22]

The lasting impact of the Eisenach rules demonstrates the influence of Germany on Scandinavian church architecture through the rest of the century, especially in Norway. City churches in Germany designed by Johannes Otzen (1839-1911) often served as models and sources of inspiration for this type of architectural practice. Otzen was a leading authority in Lutheran architecture, designing large churches in the Hanover Gothic Revival tradition, usually built of high quality red brick. Many of the fast growing cities in Scandinavia now got one or several cathedral-looking churches in the style that had originated in Otzen's Lutheran homeland.

These new churches by Otzen and his many followers managed to combine the longitudinal plan with wide and short transepts and a wide chancel which opened towards the nave, revealing the service at the altar for the many members gathered for service in these vast spaces. The buildings were still composed from clearly distinct volumes such as nave, chancel and sacristy as prescribed by the Eisenach rules, and these distinctions were clearly visible both inside and outside in accordance with the rules. These churches were thoroughly designed for the formal purpose of a ceremonial liturgy dominated by Lutheran Orthodoxy, and they may well be seen as the materialisation of the Eisenach rules.

At the end of the nineteenth century Scandinavia developed its own National Romanticism in architecture. In Norway this was derived in particular from the forms of medieval stave churches, with characteristic dragons' heads prominent above the gables, and for that reason named the Dragon style. These national gems became models for many new churches, and somewhat surprisingly, also for the Catholic churches of the new and very small Catholic congregations in the towns of Porsgrunn and Fredrikstad. [Ill. 3.5-5] By choosing this local style instead of the international neo-medievalism of this period, these Catholic church buildings could not only be associated with the Norwegian fashions and nation building of the time, but also demonstrated connections back to the specific Catholic traditions of the nation.

As in the rest of Europe, the Scandinavian countries had a rich architectural heritage from the Middle Ages which was rediscovered under influence of Romanticism during the first half of the nineteenth century. The churches, and not least the cathedrals, played an important part in this heritage and were often also among the first to be restored, meaning they often were stripped of additions and furnishings from the centuries that had followed the Reformation. In these countries, dominated by their national Lutheran Churches, it appears that the symbolic content of these restorations was founded more on historical glory than on religion. The question of the restoration of these buildings as Catholic churches had not arisen.

3.5-5 *Catholic Church in Porsgrunn, Norway, by Haldor Børve, 1899.* [Photo J. Chr. Eldal, 2013]

18 Kaiser, "Das sogenannte Eisenacher Regulativ", 114-118.
19 Eldal, *Med historiske forbilder. 1800-tallet*, 40-41.
20 Lindahl, *Högkyrkligt, lågkyrkligt, frikyrkligt*, 96.
21 Ibid., 88-101.
22 Kliefoth was especially influential in Theology at the University of Lund in Sweden: see Fischier, "Theodor Friedrich Detlev Kliefoth", 267-268.

23 "The Nordic Countries", 233-238, 252-253, 258-259, 263-270.
24 Ropeid, "Misjon og bedehus", 216.

Spaces for revival – praying house and mission house

During times when the national churches still were operating chiefly as monopolies in religious life, there were potential for tensions between different groups of people, depending on the degree of Christian engagement and belief. Many people gathered in private homes for the study of scripture, devotion and revival. This was their primary scene for piety, but these groups still sought out the church building itself for the sacraments and the religious ceremonies. By the middle of the nineteenth century the revivals had led to the organisation of new societies in all three Scandinavian states. There had for some time existed local mission societies, both the 'inner' mission working in the immediate neighbourhood, and the 'outer' which was funding and organising mission overseas. Revivals within both these groups were usually important issues.[23]

The local mission societies gathered in larger, regional and nationwide associations from around the middle of the century. At about the same time, the local societies themselves started building their own houses for these gatherings, taking over from what had been home meetings. In rural districts these houses were very modest and often small; the very first of them was built in Norway in 1842.[24] Inside they would have one big room for the meetings, and perhaps a small kitchen for preparing simple meals and making coffee. The required fittings were a lectern for the preacher and simple benches for his audience. In Norway these houses were usually termed a 'bedehus' (praying house) after a biblical term for devotional meeting-houses, while the term 'mission house' is common in Sweden and Denmark.

These houses can be found everywhere in the Scandinavian countryside. The typical praying house was erected by a group of people seeking company for revivals and the study of scripture who still belonged to the Lutheran state church, but was often in opposition to the academic pastor officiating in the local church.

In more populous areas, chiefly in the cities, these mission houses could reach considerable dimensions and demonstrate various architectural pretensions. In Swedish towns especially, impressive buildings were erected for the purpose, more and more so as the century progressed. These larger buildings followed much of the basic English Methodist design. Within a rectangular floor plan they had galleries on at least three sides, and sometimes over several storeys. On the fourth and shorter side there would usually be a podium for the leaders or elders to sit. Above them, a platform with a lectern provided a space for the preacher to perform in a much more active and lively way than was possible for a pastor in the more formal and ritualising church pulpit. There was a tendency towards centrality in the interior space, shortening the central axis and placing most of the audience close to the preacher.

One of the largest and most important mission houses in Stockholm was the Blasieholmen Church, which stood from 1864-1967 and had space for a congregation of 3,000. [Ill. 3.5-6] It was founded by the pastor and prosperous revivalist Gustaf Emanuel

3.5-6 Interior of the Blasieholmen Church, Stockholm, Sweden. Engraving by E. Beer, published in Ny Illustrerad Tidning, *2 Dec. 1876.*
[Stockholm, Stockholmkällan]

Beskow. The young architect G.E. Sjöberg designed the building following Beskow's description of Spurgeon's Baptist Tabernacle in London which he had seen for himself. The Blasieholmen Church was formally an annex of a city church belonging to the Church of Sweden, and Pastor Beskow held his services here every Sunday beside his large revivalist meetings which were open for everyone.[25]

In Sweden many mission groups originating within the national state church broke free from their original organisation and joined another nationwide association. Hence these groups were transformed into congregations receiving the sacraments together and their mission houses were transformed into revivalist mission churches. An altar was added, but usually without rail and kneeling bench because in these churches the act of holy communion was no longer performed around the altar: instead, assistants brought the wine and bread to the benches.

Another line of development in the design of mission houses can be seen in the transition from a simple and undecorated interior to the practice during the last decade of the century of permitting an image of Christ and, later, even more pictorial art. The Swedish Mission Church of Eskilstuna even went through an architectural transformation, from being a profane-looking meeting house of the 1880s into a Gothic Revival church about 1900.[26]

Human contact and social engagement

In Denmark the inner mission did not grow to the same extent as in Sweden and Norway. But there was another dominant group of broad revivalism emerging from the Lutheran state church. It was called *Grundtvigianism* after the Pastor N.F.S. Grundtvig (1783-1872) and was far less orthodox, and did not share the emphasis on judging and dividing between the saved and the lost souls which was otherwise such an important issue in the inner mission. Grundtvigianism

had a much more human approach, giving people time to learn. The congregation was central in Grundtvig's concept of the church. He found the 'living word', the spoken word within the congregation, as important as scripture. The sacraments were important, but Grundtvigianism was not really 'high church' because it bestowed limited importance onto the priesthood.[27]

New and more liberal legislation in Denmark from the middle of the nineteenth century permitted the foundation of new congregations within the national church. A group following the teachings of Grundtvig built the Immanuel Church in the suburb of Frederiksberg in Copenhagen at the beginning of the 1890s. The church was designed by the architect Andreas Lauritz Clemmensen (1852-1928) in close collaboration with two famous artists in the congregation who were engaging seriously with church art, the brothers and painters Joakim (1856-1933) and Niels Skovgaard (1858-1938). An integrated part of the building programme was to express the ideas of Grundtvigianism.[28] [Ill. 3.5-7]

3.5-7 Immanuel Church, Frederiksberg, Denmark, by A.L. Clemmensen, 1892-1893.
[Photo J. Chr. Eldal, 2013]

25 Lindahl, *Högkyrkligt, lågkyrkligt, frikyrkligt*, 40-47.
26 Ibid., 54-59, 131-141.
27 See also Stidsen, "The Dynamics of Reform of Piety in Denmark", 273-275.
28 Kjær and Grinder-Hansen, *Immanuelskirken*, 87-88.

307

Like most churches of the period, this church was designed in a medieval style, and its red brick was a quite common and traditional building material. But the ordinary stops there. The building is designed as a single monolithic block, with a *campanile* standing separately to the side. There is no division in the external walls between the nave and the rounded chancel. Unity has replaced the multitude of added and clearly identifiable building parts that had represented the architectural hierarchy that had been essential in the Eisenach rules.

The new unity is revealed even further inside. Nave and chancel walls glide over one another here too; there is one single ground floor level without stairs or any hierarchy of heights. The walls reach into the vaults without any emphasis on the boundary between these basic elements of defining space. Galleries surround the whole room, creating space for pews even above and around the altar. It is easy to identify design elements from the Arts and Crafts movement in this church as well as from the feeling for form in the emerging Art Nouveau style of this period. Symbolic elements can be seen in the design of the lighting, through the windows high up in the vaulting and the skylight above the altar. To these novelties can be added the unity created within this interior which ends most of the traditional hierarchic division of space between congregation and officiator. This was also a theme in the altarpiece where the painting depicting baptism on Pentecost Sunday also portrays several congregation members actually enacting the biblical scene. Unity in architecture and between the congregation and officiator went on to be an important question in the following century, but not the only one and not always the most important.

At this time there were several active church building initiatives in the fast growing metropolis of Copenhagen. Social problems, a great shortage of churches and a fear of proletarianisation and the abandoning of the church were reasons for initiating the Church Foundation (Kirkefondet) in Copenhagen in 1891. This initiative came from a group of young academics, partly connected to Grundtvigianism, who set up a new private organisation to build, own and maintain churches, including hiring pastors to serve within the body of the state church. This new programme aimed to cater to spiritual, social and material distress in the big city, especially in the slums and poorer urban areas. Important were Sunday schools, various kinds of meetings, healthcare and the diaconate. A congregation of modest size was important to ensure contact and relations with the whole and every part, and it was a condition that the pastor took part in the life and activities of the congregation. Before 1940 this foundation alone built 26 new churches in Copenhagen, all financed by private fund-raising.[29]

These churches, being smaller than many of the earlier city churches, naturally had less of the cathedral look which had for some time been dominant and was now going slowly out of fashion. After 1900, younger stylistic models such as those based on Renaissance and Baroque forms took over from medievalism and they were also usually deeply influenced by National Romanticism. If to some degree simpler and cheaper than many of their predecessors, these buildings were still designed by first-class architects and with significant architectural character. The real novelty in these churches, however, was the new premises needed for the social activities.

On expensive central city ground the sites were often necessarily small, and consequently the spaces for different activities had to be added vertically over several storeys. An example of this is the Elias Church from 1908 by the architect Martin Nyrop (1849-1921) who had designed the famous city hall of Copenhagen a few years earlier. A monumental stair leads from the market place at the front of the building up to the main entrance and the sanctuary. A meeting hall was located in the crypt while a sacristy was placed below the chancel. This arrangement may well have been influenced by the larger meeting houses as well as by the United

29 Gravgaard, *Storbyens virkeliggjorte længsler*, 14, 19-20.

States where meeting spaces of this kind in church crypts were quite common at this time. [Ill. 3.5-8]

The ideas behind this Copenhagen programme also spread to the big cities of Sweden and Norway. The Matthew Church from 1901 in Stockholm is one example, with space for new functions in the crypt below the sanctuary.[30] In Oslo several so-called 'small churches' were built around 1900. They also accommodated an apartment for the pastor and a small flat for the deaconess to live amid the vulnerable herd. As in Copenhagen, these churches were built in close collaboration with the inner mission.[31]

These new 'small churches' also became popular during the first decades of the twentieth century in suburbs where social problems were not the issue; buildings for smaller congregations answered the requirement for closer contact between all members. Additional space for new activities, combined with flexibility, provided the new solution. Meeting rooms could be separate or opened towards the sanctuary using folding walls when needed. Wings with meeting spaces, offices and sometimes living quarters for pastors and personnel could be added to the sanctuary on the same level when building land was not too expensive. With historicism and National Romanticism still dominating stylistically, these buildings could be composed of a stylistic mix giving an impression of the remains of a medieval monastery transformed and modernised by the Lutherans after the Reformation.[32]

Revival of centralising plans

The 1890s brought a radical new church plan to Stockholm when the Trinity Methodist Church was designed from 1893-1894 with a so-called 'fan plan'. That means the whole interior was organised like a fan or a sector of a circle, radiating from the lectern. The seating followed the centralising composition, with curved benches placed concentrically around the lectern as a focus. This kind of church

plan was soon also used in a Baptist church in Stockholm.[33] [Ill. 3.5-9]

Similar plan types had been developed by Evangelical denominations in the United States during the second half of the nineteenth century.[34] When the Stockholm Methodists built their Trinity Church, they were probably influenced by their fellows in America. During this period of mass emigration to America there was also much traffic the other way, not least with preachers of any denomination, many of them as missionaries to the Old World, bringing with them new and effective practices.

It took a long time, until the 1950s, for the national churches in Scandinavia to adopt such radically new church plans. In Germany, however, there had always been opposition to the 'Eisenach Regulativ' from groups which found it disturbingly Catholic rather than essentially Evangelical. An alternative was formulated in 1891 in the 'Wiesbaden Programme', which demanded much more focus on the sermon and axial placing of the pulpit.[35] The programme was realised by the architect Johannes Otzen for the Ring Church in Wiesbaden, 1893-1894,

3.5-8 Elias Church at Vesterbros Torv, Copenhagen, Denmark, by Martin Nyrop, 1906-1908.
[Wikimedia Commons; photo 2008]

30 Lindahl, *Högkyrkligt, lågkyrkligt, frikyrkligt*, 122. See also, Jarlert, "Political Reform in Sweden", 235-237.
31 Eldal, *Med historiske forbilder. 1800-tallet*, 53.
32 Ibid., 220.
33 Lindahl, *Högkyrkligt, lågkyrkligt, frikyrkligt*, 153-154, 160-161.
34 Kilde, *When Church Became Theatre*.
35 Hammer-Schenk, "Kirchenbau", 507.

3.5-9 Plan of the Trinity Methodist Church near Östermalmstorg Square in Stockholm, Sweden, 1893-1894. [After Göran Lindahl, Högkyrkligt, lågkyrkligt, frikyrkligt i svensk arkitektur 1800-1950 (Stockholm, 1955)]

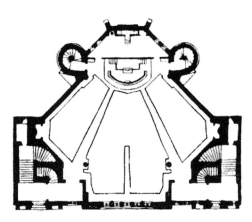

[Ill. 3.5-12-13] with a plan very similar to the contemporary Trinity Methodist Church in Stockholm and what was already common in America. The 'Wiesbaden Programme' had some influence in Germany, but only to a smaller degree among Lutherans in Scandinavia.[36] Here square and rectangular plans continued as the norm, but during the following decades there was a distinct tendency towards wider interiors with shorter naves, usually with a closer connection between the choir and the nave.[37] In the Scandinavian national churches there was not even a return to the axial placing of the pulpit which had some legitimacy in their own history.

The pictorial arts

The Lutheran Church welcomes the pictorial arts. Contrary to other major reformers, Martin Luther accepted them, but at the same time also established significant distinctions from Catholic practice. The Lutheran Reformation was based on scripture and accepted the importance of the arts, not least in the education of the masses which at this time were basically illiterate. Hence the Lutheran Reformation did not usually involve iconoclasm; themes and motifs which were not based on scripture were however considered inappropriate. Besides, material objects could not any longer be considered holy and by no means be objects of worship.[38]

The end of the eighteenth century saw a significant decrease in the use of pictorial arts. Large paintings were still being produced as altarpieces, and sometimes sculpture seems to have been preferred over painting. More common was that both these artistic disciplines gave way to a simple cross which now became the most widespread decoration to accentuate the altar in the many new churches being built. This was seen both in the many new countryside churches in Sweden from the end of the eighteenth century onwards and in Norway from the second quarter of the nineteenth century. And in both countries altar and cross were usually further accentuated by a monumental portal or a similar architectural element. [Ill. 3.5-1]

In Sweden these altar crosses were usually decorated with one or more elements representing Christ's Passion, such as the shroud hanging from the arms of the cross, with or without the crown of thorns. In Norway a single cross was used without further decoration. In 1829 the architect Linstow recommended a gilded cross as an altar piece in his pattern book for churches in Norway, commenting that this would be better than one with a painting when a capable artist could not be afforded, as would usually be the case.[39] His major concern was artistic quality rather than a specific kind of artwork or symbol.

If sculptures were not quite common as altar decorations, there was still one particular sculpture from the early nineteenth century which was copied in enormous numbers far into the following century for use in churches and in private homes. This was the giant sculpture of Christ by the Dane Bertel Thorvaldsen, originally designed in his studio in Rome in 1821-1824 for the new Christiansborg Palace Church in Copenhagen and later moved to the Copenhagen Cathedral.[40] [Ill. 3.5-2] With its peaceful expression and the welcoming pose of the arms this sculpture provided a psychological interpretation of Christ which had enormous impact on Christians and Christian art far beyond Lutheran circles.

---

36 Genz, *Das Wiesbadener Programm*.
37 Malmström, *Centralkyrkor inom svenska kyrkan*, 253-342.
38 Christie, *Den lutherske ikonografi i Norge*, I, 99-106 (English summary, I, 190-191).
39 Linstow, *Udkast til Kirkebygninger*, 21.
40 "Christiansborg Slotskirke II", 252.

Towards the middle of the nineteenth century, paintings were again preferred and widespread as altar pieces when something more artistic than a simple cross could be afforded. The design would normally consist of one large painting within a monumental frame.

The biblical basis for Lutheran church art was also discussed in the German Lutheran meetings in Eisenach. In the 'Eisenach Regulativ' from 1861 it had been decided that altars should have a crucifix, and if there also was a sculpture or a painting, it should depict a central motif in the history of salvation.[41] Popular motifs in these new altar paintings were, especially, the Resurrection, the Ascension, Christ in Gethsemane, the Baptism of Christ and Christ on the Cross. They were disseminated through large numbers of copies, often following German originals of the Romantic Düsseldorf School or their Scandinavian followers.[42] When Naturalism and Realism emerged as new ideals in the pictorial arts during the 1870s and 1880s, the climate for creativity in religious art became complicated. Towards the end of the century, new trends such as Symbolism and neo-Romanticism emerged, both creating new space and a demand for spiritual content and hence also better conditions for religious art.

The scene for the new direction in Scandinavian religious painting was the cathedral in Viborg, Denmark, which had been rebuilt in 1863-1876 to form a complete Romanesque church. The whole wooden ceiling above the nave had been decorated with paintings more or less copied from the medieval church of Saint Michael in Hildesheim, Germany, both its ornaments and several of its biblical scenes. Decorations of the walls had also been planned, and some temporary work was executed on the plastered and still damp walls behind the altar. After modern heating was installed in 1888, the walls finally started drying and permanent decorations could be planned. Towards the mid-1890s it became clear that the Danish state Church Ministry would finance such a project, because by now it was obvious that the country had found the right artist to master this vast task. That artist was the painter Joakim Skovgaard (1856-1933). He had travelled in both Italy and Greece, and large parts of the frescoes in Viborg clearly demonstrate how his studies of buildings and costumes from Italian Renaissance paintings were used to create historical distance in his own biblical scenes. There are also obvious influences from Byzantine and medieval art. His work included frescoes on all the walls, making use of many sources of inspiration in composition and detail, and united into a whole by line and colour.[43] Skovgaard also designed eight cathedral lamps for Viborg consisting of large bronze angels, each holding two rims with electric bulbs.[44] It was more of a decorative than really enlightening use of the then new, challenging and promising power of electricity.

The monumental decorative work in Viborg was completed in 1906. It was from the very beginning considered an artistic and national success, and very soon it also inspired similar works in Norway and Sweden. In Oslo the artist Emanuel Vigeland (1875-1948) furnished the choir with frescoes in the just finished church at Vålerenga in Oslo. The work was executed in 1906-1909 and comprised a monumental Crucifixion scene in the apse and the Last Supper on a side wall while the vaults were covered by painted ornament. Vigeland also designed a chandelier for the church in 1909, in the form of a three-dimensional cross, to be lit from the inside.[45] In Sweden the painter Olle Hjortzberg executed several large church decorative schemes from about the same time, combining ornament and figure scenes under the influence of Byzantine and medieval art.[46]

Stained-glass windows which had been so prominent in medieval churches gained new popularity during the nineteenth century, not least as part of the Gothic Revival and the restoration of old cathedrals. These windows could be designed in simple or complicated patterns and with ornaments as well as providing space for pictorial decoration more or less following a considered theological ico-

41 Seng, *Der evangelische Kirchenbau im 19. Jahrhundert*, 277.
42 Uberg, *Jesus det eneste*, 68-72.
43 Madsen, *Kirkekunst i Danmark*, III, 11-12; Vellev, *Joakim Skovgaards fresco-malerier*, 7-15.
44 Vellev, *Joakim Skovgaards fresco-malerier*, 22-23.
45 Albrektsen, "Emanuel August Vigeland", 366-367. The frescoes were destroyed by fire in 1979.
46 Ahlstrand, "Kyrkligt monumentalmåleri", 351; Schiller, *Olle Hjortzberg*.

3.5-10 Interior of the Bragernes Church in Drammen, Norway. [Wikimedia Commons; photo Oddbjørn Sørmoen, 2004]

nography. Here too the scenes could be copies of the same paintings as in altar pieces.

During the second half of the nineteenth century all Scandinavia appears to have imported whole windows with biblical scenes framed by medieval ornament from Germany. Among these early imports from the 1870s are windows from the firm of Dr Heinrich Oidtmann in Linnich, Germany, where a technique for printing on glass was invented.[47] The restored Nidaros Cathedral in Trondheim, Norway, imported some windows from both Oidtmann and Cologne in about 1880. About the same time, and again around 1890, King Oscar II of Sweden and Norway donated a large group of windows to this cathedral to commemorate his coronation there as king of Norway. These windows were painted in London with motifs sketched by the restoration architect Christian Christie in Trondheim. Among the biblical motifs were also scenes from the story of the national saint, St Olav, who had converted Norway to Christianity and was buried in this church.[48] Originally a Catholic saint, his role now was seen as that of the builder of the nation. Imported windows from Germany and Scotland from around 1900 have also been identified, as well as a work from 1903 by the renowned Hungarian stained glass artist Miksa Roth.[49]

Domestic production of pictorial stained glass in Scandinavia seem to have started in Sweden where the Gothenburg decorative painter Reinhold Callmander (1840-1922) made designs for stained glass and established his own firm in 1888. He delivered windows to Uppsala and Karlstad Cathedrals and numerous other churches in Sweden.[50] During the early twentieth century, several artists started designing stained-glass windows for churches, perfecting the techniques and not least developing more or less personal styles liberated from the production of copies. Some of these artists also contributed large commissions in the other Scandinavian countries, for example the Dane Joachim Skovgaard in Denmark and Sweden and the Norwegian Emanuel Vigeland in all three countries.

47 "150 Jahre Glasmalerei in Linnich".
48 Faye, *Glassmaleriene i Nidaros Domkirke*, I, 9-21.
49 In Denmark: two windows from 1902 by Mayersche kgl. Hofkunstanstalt, Munich, in Trinitatis Church, Fredericia, (see "Trinitatis kirke", 304-305); in Norway: two windows from 1901 by Meikle & Co., Glasgow, in Tjøme Church and one window from 1903 by Miksa Roth in Fagerborg Church, Oslo, Norway.
50 "C Reinhold C Callmander" and "Carl Reinhold Constantin Callmander".

BIBLIOGRAPHY

"150 Jahre Glasmalerei in Linnich: Die Glasmalereiwerkstatt Dr. Heinrich Oidtmann 20. Oktober 2007 - 9. März 2008. <http://www.glasmalereimuseum.de/DGML_DE/DGML_DE.htm> (1 june 2013).

Ahlstrand, Jan Torsten. "Kyrkligt monumentalmåleri". In: *Konsten 1890-1915*. Signums svenska konsthistoria, 11. Lund, 2001, 351.

Albrektsen, Lau. "Emanuel August Vigeland". In: *Norsk kunstnerleksikon*, 4. Oslo, 1986. 365-372.

Alm, Göran. "Arkitekturen och inredningskonsten". In: *Karl Johanstidens konst*. Signums svenska konsthistoria, 9. Lund, 1999, 35-115.

Aubert, Andreas. *Professor Dahl*. Kristiania, 1920.

Bjerkek, Ole Petter. "Alexis de Chateauneuf". In: *Norsk kunstnerleksikon*, 1. Oslo, 1982, 395-396.

Breistein, Ingunn Folkestad. "Reform of Piety in Norway, 1780-1920". In: Anders Jarlert, ed. *Piety and Modernity. The Dynamics of Religious Reform in Northern Europe, 1780-1920*, 3. Leuven, 2012, 307-325.

"C Reinhold C Callmander". In: *Svenskt Biografiskt Lexikon*, 7. Stockholm, 1927, 211.

"Carl Reinhold Constantin Callmander". In: *Svenskt konstnärslexikon*, 1. Malmö, 1952, 270.

"Christiansborg Slotskirke II". In: *Danmarks Kirker. København*, I.5. Copenhagen, 1983, 177-280.

Christie, Sigrid. *Den lutherske ikonografi i Norge inntil 1800*. 2 vols. Oslo, 1973.

Eldal, Jens Christian. "Et mangfold av kirker". In: Elisabeth Seip, ed. *Chr. H. Grosch*. Oslo, 2001, 214-283.

Eldal, Jens Christian. *Med historiske forbilder. 1800-tallet*. Kirker i Norge, 3. Oslo, 2002.

Eldal, Jens Christian, *Brytning, påvirkning, endring: Høy- og lavkirkelig materiell kultur på 1800- og tidlig 1900-tall*. In: *Fortidsminneforeningen, Årbok 2020*, 71-98.

Faye, Audhild. *Glassmaleriene i Nidaros Domkirke*. 2 vols. Trondheim, 2000.

Fischier, P. "Theodor Friedrich Detlev Kliefoth". In: *Nordisk familjebok*, 14. Stockholm, 1911.

"Frederiksberg kirke". In: *Danmarks Kirker. København*, 3. Copenhagen, 1966-1972.

Fritsch, Karl Emil Otto. *Der Kirchenbau des Protestantismus von der Reformation bis zur Gegenwart*. Berlin, 1893.

Genz, Peter. *Das Wiesbadener Programm: Johannes Otzen und die Geschichte eines Kirchenbautyps zwischen 1891 und 1930*. Kiel, 2011.

Gravgaard, Anne-Mette. *Storbyens virkeliggjorte længsler. Kirkerne i København og på Frederiksberg 1860-1940*. Copenhagen, 2001.

Hammer-Schenk, Harold. "Kirchenbau". In: *Theologische Realenzyklopädie*, 18. Berlin-New York, 2000.

Jarlert, Anders. "Political Reform in Sweden". In: Keith Robbins, ed. *Political and Legal Perspectives. The Dynamics of Religious Reform in Northern Europe, 1780-1920*, 1. Leuven, 2010, 225-239.

Kaiser, Paul. "Das sogenannte Eisenacher Regulativ von 1861: ein kirchenrechtliches Phantom 1994". In: Klaus Raschzok and Reiner Sörries, eds. *Geschichte des protestantischen Kirchenbaues: Festschrift für Peter Poscharsky zum 60. Geburtstag*. Erlangen, 1994, 114-118.

Kilde, Jeanne Hallgren. *When Church Became Theatre: The Transformation of Evangelical Architecture and Worship in 19th-Century America*. New York, 2002.

Kjær, Ulla, and Poul Grinder-Hansen. *Immanuelskirken*. Copenhagen, 1993.

Lindahl, Göran. *Högkyrkligt, lågkyrkligt, frikyrkligt i svensk arkitektur 1800-1950*. Stockholm, 1955.

Lindblom, Andreas. *Sveriges konsthistoria från forntid till nutid*. Vol. 3. Stockholm, 1946.

Linstow, H.D.F. *Udkast til Kirkebygninger paa Landet i Norge*. Christiania, 1829.

Madsen, Herman. *Kirkekunst i Danmark*. 3 vols. Odense, 1964-1966.

Mai, Hartmut. *Der evangelische Kanzelaltar: Geschichte und Bedeutung*. Halle, 1969.

Malmström, Krister. *Centralkyrkor inom svenska kyrkan 1820-1920*. Stockholm, 1990.

Ropeid, Andreas. "Misjon og bedehus". In: *Norges kulturhistorie*, 4. Oslo, 1980, 195-218.

Schiller, Harald. *Olle Hjortzberg: en konstnärsbiografi*. Malmö, 1954.

Seng, Eva-Maria. *Der evangelische Kirchenbau im 19. Jahrhundert: die Eisenacher Bewegung und der Architekt Christian Friedrich von Leins*. Tübinger Studien zur Archäologie und Kunstgeschichte, 15. Tübingen, 1995.

Stidsen, Johs. Enggaard. "The Dynamics of Reform of Piety in Denmark, c 1780-1920". In: Anders Jarlert, ed. *Piety and Modernity. The Dynamics of Religious Reform in Northern Europe, 1780-1920*, 3. Leuven, 2012, 265-285.

"The Nordic countries". In: Joris van Eijnatten and Paula Yates, eds. *The Churches. The Dynamics of Religious Reform in Northern Europe 1780-1920*, 2. Leuven, 2010, 227-276.

"Trinitatis kirke". In: *Danmarks Kirker. Vejle Amt*, 1. Copenhagen, 2006, 283-354.

Uberg, Inger Hjørdis Ulla. *'Jesus det eneste':Christen Brun og alterbildene i tid og tro 1856-1905*. Master thesis, University of Oslo, 2002.

Vellev, Jens. *Joakim Skovgaards fresco-malerier i Viborg Domkirke*. 2nd ed. Viborg, 1988.

4.
MATERIAL REFORM
IN EVERYDAY RELIGION

Introduction

Peter Jan Margry

Private religious objects, as forms of the materialisation and representation of everyday religious practices in the personal environment, have long been widespread throughout the world. During the nineteenth century, however, as a result of new production processes, religious objects proliferated in even greater quantities. Despite their new 'industrial' background, these personal mementos or tokens with sacred agency were cherished as they were often cheap, easy to keep, and, above all, widely available to the faithful.

These nineteenth-century changes and reforms were the hinges on which popularisation and massification in the production and distribution of religious objects in everyday life turned. The stipulation 'in everyday life' in connection to religious objects entails that the current section deals with religious materiality to the extent that it exists and is used by Christians in daily life, usually in the home or in the personal environment. This also implies that this section does not concern itself with the objects used in the context of the formal church and its intra- or extramural liturgy. Hence, buildings – churches, chapels and their ornamentation –, liturgical objects, and materiality related to the church services, to funerals and processions feature rarely or not at all.

Within the context of the volume as a whole, the current fourth section confronts the material cultures of a group of North-Western European countries with one another, and this during a relatively long period, from the late eighteenth century up to the first decades of the twentieth century. It tries to detect common threads, variations, and local characteristics, and attempts to explain changes and the effects these had during that period.

Although the long nineteenth century is regarded as a time of general change towards industrial processes and towards the renewal and mass production of goods and objects, it must be observed that a certain mass production of devotional objects had been occurring since as early as the Middle Ages: ranging from pilgrim signs, pocket crosses or neck pendants, devotional pins and prints to bibles and holy water containers.[1] Rosaries became immensely popular in the seventeenth and eighteenth centuries. Yet the thesis underlying the current section is that the long nineteenth century was constitutive for modern patterns in and structures of personal religiosity and its material culture. Various factors, both changes and reforms, can be identified in relation to these processes, as will be analysed in the following national contributions.

In countries or regions where industrialisation occurred relatively late, as for example Ireland and the Netherlands, the economy began to thrive in the second half of the century, generating more disposable income that people could spend on material religion. In these two countries this development coincided with a late Catholic revival. Up to that point, both countries remained relatively devoid of religious material culture, with landscapes seemingly stripped of Catholic culture, as travellers were able to observe around the mid-nineteenth century. Their backwardness also implied that production sites and sales outlets were rare, a situation that applied also to Britain and Scandinavia. Most of the products were imported and sold

1   Koldeweij, *Geloof & Geluk*.

through itinerant vendors or during missions at which religious orders sold rosaries, medals, and scapulars.

Some of the concluding observations in the following chapters address the invention and dissemination of easier and cheaper printing technologies, while at the same time low-cost paper made from wood pulp became available. This affected the development of religious material culture in two ways: on the one hand the cheap mass production of religious and devotional booklets, bibles, and prints brought these objects within the reach of the masses; on the other this also led to a sharp increase in the popularity of newspapers, journals, and illustrated magazines, and these constituted a new opportunity to enhance awareness of the availability and possibilities of religious objects, creating an even larger market. This market came about not only through innovations in the publication process, but also through more general reinventions of production processes as a result of the industrial revolution. Industrialisation would affect nearly all religious consumer products, creating a global market, which was initiated and controlled in and by Western countries, and not only by countries in North-Western Europe.

A number of other developments and reforms should be mentioned as having affected Catholic material culture especially. One is the final victory of the Tridentine reformation in the nineteenth century, ushering in a more universal Catholicism, strongly directed from its centre of power in Rome. This 'papal nationalism', countering state nationalism in Europe, turned the Vatican into the centre of authority, and it was exported across the globe as ultramontanism. Papal centralism also propagated general devotions, turning these into worldwide movements (the Holy Family, since 1845; May the month of Mary, since 1865; Our Lady of Perpetual Succour, especially after 1865; October the month of the Rosary, since 1883; the Sacred Heart, especially after 1899), creating additional target markets for mass-produced religious objects. Another reform that is important in relation to the geographical outlook of this book, was the emancipation of Catholics in countries like Ireland, England and Scotland, slowly starting there at the end of the eighteenth century and fully accomplished by the Roman Catholic Relief Act of 1829, leading ultimately to the restoration of the hierarchy in England and Wales in 1850, and in Scotland as late as 1878. In the Netherlands, the freedom of (institutional) Catholicism came with the Dutch version of the liberal revolutions of 1848: the removal of constitutional disabilities opened the way to the restoration of the hierarchy and created more possibilities for Catholics to produce and buy belief-related material objects, although it remained forbidden to erect or display religious symbols (crosses) or objects (like rosaries) in public.

In addition to the 'Roman' cults, another incentive for the increase in the production and spread of religious objects was the boom in national Marian devotions. Various national cults sprung up, more or less from the grassroots, from the 1830s onwards, when apparitional Marianism started to develop into a major devotional pillar in Europe. It resulted in the rise of major Marian pilgrimage sites (Paris, La Salette, Lourdes (Immaculate Conception), Pontmain, Knock, Marpingen, Pompeii, Fátima etc.), and hundreds of smaller ones in their slipstream, including many filial grotto shrines of Lourdes. It was an era that became typified as the Age of Mary and celebrated as the time of the *grands pèlerinages*, not only to Marian shrines but also to those of important national saints. The fact that so many new sacred sites arose also created a market for new genres of religious souvenirs and expressions of votive offering.

It is important to examine the flows of international and transnational trade and fashion, which demonstrate once again that, when it comes to religious objects, the geographical boundaries observed in this volume are arbitrary. As an artistic style, neo-Gothic became extremely popular, initially for Christians in general, later appropriated

317

specifically by Catholics. Originating in eighteenth-century England, the Gothic Revival spread across Europe, especially in the Catholic areas of Central and North-Western Europe. It became the dominant style for church buildings, printed material and statues etc. up to the beginning of the twentieth century.

The influence of France on the rest of Europe is key to understanding the renewal of genres, styles, and forms or materiality of religious objects. The Saint-Sulpice neighbourhood in Paris was the main cradle of innovations in devotional materiality, in particular of the painted plaster statue and the small printed prayer card, which both conquered the world. The specific, sentimental Saint-Sulpice style remained highly popular between 1840 and 1930. Some years previously, Paris had already become the origin of a successful movement related to one specific new religious object: the Miraculous Medal. In the first five years of its existence after 1832, twenty million of these medals were sold. The medal stood in a tradition of devotional objects with a communicative function, but was individualised to the Parisian apparitional shrine of the Rue du Bac. Worn around the neck or kept in one's pocket, it gained worldwide fame for its protective powers. Factories for industrially produced rosaries flourished around Ambert and in the wider Auvergne region since the mid-nineteenth century. Some of these factories produced tens of millions of rosaries each, mainly for export.

Paris was not the only place to function as an exemplary production base for plaster statues and other objects: major places of pilgrimage like Kevelaer and Altötting in Germany or Lourdes in France became production centres in their own right, exporting their specific religious forms and visuals to wholesalers and licensed smaller producers elsewhere in Europe. The huge success of the everyday devotional object was due to their cheap price in combination with new and attractive forms and new bourgeois styles. Prosaic mass-produced saintly simulacra of painted plaster retained their popularity from the last quarter of the nineteenth century until the beginning of the 1960s, when demand suddenly evaporated due to the 'religious revolution' of that time.

Material objects and associated practices were influenced by foreign cultures or tastes, but they could themselves also have an impact on national cultures. The Advent wreath, for example, began in Germany as a typically Evangelical phenomenon, but ended up at the beginning of the twentieth century as a supra-confessional practice, also conquering Catholic homes, ultimately not only in Germany but also in border areas and neighbouring countries. A similar process of acculturation happened to what could be called the Protestant family 'altar', the Christmas Nativity scene, which was likewise introduced in the early nineteenth century, and subsequently managed to penetrate the German Catholic home around 1900, as well as in the Netherlands, Belgium, and Scandinavia. In Britain, the celebration of Christmas was regarded as unbiblical in the Puritan tradition, but since the late 1840s carol singing, Christmas pudding and Christmas trees slowly became ubiquitous in English homes. Prince Albert personally introduced the decorated German Christmas tree to the United Kingdom, about a decade after it came to the Netherlands. For the Anglican Church, Protestant imagery was mainly sourced in Germany and the Netherlands. For Catholics, Victorian piety was infused with nostalgia for the Middle Ages. Around 1840-1860, the Oxford Movement created a Catholic devotional revival using materiality and symbols related to devotions propagated by the Vatican. Related imagery and prayer cards were mainly imported from France and Belgium.

During the second half of the nineteenth century, the mass production of commercialised religious material culture became a Europe-wide industry in which designs and fashions became more and more uniform in most of Europe, also due to the universal appeal of a shrine like Lourdes. As a result of this universality and flat uniform mass character, these 'industrial' products became the subject of criticism. They were dismissed as imitations, as false and inauthentic, as pandering to the 'bad taste' of the common people who bought them. Saint-Sulpice-style products were also ridiculed because of their presumed sentimentality. But it is important to realise that sentiment has a strong place in the practice of religion, affording an intimate and particular value to religious objects that can gain power or agency, even in mass-produced forms.[2] Clerics and artists were the main voices to claim that such products were not fit for religious purposes. However, they were fighting a rearguard action as industrial production led to the 'democratisation' of the 'material sacred'. A greater number and variety of religious objects came within the reach of believers, and as consumers of those objects, believers were better able to create their religious identities, personally and at home. In addition, William Christian has pointed to the importance of the rise of photography and the production of devotional postcards. As photography in itself became an acknowledged proof of reality, it also began to be used for the purposes of convincing people on issues of the sacred.[3] Just as previously ex-voto paintings often showcased divine interventions, the millions of postcards that were produced from the 1890s onwards also started to represent saintly visions or miracles in composite images or as photomontage, thus providing a window into the modern world and the imagination of the religious. They were a meaningful complement to devotional or prayer cards, which were the most common devotional print in the nineteenth century, but which only showed *drawings* of Christ, Mary, the saints, holy sites or the supernatural.

While universality in style prevailed, national differences never disappeared. Thus in North-Western Europe, the Catholic practice of wearing gospel texts around the neck or have them sewn into clothes as curative or preventive tools was typical for Ireland. In Britain, William Hunt's iconic painting 'The Light of the World' (1852) became extremely popular, especially after the printing of engraved copies in 1860. [Ill. 4.1-10]

The hierarchical Catholic Church used religion and devotion as a structure for the basic social unit of the family. Around 1900 this strategy succeeded in penetrating the Catholic home with the devotions (and statues and altars) of the Holy Family and the Sacred Heart. In countries like Ireland, the Netherlands and Belgium, the conquest of the home especially of statues of the Sacred Heart was widespread.

Interestingly, an increase in material culture can also be observed at this time within Protestantism, extending beyond the Bible, prayer books, and the Nativity scene. Protestants also understood the importance and impact of religious objects, especially in relation to re-confessionalisation, confessional identity politics, and pious identification. At least in the Netherlands, the 'disruptive' Bible was domesticated for use in modern family life, by applying an ideology of religious disciplining in the private environment comparable to that which Catholicism used in relation to religious objects. Dutch Protestants tried to copy the highly successful Catholic devotionalisation process.[4] As a result, 'saintly' portraits of mediators of the Bible – from the great Reformers to successful national ministers – entered the home, as did decorative wall plates with texts from the Bible, tear-off calendars, and lithographs of the "broad and narrow path", a visual warning summary of how to behave in everyday life. [Col. ill. 13] In Britain too, the home became a target of evangelism. This country experienced a second Reformation in the first half of the nineteenth century as Bible societies and the Sunday school movement helped to turn it into a deeply religious society, bringing a bible into every household and connecting this book to family events, but also still to local superstitions.

In general, research of religious objects and their use in the long nineteenth century is not easy, as sources and descriptions of personal material culture and its uses are

2   Primiano, "Kitsch", 287-288, 295, also quoting David Morgan.
3   Christian, *Divine Presence*, 97-106.
4   Margry, "Dutch Devotionalisation".

rather scarce until the 1860s, as the following chapters show. Little is known about religious material culture in Scandinavia in particular. Problems especially beset the study of material culture and folk piety in everyday life in Scandinavia in the nineteenth century. In the Protestant Scandinavian state churches, material culture was not regarded as important at this time. What was significant, Anders Gustavsson explains in his outline of the meagre results of his study, was the 'Word' in the form of sermons and daily prayer at home. The Catholic prints imported from Germany at the end of the nineteenth century, found in the houses of Scandinavian Catholics, formed an exception.

By contrast to Scandinavia, religious objects were abundantly present in the Catholic parts of Germany, as they were in other European Catholic countries. But abundance does not necessarily imply that there is a lot of information to hand. In general, mass-produced cheap everyday items are often harder to find than costly and artistic objects, and descriptions are rarer. A German author like Montanus is an exception in that he depicted the material culture of the pilgrimage to Walldürn's Holy Blood relic in the 1870s. In the stalls of this town he observed a great variety of statues and crucifixes in various materials, wax figures and candles, paper pennants, medals and rosaries, images etc. He not only mentioned the objects, but also discussed the practice of their use and stated that in the period of the *Kulturkampf* such objects could be found in all Catholic rural homes. Rural German Catholics also wore them around their necks, both men and women, and both young and old.[5]

In addition to such descriptions, photographers appeared in the home or at shrines in the last quarter of the nineteenth century. They acted as ethnographers, taking pictures of what had never been visually recorded before; their images, whether published as postcards or not, can greatly assist research into religious material culture in everyday life. The mediatisation of religion through radio and film became common at the end of the long nineteenth century, adding additional sources.

In countries like Britain, Germany, Belgium and the Netherlands, Catholic materiality, also taken as a form for commercialised popular culture, sometimes became too Catholic even for Catholics themselves.[6] In the second half of the nineteenth century, more markedly so during the *Kulturkampf*, and up to the first decades of the new century, this gave rise to Catholic movements of cultural improvement. In line with modernist thought, these regarded the existing creative religious canons of Catholic culture as too constraining and pressed for more artistic freedom. They were only successful to a limited extent, and the dominance of ultramontane Catholicism and its widely appreciated styles was too great to be easily overturned. That would only happen another four decades later, this time at the behest of the Vatican itself.

5   Montanus, *Eine Wallfahrt nach Walldürn*, 152-154.
6   Dalton, *Catholicism, Popular Culture, and the Arts in Germany*, 232-233.

BIBLIOGRAPHY

500 Jahre Rosenkranz: 1475 Köln 1975. Cologne, 1975.

Aka, Christine, Claudia Kressin and Elisabeth Maas. *Fromme Sachen. Religiöse Kultgegenstände aus niederrheinischen Privathäusern*. Xanten, 2015.

Berthod, Bernard, and Elisabeth Hardouin-Fugier. *Dictionnaire des objets de dévotion dans l'Europe catholique*. Paris, 2006.

Christian Jr., William. *Divine Presence in Spain and Western Europe 1500-1960: Visions, Religious Images and Photographs*. Budapest, 2012.

Dalton, Margaret Stieg. *Catholicism, Popular Culture, and the Arts in Germany, 1880-1933*. Notre Dame, IN, 2005.

Dühr, Elisabeth, and Markus Groß-Morgen. *Zwischen Andacht und Andenken. Kleinodien religiöser Kunst und Wallfahrtsandenken aus Trierer Sammlungen*. Trier, 1992.

Eriksen, Anna. "Our lady of Perpetual Help: Invented Tradition and Devotional Success". *Journal of Folklore Research*, 42 (2005), 295-321.

Heiman, Mary. "Catholic Revivalism in Worship and Devotion". In: Sheridan Shelley and Brian Stanley, eds. *The Cambridge History of Christianity. World Christianities c. 1815 - c. 1914*, vol. 8. Cambridge, 2006.

Heldaas Seland, Eli. "19th Century Devotional Medals". In: Henning Laugerud and Laura Katrine Skinnebach, eds. *Instruments of Devotion: The Practices and Objects of Religious Piety from the Late Middle Ages to the 20th Century*. Aarhus, 2007, 157-172.

Heldaas Seland, Eli. "The visual rhetoric of medals representing nineteenth-century Maria apparitions". In: Henning Laugerud and Salvador Ryan, eds. *Devotional Cultures of European Christianity, 1790-1960*. Dublin, 2012, 75-95.

Koldeweij, Jos. *Geloof & Geluk. Sieraad en devotie in middeleeuws Vlaanderen*. Arnhem, 2006.

Laugerud, Henning, and Laura Katrine Skinnebach, eds. *Instruments of Devotion: The Practices and Objects of Religious Piety from the Late Middle Ages to the 20th Century*. Aarhus, 2007.

Laugerud, Henning, and Salvador Ryan, eds. *Devotional Cultures of European Christianity, 1790-1960*. Dublin, 2012.

Margry, Peter Jan. "Dutch Devotionalisation. Reforming Piety: Grassroots Initiative or Clerical Strategy?" In: Anders Jarlert, ed. *Piety and Modernity*. The Dynamics of Religious Reform in Northern Europe, 1780-1920, 3. Leuven, 2012, 125-156, 187-190.

Martini, Rodolfo. *Medaglia devozionale cattolica moderna e contemporanea in Italia ed Europa, 1846-1978*. 5 vols. Milan, 2009.

McDannell, Colleen. *Material Christianity: Religion and Popular Culture in America*. New Haven CT, 1995.

Montanus, C. *Eine Wallfahrt nach Walldürn*. Edited by Henner Niemann and Manuel Trummer. Obernberg am Main, 2016 [1878].

Perrin, Joël, and Sandra Vasco Rocca, eds. *Thesaurus des objets religieux. Meubles, objets, linges, vêtements et instruments de musique du culte catholique romain*. Paris, 1999.

Primiano, Leonard Norman. "Kitsch". In: John C. Lyden and Eric M. Mazur. *The Routledge Companion to Religion and Popular Culture*. London, 2015, 281-312.

Proctor, Robert, and Ambrose Gillick. "Pilgrimage and Visual Genre: The Architecture of Twentieth-Century Roman Catholic Pilgrimage in Scotland". *Material Religion*, 15 (2019), 456-487.

Thijs, Alfons K.L. *Antwerpen, internationaal uitgeverscentrum van devotieprenten, 17de-18de eeuw*. Leuven, 1993.

Vandenbroeck, Paul, ed. *Backlit Heaven: Power and Devotion in the Archdiocese*. Mechelen-Tielt, 2009.

4.1
Victorian Piety and the Revival of Material Religion in Britain

Mary Heimann

Britain in the 'long' nineteenth century, though now remembered for its supposed secularisation, seemed more striking, at the time, for its intense religious activity and many public expressions of Christian faith. Outward signs of inner Christian piety – Protestant and Catholic – increased dramatically across the British Isles between 1780, the year of the anti-Catholic Gordon Riots, and 1920, the year that the Church in Wales was disestablished. Protestant revivalism from the 1780s, followed by Catholic renewal from the 1830s, combined to give a new religious aesthetic to Christian practice in Britain. The result was a distinctively Victorian piety, sentimental or even mawkish to modern tastes, that was strongly influenced by Evangelical attitudes towards conversion and atonement, infused with Romantic nostalgia for the Middle Ages and touched by traditionally Catholic ideas of the sacramental. Spirituality became more rooted in the material as religious fashion shifted from a characteristically eighteenth-century 'rational' approach, based largely on written texts, to a more folksy nineteenth-century approach, in which Evangelical emphasis on religious feeling, Catholic revivalism, Romantic reverence for holy objects and places, sentimental focus upon the home and desire for tangible 'proofs' of the supernatural combined to make religious experience into something increasingly woven into the everyday and apprehended by the senses as well as by heart, mind and soul.

Material objects believed to symbolise, embody or evoke Christian piety ranged from devotional and liturgical aids to sacred places and from holy images and books to religious artefacts and plaster statues. Organ music, incense, religious pictures, candles, bell ringing, holy water and congregational hymn singing framed worship and religious devotions and set them apart from secular entertainments. Revivalist missions, open-air sermons, public confessions, recitations of the rosary, temperance pledges, religious processions, pilgrimages, Bible salesmen, carol singing, Salvation Army bands and much else besides brought religion out of doors and into the country's high streets and village greens. Explicitly Christian architectural styles, at first used only for ecclesiastical purposes, came to seem appropriate for charitable, municipal, educational and other public buildings, including the newly rebuilt Houses of Parliament. Clergymen, who had once simply dressed as respectable gentlemen, adopted clerical uniform, including the Roman collar, as a mark of their 'professional' status. Nuns and monks, dressed in the distinctive habit of their particular religious order, by their physical presence reminded Victorians of the medieval origins of colleges, schools and hospitals as well as convents and monasteries. Children, organised into societies ranging from the Boy Scouts to the Children of Mary, carried banners or wore distinctive uniforms: the boys dressed in pseudo-military attire, prepared to serve God, Queen and country; the girls in chaste white dresses with a blue sash, the colour associated with the Blessed Virgin Mary. The interiors of parish churches, once white-washed and plain, were painted in bright colours, filled with flowers, lit with candles, covered with memorials and decorated with stained glass, statues and paintings.

4.1-1 'Father reading the Bible to his children', a popular widespread nineteenth-century engraving of Jean-Baptiste Greuze's Père de Famille *(1755). [Private collection]*

Home life, which was punctuated by morning and evening prayers, Bible-reading, the saying of grace before meals, the keeping of the Sabbath, the following of the feast and fast-days of the liturgical year, became more distinctively and tangibly Protestant or Catholic through the display in the home of such items as holy pictures, crucifixes, Lourdes water or family Bibles, the wearing of special clothes on the Lord's Day, the eating of fish on Fridays, and many other denominationally distinct domestic rituals. [Ill. 4.1-1] Christian rites of passage, such as baptism, First Commun-ion, weddings and funerals, loomed large in the social calendar. Rites of mourning were elaborately observed and cemeteries, set out to mirror the social distinctions of the living, took over vast urban spaces, such as at Highgate cemetery in London or the Necropolis in Glasgow. Increasingly elaborate and ritualised celebrations of Christian holidays, especially Christmas, mingled with commercialism and became, like the Sunday roast, a touchstone of respectable middle-class family life.

The material side of religion, which had been attacked during the sixteenth-century Reformation, suppressed by the Puritans in the seventeenth century and scorned by Deists in the eighteenth century, had long been absent from the religious scene in Britain. It came back with a vengeance in the nineteenth century. This broad shift in religious sensibility and taste, which owed a great deal to the Romantic Movement and had clear parallels in contemporary revivals on the Continent, most notably the German Protestant Pietist and French Catholic ultramontane movements, was particularly intense in the British Isles. The change in British attitudes can be explained in part as an emotional reaction, after the shocks of the French Revolution, to the overweening confidence that had been placed on reason during the eighteenth-century Enlightenment, but widely discredited after regicide, secularisation, war and terror. It can also be understood as a Romantic return to the simple, rustic piety cherished in the poems and songs of William Wordsworth or Robert Burns, together with an awe and love for the Middle Ages as inspired by the writings of Sir Walter Scott. It can also be seen as a consequence of the gradual withdrawal of the state church in the face of increased religious competition, Protestant and Catholic, across the British Isles over the course of the 'long' nineteenth century.

From church establishment to religious pluralism

The nineteenth-century religious boom in Britain was accompanied by sharp population increases, the weakening of its two established churches, and a strong growth in denominational competition. In 1780, the Church of England still dominated the religious landscape of England and Wales. It was the Anglican Church, with its tasteful ceremonial, familiar liturgy and *Book of Common Prayer*, its Oxford-trained clergymen and gentlemen bishops, its distinctive blend of privilege, duty and quiet piety, that spoke for the nation and set the religious tone. The mid-eighteenth-century Methodist and early-nineteenth-century Evangelical movements within the Church of England, whose fire was ultimately to affect all the Christian denominations, had not yet been fully accepted in polite society. This was to change after the Methodist church broke away from the Church of England at the end of the eighteenth century and the Evangelical wing took its place within the Anglican establishment from the first decade of Victoria's reign.

Roman Catholicism, which in 1780 was practised in Britain by a minority of so-called 'Recusants' or 'Old Catholics' to be found mainly in little pockets in London, Yorkshire, Lancashire and in the western Highlands and Islands of Scotland, offered no serious challenge either to the established Church of England or to the established Church of Scotland. In 1800, when the combined population of England and Wales was estimated at 8.9 million and the population of Scotland at roughly 1,610,000, there was as yet no visible Catholic community in Wales, fewer than 100,000 practising Catholics in England and barely 30,000 in Scotland. Old Catholics, conscious of being in a tiny, recently persecuted minority, were cautious and tactful in their articulation of the faith. Recusants ordinarily spoke of going to 'prayers' rather than to 'Mass', for example, and characteristically referred to themselves as 'Christians' rather than as 'Catholics'.[1] *The Garden of the Soul*, the English Catholic prayer book first compiled in 1740 by London vicar-apostolic Richard Challoner and used by recusants throughout the British Isles, described itself simply as being for the use of "Christians who, living in the world, aspire to devotion".[2] [Ill. 4.1-2] It was not until the 1830s and 1840s that Ambrose Phillips de Lisle and Father Ignatius Spencer began to promote the use of prayers "for the conversion of England" or to insist on importing Italian devotions into English Catholic churches. Within a generation, some of these devotions and practices had become a standard part of nineteenth-century Catholic worship throughout Britain, helping to sharpen a sense of denominational difference that was being simultaneously emphasised in a myriad of other ways, not only in catechisms and prayerbooks, but especially through the spread of Catholic schools and exclusively Catholic social, charitable and devotional societies.

Between 1780 and 1920, the Church of England, which was Anglican in theology, gradually gave way to reformist pressure, led by Nonconformist, Dissenting and Catholic lobbies, to remove most of its special privileges as the 'national' and 'established' Church of England and Wales. Britain's other established church, the Church of Scotland, which was Presbyterian, lost its hold over the 'Free Church' in the Disruption of 1843 and, from 1847, had to compete not only with the Free Kirk but also with the United Presbyterian Church. In Wales, which did not have its own national, established Church, the Church of England similarly lost out to dissent, especially Calvinist Methodism and Welsh Presbyterianism, over the course of the first half of the nineteenth century. By the last decade of the nineteenth century and first decade of the twentieth, separation from the 'English' Church had become the goal of most Welsh Nonconformists, and four separate Welsh Disestablishment bills were put before Parliament.[3] From the middle of the nineteenth century, Britain's established churches also had to cope with sharply increasing competition from the Catholic Church, whose ecclesiastical hierarchy was formally 'restored' to England and Wales in 1850 and to Scotland in 1878.

The long, drawn-out battle that took place over the course of the 'long' nineteenth century over the status of the dissenting and established churches of England and Scotland turned Victorian Britain into a religious marketplace that ended by offering a greater array of liturgical and devotional choice – Protestant and Catholic – than perhaps any other Christian country in Europe. Earnestly proselytising denominations and sects often condemned, but also copied from, one another as each sought the most effective methods to transmit its own, denominationally distinct slant on the universally Christian message of salvation. This denominational competition intensified outward religiosity as a variety of methods were sought to 'convert' nominal Christians to earnest religious practice. The new religiosity in turn left material traces, tangible objects of a symbolic kind, that help to illuminate the sensibilities and religious experiences of a variety of Victorian and Edwardian Christians. Material religion was especially pronounced in Catholic revivals, both Roman Catholic and Anglo-Catholic, which gloried in the tactile and sensual aspects of church worship and decoration; but was also present, for example in Bible pictures and religious keepsakes, among Protestant congregations.

In 1780, the Church of England arguably had legitimate claims to its established status in England. After all, in England – despite the presence of a significant minority of

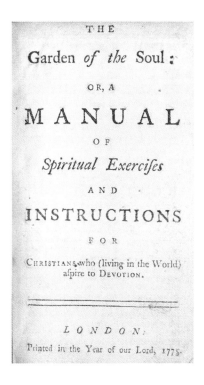

4.1-2 Cover of the English Catholic prayer book The Garden of the Soul, *compiled by Richard Challoner (ed. 1775).*
[www.archive.org]

1   Bossy, *The English Catholic Community*, 364.
2   Challoner, *The Garden of the Soul*.
3   Robbins, "Religion and Community in Scotland and Wales", 376.

Quakers, Catholics, Jews, Unitarians, Congregationalists, Methodists, Baptists, and other Nonconformists and Dissenters – a clear majority of the population identified themselves as Anglican and chose to attend services – or at least to be married, buried or have their children christened in – the local parish church. The case was less clear-cut in Scotland where, even though the established Church of Scotland was Presbyterian in structure and more Calvinist in theology than the English Church, a sizable proportion of the population preferred to worship in alternative 'free' churches. In Wales, too, perhaps as many as half the people already attended Nonconformist or Dissenting services rather than those offered by the established 'Church of England in Wales'. But in Ireland, which had become bound to Great Britain through the Act of Union of 1800, it was impossible to defend the constitutional position on common-sense grounds. It was therefore in Ireland, where three-quarters or more of the population was made up of Catholics who refused to attend services offered by the Anglican 'Church of Ireland', and even the Protestant minority was mainly Presbyterian, that the requirement to support the Church of England seemed the most arbitrary and was the most widely resented.

The anomaly of Ireland, together with pressure from an increasingly vocal, self-confident and growing Nonconformist and Dissenting lobby in England and Wales, led the Westminster Parliament, over the course of the 'long' nineteenth century, gradually to ease the laws that since the seventeenth century had sought to restrict the influence of Roman Catholics, Dissenters and Nonconformists in public life. In Scotland, Calvinist, Presbyterian and Evangelical Nonconformists and Dissenters, followed by Catholics, similarly forced open the religious marketplace and pushed the Presbyterian Church of Scotland onto the defensive. Sustained public debate over theological questions, accompanied by the gradual lifting of religious restrictions and a sharp increase in evangelism and religious revivalism, led to what can almost be described as a second religious Reformation across Victorian Britain. Sparked by late-eighteenth-century Evangelicalism, spread by mid-century revivalist fervour, aided by Irish immigration in the 1840s and sustained by interdenominational competition, this Second Reformation turned Victorian and Edwardian Britain into an exceptionally active, energetic and visibly religious society.

Changes in religious expression that took place in nineteenth-century Britain were enabled, though not caused, by a series of parliamentary and church reforms that gradually wrested control from England to the other parts of the British Isles, and from the established Church of England to old and new religious Nonconformists and Dissenters. These changes began with piecemeal religious reforms undertaken in the late eighteenth century to pacify Ireland (the Catholic Relief Acts of 1778, 1791, 1793) and gained momentum with the repeal of the Test and Corporation Acts in 1828, the passing of the Catholic Emancipation Act in 1829, and the passing of the Great Reform Act of 1932 that gave the Protestant Nonconformist and Dissenting lobby a greater voice in Parliament. Between roughly 1836 and 1906, Dissenters' principal grievances were gradually rectified through the introduction of the civil registration of births, marriages and deaths (1836), the Burials Act (1880), the admission of Nonconformists to degrees at the universities of Oxford and Cambridge (1854 and 1856, respectively) and to teaching posts and College fellowships (1870) and through the amendments to the 1870 and 1902 Education acts that gradually removed the Anglican monopoly over the state-funded religious education of schoolchildren.[4]

By 1920, only a very few Dissenting, Nonconformist and Catholic legal or political grievances still remained. Prejudices and mutual suspicions naturally took longer to fade: overt sectarianism continued to flourish not only in Northern Ireland, where it became notorious; but also in other areas of denominational and ethnic tension, such

4   Knight, *The Church in the Nineteenth Century,* 23-26.

as Liverpool, Manchester and Glasgow. The Church in Wales was formally disestablished in 1920, marking an end to the vestiges of Anglican control over Wales; the Presbyterian Church of Scotland, which had been similarly upstaged by rival denominations, was disestablished a few years later, in 1929. The Church of England, although it retains its special status as England's established church to the present day, was from the second half of the nineteenth century divided into *de facto* High, Low and Broad Church groupings. This meant that Anglicans often had more in common, in their theological understandings and style of worship, with denominations outside the Church of England than they had with each another. Both the Church of England and the Church of Scotland also faced what had become serious denominational competition from the English and Scottish branches of the Roman Catholic Church. How this extraordinary change in the British religious landscape came about had a great deal to do with both Protestant evangelicalism and Catholic revivalism.

Evangelical Revival

The Evangelical Revival of the late eighteenth and early nineteenth century revolutionised the way in which the Christian faith came to be practised and understood by many of its most vocal and energetic adherents. The 'Methodist' movement led by Anglican clergyman John Wesley in the eighteenth century had touched a group of especially earnest and energetic Anglican 'saints' who won a strong following among the poorer classes in the industrial villages of northern England and the eastern seaboard of the United States. Initially disdained and ridiculed by Georgian gentlemen and ladies as 'enthusiasm' (fanaticism), from the turn of the nineteenth century Evangelicalism, called 'vital religion' or 'seriousness' by its advocates, set the new religious tone that was to become so characteristic of the Victorian period and which gradually made overt religious intensity, active proselytising and direct appeals to the emotions respectable.

From about the last decade of the eighteenth century, leading Evangelicals such as William Wilberforce, Hannah More and others rejected what they saw as the complacent and undemanding approach taken to faith by self-styled Christians in polite society, complaining that it was too easy simply to give one's vague assent to the doctrines and morality of Christianity. What was needed, they argued, was a complete revolution of the heart in which Christ, as Hannah More put it, was made "the principle of all human action, the great animating spirit of human conduct".[5] On his twenty-first birthday, in 1807, Edward Bickersteth, who was later to become renowned as a leading Evangelical preacher of the high Victorian period, confided to his diary, with characteristic sense of urgency: "Eternity is at stake, and I am trifling away the salvation of my soul. My soul asks the question, what shall I do to be saved?"[6]

'Conversion' to an earnest faith meant more to Evangelicals than simply seeking baptism or trying to follow Gospel injunctions. It also meant persuading nominal, lukewarm, indifferent or complacent Christians – initially the socially and materially advantaged, later the poor and disadvantaged, too – to take their own Christian faith more seriously, to make their vows and confessions and prayers more real. Early Evangelical treatises that targeted the well-to-do included Thomas Gisborne's *Enquiries into the Duties of Men in the Higher and Middle Classes of Society* (1775) and *Enquiry into the Duties of the Female Sex* of 1797 together with Hannah More's *Thoughts on the Importance of the Manners of the Great to General Society* (1787) and *Christian Morals* of 1813 and William Roberts' *Portraiture of a Christian Gentleman* (1829).

The first Evangelical tract to reach a mass middle-class audience was John Angell James' *The Anxious Inquirer after Salvation*, which became an instant bestseller after its publication in 1834. "You have lately been

---

5 More, *An Estimate of the Religion of the Fashionable World*, 146.
6 T.R. Birks, *A Memoir of the Revd E. Bickersteth* (1852), I, 39 as cited in Bradley, *The Call to Seriousness*, 20.

4.1-3 Portrait of John Angell James (engraving by J. Cochran, after H. Room) and cover of the sixth edition of his The Anxious Inquirer after Salvation (1835).
[London, National Portrait Gallery: NPB D8559; London, British Library]

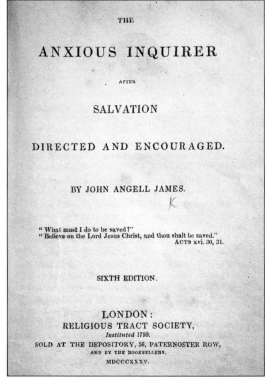

awakened, by the mercy of God", it began, "to ask, with some degree of anxiety, that momentous question, 'What shall I do to be saved?'" "No wonder," it continued, "you should be anxious; the wonder is, that you were not concerned about this matter before, that you are not deeply solicitous now, and that all who possess the word of God do not sympathise with you in this anxiety."[7] James, who was Congregational minister at Carr's Lane, Birmingham, used this kind of immediate, personal rhetoric to bring his listeners to a horrified sense of their own sinfulness and so to seek Jesus and throw themselves on God's mercy. As James reassured those tempted to despair: "Millions in heaven are already saved, and myriads more are on the road to salvation. God is still willing and Christ is still as able to save you as he was them."[8] [Ill. 4.1-3]

Evangelical 'conversion' typically led not only to more frequent and fervent prayer and self-scrutiny and to the active cultivation of virtues such as honesty, sobriety, chastity and the attempt to avoid such vices as gluttony, avarice, idleness, intemperance and pride, but also to active engagement in the world through philanthropy and charity. The sorts of techniques being revived within the Church of England by the Evangelical movement – including the public confession of sins to seek forgiveness, the use of hell-fire sermons to stir consciences, and the vehicle of open-air prayermeetings to express praise, joy and thanksgiving – had obvious precedents in the Calvinist, Methodist, Baptist and other Low Church Protestant traditions. What is less often noticed is that these Protestant revivals, with their strong emphasis on the need for individual salvation and saving grace, also had clear parallels with the 'missionary' techniques being popularised in England, Wales and Scotland from about the same time by Catholic religious orders such as the Passionists, Redemptorists, Marists and Jesuits. Catholic missions, a pronounced feature of Irish Catholic life in the second half of the nineteenth century, were nearly as prominent a feature in the rest of the British Isles, where they targeted not only locals, but also large numbers of nominally Catholic Irish immigrants who had fled the Great

7 James, The Anxious Inquirer after Salvation (1834). There were many subsequent editions.
8 Ibid.

Famine of 1845-1849 and sought work in England, Scotland or Wales. Revivalist meetings were intended to lead penitents to denominationally specific ends (baptism or the renewal of baptismal vows in the Protestant case and confession and regular Mass attendance in the Catholic). There was nevertheless a strong family resemblance between the techniques, language and atmosphere of Protestant and Catholic revivals that suggests at the very least shared religious tastes between sharply opposed Christian denominations.

The Bible

Evangelism meant seeking to convert. As a first logical step, this meant spreading the 'Good News' by bringing the Bible – the all-important Word of God – to those who remained ignorant of it. The Sunday School movement, as launched by the Evangelical Hannah More at the turn of the century, set out to teach poor children to read rather than to write, since its primary purpose was to ensure that even ragged factory girls and the rural poor were able to read their Bibles. [Ill. 4.1-4] This followed the logic of the Welsh circulating schools, devised by Griffiths Jones, in which teachers visited a parish for just three months, teaching as many pupils as possible in the shortest amount of time.[9] "The grand object of instruction" at Sunday School, as Hannah More explained to a friend, "is the Bible itself … the great thing is to get it faithfully explained, in such a way as shall be likely to touch the heart and influence the conduct."[10] In 1804, the British and Foreign Bible Society was founded, initially to ensure that God's word was spread more widely among Welsh-speakers, where demand for personal Bibles outstripped supply and the story of Mary Jones, 'the little girl without a Bible' became a legend. It was responsible for producing over 100 editions of the Welsh Bible over the course of the nineteenth century.[11] The Society was able to capitalise on the technical advances of 'stereotyping' in printing that sharply brought down the cost of typesetting. This enabled the Church of England's King James, or 'Authorized Version', of the English Bible to be translated into foreign languages and distributed cheaply around the world as well as at home. With characteristically grand Evangelical ambition, the Bible Society sought to ensure that every living person in the world, however poor, remote or uneducated, would eventually own his or her own, personal copy of the Bible. [Ill. 4.1-5]

Differences over theological emphases in different collections and translations of sacred scripture led to competition among rival editions of the Bible. In 1825, the Glasgow and Edinburgh branches withdrew from the British and Foreign Bible Society over a controversy about the inclusion of the *Apocrypha* and Metrical Psalms, becoming what later became known as the Scottish Bible Society. A similar controversy in 1831 led to the secession of the Unitarians, who formed their own Unitarian Bible Society. Richard Challoner's translation of the Bible for the use of English-speaking Catholics,

4.1-4 Sunday School class in a poor district in London. Engraving, 1873. [World History Archive: WHA-004-0132]

9 White, *The Welsh Bible*, 62-63.
10 *The Mendip Annals*, ed. A. Roberts (1859), 8, as cited in Bradley, *The Call to Seriousness*, 45.
11 White, *The Welsh Bible*, 103-104. The first full Welsh translation was published in 1588, twenty-three years before the emergence of a single standard English 'Authorized version' (1611).

329

4.1-5 Bible edition by the British and Foreign Bible Society, 1885. [Private collection]

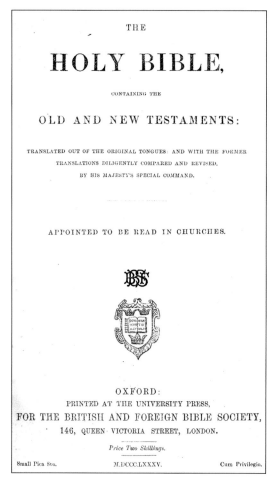

12 McDannell, *Material Christianity*, 73, 77, 81.

13 Opie and Tatem, eds., *A Dictionary of Superstitions*, 23.

the Douai-Rheims Bible of 1752 (which borrowed heavily from the King James version), remained the standard Bible for British Catholics throughout the nineteenth century. Successive nineteenth-century editions of the Douai Bible, however, increasingly emphasised Catholic points of difference from the King James version; and Challoner's translation was eventually superseded in 1913 by the first in what was to become a series of distinctively 'Westminster versions' of Holy Scripture for the use of Catholics in Britain. One result of this evangelical effort was that knowledge of the Bible spread spectacularly over the course of the nineteenth century, achieving one of the Victorians' most cherished goals. At the same time, denominational barriers became sharper and more distinct as more and more rival versions of the Bible came into circulation, each authorised only for its particular sector of the Christian population.

Bibles, which were often imposing physical objects, took on special significance in the Victorian home as well as in church. Important family events, such as births and deaths, were recorded in their pages. Objects of sentimental value, such as a flower from a wedding or the lock of a baby's hair, were often pressed within its pages. As Colleen McDannell has pointed out, images of the family gathered to listen to Father authoritatively reading from the Bible in the kitchen, as in the widely reproduced nineteenth-century engraving of Jean-Baptiste Greuze's *Père de Famille*, or else in the front parlour (as in the accompanying illustration to 'Evening Devotions' in *Godey's Lady's Book*) became a commonplace of Victorian sentimental domestic art. [Ill. 4.1-1] Similarly stereotyped images of a gentle mother listening to her child's bedtime prayers, or tenderly reading the Bible to a child, perhaps with an arm draped about the little one's shoulders, complemented the male stereotype of the authoritative *paterfamilias* with the female stereotype of the 'angel in the house'.[12] In some Nonconformist homes, enormous, leatherbound copies of the Good Book were made into venerable objects that were placed on a lectern or table in the front parlour, a room set aside for Sunday visitors rather than for everyday use.

Superstitions were often attached to the Bible. In the Scottish countryside, according to Robert Burns, Bibles were sometimes used for divination. The notion that an open Bible would help a woman in labour and protect her newborn baby from harm appears to have been widespread in the Scottish Highlands and in the slums of Glasgow.[13] The common English superstition that anyone who dared to perjure himself when swearing on a Bible would be struck dead is tacitly acknowledged to this day in the courtroom practice of taking the oath before giving testimony. By the late 1860s, Bible Women were being paid ten shillings a week to take Bibles to the poorest areas of London and persuade the destitute to buy a Bible for a shilling, paid in weekly instalments of a penny.[14] By the end of the nineteenth century and beginning of the twentieth, armies of clergymen, Bible women and door-to-door salesmen had ensured that just about every household in Britain possessed a copy of the Bible – even in homes where not everyone was capable of reading it. The crusade was carried on, throughout the twentieth and into the twenty-first century, by the American Gideon society, which sought to place a free Bible in every hotel room across the United States and its hotels abroad; and by the Church of the Latter-Day Saints (Mormons), whose distinctive version of the Bible included their own, additional 'Book of Mormon'. By the end of the nineteenth century, Bibles had become at once much more accessible and widespread, but also more denominationally distinct – and sometimes divisive – than at its beginning. The sense of denominational difference was only sharpened by controversies over literal readings of Genesis, the humanity of Jesus and other disputes in Biblical Criticism, often brought over from Germany and France, that preoccupied the Victorians from the 1830s to the 1880s, and were given added impetus from the 1860s in the wake of the publication of Darwin's *On the Origin of Species*.[15]

Church architecture and decoration

The most obvious material change in the religious landscape of Great Britain over the course of the 'long' nineteenth century was the sheer increase in the number of church, chapel and other Christian buildings that sprang up in towns and across the countryside as each denomination sought to keep up with population increases and the dislocation of people associated with immigration and industrial and urban sprawl. In 1818, Parliament voted that a million pounds be spent on restoring and building churches, mainly in the north of England where the accelerated population of the industrial towns had outstripped existing structures. This led to a boom in church building. In the 29 years between 1801 and 1830, for example, just 447 Church of England churches were built or rebuilt; but in the 24 years between 1851 and 1875 the figure had jumped to 2,438.[16] The style in which the Church Commissioners chose to build these new churches and attached ecclesiastical buildings was English Gothic.

Georgian neoclassicism, which had dominated eighteenth-century taste, was emphatically rejected by the Victorians as a pagan style, inappropriate for a Christian country, "What have we, as *Christians*", as Augustus Welby Pugin, one of the most influential architects of the early Victorian age, put it, "to do with all those things illustrative *only of former error*? Is our wisdom set forth by the owl of Minerva, or our strength by the club of Hercules? What have we (who have been redeemed by the sacrifice of our Lord himself) to do with the carcasses of bulls and goat?"[17]

Although it was widely agreed that the specifically Christian architecture of the Middle Ages contained the most appropriate set of symbols to reiterate ancient Christian values, this still left open the possibility of choosing from a number of possible styles. The early English style of Gothic was judged by most Victorians too crude and heavy, too obviously influenced by its Norman antecedents, a style in its 'infancy'; whereas fifteenth-century 'decorated' Gothic was argued to be in its corruption and decay. Only the middle style, fourteenth-century 'pointed' English Gothic, was argued to be at the prime of life, at its most ripe and (favourite word) 'manly'. In 1834, Pugin's love of 'pointed' Gothic went so far as to persuade him to convert from Anglicanism to Catholicism on the grounds "that the Roman Catholic Church is the only true one, and the only one in which the grand and sublime style of church architecture can ever be restored".[18] Two years later, he brought out his polemical, hugely influential tract contrasting the supposed ugly and heartless utilitarianism of

14 Bradley, *The Call to Seriousness*, 48.
15 For a concise account of 'Science and Religion', see Heimann, "Christianity in Western Europe from the Enlightenment", 490-497.
16 See Parsons, "Reform, Revival and Realignment", 25, note.
17 Pugin, *The True Principles of Pointed or Christian Architecture*, 54.
18 As cited in Clark, *The Gothic Revival*, 169.

nineteenth-century English architecture and society with the supposed Christian charity and inclusiveness of medieval times as *Contrasts: or A Parallel Between the Noble Edifices of the Fourteenth and Fifteenth Centuries and Similar Buildings of the Present Day. Shewing the Present Decay of Taste*. The message was one that led to increased interest not only in medieval architecture, but also in medieval art, decoration and, by extension, theology, spirituality and liturgy.

Liturgical renewal and ritualism

As John Henry Newman, a clergyman don responsible in the 1820s and 1830s for recruiting and training the next generation of Anglican clergymen, later wrote in his spiritual autobiography, the Church of England then seemed in "general need of something deeper and more attractive than what had offered itself elsewhere".[19] The Anglican church, Newman argued, "must have a ceremonial, a ritual, and a fullness of doctrine and devotion… if it were to compete with the Roman Church with any prospect of success", since the Roman Catholic Church "alone, amid all the errors and evils of her practical system, has given free scope to the feelings of awe, mystery, tenderness, reverence, devotedness, and other feelings".[20] John Keble's *The Christian Year* (1827), the work of a young Oxford theologian that offered Romantic Christian poetry for every Sunday in the year, sought to fill the gap that Newman and other Anglicans sensed. *The Christian Year*, though initially considered effeminate by some old-school Anglicans, went into over one hundred editions and quickly became "not only a cherished classic" but also a "sacred book" to be placed beside Bible and Prayerbook in the Anglican canon.[21]
[Ill. 4.1-6]

In 1833, after what appeared to a circle of Oxford-based Anglican clergymen to be the latest in a series of alarming instances of governmental interference in the established Church of England (the suppression of some bishoprics in Ireland), John Keble launched what came to be known as the Tractarian or Oxford Movement by preaching at the university church in Oxford on the theme of 'National Apostasy'. The series of polemical essays that followed, all published by Oxford clergymen dons between the years 1833 and 1845 as 'Tracts for the Times', earned their authors the scornful name of 'Tractarians' after their methods or 'Puseyites' after Edward Bouverie Pusey, their leader; it has more commonly been known since as the 'Oxford Movement'. Those within the Church of England who remain inspired by its theological, devotional and ritual reforms, and are sometimes called 'Ritualists', are better known today as 'High-Church Anglicans' or 'Anglo-Catholics'.

The *Tracts for the Times* were prompted by what seemed to their Anglican authors to be the imminent threat of Church disestablishment in the face of persistent Nonconformist and (Roman) Catholic pressure. They therefore initially focussed a good deal of their attention on the sinfulness of the interference in spiritual matters by outside bodies and the dangers inherent in the separation of church from state. But they justified the privileged position of the Church of England on grounds that were theologically contentious, namely that the Anglican Church was unique among all other Christian churches in Britain in alone preserving the continuity of apostolic succession. To Newman and Keble in particular, the best defence of the Church of England lay in the claims for its catholicity or universality, and they returned to the Anglican divines of the sixteenth and seventeenth centuries to find grounds for affirming its status as the true church of Christendom.

The broadly Catholic arguments with which even the earliest *Tracts for the Times* tried to justify the position of the Anglican Church quickly hit a nerve with those Evangelical clergy whose own defence would naturally have been Protestant. Low Churchmen's emphasis on the priesthood of all believers and deep mistrust of any resemblance to the Roman Catholic Church, symbol to

19 Newman, *Apologia Pro Vita Sua*.
20 Ibid., 262.
21 Shairp, "Introduction", ix.

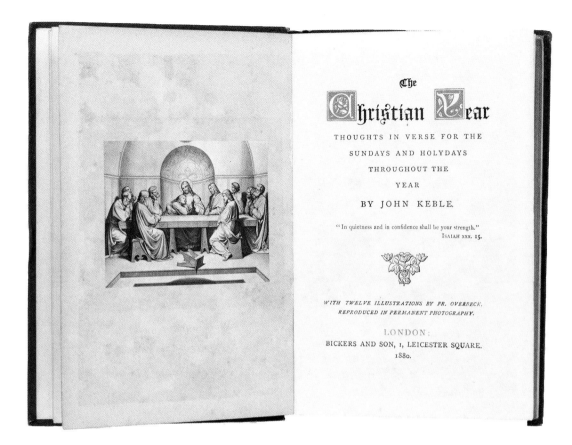

4.1-6 1880 edition of John Keble's The Christian Year, *with illustrations by the 'Nazarene' Friedrich Overbeck. [Private collection]*

them of all that was corrupt in Christendom, led them to react swiftly to what they saw as the theological errors of the Oxford men. As the Evangelical newspaper the *Christian Observer* began to critique what it termed the "extraordinary doctrines" of the Tractarians, unprecedented numbers of undergraduate students continued to flock to Newman, Pusey and Keble's lectures and the fame (or notoriety) of the *Tracts for the Times* to spread. Increasingly, the *Tracts for the Times* were moving towards a full-blown defence of the Anglican position as what Newman termed a *Via Media*, or middle way, between what he presented as the twin extremes of 'Popery' (Catholicism) on the one hand, and 'Puritanism' (Calvinism) on the other. In the attempt to show that the English church, not the Roman, was the true descendant of the ancient church, Tractarians revived many practices that had been unknown in England since the seventeenth century and which smacked of 'popery' even to mainstream Anglicans. Lights, altartables, incense, clerical dress, indeed most of the trappings of medieval Catholicism, began to be restored to showpiece Tractarian churches like St Mary's in Oxford, amid an increasing public unease which, by the 1840s, had turned to a storm of controversy and publicity.

Architectural and liturgical enthusiasm for Gothic revival and neo-medievalism spread to parish churches around the country, and also to the other ancient English university, the University of Cambridge. In 1839, John Mason Neale and Benjamin Webb formed the Cambridge Camden Society, whose aim was to build new churches in the style of fourteenth-century Gothic and to restore existing churches to a more Catholic use, by removing the focus from the pulpit (which implied the Protestant function of a preachinghouse) to the sanctuary and altar (which placed emphasis on the sacrament of holy communion as a sacrifice). The dangers were becoming apparent. As a Protestant minister warned, in a published sermon of 1844: "as Romanism is taught analytically

333

at Oxford, it is taught artistically at Cambridge... it is inculcated theoretically at the one university and it is sculptured, painted and graven at the other".[22] Like Pugin and the Tractarians, the Camdenians continued in a Catholic direction. Neale not only published translations of hymns from the ancient Eastern churches but, from the 1840s onwards, actually went so far as to begin re-establishing religious communities within the Church of England. This was at the same time that a bewildering variety of Roman Catholic orders – English, Irish, French, Belgian, Italian and other – were rapidly being deployed around the British Isles to cope with population increases, especially through Irish immigration, into the great industrial cities of northern England and the central belt of Scotland. It was also a decade of widespread revivalist missions, Protestant and Catholic, which charged the religious atmosphere and sometimes stoked sectarian fires.

In 1841, Newman published his famous Tract 90 that actually stated outright that the articles of the Church of England were "patient of [i.e. open to] a Catholic interpretation".[23] In the storm of controversy that followed, and the official condemnation of the Tract by the University of Oxford, Newman gradually gave up his university position and withdrew to Littlemore, a few miles away from the city. Four years later, he shocked not only Evangelicals but also his High-Church friends, by being received into the Catholic Church, an act that ended the Tractarian Movement and led to a major theological crisis within the Church of England. A significant number of Newman's followers, W.G. Ward and Frederick Faber among them, followed his example and left the Church of England to be received into the English Catholic Church, beginning a tradition of high-profile British converts to Rome.[24] Those who stayed behind, most notably John Keble and Edward Bouverie Pusey, remained as leaders of the High Church, 'Anglo-Catholic' or ritualist wing within the established church. One of the Oxford Movement's long-term legacies was to leave the Church of England divided into Low, Broad and High Church groupings that sometimes had more in common with outside denominations – Protestant Nonconformist or Roman Catholic – than with each other. On the other hand, more intense Anglican participation in church, thanks to both Evangelical and Catholic revivals, had become the norm. In the 1830s, for example, most Anglican churches offered communion just four times a year. By the end of the century, weekly communion was the norm for all Anglican places of worship. In Low Church parishes, communion might be followed by prayer-meetings, revivalist missions and Bible study groups; in High Church parishes, it might be supplemented by Matins, Lauds, Evensong and all the other daily offices that had once been the preserve of Catholic monasteries and convents.

Catholic Revival

At just about the same time that the Evangelical Revival and Oxford Movements were converting the British establishment to a more intensely religious life, the Roman Catholic population of the British Isles increased so sharply – largely through Irish immigration in the 1840s – that British Catholicism came out of the shadows and took its place as yet another denomination that needed to be reckoned with politically and practically.[25] By mid-century, the Vatican agreed to remove Britain's status as a 'missionary' territory and to allow a fully-fledged ecclesiastical hierarchy formally to represent and cater for its Catholic populations. The Catholic hierarchy was duly 'restored' to England and Wales in 1850 and, after further campaigning, to Scotland in 1878. Although the 'restoration of the ecclesiastical hierarchy' meant little more, in practice, than allowing Catholic 'vicars-apostolic' to be called 'bishops' and 'missionary territories' to become 'dioceses', a triumphalist speech made by the English Catholic archbishop Nicholas Wiseman 'out of the Flaminian Gate' in

---

22 As cited in Clark, *The Gothic Revival*, 228.
23 [Newman], *Tract 90. Remarks on Certain Passages in the Thirty-Nine Articles*. See also Pusey, *The Articles treated on in Tract 90 [by J. H. Newman]*.
24 Gordon-Gorman, *Converts to Rome*, listed approximately 4,000 converts to Catholicism during the half-century that followed the Oxford Movement.
25 Reliable, clear-cut figures for the number of Anglicans, Catholics, Presbyterians, Baptists, Methodists and other Nonconformist and Dissenting Christians living in nineteenth-century Britain do not exist. Apart from inconsistencies in the gathering of statistical data, the nature of the information gathered does not always allow for the comparison of like with like across denominations. The most reliable estimates for overall figures and patterns of growth can be found in Currie, Gilbert and Horsley, *Churches and Churchgoers* but are too lengthy and discursive to be reproduced here.

Rome and subsequently reported in alarmist terms by the British press prompted widespread fears that this 'papal aggression' was only the first step in a plot to overturn Britain's hard-won Protestant settlement. Violent anti-popery riots followed, lasting for days in London and other major cities.

The fear of Catholicism became widespread in Britain at mid-century partly because of the notion of 'papal aggression', but also because of a brisk trade in salacious tales of young girls supposedly walled up in convents or held captive by wily Jesuit priests, together with the active promotion of such fears through the lecture tours and polemical pamphlets put out by energetic anti-Catholics such as Mr Newdegate.[26] Catholicism was also seen as threatening because of the scale of Irish immigration of the 1840s, because the Oxford Movement had resulted in the sensational conversions of a number of prominent Anglican clergy, because there was a visible increase in Catholic buildings – including churches, schools and religious houses – and because a great deal of public Catholic worship and devotion seemed foreign and alien to local Protestant sensibilities. Only in the longer term did the restoration of the Catholic hierarchy give Catholics and others the sense that Catholicism in Britain was for the first time since the Reformation being treated as an 'official' religion, a legitimate denomination rather than a treasonous sect.[27]

Devotional revolution

In the 1840s and 1850s, during what has come to be known as the Catholic Revival, the tone and presentation of the Catholic message as preached across the British Isles changed. Going to confession and taking the Blessed Sacrament stopped being treated as fearful privileges to be reserved for the most solemn occasions in the liturgical year, but became a weekly – or even daily – habit for those who aspired to holiness. Hagiographies began to stress, rather than to seek to explain away, wonders and miracles surrounding the lives of the saints. Clergy, formerly treated as little different from other professionals, came increasingly to be set apart as different, as holy. The previously notorious Jesuits and a range contemplative orders, whose very right to exist had been widely questioned during the Enlightenment, were now held up to ad-

4.1-7 Hymn 'God bless our Pope', written by Nicholas Wiseman.
[Sunday School Hymn Book, 1907, 47]

26 See Arnstein, *Protestant versus Catholic in Mid-Victorian England*.
27 Wolffe, *God and Greater Britain*, 49-62.

28 All Catholic churches in England and Wales advertised their mass times and extra-liturgical services in annual editions of *The Catholic Directory and Annual Register*. It is from these figures that the percentages cited here have been calculated.
29 For the exact figures, see table 1, appendix 1 and figures 1-14, appendix II, in Heimann, *Catholic Devotion in Victorian England*, 174-190. The results are discussed on pp. 40-45 of the same work. See also Aspinwall, "Catholic Devotion in Victorian Scotland", 32-33.
30 Heimann, *English Catholic Devotion*, 44.

4.1-8 Cover (detail) of the Boys' Brigade Gazette, 1883.
[www.thebbmuseum.org]

miration as among the most spiritually advanced. The papacy, personified in the person of Pio Nono (Pius IX), the 'Prisoner in the Vatican', became the object of empathetic prayers, Peter's Pence collections and rousing English Catholic hymns such as 'God Bless Our Pope'. [Ill. 4.1-7]

Together with changes in the tone and emphases in Catholic preaching and hagiography in the British Isles came a dramatic rise in the provision and popularity of a whole range of extra-liturgical practices known as devotions, some of which had a distinctly medieval flavour. Whereas only a tiny fraction of Catholic churches in Britain up to the 1840s had offered Benediction of the Blessed Sacrament (a distinctively English Catholic version of a service culminating with the blessing of the congregation by the Blessed Sacrament in an elaborate monstrance), by 1900 nearly 90% of all English Catholic churches catered for weekly, or even daily, Benediction of the Blessed Sacrament, the most popular slot being 7 or 8 pm on Sunday evening. Similarly, the service of the Rosary, another Catholic devotional extra in which the congregation, usually led by a priest, recited the Dominican rosary of 15 decades, had been scarcely represented in the Catholic churches of England, Scotland and Wales up to the 1840s; by the end of the century, however, it was offered by 80% of all churches.[28] The Franciscan Lenten devotion known as the Stations or Way of the Cross (*via crucis*), in which the penitent empathetically meditates on the stages of Christ's suffering and crucifixion, became available in all dioceses – and perhaps as many as a fifth of all churches – by the 1860s, though it did not complete its spread to more or less all Catholic churches until about the middle of the twentieth century.[29] Devotions to the Sacred Heart of Jesus, a pious practice closely associated with contemporary French Catholic spirituality and whose special Mass and Office of the feast was extended to the whole Church by Pius IX in 1856, became more prominent in English Catholic prayer books from about 1875.[30]

Catholic devotions were spread and promoted with particular effectiveness through an increasingly vast network of Catholic schools and a host of exclusively Catholic devotional clubs, associations and societies known as confraternities, sodalities or guilds, whose revival and rapid spread from the 1850s was another marked feature of nineteenth-century Catholicism. Some of these societies, known as Third Orders, offered lay Catholics the opportunity to take part in the religious life of a chosen religious order, most commonly the Order of St Francis or the Order of St Dominic, yet without committing themselves so far as to become actual novices. Those who took their status as a 'tertiary' seriously might choose to wear a scapular, or symbolic yoke, of their chosen order underneath their clothes, or perhaps to keep a discrete 'rosary ring' or rosary beads in their pocket for counting off their Hail Marys and Our Fathers. Other devotional societies, such as the Children of Mary or the Catholic Boys' Brigade [Ill. 4.1-8], were aimed at young girls or boys (the sexes were strictly segregated) with an eye to keeping them chaste and pious through the particularly tricky stage of adolescence. Still other Catholic confraternities, such as the Society of St Vincent de Paul, existed primarily to help the poor; or, like the Temperance Guild of Our Lady and St John or the Association

of the Cross, to combat a specific social evil, alcoholism in this case, through the use of distinctively Catholic prayers and devotional practices.

The vast majority of devotional societies, which consisted of a bewildering variety of Rosary, Blessed Sacrament, Sacred Heart, Holy Family, Immaculate Conception, Immaculate Heart, Way of the Cross, Precious Blood and countless other confraternities, sodalities and guilds, were explicitly spiritual rather than social in that they sought to focus their members' attention on a particular devotional practice and, through it, to strengthen commitment to a discrete aspect of Catholic doctrine. The spread of devotional societies, especially through parish churches and convent schools, led to the increased use of images such as the 'miraculous medal', the Sacred Heart and the Holy Family, all of which were often included in prayer books and appendices to catechisms from the 1870s. Images of St Bernadette, bottles of Lourdes water and replicas of the Lourdes grotto came to Britain, by way of France, somewhat later, starting in the 1880s (which was also when the first English Catholic pilgrimages to Lourdes began to be held), and reached new heights of popularity in the first half of the twentieth century.

At the same time that Catholic expectations of worship and devotion were becoming more intense and demanding, Catholics were becoming increasingly segregated from non-Catholics. Educated separately wherever possible, strongly discouraged from marrying outside the fold, and urged to participate more frequently in denominationally specific rites of passage and communal events such as retreats, processions and pilgrimages, Catholics found their everyday experience to be increasingly different from that of non-Catholics.[31] This 'cradle-to-grave' Catholicism created what has also been called 'the Catholic ghetto', a network of educational, recreational, religious, charitable and welfare provision that effectively separated Catholics and Protestants from each other at the same time that, paradoxically, their religious tastes,

sensibilities and morality were growing to have so much in common.

Holy pictures

Holy pictures used for contemplation by British Christians were often imported from the Continent: French and Belgian images were especially widespread among Catholics, German and Dutch designs among Protestants. The Nazarene style, which combined the ideals of classicism and the early Italian Renaissance, became the favourite idiom, in Britain as on the Continent, in which to paint nineteenth-century popular religious images, from distinctly Catholic images of the Blessed Virgin Mary, Sacred Heart or the saints to Bible illustrations of the Good Shepherd aimed at Protestants. [Ill. 4.1-9] This was the style in which the vast majority of prayer cards, holy pictures and pious reproductions to be displayed in the home were painted or drawn, and in which devotional objects sold at Catholic sites of

4.1-9 Nineteenth-century French devotional image (in English) of the Good Shepherd.
[Leuven, KADOC-KU Leuven]

31 See Tenbus, *English Catholics and the Education of the Poor*.

32 von Achen, "Fighting the Disenchantment of the World", 138.
33 See <http://www.19thc-artworldwide.org/autumn03/73-autumn03/autumn03article/273-unwilling-moderns-the-nazarene-painters-of-the-nineteenth-century>.
34 White, *Frost in May*, 45-46.

4.1-10 Engraving of William Holman Hunt's 'The Light of the World'. [Private collection]

pilgrimage were usually portrayed. "Even in neo-Gothic altarpieces, or on holy cards with Gothic framing", as von Achen points out, "the pictures themselves most often do not appear in Gothic style, but in this tradition of the Nazarene movement in which sweeter versions of classicist features, perhaps in medieval costumes, lived on through the nineteenth century."[32]

Although now largely forgotten in Britain, the Nazarene circle of German painters, and especially Friedrich Overbeck, were highly prized by the Victorians for their view of the function of art as moral and religious. Their work can be shown to have directly influenced Charles Eastlake, a president of the Royal Academy and the first director of the National Gallery in London, as well as the pre-Raphaelite brotherhood, most notably Holman Hunt and Ford Madox Brown. Indeed, when the manuscript of what was eventually published as the first volume of Ruskin's *Modern Painters* was first offered to the London publisher John Murray in the 1840s, he is said to have turned it down with the comment that he might have been interested if Ruskin had offered him a book on the Nazarenes instead.[33]

Sunday School religious pictures were didactic, but also sentimental and designed to be approachable and accessible. While God the Father, a stern patriarch, might be too frightening to approach directly, Jesus meek and mild carrying a woolly lamb on his shoulders or 'suffering the little children' to come unto him could be turned to with confidence. For Catholics, a similar contrast was drawn between God the Father and God the Holy Ghost, who a convent schoolgirl remembered as "awe-inspiring conceptions, Presences who could only be addressed in set words and with one's mind, as it were, properly gloved and veiled", as opposed to "Our Lady and the Holy Child and the saints" to whom she felt able to speak "as naturally as to her friends".[34] The notion of the Blessed Virgin Mary in particular as a beautiful, comforting, gentle and forgiving intercessor,

a loving mother who would not scold, was especially attractive to nineteenth-century sensibilities, and may help to account for the sharp rise in both Marian devotion and the sacrament of Penance (confession).

The single most popular painting of the late Victorian period, 'The Light of the World' by William Holman Hunt, one of the pre-Raphaelite brotherhood, was closely based on the Nazarene painter Philipp Veit's similar depiction of 1824. Holman Hunt's famous image of Christ knocking at a door, originally painted between 1851 and 1853 and recopied in life-size between 1900 and 1904, was taken on a tour of the colonies in 1905 where it is estimated to have been seen in the flesh by about 7 million people. 'The Light of the World', as iconic and well-known a painting in the late nineteenth century as

the Mona Lisa became in the twentieth, was in effect a sermon in oils, a religious commentary on Revelation chapter 3, verse 20: "Behold, I stand at the door, and knock: if any man hear my voice, and open the door, I will come to him and will sup with him, and he with me." The invitation was not so much to aesthetic appreciation as to religious conversion. After engravings of the painting were taken and published in 1860, the image came to be extremely rapidly reproduced. Maas has found that, within a decade, nearly every home in the United Kingdom, as well as many throughout the colonies, possessed a copy of this most iconic and sentimental Christian image.[35] [Ill. 4.1-10]

Christmas

Christmas, which had been banned entirely during the seventeenth-century Interregnum of 1649-1660 on the grounds that it was 'popish' and 'unbiblical', continued to be viewed with suspicion in the Puritan and Calvinist traditions, but steadily increased in importance among Anglicans in particular. Modern English Christmas celebrations – including mince pies, Christmas trees, carol singing, seasonal pantomimes, rich neo-medievalism and the exchanging of cards – date from the 1840s. The sudden fashion for Christmas trees is attributed to Queen Victoria's consort, Prince Albert, who brought a number of German Christmas traditions, including the decorated Christmas tree, into the royal household in the 1840s. The first Christmas card is claimed by the Victoria and Albert museum to have been sent in 1843, the same year that Charles Dickens published *A Christmas Carol*. The sudden boom in special supplements and editions of serials and magazines such as *Household Words* and *All the Year Round* show that a Christmas market also developed rapidly from the 1840s. By 1848, when the *London Illustrated News* published a drawing of the royal family celebrating Christmas together around a decorated tree, the scene already looks like a modern English Christmas. By 1861, Mrs Beeton's *Book of Household Management* included a recipe for 'Christmas cake' (though not yet for a steamed 'Christmas' plum pudding) and declared that "a Christmas dinner with the middle classes of this empire, would scarcely be a Christmas dinner without its turkey; and we can hardly imagine an object of greater envy than is presented by a respected portly pater-familias carving, at the season devoted to good cheer and genial charity, his own fat turkey, and carving it well."

Continued hostility to Christmas from the Free Church and indifference on the part of the Presbyterian Church of Scotland meant that Christmas Day, which remained overshadowed by Hogmanay (New Year's) north of the border, did not become a public holiday in Scotland until as late as 1958. The Chapel of King's College, Cambridge, first brought in its now internationally famous 'Festival of Nine Lessons and Carols' in 1918; the service was first broadcast to the nation in 1928. The monarch's Christmas Day message was begun by King George V on 25 December 1932 and continued nearly every year thereafter. These radio and television rituals sealed the importance of Christmas by reminding the public of the monarch's continued headship of the Church of England and the British establishment's continued recognition of Britain as a Christian country.

Conclusion

Over the course of the 'long' nineteenth century, a series of government-led reforms gradually removed the monopoly over religious worship, education and welfare that had once been the preserve of the established churches of Great Britain. Catholic Emancipation and the opening up of state-funded institutions to dissenters, Nonconformists and Roman Catholics led not only to the disestablishment of the Irish, Welsh and Scottish churches, but also to the creation

35 Maas, *Holman Hunt and the Light of the World*, 73-76.

of a religious marketplace in which each denomination and sect sought to attract new adherents. The result was an atmosphere of fierce denominational competition that was simultaneously characterised by a lively sense of trans-denominational religious revival. This revival in turn gave the Victorians and Edwardians much of their characteristic air of piety, prudery, earnestness, public-spiritedness and missionary zeal.

By 1920, Anglican, Catholic and Nonconformist places of worship had come to express their differences of theological emphasis and spiritual mood outwardly as well as inwardly. This was not only a question of pamphlet wars among clergymen or sectarian folk prejudices among the laity, but also of concrete expressions of material difference that could be apprehended by the senses. Anglican churches typically advertised their claim to apostolic succession by building in fourteenth-century 'pointed' English Gothic, whereas 'Low' Church Presbyterian, Baptist and Unitarian chapels favoured plain styles that gave precedence to light, symmetry and the pulpit. Catholic churches, whether Roman Catholic or Anglo-Catholic, underlined their claim to belong to the universal Catholic Church by building in Romanesque, Byzantine, French or English Gothic style; by providing frequent communions, Benediction and recitation of the Rosary; by catering for confession; by decorating their interiors with images of the Sacred Heart, plaster-cast statues of the saints, and perhaps a replica of the grotto at Lourdes; by covering church walls with the fourteen Stations of the Cross; and by routinely including holy water stoups, candles and incense. Denominational affiliation could also be expressed through food, whether by eating fish on Fridays or tucking into Hot Cross buns at Easter or plum puddings at Christmas. By the end of the 'long' nineteenth century, denominational differences in Britain were no longer simply expounded in words as written in pamphlets and treatises or shouted out on street corners. They were also felt, heard, smelled, seen and tasted.

BIBLIOGRAPHY

Arnstein, Walter L. *Protestant versus Catholic in Mid-Victorian England: Mr Newdegate and the Nuns.* New York, 1982.

Aspinwall, Bernard. "Catholic Devotion in Victorian Scotland". In: Martin Mitchell, ed. *New Perspectives on the Irish in Scotland.* Edinburgh, 2008, 32-43.

Bossy, John. *The English Catholic Community 1570-1850.* London, 1975.

Bradley, Ian C. *The Call To Seriousness: The Evangelical Impact on the Victorians.* New York, 1976.

Chadwick, Owen. *The Victorian Church.* 2 vols. London, 1971 [1966].

Challoner, Richard. *The Garden of the Soul: A Manual of Spiritual Exercises and Instructions for Christians, Who, Living in the World, Aspire to Devotion.* London, 1740.

Clark, Kenneth. *The Gothic Revival: An Essay in the History of Taste.* London, 1950.

Currie, Robert, Alan Gilbert and Lee Horsley. *Churches and Churchgoers: Patterns of Church Growth in the British Isles since 1700.* Oxford, 1977.

Gilley, Sheridan, ed. *Victorian Churches and Churchmen: Essays Presented to Vincent Alan McClelland.* Woodbridge (Suffolk) - Rochester (NY), 2005.

Gilley, Sheridan, and W.J. Sheils. *A History of Religion in Britain: Practice and Belief from Pre-Roman Times to the Present.* Oxford, 1994.

Gordon-Gorman, William. *Converts to Rome: A Biographical List of the More Notable Converts to the Catholic Church in the United Kingdom during the Last Sixty Years.* London, 1910.

Heimann, Mary. *English Catholic Devotion, 1850-1914.* D.Phil. thesis, University of Oxford, 1992.

Heimann, Mary. *Catholic Devotion in Victorian England.* Oxford, 1995.

Heimann, Mary. "Christianity in Western Europe from the Enlightenment". In: Adrian Hastings, ed. *A World History of Christianity.* London, 1999, 458-507.

Herringer, Carol Engelhardt. *Victorians and the Virgin Mary: Religion and Gender in England, 1830-85.* Manchester, 2008.

James, John Angell. *The Anxious Inquirer after Salvation.* 6th ed. London, 1835 [1834].

Jarlert, Anders, ed. *Piety and Modernity.* The Dynamics of Religious Reform in Northern Europe 1780-1920, 3. Leuven, 2012.

Keble, John. *The Christian Year.* London-New York, n.d. (originally published in 1827).

Kehoe, S. Karly. *Creating a Scottish Church: Catholicism, Gender and Ethnicity in Nineteenth-Century Scotland.* Manchester-New York, 2010.

Knight, Frances. *The Church in the Nineteenth Century.* London-New York, 2008.

Larkin, Emmet. "The Devotional Revolution in Ireland, 1850-75". *American Historical Review*, 77 (1972), 625-652.

Laugerud, Henning, and Salvador Ryan, eds. *Devotional Cultures of European Christianity, 1790-1960.* Dublin, 2012.

Maas, Jeremy. *Holman Hunt and the Light of the World.* Aldershot, 1984; 1987.

McDannell, Colleen. *Material Christianity: Religion and Popular Culture in America.* New Haven-London, 1995.

More, Hannah. *An Estimate of the Religion of the Fashionable World.* 1791; 1808 edition.

[Newman, John Henry]. *Tract 90. Remarks on Certain Passages in the Thirty-Nine Articles.* London, 1841.

Newman, John Henry. *Apologia pro Vita Sua.* New York, 1956 [1864].

Opie, Iona, and Moira Tatem, eds. *A Dictionary of Superstitions.* Oxford, 1989.

Parsons, Gerald. "Reform, Revival and Realignment: The Experience of Victorian Anglicanism". In: Gerald Parsons, ed. *Religion in Victorian Britain.* Vol. 1. Manchester, 1988, 14-66.

Parsons, Gerald. "Victorian Britain's Other Establishment: The Transformations of Scottish Presbyterianism". In: Gerald Parsons, ed. *Religion in Victorian Britain.* Vol. 1. Manchester, 1988, 117-145.

Pugin, A. W. N. *The True Principles of Pointed or Christian Architecture.* New York, 1973 [London, 1841].

Pusey, Edward Bouverie. *The Articles treated on in Tract 90 [by J. H. Newman] reconsidered and their interpretation vindicated in a letter to ... R. W. Jelf. ... With an appendix from Abp. Ussher on the difference between ancient and modern addresses to Saints.* Oxford-London, 1841.

Robbins, Keith. "Religion and Community in Scotland and Wales". In: Sheridan Gilley and W.J. Sheils, eds. *A History of Religion in Britain: Practice and Belief from Pre-Roman Times to the Present.* Oxford, 1994, 363-380.

Shairp, John Campbell. "Introduction". In: John Keble. *The Christian Year.* Everyman's Library. London-New York, n.d.

Tenbus, Eric G. *English Catholics and the Education of the Poor, 1847-1902.* London, 2010.

Von Achen, Henrik. "Fighting the Disenchantment of the World: the Instrument of Medieval Revivalism in Nineteenth-Century Art and Architecture". In: Henning Laugerud and Salvador Ryan, eds. *Devotional Cultures of European Christianity, 1790-1960.* Dublin, 2012.

Waugh, Evelyn. *Brideshead Revisited: The Sacred and Profane Memories of Captain Charles Ryder.* London, 1962 [1945].

White, Antonia. *Frost in May.* London, 1978 [1933].

White, Eryn. *The Welsh Bible.* Stroud, 2007.

Wolffe, John. *God and Greater Britain: Religion and National Life in Britain and Ireland 1843-1945.* London-New York, 1994.

4.2
Reform and Change in Material Expressions of Catholic Devotion in Ireland

Patricia Lysaght

Background

The nineteenth century has been identified as the period during which the religious attitudes and behaviour constituting the religious pattern of Irish society in the twentieth century was shaped. It was in the nineteenth century that the Tridentine pattern of religious practice which was "centred on regular sacramental practice based on sufficient catechetical instruction within the framework of the parish under the direction of the parish priest" with the bishop as the lynch-pin of the system, became firmly established throughout Ireland.[1] The Tridentine pattern had been longest established in the towns, and, in the second half of the nineteenth century, it spread from there to become and to remain the general pattern of Irish Catholic culture.

It had taken almost three centuries for Tridentine Catholicism to become predominant in Ireland due to the effects of conquest by the English monarchy, the development of the state-sponsored English Protestant Reformation in Ireland and its effect on Catholic Church structure, personnel and catechesis, and ongoing penal legislation to the late eighteenth century, until Catholic emancipation was achieved in 1829.

The sixteenth century was witness to the English military conquest of Ireland, the introduction of the English Reformation and the development of the Irish Counter-Reformation movement. The Reformation had only limited success in Ireland. The conversion mission of the state-sponsored reformed church, the Church of Ireland, was essentially a failure with regard to the population in general. This was primarily because the first concern of the English Tudor monarchs and their successors was to militarily subdue the country and to impose linguistic change, as well as change in "manners, order and apparel", thus forging a "necessary link between Anglicization and reformation", rather than to apply general coercive enforcement of English Reformation practice.[2] Attempts at large-scale religious conversion to Protestantism was thus relegated to second place even though enabling legislation was enacted. In 1536, the monarch Henry VIII of England was declared "the only Supreme Head on Earth of the whole church of Ireland" by the 'Reformation Parliament' in Dublin. In 1537 acts of parliament against the authority of the Pope and for suppression of the monasteries, were passed. But no serious attempts to impose Reformation statues in Ireland were made until the 1570s, by which time a well-organised and effective Counter-Reformation movement was in operation. Reformation policy and practice of the sixteenth century had shaken the Catholic Church in Ireland to its roots, and the political climate during the following two centuries was not conducive to reorganisation, re-entrenchment and stability.

The seventeenth century was a period of immense political, social and cultural upheaval in Ireland. Part of the province of Ulster was settled by Scots and English immigrants. The subsequent Rebellion in 1641 of the native Irish against those settlers developed into nine years of war, ending in defeat for them, followed by confiscation of virtually most Catholic property and land. Ownership of land was thus transferred to

4.2-1 Sodality of the Children of Mary, Mullinavat, 1915.
[Dublin, National Library of Ireland; photo A.H. Poole]

1 Corish, *The Irish Catholic Experience*, 103-105.
2 Ford, *The Protestant Reformation in Ireland*, 26-27; Hayes-McCoy, "The Tudor Conquest", 180; Ó Fiaich, "The Language and Political History", 104.

the new Protestant proprietors who became the new landlord elite and a minority religious class, with the majority of the Catholic population essentially constituting their tenantry. Even though persecution of Catholic clergy was practised, there was no effective mission to convert the population at large to Protestantism. From a purely practical point of view, there was nothing to be gained from converting the Catholic poor to Protestantism since the ownership of land, the source of wealth and power, was already in Protestant hands.

The defeat of the Catholic James I of England, by William Prince of Orange in 1690, signalled the defeat of the Catholic cause and ensured Protestant succession in England and, for the following two centuries, Protestant dominance in Ireland. 'Popery in the gross' was considered a political threat to the Protestant land settlement in seventeenth-century Ireland and this led to the enactment of far-reaching anti-Catholic laws (Penal Laws). These laws were ultimately ineffective due to the lack of political will to stringently apply them. By the end of the eighteenth century less than five per cent of Irish land was in Catholic hands. The Catholic Relief Acts of 1778, 1782 and 1793 removed the principal restrictions of the Penal Laws on the ownership of land, the activities of priests and bishops, and on Catholic education. Full Catholic emancipation was however not achieved until 1829.[3] Forty years later, an act which dealt with the disestablishment and disendowment of the Protestant Church of Ireland was passed and came into effect on 1 January 1871.

These centuries of great political, religious, social and cultural turmoil in Ireland inevitably fundamentally affected the Catholic church establishment, which was already in need of reform and renewal in the sixteenth century. The impact of the Reformation had brought into focus many serious weaknesses in church organisation, and also in the quality of catechetical instruction and discipline, among both clergy and laity. While the church endeavoured to organise itself along Tridentine lines it lacked infrastructure and sufficient clergy to provide the necessary guidance and catechesis during much of the period. As a result, there was serious disruption of catechesis, and the Catholic hierarchy was hindered in its efforts to bring within the contemporary ambit of the church a whole range of beliefs and observances, especially the more public ones, such as those connected with wakes, patterns and pilgrimages, which were only partly, if at all, sanctioned by the church authorities.

This situation deteriorated in the late eighteenth and early nineteenth century due to a degree of lax internal church discipline and unprecedented population growth – from c. 4.5 millions in 1791 to 8.1 millions in 1841, of which 81% were Catholics.[4] Four-fifths of these lived on the land, most at subsistence level especially in the west of the country, but to varying degrees elsewhere also. This segment of the population, largely dependent on the potato for food, became increasingly at risk prior to the Great Famine of 1845-1850, and it was also among this group that "the influence of official Catholicism was weakest".[5] It was at this segment of the population on the periphery of the Catholic Church's catechetical programme, and largely residing in some of the most disadvantaged areas of the west and south-west of the country, that a well-organised, well-funded and determined campaign of evangelisation by Protestant societies emanating from England, and dedicated to the conversion of Irish Catholics, was directed, for almost forty years (c. 1820-1860). This missionary conversion movement – known as the 'Second Reformation' or the 'Bread and Butter Reformation' – had considerable human and financial resources at its disposal, and the religious instruction was provided, where necessary, through the medium of the Irish language. Bible teachers were trained and supported (800 in the years 1818-1827 alone), as well as itinerant preachers, many of whom were fluent Irish speakers drawn from the Catholic community. Large numbers of Protestant bibles, in Irish as well as

---

3 Corish, *The Irish Catholic Experience*, 123-150; Wall, "The Age of the Penal Laws"; McDowell, "The Protestant Nation"; Whyte, "The Age of Daniel O'Connell".
4 Connolly, *Priests and People in Pre-Famine Ireland*, 58-73.
5 Connolly, *Religion and Society in Nineteenth-Century Ireland*, 53-54.

in English, and free elementary education, were offered to those prepared to accept the religious instruction that accompanied it.[6] But the campaign was disastrous from many points of view. It stirred old memories of the persecution of priests, confiscation of land, penal legislation, and domination by a Protestant religious minority – the latter perceived as being linked to the distribution of food for religious conversion purposes during the Great Famine.

Although some pockets of Protestantism were established as a result of the 'Second Reformation', the endeavour was ultimately unsuccessful and went into decline after the middle of the nineteenth century. Its demise was hastened by the successful adoption by the Catholic establishment of measures similar to its own, such as the provision of books for the laity. While Catholic books, including sermon books for the clergy in the English and Irish languages, were published in Ireland in the eighteenth and early nineteenth centuries, further efforts were made to provide a literature for the Catholic laity in general – at least for those who could read.[7] Thus the Catholic Book Society was set up in 1827 to print and distribute Catholic literature, including schoolbooks, as cheaply and as widely as possible. Lists of books available from the Catholic Book Society appeared in various issues of the *Irish Catholic Directory*. The Catholic Society for Ireland was formed in 1835 with the aim of promoting parochial libraries, co-ordinating the work of sodalities and the Confraternities of Christian Doctrine, and the distribution of Catholic literature, free of charge where necessary. The weekly newspaper, *The Irish Catholic*, first published in 1888, is still in existence. The parish mission movement from the 1840s led by various religious orders, such as the Vincentians, Dominicans and Franciscans, also constituted a counter-attack against the 'Second Reformation', and the National Schools system established in the 1830s, which became increasingly under the control of the Catholic clergy, also enabled more effective and more widespread catechesis to be carried out.[8]

Thus the 'Second Reformation' acted as a further stimulus to the internal reform and renewal already underway in the Catholic Church in Ireland in the mid-nineteenth century, as a new generation of reforming bishops set themselves the task of tightening discipline, imposing higher standards on the lower clergy in the performance of their religious duties, and in delivering instruction and knowledge to the laity. The Synod of Thurles (1850) – "the first national assembly of the Irish church for almost 700 years – introduced a comprehensive and up-to-date code of ecclesiastical law, summarising and consolidating the reforms of the preceding fifty years". Thereafter, the full pattern of Tridentine Catholicism, which had been difficult to implement in Ireland, would become the norm, as was the case in Catholic Europe.[9]

Thus Catholic religious practice was becoming more institutionalised and centred mainly on the parish church, except for the sacrament of penance which still clung to the bi-annual 'stations' – religious services held in private houses. The traditional funeral Mass which was also usually held in the home of the deceased, was henceforth to be held in the church. This change was introduced in the ecclesiastical province of Dublin in the 1850s but its progress was slow and uneven elsewhere, especially in more remote parts of rural Ireland. This was the case even though the new Roman Code of Canon Law of 1918 laid down that funerary rites and the funeral Mass should take place in the church setting.

The parish missions also helped to concentrate Catholic religious practice in the parish church. Parish missions led by visiting preachers of many religious orders, including the Vincentians, Redemptorists, Dominicans and Passionists, commenced in the 1840s, gained momentum from the 1850s, and persisted strongly throughout the remainder of the nineteenth century and beyond. This becomes evident from a survey carried out by the Bishop of Kerry, John Coffey, in 1890, by means of a questionnaire issued to the

6 de Brún, "Irish Society Bible Teachers"; "Scriptural Instruction in the Vernacular"; for a recent assessment of the 'Second Reformation in West Kerry 1925-1945', benefitting, thanks to digitasation, from access to rich contemporary sources, see MacMahon, *Faith and Fury*.
7 Ó Súilleabháin, "Catholic Sermon Books Printed in Ireland"; Id., "Catholic Books Printed in Ireland".
8 Connolly, *Priests and People in Pre-Famine Ireland*, 86-87; Corish, *The Irish Catholic Experience*, 165-166, 178, 188, 205-206; Fuller, *Irish Catholicism since 1950*, xxii. Cf. O'Donovan, *Stanley's Letter*, 28-31, 112-113.
9 Fuller, *Irish Catholicism since 1950*, xxvii-xxviii; Corish, *The Irish Catholic Experience*, 201.

10 de Brún, "Kerry Diocese in 1890".
11 Donnelly, "The Marian Shrine of Knock", 63-67; Corish, *The Irish Catholic Experience*, 210-211.
12 De Brún, "Kerry Diocese in 1890". Founded in Rome in 1563, the Sodality of the Children of Mary had, during the nineteenth century, become "one of the largest religious organizations in the world". Introduced into Ireland by the Jesuits in 1598, the Sodality became very prominent in convent schools throughout the country in the nineteenth century (Donnelly, "The Marian Shrine of Knock", 62).
13 Connolly, *Religion and Society in Nineteenth-Century Ireland*, 54; Corish, *The Irish Catholic Experience*, 167-170, 211-212.
14 McGrath, "The Tridentine Evolution of Modern Irish Catholicism".

parish priests of his diocese. The responses to the question (no. 23) 'Give date of last Mission in your Parish' from the forty-nine parishes involved, show that a mission had been held in the vast majority of them (39) during the previous ten years, with nine having had missions during the previous seventeen years, and there were just five parishes in which no missions had been held.[10]

These missions served also to foster private devotions through the blessing of medals, rosary beads, the brown scapular, and religious images, and by encouraging enrolment in a variety of devotional confraternities and sodalities.[11] Bishop Coffey's Survey gives an indication of confraternities or sodalities that were being established in a rural diocese in the second half of the nineteenth century. Among these was the Confraternity of the Living Rosary which had been set up in nine parishes between 1860 and 1890. The Confraternity of Our Lady of Mount Carmel (Scapular Confraternity), already established in a parish in the diocese in 1825, experienced further expansion in the 1870s and 1880s, as did the Sodality of the Children of Mary.[12] The Sodality of the Sacred Heart was also set up in a number of parishes between 1884 and 1890, and here the importance of the mission in providing impetus for the creation of confraternities is also indicated by means of the Survey. In 1890, for example, the Sodality of the Sacred Heart had been established in a particular parish during a mission which had been held just two weeks previously. The Confraternity of the Holy Face had also been "lately" established in the same parish with "very large numbers" enrolling as members. Other devotions centred on the church, under clerical control, included Benediction, the 'Forty Hours' Adoration of the Blessed Sacrament, and the devotion of the 'Nine Fridays' in honour of the Sacred Heart – which had become almost universal by 1890, and which involved confession and Holy Communion on nine consecutive Fridays, and which also promoted devotion to the 'Holy Hour'.[13] [Ill. 4.2-2]

Thus, by the end of the nineteenth century the Catholic Church, as the majority church in Ireland, had developed into a well-organised, independent and powerful institution, affecting, though not entirely displacing, attitudes to traditional folk beliefs and practices which had interacted with the doctrines and rituals of official Catholicism over the centuries, to form the traditional world view of the vast majority of the people of Ireland until relatively recent times. The Tridentine evolution of Irish Catholicism had occurred and was to remain firmly in place until the holding of the Second Vatican Council in 1962.[14]

Religious material culture

Within the broader picture of the position of the Catholic church establishment in the context of the political, religious, social and cultural situation in Ireland in the seventeenth, eighteenth and early nineteenth centuries, religious material culture receives only sporadic and scattered men-

4.2-2 Cover of a leaflet on the devotion of the Holy Face, published by the Irish Messenger Office.
[Private collection]

tion. Catholic families, who sent sons to be educated in the Irish Colleges in Catholic Europe in Counter-Reformation and later times, would have received personal and household religious and devotional objects, such as crucifixes, rosary beads, scapulars and prayer books, from the Continent. That clergy returning from Continental Europe at that period brought items such as these with them is evident from a number of sources. The existence of crucifixes in private households is attested for the mid-seventeenth century, in the well-to-do barony of Forth in the south-east of Ireland. Crosses in public places are also mentioned at this time in the context of the conquest of the country by English parliamentary forces, led by the Puritan Oliver Cromwell, when such religious artefacts were destroyed:

> very many crosses in public roads, and crucifixes, in private houses and chapels in the said barony kept, builded of stone, timber or metal, representing the dolorous passion of our Saviour Jesus Christ, which, wherever found, were totally defaced, broken or burned by Cromwellian soldiers.[15]

The use of 'manuals of prayer' by the laity for Sunday vespers in Wexford town is referenced for the mid-seventeenth century, and a family prayer book by a county Kilkenny family for the listing of births and deaths from the mid-seventeenth century to the middle of the eighteenth century, is also attested.[16]

The continuing population increase in the eighteenth century – from about four and half million people in 1791 to more than eight million in 1841, on the eve of the Great Famine (1845-1850), dramatically increased the number of the rural poor, who were essentially unable to offer financial support to the Catholic church establishment, and who were also most unlikely to have had much in the way of material devotional aids – apart possibly from rosary beads, the brown scapular, and some blessed medals.

Even church buildings, their religious material culture, and religious services, could be quite inferior or even lacking. While church building, especially in some urban centres, was progressing in the late eighteenth and the first half of nineteenth century, many areas of rural Ireland were without churches, and even those which existed were often of poor construction, unadorned, and with little furniture, some even without a railed-in sanctuary or a sacristy for the priest to vest for Mass.[17] These were essentially Mass houses, built to protect the participants from the elements, and many were without baptismal fonts, requiring that baptisms be performed in the priest's house or in the home of the child, and as facilities for the reservation of the Blessed Sacrament in churches were not always present, it, too, was often kept in the priest's house.[18] Even the priest's vestments, altar cloths and furnishings, were often in a poor condition, "and the use of candles, incense, music and devotional images was rare outside the larger towns and a few other areas of advanced liturgical development".[19] Religious services which were non-obligatory, such as Benediction and the Stations of the Cross, were not available in all parishes. While engaged in a mission in Enniskillen in 1852, an Austrian Redemptorist learned that the people had never experienced Benediction of the Blessed Sacrament or incense wafting from a thurible.[20] An insight into the relative absence of religious objects, such as Christmas crib figures, even in the context of the principal church – the Pro-Cathedral – in the capital city, Dublin, in the mid-nineteenth century, is the request for crib figures from the Archbishop of Dublin, Cardinal Cullen, on 15 January 1856, to Tobias Kirby, Rector of the Irish College in Rome. Stating that he proposed to erect a crib in the pro-Cathedral in Dublin the following year, Cullen wrote: "If you see a few good shepherds or angels going astray in any old shop, send them to us. Such things cannot be found here."[21] But many such objects did become available later as is evident from advertisements for religious artefacts in *The Catholic Directory* in the late nineteenth century. [Ill. 4.2-5]

15 Corish, *The Irish Catholic Experience*, 119.
16 Ibid., 133; <http://pilgrimagemedievalireland.com/>.
17 Corish, *The Irish Catholic Experience*, 175-176.
18 Ibid., 175-176.
19 Connolly, *Religion and Society in Nineteenth-Century Ireland*, 49.
20 Ibid., 48-49.
21 Corish, *The Irish Catholic Experience*, 212.

Bohemia and some parts of Austria". He goes on to point out how different in fact the situation was, noting the absence of "remarkable ecclesiastical buildings", except for the Dublin and Armagh cathedrals. He then remarks that if the Bohemians had a saint as famous as St Patrick "they would have erected a thousand statues to his honour in all corners of the land", while in Ireland "there are scarcely two statues of St Patrick". He adds: "In short, the whole land seems as if it were stripped of every blossom of Catholicism, and as if Protestantism had entirely done away with all those hated crosses and signs of image-worship."[22]

An aspect of social behaviour which was considered to be in much need of reform in the early nineteenth century was the general lenient attitude towards excessive alcohol consumption. Temperance societies were set up to tackle the problem of drunkenness, especially among the urban and rural poor. Among the most significant was the Cork Total Abstinence Society founded in 1836 in Cork city by the Capuchin priest Theobald Mathew. [Ill. 4.2-3] Again, Kohl, who witnessed Father Mathew's work during his travels in rural Ireland, has left a description, not only of the temperance movement itself and its effects, but also about the visual emblems associated with it. At Kilrush, county Clare, he heard Father Mathew address the people and he also observed the distribution of temperance medals among those who attended and took 'the pledge' in the 1840s:

4.2-3 *Theobald Mathew wearing the Cork Total Abstinence Society Medal.* [Washington, Library of Congress: LC-DIG-pga-01772]

During his sojourn in Ireland in the mid-nineteenth century, the German Lutheran traveller, Johann Kohl, remarked on the virtual absence of public religious material culture at that period. He commented in 1844 that in view of the strong attachment of the Irish to the Catholic religion, one would expect to find the "whole land full of priests, nuns, monks, churches and cloisters; and expect to find crucifixes, crosses, and images on all the roads; in a word, that Ireland has, in this respect, the same appearance as

At nine o'clock on the following morning, Father Mathew was again at his post. This time, however, the scene of his labours was the church, where he read mass, and then distributed temperance medals to some hundreds of persons who presented themselves for that purpose. This medal is a round piece of pewter, about the size of a five-franc piece. Upon it are stamped the words of the pledge, which are to the effect, that the holder will abstain from all intoxicating liquors, and do all in his power to dissuade others from using them. Some persons, as I have said, wear

22 Kohl, *Travels in Ireland*, 182-183.

them constantly as a kind of amulet. They frequently hang them around the necks of their children, who are admitted into the society long before they know any thing of intoxicating liquors … The wealthy have silver medals, which they wear on festive occasions. Along with this medal each person receives a paper, a sort of diploma, or certificate of admission into the society. In Ireland this medal is called 'the pledge,' and to 'take the pledge' means the same as to become a member of the society. On the other hand, to 'break the pledge' means to break the vow, and again return to intemperance …[23]

Kohl goes on to say that some beggars had joined the temperance movement, as the wearing of their temperance medal improved their chance of getting alms as they were thought to make good use of money received. He also noted that some people regarded the medal as a sort of talisman, imagining it to be imbued with beneficial and protective powers because it had been blessed by Father Mathew.

The English travellers, Mr. and Mrs. S. C. Hall, also visited Fr. Mathew during their visit to Cork in the autumn of 1840, and they too saw him administer 'the pledge', after which a medal and a card were given to each new member. The Halls provide an engraving of the front and back of the medal. The words of the pledge are engraved in a cross shape on the front of the medal, and around the edge is written: "Cork Total Abstinence Society Founded 10 April 1836" and "The Very Revd. T. Mathew President". The Halls go on to describe the very direct and emotive message of the card:

> The card is a copy of the medal, with the addition of two prints, one of 'Temperance,' picturing a happy cottage home, surmounted by a bee-hive; the other of 'Intemperance' describing a wretched hovel and its miserable inmates; above it is a lighted candle, into the flame of which a poor moth rushes, and a bottle, round which a serpent coils. It contains also a passage from the Acts, 'He reasoned of righteousness, temperance, and judgement to come.'[24]

The Halls also state that special powers of healing and protection were being attributed to Father Mathew: "many of the pledged believe that Mr. Mathew possesses the power to heal diseases and preserve his followers from all spiritual and physical dangers, an error which Mr. Mathew does not labour to remove, although he is, certainly, not charged with having striven to introduce or extend it". In the nineteenth century, statues of Father Mathew were unveiled on St Patrick's Street, Cork (1864) and O'Connell Street, Dublin (1893), where they still stand.

Another, and more enduring temperance movement, The Pioneer Total Abstinence Association of the Sacred Heart, was established in Dublin in 1898, almost fifty years after Father Mathew's death. [Ill. 4.2-8] An organisation for Catholics, those who join (known as 'taking the pledge') agree to abstain from all alcoholic drink, and devotion to the Sacred Heart of Jesus is encouraged. 'Pioneers' as the members of the Association are known, wear a lapel pin called a 'Pioneer Pin', bearing an image of the Sacred Heart. This is worn by both men and women. [Ill. 4.2-4] The Association is still active today among all age groups and has an extensive international network. The Association pub-

23 Ibid., 106-107.
24 Hall, *Ireland*, I, 42-43.

4.2-4 *The Pioneer Pin of an Irish Chaplain William J. G. Doyle of the Jesuit Order who was killed in the Battle of Ypres on 16 August 1917. His Pioneer Pin, Agnus Dei, Miraculous Medal, and other blessed objects were recovered by a fellow chaplain on his death.* [Irish Jesuit Archives, Dublin]

RELIGIOUS ARTICLES

FOR

CATHOLIC CHURCHES, COMMUNITIES, CONVENTS, &c.

MAISON FRANCAISE

(French House).

OFFICES:

7 WELLINGTON QUAY,	12 Rue Duguay Trouin,
DUBLIN,	PARIS,
Near Essex Bridge.	*Near St. Sulpice's Church.*

MONSIEUR L. GUERET,

Publisher and Manufacturer in Paris.

RESPECTFULLY begs to inform the Roman Catholic Clergy, Heads of Religious Houses, Convents, &c., that he is able to offer them a large and selected stock of Religious Goods, such as Lace Pictures for Prayer-books; Beautiful Emblems, embroidered on rice paper, and others printed; Pictures in Sheets, New Chromos in Sheets, large plain, coloured and black ground Pictures of all kinds of subjects, with or without frames. Sheets of Hearts, red, blue, and purple; small and large Stations of the Cross in Oil Paintings, also in plain; coloured and black ground Engravings framed. Mortuary Cards in Sheets, or printed by hundred or half hundred. Scapulars; Standing Lamps of every colour; Branches for Benediction, with 3, 5, 7, 12 lights. The best Incense of Jerusalem, guaranteed to be of the same quality used in Rome and all the Churches on the Continent. Brass and Silver Beads and Medals; Pearl Crosses and Medals for School Distribution, Pictures, Medals, and Statues of Our Lady of Lourdes. Handsome Crucifixes, coppered, bronzed, and gilt, also in plastic and Ivory; Irish Lockets, and sets of Green Enamelled Shamrocks. Altar Lights; Cruets; Ornamental Chapels in carved wood for private Oratories; Holy-water Fonts; Glass Shades; Large Statues in plaster and terra-cotta; Small Statues in French plastic and biscuit; Vases for Natural and Artificial Flowers; Candlesticks in bronze and silvered glass; Cribs in plaster and plastic of every size and price. Infant Jesus in Wax; Hearts, Crowns, and Monograms; Articles of Paris for Bazaars.

N.B.—Orders by Post punctually executed, and forwarded to any part of Ireland *carriage free, when amounting to £6*. Large Statues and Heavy Bronzes excepted.

☞ Special prices for the Clergy and Religious Communities.

WHOLESALE AND RETAIL,

7 WELLINGTON QUAY, 7

Near Essex Bridge.

---

lishes a monthly magazine called *The Pioneer*, founded in Dublin by the Jesuit priest, Fr. James Cullen, in 1899.

While religious attitudes and practices of Irish society in the second half of the nineteenth century were gradually remoulded along Tridentine lines, prior to that period the sacraments of baptism, matrimony, penance and the Eucharist were, of necessity, frequently celebrated in private houses, due to non-existent or poor church facilities in some areas of the country. This presupposes that the priests had appropriate travel kits for the celebration of Mass and for the administration of the various sacraments administered in the non-church setting. There is evidence from the oral tradition that Mass kits, as well as vestments, were left in private houses for both safe-keeping and in order to be available for the next occasion when Mass would be celebrated in the locality.

With the growing prosperity of the Catholic community, especially among tenant farmers and the urban merchant class, in the second half of the nineteenth century, church building and refurbishment were progressing, "with a new emphasis on magnificence and external display" especially in urban settings.[25] Thus, the physical surroundings for the celebration of Mass, for the administration of the sacraments, and for devotions of various kinds, also improved during these decades, in the form of better church buildings, decoration, religious artefacts, vestments, and church furniture. The presence of a range of suppliers of religious articles for churches, communities and convents, in Dublin, but who also serviced other parts of the country, reflects this situation. This is evident, for example, in an advertisement which appeared in *The Catholic Directory* for 1873. [Ill. 4.2-5]

In addition, a range of auxiliary church services such as Benediction, Stations of the Cross, novenas and processions, lay confraternities and sodalities, increased in number in the late nineteenth century, and with them an associated material culture of medals, badges and banners.

Particular devotions

The rosary

The rosary, as a sequence of prayers (Our Father, Hail Mary, Glory be to the Father), and as a string of beads used to count the prayers, is a distinctive element of Marian devotion in Ireland. Marian devotion has been part of Irish spirituality since the early centuries of Christianity in the country, and was strongly nurtured by the apparitions of Our Lady at Knock in 1879. [Ill. 4.2-6]

In pre-Reformation times, the Dominicans had about thirty-eight monasteries in various parts of Ireland and were thus in a strong position to ensure widespread propagation of the rosary devotion in the country. This position was strengthened towards the end of the sixteenth century when the Dominican bishop of Clonfert got permission to set up the Confraternity of the Holy Rosary in his diocese. The practice of the rosary was further strengthened by other Marian devotions such as the Sodality of the Blessed Virgin, established by the Jesuits in Limerick and Kilmallock in 1565. This sodality – which included the daily recitation of the rosary as a family prayer – was widely distributed in Ireland in the seventeenth century and played an important role in Counter-Reformation spirituality in the country.[26] In the political and religious turmoil of the seventeenth century, private devotion was relied on to such an extent that the rosary became the principal Marian devotion in Ireland at the time.[27] This was due in large measure to the sustained efforts of the Dominican fathers, who had become known as the Rosary Fathers (*Aithreacha an Phaidrín*). The importance of the rosary as a national prayer is indicated by the direction of the Provincial Council of Armagh in 1642 that the rosary should be said every evening for the good of the country.[28]

Rosary beads are mentioned in relation to lay people since the seventeenth century.[29] Rosaries were brought to Ireland by clergymen returning from the Continent and by other travellers, such as visiting Irish officers from the French and Austrian armies.[30] Spanish influence is also discernible due to Irish priests trained at the Irish colleges in Spain returning to the home mission in Ireland, and also to trade links between the two countries, from the late sixteenth century onwards. This is evident in surviving silver rosaries, while amber, often used to make rosaries in Ireland, was probably bought from Spanish sailors at the port of Galway.[31] The port towns of Dublin, Waterford, Kinsale, Cork, Limerick and Galway were, in the eighteenth century, centres of rosary manufacture, and all except Kinsale had a Dominican monastery.[32]

Rosary beads could also be valuable, like the so-called, Galway rosaries consisting of fifteen decades of large amber beads and large silver crosses, examples of which adorn seventeenth-century wooden statues of the Madonna, the so-called 'Rosary Madonnas', in Galway and Limerick, which are among the surviving pre-eighteenth-century statues

4.2-5 (Left page) advertisement for Catholic religious objects by Maison Française (French House) with offices in Dublin and Paris.
[The Irish Catholic Directory (Dublin, 1873)]

4.2-6 Devotional image on the apparition of Our Lady at Knock.
[Leuven, KADOC-KU Leuven]

25 Connolly, *Religion and Society in Nineteenth-Century Ireland*, 54.
26 Concannon, *The Queen of Ireland*, 134-135; Corish, *The Irish Catholic Experience*, 93; O'Dwyer, *Mary*, 209, 214-215, 293.
27 Corish, *The Irish Catholic Experience*, 133.
28 O'Dwyer, *Mary*, 218.
29 Carrigan, *The History and Antiquities of the Diocese of Ossory*, I, 122; II, 397: a five-decade rosary appears in a mortuary sculpture (1608) in the Cistercian Abbey of Kilcooley, and in the will (1693) of Bishop James Phelan, Kilkenny, monies were bequeathed to certain lay people to buy 'Rings or Beads'.
30 Concannon, *The Queen of Ireland*, 125-126.
31 McGuire, "Old Irish Rosaries", 98-99.
32 O'Dwyer, *Mary*, 222.

of Our Lady.[33] Rosary beads with crosses and *paternoster* beads of gold, are known at this period, but rosaries made entirely of silver were common in the seventeenth, eighteenth and nineteenth centuries among prosperous members of society.[34]

Of assistance to the Counter-Reformation movement in Ireland and for catechesis, was the publication of devotional works and catechisms for the Irish church by Irish monks and priests on the European Continent. The catechism by Andrew Donlevy first published in Paris in 1742, mentions the importance of the rosary as a supplicatory prayer and as a form prayer for those who could not read.[35] He presumes that rosary beads will be in use as he states that, to begin, the Sign of the Cross is followed by the Apostles' Creed said on the cross of the beads, a *Paternoster* is said on each large bead and an *Ave Maria* on each small bead, and to conclude, three *Paternosters*, three *Aves* and the Creed are said, followed by the Sign of the Cross as at the beginning.[36]

By the middle of the eighteenth century the rosary, according to the Archbishop of Cashel, "was duly observed by most of the people".[37] This observation is supported by Bishop Moriarty of Kerry, in his Allocution to the Clergy, Diocesan Synod, 1867, when he stated: "This devotion has had in later years, most wonderful development". He urged the clergy to promote the recitation of the rosary as a family prayer, and as a communal prayer by reciting it in the church before Mass on Sundays, and to establish confraternities of the Blessed Virgin in every parish.[38] Catholic Emancipation in 1829, the introduction of the Sodality of the Living Rosary into Ireland "in aggregation with the Arch-Confraternity of the Immaculate Heart of Mary, Refuge of Sinners, in Paris", by Archbishop Daniel Murray of Dublin, in 1841, and the advent of the parish missions, during which the Litany of the Blessed Virgin and the rosary were said, contributed significantly to the enthusiasm for and the spread of the rosary devotion throughout Ireland in the late nineteenth and early twentieth centuries.[39] That the rosary beads, and thus also the rosary devotion, were of special importance for Irish families is also evident from the works of a variety of artists mainly from the second half of the nineteenth century and early part of the twentieth, who depict rosary beads hanging in Irish rural kitchens.[40]

In the twentieth century, other factors contributed to the propagation of the rosary. These included the founding of the Catholic association called the Legion of Mary in Dublin in 1921 which involves recitation of the rosary. Of special importance was the Rosary Crusades of the Dominican Order, which included enrolment in the Confraternity of the Most Holy Rosary and the Golden Rose (the emblem of the Confraternity), and the Family Rosary League of the Rosary Apostolate of the Dominican Order.[41]

Rosary beads in common use in the late nineteenth and early twentieth century were made of a variety of substances. Few of those made of wood survived. Those made of horn were more durable and long-lasting. Stones of fruit were also used for this purpose and in the National Museum of Ireland there is a rosary beads made of chestnut seeds said to have belonged to Father Mathew, the nineteenth century 'Temperance Priest'. Rosaries were purchased at missions and blessed by the preachers. Hung up in the kitchen near the hearth, the blessed rosary beads was thought to protect the house and its occupants in a general sense, and if carried on the person, it was regarded as a safeguard against supernatural beings and forces, especially at night.[42]

The brown scapular

In addition to the rosary, devotion to the brown scapular, the Scapular of Our Lady of Mount Carmel, was one of the most widespread Marian devotions in Ireland, and it was propagated by the Carmelite Order. The popularity of the scapular was linked to the scapular promise – that whoever dies clothed in the habit will not suffer eternal fire – and

---

33 Pochin Mould, *The Irish Dominicans*, 122, Fig. 54, 239-241.
34 McGuire, "Old Irish Rosaries", 99. Recent excavation in Ballinasloe, Co. Galway, revealed skeletons dating to between 1479-1638, one of which had a five-decade bone rosary beads wrapped around its feet. (rte.ie/news/Connacht/2021/0923/1248628-ballinasloe-history/).
35 *An Teagasg Críosduidhe, Do réir Ceasda agus Freagartha/The Catechism, or Christian Doctrine, by Way of Question and Answer*.
36 Donlevy, *An Teagasg Críosduidhe*, 391-395.
37 Corish, *The Irish Catholic Experience*, 133.
38 Moriarty, *Allocutions to the Clergy and Pastorals*, 184-186.
39 O'Dwyer, *Mary*, 261; Donnelly, "The Marian Shrine of Knock", 63-64.
40 Kinmonth, *Irish Rural Interiors in Art*, 59, Fig. 55; 62, Fig. 58; 67, Fig. 62; 134, Fig. 136; 134-135, Fig. 137; 161-162, Fig. 165; 163, Fig. 166; 168, Fig. 169; 184-185, Figs. 182, 183; 188, Fig. 186; 231, Fig. 223.
41 Lysaght, "Attitudes to the Rosary and its Performance in Donegal", 19-20.
42 Lysaght, "The Uses of Sacramentals", 195-196. Cf. also note 34.

the Sabbatine privilege (1322) – that the Blessed Virgin Mary will assist the souls of deceased members of the confraternity especially on Saturday, the day especially dedicated to her.[43] An integral part of the scapular devotion was, and is, the wearing of the brown scapular. This small garment, made of two pieces of brown woven wool, joined by string, is blessed by a priest, and worn over the shoulders. It is an attenuated version of the large cloth scapular (Latin: *scapula*, 'shoulder') of the Carmelite habit, and it is worn by the laity who wish to be associated with the Carmelite Order as members of the scapular confraternity.[44] This reduced version of the Carmelite scapular became very popular in Europe, and during his visitation in Spain and Portugal in 1566-1567, the prior general of the Carmelite Order, John Baptist Rossi, said that he distributed about two hundred thousand scapulars and letters of confraternity.[45]

It is probable that the Confraternity of the Brown Scapular was established in Dublin by 1728. By 1786, an Arch-Confraternity of Our Lady of Mount Carmel (Scapular Confraternity) was in existence, when monthly sodalities were introduced. The closing decades of the eighteenth century and the early nineteenth century were periods of great enthusiasm for the scapular devotion in Ireland, some of it undoubtedly linked to belief in the protective power of the scapular itself. [Ill. 4.2-7]

Writing in 1801 about different rebellions in Ireland, Richard Musgrave stated that bags of scapulars were sent to markets in counties Mayo and Sligo in the western part of Ireland (presumably from the Carmelite centres in Dublin) for purchase by the people. He also made a particular connection between the wearing of the brown scapular and the rising of the United Irishmen in the west of the country in 1798, in terms of a sense of mutual recognition and protection which it was believed to afford. In connection with a landing of the French force to lend assistance to the Irish, Musgrave wrote:

4.2-7 *The Brown Scapular of Our Lady of Mount Carmel.*
[London, Welcome Collection]

Another circumstance which contributed to promote the cause of rebellion in these counties, and to cement its votaries, by a bond still more binding than the oath of the united irishmen or defenders, was the propagation of the mysteries of the Carmelites among Roman catholicks. (…) This [i.e. the Scapular] soon became the signal by which those of the true faith were to know each other, and the rallying point for those devotees who carried on the crusade against the hereticks; and a shop was opened after the landing of the French, where all the sons of Erin, with their pikes in their hands, were supplied with scapulars at regulated prices. These were intended, not only to unite them more strongly against the common enemy, but to arm them with fresh courage, and protect them from danger in the hour of trial.[46]

The closing decades of the eighteenth century and the early decades of the nineteenth century were times of keen devotion to the

43 Smet, *The Carmelites*, II, 222-224.
44 Barry, *Carmel*, 6; Attwater, *The Catholic Encyclopaedic Dictionary*, 466; 476.
45 Smet, *The Carmelites*, II, 224.
46 Musgrave, *Memoirs of the Different Rebellions in Ireland*, II, 115, 117; O'Dwyer, *Mary*, 251; see also Costello, "Little's Diary of the French Landing in 1798", 64-67, 88-89, 122; cf. McCaffrey, *The White Friars*, 439-440.

brown scapular. In 1799 a treatise on the Confraternity of Our Lady of Mount Carmel, commonly called the Scapular, was published in Dublin.[47] Between 1808 and 1820 at least three books dealing with the scapular devotion where published in Ireland by the Carmelite Order, and around 1840 "a great wave of enthusiastic devotion to Our Lady through the brown scapular" is said to have manifested itself, and faculties "to bless scapulars were requested regularly by diocesan and regular priests".[48] The parish missions from the mid-nineteenth century contributed significantly to the spread of the devotion and the brown scapular was promoted by religious orders other than the Carmelites, such as the Redemptorists, who were empowered to bless it, in the course of mission work. Scapulars were available for purchase during the mission and they were blessed in abundance by the preachers towards the end of the event. By encouraging people to enrol in pious associations such as the Sodality of the Brown Scapular, the missioners sought to perpetuate the upsurge in piety among the laity evident during the mission.[49] A survey of his diocese by the Bishop of Kerry in 1890, carried out through his parish priests, shows how popular and widespread devotion to the brown scapular was in rural Ireland at the end of the nineteenth century.[50]

The continuing importance of the parish mission for the spread of brown scapular enrolment and devotion until well into the twentieth century is evident also from oral tradition. Also apparent from the oral tradition is a corpus of scapular prayers and poems in the Irish language. These were part of the private devotion of the people in Irish-speaking areas of the country and nourished a personal spirituality. A prayer in the Irish language entitled *Ortha an Scabaill*, the 'Scapular Prayer' was still known by young and old in county Donegal in the mid-twentieth century.[51] This prayer includes a clear statement of the scapular vision and promise. It explains the significance of the brown scapular devotion to the individual and contains an exhortation to lead a worthy life, pointing out that enrolment in the scapular is not a guarantee of the privilege of a happy death but that this depends on the devout wearing of the scapular in honour of the Blessed Virgin, fasting, bearing suffering in silence and with resignation, devoutly observing the five major feast days in honour of Our Lady, and having recourse to the Virgin Mary for guidance along the road of life towards the kingdom of glory. The prayer also emphasises Marian devotion, obedience to the clergy, and the reception of the sacrament of penance, and it was probably an important means of providing instruction for, and imposing discipline on the laity, in the often difficult circumstances of the Catholic Church in Ireland in the eighteenth and nineteenth centuries.

Side by side with this strict declaration of the scapular vision and promise, and the conditions under which the promise may be obtained, are oral anecdotes about the miraculous powers of the scapular. These anecdotes mirror those found in Carmelite literature, which in turn reflects European scapular tradition of the sixteenth and seventeenth centuries. They may also echo a perception of protectiveness inherent in the Irish-language designation for the brown scapular 'Brat Muire', 'Mary's Cloak'.[52] The miraculous protective power attributed to the scapular in Carmelite literature against the dangers of the sea was singularly adapted by the people living along the west coast of Ireland to the requirements of maritime communities, who sought protection through it from the perils of the sea while fishing in their light crafts. The confidence that people had that the scapular would protect them from drowning is evident in the following narrative from the western part of county Kerry:

> I often heard that anyone who would be enrolled in the scapular would not be drowned. There was a man in this village, Séamas Ó Curráin, Seán Joan's father. He was out on Carraig Dhubh in a currach … And the currach overturned on him, and

---

47 O'Dwyer, *Mary*, 248.
48 de Hindeberg, *Paidreacha na nDaoine*, 85; *Seventh Centenary Souvenir*, 35.
49 Donnelly, "The Marian Shrine of Knock", 63-64.
50 de Brún, "Kerry Diocese in 1890"; cf. Moriarty, *Allocutions to the Clergy and Pastorals*, 185.
51 Lysaght, "The Uses of Sacramentals", 206-207.
52 Pochin Mould, *The Irish Dominicans*, 87.

it was a long time before help could go to it. But he stayed on the top of the tide and he was saved. It was said that it was the blessed objects which he had around his neck that kept him afloat. He had an Agnus Dei, and a scapular, and other blessed medals around his neck.[53]

Also connected to enrolment in the brown scapular was the tradition of clothing a dying person in the brown habit which had a large cloth scapular, linked to the Carmelite habit.[54] In this way, the requirement to be clothed in the scapular at death in order to receive the Scapular Promise – protection from eternal fire – was considered to be fulfilled. A twentieth-century narrative emphasising the protective power of the habit with the scapular, tells of a man who was buried in a habit originally intended for his wife. The habit was too short and the lower part of his limbs was exposed. "After his death he appeared to his wife and friends and told them that he was saved and very happy, and that he had a very easy passage through Purgatory due to the habit which he wore, except for the lower part of his limbs which was unprotected by the habit, and consequently experienced some suffering." On the other hand, some elderly people were reluctant to be enrolled in the brown scapular, fearing that unless both husband and wife were enrolled they would not be together in the next life. Elderly men were also afraid to be dressed in the brown habit at death as they feared they might not be recognised by their deceased spouses or relatives on 'the other side'.[55]

Belief in the efficacy of the scapular in extinguishing fire – by throwing the blessed scapular on the conflagration – was also widespread in the nineteenth century, and this remained firmly established in the oral tradition in Ireland into the twentieth century.[56]

Devotion to the Sacred Heart of Jesus

The medieval European devotion to the humanity of Jesus under the symbol of the Sacred Heart was to be found in Cork in the late eighteenth century and in Dublin in the early nineteenth century.[57] On Passion Sunday 1873, the bishops of Ireland formally consecrated the country to the Sacred Heart of Jesus. Devotion to the Sacred Heart, which became very popular throughout the country, was promoted especially by the Vincentian Fathers who had set up a branch of the Confraternity of the Sacred Heart at the Church of St Peter in Phibsborough, Dublin. They also sought to set up branches of the Confraternity in places in which they gave missions.

The raising of the status of the Confraternity to that of an Arch-Confraternity by Pope Leo XIII imparted to it "all the indulgences enjoyed by the Archconfraternity of S. Maria della Pace in Rome" and gave "the Vincentians authority to affiliate those confraternities promoted by them in the exercise of their ministry, and to communicate to them the same indulgences".[58] There were male and female branches of the Confraternity. The personal emblem of membership in the Confraternity of the Sacred Heart was the Confraternity Medal, which members were obliged to wear at the monthly meeting and at the monthly Mass of the Confraternity. Women members wore the medal on a red ribbon around the neck and men wore it on a short ribbon which was attached to the coat lapel.[59] Devotion to the Sacred Heart involved frequent communion, especially on the First Friday of each month, and also attendance at a monthly 'Holy Hour' for meditation on Christ's suffering in the garden of Gethsemane. By the 1890s the devotion of the "Nine First Fridays" in honour of the Sacred Heart had become almost universal in Ireland. From a practical point of view, the Sacred Heart devotion promoted monthly confession and communion based in the church premises under the control of the clergy, among the laity.[60] In addition to

53 Lysaght, "The Uses of Sacramentals", 214.
54 Pochin Mould, *The Irish Dominicans*, 87-88.
55 Lysaght, "The Uses of Sacramentals", 211-212.
56 Concannon, *The Queen of Ireland*, 211-212; Lysaght, "The Uses of Sacramentals", 216.
57 McGrath, "The Tridentine Evolution of Modern Irish Catholicism", 518; Corish, *The Irish Catholic Experience*, 234.
58 C.M., "The Confraternity of the Sacred Heart", 232.
59 Ibid., 238.
60 Corish, *The Irish Catholic Experience*, 234.

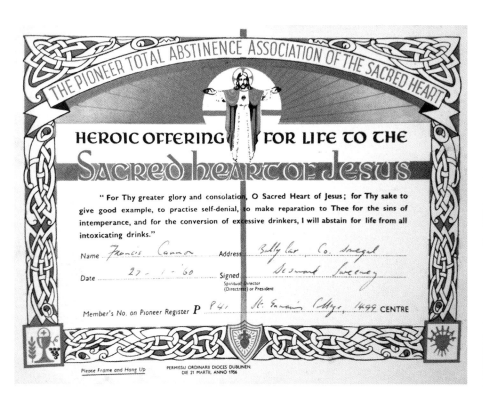
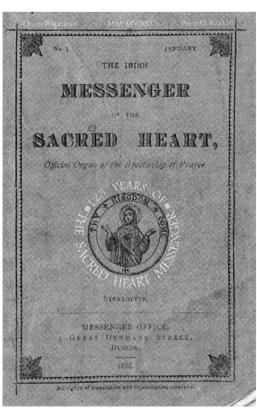

4.2-8 Certificate of membership of The Pioneer Total Abstinence Association of the Sacred Heart.
[Private collection]

4.2-9 First issue cover of The Irish Messenger of the Sacred Heart *(1888), 125th anniversary facsimile.*
[www.corjesusacratissimum.org]

61 Kinmonth, *Irish Rural Interiors in Art*, 184-145, Figs. 182-183; see also 69-70, Fig. 65; 163, Fig. 167.
62 Kinmonth, *Irish Country Furniture*, 192, Fig. 308; 194, Fig. 313.
63 Kinmonth, *Irish Rural Interiors in Art*, 70-71 and Fig. 66; Id., *Irish Country Furniture*, 193, Fig. 312.

the work of the Vincentians, devotion to the Sacred Heart was promoted by the League of the Sacred Heart which was also known as the Apostleship of Prayer, led by the Jesuits. This was done especially through the publication, the *Irish Messenger of the Sacred Heart*, founded in 1888 by Fr. James Cullen, S.J., director of the Apostleship of Prayer. [Ill. 4.2-9] *The Messenger* remains one of the most popular Catholic publications in Ireland today. The practice of consecrating families to the Sacred Heart was widespread in Ireland until about the second half of twentieth century. Prints of the Sacred Heart were to be found in Irish homes especially from the second half of the nineteenth century onwards. In a number of paintings by nineteenth- and early-twentieth-century artists a picture of the Sacred heart in the home is depicted. One such work by Aloysius O'Kelly, entitled 'Mass in a Connemara Cabin' (1883), shows a Sacred Heart print attached to a kitchen wall. In an early-twentieth-century depiction of the kitchen of a prosperous farmhouse, a large framed

print of the Sacred Heart flanked by a pair of candles in brass candlesticks, is to be seen.[61] Later, a type of Sacred Heart shrine consisting of the framed Sacred Heart picture with a small, oil-burning, red-globed votive or 'Sacred Heart Lamp' placed on a pedestal before it, became a common and much-loved feature in Irish Catholic homes.[62] In the twentieth century, as rural electrification became available, the oil lamp with its red globe was superseded by a small electric light bulb with a cross shape inside, and this, together with the Sacred Heart picture, remains a feature of many Irish homes to the present day.[63]

When saying the rosary it was customary for the family to kneel facing the Sacred Heart picture and lamp. In the twentieth century, a small metal Sacred Heart shield was attached externally to the entrance door of the house as a form of protection for the family, and a cardboard version, including the promise: "I will bless the homes in which the image of my heart shall be exposed and honoured", to be attached internally to the reverse of the door, is still available. In cemeteries, too, the influence of devotion to the Sacred Heart became and remains very much in evidence. An image of the Sacred Heart (with a wound on the right-hand side, surrounded by the crown of thorns and surmounted by flames) became very popular in funerary monuments, particularly in Celtic Cross-style gravestones, from the late nineteenth century onwards. A Sacred Heart picture, together with medals, including such as the miraculous medal, were often attached to children's cribs to protect them from supernatural beings.

Gospel / Leabhar Eoin / *St John's Gospel*

Reference to the wearing of a gospel for protective and curative purposes is to be found as early as the late eleventh century in Ireland. According to a text dated on linguistic grounds to that period, a scholar about to set out on a long journey had *soscéla* 'gospels' placed around his neck by his monastic tutor, presumably to afford him protection on his travels.[64] There are frequent references to the wearing of a 'gospel' in nineteenth-century Ireland. One writer described it as "… a text of Scripture written in a particular manner, and which has been blessed by a priest. It is sewed in red cloth and hung about the neck as a cure or preventive against various diseases, etc. Few Irish peasants will be found without a 'gospel'".[65] That the 'text of scripture' was in fact John I: vs. 1-14 is widely attested in the oral accounts. In Irish-speaking areas it was thus known as *Leabhar Eoin* (St John's Gospel). Its efficaciousness against sickness and as a form of protection against supernatural beings are also emphasised. The Gospel was widely known throughout the country and commonly worn, and there is frequent reference to it especially in the western parts of Ireland, in the nineteenth and early twentieth centuries. The following account from county Kerry is indicative of this:

> Should a young man or a young woman or a child become ill someone would go to the priest to fetch the *Leabhar Eoin*. This involved the priest writing Verses 1-14, Chapter 1 of the Gospel according to St. John in Latin (i.e. '*In principio erat verbum*', etc.) on a piece of paper. Any scrap of paper would do. The paper would be placed in a small cloth purse and put around the neck of the sick person. It is said that the *Leabhar Eoin* is possessed of great power and cured many a person.[66]

The Gospel or *Leabhar Eoin*, if sewn into a child's clothing, was considered to provide protection from abduction by supernatural beings and also from the effects of the 'evil eye'.[67] In view of the trust and confidence which people placed in the Gospel as a means of healing and protection, great care had to be exercised by the priest when writing out the text in Latin, because if he made a mistake while doing so, the person for whom it was being written was thought to be in grave danger of death or of some other serious misfortune. Its correctness could be tested by throwing it in the fire since traditional belief held that a correctly-written Gospel was impervious to fire.[68]

Recourse to the *Leabhar Eoin* in the case of sickness – even by those who had emigrated to the Unites States of America, who would ask their family at home to get a Gospel from the priest for them – still remained part of popular practice until well into the twentieth century, and it is clear that at least some priests were still willing to provide it at that period.[69] A donation was given to the priest for the Gospel; in fact people felt that it would not be efficacious otherwise.

Conclusion

The nineteenth century is generally recognised as the century during which the Tridentine pattern of Catholic religious practice became established in Ireland. That it had taken so long for this pattern to be established is explained against the background of developing political, religious and

[64] Meyer, *Aislinge Meic Conglinne*, 10, 135.
[65] Croker, *Fairy Legends and Traditions of the South of Ireland*, 163.
[66] Tyers, *Malairt Beatha*, 63-64; translated from Irish. Cf. Ó Crualaoich, "An Leabhair Eoin".
[67] Lysaght, "The Uses of Sacramentals", 200.
[68] An Seabhac, "Sidhe agus Púcaí", 324, 329; see also the narrative from Kerry: Tyers, *Malairt Beatha*, 65-66.
[69] Tyers, *Malairt Beatha*, 65-66.

demographic situations in Ireland from the sixteenth century to the nineteenth. Full Catholic Emancipation was achieved in the early nineteenth century (1829) but the state church was not disestablished until 1871. The previous centuries of turmoil adversely affected the ability of the Catholic Church to undergo the reform and renewal necessary to organise itself successfully along Tridentine lines. Unprecedented population growth from the 1790s to the 1840s, which saw almost a doubling of the population, especially among those at subsistence level, substantially aggravated this predicament. But faced with the threat to Catholicism from evangelical groups of the Church of Ireland and the Church of England, from 1820-1860, especially among the impoverished rural population, the Catholic Church establishment sought, through the promotion of various societies and the national school system, to make catechesis and Catholic literature more widely available to the laity. Thus, this 'Second Reformation' stimulated the Catholic Church establishment towards internal reform and renewal along Tridentine lines, something which was accelerated by the disaster of the Great Famine (1845-1850) as this resulted in a population decease of about two millions, thus essentially relieving pressure on church infrastructure and the clergy.

The demographic and social change effected by the Famine and the economic improvement which materialised in the second half of the nineteenth century, gave rise to a newly-prosperous middle-class laity, more financially secure and conventional in outlook, and better able to support a more orthodox and conservative church establishment. The parish missions from mid-century, the establishment of sodalities, confraternities and other communal devotions centred on the church, meant that by the end of the nineteenth century the Tridentine form of Catholicism had finally become predominant in Ireland.

Sources provide evidence that religious material culture was in short supply among the laity in general before the early decades of the nineteenth century; likewise, the very poor condition of the religious material culture of some churches, or even the lack of items such as baptismal fonts, is also indicated.

The increased prosperity of the merchant and farming classes after the mid-nineteenth century Great Famine enabled them to provide strong financial support for the Catholic Church. This was reflected in an increase in new church buildings and refurbishment, and in the availability of a range of religious objects along continental lines for both public worship and private devotion, as advertised in various issues of *The Irish Catholic Directory*, in the second half of the nineteenth century. The ability to purchase expensive devotional aids such as silver rosary beads and medals, pearl crosses for distribution in schools, and green enamelled shamrocks, all point, not only to increased prosperity among this section of society, but also to a continuing desire for, and the use of religious material culture in a personal and private capacity.

Reform societies, such as the Total Abstinence Societies had an associated material culture of badges to be worn in public, as did the many confraternities and sodalities that were formed throughout the country especially in the second half of the nineteenth century. The brown scapular devotion was, in addition to the rosary, one of the most widespread Marian devotion in Ireland. At the end of the nineteenth century, the Sacred Heart devotion had become widespread in Ireland with an associated material culture including a type of Sacred Heart shrine in a prominent position in the home.

BIBLIOGRAPHY

An Seabhac. "Sidhe agus Púcaí". *Béaloideas*, 3 (1932), 324, 329.

Attwater, Donald, ed. *The Catholic Encyclopaedic Dictionary*. London, 1931.

Barry, Gabriel. *Carmel*. May-June, 1998.

Carrigan, William. *The History and Antiquities of the Diocese of Ossory*. 4 vols. Dublin, 1905.

C. M. "The Confraternity of the Sacred Heart". *The Irish Ecclesiastical Record*, 56 (1940), 232-243.

Concannon, Mrs. Thomas. *The Queen of Ireland: An Historical Account of Ireland's Devotion to the Blessed Virgin*. Dublin, 1938.

Connolly, Sean J. *Priests and People in Pre-Famine Ireland 1780-1845*. Dublin, 1982.

Connolly, Sean. *Religion and Society in Nineteenth-Century Ireland*. Dundalk, 1987.

Corish, Patrick J. *The Irish Catholic Experience: A Historical Survey*. Dublin, 1986.

Costello, Nuala, ed. "Little's Diary of the French Landing in 1798". *Analecta Hibernica*, 11 (July 1941), 57-168.

Croker, T. Crofton. *Fairy Legends and Traditions of the South of Ireland*. Part 2. London, 1828.

de Brún, Pádraig. "Irish Society Bible Teachers, (1818-1827)". *Éigse. A Journal of Irish Studies*, 19 (1983), 281-322; 20 (1984), 34-92; 21 (1986), 72-149; 22 (1987), 54-106; 23 (1989), 80-82 (Bíoblóir Á Chosaint Féin); 24 (1990), 70-120; 25 (1991), 113-149; 26 (1992), 131-172.

de Brún, Pádraig. "Kerry Diocese in 1890: Bishop Coffey's Survey". *Journal of the Kerry Archaeological and Historical Society*, 22 (1989), 99-180.

de Brún, Pádraig. *Scriptural Instruction in the Vernacular. The Irish Society and its Teachers 1818-1827*. Dublin, 2009.

de Hindeberg, Piaras. *Paidreacha na nDaoine (Traditional Prayers)*. PhD thesis, National University of Ireland. Dublin, 1942.

Donlevy, Andrew. *An Teagasg Críosduidhe, Do réir Ceasda agus Freagartha. The Catechism, or, Christian Doctrine, By Way of Question and Answer*. Dublin, 1848. 3rd edition.

Donnelly, J.S. Jn. "The Marian Shrine of Knock: The First Decade". *Éire-Ireland*, 28 (Samhradh-Summer 1993) 2 [St. Paul, Minnesota, USA]), 54-99.

Ferriter, Diarmaid. *A Nation of Extremes. The Pioneers in Twentieth Century Ireland*. Dublin, 1998.

Ford, Alan. *The Protestant Reformation in Ireland, 1590-1641*. Dublin, 1997.

Fuller, Louise. *Irish Catholicism since 1950: The Undoing of a Culture*. Dublin, 2002.

Hall, Mr. and Mrs. S.C. *Ireland: Its Scenery, Character, &c*. 3 vols. London, 1841-1943.

Hayes-McCoy, G.A. "The Tudor Conquest (1534-1603)". In: T.W. Moody and F.X. Martin, eds. *The Course of Irish History*. Cork-Dublin, 1994 (revised edition of 1967), 174-188.

Irish Catholic Directory, The. Dublin, 1839, 1873.

Kinmonth, Claudia. *Irish Country Furniture 1700-1950*. New Haven, 1993.

Kinmonth, Claudia. *Irish Rural Interiors in Art*. New Haven, 2006.

Kohl, Johann George. *Travels in Ireland*. London, 1844.

Lysaght, Patricia. "The Uses of Sacramentals in Nineteenth- and Twentieth-Century Ireland. With Special Reference to the Brown Scapular". In: Nils-Arvid Bringéus, ed. *Religion in Everyday Life*. Stockholm, 1994, 187-222.

Lysaght, Patricia. "Attitudes to the Rosary and its Performance in Donegal in the Nineteenth and Twentieth Centuries". *Béaloideas*, 66 (1998), 9-58.

MacMahon, Bryan. *Faith and Fury. The Evangelical Campaign in Dingle and West Kerry 1825-1845*. Dublin, 2021.

McCaffrey, R. *The White Friars*. Dublin, 1926.

McDowell, R.B. "The Protestant Nation (1775-1800)". In: T.W. Moody and F.X. Martin, eds. *The Course of Irish History*. Cork-Dublin, 1994 (revised edition of 1967), 232-247.

McGrath, Thomas G. "The Tridentine Evolution of Modern Irish Catholicism, 1563-1962: A Re-examination of the 'devotional revolution' thesis". *Recusant History*, 20 (1991), 512-523.

McGuire, Edward A. "Old Irish Rosaries". *The Furrow*, 1954, 97-105.

Meyer, Kuno. *Aislinge Meic Conglinne: The Vision of MacConglinne*. London, 1892.

Moody, T.W. "Fenianism, Home Rule, and the Land War (1850-91)". In: T.W. Moody and F.X. Martin, eds. *The Course of Irish History*. Cork-Dublin, 1994 (revised edition of 1967), 275-293.

Moody, T.W., and F.X. Martin, eds. *The Course of Irish History*. Cork-Dublin, 1994 (revised edition of 1967).

Moriarty, Right Rev. Dr. *Allocutions to the Clergy and Pastorals*. Dublin, 1884.

Musgrave, Richard. *Memoirs of the Different Rebellions in Ireland*. Vol. 2. Dublin, 1802.

Ó Crualaoich, Gearóid. "*An Leabher Eoin*: The *In Principio* Charm in Oral and Literary Tradition". In: Iloma Tuomi, John Carey, Barbara Hillers, Ciarán Ó Gealbháin, eds. Cardiff, 2019, 177-187.

O'Donovan, Patrick F. *Stanley's Letter. The National School System and Inspectors in Ireland 1831–1922*. Galway, 2017.

O'Dwyer, Peter. *Mary: A History of Devotion in Ireland*. Dublin, 1988.

Ó Fiaich, Tomás. "The Language and Political History". In: Brian Ó Cuív, ed. *A View of the Irish Language*. Dublin, 1969, 101-111.

Ó Fiannachta, Pádraig. "Seanmóireacht Ghaeilge san Ochtú agus sa Naoú hAois Déag" (Irish-language Preaching in the Eighteenth and Nineteenth Centuries). *Irishleabhar Mhá Nuad*, 1983, 141-149.

Ó Súilleabháin, An tAth. Pádraig. "Catholic Sermon Books Printed in Ireland, 1700-1850". *The Irish Ecclesiastical Record*, 99 (January-June 1963), 31-36.

Ó Súilleabháin, An tAth. Pádraig. "Catholic Books Printed in Ireland 1740-1820 containing lists of Subscribers". *Collectanea Hibernica*, 6-7 (1963-1964), 231-233.

Pochin Mould, Daphne D.C. *The Irish Dominicans*. Dublin, 1957.

Seventh Centenary Souvenir 1271-1971. Dublin, n.d.

Smet, Joachim. *The Carmelites: A History of the Brothers of Our Lady of Mount Carmel. 2: The Post Tridentine Period 1550-1600*. Darien, Ill., 1976.

Tyers, Pádraig. *Malairt Beatha*. Dún Chaoin, 1992.

Wall, Maureen. "The Age of the Penal Laws (1691-1778)". In: T. W. Moody and F.X. Martin, eds. *The Course of Irish History*. Cork-Dublin, 1994 (revised edition of 1967), 217-231.

Whyte, J.H. "The Age of Daniel O'Connell (1800-47)". In: T.W. Moody and F.X. Martin, eds. *The Course of Irish History*. Cork-Dublin, 1994 (revised edition of 1967), 248-262.

4.3
The Material Expression of Everyday Religion in Belgium

Tine Van Osselaer

Influenced by the changing relations between Church and society on a national as well as an international Roman Catholic scale, everyday religion found its material expression at different levels of the Catholic community. In order to grasp the changes of the period 1780-1920, this article focuses on three of these levels. The first paragraph diachronically summarises the evolution of Belgian Catholicism by focusing on the level of the Christian community and indicating innovations in its material culture. The chronology sketched in this first part is referred to in the next sections that zoom in on the Christian family, the Catholic individual and on the ways in which the material innovations influenced their religious practices.

A Christian community

Criticism and creativity (1780-1830)

In the first period, ranging from 1780-1830, religious reforms were instigated by the subsequent governments that ruled over the Southern Netherlands. The Josephistic reforms, introduced in the last years under Austrian rule (1780-1795), fit the ideas on Enlightened Christianity and strongly opposed the 'excesses' of popular Catholicism. Restrictions were imposed on everyday religion (for example the number of feasts) and its material expressions (it was no longer allowed to carry images during processions).[1] During the subsequent French rule (1795-1815), with its 'cult of reason', religion was regarded as superstitious and atavistic, and eventually confined to the private sphere.

The symbolic weight of the material expressions of religion was deemed considerable. In the 1790s, for instance, crucifixes, Marian statues and the like were removed from the public spheres.[2] Still, this stripping of the public spheres represented only one side of the events: within the more private spheres of the home these years proved to be a time of creativity. While the churches were now forbidden territory for the clergy, the faithful opened up their houses for illegitimate masses and developed new means to support their pastors. The 'altars' produced in this period form eloquent illustrations of how religion re-emerged or, rather, survived via people's creativity and will to remain faithful to their religion. The boundary between sacred and profane objects became literarily blurred. A bridal suitcase, for instance, could be loaded with religious meaning when it was turned into an altar during illegitimate masses. Likewise, special closets with built-in altars were invented, as were portable altars that could be turned into a bread-box or book.[3] Norbertus Heylen, a Norbertine Father and pastor of Grimbergen, for example, documented these practices when he wrote down his experience of the French occupation: "(…) On the 17th of September 1797, we went to read mass in the parsonage, and read it on the commode above, in the first room against the stairs of the left side."[4] In the United Kingdom of the Netherlands (1815-1830), the public expression of piety was restricted as well even though King William I granted freedom of religion.

4.3-1 Children playing mass, Turnhout, 1905.
[Private collection]

1. Roegiers, "Routine, reorganisatie en revolutie", 265.
2. Tihon, "De restauratie", 9-10.
3. E.g. in the museum of Overmere. Penne, *Overmere*, 10-12.
4. "(…) Den 17. Sept. 1797 hebben wij gaen mis lessen in de Pastorij, en leesden die op 1 Commode boven in de eerste kaemer tegen den trap van den slinken kant." Borremans, Borremans and Boschmans, *Kroniek van Norbertus Heulen*, 131.

5   Majerus, "Plus près de vous mon Dieu …", 253.
6   Viaene, "De ontplooiing van de 'vrije' kerk", 54. This power of the written word becomes also apparent in the textual messages applied to pillows or cloth roles. Pirotte, "L'univers des objets", 143; Morgan, *Religious Visual Culture*, 66-68.
7   Scaillet, "La religion populaire", 114; Dirkse, "Hier woonden katholieken", 47.
8   "C'est le triomphe de la confiture!'" Léon Gautier in 1876 (French Catholic) cited in Pirotte, "L'univers des objets", 150. Id., "L'image et le sacré", 75.
9   Viaene, "De ontplooiing van de 'vrije' kerk", 82.
10 De Maeyer, "Léon XIII", 304-305; Viaene, "De ontplooiing van de 'vrije' kerk", 94-96; Id., *Belgium and the Holy See*, 146.
11 Grand-Carteret, *Contre Rome*, 37.

4.3-2 Poster 'God sees me. No swearing here'.
[Leuven, KADOC-KU Leuven]

New materials, new means and on a new scale (1830-1880)

The years after the declaration of Belgium's independency (1830) compensated for the decades of restriction. Using the increased legal room to manoeuvre, the Catholic Church wanted to make up for the losses of the previous years and in the next decades they build chapels and churches, reorganised ecclesiastical structures and created new parishes. Aiming at a popular ground for religion in a secularised society, the clergy embraced popular religion and 'clericalized' it. This demonstrative popular religion was to express the Church's popular resonance and the religious revitalisation.

The clergy tried to win people for religion via, for example, *volksmissies* (popular missions) that were organised all over the country. The missionaries tried to bring the various parishes back to more pious ways, and they took care to stage this collective atonement of the Christian community and, most importantly, to create a physical reminder. So-called missionary crosses were erected during impressive public ceremonies. As such, the temporary gatherings of repentance were supplemented by more long-lasting symbolic representations and commemorations of these new intentions (renewal of baptismal vows, dedication to Mary).[5] What is more, in the aftermath of the missions, numerous Catholics took home a poster stating: "Here is no cursing allowed" indicating that their intentions ideally also had an effect in the more private sphere of their homes. These posters are, as Vincent Viaene has indicated, an eloquent example of the oral quality and magical power of the printed word.[6] [Ill. 4.3-2]

The clergy, increasingly interested in keeping or (bringing) all the faithful in the Catholic fold, stimulated a Catholic group culture, promoted a Catholic lifestyle and mobilised their flock for mass devotions. In this latter aspect, they could benefit from the new production processes that developed around the middle of the nineteenth century. These enabled a mass-production of devotional objects and thus also their mass-consumption. Production centres developed within Belgium (e.g. Maison Gérard in Namur, Maison Haenecour in Anderlecht and Vermeeren-Coché in Brussels[7]), but a high number of the devotional objects was imported from other countries as well. This transnational circulation of various statues, cards and so on stimulated also a certain uniformity in style. Most often it has been referred to as the so-called Saint-Sulpice style since one of its most famous production (and distribution) centres lay in this Parisian quarter. However, the style was unanimously applauded to and incited vehement critiques among some Belgian Catholics, for instance at the Catholic Congresses of Mechelen (1860s). Its adversaries criticised it as sentimental, inauthentic and of mediocre quality. One commentator even called it the "triumph of marmalade" (1876).[8] What is more, even though there was a certain uniformity in style, diversity still reigned over the devotional prints of the time, for instance in their presentation of Jesus or Mary. The new 'national' (romanticising the nation's past) neo-Gothic style also gained importance.[9] While it benefitted from the ('modern') mass-production processes, the style idealised the piety of the Middle Ages.

The large-scale potential of the mass-production processes also supported new emphases in Catholic culture. They played an important role in the promotion of certain devotions (such as the cult of the Sacred Heart and of Our Lady of Lourdes) and contributed to the staging of the pope. The latter fit in with the institutional centralisation of Rome and the papal devotion that developed within the internationally oriented 'Romanised' devotional culture. Rome embraced new techniques and apart from devotional cards in a neo-medieval style, images with a photo and the signature of the pope circulated world-wide. These and other means, as for example, St Peter's pence (a financial contribution created in 1860) supported the pope's increasing heroisation and enabled the faithful to feel personally involved with his cause.[10] Still, this materialisation of the pope's cause also triggered severe protest and numerous Belgian anti-clerical, anti-papist cartoons document the criticism and mockery that the St Peter's pence caused.[11] [Ill. 4.3-3]

Although clergy eagerly engaged in the distribution of these low-cost devotional objects, one of the most important innovations in the late nineteenth century was the creation of shops specialised in devotional objects (replacing the older 'colporteurs'). Advertising their products in the newly created religious periodicals, they could reach a wide audience. Accordingly, some scholars have indicated that the most shocking in the distribution of the Saint Sulpice style was the high amount of objects sold in that same Parisian corner.[12] In this 'commodification' of religion (as Arie Molendijk has called it) the churches lost their monopoly on religion as various organisations and commercial undertakers took charge of the market and tried to listen to the demands of the consumers.[13]

New techniques and materials were used, lowering the costs of the traditional gamma of religious articles but also enabling new symbioses. Among the most telling examples of the time are the small-scale replicas of the Massabielle grotto that floated Catholic landscapes from the second half of the nineteenth century onwards. These material reminiscences of Mary's visit to Bernadette in Lourdes (1858) benefitted from the popularity of romanticist grotto-formations in the landscape architecture of the time. At

4.3-3 Cartoon critisizing St Peter's pence, c 1875.
[Brussels, Royal Library, Graphic collection: S II 144524]

12 Rooijakkers, "De dynamiek van de devotionalia", 97; Pirotte, "L'univers des objets", 141.
13 Molendijk, "Inleiding", 9.

4.3-4 Postcard of Belgian Lourdes pilgrimage holding mass in train. [Collection Tine Van Osselaer]

Modern means and militantism (1880-1920)

This unifying quality also showed in the mass manifestations that were organised since the late nineteenth century. In the midst of the so-called 'culture wars', most often identified as a battle between Liberals and Catholics, it became important to show the mobilisation potential of (Belgian) Catholicism. With a 'turn to the people', the Catholic elite and the Church tried to face the social tensions triggered by an increasing industrialisation and urbanisation, and to counter the lures of Socialism. The devotional accents in this search for popular support lay on the Eucharist, the Sacred Heart and Mary. For the coronations of statues of the Virgin Mary, for instance, thousands of people were summoned via diverse media such as pastoral letters and tracts as well as posters and press. As Jan De Maeyer has noted, the public part of this ceremony (often a collaboration between local authorities and the clergy), and more particularly the historical part of the parade, aimed at legitimising the event by pointing at the historical importance of the religious site. At the same time however, the parade also served to encourage the spectators to let go of their prejudices and thus functioned as a religious socialisation.[14] The mass manifestations often left not only a lasting impression, but also a physical reminder. The Sacred Heart ceremonies – organised at the level of the parish or town – for instance, focused on the installation of a Sacred Heart statue or its crown.[15] As the missionary crosses before them, these images thus continued to remind the communities of the promises made on these occasions. Moreover, as these were often festivities in which the whole community was involved, the celebration was not limited to the communal terrains. On these occasions, Catholic families took care to decorate the 'public' side of their homes, that is the façade, festively with flowers, slogans and their own statue of the Sacred Heart. The presence of the later indicated that they, as a Christian

first, they were erected primarily in cloister and church gardens and on churchyards. After a while, however, the faithful started to construct them in their own backyards. This was, for example the case in Oostakker, where the replica Lourdes-grotto developed into an important religious site after the miraculous cure of Pieter De Rudder in 1875. These constructions, made from concrete and rock formations, exemplify how industrial materials were easily integrated in the production of religious objects. Furthermore, similar to what we have seen in the first period, a religious meaning could be added to more 'profane' things, even to those that, according to some, symbolised 'modernity'. One of the most significant examples are the pilgrimage trains that were constructed in such a way that they were fit to hold a mass in. Enabling the faithful to travel quickly and comfortably to (national or international) pilgrimage sites, these trains thus offered the ambulant faithful a site for worship and moments of gathering together also across national borders. [Ill. 4.3-4]

14 De Maeyer, "Les couronnements en Belgique".
15 Mayeur, Bouchez and De Paepe, *OnGELOOFlijk!*, 52-53.

family had accepted Christ's rule as king over their family, nation and society as a whole. 'Public' and 'private' Catholic identity coincided, especially on the level of the family.

The Christian community stretched beyond national and European borders. Playing upon exoticism, sentimentalism and proselytising discourses, the missionary enterprise also had its effect on the material culture of Belgian Catholicism. As Jean Pirotte has indicated, missionary movements used numerous (modern) means to create an atmosphere that was favourable of the missions. There were missionary periodicals, calendars, almanacs, but also small money boxes in the shape of a little black boy that nodded its head whenever someone put a coin in. [Ill. 4.3-5] Apart from these images and means created for the promotion of the missions, the clergy also succeeded in mobilising Belgian Catholics to collect 'used' material for the missions.[16] Jean Pirotte and Claude Soetens refers to the so-called *Chiffoniers du Bon Dieu* (rag-and-bone men of the Good Lord) who were created in the seminar of Namur in 1888 and collected stamps and 'gilded paper' all over Belgium. He indicates that whereas selling and recycling this material most probably helped to fund missionary activities; the goal was primarily to raise the awareness of Belgian Catholics for the missions.[17] These initiatives form a perfect example of how 'everyday' used objects could gain a new meaning via actions of the laity (collecting) that were carried out in order to benefit a higher goal (the Catholic missions) and counted on modern processes (recycling).

The most vehement change in the political context and action radius of Belgian Catholicism at the start of the twentieth century was of course the Great War. During the years of warfare, the Catholic Church stimulated a syncretism between national and religious feelings. This blending was most explicitly phrased in Cardinal Mercier's letter, "Patriotism and Endurance", of Christmas 1914 in which he suggested building a basilica in honour of the Sacred Heart as a

4.3-5 St Anthony moneybox for the missions. The little black boy nods gratefully when coins are offered.
[Leuven, KADOC-KU Leuven: BE-942855-2471-20]

sign of gratitude (for the future victory). This devotion, and its nationalist undercurrent, materialised also in the amulets some of the Belgian soldiers wore on their uniform (as did soldiers from other countries): an image of the Sacred Heart against the background of the national flag.[18]

A Christian family

Up till now, focus has been on the Christian community, this consisted however of smaller unities: the Catholic families. Also on this level, the material expression of everyday religion was very diverse, subject to changes in the production processes, and depended on and contributing to new emphases in national and international Catholicism.

16 Pirotte, "L'image et le sacré", 73.
17 Pirotte and Soetens, "Les missions", 694.
18 *Gott mit uns*, 19; Van Osselaer, "Missing in Action?".

19 Nissen, "Zoals in het huisje van Nazareth …", 147; Margry, "Persoonlijke altaren", 54; Van Osselaer, "Introduction".
20 Van den Heuvel, "Volksdevotie en vroomheid", 462.
21 "Ce sont des objets à toucher, à fabriquer et à manipuler dans le culte domestique." Pirotte, "L'image et le sacré", 84.

4.3-6 Devotional objects at home, Ghent. Photo, 1929.
[Leuven, KADOC-KU Leuven: KFB1226]

New possibilities

Popular Christianity was influenced by and contributed to the domestic ideology that was on the rise since the nineteenth century. This idealisation of the Christian home and family was stimulated by the Belgian bishops and the Catholic elite primarily since the second half of the nineteenth century. They worried about the increasing urban masses and the little care these seemed to have for the Church's marital proscriptions. In their opinion, the Catholic family was the corner stone of a Christian – hence stable – society.

In the course of the nineteenth century, devotional objects increasingly entered Catholic homes, characterising their inhabitants as a Christian family. They were a visual reminder of Catholic ideology, testimonies of the rising importance of certain cults and remembrances of solemn occasions (and the promises they entailed). The religious revival of the nineteenth century and the sacralisation of the family were supported by the new possibilities in the industrial production of devotional objects. New procedures lowered the costs of these printed images and plaster statues and thus brought their possession within the reach of also the less prosperous families. Saints' images – made of wood, biscuit, porcelain but above all also plaster – entered the living rooms *en masse* during the nineteenth century.[19] Prominently present in the home decoration (a crucifix above the hearth for instance), they were ideally located in places where they were visible for all to see. Some of them were intended to protect the home and – as the palm branch taken home on Palm Sunday – bring God's blessing over the house. Others aimed at stimulating a family's religious routines. Holy-water fonts, for instance, invited those who passed by them to swiftly cross themselves while parents plunged in their fingers when blessing their children before they went to sleep.[20] [Ill. 4.3-6]

The images of Saints and other devotional objects were grouped together in the cultic centre of the home and flanked by candles. The quality of the images and the way they were presented (e.g. under a bell-glass) hinted at the social status of the family. [Col. ill. 14] Nonetheless, whether high-priced or cheap, they offered a physical hold and inspiration for a family's prayer. Gathering in front of these objects, a family could confirm during these rituals both its familial and religious identity. Moreover, as Pirotte has noted, religious statues and other objects were there to be "touched, fabricated and manipulated in the domestic cult". Some of the illustrations of the *livres d'heures,* for instance, were deliberately printed in black and white so that they could be coloured by the faithful.[21]

New objects

Likewise, Charles De Ribbe's *Livre de famille* or *Livre de Raison* incited family members to work together in filling out and colouring the book. Decorated in a neo-Gothic style, the book called for the involvement of all family members. These were, however, called to different tasks (in accordance with the gender ideology of the time). The *pater familias* ideally entered the requested information on the various pages whereas the female members of the family took care of the colouring of the illustrations.[22]

Apart from their religious, commemorative and decorative functions, the various objects were also part of a gift exchange among family members. Those going through Christian rites de passage such as the Holy Communion distributed cards commemorating the event. The cards were first introduced among the higher classes in the nineteenth century, in the twentieth century it turned into a custom also among the 'common' people.[23] As for the gift-exchange on these occasions: godfathers and godmothers often gave prayer books (e.g. missal) to their godchildren. Due to the lower production costs and the increasing level of education these books started to circulate in all levels of society during the nineteenth century.[24] Even though there was some rivalry from French companies, a high amount of the missals was published by specialised (lay) Belgian publishing houses such as Brepols, Spitaels and Casterman/Desclée. In the 1920s, however, abbeys entered the market (as Saint Andries in Bruges, Keizersberg in Leuven and Clervaux in Luxembourg) and started to create and publish new missals. The popular missals, produced within the context of the Liturgical Movement, enabled a more intense involvement of the parishioners in church.[25] [Ill. 4.3-7]

Family ties were supported also via the religious postcards family members sent to each other. These depicted guardian angels, children dressed as angels, Saint Nicolas/Père Noël in the presence of adults and children. The producers thereby used the new medium of photography in creative mixtures of photos and art, actors and painted sceneries. As William Christian has noted, they "encouraged the notion of absence combined with fondness" and were particularly popular in the period 1895 to the end of World War I. During the world war (the 'great post card war') the composite images changed to a more military setting but these were again combinations of living people, often soldiers, in the presence of photo-shopped or drawn supernatural beings (angels, Jeanne d'Arc, the Virgin Mary). Other cards connected "the loved ones at home to the loved ones at the front" and showed civilians praying for their soldiers whose picture is put in the upper sections of the cards.[26] The postcards were a materialisation of the love and care people had for each other and the role they assigned to supernatural beings in this relationship (guardians and stimulators of Christian feelings).

Annual religious feasts that were celebrated on the family level also stimulated family cohesion. The home decorations on these occasions were also subject to change and not devoid of transnational influence. Christmas trees, for instance, were an effect of German influence.[27] Numerous food items spiced up Catholic feasts and gathered families around the dinner table. Certain religious feasts were explicitly associated with particular food (e.g. Easter eggs, Saint Nicholas' spiced biscuits in the form of this Saint ...) or at least became so under influence of the increasing advertisement in the rising mass media. (Some food articles, such as bread of Saint Hubert gained a special meaning through benediction. They were consumed at home however. The bread of Saint Hubert was shared also with the family dog since, allegedly, this would preserve him from rage). These family feasts could even take on a rather playful character. The feast of Epiphany, for instance, included the distribution of cards that indicated the role one had to play at diner.[28] However, Catholic dietary habits included not only times of affluence but also periods of restriction. Referring to Jesus' forty days of fasting, Catholic teaching called for a special diet in the month before Easter when all meat was forbidden.

Some things were donated in a family setting, on the occasion of religious feasts, but were in fact intended at stimulating the religiosity of the individual Catholic. This was the case with religious toys as these were intended to socialise children as good Catholics (according to the respective gender

4.3-7 Title page of the 1927 edition of the first Dutch popular missal, published by the Benedictine abbey of Affligem. [Leuven, KADOC-KU Leuven: KZ22-6/ [1927]]

22 De Maeyer, "Des vierges et des manuscrits", 68.
23 Likewise, obituary cards circulated when a person died. Already in the early nineteenth century, this was habit among all layers of the population. Pirotte, "Devotieprentjes", 179-181.
24 Scaillet, "La religion populaire", 153. Replacing the 'petits livres d'heures' of old. Pirotte, "Le paysage catholique", 41.
25 Muraille-Samaran, "Recueils de prières", 150.
26 Christian, *Divine Presence*, 132, 162-164.
27 Vincent, "Le cycle des 12 jours", 41. There were references to Christmas trees in Belgian newspapers at least since the 1870s.
28 Pirotte, "L'Univers des objets", 145-146. Today one still looks for the bean in the dough that crowns one of the participants as king.

4.3-8. *Toys, including a doll dressed in religious garments, of a seven-year-old girl. Photo, c 1890.*
[Leuven, KADOC-KU Leuven: KFA 14108]

Individual Catholics

'Democratisation' and 'individualisation'

Catholic piety also found its material expressions at the level of the individual Catholics. Wearing a cross or specific garments, touching a rosary while praying, looking at devotional images: Catholic practices implied the use of all of the senses. In addition, some of these objects were also intended to support the memory of the faithful. The design of the rosaries, for instance, made them an ideal counting devise during prayer and helped the faithful to concentrate. Likewise, devotional leaflets reminded the faithful of certain prayers and of their membership of confraternities.[31] Furthermore, keeping these objects close-by could trigger certain feelings. For example, wearing small objects (e.g. an *Agnus-Dei* made of wax) as amulets, could make the carrier feel protected. This was also the case for the scapulars that were worn beneath one's clothes. The latter slowly changed form in the period that is under discussion here: whereas they used to be made of pieces of woollen cloth, in the nineteenth century it increasingly took the shape of a medal. (Moreover, their use became more widespread since one of its main limitations was deleted in the nineteenth century. In 1838 the decree that one had to be inscribed in a confraternity before one was allowed to wear a scapular was no longer valid).[32] Some of the amulets were worn in certain phases of one's life. Pregnant women, for instance, wore so-called cords of Our Lady of Deliverance in order to ensure a safe delivery or made sure that a Life of Margaret touched their belly. As noted above, soldiers wore amulets (e.g. of the Sacred Heart) during the Great War. Other small objects, such as crosses made of materials that were said to have a healing potential, were used as a remedy rather than a protection.[33] As Robert Orsi has noted, the Catholic faithful experience Divine presence in "matter, in things – first of all in the consecrated Host", but also in relics, in statues, images and so on.[34]

norms). [Ill. 4.3-8] The reason I discuss these toys here and not under the paragraph 'individual Catholics', is that playing often meant playing together. This was for example the case with the miniature mass-sets given to boys. These could contain small replica missals, chandeliers, chalices that were then used on altars constructed by handy fathers. The would-be priests were dressed in priestly garbs bought from toy producers, but more often sown by their mothers. [Ill. 4.3-1] The altars were, just like the dolls dressed in religious garments (replica-nuns) that were given to girls, nothing new in the nineteenth century. Their appearance could change however (e.g. the size of the altar and material[29]) and new inventions were included. A late nineteenth-century version of the 'magic lantern' could, for instance, contain an electric lamp which optimised the projection of the images. The basic line remained the same however, even if the material changed: via these image projectors, children could learn Biblical stories at an early age.[30]

29 Post, "Een mooi spelletje", 168.
30 Hermans and Morelli, *Speelgoed waarin je kan geloven*, 11, 21-22.
31 Scaillet, "La religion populaire", 153.
32 Spaans, "De democratisering", 36-39.
33 Pirotte, "L'Univers des objets", 142-143.
34 Orsi, "Belief", 13.

Turning the Divine into something tangible, relics (body parts of the saint or cloths that had touched his or her body) or objects that had touched these relics, were object of affection and often loaded with miraculous powers.

Joke Spaans has called this wearing of devotional objects on the body, a "body technique". It is learned behaviour, derives its meaning from the surrounding culture, it communicates and at the same time makes certain values its own (e.g. wearing a cross made someone visible as a Catholic). She emphasis that the amount of the devotional objects, worn on the body, had been rather limited and regulated before the nineteenth century. However, their distribution took a turn in the nineteenth century as scapulars and the like were increasingly propagated among all layers of society. Joke Spaans has called this evolution, the "democratisation" of the religious accessories.[35] As far as their diffusion was concerned, these objects profited from the possibilities that the mass-production of the nineteenth century entailed. As Pascal Majerus has suggested, their massification allowed not only the familiarisation but also the individualisation of religion.[36] As the production costs dropped, more individual Catholics could afford to buy religious articles. Mass production enabled mass-distribution not only of the religious accessories, but also of images, statues and so on. The Catholic faithful – if they desired so – could adorn their daily lives with religious things. Both 'in public' (in their attire or in rooms that could be entered by visitors) and, more privately, at their bedsides (e.g. in support of their evening prayers). These objects – ideally – were the material marks of a piety that did not limit itself to ritualistic performance of communal Catholic practices, but influenced the whole life of the faithful and touched their hearts.

Older traditions, new forms

Apart from the specific 'handling' of particular objects (manipulation of the Divine), one's Catholic identity could also show from the mere appearance of the faithful. The external features of a person had, long before the nineteenth century, the potential to suggest the religious convictions of the individual in question. (One of the reasons why these were forbidden at the end of the eighteenth century).[37] Small references such as a crucifix, scapular or medal, worn above or below one's clothes, made someone recognisable as a Catholic. Likewise, wearing black while in mourning; or one's Sunday best during Mass, indicates how much Catholic piety was not only a matter of right behaviour or beliefs, but also implied certain dress codes. While men were expected to attend the mass bareheaded, women were supposed to wear a veil or hat. Both dressed in their best clothes ('Sunday best') however, when going to church. What this entailed seems to have been up for some discussion. Considering the number of warnings promulgated by the bishops and popes (e.g. Pius VII and Leo XII), this was not always self-evident, especially among the female parishioners. On the 11th of January 1914 the Belgian bishops condemned indecent clothes in a communal pastoral letter. Half a year later, on the 19th of June 1914, Cardinal Mercier posted up in churches that women had to wear high-necked dresses and long sleeves if they wanted to receive communion. Apart from a too immodest dress, barely covering up their bodies, women could also dress improper by wearing too luxurious and impractical clothes. The clergy believed this to be the case when fashion dictated a kind of dress that made hard for women to enter the church pews and to kneel. This battle against fashion, was, as some commentators indicated, as "old as the church".[38] The religious dress code was, however, also subject to change. That was, for instance, the case with the white wedding dresses that symbolised the bride's purity. Introduced after World

35 Spaans, "De democratisering", 49.
36 Majerus, "Plus près de vous mon Dieu …", 262.
37 Tihon, "De restauratie (1802-1830)", 9-10.
38 Van Osselaer, *The Pious Sex*, 59.

War I, these gowns were, at first, only worn by brides of the higher classes. The lower classes, who could not afford this exuberant cost, continued to wear their black Sunday best on the occasion until World War II.[39]

What is more, the faithful could not only present themselves as good Catholics by certain bodily actions (e.g. fasting, walking …) but a person's body in itself could gain a religious meaning. The ideal of 'vicarious suffering' is of particular importance in this respect. As it became more widespread since the second half of the nineteenth century, a sick and suffering body could thereby literarily embody the patient's atonement for the sins of others. Through this physical pain and the willing acceptance of it, they turned into 'heroic victims'.[40] These new 'mystics', as the stigmatised Louise Lateau (1850-1883), stimulated new practices and as Paula Kane has noted it became customary to visit them at home (even though the Church does not approve of venerating people during their lifetime). She thereby describes how a number of (German) pilgrims after one of the stigmatic's 'passions' took care to collect fragments of Louise's blood on their handkerchiefs.[41] These pilgrims thus created their own 'relics' ensuring them, on return of their pilgrimage, of a material reminder that could be turned into religious object in its own right. The creation of these objects was possible thanks to the interplay of a nineteenth-century devotional culture focused on (female) religious suffering, a flourishing pilgrimage culture and older tradition of relics brought back from pilgrimage sites.

Miraculous cures also hinted at the Divine presence through human bodies. In the latter case, the faithful would take care to leave a material reminder of this cure at the site of the Divine intervention. These could be the crutches that were no longer needed or a plaque that summarised the event (thanking the 'responsible' divine actor). The opposite was also true however: votive candles lightened in churches and at pilgrimage sites symbolised the various wishes that the faithful requested of Heaven's inhabitants. Likewise, miniature versions of the part of the body for which one demanded Divine help were donated at the site.[42]

The miraculous cures and their narratives were age-old, but in the late nineteenth century they gained a new vigour as they stimulated the production of new objects: postcards of the *miraculé(e)s* (miraculously cured people). Depicting the cured bodies of the people involved via the new means of photography, they formed an excellent means to publicly 'prove' God's power. The cure of Pieter De Rudder near the imitation Lourdes-grotto in Oostakker (in 1875) is a case in point. His postcards were sold both in Lourdes and in Oostakker and as Suzanne Kaufmann has indicated, he became "something of a sacred icon". Furthermore, his bones (exhumed in 1899) were put on display and stirred a lot of commotion in the medical world. Plaster copies of them were sent to Lourdes where they – displayed in a special glass case – were visible for all to see.[43] [Ill. 4.3-9]

As these postcards illustrate, the faithful liked to take a reminder of these solemn sites with them on their return. The Lourdes bottles with their Virgin-like shape are the best-known examples. However, cards with Bernadette's image were quite popular as well. Claude Langlois' research on the photographs of Bernadette Soubirous (the first Saint photographed during her lifetime[44]) stipulates that these formed the answer to a request of the public that liked to see the physical traits of the visionary. He adds that these pictures (of which the first ones were taken in 1861, so a few years after the apparitions in 1858) functioned primarily as a model for engravings of which the prints could be sold by the millions.[45] No need to say that as the photography techniques changed, so did the postcards of apparition sites. In the case of Bernadette for instance, the visions had to be staged in a studio, at later sites, the pictures were taken during the apparitions.[46]

Postcards were not the only things pilgrims took home with them. Other items

---

39 Mayeur, Bouchez and De Paepe, *OnGELOOFlijk!*, 13.
40 On 'vicarious suffering', see Kane, "She offered herself up".
41 Kane, "Stigmatic Cults and Pilgrimage".
42 Candles had, of course, a whole variety of functions (Pirotte, "L'Univers des objets", 141). Bodily parts: Ibid., 142.
43 Kaufmann, *Consuming Visions*, 184.
44 Harris, *Lourdes*, 145.
45 Langlois, "Photographier des Saintes", 263.
46 See, for instance, the work of William Christian on the postcards of the Ezquioga site ("L'œil de l'esprit").
47 Dezutter, "Achterglasschilderkunst".
48 Tousaint, "Les medailles réligieuses", 132.
49 Godson, "Catholicism and Material Culture in Ireland", 38: artefacts "in some way 'reflect' social worlds" but also "constitute them".

were attached to their clothes or gear and function as a visual indication that they had visited the sanctuary. Some of them took home so-called 'pilgrimage pennants'. These paper triangles were wide-spread in Belgium (circulated the region already in the fifteenth century), whereas they can only be sparsely found in the Netherlands, France and Germany. They had coloured or black-and-white images on them and a total length of circa 25-30 centimetres.[47] Other pilgrims took home pilgrimage medals that had been circulating since the thirteenth century. New production processes developed in the nineteenth century in France and Italy enabled a mass production and hence floated the various pilgrimage sites with this imported style. During World War I, as these imports were made impossible, a Belgian firm (Maison Fonson) started to produce medals for the Belgian market that had a superior quality.[48]

Conclusion

As the above paragraphs have demonstrated, religious material culture was not a passive reflection but actively constituted and shaped its social worlds.[49] The objects enabled and produced the lived religious world, varied in meaning, function and the way the faithful handled them and were inspired by them. They could trigger a bodily response, inspire action, memories, offer a support during prayer, symbolise Catholic identity, help to delineate groups and enhance their cohesion ... As for the impact of the reforms on the diversity and the extent of material expressions, no conclusion can be deemed all-compassing, the best one can do is to hint at some trends. In the first period under discussion, 1780-1830, new political rulers instigated reforms that displayed their rather negative ideas about popular Catholicism and eventually confined it to the private sphere (banning religious symbols, both at the community and individual level). After the declaration of independence (1830), the Church promoted a 'clericalized' popular religion and also stimulated the creation of physical markers of that revival at the level of the community (missionary crosses), and family (posters against cursing). For the later nineteenth century, one of the most dominant themes in this period is the increasing 'democratisation' of devotional objects. This had an effect of the three levels of popular Christianity we discussed separately, but that were of course hard to separate from each other. The cheaper production processes developed in the nineteenth century lowered the cost of various objects. This enabled an individualisation of religious practices and beliefs, but also supported the (supranational) promotion of various ideals such as the pope as charismatic leader and the idealisation of the family. New means provided new opportunities. Yet, even when the means were absent and the space for action was restricted, as in the first period under discussion, the faithful still found a way to produce them. So, if anything, than the above paragraphs form a testimony of people's creativity in both the production and practice.

4.3-9 Postcard of the Lourdes grotto in Oostakker, near Ghent, with on the left of the gate replicas of the miraculously healed bones of Pieter De Rudder. [Leuven, KADOC-KU Leuven]

BIBLIOGRAPHY

Borremans, Hilda, Lieve Borremans and Jos Boschmans, eds. *Kroniek van Norbertus Heulen. Norbertijn en pastor van Grimbergen (1795-1818)*. Grimbergen, 2007.

Christian, William A. Jr. "L'œil de l'esprit. Les visionnaires basques en transe, 1931". *Terrain*, 30 (1998), 1-17.

Christian, William A. Jr. *Divine Presence in Spain and Western Europe 1500-1960*. Budapest-New York, 2012.

De Maeyer, Jan. "Léon XIII: 'Lumen in Coelo'. Glissements de la perception dans le contexte d'un processus de modernisation religieuse". In: Vincent Viaene, ed. *The Papacy and the New World Order: Vatican Diplomacy, Catholic Opinion and International Politics at the Time of Leo XIII 1878-1903*. Leuven, 2005, 303-322.

De Maeyer, Jan. "Des vierges et des manuscrits dans des châteaux et des abbayes. Réalité médiévale ou fiction romantique?" In: Thomas Coomans and Jan De Maeyer, eds. *The Revival of Medieval Illumination: Nineteenth-Century Belgian Manuscripts and Illumination from a European Perspective*. Leuven, 2007, 62-77.

De Maeyer, Jan. "Les couronnements en Belgique: entre dévotion populaire, tourisme culturel et stratégie ecclésiastique". In: Paul D'Hollander and Claude Langlois, eds. *Foules catholiques et régulation romaine. Les couronnements des vierges de pèlerinage à l'époque contemporaine (XIXe et XXe siècles)*. Limoges, 2011, 99-113.

Dezutter, W.P. "Achterglasschilderkunst 18e-19e eeuw. Uit Midden-Europa geïmporteerde volkskunst in Vlaanderen". In: Stefaan Top, Danny Vanloocke and Raoul Verbeure, eds. *Volksdevotie in Vlaanderen. Materiële getuigenissen van vrome huisvlijt en kunstnijverheid*. Bruges, 2000, 31-37.

Dirkse, P. "Hier woonden katholieken". In: *Vroomheid per dozijn: tentoonstelling Rijksmuseum Het Catharijneconvent Utrecht van 3 april t/m 15 augustus 1982*. Utrecht, 1982, 47-55.

Godson, Lisa. "Catholicism and Material Culture in Ireland 1840-1880". *Circa*, 103 (2003), 38-45.

Gott mit uns. De nood om te geloven. Diksmuide, 2012.

Grand-Carteret, John. *Contre Rome. La bataille anti-cléricale en Europe*. Paris, 1906.

Harris, Ruth. *Lourdes: Body and Spirit in the Secular Age*. New York, 1999.

Hermans, Roeland, and Anne Morelli. *Speelgoed waarin je kan geloven*. Leuven, 2013.

Kane, Paula. "'She offered herself up': The Victim Soul and Victim Spirituality in Catholicism". *Church History*, 71 (2002) 1, 80-119.

Kane, Paula. "Stigmatic Cults and Pilgrimage: The Convergence of Private and Public Faith". In: Tine Van Osselaer and Patrick Pasture, eds. *Christian Homes: Religion, Family and Domesticity in the 19th and 20th Centuries*. Leuven, 2014, 104-125.

Kaufmann, Suzanne. *Consuming Visions: Mass Culture and the Lourdes Shrine*. Ithaca-London, 2005.

Langlois, Claude. "Photographier des Saintes: de Bernadette Soubirous à Thérèse de Liseux". In: *Histoire, images, imaginaires (fin XVe siècle - début XXe siècle)*. Le Mans, 1998, 261-273.

Majerus, Pascal. "Plus près de vous mon Dieu … Les dévotions nouvelles dans la province de Luxembourg au XIXe siècle". In: André Neuberg, ed. *Le choc des libertés. L'Église en Luxembourg de Pie VII à Léon XIII (1800-1880)*. Bastogne, 2001, 245-265.

Margry, Peter Jan. "Persoonlijke altaren en private heiligdommen". In: Arie Molendijk, ed. *Materieel christendom. Religie en materiële cultuur in West-Europa*. Hilversum, 2003, 51-78.

Mayeur, Ruben, Hilde Bouchez and Chris De Paepe. *OnGELOOFlijk! Van hemel, hel en halleluja*. Kortrijk, 2010.

Molendijk, Arie. "Inleiding". In: Arie Molendijk, ed. *Materieel christendom. Religie en materiële cultuur in West-Europa*. Hilversum, 2003, 7-12.

Morgan, David. *Religious Visual Culture in Theory and Practice*. Berkeley, 2005.

Muraille-Samaran, Colette. "Recueils de prières, paroissiens et missels (1570-1970)". In: *Piconrue. Un musée pour le futur. Art religieux et croyances populaires en Ardenne et Luxembourg*. Bastogne, 2000, 149-158.

Nissen, Peter. "'Zoals in het huisje van Nazareth …' Over devoties en rituelen in de kring van het gezin en de religieuze aankleding van het woonhuis". *Trajecta*, 4 (1995), 141-157.

Orsi, Robert. "Belief." *Material Religion*, 7 (2011) 1, 10-17.

Penne, Frans. *Overmere. Dorp van de Boerenkrijg*. 2nd ed. Antwerp, 1968.

Pirotte, Jean. "L'Univers des objets, supports de la foi". *Lumen Vitae*, 41 (1986) 2, 139-154.

Pirotte, Jean. "L'image et le sacré. De la séduction des formes à la méditation avec le divin". In: *Piconrue. Un musée pour le futur. Art religieux et croyances populaires en Ardenne et Luxembourg*. Bastogne, 2000, 69-86.

Pirotte, Jean. "Devotieprentjes, 'media' van een religieuze volkscultuur". In: Anne Morelli, ed. *Devotie en godsdienstbeoefening in de verzamelingen van de Koninklijke Bibliotheek*. Dossier van de Koninklijke Bibliotheek Albert I, 26, Koninklijke Bibliotheek van België, ULB Centre interdisciplinaire d'étude des religions et de la laïcité. Brussels, 2005, 169-186.

Pirotte, Jean. "Le paysage catholique au XXe siècle. Des rêves de chrétienté aux prodromes de la sécularisation (1878-1960)". In: Olivier Donneau, ed. *La croix et la bannière. Les catholiques en Luxembourg de Rerum Novarum à Vatican II*. Bastogne, 2005, 11-62.

Pirotte, Jean, and Claude Soetens. "Les missions à l'époque coloniale". In: Jean Pirotte and Guy Zélis, eds. *Pour une histoire du monde catholique au 20ᵉ siècle, Wallonie-Bruxelles*. Louvain-la-Neuve, 2003, 681-707.

Post, Paul. "'Een mooi spelletje…'. Over het spelen van de mis". *Trajecta*, 4 (1995) 5, 158-179.

Roegiers, Jan. "Routine, reorganisatie en revolutie (1757-1802)". In: Jan De Maeyer, Eddy Put, Jan Roegiers, André Tihon and Gerrit Vanden Bosch, eds. *Het aartsbisdom Mechelen-Brussel: 450 jaar geschiedenis.1: Het aartsbisdom van de katholieke hervorming tot de revolutietijd 1559-1802*. Antwerp, 2009, 231-296.

Rooijakkers, Gerard. "De dynamiek van devotionalia. De materiële cultuur van het geleefde geloof in oostelijk Noord-Brabant". In: Marit Monteiro, Gerard Rooijakkers and Joost Rosendaal, eds. *Dynamiek van religie en cultuur*. Kampen, 1993, 80-106.

Scaillet, Thierry. "La religion populaire". In: Jean Pirotte and Guy Zelis, eds. *Pour une histoire du monde catholique au 20e siècle, Wallonie-Bruxelles. Guide du chercheur*. Louvain-la-Neuve, 2003, 111-160.

Spaans, Joke. "De democratisering van het religieus accessoire". In: Arie Molendijk, ed. *Materieel christendom. Religie en materiële cultuur in West-Europa*. Hilversum, 2003, 29-50.

Tihon, André. "De restauratie (1802-1830)". In: Jan De Maeyer, Eddy Put, Jan Roegiers, André Tihon and Gerrit Vanden Bosch, eds. *Het aartsbisdom Mechelen-Brussel: 450 jaar geschiedenis. 2: De volkskerk in het aartsbisdom: een vrije kerk in een moderne samenleving 1802-2009*. Antwerp, 2009, 6-33.

Toussaint, Jacques. "Les medailles réligieuses". In: *Piconrue. Un musée pour le futur. Art religieux et croyances populaires en Ardenne et Luxembourg*. Bastogne, 2000, 129-133.

Van den Heuvel, J. "Volksdevotie en vroomheid". In: Michel Cloet, ed. *Het bisdom Brugge (1559-1984). Bisschoppen, priesters, gelovigen*. Bruges, 1984, 459-472.

Van Osselaer, Tine. *The Pious Sex: Catholic Constructions of Masculinity and Femininity in Belgium, c. 1800-1940*. Leuven, 2013.

Van Osselaer, Tine. "Introduction". In: Tine Van Osselaer and Patrick Pasture, eds. *Christian Homes: Religion, Family and Domesticity in the 19th and 20th Centuries*. Leuven, 2014, 7-25.

Van Osselaer, Tine. "Missing in Action? Religion in the Great War: A Historiographical Survey of Belgium and the Netherlands". *Trajecta*, 23 (2014) 2, 239-253.

Viaene, Vincent. "De ontplooiing van de 'vrije' kerk (1830-1883)". In: Jan De Maeyer, Eddy Put, Jan Roegiers, André Tihon and Gerrit Vanden Bosch, eds. *Het aartsbisdom Mechelen-Brussel: 450 jaar geschiedenis. 2: De volkskerk in het aartsbisdom: een vrije kerk in een moderne samenleving 1802-2009*. Antwerp, 2009, 33-99.

Viaene, Vincent. *Belgium and the Holy See from Gregory XVI to Pius IX (1831-1859): Catholic Revival, Society and Politics in 19th-century Europe*. Leuven, 2001.

Vincent, Michel. "Le cycle des 12 jours". In: *Le Temps de Noël*. Liège, 1992, 27-52.

4.4
Societal Change and Shifts in the Material Expression of Devotional Catholicism in the Netherlands*

Peter Jan Margry

Religious and political context 1780-1853

In 1795, in the slipstream of the French Revolution, a 'Batavian' revolution happened in the Dutch Republic. This upheaval made the unification of the seven autonomous provinces into a single nation politically possible. It broke through the regional particularism of the *ancien régime* and set up a centralised government in The Hague. This velvet or bloodless revolution also brought freedom of religion and an apparent equality to the various religious denominations, which for the most part had suffered a more or less suppressed position since the Reformation. During the *ancien régime*, the Dutch Reformed Church had been the privileged faith, affirmed as the 'national' religion by the States General of the Dutch Republic, while Catholics and other minorities were forced to practice their beliefs in clandestine barn or house churches. The equality of faiths was explicitly written into the new national 'constitution' of 1798, a fundamental political reform that brought freedom of religious practice, although in reality certain limitations continued to exist.

The overall social and economic situation in the Netherlands at the end of the eighteenth century was affected by the fact that the heyday of the Golden Age was past. The outlying rural areas, like the Catholic south, were economically relatively underdeveloped. In addition, the two centuries-long religious suppression had also banned the free production and sale of religious objects in the country. This situation can be assessed for the beginning of the long nineteenth century by observing the still modest material religious presence in the Catholic home. Reforms and changes – political, legal, religious, and economic – during the century show how the position of Catholics changed from that of a loosely-knit, orphaned community to a national political and religious force. This contribution describes and analyses the ways this process influenced the material culture of popular Catholicism until about 1920.

As a consequence of the religious liberty of 1795, the national government decided to restore to the Catholics an important number of the medieval churches that had been sequestrated and expropriated at the end of the sixteenth century by the new Protestant rulers. Those churches had been profaned: demolished, closed, or modified into Protestant houses of worship, and they had fallen victim to iconoclasm and the stripping of their interior decorations. Sanctuaries were even completely erased, as the Protestant government did not want to risk the continuation of the loathed pilgrimage cults. Catholic signs in public spaces – crosses, statues, images etc. – were removed, resulting in the thorough desacralisation of the landscape.[1]

The 1795 restitution of churches was welcomed by Catholics, and it also confronted them with the necessity of restoring or re-decorating the buildings, which were devoid of Catholic ornamentation.[2] In the Catholic south where there were few Protestants, Catholics were able to re-appropriate their former churches quite easily, while in the centre and north of the Netherlands – where Catholics formed a diaspora – former Catho-

4.4-1 Intronisation of the Statue of the Sacred Heart in an Arnhem home by Father M. Scheijen.
[St. Agatha, Archive of the Fathers of the Sacred Hearts]

* This contribution is mainly about personal and family- or home-oriented religious material culture in everyday life. As the size of the chapters in this volume is limited, the materiality of procession culture or of the Church's life cycle rituality (funerals, weddings etc.) is not addressed; books and printed materials are discussed only to a limited extent.
1 Margry, "Imago en Identiteit".
2 For an overview of the differentiation in Christian (genres of) objects in Low Countries churches and convents, see Van Zanten, *Religieus erfgoed*.

lic churches generally remained in use by Protestants.

The lack of Catholic churches occasioned a national church building programme under the guidance of the national government. This material programme coincided with an intensive spiritual missionary campaign by religious orders, a two-pronged operation to reinvigorate the Catholic flock. Catholics also became increasingly open to a revival of extinct pre-Reformation Marian devotions and saints' cults, and were eager to embrace the newly introduced international (Roman) forms of piety. As there was no parish structure until 1853, grassroots and lay initiatives had a major part in this development. Devotions thus also gained a strong foothold in the homes of Catholics, feeding the need to acquire devotional objects.

Among Protestants, however, this dynamic caused a strong fear of new confrontations with religious materiality, symbols and rituals in public – from rosaries and statues of saints to processions and pilgrimages etc. – so that new curbs on this part of religious freedom were introduced. The Dutch liberal 'revolution' of 1848 eventually turned out to be somewhat of a double-edged sword for the Catholic community: on the one hand a new constitution enabled the restoration of the hierarchy, a change that would strongly stimulate the Catholic emancipatory movement, with the mass organisation of the Catholic laity in the so- called devotionalisation process.[3] But, on the other hand, a compromise was urged with the 'Protestant' nation in 1853. The papal bull that erected the new dioceses came as a bolt from the blue for many in the country and it sparked off a spontaneous grassroots revolt – the April movement – against the Catholic Church. The Protestant nation was disturbed by what it regarded as a global conspiracy by Rome; Protestants demanded a constitutional ban on all religious rituals in the public sphere. Both 'reforms' had their influence on material religion. It restricted the public performance and appearance of rituals even more, as all public visual references and symbols relating to Catholic rituals and devotions were once again declared taboo. '1853' symbolises the nineteenth-century watershed for Dutch Catholics, as dioceses and parish structure were restored, something made possible by the new liberal constitution.

Although the German *Kulturkampf* and the associated political anti-Catholicism of the 1870s also had echoes in the Netherlands and brought the question of public schools, public Catholicism and saints' cults onto the political agenda again, it was also the overture to a new period in which both Catholics and Protestants ultimately joined hands in a *political* move against the dominance of secular liberalism. Together they won the struggle for a denominational private school system, conveying education in a religious way. The political cohabitation between Protestants and Catholics was the start of a relatively stable era in which Dutch Catholicism ultimately became the largest religious and political community in the country, very strictly organised, and – in gratitude for the 1853 restoration – with a strong orientation towards Rome and its ultramontane policy; a situation that lasted until deep into the twentieth century.

Using all means at their disposal, Dutch Catholics realised a strong religious material presence in society. They did this in the public sphere through a vast programme of building churches, shrines and devotional chapels, and in the private sphere by introducing a great variety of devotions and their related material culture into the family home. As section 2 of this book deals with the building and decoration of churches, I will limit myself here mainly to the private sphere, the home environment.

---

3 See on this process Margry, "Dutch Devotionalisation".

The material sacred in private space

Sources for domestic devotional material culture in the long nineteenth century are scarce, and this is particularly true for its early decades. An exception for the early era are the writings of Stephanus Hanewinckel (1766-1856), who was not only a Reformed minister but also an interested cultural observer. He was stationed in the southern Catholic province of Noord-Brabant in 1798, and travelled the region far beyond the confines of his own parish, while as a rigid minister continuously expressing amazement and dismay at the "superstitious" practices he encountered among the rural Catholic population. His observations unintentionally placed him in the role of an ethnographer *avant la lettre*, albeit a very biased one. Describing the interiors of the homes of simple Catholic farmers and craftsmen, he noted that the walls of the houses he visited were often decorated with cheap woodcut prints of saints and/or of the popular Marian shrines of Handel or Kevelaer (in Germany), and he also encountered the latter two in taverns. It was less common to find a crucifix with blessed candles and a palm or boxwood sprig, whether or not in combination with a bottle of holy water.[4] Residents who had this in their homes explained that they used the holy water in case of lightning, to sprinkle the corners of the house in cruciform manner to prevent the house from being struck. For the same purpose, or for protection against evil in general, he found white crosses chalked on the exterior walls of rural houses or small wooden crosses on the roof.[5]

Hanewinckel further noted that women often wore a silver or gold cross around their necks.[6] These pendants were a traditional and widespread example of personal religious objects, as old probate inventories for the village of Oirschot also demonstrate. The cross was of course the essential symbol of Catholicism, but was also seen as a universal protective token or 'amulet' that could be used for all kinds of blessings and invocations. But the minister rarely observed statues of saints or other larger devotional objects in cottages. Church books like bibles or New Testaments were also still quite scarce. Religious statues and paintings were predominantly found in the homes of the rural elite. We do not know what the situation was at the time for urban Catholics.

According to Hanewinckel, "nearly every Catholic, man or woman" at the time was a member of a devotional confraternity.[7] Although in his abhorrence he was probably exaggerating, it is true that many families already participated in sodalities and religious associations around 1800, before the wider Catholic 'devotionalisation' process had begun.[8] The two most popular confraternities

4.4-2 'The peddler', selling rosaries and other (religious) objects in late 18th century Holland, history painting of Jan J.M. Damschreuder, 1873. [Private collection]

4   Meijneke, *Op reis door de Meierij met Stephanus Hanewinckel*, 162, 229-230, 241, 296, 326.
5   Ibid., 202.
6   Versprey, *Brabantse akkers, gezegende grond*, 67-68.
7   Meijneke, *Op reis*, 202.
8   See for the high level of confraternity membership during the nineteenth century, Margry, "Dutch Devotionalisation", 147-148.

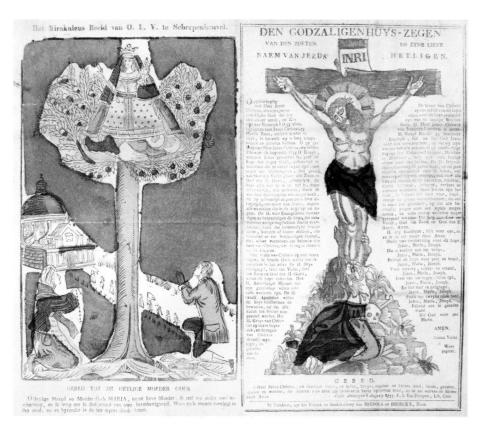

4.4-3 Houseblessing of Our Lady of Scherpenheuvel (Belgium), published by Brepols-Dierckx in Turnhout, c 1840. [Utrecht, Museum Catharijneconvent]

changed during the century, and in 1892 another ethnographer observed that there were "few houses [in Brabant] where you do not find them".[10] The pilgrimage pennon was an alternative for the house blessing, and it had a comparable function. But generally homes lacked elaborate decorations at the time.[11] [Ill. 4.4-4]

Due to the suppression of Catholics during the *ancien regime* there was very little production of devotional objects within the Republic, resulting also in the relatively infrequent presence of such items in the home. Catholics often acquired them during a foreign pilgrimage or by importing them. In the late eighteenth century, printed devotional material was still mostly imported from outside the former – 'Protestant' – territory of the Republic, with important distributors for the Netherlands being Lecuyer (Uden), Bontamps (Venlo), Brepols (Turnhout, B) and Hertsens (Antwerp, B), Schaffrath (Geldern, D), Schaaf, Verbeeck (Kevelaer, D), Pellerin (Epinal, F), and Didion (Metz, F).[12] It was not until the second half of the nineteenth century that Dutch Catholic publishers became more active and started to produce particularly devotional booklets themselves. Larger prints mainly continued to be imported from abroad or were produced on license from the foreign printers.

After the middle of the nineteenth century, small devotional prints and prayer cards became popular and began to be imported. Many of these came from Paris, often in the romantic-naturalist 'Saint Sulpice' style, so named after the street where they were produced, introducing new 'bourgeois' esthetical norms.[13]

Catholics initially obtained devotional cards in sanctuaries, from religious orders (during missions), travelling vendors or at markets. These small objects became very popular due their portable nature, low price, and the possibility of choosing cards that suited personal taste. They could likewise be used as protective sacred objects kept on one's person, while personal collections, including of obituary cards, were formed as they were accumulated in the pages of pri-

at the time were those of the rosary and pilgrimage confraternities. The latter organised the annual collective pilgrimages to two major destinations just *outside* the Netherlands, Kevelaer (Germany) and Scherpenheuvel (Southern Netherlands), a transnational travelling tradition rooted in the persecution of Catholicism during the *ancien régime* and the later ban on processions, endowed with a specific material culture.

The popularity of these pilgrimages explains the widespread diffusion of printed (copper engraved or woodcut) house blessings in Dutch homes. A house blessing consisted of a double image of one of the two Marian shrines that have been mentioned on the left and the crucified Christ on the right, accompanied by a prayer. It was actually a *centsprent* (penny print): cheap, large, expressive and often colourfully hand painted. They were affixed above the front or cellar door, or to the inside of cabinet doors, exercising from there their ascribed protective power over the home and its residents.[9] [Ill. 4.4-3] It was a practice that hardly

9   Meijneke, *Op reis*, 229-230.
10 Nissen, "'*Zoals in het huisje van Nazareth*'".
11 De Mooij, "Devotionalia en volkskunst".
12 Boerma et al., *Kinderprenten, volksprenten*, 320-322, 486-496; cf. Thijs, *Antwerpen*, 63-64.
13 Toelen, *Geloof in gips*, I, 46-47.

4.4-4 Pilgrimage pennon of the St Anthony shrine in Keldonk. Printed by J. Jongenelen in Roosendaal, around 1915.
[Collection P.J. Margry]

vate prayer books. The heyday of these cards lasted for more than a century, from about 1850 to the 1950s. Larger wall prints of saints also became cheaper and more popular, no longer mainly woodcut prints but full-colour lithographs. The prints produced by publishers like Lecuyer in 's-Hertogenbosch or Crajenschot in Amsterdam not only mirrored French or Belgian influences, but also reflected the religion of the region and the dynamics of sickness and healing by the diffusion of specific saints in print.[14] Increasingly, devotional materiality became available through specialised publishers (like Lutkie & Cranenburg), vendors and shops, especially after the 1853 restoration of the Catholic hierarchy.

Devotionalisation, popular mission, and pastoral visits

The shift in the possession and use of Catholic religious and devotional material culture more or less followed the development of the Dutch devotionalisation process since the 1830s.[15] Research in estate or probate inventories from Catholic parts of the Netherlands around the reference years of 1830, 1860, and 1890 shed light on the changes. Whereas before the 1830s, the lower and middle classes usually did not possess more than one or two printed image of a saint, Kevelaer pennon, or cross as Hanewinckel had observed earlier, after this decade, they also began to acquire three-dimensional objects. Although the inventories seem to provide a full overview of the material religion present in the home, in fact they usually only mentioned the precious objects. For example: on the few occasions that a rosary is mentioned, it was a valuable specimen in silver, while praying the rosary was already common practice before the nineteenth century. It reached a high after 1883, when Rome consecrated the month of October to the rosary. It may safely be assumed that almost every Catholic home owned at least one set of rosary beads.[16] [Ill. 4.4-5]

Similarly, cheap prints and small devotional items such as scapulars and medals hardly ever made it onto an inventory, despite their wide dissemination.[17] We know

14 Regarding Lecuyer and the land of Ravenstein and Megen, see: Rooijakkers, *Rituele repertoires*, 594-620; cf. De Mooij, "Devotionalia en volkskunst", 158.

15 This devotionalisation process is discussed in greater detail in volume 3 of this series.

16 There were 678 rosary confraternities in the Netherlands in the nineteenth century, and 522 of these were founded after 1850, see: <http://resources.huygens.knaw.nl/broederschappen>.

17 Thus in 1843 in the eastern region of Twente, the possibility to enrol in a confraternity and obtain a protective scapular sold by Jewish vendors brought a crowd out onto the streets of the town of Oldenzaal; this was unconnected to the 49 scapular confraternities that existed in the Netherlands (nearly all from after 1830), as the pope had disconnected the acquisition of a scapular from confraternity membership in 1838.

4.4-5 Collaborator of the former rosary factory in Sint Willebrord, c 1910. [Devotionalia 37 (2018) 170]

18 Heldaas Seland, "19th Century Devotional Medals", 159.
19 Arts, *Een knekelveld maakt geschiedenis*.
20 Heldaas Seland, "19th Century Devotional Medals", 170.
21 Schuurman, *Materiële cultuur en levensstijl*, 189, 193-194; Bey, "Onze woning moet om ons passen", 86.
22 Bey, "Onze woning moet om ons passen", 87.
23 The glass protected the statue in general, but also functioned as a sort of canopy honouring the sacred object. The small devotional cabinet or box containing a statuette and artificial flowers that was occasionally found around 1800 is a sort of precursor of the more popular statue glass bell variant later in the century. Contrary to the idea that it is an old form, it is a relatively young expression. These glass bell ensembles constitute the religious mirror of the secular *pendule* under glass.

that many Dutch Catholics did in fact possess such items from references in letters such as that which the apostolic vicar Den Dubbelden wrote to Pope Pius IX in 1849. Possibly exaggerating somewhat to please his addressee, he mentioned that "most of the Catholics in my vicariate of 's-Hertogenbosch wear the Miraculous Medal". The Miraculous Medal of Mary was a true, European mass cult object of which millions had been disseminated as early as the 1830s. This religious item was distributed from Paris, where the confraternity of the Sacred Heart of Mary, related to the famed apparitions of the Rue du Bac, produced the medal, initially made of copper. It functioned as a propaganda tool, as a community-making badge of the pious organisation, and, given its consecrated status, as an apotropaic or curative device for the wearer.[18] Even after death these medals had a sacred meaning: archaeological findings have established that from the second half of the nineteenth century onwards, corpses buried in an Eindhoven cemetery started to be accompanied by devotional medals or crosses as a grave goods.[19]

Later, due to new technologies and materials (the medals were made of aluminium from the late nineteenth century onwards), productions costs were reduced further and could hence easily match an equally sharp rise in mass memberships of congregations and confraternities of all kind of devotions. In 1910, medals were also allowed as substitutes for cloth shoulder scapulars, "because of the problems of wearing them" (practical and hygiene), but also to better diffuse the scapular devotion and its indulgences. The immense popularity of medalets caused the Church once again to warn against the excessive accumulation of medals, which was considered to be superstition.[20] [Ill. 4.4-6]

The Dutch Catholic community was changing, and not only because of the restoration of the hierarchy. Incentives to change also came from the improved economic position and from the technical innovations of cheap printing and mass production which affected the material culture. From the middle of the nineteenth century onwards, a majority of farms and middle-class homes in the south of the Netherlands possessed a statue of a saint (particularly of Mary), in addition to a crucifix in the house.[21] The middle classes in the Catholic province of Limburg showed more or less the same pattern, although the data seems to indicate that small farmers were less likely to own such items.[22] The new local factory of Regout in Maastricht, a major producer of porcelain and glass objects, started to remedy this from about 1850 onwards. Marian statues or crucifixes flanked by statues of Mary and Joseph, whether or not placed under a glass bell, with flower vases or candleholders on both sides, objects earlier occasionally imported from Belgium, began to be produced there for the southern Dutch market.[23]

In the predominantly Protestant central and northern parts of Netherlands – where the so-called Dutch Catholic diaspora was nonetheless growing – probate inventories of 1855-1860 list crosses, crucifixes, statues of Mary and holy water basins in homes. This implies that these statues were acquired probably years earlier, as inventories were made up after the demise of the owner of the objects.[24] However, in the north-eastern region of Achterhoek, statues and water basins often only began to appear in the inventories after 1870, and thus the purchase of them years earlier. The introduction of devotional materiality shows a northward geographical progress, from Belgium and the Rhineland via the southern Dutch provinces to the north. It coincides with the rise of popular parish missions and the foundation of devotional confraternities from the 1830s onwards, which both stimulated devotional practice and sacred material culture.

In addition to geographical differentiation in the reception of material culture, social variation is also in evidence. Outside the province of Limburg, the upper middle class or bourgeoisie (*burgerij*) seems to have begun acquiring devotional objects decades later, towards the end of the nineteenth century. This is a rare but fine example of *gehobenes Kulturgut*, probably due to accommodation behaviour among the Catholic elite, which initially did not want to be associated, within the 'Protestant' nation, with popular devotionalism. When these Catholics started to bring statues and crucifixes into their homes, they usually placed them not in the hall or in other more public areas, but only in the bedroom. This appears to endorse the idea that the Catholic elite initially dissociated itself from these items, which were regarded as sentimental and pious. They wanted or needed to behave as enlightened Dutch Catholics accommodated to Protestantism.

In modest homes and cottages, statues and other objects were usually placed in the kitchen where the family congregated, but with the advent of a dedicated 'living room' in the home, statues were moved there. In the Netherlands, it was the middle class that took the lead in the three-dimensional materialisation of Catholic devotionalism, bringing it into full connection with everyday family life. [Ill. 4.4-7]

The inexpensive production of 'basic' religious objects was ultimately the cause of the diffusion of devotional objects in the home. From the beginning of the twentieth century, most Catholic homes had holy water basins and crucifixes in the bedrooms,

4.4-6 *Home composed accumulation of devotional medals on a fabric surface. Also a faded protective saintly figure printed on silk is sewn on the backside. Belgium, c 1920.*
[Collection P.J. Margry]

stimulating more frequent prayer and piety practices on an individual basis. Devotional objects also became personalised, as framed first Holy Communion certificates, often in the form of chromolithographs, and confraternity membership certificates found their way onto the walls of the home following the French example. This was the case mainly after 1880 and more strongly so after 1900, coinciding with the start of Pope Pius X's Eucharistic campaign or reform. Instead of or in addition to a certificate, German- or Regout-produced porcelain breakfast sets (a plate with cup and saucer called a 'dejeuneetje')[25] also became a popular personal memento in the new century, often presented to the communicant in combination with their first prayer book or personal rosary.

While prints and crucifixes were meant to be hung on walls, statues, flower vases and candleholders needed a surface to stand on. The appearance of three-dimensional objects in the home necessitated a conscious process of creating a place for these newly acquired objects, a location for the sacred as a spatial precondition for the creation of home altars. In the second half of the nineteenth and in the early twentieth century, again due to the reviving economy, the amount of furniture even in modest households began to grow,

24 The data which make this process visible can be found in the online database of probate inventories of the Meertens Institute </www.meertens.knaw.nl/boedelbank/>. See especially those from Lichtenvoorde and Medemblik. Crucifixes were already found earlier in the Catholic south.
25 A symbolic gift referring to the duty to abstain from food and drink before communion and have breakfast afterwards.

4.4-7 Frans and Mie Jansen making music in their home in Tilburg, with various religious statues and wall decorations in the background, 1901. [Tilburg, Municipal Archive; photo Henri Berssenbrugge]

26 Cajetanus, *Het huisgezin en de godsdienst*, 157-158.

including chests of drawers and sideboards, which, unlike traditional cabinets, and like chimneys, were very well suited for the installation of a home altar in a practical and reverent way. In line with this, the Church recommended that Catholic families should have at least one statue in the home, as a focal point for prayer and devotion.[26]

The Church's strategy was meant to bring Catholicism into the home and to gradually turn families into the basic religious unit of society and of the Church. Rome's policy impelled families to engage jointly in devotional practices at home. This was a form of private religious practice, but at the same time it was a domestic preparation for the formal liturgy and for reflection on Catholic life in general. The home altar seemingly suited this purpose perfectly. The home altar and the other objects derived their sacredness from a blessing and rom prayer. The word altar might also suggest the presence of relics, but private possession of bodily remains was not allowed and relics were difficult to obtain until the personal relic card became popular at the end of the nineteenth century. This was a small devotional protective card to which a tiny piece of cloth was usually attached, sometimes part of the original clothing of the saint, but more often a cloth that had been in contact with the saint him- or herself or with objects that they had worn or possessed, so-called second- or third-class relics.

The family was thus moulded into a 'household of faith', to apply Ann Taves's expression, in a material and spiritual manner. This societal nucleus was stimulated from the moment that Christmas was positioned as a family feast, a few decades later spatially situated around a decorated and lit Christmas tree in the home. The tradition of the Christmas tree was brought to the Netherlands by German immigrants and merchants in the middle of the nineteenth century. Its introduction was initially opposed as a 'pagan' remnant contrary to Catholic theology. This inhibition was neutralised through the insertion of Christian symbolism: an altar-like ensemble of the Holy Family, arranged around the manger in a stable and surrounded by animals, shepherds and the three Magi. This Nativity scene make it possible to visualise and convey the Christmas message to children more effectively. It was only after 1900 that Nativity scenes became more generic, as dozens of small statue factories started producing affordable figurines. By the 1920s the presence of a Nativity scene had become universal among Catholics in the Netherlands. The Church had lost its battle over the tree, which had become a standard Christmas feature for Catholics too. Similarly, the semi-profane children's feast of the Dutch *goedheiligman Sinterklaas* functioned as a popular family feast, while playfully teaching children to ask the saint to produce 'miracles' – i.e. to send (religious) presents through the chimney – on the feast of Saint Nicholas.

The formal instrument that the Church used to carry out its family project was the Archconfraternity of the Holy Family. Since about 1850, families in the Netherlands were stimulated to enrol as a unit and to live a truly Christian life. Children especially were addressed to familiarise them with the mysteries of Catholicism and its religious life. The confraternity therefore propagated a 'child-focused' copy of the real liturgy: since the 1890s children were encouraged to participate in Child Jesus (*H. Kindsheid*) processions, dressed up and equipped with appropriate accoutrements, all under the supervision of a child-pope, as if it were the 'adult' version. [Ill. 4.4-8]

Everyday life and religious practice became more and more intertwined through such interactions between the home and the church. This also came to the fore perfectly in the fascination for another dramatic and theatrical aspect of Catholicism: the boys' game of 'playing Mass'. This imitative practice arose in the last decades of the nineteenth century, and became quite popular in (upper) middle-class families in the first three decades of the twentieth century. Boys used substitute miniature altars with the whole panoply of small sacred vessels and vestments, while, to a lesser extent, girls played with religious doll houses inhabited by dolls dressed as sisters of various congregations.[27] (See also ill. 4.3-1 and 4.3-8.)

In the meantime, sideboards had become ubiquitous in the living room, a necessity for the correct display and bricolage of religious objects. The rise of the home altar required a protected and reverent central place. This corresponded with the launch of the Sacred Heart devotion at the beginning of the twentieth century. The devotion to the Sacred Heart was strongly promoted by the Vatican. Along with the cult of Mary, the domestic veneration of the Sacred Heart became the most successful home devotion in the Netherlands. Its domestic success was a kind

4.4-8 Framed Holy Family chromolithography, c 1880.
[Collection P.J. Margry]

of repetition of the methods used previously to involve the whole family in the religious and devotional domain, as had been done in the 1850s through a national network of the Holy Family associations. The popular illustrated magazine *Katholieke Illustratie*, a materialised expression of Catholic culture, helped Catholics by portraying examples of how to assemble a home altar. [Ill. 4.4-1]

There was already a tradition of consecrating nations and peoples to the Sacred Heart, but in 1907, after a pilgrimage to the Sacred Heart shrine in Paray-le-Monial, the idea gained ground in Rome that the Sacred Heart should be consecrated or enthroned in society and, in particular, in every household. After 1910, this objective was aggressively pursued in the Netherlands both as regards its collective and its domestic aspect.[28] The former involved the communal, parochial erection of a statue of the Sacred Heart in the open air in some public location in the town or village, often in front of the church or another religious institution.[29] Although this was a collective ceremony and a public memorial, individuals could subscribe beforehand to the movement and donate money to help realise the community

27 Post, "An excellent game…"; Hermans and Morelli, *Speelgoed*, 21-31.
28 See on the start of the family enthronement movement in the Netherlands by Mateo Crawley-Boevey: "Mijn afscheid van Nederland", *De Tijd. Godsdienstig-staatkundig dagblad*, 15 April 1916, and Benedict XV's letter supporting the pioneering work by Crawley-Boevey SSCC, printed in Kaptein, *Intronisatie*, 7-11; cf. on the very start of the movement in Rome: Menozzi, *Sacro Cuore*, 255-293.
29 Morgan, *The Sacred Heart of Jesus*, 30-38.

4.4-9 Intronised statue of the Sacred Heart in an Arnhem home.
[St Agatha, Archive of the Fathers of the Sacred Hearts]

30 Subscriptions and donations were published in Catholic newspapers, for example: "Inschrijving voor het standbeeld voor het H. Hart", *Nieuwe Tilburgsche Courant*, 27 June 1917, 1 March 1918, 12 June 1918.

31 Statues conformed to the nineteenth-century 'French' iconography with the heart upon the chest of a tender and inviting Jesus, to accommodate the more family- and school-oriented form of devotion, cf. Morgan, *The Sacred Heart of Jesus*, 23-24.

statue.[30] The domestic version of this devotional policy involved the aim of enthroning a statue of the Sacred Heart in every Catholic home, in a 'place of honour', in practice usually a table or sideboard in the living room.[31] To this end the statue (or framed printed image) had to be personally 'enthroned', placed and blessed, by a priest in the presence of the whole family, which collectively had to vow to keep the statue in its home, venerate it, and pray before it, and which had to promise to live a Catholic life, keeping all the Christian virtues. The family as a whole had to sign a contract, dedicating itself fully to the Sacred Heart, acknowledging him as a friend and peacekeeper of the home, but also as Christ the King of society at large. His holy image was to be honoured with candles (later also replaced by an electric lamp) and, on the first Friday of the month, with fresh flowers. In return, he was supposed to bestow abundant blessings upon the home.[32] [Ill. 4.4-9]

Stimulated by the Vatican through a papal indulgence in 1915, and by the increasing availability of affordable plaster statues suitable for a desktop altar setting, within a decade the Sacred Heart Enthronement Work became a movement with a strong presence, bringing the statue into nearly every Dutch Catholic home.[33] A sign was put up at the front door of homes where enthronement had taken place to show publicly that this family was devout and faithful. In addition to these domestic statues, large public statues were also erected in most Catholic towns and villages in the 1920s.[34]

However, the enthronement of the Sacred Heart statue competed with the devotional ensemble around the Virgin Mary that was already present in many homes. This had been the case especially since 1865, when the celebration of the Marian month of May (later also October as the month of the rosary) was introduced. Increasingly, on feasts of Mary her statue was adorned with flowers and candles. This stimulated the shift from her hitherto customary place in the family kitchen to the more dignified living room, where the sideboard became the cultic centre of the family. Other objects to be found there were mementos of the deceased, prayer cards, and to a lesser extent, statues of the Holy Family, or some other beloved saint. [Ill. 4.4-10] Bottles containing a crucifixion scene and the *Arma Christi* gained popularity from the late eighteenth century on. [Ill. 4.4-11] On Palm Sunday, the palm frond was blessed and brought home where it was affixed to the cross in every room, still used to protect against a lightning strike. In the second half of the century the popularity of the patron saint of protection against lightning, Donatus, quickly increased. A special prayer to Saint Donatus and the veneration of his image were additional prophylactic instruments against lightning.

4.4-10 Home wall decoration membership print of the Society of the Sacred Heart of Jacoba van Leur in Utrecht, 1908.
[Collection P.J. Margry]

In comparison to earlier devotions practiced at home, the Church's involvement with daily family life was further reinforced, as this time the Church often succeeded in having the parish priest or curate gain entry to the family home for the house blessing. The yearly pastoral home visit intensified the personal relationship between family and parish clergy, especially after 1900 when these visits became more 'conversational' (instead of simply administrative).[35] Such home visits were typical for religiously mixed countries. It gave the parish clergy an authorised control of family life and, in this case, also an instrument for steering domestic devotions towards a more Christ-centred piety, while focusing on human sinfulness.

Up until the restoration of the Catholic hierarchy in 1853 Dutch Catholics had long desired full inclusion in the wider Church. They were therefore particularly sensitive towards newly introduced pastoral care and to Rome and its central policy. They cultivated a more than average 'idolatry' for the figure of the pope. Devotions stimulated or introduced by the pope were immediately embraced, like the devotion to Our Lady of Perpetual Succour which was renewed in 1867, leading to the introduction of the very popular framed reproduction of the icon in the home, as well as to terracotta plaques that could be cemented onto the façade of the house, publicly showing their fidelity to catholicism.

Photography and new printing techniques (lithographs) facilitated a new manner of devotional communication and piety. Life-like portraits of popes, bishops, and popular missionary preachers like the Redemptorist Father Bernard Hafkenscheid of Amsterdam (1807-1865), became popular images that could be affixed to the living room wall. The reduction of the cost of paper and printing that took place in the second half of the century created an enormous boost in the production and sale of devotional books, prayer books, and the many confraternity booklets related to the exponential growth of religious associations, particularly widespread after the 1880s (more than 7,000 confraternities, alone in the Netherlands). At the time, illustrated magazines presented new possibilities for the mediatisation of new visual formats. With their often ideal-type illustrations they were meant to inspire Catholic families in various ways, for instance by giving suggestions on the best way to create and decorate their own home altar.

The Netherlands was an important market for small porcelain statuettes and water containers up to the first quarter of the twentieth century. [Ill. 4.4-14] At that point the market was taken over by plaster, glass or metal objects. Larger statues and objects were usually made from wood or terracotta until the last quarter of the nineteenth century. From that period on, they were increasingly rendered in plaster cast, with statues for outdoor use in limestone or, for cheaper editions, in concrete. These kinds of images proved to be not only a cheap alternative for private homes, but also for the many new churches that needed a less expensive interior or exterior décor.

32 To enhance the commitment of children to the devotion their baptismal candle was placed and lit next to the statue on their birthday: Palm, *Moederkerk*, 219.
33 From 1916 onwards, various Dutch booklets in several print runs were published on how to perform the enthronement and the devotion to the Sacred Heart.
34 Egelie, *Beeld van het Heilig Hart*.
35 Caspers, "Het jaarlijks algemeen huisbezoek"; Leenders, *"Zijn dit nu handelwijzen van een herder...?"*, 144-149.

4.4-11 Bottle with the Arma Christi in miniature, Belgian origin, c 1875. [Collection P.J. Margry]

Twentieth-century change

Around the middle of the nineteenth century, critics first began to pour obloquy upon the 'ugly', 'non-artistic', or sentimental religious objects and articles that were for sale, which they regarded as an example of the downside of the commodification of holy places. But it was during the first decades of the twentieth century that this church-internal call for artistic reform was at its strongest. Sentimental, cheap objects were regarded as contrary to the inherently sacred character and spiritual purposes of religious art. Artists mocked them by calling them 'Kevelaer style' ('kitsch' in current terminology), after the popular Marian shrine and its many manufacturers and shops with cheap religious paraphernalia near the Dutch-German border, a shrine then still more popular than Lourdes.[36] The mass pilgrimages of those days played an important role in the production and dissemination of devotional objects. The use of tin plate, plaster and other new mass production materials stimulated consumer-oriented creativity and pricing in the design of devotional objects. Despite the criticism, the variety and number of devotional objects continued to rise. Pilgrims wanted to bring back an object related to the sacredness of the pilgrimage shrine to keep in their homes, in the same way that they had brought house blessing prints home. The power attributed to such objects was crucial to them, and they set much less store by any possible high-culture aesthetics. Pilgrims just wanted to bring home a meaningful souvenir, a sacred representational object from the shrine. [Ill. 4.4-12]

Many small factories were situated near their main market, the Catholic south, offering Catholics 'piety by the dozen'. The design still often reflected foreign influence, as many Italian and Belgian plaster workers came to the Netherlands as moulders, but also because the material culture increasingly used 'universal' templates. The heyday of plaster cast statues, and in fact of most religious paraphernalia, ran from about

36 Smits, "Boerenkunst".

1900 until the 1950s. Not surprisingly, this was the same time that community- and family-oriented Dutch devotionalism was at its peak, a phenomenon now often referred to – nostalgically – as the era of the 'Rich Roman Catholic Life' (*Rijke Roomsche Leven*). This concept denotes the period when Dutch Catholics' everyday lives were steeped in a highly inward-looking and instrumentalised form of ultramontane-inspired devotionalism, in which rituality and religious material culture played a decisive role.[37]

During the inter-war years, the border town of Venlo was the Dutch centre of the mass production of statues, influenced by German craftsmanship. The oldest and by far the largest factory of the country was Gerard Linssen's, established in 1893. In addition to various smaller factories, north Limburg and east North-Brabant, as well as The Hague (Antheunis, 1893) and Amsterdam (Van Paridon, 1900) also became important production centres.[38] By this time, the clergy generally judged the resulting products as 'inferior' or 'sentimental', but to little effect, as the industry was lay-controlled. In fact, the manufacturing process was mainly in the hands of non-Catholics. In a historical expression of anti-Semitism, some critics blamed the often Jewish owner-producers for the tacky design and materialism of their products.[39] Again, the faithful had a different view. While the Church was worried about the poor and cheap quality of these objects, the consumers actually adhered more precisely to the Church's teachings by not taking the seemingly inappropriate visual images too literally, but regarding them as a means to practice devotion and give this a personal meaning. Mass production also facilitated an unprecedentedly wide choice of cult objects, reflected in the mass popularity of shrines and saints at the time: statues of the Sacred Heart, the Holy Family, the Child Jesus, Anthony of Padua, Gerard Majella, and Theresa of Lisieux were the most popular, but the Linssen factory, for example, could deliver plaster statues of at least 3,000 different saints. [Ill. 4.4-13]

4.4-12 Salt, pepper and mustard set as pilgrimage souvenir from the sanctuary of the Gorcum Martyrs in Brielle, c 1890.
[Collection Historisch Museum Den Briel]

The popularity of Marian devotion created a steep rise in the demand for rosaries around 1900, creating possibilities for competition with French production in Dutch local cheap labour areas. This is what the factory opened in the village of Sint Willebrord in 1909 did; the branch it opened just across the border in Putte in 1912 served the vast Belgian market. Interestingly, only few people worked in the factory itself, where the preparatory processing of the material was carried out. The intensive manual labour of 'turning' and 'chaining' the chaplet was outsourced as home manufacturing.

The material sacred in the public space

To give an idea of the magnitude of the Dutch Catholic church building campaign for the rapidly growing flock, it may suffice to point to the diocese of Haarlem as an example for the western Dutch provinces. Between 1795 and 1920 more than 300 new churches were built in that diocese alone. For the whole country (which at the time numbered approximately 1,100 parishes) hundreds of additional churches were needed, and many more had to be restored

37 De Coninck and Dirkse, *Roomsch in alles*.
38 An overview of Dutch factories can be found in: Toelen, *Geloof in gips*, I, 65-80.
39 Zijp, *Vroomheid per dozijn*, 59-60.

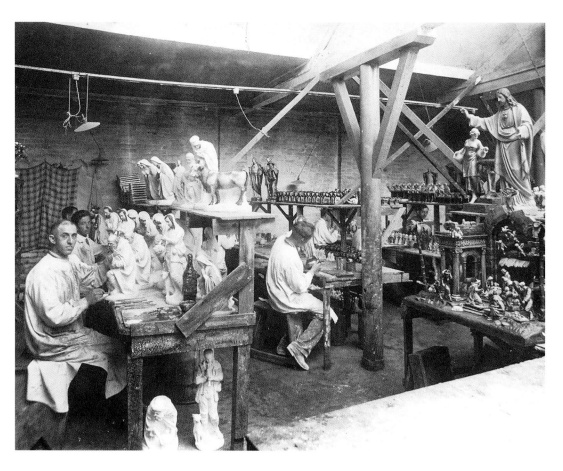

4.4-13 The painting (polychromy) of plaster casted saintly statues in the St Joseph Factory in Venlo, around 1900. [Courtesy family Alsters, Venlo]

or enlarged. In 1912 the country numbered approximately 1,300 parish churches, a figure that would grow even further after 1920.

This building programme was aligned with a strong desire for indigenous pilgrimage shrines which would not require foreign travel, as pilgrims had had to do in the past. Throughout the country, priests and laypeople tried to create sanctuaries, preferably based on existing traditions of former medieval shrines, but mostly as new shrines created from scratch. The Dutch *bouwpastoor* or 'building parish priest', the priest who built and raised funds for his own new parish church, was the model par excellence of entrepreneurial Dutch Catholicism. To attract parishioners to his church, he often decided to introduce the cult of a saint with a proven track record in miracle working for humans and for cattle, hoping thus also to attract votaries from the wider region to pray to 'his' Mary, St Cornelius or St Roch, to name only a few of the popular patron saints. He could then expect to receive higher revenues from the offerings in the local church, which would finance the building, support the priest, realise rich interior decoration and keep the devotion alive.

A special way of stimulating devotions through material culture could also be set up by lay initiatives. The early-twentieth-century Church Building Foundation financed by the wealthy Rotterdam stockbroker Joannes Grewen is an example. Grewen's personal devotion to Anthony of Padua caused him to create a fund from which dozens of parish churches dedicated to Saint Anthony could be built, in order to stimulate popular devotion to this saint in the vicinity, and some of them became real shrines.[40]

Church and chapel decoration also took place in a performative, improvised way by the faithful themselves. When shrines proved to be effective or successful, people made votive offerings to express their thanks or to try to obtain the intercession of the saint.

40 Margry, "Bouwen onder Antonius".

Unlike elsewhere in Europe, offerings of votive paintings were not typically made in the Netherlands, but simple ex votos, such as representations in silver or silver plate (and formerly also in wax) of religious symbols (a cross or a heart), human body parts, cattle and houses, etc. according to the graces received, were common, along with more generic offerings such as candles, food, and money.[41] As the devotional annual cycle brought new ex votos every year, older ones had to go: they were simply discarded or melted down for sale. In the last quarter of the century, ex voto tiles with inscriptions after the French example became popular. The vast tile walls in the Marian shrines of Sittard and Roermond are fine illustrations of this.

The popularity of the cult of Our Lady of Lourdes picked up speed in the Netherlands after the first national pilgrimage to this Southern French shrine was organised in 1873. It stimulated Catholics at home to build hundreds of concrete copies of the grotto, starting with that of Maastricht-Sint Pieter in 1874. These grottos were created by specialised *rocailleurs* or 'grotto makers', usually on the premises of a parish church or monastery. No fewer than seventeen imitation grottos became independent active filial pilgrimage shrines, often under the name of 'Little Lourdes' or 'The Lourdes of the North'. The popularity of devotion to Our Lady of Lourdes also saw the rise of new genres of home devotional objects, such as tin containers for Lourdes water, miniature table grottos, luxury prints framed in bulbous glass, and even 'frivolous' illuminated music boxes that played the Lourdes Hymn. [Ill. 4.4-15]

After the restitution of the medieval churches to the Catholics – parishes were not created until 1853 – their financial situation did not allow them to fully furnish and decorate a church. Although liturgical services could be held again in churches as they were, it did not immediately bring back the former splendour and a material setting adapted for the broad variety of Catholic devotional practices. One of the new ways to decorate churches and equip them for devotional use was the popular confraternity of Perpetual Adoration of the Blessed Sacrament. After the first group was instituted in Rotterdam in 1859, this sodality grew within a year to a thousand members, spreading out rapidly all over the country. In 1909 it had fifteen sections with more than 40,000 members. Supported by the congregation of the Sisters of Perpetual Adoration of the Blessed Sacrament, it gave a practical impetus to lay commitment, not only to the veneration of the Sacrament and reparation, but also to gifts in kind, money and labour to help decorate poor churches and adorn them with the necessary devotional and liturgical objects. In practice, it depended mostly on the efforts and networks of the parish priest.

The church boom created a corresponding upsurge in artistic and decorative ateliers that produced dedicated statues, pulpits, altars and confessionals. The rising popularity ever since the mid-nineteenth century of the devotion of the Way of the Cross stimulated every parish to have one installed in the church. The larger interior decoration pieces for churches, including statues and all kinds of church furniture, etc., were usually made in the workshops of religious art that were attached to the many architects' firms from the middle of the nineteenth century onwards. The most important were those of Cuypers/Stoltzenberg (Roermond/Amsterdam), Tepe (Amsterdam), Margry (Rotterdam) and Brom (Utrecht). Moving northwards from the south, especially via the city of Roermond – where the Cuypers/Stoltzenberg firm was based –, stylistic (neo-Gothic) and technological influences from Antwerp, Leuven and Paris penetrated the Netherlands.[42]

Because of usually Gothic architecture, the restitution of the old churches constituted an unintentional overture to the powerful symbolic and physical presence that Catholics would regain in the Dutch public space over the following years. For non-Catholics, the Netherlands was a 'Protestant' landscape in which Catholic rituality, bell ringing, crosses and, increasingly, the neo-Gothic

4.4-14 Porcelain statue of St Anthony of Padua (No. 1260 B), combined with a water reservoir for a flower in the back, c 1875.
[Collection P.J. Margry]

41 Margry, "De Ex voto's van St. Markoen te Dorst"; Zuring, "Ex-voto's in Noord-Brabant"; Hendriks-Craenmehr, "Een aandenken uit Sittard".
42 Schiphorst, "Jean Lauweriks".

4.4-15 Metal Lourdes water container, c 1910. (See also col. ill. 15.) [Collection P.J. Margry]

style appeared as disturbing intrusions. The silent appropriation of that style by Dutch Catholics around the 1850s initiated a stream of neo-Gothic building activities. Hundreds of church towers or massive monasteries appeared in the city and landscape. Having been appropriated by Catholics as their revivalist style, neo-Gothic became the quintessentially Catholic form of architecture. All buildings designed in this style were automatically identified as iconically Catholic.

The Guild of Sint Bernulphus was created in 1869 as a church organisation to enhance interest in and respect for medieval art and architecture, and to spread knowledge of, and stimulate the flourishing of contemporary religious art.[43] Its focus was on the clergy and the laity (art practitioners), and it was closely related to the revival of Catholicism in the Netherlands and the need for buildings and decoration; the Guild rigidly propagated the neo-Gothic style.

Once the devotionalisation process came to full fruition, the neo-Gothic style quite abruptly became outdated. Like in other countries in Europe, renewal and change in the arts were pursued in the Netherlands by movements of new generations of Catholics, who began to urge modernisation around 1900. Since 1911, criticism of the strict stylistic rules for artists emanating from Rome had been voiced by the new Catholic artists' society *De Violier* based in Amsterdam. This society stressed the necessity of giving way to new artistic styles. It wanted to break through the hegemony and repetitiveness of the neo-Gothic style, and stimulate and propagate better taste in various other expressions of the arts, against the mass-produced conformity of the neo-Gothic which had lost its expressiveness, and the dominance of architects vis-à-vis independent artists and decorators. They favoured the German Beuron School of monochrome and stylised sculpture over the bright and flamboyantly coloured classical design. After the First World War, there was a definite breakthrough of modernisation. One striking event which can symbolise the shift is the rigorous iconoclasm that occurred in the architect Jos Margry's atelier for religious art in Rotterdam in the early 1920s. The architect permitted his children to smash the unblessed stock of outdated and unsaleable neo-Gothic cast statues.

At that time the Catholic community consisted of an impressive organisational infrastructure as one of the two main societal pillars of Dutch society. Given that Catholics formed a single hierarchical church, unlike their denominationally divided Protestant counterparts, their pillar became the most highly organised one. The political victory of the confessional parties and the introduction of universal suffrage in 1917 symbolised a new era. Religion had become the defining element of identity, much more so than class or region. Stylistic changes heralded in the new era.

Modern means for spreading the faith in the form of wireless radio sets were not introduced on a large scale in the Netherlands within the time frame of this volume. It was only in 1925, one year after the Protestant broadcasting corporation, that a Catholic equivalent was established under the supervision of the bishops.

---

43 Looijenga, *De Utrechtse school*; *Het Gildeboek*; Toelen, *Geloof in gips*, I, 49-51. See also the contribution by Antoine Jacobs in this publication (1.3).

Reform and material popular religion: evaluation

Reform within the material expression of Catholicism in the Netherlands is deeply connected to changing power relations between the Church and the state during the long nineteenth century, pivoting around the proclamation of freedom of religion (1795/1798) and the restoration of the hierarchy in 1853. Religious freedom opened the way for the emancipation of the large Dutch Catholic minority, a process of self-realisation and expression. Initially the physical accommodation in church buildings of the 'orphaned' Catholic liturgy and devotion on a national scale was crucial, an expedient necessary to allow for the start of the devotionalisation process in place after the 1830s. In this way the Dutch Catholic community gradually became hyper-organised in local, regional and national devotional networks of confraternities, whether or not connected to local shrines of saints, and in national devotional associations.

At the beginning of the long nineteenth century, religious material culture among Catholics was rare, mainly due to the suppression of their religion. This slowly changed thanks to the improving economic situation and the organised import of objects from abroad. After 1853, in the context of the restoration of the Dutch church province and the process of devotionalisation, a broad variety of devotions, saints' cults and shrines was introduced, in combination with huge numbers of mass-produced devotional objects. These objects were still mostly imported or made by immigrant producers. Towards the end of the nineteenth century, the Dutch hierarchy had fully succeeded in bringing the liturgy and devotion into the Catholic home, connecting the whole family into a tight-knit structure of devotion and religion. 'Industrial' devotional material culture found its way into the heart of the family home in various forms and in great numbers. Around the turn of the century, a substantial part of the production of devotional goods was done in the Netherlands itself, to serve the vast Dutch Catholic market directly; a market not yet satisfied at the beginning of the twentieth century. Despite early twentieth-century modernism and criticism of the neo-style straitjacket of Catholic materiality, until deep into the twentieth century the majority of the Catholic community continued to buy and use religious paraphernalia and statues in their mass-produced form, in a design still dating mostly from the second half of the preceding century.

BIBLIOGRAPHY

Arts, Nico, ed. *Een knekelveld maakt geschiedenis. Het archeologisch onderzoek van het koor en het grafveld van de middeleeuwse Catharinakerk in Eindhoven, 1200-1850*. Utrecht, 2013.

Bey, Jette. *"Onze woning moet om ons passen". Huiselijkheid en inboedel in Limburg in de negentiende eeuw*. Diss. doct. University of Nijmegen, 2000.

Boerma, Nico, Aernout Borms, Alfons Thijs and Jo Thijssen. *Kinderprenten, volksprenten, centsprenten, schoolprenten. Populaire grafiek in de Nederlanden, 1650-1950*. Nijmegen, 2014.

Cajetanus, Fr. *Het huisgezin en de godsdienst*. Amsterdam, 1895.

Caspers, Charles. "Het jaarlijks algemeen huisbezoek in katholiek Nederland rond de eeuwwisseling". *Trajecta*, 4 (1995) 2, 122-140.

De Coninck, Pieter, and Paul Dirkse. *Roomsch in alles. Het rijke roomse leven 1900-1950*. Zwolle, 1996.

Dekker, A.J. "De opkomst van de kerstboom en kerstviering in Nederland (ca. 1835-1880)". *Volkskundig bulletin*, 8 (1982), 124-179.

De Mooij, Charles. "Devotionalia en volkskunst". In: Charles de Mooij and Renate van de Weijer, eds. *Rijke oogst van schrale grond. Een overzicht van de Zuidnederlandse materiële volkscultuur ca. 1700-1900*. Zwolle, 1991, 145-163.

Dibbits, Hester. *Vertrouwd bezit. Materiële cultuur in Doesburg en Maassluis 1650-1800*. Nijmegen, 2001

Dohms, Peter. *Die Wallfahrt nach Kevelaer zum Gnadenbild der 'Trösterin der Betrübten'. Nachweis und Geschichte der Prozessionen von den Anfängen bis zur Gegenwart*. Kevelaer, 1992.

Donkers, Geert. "De Katholieke Kunstkring De Violier, 1901-1920". *Trajecta*, 10 (2001), 112-135.

Egelie, Godfried C.M. *Beeld van het Heilig Hart in Limburg. Religieuze en sociale betekenis van de verering in de twintigste eeuw*. Zutphen, 2004.

Gedenkboek (1919-1929). Feestuitgave bij het zestigjarig bestaan van het St. Bernulphusgilde. Special issue of *Het Gildeboek. Tijdschrift voor kerkelijke kunst en oudheidkunde*, 12 (1929) 3-6.

Het Gildeboek. Feestuitgave van het St. Bernulphusgilde, 28 november 1869-1919. Special issue of *Het Gildeboek. Tijdschrift voor kerkelijke kunst en oudheidkunde*, 2 (1919) 3-4.

Heldaas Seland, Eli. "19th Century Devotional Medals". In: Henning Laugerud and Laura Katrine Skinnebach, eds. *Instruments of Devotion: The Practices and Objects of Religious Piety from the Late Middle Ages to the 20th Century*. Aarhus, 2007, 157-172.

Helsloot, John I.A. "De kerstboom prijkt, 't is kinderfeest. Kinderen en Kerstmis tussen 1840 en 1960". In: Sijbolt Noorda and Christien Oele, eds. *Er is een kindeke... De geboorte van Jezus in de Nederlandse cultuur*. Amsterdam, 2004, 123-146.

Hendriks-Craenmehr, Mariska. "Een aandenken uit Sittard. Devotionalia ter ere van Onze Lieve vrouw van het Heilig Hart". In: Charles Caspers, Wolfgang Cortjaens and Antoine Jacobs, eds. *De basiliek van Onze Lieve Vrouw van het Heilig Hart te Sittard. Architectuur, devotie, iconografie*. Sittard, 2010, 199-213.

Hermans, Roeland, and Anne Morelli. *Speelgoed waarin je kan geloven*. Leuven, 2013.

Jacobs, Jan, Lodewijk Winkeler and Albert van der Zeijden, eds. *Aan plaatsen gehecht. Katholieke herinneringscultuur in Nederland*. Nijmegen, 2012.

Jentjens, Leonard. *Van strijdorgaan tot familieblad. De tijdschriftjournalistiek van de Katholieke Illustratie 1867-1968*. Amsterdam, 1995.

[Kaptein], Joachim. *Intronisatie van het Allerheiligste Hart van Jezus in de woningen door de plechtige toewijding der huisgezinnen aan dit Goddelijk Hart*. Den Bosch, 1916.

Knippenberg, Willy H. Th. *Devotionalia. Religieuze voorwerpen uit het katholieke leven*. 2 vols. Eindhoven, 1985²-1986.

Knippenberg, Willy H. Th. "De verering van het Heilig Hart van Jezus". In: *Volkscultuur in Brabant. 2: Leergang Volkskunde 1988*. Utrecht, 1990, 7-22.

Koenders, A. *Over scapulieren en scapuliermedailles*. Venlo, 1912.

Landheer, Hugo. *Kerkbouw op krediet. De financiering van de kerkbouw in het aartspriesterschap Holland en Zeeland en de bisdommen Haarlem en Rotterdam gedurende de periode 1795-1965*. Amsterdam, 2004.

Leenders, Jos M.M. *'Zijn dit nu handelwijzen van een herder...?' Hollands katholicisme 1840-1920*. Nijmegen, 2008.

Looijenga, Arjen Johan. *De Utrechtse School in de neogotiek. De voorgeschiedenis en het Sint Bernulphusgilde*. Leiden, 1991.

Manning, A.F. *Zestig jaar KRO. Uit de geschiedenis van een omroep*. Baarn, 1985.

Margry, Peter Jan. "De ex-voto's van St. Markoen te Dorst. Enkele opmerkingen bij het gebruik van geloftegeschenken als historische bron". *Brabants Heem*, 38 (1986), 245-258.

Margry, Peter Jan. "Bouwen onder Antonius. Devotionalisering via de Bossche Kerkbouwstichting". In: Leon van Liebergen and Wouter Prins. *Antonius. De kleine en de grote*. Uden, 1995, 25-35.

Margry, Peter Jan. "Imago en identiteit. De problematische manifestatie van 'het katholieke' in de Nederlandse samenleving rond het midden van de negentiende eeuw". In: Jurjen Vis and Wim Janse, eds. *Staf en Storm. Het herstel van de bisschoppelijke hiërarchie in Nederland in 1853: actie en reactie*. Hilversum, 2002, 64-86.

Margry, Peter Jan. "Sakrale materielle Kultur in den Niederlanden der Gegenwart: Persönliche Altäre und private Heiligtümer". *Rheinisches Jahrbuch für Volkskunde*, 35 (2003/2004), 247-263.

Margry, Peter Jan. "Practicing Religion in Private: The Home Altar". In: Paul Post, Arie L. Molendijk and Justin E.A. Kroesen, eds. *Sacred Places in Modern Western Culture*. Leuven, 2011, 227-233.

Margry, Peter Jan. "Dutch Devotionalisation. Reforming Piety: Grassroots Initiative or Clerical Strategy?" In: Anders Jarlert, ed. *Piety and Modernity*. The Dynamics of Religious Reform in Northern Europe, 1780-1920, 3. Leuven, 2012, 125-156, 187-190.

Margry, Peter Jan, and Charles Caspers. *Bedevaartplaatsen in Nederland*. 4 vols. Amsterdam-Hilversum, 1997-2004.

Mariman, E.C.M. *Van rozenkransen, rozenhoedjes en andere katholieke bidsnoeren*. Maastricht: eigen beheer, n.d.

Mariman, Edwin. "Rozenkransmakers in onze regio". *Devotionalia*, 37 (2018), 166-172.

Meijneke, Frank C., ed. *Op reis door de Meierij met Stephanus Hanewinckel. Voettochten en bespiegelingen van een dominee, 1789-1850*. Tilburg, 2009.

Menozzi, Daniele. *Sacro Cuore. Un culto tra devozione interiore e restaurazione cristiana della società*. Rome, 2001.

Morgan, David. *Visual Piety: A History and Theory of Popular Religious Images*. Berkeley, 1998.

Morgan, David. *The Sacred Heart of Jesus: The Visual Evolution of a Devotion*. Amsterdam, 2008.

Nissen, Peter J.A. "Mobilizing the Catholic Masses through the Eucharist: the Practice of Communication from the Mid-19th Century to the Vatican Council". In: Charles Caspers, Gerard Lukken and Gerard Rouwhorst, eds. *Bread of Heaven: Customs and Practices Surrounding Holy Communion: Essays in the History of Liturgy and Culture*. Kampen, 1995, 145-164.

Nissen, Peter J.A. "'Zoals in het huisje van Nazareth...'. Over devoties en rituelen in de kring van het gezin en de religieuze aankleding van het woonhuis". *Trajecta*, 4 (1995), 141-157.

Palm, Jos. *Moederkerk. De ondergang van Rooms Nederland*. Amsterdam, 2012.

Post, Paul G.J., ed. *Verbeelding van vroomheid. De devotieprent als cultuurwetenschappelijk bron.* Thematic issue of *Volkskundig Bulletin*, 16 (1990) 3, 251-402.

Post, Paul. "'An excellent game...' On playing the Mass". In: Charles Caspers, Gerard Lukken and Gerard Rouwhorst, eds. *Bread of Heaven: Customs and Practices Surrounding Holy Communion. Essays in the History of Liturgy and Culture.* Kampen, 1995, 185-214.

Rooijakkers, Gerard. "De dynamiek van devotionalia. De materiële cultuur van het geleefde geloof in oostelijk Noord-Brabant". In: Marit Monteiro, Gerard Rooijakkers and Joost Rosendaal eds. *Dynamiek van religie en cultuur.* Kampen, 1993, 80-106.

Rooijakkers, Gerard. *Rituele repertoires. Volkscultuur in oostelijk Noord-Brabant 1559-1853.* Nijmegen, 1994.

Schiphorst, Lidwien. "Jean Lauweriks, vanaf 1854 eerste beeldhouwer in het atelier Cuypers/Stoltzenberg. Een kunstenaar in dienst". *Spiegel van Roermond. Jaarboek voor Roermond*, 2010, 104-115.

Schuurman. Anton J. *Materiële cultuur en levensstijl. Een onderzoek naar de taal der dingen op het Nederlandse platteland in de 19e eeuw: de Zaanstreek, Oost-Groningen, Oost-Brabant.* Wageningen, 1989.

Smits, K. "Boerenkunst". *R.K. Boeren en Tuindersstand*, 25 april 1940.

Stal, Annie. "'De offerstenen die hier prijken... 't zijn huldeblijken'. De votiefteksten in de basiliek". In: Charles Caspers, Wolfgang Cortjaens and Antoine Jacobs, eds. *De basiliek van Onze Lieve Vrouw van het Heilig Hart te Sittard. Architectuur, devotie, iconografie.* Sittard, 2010.

Taves, Ann. *The Household of Faith: Roman Catholic Devotions in Mid-Nineteenth-Century America.* Notre Dame, 1986.

Thijs, Alfons K.L. *Antwerpen, internationaal uitgeverscentrum van devotieprenten, 17de-18de eeuw.* Leuven, 1993.

Toelen, Ans. *Geloof in gips. Massaproductie van religieuze voorstellingen.* 4 vols. Unpublished MA thesis Nijmegen University. Tilburg, 1992.

Van den Berg, Arie, and Gerard Rooijakkers. "Een prentenmaker zonder pers. De houtsneden van Philippus J. Lecuyer te Uden en 's-Hertogenbosch, 1772-1774". *Volkskundig Bulletin*, 16 (1990) 3, 254-309.

Van der Hoek, Ragdy. *De hemel in gips. Schets van de religieuze beeldenindustrie in Venlo.* Venlo, 2008.

Van Liebergen, L.C.B.M., ed. *Volksdevotie. Beelden van religieuze volkscultuur in Noord-Brabant.* Uden, 1990.

Van Osselaer, Tine. "Home is where the Heart is: The Sacred Heart Devotion in Catholic Families in Interwar Belgium". in: Tine van Osselaer and Patrick Pasture, eds. *Christian Homes: Religion, Family and Domesticity in the 19th and 20th Centuries.* Leuven, 2014, 159-178.

Van Rooden, Peter. "Long-term Religious Developments in the Netherlands, c. 1750-2000". In: Hugh Mcleod and Werner Ustorf, eds. *The Decline of Christendom in Western Europe, 1750–2000.* Cambridge, 2003, 113-129.

Verspaandonk, J.A.J.M. *Het hemels prentenboek. Devotie- en bidprentjes vanaf de 17e eeuw tot het begin van de 20e eeuw.* Hilversum, 1975.

Versprey, Johan. *Brabantse akkers, gezegende grond. Archeologische begeleiding van munitiesanering en onderzoek naar het gebruik en de beleving van de Oerlese akkers, gemeente Veldhoven.* Amsterdam, 2013.

Wintle, Michael. *Pillars of Piety: Religion in the Netherlands in the Nineteenth Century, 1813-1901.* Hull, 1987.

Wintle, Michael. "The Netherlands". In: Sheridan Shelley and Brian Stanley, eds. *The Cambridge History of Christianity. World Christianities c. 1815 - c. 1914*, vol. 8. Cambridge, 2006, 333-341.

Zanten, Mieke van. *Religieus erfgoed uit kerken en kloosters in de Lage Landen. Geïllustreerd lexicon van Nederlandse en Vlaamse termen.* Zutphen, 2008.

Zijp, Robert P., ed. *Vroomheid per dozijn.* Utrecht, 1982.

Zuring, Jan. "Ex-voto's in Noord-Brabant". *Brabants Heem*, 43 (1991), 93-104.

MEN VIND IN DEN BYBEL, DE NAAM *JEHOVAH* of *HEERE*,

6855 Maal, het middelste staat 2 Chron. 4, Vers 16.

Boeken .... 66.
Capittels .... 1189.
Verzen .... 31192.
Woorden .... 773692.
Letters .... 3566480.
Het woord Ende .... 46227.
Het middelste Capittel is Psalm .... 117.
Het middelste Vers is Psalm 101 Vers .... 8.

IN DE APOCRYPHE BOEKEN,
Capittelen .... 180.
Verzen .... 6081.
Woorden .... 152185.

Het Heilig Bijbelwoord is ons veel grooter schat,
Dan 't gantsch Geschapendom, met al haar heil bevat.

BY J. SCHEFFERS.

Men vind in 't Oude Testament.
Boeken .... 39.
Capittels .... 929.
Verzen .... 23213.
Woorden .... 592419.
Letters .... 2728100.
Het woord Ende .... 35543.
't Middelste Boek is Proverbia.
't Middelste Capittel is Job 29.
De 2 Middelste Verzen zyn 2 Chr. 20, Vers 17 en 18.
Het Kleinste Vers is 1 Chron. 1, Vs. 1.

God heeft aan Israel geschonken,
Vijf Boeken; Mozes vast geklonken,
't Boek Jozuä, der Richtren stand.
't Geval van Ruth, in 't Heilig Land.
Twee heeft 'er Samuel beschreven:
De Konings Boeken daar beneven.
Chronica, Esra, hoog geacht;
Nehemia, vol Geest en kracht.
't Boek Ester, Job en dat der Psalmen.
Geeft ons na droefheid, vreugde galmen.
De Spreuken, Prediker, 't hoog gedigt;
Gaf groot Vorst Salomon, in 't ligt.
Jezaiäs Euängelie Chooren:
Jeremiä deed Gods reede hooren;
Zijn klaag-gezangen zijn vol druk;
Ezechiël, meld van 's Volks geluk.
Een Daniël, heeft wat groots geschreven.
Hozea, Joël, hoog verheven:
Niet minder Amos, Gods Propheet!
Obadja, Jona, Micha, weet
Met Nahum, schrik en troost te melde.
Daar Habakuk Gods wraakzwaard stelde.
Zephanja, blaasd de boet Bazuin;
Haggai, schildert Sions Kruin;
Laat Zachariä, U verblijen,
Roemd Maleächis Profezijen;
Dien Sluiter van het Oud Verbond;
Wijst ons op Christus tijd en stond.

Men vind in het Nieuwe Testament.
Boeken .... 27.
Capittels .... 260.
Verzen .... 7979.
Woorden .... 181253.
Letters .... 838380.
Het woord Ende .... 10684.
Het Middelste Boek is 2 Tessalon.
De twee Middelste Capittels zijn Rom. 13 en 14.
't Middelste Vers is Hand. 7, Vers 7.
Het Kleinste Vers is Joh. 11, Vers 35.

God heeft in 't Nieuw Verbond gegeven:
Vier Boeken van Vorst Jezus Leven;
En een van zijn Aposteldom,
Dan volgen Paulus brievendrom,
Aan Romes en Chorinthes Kerken;
Galaten, stigt hij door zijn werken:
Ephezen en Philippis Stand.
Groeid door zijn brieven hand voor hand;
Hij schreef ook aan de Collossensen,
Een Leerbrief als aan Christen menschen
Der Thessalonicensen Kerk;
Vercierde hij, met Christus merk.
Hij heeft aan Timothe, geschreven,
Aan Titus een, vol geest en Leven.
Aan Philemon, met kragt van reen,
Groot is zijn brief, aan de Hebreen.
Jacobus brief, leerd Christi werken.
Een Petrus stigt, verstrooide Kerken.
Johannes brieven, hoog geacht;
Met Juda's brief, zijn vol van kragt.
Het Openbarings boek, beschreven
Door Godlijk ligt, in Geest verheven:
Betreft de Kerk van 't Nieuw Verbond,
Hier op dit Aardsche Wisselrond.
Gelukkig zij, die dit bewaaren:
De Geest en Bruid zal 't ons verklaaren
Haar naam blijft zalig ongestoord,
Johannes sluit het Bijbelwoord.

4.5
God's Word Materialised

The Domestication of the Bible in Dutch Protestantism

Fred van Lieburg

In 1837, a theology student in Leiden, Nicolaas Beets (1814-1903), wrote his sketches of daily life in the Netherlands, which, published as the bestseller *Camera Obscura*, are said to be a mirror of the typical bourgeois life in the early nineteenth century. Among the vivid atmospheric sketches of the time is a passage in the chapter on the Stastok family, in which the main character ends up in the farmstead of a wealthy couple. In the main room was a stately bed and a Frisian clock on the wall, a draughtboard and four paintings, "not to mention one of those tables that could be called abbreviated editions of Trommius and on which one could read how many chapters, how many verses, and how many 'ands' there were in the Bible and many other things worth knowing. One such table had a guilded frame."[1]

Abraham Trommius (1633-1719) was the compiler of a concordance of the Dutch *Statenbijbel* or States Bible, the Authorised Version of the Bible of 1637.[2] He did generations of preachers and other zealous students of the Bible a great service with this tedious, painstaking work. His concordance became a household name, not to say an item – 'the Trommius'. Beets referred to excerpts with statistical data on the text of the Holy Scripture that apparently circulated. The 'table' that he mentioned can easily be identified as a cardboard card that was supposedly sold for the first time in Rotterdam in 1820. The text consisted of a list of statistical trivia about the Bible and the 'apocryphal' deuterocanonical books, framed by two poems on all the books of the Old and New Testaments. In the middle was a two-line moral: "The Holy Biblical Word is a much greater treasure for us / than the whole of creation with all its happiness".[3]

It is not that easy to clarify the function of this picture in the early nineteenth century. Of course, the numbers and poems reflect, on the one hand, the temporally and spatially unlimited human need for order, quantification, and curiosity. Such lists have been compiled from sacred or authoritative texts throughout the centuries by pious or not so pious numbers aficionados. Around 1780, a Swedish traveller met a man in Holland who had copied the Bible and took the 'useless trouble' of counting the chapters, words, and letters of each book.[4] The above-mentioned table from 1820 is allegedly derived from a foreign source.[5] We can also refer to the how people dealt with sacred texts as magical objects that could give people personal messages. For example, in resorting to bibliomancy ('choosing' Bible texts at random to get a divine message), a text is no longer

---

1. Hildebrand, *Camera Obscura*, 100 ("om niet te spreken van een dier tabelletjes, welke men verkorte uitgaven van Trommius zou kunnen noemen, en waarop men lezen kan hoeveel kapittels, hoeveel verzen, hoeveel ende's in den bijbel staan, en dergelijke wetenswaardige dingen meer. Zulk een hing er in een verguld lijstje.")
2. Trommius, *Volkomene Nederlandtsche Concordantie.*
3. "Het Heilig Bijbelwoord is ons veel groter schat, / Dan 't Gansch Geschapendom, met al haar heil bevat." The Meertens Institute holds a copy of the table, printed

4.5-1 Eighteenth-century penny print containing a poem on the bible, published by J. Scheffers.
[Amsterdam, Meertens Institute]

by Johannes Scheffers in Rotterdam early in the nineteenth century (Collectie 42:59, no. 2). See also Zijp, "Wandteksten", 70; a picture in Mönnich and Van der Plas, *Het Woord in beeld*, 152.

4. Björnståhl, *Reize door Europa en het Oosten*, 273: "Ik zag ook nog een ander handschrift van Claas Commers van der Mark, die den Neêrduitschen bijbel zelf afgeschreven, en zig de nutlooze moeite gegeven heeft, van de kapittels, versen, worden en letters in elk boek van denzelven te tellen: de Psalmen bestaan dus uit 150 kapittels, 2527 versen, 41644 woorden en 195459 letters e.z.v.; eindelijk heeft hij het geheele oude en nieuwe testament tezamen gerekend; in het jaar 1761, toen hij deze vrugtlooze en vervelende rekening begon, was hij zeven en zestig jaaren oud."
5. Eisfeld, *Lebenserinnerungen von Paul und Sophie Schönwälder*, 57 (note from 1878): "Am 8.4.1820 war in einem märkischen Wochenblatt zu lesen: Die ganze Bibel enthält 31.173 Verse, 773.692 Wörter, 3.566.480 Buchstaben. 'Ja' kommt 6855-mal vor, 'nein' 46227-mal. Das mittelste Kapitel der ganzen Bibel ist Psalm 117, der mittelste Vers Kapitel 101 Vers 8. 3 Jahre hat ein Amerikaner mit Zählen täglich 8-9 Stunden zugebracht."

an organic unity but a materialised sacrality.[6] Thus, the Bible can also be the object of naive lists, not to mention acrobatic numerology in order to analyse world history or to predict the end of time. [Ill. 4.5-1]

Homo religiosus can disguise himself as *homo ludens*, but he can just as easily present himself as *homo civilis*. Precisely at the beginning of the nineteenth century, a view of the Bible as the 'book of civilisation' began to emerge. Bible societies that were formed in a number of European countries and colonies following the British model propagated the spread of God's Word as a tool that had the power in itself to revitalise Christians and to convert those of other faiths or 'heathens' into morally disciplined citizens of nations and the world.[7] The concentration on the Bible text as such, without any confessional coloured notes and commentary, functioned as a tool to help in the formation of a universal Christian civil religion. The major changes in politics, in ecclesiastical and socio-economic areas, however, forced a free market with a wide diversity in new worldview subcultures, as treated in detail in other volumes of this *Dynamics of Religious Reform* series.

This chapter looks at the material dimension of the religious transformation between 1780 and 1920, and focuses on Dutch Protestantism – as a counterpart to the contribution by Peter Jan Margry on Dutch Catholicism (and a supplement to my earlier contribution on general changes in Protestant piety in the Netherlands in volume 3).[8] There is not much research available on which such a study can be based, although a Dutch volume on material Christianity in Western Europe (2003) contained a few articles on the Protestant use of the Bible, while the historian John Exalto delivered some contributions to Protestant reading culture and visual piety.[9] In this chapter, the thematic focus on the Bible – as text and as book – serves to illustrate a development that can, in the end, be characterised as 'domestication'. Domestication implies then the growing role of Bible-related objects in the devotional home culture, resulting in an integration of public and private spheres among large groups of believers. In addition to textual expressions of this, we will also discuss visual representations, whereby the visualisation concerns both the content of the Bible itself and the Protestant 'servants of the divine Word'.

Bible texts distributed

Historians of culture have extensively researched archives in the Netherlands on estate inventories from the early modern period and made them available to the public.[10] These official descriptions of household possessions suggest that Bibles, prayer books, and other (theological, catechetical, or devotional) books were – until far into the eighteenth century – the most important and widespread religious objects in the homes of ordinary Dutch citizens and farmers. Indeed, durable goods are predominant in these sources, and cheap prints and other disposable material or worthless artefacts are missing. But for the typical Protestant family, it is plausible that, in any case, it would have had a complete, more or less beautifully bound Bible (the Dutch States Bible for the Reformed and Remonstrants; specific translations for Lutherans and Mennonites) that was used for the daily Bible readings at the dinner table. Smaller (partial) editions of the Bible – like religious books – were used more for personal devotion.

In 1812, the Netherlands Missionary Society, founded in 1797 and as much concerned about the Dutch people living next door as it was about heathens in distant countries, did a survey to determine the extent of Bible possession in the Netherlands and concluded that there was no remarkable lack, even among the poor. When Robert Pinkerton, the agent for the British and Foreign Bible Society, visited Holland in 1814 to help set up a Dutch counterpart, he was informed that there was a market for Bibles here. About thirty years later, the establishment of a British sales outlet in Amsterdam

---

6   Cf. Van Lieburg, "De Bijbel als orakelboek"; Id., "Direkte Gotteserfahrung".
7   Van Lieburg, *De wereld in*.
8   Margry, "Dutch Devotionalisation"; Van Lieburg, "Reforming Dutch Protestant Piety".
9   Molendijk, *Materieel christendom*; Exalto, *Wandelende bijbels*; Id., "Religious Visual Culture in the Private Space". For the early modern period, see Maan, "Material Culture".
10 See the online inventory of the Meertens Institute in Amsterdam <www.meertens.knaw.nl/boedelbank/>; Dibbits, *Vertrouwd bezit*, 285, 293; Kamermans, *Materiële cultuur in de Krimpenerwaard*, 129-134.

and the introduction of salesmen in various Dutch cities proved to be very successful in selling cheap Bibles. The Netherlands Bible Society was thus shown up, but it recovered sufficiently to become the market leader at the end of the nineteenth century. To stimulate Bible reading at home, the Society became famous from 1858 on by offering free Bibles to newlyweds at local branches. Ministers presented the Bibles during the wedding ceremony as an initiative for the basis of a good Protestant family. This large-scale practice of boosting civil religion was discarded around 1920 as out of date.[11]

In addition to Bibles, 'prayer books' were a constant item in the possessions of – at least – Dutch Protestants. These prayer books sometimes contained a complete Bible or the New Testament, as well as the rhymed psalms that were sung in the worship services (the rhymed version issued by the state was generally used from 1773 to 1967), as well as some standard confessional, catechetical, and liturgical texts that were used in church and school. The material appearance of these prayer books was just as important as their content. Because of their public use and the resultant social exposure, they were often decorated with gold, silver, or copper locks and corner brackets.[12] Today, every Dutch person still knows the children's song: "Altijd is Kortjakje ziek, midden in de week, maar 's zondags niet" (Kortjakje is always sick during the week, but not on Sundays). Earlier eighteenth-century versions that spoke of Kortjakje as a lower-class girl who spent her Sundays drinking gin were replaced over the course of the nineteenth century by a variation that referred to a nice, civilised girl's going to church on Sunday: "'s Zondags gaat zij naar de kerk, met een boek vol zilverwerk" (On Sundays she goes to church, with a book [bible] with silver ornamentation.)[13]

A new phenomenon in the mass production of texts and books was the tear-off calendar, which consisted of a book block from which every day one could tear off a page with the date (and other specifics about that day) on the front and a memorable text, often in the form of a serial story, on the back. The religious, Protestant variant contained Bible passages or meditative, edifying or uplifting, and always pious (miracle) stories, proverbs, and poems. The tear-off calendars could be hung on a board on the wall, and such boards were usually decorated with an artful, colourful painting, often from the Bible. The oldest Dutch tear-off calendar, which followed the British design, dated fom 1867, and around 1920, there had to have been at least fifteen Protestant versions on the market.[14] They also enjoyed wide circulation. At that time, the Vereniging tot Verspreiding der Heilige Schrift (Society for the Distribution of Holy Scripture), a popular competitor of the Netherlands Bible Society that was founded in 1923, published a tear-off calendar with a print run of 26,000 copies.[15]

Another development that brought the biblical texts in pithy form into the daily life of continually more people was the popularisation of decorative plates and ornamental texts.[16] [Ill. 4.5-1 & 4.5-2] These objects recall the text boards that were introduced in many Protestant church buildings since the Reformation to replace, as it were, the paintings of the saints.[17] In the late nineteenth century, the production of small-scale boards for the home began to take off.[18] The texts were often written on cheap cardboard or burned

4.5-2 'Calvinistic' admonition ("Do not complain but bear, and ask for strength") as home wall decoration produced for Dutch protestants, sold by the Amsterdam Paulus Association, c 1920. The line was taken from a poem of the Dutch writer Nicholas Beets. [Collection P.J. Margry]

11 Van Lieburg, *De wereld in*.
12 Van Noordwijk, *Zondags zilver*; Id., *De erfenis van Kortjakje*; Id., *Zilver voor de Zondag*.
13 Van Vloten and Brandts Buys, *Nederlandsche baker- en kinderrijmen*. See also the online inventory of the Meertens Institute in Amsterdam <www.liederenbank.nl/>.
14 Van Gelderen, *Filippus*.
15 Fikse-Omon, *Papieren evangelisten*, 86.
16 Morgan, *The Lure of Images*, 221.
17 Steensma, *Protestantse kerken*, 163-216; Van Swigchem, Brouwer and Van Os, *Een huis voor het Woord*, 269-281.
18 Zijp, "Wandteksten"; Fikse-Omon, *Papieren evangelisten*, 85. See also Dane, "Goed, fraai en goedkoop".

into a wooden plate or plank: for those well off there were black velvet text plaques with gold letters or wall plates in beaten out copper. These plates often displayed Bible texts that played a role in one's baptism, leaving (Sunday) school, confession, marriage or a marriage anniversary – usually with the date and possibly names. Being confronted daily with such plaque or plate helped to train one in personal piety as a reminder of important moments or to urge one to action in the present.

Bible stories visualised

Although Protestantism – particularly Calvinism, more than Lutheranism or Mennonism – is often viewed as hostile to art or images, it had however no theological or practical objection to depictions of created reality in whatever form. The prohibition against images in the Decalogue obtained only for the visualisation of God (not of Jesus as a human being) and for the function of images in personal devotion. Images of Christ, Mary, saints, or other people, could not be used as the object of worship or as a means for worshipping God. In contrast to Catholicism, Protestantism was reserved with respect to an exuberant religious image culture, but, in a strict sense, there was no objection in Protestantism to art forms like painting, sculpting, engraving, and casting nor to artistic depictions of angels, people or animals. All of these could be found in the Dutch Republic – both in Protestant, formerly Catholic church interiors and Protestant living rooms as well as in illustrated Bibles and books – and that practice continued into the nineteenth century.[19]

A good testimony to the hybrid image culture in which biblical depictions were frequent though not dominant can be found in the tile tableaux (Delftware) in the homes of the middle class and farmers. In the seventeenth and eighteenth century, the Netherlands were the market leaders in this field. Those tiles were cemented into the chimneys of many a living room or the walls and ceilings of rooms and kitchens with depictions of trades, games, or village scenes, as well as biblical figures and stories. For religious themes, tile painters made demonstrable use of various Bibles containing prints or plates that were in circulation at the time. Sometimes, a big tile tableau resembled a Bible visualised in stone, like the panel of 84 tiles that told the story 'From Paradise to Resurrection'. Blue was the primary colour used for tile painting until about 1760 and after that purple, brown, or even polychrome became fashionable. After 1800 there was a steep decline in the production of tiles. Of the eighty tile factories at that time in the Netherlands, only two remained. Wherever these long-lasting tile walls were found, they were often left intact as historical relics.[20]

Material depictions of the biblical content in the home – on tiles, as well as on furniture and tableware – did not seem to have any specific devotional function until late in the nineteenth century.[21] They articulated the unity of the Christian view of the world in daily life; images were not intended, after all, to have any kind of far-reaching role in personal faith experience in Protestantism. The development of confessional subcultures in the second half of the nineteenth century would give an undeniable stimulus to devotionalisation. The mass production of Bibles and books for a selective public meant that the image could not remain outside religious identity politics. There was also an increase in the number of areas in which religious, biblically oriented material was offered. Protestant Sunday schools for example offered accessible and evangelically oriented education to children from the poorer classes (supported nationally by the Nederlandse Zondagsschool Vereniging (Netherlands Sunday School Society) of 1865 and the Gereformeerde Zondagsschoolvereniging Jachin (Reformed Sunday School Society Jachin) of 1871). Subsequently, the number of independent Christian elementary schools (since 1917 entitled to the same government financial support as public neutral schools)

---

19 Cf. Van Asselt, "The Prohibition of Images and Protestant Identity".
20 Pluis, *Bijbeltegels*.
21 See the catalogue of an Utrecht exhibition: Kootte, *De bijbel in huis*.

grew in which visualisation of the Bible for children was an important didactic aid, in accordance with the general pedagogic ideal of 'visual education'.

In 1867, the first Dutch version of the cheap and coloured lithography of the 'broad and narrow way' was printed. It became one of the popular images within Dutch Protestantism. [Ill. 4.5-3] The plate was a contemporary depiction of the old motif of the two paths in human life: the broad, which offers a great deal of amusement and entertainment but leads to hell, and the narrow, which leads via many trials and hardships to heaven. Originating in German Württemberg Pietism (1863), the plate also became known in the Anglo-Saxon world from 1883 on after the open-air preacher Gawin Kirkham became acquainted with it when preaching in Amsterdam and The Hague. The plate often hung in catechism classrooms, Sunday schools, and deaconess hospitals as well as in living rooms. Many children looked fearfully at the fires of hell, while others faithfully learned by heart the Bible texts that were cited in various scenes. In general, the depiction was a far-reaching indoctrination of the biblicist two-paths theology. It made a strong visual appeal to the viewer to figure out on what path he was or what phase of the route, whether he had to go back or had to persevere in his present way of life.[22]

In 1887 the publisher of Protestant children's books in Nijkerk, G.F. Callenbach (1833-1917), started to expand his stock with visual material, inspired – as he said himself – by the American products of the Providence Lithograph Company. He began with children's books containing colourful illustrations of which several copies were ordered by Sunday school boards at one time to be handed out at Christmas celebrations or other occasions. Wall texts printed in colour quickly followed, as did Bible and missionary prints. This was in turn followed by a large Christmas print of the child Jesus in the crib, surrounded by Mary and Joseph and by the wisemen from the east, available in a black-and-white and colour editions, "a

4.5-3 *Dutch version of the popular lithography 'The broad and narrow way'. (See for the English version, col. ill. 13.)* [Private collection]

true gem for many a room". In 1910, Callenbach introduced a cut-out of the tabernacle and in 1915 two new 'cut-outs' of an oriental sheepfold and an oriental farmer's home. The small cards with biblical depictions that served as 'reward pictures' in countless (Sunday) schools were a continuing success. The role of the image in religious indoctrination had undeniably penetrated Protestantism to a large extent at that time.[23]

Bible interpreters portrayed

During the peak period of the confessional age, a print circulated in Europe on the theme "the light is placed on the candlestick," which had been published by an English bookseller around 1650. The print showed a table with a row of Reformers on the one side – Luther, Calvin, Melancthon around a Bible with a burning candle. On the other side of the table was the pope, a cardinal, a monk, and the devil itself who were attempting in vain to blow the candle out, a symbol of the light of the Holy Spirit in the Word of

22 Mönnich and Van der Plas, *Het Woord in beeld,* 144-145; Lang, "Geschichte und Konzeption von Charlotte Reihlens Zwei-Wege-Bild"; Van Lieburg, *Opwekking van de natie,* 165-167.
23 Dane, "Goed, fraai en goedkoop".

God. This print was reprinted various times in the Dutch Republic, suitable for hanging on the wall as an emblem of the Protestant Reformation. A good addition was a portrait gallery on the wall in the picture with other figures (for example Philips Marnix van St. Aldegonde) that fit into the Dutch perception of Reformation history. There is even a Delft plate from 1692 on which the gallery is supplemented by subtle references to contemporary discussions in theology and philosophy in the Dutch Republic.[24]

This Reformation print appears to fallen out of favour in the eighteenth century but would be reproduced in the time of reconfessionalisation in the nineteenth century. The notion of reference to confessional identity in the home is striking. Aside from specific historical episodes, this was expressed in individual portraits of ministers, who were servants of the Word in specific stands or were icons of a certain theological orientation in the national church. Such portraits were found in books but were also marketed separately with the possibility of framing and exhibiting in private homes. In a large city like Amsterdam, prints with several portraits of then active ministers were being produced. In addition, there were quite a number of portraits of the great Protestant Reformers (Menno Simons, Martin Luther, and John Calvin) and various ministers circulating, in some cases as paintings but much more often as relatively large prints. The religious function of these images has to be sought in a mixture of confessional identity, local connectedness, and personal identification with – or in imitation of – a more or less universal Christian spirituality and subdued piety.

Over the course of the nineteenth century, Dutch Protestantism extended its range of confessional icons with figures who primarily represented a specific spiritual, ideological, and political orientation. Labels like the Protestant Réveil, the anti-revolutionary, Christian-historical or neo-Calvinistic movements dominated with respect to these orientations, but important public representatives of a classical Christian, biblical worldview were, in any case, the authors Willem Bilderdijk, Isaac da Costa, and politician Guillaume Groen van Prinsterer. Illustrative for this widening as well as for a material enrichment is a bookcase that was offered in 1890 by the supporters of the Anti-Revolutionary Party to 'their' Minister of Colonies, Levinus W.C. Keuchenius (1822-1893). This bookcase, filled with works by Reformed writers from the sixteenth to the nineteenth century, was ornamented with two Protestant figures and with a bronze bust of Groen van Prinsterer by the sculptor Bart van Hove.

Among the newest heroes of orthodox Protestantism in the late nineteenth and early twentieth century was Abraham Kuyper (1837-1920), who, in various roles of preacher, journalist, politician, professor, launched the national mobilisation of traditional Reformed people. He can also be used as an illustration of the acceptance of the art form of the bust in a religious subculture that actually wanted little to do with images, let alone sculptures. He even wrote in his famous Stone lectures: "Calvinism has never burned its incense upon the altar of genius, it has erected no monument for its heroes, it scarcely calls them by name."[25] In his house, in the meantime, was a large bust of Calvin, commissioned by a group of friends from a German sculptor and offered to him at his 25th wedding anniversary.[26] In 1905, as prime minister, he allowed a marble bust of himself to be made by the prominent artist Toon Dupuis. After his death in 1920, it was completely normal for people to be able to buy bronze and copper plaques with his profile.[27] [Ill. 4.5-4]

The greatest breakthrough in the material image culture of the nineteenth century is to be attributed, of course, to photography, which penetrated all strata and persuasions in society. For the top stratum of the Protestant world, this meant first of all the diversification and democratisation of the minister's portrait. The classic depiction of the expositor of the Word and pulpit orator, with his official robes and with Bible

---

24 Spaans, "Faces of the Reformation".
25 Kuyper, *Het Calvinisme*, 16 ("Het calvinisme heeft nooit zijn wierook voor het genie ontstoken, het heeft geen standbeeld voor zijn helden opgericht, ternauwernood noemt men hun namen.").
26 *De Bazuin*, 6 juli 1888.
27 The plaque of Kuyper was designed by Johannes Cornelis Wienecke and was produced and sold by Hotzo Spanninga at Joure.

4.5-4 Buste of John Calvin, possessed by Abraham Kuyper.
[Amsterdam, University Library Vrije Universiteit Amsterdam]

and book nearby, was broadened to include scenes of his life in his study, with his family in the garden, or with his church council in the council room, with the ministers' society in a city or region. When ministers were installed or left, reproductions of such photographs found their way into the hands of congregational members. At the same time, the minister lost his monopoly on being the image-bearer of the tradition of the Word. Church councils, the boards of all kinds of societies, such as those of the Christian boys' and girls' societies, posed for the photographer. Thus, the deep anchoring of religion in the daily life of (Protestant) Dutch people in image and the material was established by the participants themselves who wanted to be appreciated and remembered by succeeding generations.

Conclusion

We began this chapter on the material conditions of the *homo religiosus* within Dutch Protestantism with an example of an overview of numbers from the Bible that appeared on the market from the late eighteenth century on. In the early twentieth century, the *homo ludens* could also play a card game that was specially devoted to the Bible. Curiously enough, this *Biblisches Quartettspiel* (Biblical Happy Families Game) was introduced by a German Talmud teacher in 1920, Simon Unna in Frankfurt am Main.[28] Perhaps under the influence of this Jewish inspiration, the Protestant bookseller and Bible salesman Nicolaas Rot (1880-1925) followed shortly thereafter with a Dutch version. In his hometown of Apeldoorn, Rot was a leader of the Plymouth Brethren, thus a member of an international revival movement. His "biblical Happy Families game" also contained cards with people and texts from the New Testament.

It is remarkable that in contemporary Protestantism the phenomenon of a card game that used the Bible is viewed critically. A review in the *Algemeen Weekblad voor Christenen en Cultuur* (General Weekly for Christians and Culture) in 1929 criticised the biblical Happy Families game for children issued by the orthodox Protestant publisher Marcelis Bredée (1854-1947) in Rotterdam: "Are there really Christian parents who would allow the Bible to be misused in this way in their home? The intention may be good, but ... that can't be!"[29] What seemed to one group to be a good means to practise and expand one's religious knowledge was an inappropriate mingling of the profane and religious sphere for another. Paradoxically enough but not theologically incomprehensible, liberalism can be associated with the dematerialisation of the spiritual life, whereas Christians faithful to the Bible made ready use of material aids for raising and educating their children.

The reference to the 'home circle' points in the meantime to the broad acceptance of

28 Publisher was Nicolaas Bamberger in Bad Kissingen. Object in Leo Baeck Institute, New York (partner in Center for Jewish History). A positive commentary can be found in *Nieuw Israelietisch Weekblad*, 12 March 1920.

29 Cited in *Nieuwe Rotterdamsche Courant*, 9 July 1929 ("Zouden er werkelijk christenouders zijn, die toelaten, dat in hun huiskring de Bijbel op deze wyze wordt misbruikt? De bedoeling zal wel goed zyn, maar... – dat moet toch niet!").

the unity of the public and private sphere, in the church and religious life as well. The general rise of the 'domestication' during the nineteenth century, which resulted in the cultural civilisation offensives and responses to the effects of industrialisation, pauperisation, and women's emancipation is again illustrated in this contribution on Dutch Protestantism. According to the standard hypothesis, we can see a process of 'devotionalisation' here just as we can in Roman Catholicism in various Protestant denominations and subcultures. The material shape of that development was the consequence of the enormous growth in the production of Bibles, books, plates, prints, and other data carriers. Supply and demand stimulated each other, and the consumption of these products outside the traditional spaces of church and (Sunday) school penetrated irresistibly into the literal and figurative private rooms of daily existence.

For convenience's sake, we have focused on the objects and subjects of word and image that the Word mediated in the sacral sense – Bibles, books, wall plates, prints and even sculptures. The card game was also discussed, and in my 2013 contribution to this series, the advent of the Christmas tree in nineteenth-century Protestant living rooms was recalled. Music instruments should not be overlooked to the extent that they were also involved in the movement of sacralisation and essentialisation of music. In imitation of the pipe organ (church or cabinet organ), the harmonium became more popular in private homes and stimulated vocal piety. Abraham Kuyper articulated that in a striking way to his supporters in 1891: "The increasing use of the organ in Christian circles promotes decent singing extraordinarily, and it is to be desired that, in the circles of our people the worldly piano will be moved more to the background so that the organ can again be given a place of honour."[30] Protestant organ and music sellers nurtured this desire.

Just like religiosity simulated domestication, domestication stimulated religiosity in a spiritual and material sense.[31] As cultural symbols of religious identities, material artefacts supported the religious shape of everyday life.[32] This interaction was not typically Dutch; confessional differences are just as undeniable as those between Catholic and Protestant church interiors. The Catholic home religion was practised in a sacral space around an image of Mary, surrounded by crucifixes and devotional prints.[33] The Protestant living room had its wall symbols, possibly a lectern for and with the Bible, a bust or a harmonium but lacked an acknowledged cultic centre. That cultic centre here was rather the daily Bible reading, regular prayer and singing, the rhythm of the mediation of salvation through the Scripture, in text, image, or, in the final instance, the spiritual depiction of the incarnate Word.[34]

---

30 *De Heraut,* 11 October 1891 ("Het toenemend gebruik van het Orgel in de Christelijke kringen bevordert het behoorlijk zingen ongemeen, en het ware te wenschen, dat men in de kringen van ons volk de wereldsche piano al meer op den achtergrond deed treden, om het Orgel weer in eere te brengen."). Cf. Köhle-Hezinger, "Das Harmonium".
31 Hall, "Sweet Home"; Morgan, *The Lure of Images,* 103-134.
32 Cf. Nissen, "Percepties van sacraliteit", 263-264.
33 Nissen, "'Zoals in het huisje van Nazareth…'".
34 Cf. Morgan, *Visual Piety,* 182.

BIBLIOGRAPHY

Asselt, Willem J. van. "The Prohibition of Images and Protestant Identity". In: Willem J. van Asselt et al., eds. *Iconoclasm and Iconoclash: Struggle for Religious Identity*. Leiden-Boston, 2007, 299-311.

Björnståhl, J.J. *Reize door Europa en het Oosten. Vijfde deel, bevattende Het dagboek der reize door Zwitserland, Duitschland, Holland en Engeland*. Utrecht-Amsterdam, 1783.

Dane, Jacques. "'Goed, fraai en goedkoop.' De zondagsschool en de verbeelding van Gods woord (1880-1940)". In: Arie L. Molendijk, ed. *Materieel christendom. Religie en materiële cultuur in West-Europa*. Hilversum, 2003, 129-145.

Dibbits, Hester. *Vertrouwd bezit. Materiële cultuur in Doesburg en Maassluis 1650-1850*. Nijmegen, 2001.

Eisfeld, Helmut, ed. *Lebenserinnerungen von Paul und Sophie Schönwälder [1836-1895]*. Röttenbach, 2006.

Exalto, John. *Wandelende bijbels. Piëtistische leescultuur in Nederland 1830-1960*. Zoetermeer, 2006.

Exalto, John. "Religious Visual Culture in the Private Space: The Living Room in Late Nineteenth- and Early Twentieth-Century Dutch Protestantism". *Trajecta*, 25 (2016), 217-237.

Fikse-Omon, Katinka. *Papieren evangelisten. Van VVHS en BKV naar Ark Mission 1913-2013*. Amsterdam, 2013.

Gelderen, J. van. *Filippus, gereformeerd traktaatgenootschap 1878-1978. Fragmenten ontleend aan het uitgavenfonds van "Filippus"*. Hattem, 1978.

Hall, Catherine. "Sweet Home". In: Michelle Perrot, ed. *Histoire de la vie privée*. 4: *De la Révolution à la Grande Guerre*. Paris, 2000, 53-88.

Hildebrand [pseudonym of Nicolaas Beets]. *Camera Obscura*. Haarlem, 1839.

Jarlert, Anders, ed. *Piety and Modernity. The Dynamics of Religious Reform in Northern Europe, 1780-1820*, 3. Leuven, 2012.

Kamermans, Johan A. *Materiële cultuur in de Krimpenerwaard in de zeventiende en achttiende eeuw. Ontwikkeling en diversiteit*. Wageningen, 1999.

Köhle-Hezinger, Christel. "Das Harmonium oder: Frommes Schwellen, sanfte Bewegung". In: Siegfried Becker et al., eds. *Volkskundliche Tableaus. Eine Festschrift für Martin Scharfe zum 65. Geburtstag von Weggefährten, Freunden und Schülern*. Münster etc., 2001, 183-202.

Kootte, T.G., ed. *De bijbel in huis. Bijbelse verhalen op huisraad in de zeventiende en achttiende eeuw*. Zwolle-Utrecht, 1991.

Kuyper, Abraham. *Het Calvinisme. Zes Stonelezingen, in October 1898 te Princeton (N.-J.) gehouden*. Amsterdam, 1899.

Lang, Friedrich Gustav. "Geschichte und Konzeption von Charlotte Reihlens Zwei-Wege-Bild". *Blätter für württembergische Kirchengeschichte*, 110 (2010), 305-367.

Lieburg, Fred van. "De Bijbel als orakelboek. Bibliomantie in de protestantse traditie". In: Arie L. Molendijk, ed. *Materieel christendom. Religie en materiële cultuur in West-Europa*. Hilversum, 2003, 81-105.

Lieburg, Fred van, ed. *Opwekking van de natie. Het protestantse Réveil in Nederland*. Hilversum, 2012.

Lieburg, Fred van. "Reforming Dutch Protestant Piety, 1780-1920". In: Anders Jarlert, ed. *Piety and Modernity. The Dynamics of Religious Reform in Northern Europe, 1780-1820*, 3. Leuven, 2012, 157-185 and 187-190.

Lieburg, Fred van. "Direkte Gotteserfahrung. Pietismus und Bibliomantie". *Pietismus und Neuzeit. Ein Jahrbuch für die Geschichte des neueren Protestantismus*, 39 (2013), 298-314.

Lieburg, Fred van. *De wereld in. Het Nederlands Bijbelgenootschap 1814-2014*. Amsterdam, 2014.

Maan, Tony. "Material Culture and Popular Calvinist Worldliness in the Dutch 'Golden Age'". *History Compass*, 9 (2011), 284-299.

Margry, Peter Jan. "Dutch Devotionalisation. Reforming Piety: Grassroots Initiative or Clerical Strategy?" In: Anders Jarlert, ed. *Piety and Modernity. The Dynamics of Religious Reform in Northern Europe, 1780-1820*, 3. Leuven, 2012, 125-156 and 186-187.

Molendijk, Arie L., ed. *Materieel christendom. Religie en materiële cultuur in West-Europa*. Hilversum, 2003.

Mönnich, C.W., and Michel van der Plas. *Het Woord in beeld. Vijf eeuwen Bijbel in het dagelijkse leven*. Baarn, 1977.

Morgan, David. *Visual Piety. A History and Theory of Popular Religious Images*. Berkeley etc., 1998.

Morgan, David. *The Lure of Images: A History of Religion and Visual Media in America*. London-New York, 2007.

Nissen, Peter. "'Zoals in het huisje van Nazareth...'. Over devoties en rituelen in de kring van het gezin en de religieuze aankleding van het woonhuis". *Trajecta*, 4 (1995), 141-157.

Nissen, Peter. "Percepties van sacraliteit. Over religieuze volkscultuur". In: Ton Dekker, Herman Roodenburg and Gerard Rooijakkers, eds. *Volkscultuur. Een inleiding in de Nederlandse etnologie*. Nijmegen-Amsterdam, 2000, 231-281.

Noordwijk, Bernard van. *Zondags zilver. Drie eeuwen versierde kerkboekjes*. Heerenveen, 2006.

Noordwijk, Bernard van. *De erfenis van Kortjakje. 250 jaar boekjes vol zilverwerk*. Kampen, 2009.

Noordwijk, Bernard van. *Zilver voor de Zondag. "Boecxkens met pragtigh sluytwerck"*. Heerenveen, 2013.

Pluis, Jan. *Bijbeltegels / Bibelfliesen. Bijbelse voorstellingen op Nederlandse wandtegels van de 17e tot de 20e eeuw / Biblische Darstellungen auf Niederländischen Wandfliesen vom 17. bis zum 20. Jahrhundert*. Münster, 1994.

Spaans, Joke. "Faces of the Reformation". *Church History and Religious Culture*, 97 (2017), 408-451.

Steensma, Regnerus. *Protestantse kerken: hun pracht en kracht*. Gorredijk, 2013.

Swigchem, C.A. van, T. Brouwer and W. van Os. *Een huis voor het Woord. Het protestantse kerkinterieur in Nederland tot 1900*. The Hague - Zeist, 1984.

Trommius, Abraham. *Volkomene Nederlandtsche Concordantie ofte Woordt-register des Nieuwen [resp. Ouden] Testaments*. Groningen, 1672 resp. 1685-1691.

Vloten, J. van, and M.A. Brandts Buys. *Nederlandsche baker- en kinderrijmen [1871/1872]*. Rotterdam, 1995.

Zijp, Robert P. "Wandteksten, een teken aan de muur". In: Robert P. Zijp, ed. *Vroomheid per dozijn*. Utrecht, 1982, 68-72.

Erinnerung
an die erste heilige Communion.

Laßt' mit frommem Sinn uns ehren
Jesum, unser höchstes Gut,
Denn er will uns selbst hier nähren
Durch sein eig'nes Fleisch und Blut.

Das allerheiligste Altars-Sakrament, habe ich zum **erstenmal** empfangen, den 16ten April im Jahre 18 50 in der Pfarr-Kirche zu St. Amas zu Ofen

Tausck Elise

P. Franz Sales m/p

4.6
Pious Things

Popular Religiosity of the Nineteenth Century from the Perspective of Material Culture in Germany

Dagmar Hänel

The 'long nineteenth century', the period between approximately 1780 and 1914 is of great importance for the development of modern society.[1] Religion, especially in terms of its institutions, its interpretation in everyday culture and its representation is amongst the central areas of discourse of this time and is summarised by the term 'secularisation'.[2] While this process seems clear on the institutional level, there is a manifold difference in the field of popular religiosity, where one finds religious practices handed down from the *ancien regime* as for instance pilgrimages to Kevelaer and Altötting, alongside new established cults of the Immaculata, based on the model of Lourdes and the Sacred Heart of Jesus. Statues of saints and religious pictures become mass products with various functions in community life and in the mission, which is once again in revival, as well as in domestic and individual piety. It is exactly the material culture of popular piety which shows the effectiveness of religious belief systems in everyday life.[3] 'Pious things', however, also show the variety and heterogeneous nature of this phenomenon. In order to make this variety manageable, examples are categorised according to public and private areas, as well as to the social contexts of community and family. Before a concluding summary, individual religious objects are described in brief.

Religiosity in the nineteenth century in Germany

The theme and area to be described for the defined time period are by no means clear. While it is hoped that the theme of 'religion', or rather 'popular religiosity' through the perspective of material culture can be worked out more clearly below, it is necessary to describe in brief and limit the spatial reference to a nation state which exists only from the end of the period of investigation.

In the nineteenth century, the small states which had historically developed within the Holy Roman Empire of the German Nation transform themselves under the leadership of Prussia into a nation state (the state was founded in 1871). Religion and religious denomination play important roles in this process of nation building. In the following account the individual states are not specified, but the main directions of development which they have in common are described. A spatial focus is the Rhine Province, as the religious conflict situation between church and state is particularly evident here, and at the same time the Rhine Province, together with the neighbouring state of Westfalia, represents the most comprehensive cultural transformation as a result of industrialisation (mining and steel industry in the Ruhr region and in the Saarland, the textile industry in the Rhineland and Westfalia). The conflict situation between church (especially the Catholic Church) and the state is not an innovation which begins with the dominance of Prussia in 1815, but it is something which has its roots in the confessionalisation processes of the sixteenth and seventeenth

4.6-1 German first communion remembrance print for Elise Tausch, 16 April 1850.
[Collection P.J. Margry]

1 Bauer, *Das "lange" 19. Jahrhundert*.
2 McLeod, *Secularisation*.
3 Basic comparison on this: Korff, "Zwischen Sinnlichkeit und Kirchlichkeit"; Pieske, *Bilder für jedermann*; Kriss-Rettenbeck, *Ex Voto*; Mohrmann, *Individuum und Frömmigkeit*; Scharfe, *Über die Religion*.

4.6-2 Saint Catharine painted on glass (Hinterglasschilderung), home wall decoration from Bayern, c 1800. [Collection P.J. Margry]

centuries. For the late eighteenth century, it can be stated that the position of the church is characterised by the beginnings of the Enlightenment, which takes a critical view of traditional forms of piety, especially those of Catholic origin, such as pilgrimage and the veneration of saints, and rejects them as latently 'superstitious'.[4] Alongside this, however, a Catholic renewal movement is growing up, which promotes traditional forms of piety, and whose influence clearly increases in the course of the nineteenth century by measures such as mission work and the founding of religious congregations.[5] [Ill. 4.6-2]

Werner Blessing summarises basic constellations of everyday religious culture and in addition to a town – country difference, also points to the importance of denominational differences. Both Reformed and Lutheran parishes were "concentrated on Christ and the Bible, prayer and chorale, and therefore had a close connection to the pastor and church rules, in other words to a leading figure who was bourgeois by origin and habitus"[6]. In contrast to that, Catholic parish priests were mainly from rural or artisan families, the religious life of Catholicism was more sensuous represented in rituals and images. Within the context of the founding of the *Reich* and the process of nation building, the question of religious denomination is increasingly politicised and represented in the *Kulturkampf* right down to the level of family and private piety. In the German *Reich*, there is not only a denominational split but also a social one: especially the rural, agrarian regions of the middle and southern areas have a mainly Catholic population and are characterised by poverty.

In the course of the internal immigration caused by industrialisation, masses of the uneducated, socially weak population groups migrate to the industrialised centres (for example in the Ruhr region and the Saarland). Here, and in the cities, they meet the Protestant elite: civil servants, factory owners, academics, who not only stand as representatives for the Prussian state and the modern world, but also for the 'wrong' denomination. With the help of denominational polemics on both sides, powerful stereotypes of the 'uneducated, superstitious Catholics' on the one side and the 'liberal-modernist, anti-church Protestants' on the other side are popularised and used ideologically in the *Culture Wars*.[7]

Three phases can be discerned for specific manifestations of popular religious culture:
1. Enlightenment and Catholic restoration (approx. 1780-1815),
2. Denominational conflicts in Prussia (approx. 1815-1870),
3. Kulturkampf in the Empire (approx. 1870-1880).

Through all three phases there runs the increasing industrialisation and the rise of the bourgeoisie with the enforcement of a specific set of values as guiding processes in the context of social and cultural change.

A fourth and final phase, which brings the nineteenth century to a close, is the beginning of the First World War: here the nation is sanctified and Reich and Kaiser are presented as integrating institutions which rise above religious denominations. Specific material testimonies can be read as paradigm symbols for the transformation of these conflicts and the underlying religious thought patterns into daily cultural practice.

---

4   For the term 'superstition' and the relevant discourses, see Daxelmüller, "Volksfrömmigkeit" and Hänel, "Frömmigkeit im Transit?".
5   Cf. Kotulla, *"Nach Lourdes!"* and Klosterkamp, *Katholische Volksmission*.
6   Blessing, "Reform, Restauration, Rezession", 99.
7   For the culture battle in Prussia, see Clark and Kaiser, *Culture Wars*.

Religion in the public sphere

It is obvious that in a time which is characterised by conflict between state and church institutions, the public sphere gains importance as a cultural area for both subtle and explicit representation of symbolic negotiating processes. Pilgrimages, for example the massive pilgrimage to the Robe of Jesus in Trier in 1844, and even more so in 1891, become demonstrations of Catholic piety against state repression of the faith.[8] Pilgrims 'conquer' streets and public squares and show a collective presence by their large numbers. The crosses, statues of saints, pictures and pilgrimage flags carried in the pilgrimage procession are a visual sign of the sacred in profane places. Songs and prayers are acoustic signs of the appropriation of space. The increase in religious expressions can be read as a reaction to the growing state repression in the context of the Culture Wars.[9]

Another kind of public space in which religion manifests itself in many ways, both material and ritual, is the cemetery. The nineteenth century brings with it many changes in burial practices.[10] In the French occupied parts of the empire, for example in the Rhineland and in Westfalia, French law is applied to burial practices. Burials within the church premises became forbidden, burials were put under the control of communities from an organisational and financial point of view, and many new cemeteries are created outside city limits and made subject to hygiene and medical conditions.[11] The Prussian reforms entrench these developments after 1815 and strengthen the enlightenment-scientific aspect with the introduction of the autopsy and the morgue.[12] Cremation becomes a subject of conflict between denominations: this is promoted above all in educated, urban middle-class circles, which are enlightened and liberal, this new practice of funeral culture provokes, however, opposition in Catholic traditionalism.[13] The sanctions even extend to excommunication.[14] The materials and design of the crematoria built

4.6-3 The Angel (galvanoplasty) based on the model of Adolf Lehnert is widely distributed throughout Germany. This example stand on a gravestone from the Lindener Berg cemetery in Hannover. [Wikimedia Commons; photo Ra Boe, 2006]

in the nineteenth and early twentieth century suggest sacred buildings,[15] and at first the introduction of cremation had only a minor effect on the cemeteries. Technical innovations in production and material have a stronger influence on tomb and grave design: the new technique of galvanoplasty becomes an industrial mass product. In sepulchral culture, this technique becomes important for a mainly bourgeois mourning culture. Figures of mourning women and angels were especially popular, and the imagery of the cemeteries in the nineteenth century shows a romantically transfigured view of death and the hereafter, symbolised in the antique looking forms of broken columns and Greek temple architecture, with butterflies and mourners. [Ill. 4.6-3] Neo-Gothic elements were also very popular, this also express a shift towards medieval religious symbolism, which was

8 Cf. Clark and Kaiser, *Culture Wars*; Korf, "Formierung der Frömmigkeit"; Blackbourn, *Marpingen*.
9 Cf. Clark and Kaiser, *Culture Wars*.
10 Cf. basically the following: Ariès, *Geschichte des Todes*; Fischer, *Vom Gottesacker zum Krematorium*; Denk and Zieserner, *Der bürgerliche Tod*.
11 Cf. Ariès, *Geschichte des Todes*; Fischer, *Vom Gottesacker zum Krematorium*.
12 Hänel, *Bestatter im 20. Jahrhundert*, 41-44.
13 Fischer, *Vom Gottesacker zum Krematorium*; Thalmann, *Urne oder Sarg*.
14 In 1886, the Catholic Church issues a ban on cremation, which also forbids any participation by the clergy in any such funeral.
15 The first crematorium in Germany is built in Gotha, and the first cremation takes place there in 1878: Fischer, *Vom Gottesacker zum Krematorium*, 209f.

407

promoted by romanticism. This use of sacred forms, like the many tomb structures using church architecture, is a reaction to the loss of the use of churches for burials.

The cemetery of the nineteenth century was moreover a place of social distinction, and by using a recognised pictorial scheme in the design of the grave, a family sees itself as enlightened, bourgeois and modern.[16] It did not make much difference for its symbolic value whether an investment was made in a stone monument on the grave, or whether a galvanoplastic item is bought from a catalogue. Social lower classes are represented rather rarely in civil grave design. Their dead are buried in graves in rows, without much form of decoration. Gravestones are often marked with a cross, or are erected directly in the form of a cross. Wooden crosses and statues of Mary, the latter often as cheap plaster figures were widespread.

The changes in the material design of the cemetery as a place to represent mourning and remembrance culture clearly show the assertion of bourgeois views of the world and aesthetics. Religion, especially in its institutionalised form as the church, is pushed from the cemeteries and the burial culture to the sidelines, and new professions such as funeral directors take over central functions of social networks like the neighbourhood and the clergy. This process started in urban surroundings and escalated also in rural regions during the century. The material design of the cemetery, however, draws on religious motifs, from neo-Gothic architecture to the mourning angel.

Community life

Central areas of religious life in the church communities take place in public. Feasts during the course of the year, with their traditional practices such as processions, blessings, pilgrimages, but also with fairs connected to religious festivals point to the public character of religion and certain forms of piety.[17] The Sunday service with its social implications and other supplementary factors are also part of this. It is in the conflict between state and church that these public events of religious life become sensitive conflict areas.

This conflict becomes clear in relation to the question of how to handle Sundays and holidays in the context of industrial work. By the beginning of the nineteenth century, various Catholic holidays were no longer recognised appropriately. Thus, in the context of French occupation, the number of (non-working) holidays was reduced to four (Christmas, New Year, Easter Monday, Assumption). After 1815, this restriction was partially maintained by the Prussian authorities, although there were different regulations in the various regions. This situation brought the issue of the relevance of 'Sundays and Holidays' within a denominational polemic. The reactions to the state influence on the practice of religion differ – they range from acceptance to resistance, and even the clergy were divided in their actions. The 'Holiday Contract', which was negotiated between Prussia and the Vatican in 1829, was only a superficial solution: fourteen Catholic holidays were recognised, but not as non-working days. In a pastoral letter, Archbishop Count Spiegel of Cologne allows believers "to go to work after attending early morning mass".[18] This is a reflection of the need of the industry to keep machines and furnaces running continuously. Economic interests outweigh religious ones, an undisturbed working life outweighs the life of the community.

The clergy tried to counteract the diminishing connection of its following to the church through missionary activities. Parish missions by Jesuits or other orders led to a revival of piety, above all because new devotions inspired by romanticism, Sacred Heart of Jesus worship and a revival in veneration of the Virgin Mary, due to apparitions in France, which inspired later ones in Belgium and Germany, fell on fertile ground.[19] Virgin Mary and Sacred Heart of Jesus devotions, rosary prayers and other forms of piety were

16 Fischer, *Vom Gottesacker zum Krematorium*.
17 Kriss-Rettenbeck emphasises the public nature of votive offerings as actions with a legal character: Kriss-Rettenbeck, *Ex voto*, 303.
18 Sperber, "Der Kampf und die Feiertage in Rheinland-Westfalen", 130; Id., *Popular Catholicism*.
19 For Sacred Heart of Jesus worship in the nineteenth century, see Morgan, *The Sacred Heart of Jesus*; Busch, *Katholische Frömmigkeit* and Schlager, *Kult und Krieg*. For the appearances of the Virgin Mary in Lourdes, see Harris, *Lourdes*; Kotulla, *"Nach Lourdes!"*

4.6-4 Devotional image of the Sacred Heart of Jesus.
[Bonn, LVR-Institut für Landeskunde und Regionalgeschichte]

4.6-5 Devotional image of the apparition of the Virgin Mary in Lourdes.
[Bonn, LVR-Institut für Landeskunde und Regionalgeschichte]

above all supported and popularised by community groups and religious brotherhoods and sisterhoods. In 1856, Pope Pius IX introduced the solemnity of the Sacred Heart of Jesus on the third Friday after Pentecost. The first Friday in the month counts as Sacred Heart of Jesus Friday, on which there are masses and blessings for the sick, the Blessed Sacrament is displayed and the sacramental blessing is dispensed. In 1875, the German episcopate dedicated the German Empire to the Sacred Heart of Jesus and in 1899, Pope Leo XIII dedicated the entire world to the Sacred Heart of Jesus.[20] [Ill. 4.6-4 & Ill. 4.6-5]

The events in Marpingen in the Saarland show how influential the images and stories of the appearance of the Virgin Mary in Lourdes, popularised all over Europe, were on people's world of imagination, and how useful they were in the political and ideological battle. In 1876, three children reported a total of eleven appearances by the Mother of God, who appeared here in the form of the Immaculata, the Immaculate Conception, as in the narrations successfully handed down, especially from Lourdes. As soon as the first appearance was made known, a stream of pilgrims broke upon the mining and farming village, stories of healing promoted the popularity of the place. In Marpingen, the Prussian authorities came down hard on the "hair-raising belief in ghosts"[21]: the authorities used military power against the pilgrims, the children were taken from their parents and accommodated in a Protestant educational establishment for several months. In addition, the attitude of the parish priest and the episcopal administration in Trier, which ranged from wait-and-see to rejection, contributed to the rejection of the pilgrimage (at that time the bishop's seat was vacant, Prussia and the Vatican were arguing about the appointment and the acceptance). The study by David Blackborn shows the relationships of social problems and crisis in the context of industrialisation and impoverishment of the region to the strengthening of the cult of the Virgin Mary according to the French model,

20 Art, "Herz Jesu", 52.
21 Frohschammer, "Die Glaubwürdigkeit der Wunderheilungen", 167.

and shows their ideological meaning and usefulness in the *Kulturkampf*.[22]

The increase in worship of Saint Joseph can also be interpreted in the context of industrialisation. Joseph, who at best has a peripheral role in the New Testament as the betrothed of Maria and the foster father of Jesus, becomes 'Joseph the Worker' and an integrating figure for Catholic industrial workers.[23] The iconography of this saint[24] changes here: in the Middle Ages and in the Baroque period, Joseph was depicted as an old man and placed in the nativity scenes next to or behind the crib, or was shown with only sparse, white hair, leading a donkey on the flight to Egypt, while the 'new' Joseph is younger and is shown as a craftsman with his tools.[25] [Ill. 4.6-6]

May 1st becomes his commemoration day – this date can also be read in the context of the beginning of the workers' movement, the social question, and the attitude of the church as a deliberate counterpoint and an attempt to bind the workers to the church and community life.[26] This attempt is not very successful, and on the contrary, it is clear that the Catholic Restoration and the introduction of the new emotional devotions appeal to and reach women in the main, while men have other priorities.[27]

On the Evangelical side as well, the clergy battles against the increasing distance between the population and the church. The 'internal mission', with institutions such as the 'Rauhes Haus'[28] and the deaconesses, took on the modernity, which, with industrialisation and social deprivation, was seen as anti-faith, using similar strategies to those of the Catholic Church: ritualising, emotionalising, religious education for the people. In this connection, quite new forms of material religious practice emerged, such as the Advent wreath, which was first used as a pedagogical tool by Johann Heinrich Wichern in 1839 as a symbolic representation of the time of Advent. In contrast to present-day practice Wichern still placed a candle for every day on a wooden wheel, whereby the Sundays were represented by bigger candles. In the

4.6-6 *Devotional image of Saint Joseph the Worker. (See also col. ill. 16.)*
[Bonn, LVR-Institut für Landeskunde und Regionalgeschichte]

'Rauhes Haus' in Hamburg, a Protestant educational establishment led by Wichern, light symbolic of the Advent wreath was used as training for religious practices.[29] In a reduced form with four candles, the Advent wreath spread throughout all Germany within a few decades. The Advent wreath decorated family tables in both bourgeois and rural areas, as well as in Protestant churches and, after World War I, also in Catholic churches and community halls. In the course of the establishment of the bourgeois Christmas time, it became an important part of the sensuous comprehensible preparation.[30] The advent wreath is in addition an example of how religious objects from the public spaces of the churches and communities migrate into the intimacy of the family and private life.

The privatisation of piety: the Christian family

It was not only Wilhelm Heinrich Riel who thought of the family as the nucleus of the nation.[31] The Christian churches also define the family as the cornerstone of their community. Thus the nineteenth century is characterised by a reinterpretation of the social family ideal: the new working and living conditions of the industrialised world promote a bourgeois family idyll, which can only seldom be lived out in reality. Women's and children's work, impoverishment and the loss of traditional social networks formed the background to the everyday reality of family life. It is in the urban bourgeoisie above all that a retreat into the private and into the introduction of new roles for the family and the sexes can be seen. Here, religiosity becomes an element of a bourgeois value system, a process that however can be described as supra-denominational, but at the same time, it implies a certain distancing from the rules of the institutionalised church and community life. The introduction of this bourgeois family ideal is especially apparent in the context of the transformation of annual religious practices: Christmas and Easter, as central Christian celebrations, are redefined as bourgeois family celebrations and are equipped with new symbols (Father Christmas, Baby Jesus, and Easter Bunny) and with new rituals (Christmas tree and decorations, the exchange of gifts, hunting for eggs).[32] This redefinition spreads in the society during the nineteenth century. One main element is, that the celebration of the birth of Christ is no longer the church service in the parish. Thus the bourgeois Christmas celebration, with rituals developed here, and with specific gifts, stories and images is an important element in establishing and incorporating bourgeois values and roles within families.[33] [Ill. 4.6-7]

Apart from the slow transformation of church customs into bourgeois, profane family celebrations, a tendency for the privatisation of religiosity at other levels and in other

4.6-7 Preparation of the Christmas tree. Drawing from the popular bourgeois journal Die Gartenlaube.
[Private collection]

22 Cf. Blackborn, *Marpingen*.
23 Döring, *Heilige Helfer*, 84-87.
24 Joseph is also an important part in the devotion of the 'holy family'. Its iconography refers to bourgeois imagination of an ideal family with its values of diligence, piety and order.
25 The iconography of the 'young' Joseph as a manual labourer begins as early as the sixteenth century, but is increasingly popularised in the nineteenth century by the industrial mass production of printing and plaster statues. Art, "Mann Marias".
26 Korff, "'Heraus zum 1. Mai'".
27 Busch, "Die Feminisierung der ultramontanen Frömmigkeit".
28 'Rauhes Haus' was founded in 1833 in Hamburg as a social service institution. It sheltered children and young people, especially mentally handicapped and disturbed or juvenile delinquents. The aim of the founder, Johann Heinrich Wichern, was the social rehabilitation by education, piety and practices of bourgeois order.
29 Bausinger, "Der Adventkranz".
30 Gajek, "Erst eins, dann zwei, dann drei, dann vier…".
31 Riehl, *Die Familie*.
32 Weber-Kellermann, *Die deutsche Familie*; Id., *Saure Wochen, frohe Feste*.
33 Eberspächer, "Lichterglanz und Kinderglück".

4.6-8 Picture of the guardian angel, a popular wall decoration.
[Bonn, LVR-Institut für Landeskunde und Regionalgeschichte]

social groups is also apparent. The private sphere of family life is increasingly decorated with religious illustrations and furnishings. The technical innovation of industrialisation leads to mass production in the area of religiosity as well. Statues of saints made of plaster, often brightly painted, are integrated into domestic altars and publicly displayed in windows and makeshift altars in front of the home during processions and pilgrimages. Immaculata and Sacred Heart of Jesus figures are very popular. So the mass production of this artefacts indicates the popularity of the new resurgent romantic-emotional devotions.

It is not only the figurative representations of the sacred which becomes cheap by mass production and thus available for all classes. The mass production of pictures also increases massively and cheap prints flood the market, the most popular subjects being religious ones.[34] The latest miracles of the appearance of the Virgin Mary as well as the Sacred Heart of Jesus in Nazarene style were included in this.[35] A popular, supra-denominational subject is the guardian angel, a few standard versions of which decorate bedrooms, hallways, but above all children's rooms in the bourgeois homes of both Protestants and Catholics.[36] [Ill. 4.6-8]

Frequently, complete ensembles of devotional objects are put together, which create sacred rooms within the private sphere: holy figurines, cross, candles, and in addition pictures of the saints and rosary are staged on sideboards or tables, with a Bible or devotional book added, a holy water container hangs on the wall. In rural areas, the symbolic or pictorial presence of the saints is intended to extend their protection to the livestock: consecrated palm branches or bunches of herbs hang on the door of the animal shed,[37] and pictures and statues of the patron saints of livestock are fixed in or on the animal sheds. The mass production of cheap religious objects shows their 'setting in life', which is predominately located in the private sphere of family life.

The world of objects of individual piety

The way people use material culture in order to establish a personal relationship with the sacred, is quite heterogeneous and individual. Religious everyday culture appears too differentiated, and attributions of which things and which actions can create a religious relation are highly subjective. In addition, the attribution made by oneself may vary from the attribution made by others: something which can be obvious religious behaviour for the person himself, may appear to some clergy in the tradition of the Enlightenment to be actions related to magic and 'superstition'.[38]

One example is the rosary devotion. The rosary in fact is one of the most personal religious objects. From the early Middle Ages this object develops from a prayer cord with mostly ten balls to its actual form which was generated in early fifteenth century. It is organised in 59 balls of two different sizes

34 Brückner, *Populäre Druckgraphik Europas.*
35 Brückner, *Elfenreigen – Hochzeitstraum.*
36 Bringéus, *Volksfrömmigkeit,* 64-89.
37 Döring, *Rheinische Bräuche durch das Jahr,* 141, 311f.
38 Scharfe, *Über die Religion.*

in a circle, counting each ten of Ave-Maria and one Lord's Prayer and three plus one balls with a cross to start the rosary prayer.³⁹ The rosary is one of the traditional religious items becoming very popular in the late nineteenth century. Pope Leo XIII supported the rosary with eleven encyclicals from 1883 to 1898,⁴⁰ his motivation is connected with a strong engagement for Marian devotion, especially in the context of the apparitions in Lourdes (1858). With the official support of the rosary devotion, this ritual on the one hand belongs to the sphere of community life, in Marian devotion and pilgrimage. In many Catholic regions the rosary prayer was among the indispensable mourning rituals in case of death.⁴¹ However, individual prayer and private devotion was also carried out with the rosary. It was an object of great emotional value, it was often a gift from a godfather on the occasion of communion or confirmation, it was a reminder of the central initiation rituals of life and accompanied the person through life – even up to death, as the rosary was put in the grave with the deceased.

Popular graphic reproductions could also be important for individual piety: pictures of saints and obituary pictures were kept in albums, prayer books, boxes and drawers. [Ill. 4.6-1] Pictures of saints and pilgrimage medals were given as presents, souvenirs of pilgrimages, memorabilia or decoration. In individual use, they were often believed to have the properties of amulets: for example, images of the Sacred Heart of Jesus were not only intended to stimulate the soldier to prayer and remind him of religion while on campaign, but also to confer the protection of the saints upon him. Gottfried Korff coined the term 'Allies in Heaven' for the variety of popular religion during the First World War.⁴²

4.6-9 "Totenzettel", prayer card for a fallen soldier in the First World War. [Bonn, LVR-Institut für Landeskunde und Regionalgeschichte]

Summary and outlook

The inventory of religious objects grew massively in the nineteenth century. Industrial mass production made available statues, pictures, devotional objects and books in previously unimaginable quantity and variety at ever lower prices. People used these objects as piety is increasingly lived and expressed in private and in order to accompany everyday life with religious furnishings. In addition, new cults (Sacred Heart of Jesus, Lourdes) which have a relation to romantic ideals of emotional expressions are spread out. Their great popularity is shown in the mass material representations.

Conflicts between state and Catholic Church accompanied believers throughout the nineteenth century, currently in the last third of the century in the *Kulturkampf*. At the level of popular religiosity, pilgrimages and processions become demonstrations of the power of Catholicism just as much as a subject of denominational – polemical publicity. In this, the actions of the Catholic

39 Frei and Bühler, *Der Rosenkranz*.
40 Ibid.
41 Hänel, *Letzte Reise*.
42 Korff, *Alliierte im Himmel*, 1.

Church were quite ambivalent in its efforts "to control popular piety, to form it, and in phases, to use it for agitation".[43]

From 1878, the *Kulturkampf* was step by step brought to an end. Probably the most important motivations for compromise and understanding between the churches, the Centre Party, and the Prussian State were Bismarck's internal political interests: in order to achieve the Socialist Laws, he needed a broad majority in the parliament. With the outbreak of the First World War, the denominational conflicts were completely put to one side.[44] [Ill. 4.6-9]

The national appeal included all denominational, political and social differences under the national roof. Just like the brothers, fathers, husbands and sons in the field, so by August 1914 at the latest, the Kaiser was no doubt included in individual prayers of many people for protection and assistance. This connection of nation, cult of the Kaiser, and religion also has meaning for the culture of remembering death in war: in the formula "Fallen for Kaiser and Fatherland", the sanctification of the nation coagulates in the culture of monuments and remembrance at the beginning of the twentieth century.

---

43 Freytag, *Aberglauben im 19. Jahrhundert*, 67.

44 "I no longer know any parties, I just know Germans! As a sign that you are firmly resolved, without party differences, without differences of origin or religious denomination, to stick with me through thick and thin, through hardship and death, I request the party leaderships to step forward and give me this in my hand". The speech of Wilhelm II in the Reichstag on 4th August 1914 was an explicit appeal to end the *Kulturkampf*.

BIBLIOGRAPHY

Ariès, Philippe. *Geschichte des Todes*. 9th edition. Munich, 1999.

Art, Jozef. "Herz Jesu, Herz-Jesu Verehrung". In: *Lexikon für Theologie und Kirche*, 5. Freiburg, 1996, 51-58.

Art, Josef. "Mann Mariens". In: *Lexikon für Theologie und Kirche*, 5. Freiburg, 1996, 999-1003.

Bauer, Franz J. *Das "lange" 19. Jahrhundert (1789-1917). Profil einer Epoche*. Stuttgart, 2004.

Bausinger, Hermann. "Der Adventskranz. Ein methodisches Beispiel". In: Martin Scharfe, ed. *Brauchforschung*. Darmstadt, 1991, 225-255.

Blackborn, David. *Marpingen: Apparitions of the Virgin Mary in Bismarckian Germany*. Oxford, 1993.

Blessing, Werner K. "Reform, Restauration, Rezession". In: Wolfgang Schieder, ed. *Volksfrömmigkeit in der modernen Sozialgeschichte*. Göttingen, 1986, 97-122.

Bringéus, Nils-Arvid. *Volksfrömmigkeit. Schwedische religionsethnologische Studien*. Münster, 2000.

Brückner, Wolfgang. *Elfenreigen – Hochzeitstraum. Öldruckfabrikation 1880-1940*. Cologne, 1974.

Brückner, Wolfgang. *Populäre Druckgraphik Europas. Deutschland vom 15. bis zum 20. Jahrhundert*. Munich, 1975.

Brückner, Wolfgang. *Wallfahrt – Pilgerzeichen – Andachtsbild. Aus der Arbeit am Corpuswerk der Wallfahrtsstätten Deutschlands. Probleme, Erfahrungen, Anregungen; mit Katalog und Abbildungen der baden-württembergischen Wallfartsbildchen in der Sammlung Hofmann, Würzburg*. Würzburg, 1982.

Brückner, Wolfgang, and Wolfgang Schneider. *Hinterglasbilder aus den Sammlungen der Diözese Würzburg*. Würzburg, 1990.

Busch, Norbert. "Die Feminisierung der ultramontanen Frömmigkeit". In: Irmtraud Götz v. Olenhusen, ed. *Wunderbare Erscheinungen. Frauen und katholische Frömmigkeit im 19. und 20. Jahrhundert*. Paderborn, 1995, 203-219.

Busch, Norbert. *Katholische Frömmigkeit und Moderne. Die Sozial- und Mentalitätsgeschichte des Herz-Jesu-Kultes in Deutschland zwischen Kulturkampf und Erstem Weltkrieg*. Gütersloh, 1997.

Clark, Christopher, and Wolfram Kaiser, eds. *Culture Wars: Secular-Catholic Conflict in Nineteenth-Century Europe*. Cambridge, 2003.

Daxelmüller, Christoph. "Volksfrömmigkeit". In: Rolf W. Brednich, ed. *Grundriss der Volkskunde. Einführung in die Forschungsfelder der Europäischen Ethnologie*. Berlin, 2001, 491-513.

Denk, Claudia, and John Ziesemer, eds. *Der bürgerliche Tod: Städtische Bestattungskultur von der Aufklärung bis zum frühen 20. Jahrhundert*. Regensburg, 2007.

Döring, Alois. *Rheinische Bräuche durch das Jahr*. Cologne, 2006.

Döring, Alois. *Heilige Helfer. Rheinische Heiligenfeste durch das Jahr*. Cologne, 2009.

Eberspächer, Martina. "Lichterglanz und Kinderglück. Zur Entwicklung der Familienweihnacht". In: Nina Gockerell, ed. *Weihnachtszeit. Feste zwischen Advent und Neujahr in Süddeutschland und Österreich 1840-1940*. Munich, 2000, 11-17.

Fischer, Norbert. *Vom Gottesacker zum Krematorium. Eine Sozialgeschichte der Friedhöfe in Deutschland*. Cologne, 1996.

Frei, Urs-Beat, and Fredy Bühler, eds. *Der Rosenkranz. Andacht – Geschichte – Kunst*. Bern, 2003.

Freytag, Nils. *Aberglauben im 19. Jahrhundert. Preußen und seine Rheinprovinz zwischen Tradition und Moderne (1815-1918)*. Berlin, 2003.

Frohschammer, Jakob. "Die Glaubwürdigkeit der Wunderheilungen in Lourdes und Marpingen". *Die Gartenlaube*, 10 (1878), 164-167.

Gajek, Ester. "'Erst eins, dann zwei, dann drei, dann vier…' Von Adventskränzen, Strohhalmkrippen und Adventskalendern". In: Nina Gockerell, ed. *Weihnachtszeit. Feste zwischen Advent und Neujahr in Süddeutschland und Österreich 1840-1940*. Munich, 2000, 19-34.

Hänel, Dagmar. *Bestatter im 20. Jahrhundert. Zur kulturellen Bedeutung eines tabuisierten Berufs*. Münster, 2003.

Hänel, Dagmar. *Letzte Reise. Vom Umgang mit dem Tod im Rheinland*. Cologne, 2009.

Hänel, Dagmar. "Frömmigkeit im Transit? Populäre Religiosität und Raumkonzepte am Beispiel des Wallfahrtsortes Lourdes". In: Ruth-E. Mohrmann, ed. *Alternative Spiritualität heute*. Münster, 2010, 93-112.

Harris, Ruth. *Lourdes: Body and Spirit in the Secular Age*. London, 1999.

Klosterkamp, Thomas. *Katholische Volksmission in Deutschland*. Leipzig, 2002.

Korff, Gottfried. "Formierung der Frömmigkeit. Zur sozialpolitischen Intention der Trierer Rockwallfahrten 1891". *Geschichte und Gesellschaft. Zeitschrift für Historische Sozialwissenschaft*, 3 (1977), 352-382.

Korff, Gottfried. "Zwischen Sinnlichkeit und Kirchlichkeit. Notizen zum Wandel populärer Frömmigkeit im 18. und 19. Jahrhundert". In: Jutta Held, ed. *Kultur zwischen Bürgertum und Volk*. Berlin, 1983, 136-148.

Korff, Gottfried. "'Heraus zum 1. Mai'. Maibrauch zwischen Volkskultur, bürgerlicher Folklore und Arbeiterbewegung". In: Richard van Dülmen and Norbert Schindler, eds. *Volkskultur. Zur Wiederentdeckung des vergessenen Alltags (16.–20. Jahrhundert)*. Frankfurt, 1984, 246-281.

Korff, Gottfried, ed. *Alliierte im Himmel. Populare Religiosität und Kriegserfahrung*. Tübingen, 2006.

Kotulla, Andreas J. *"Nach Lourdes!" Der französische Marienwallfahrtsort und die Katholiken im Deutschen Kaiserreich (1871-1914)*. Munich, 2006.

Kriss-Rettenbeck, Lenz. *Ex Voto. Zeichen, Bild und Abbild im christlichen Votivbrauchtum*. Zürich-Freiburg, 1972.

McLeod, Hugh. *Secularisation in Western Europe 1848-1914*. London, 2000.

Mohrmann, Ruth-E., ed. *Individuum und Frömmigkeit. Volkskundliche Studien zum 19. und 20. Jahrhundert*. Münster, 1997.

Morgan, David. *The Sacred Heart of Jesus: The Visual Evolution of a Devotion*. Amsterdam, 1998.

Pieske, Christa. *Bilder für jedermann. Wandbilddrucke 1840-1940*. München, 1988.

Riehl, Wilhelm Heinrich. *Die Familie. Die Naturgeschichte des Volkes als Grundlage einer deutschen Sozial-Politik*, 3. 11th edition. Stuttgart, 1897.

Scharfe, Martin. *Über die Religion. Glaube und Zweifel in der Volkskultur*. Cologne, 2004.

Schlager, Claudia. *Kult und Krieg. Herz Jesu – Sacré Cœur – Christus Rex im deutsch-französischen Vergleich 1914-1925*. Tübingen, 2011.

Sperber, Jonathan. *Popular Catholicism in Nineteenth-Century Germany*. Princeton, 1984.

Sperber, Jonathan. "Der Kampf und die Feiertage in Rheinland-Westfalen 1770-1870". In: Wolfgang Schieder, ed. *Volksfrömmigkeit in der modernen Sozialgeschichte*. Göttingen, 1986, 123-136.

Thalmann, Ralf. *Urne oder Sarg. Auseinandersetzungen um die Einführung der Feuerbestattung im 19. Jahrhundert*. Bern, 1978.

Weber-Kellermann, Ingeborg. *Die deutsche Familie. Versuch einer Sozialgeschichte*. Frankfurt am Main, 1974.

Weber-Kellermann, Ingeborg. *Saure Wochen, frohe Feste. Fest und Alltag in der Sprache der Bräuche*. Munich, 1985.

4.7
The Impact of Religious Reform on the Material Culture of Popular Piety in Scandinavia

Anders Gustavsson

My contribution deals with the impact of religious reform on the material culture of popular piety at the hand of some examples in Scandinavia. However, in the Protestant Scandinavian state churches of the nineteenth century material culture has actually no importance.[1] The important thing in those churches was the word in the form of sermons and daily prayer in the homes. The focus will then be here on religious revival movements of the latter half of the nineteenth century. Since these movements have left written documents in the form of protocols, with which one can follow discussions and decisions brought about by new material culture. Popular piety within the Protestant state churches, where there are few documents from the nineteenth century, is much more difficult to follow than within revival movements.[2]

In Denmark and Norway, the religious revival movements remained within the state church, while in Sweden several free-church movements developed. During the 1800s, those included baptism and the Swedish Mission Society, founded in 1878. In Denmark, there existed a liberal and nationalistic movement known as *Grundtvigianism* with the general slogan "First – a human being and then – a Christian". Another movement, the Home Mission, was pietistic; it attached more importance than Grundtvigianism to its members' lifestyles, not just to their faith.

Sunday work in a new social context

When new technology began to be used in agriculture and fishing, the issue of abandoning Sunday as a day previously ascribed for rest was brought to the fore. In Danish fishing, this issue became topical at the end of the 1800s, when larger boats which could visit more distant fishing grounds were used. Such boats were away from home for several weeks and therefore also on Sundays; this had not occurred before. Grundtvigianism did not mind the new practice of Sunday fishing. By contrast, the Home Mission did not accept this trend, referring to the third Commandment in the Bible. When the Home Mission gained ground among the Jutland fishing population, it was largely the issue of Sunday fishing that prevented the cooperation of joint owners of vessels. It became a matter of faith for Home Mission fishermen to refuse sailing on Sundays. In Esbjerg in south-western Jutland, the 'Sunday boats' of the Home Mission fishermen were a distinctive element of the fishing fleet, and they usually lay near each other at the so-called 'evangelical pier'. The biblical names Zoar, Hebron, Maran-Atha, Ebenezer, Saron, Immanuel and Bethesda were common on boats owned by Home Mission members. These fishing boats were striving to get at home before Saturday midnight; they usually lay at anchor offshore and kept Sabbath there. The issue of observing the Sabbath determined whether one would be counted as a member of the community of believers or not.

When dairies were started in Denmark, they used to take milk on Sundays. This was

4.7-1 *After the Sunday service in Morlanda church in western Sweden around 1900. Outside the gateway one can observe four women: three of them wear the old black headscarf while the fourth one has a decorated hat on her head, which at that time was a sign of higher social position.*
[Private collection]

1   With as only exception the Catholic oil prints imported from Germany in the late nineteenth century.
2   A major source, the reports from the clergymen, every sixth year in the nineteenth century, hardly mention (material) folk piety in the homes. It is only for the mid twentieth century that there is more information on Swedish material culture. In 1942 the church historian Hilding Pleijel established the Church History Archives in Lund. He sent out students and young scholars to collect reports about folk piety from different parts of Sweden. For Denmark and Norway no such archives exist.

acceptable for Grundtvigianism, but not for the Home Mission. For farmers belonging to the Home Mission the issue of delivering milk to dairies on Sunday became an indicator of religious persuasion similar to that of no-fishing-on-Sundays for fishermen. This issue was brought up in the 1880s when evangelical groups in Copenhagen founded the Association for the Promotion of the Rightful Observance of Sunday. One statement from the narratives of the time exemplifies the attitude to this issue: "We cannot sin against God's Commandment". In the 1890s, the Sunday closing of dairies gained ground. Approximately 100 cooperative dairies which until the 1940s either completely or partially limited their operations on Sundays were, with few exceptions, located in north-western and central Jutland where the Home Mission was strong. These dairies were called Sunday rest.

In Sweden, a similar question arose about grain milling on Sundays when more need of flour to people and cattle was experienced owing to the expanded and improved efficiency of agriculture. Before the time of electricity water and windmills were entirely dependent on access to water and wind. It might be tempting to grind on Sundays if for a long time there had been a shortage of water and wind. The nineteenth-century farmer Jakob Jonsson, inspired by a revival movement within the state church, repudiated from grinding on Sundays for religious reasons. Saturday midnight was seen by him as a boundary that God had set. Working until midnight on Saturday evening was of special importance for him when it rained after a lengthy period of dry weather and there was ample water to drive the farm's two water-powered mills. On Saturday 24 May 1873, he noted that "we were able to mill grain on both mills towards evening and then until midnight, and if it hadn't been Sunday the day after, we would have continued the milling longer". Jonsson placed the sanctity of Sunday in a larger religious context going back to the story of Divine Creation. At the time of Christmas holidays, New Year and 12th Night in 1872-1873, a lot of water ran through the millstream. In motivating his resting from work during Sundays and holidays, Jonsson reflected on how nature herself benefited from being allowed to rest. "It seems that the Lord of Nature, the God and Creator of us all, wishes even water (millwater) to hold a day sacred and to rest on the Sabbath so that it might run in its natural course free and unhampered, that is to flow unchecked in its natural channel on and in the earth and not in those passages invented by man that sometimes lead it above the surface of the earth so that the higher fall can power the assembled wheelwork." God assumes responsibility for nature by protecting it, and man must also show consideration and respect for this in spite of new technological innovations. This type of reasoning testifies to a religious basis of the early milieu awareness.

Celebration of life cycle ceremonies

In earlier times women about six weeks after childbirth would go through a religious ritual called Churching of Women. This ritual began gradually disappearing during the second half of the nineteenth century. Communities in which this ritual disappeared earliest were under the impact of emerging industrialism. This applies, among other things, to the region of Skåne in southern Sweden. Thus, in the station resort Örkelljunga, the declining rate of churching rituals from 1894 could be related to the fact that the railway came there that year when new people moved in there. In the similarly Scanian place Örtofta, families who were the first to abandon the ritual consisted of employees at the railway station and the sugar mill. These were the wives of station men, repair technicians, a manager, a chemist and engineers who had moved from other locations.

Memorials to the dead also changed from the mid-1800s. The previously used wooden crosses were increasingly replaced by iron

crosses of a much longer duration. Through this innovation it became possible not only to design texts but also to use image motifs, a practice unobservable before. These texts and images give an idea of how people perceived mortality and death. Thoughts of the life transience as well as beliefs about existence after death expressed on memorials in places associated with revival movements can be compared to those in places unmarked by revivalist movements. Thus, one of the iron crosses in Röra churchyard in western Sweden was raised to commemorate Johan Henriksson, the Member of Parliament who died in 1867. The text on the cross was taken from Psalm 144: 4: "Man is like to vanity, his days are as a shadow that passeth away". This inscription refers only to the transience of life. However, at the bottom of the cross, an angel holding a triumphal wreath is depicted; this image must be a symbol of existence after death. The same thing can be said about the old Christian symbol of belief, hope and charity pictured as a cross, an anchor and a heart intermingled in each other. This symbol is engraved at the top of this iron cross. During the late 1800s iron crosses were often replaced by tombstones of granite. At that time the granite industry came up, and there was even more room on the stone for engraving texts and picture symbols. [Ill. 4.7-2]

Religious motifs at home

In Catholic parts of Germany mass-produced religious pictures, known as oil prints, were spread on a large scale during the late 1800s. Many pictures of this type were also imported into Protestant homes in Sweden. In this way pictures with Catholic-inspired designs were hanging in homes of people involved into inner church revival movements. Those were pictures of the thorn-crowned Jesus' heart and images of Mary with a halo or sword-pierced heart. A woman born in 1902 told: "At my grandparents' home in the early 1900s there were pictures of the Virgin Mary and the thorn-crowned Christ". These religious oil prints usually hang in a sleeping room. The devotional aspect of those pictures was obvious. It is interesting that their Catholic symbols did not seem to have been either discussed or been questioned in those Lutheran homes. It is not certain whether people who bought these pictures were aware of the nineteenth-century Catholic ideology that lay behind the motives, namely, the cults of 'the Sacred Heart of Jesus' and 'the Immaculate Heart of Virgin Mary'. However, the same devotional image could be perceived differently when hanging at a Catholic home in Germany or a home of Protestant revival movement members in western Sweden. It is interesting that the adaption of these new oil prints did not question their religious background. [Ill. 4.7-3]

By contrast, during the early 1900s, members belonging to different free churches repudiated motives that were perceived as Catholic. When a Swedish farmer born in 1911 bought a farm, there were religious pictures from the former owner. He declared, "the Madonna, we took it out immediately. There is no confidence in her." Members belonging to free churches chose to buy not oil

4.7-2 The granite gravestone with the engraved reference to the Book of Psalms, chapter 39, verse 6, commemorates the farmer Gustaf Andersson and his wife Johanna, who both died in 1871.
[Photo Anders Gustavsson]

4.7-3 *The Virgin Mary with the burning sword-pierced heart banded with roses and the thorn-crowned Christ in a Lutheran home in western Sweden at the end of the nineteenth century.* [Private collection]

prints but mass-produced pictures with religious texts sold by the Swedish mail-order company Åhlén & Holm founded in 1899. The texts on such pictures were considered as more important than picture motives.

The practice of the Christmas crib was also introduced to Sweden from Germany at the end of the nineteenth century. In the beginning, due to its supposed Catholic origin, the crib was sometimes regarded with suspicion. Later on, in the early 1900s, the crib was accepted and became particularly popular among higher social classes in big cities and at clergymen's homes.[3]

Women's clothing in public meeting rooms

When at the end of the nineteenth century some women in the Swedish society began to wear industrially-produced hats, women within the inner church revival movement in western Sweden, named *schartauanism*, went on wearing their traditional black headscarf when visiting the church. It was important for these lay women to keep this custom as the black head-cloth was part of their worship wear. Later on this custom successively disappeared among younger women, and hats became their usual head-cloths. Older women, on the contrary, chose to wear the traditional black headscarf for the rest of their life; they strived against novelties in head covering, in rural areas as well as in towns. Thus the new type of head covering was only accepted by a younger generation within the revival movement. [Ill. 4.7-1]

In the early 1900s, women's clothing and hairstyle at public meetings in mission houses of the free churches were under control of regulations common in the revival movements both in Sweden and Norway. So it was not easy for female members to follow new trends in their outerwear. This is, for example, reflected in debates and sanctions of the mission church on the island of Smögen which was founded in 1879. Many sets of its minutes state that the chairman of the board or the pastor had received information from this or that member about someone else's wrongdoings. Thus, at the community meeting in 1912 a male member of the congregation argued: "The way our sisters show their bare arms and wear low-cut blouses, as well as extremes of their hairstyle is indeed a disgrace to the Lord's cause". Other male members expressed themselves in a similar fashion. For instance, one of them maintained that "after a meeting at which the song society performed, he heard strong complaints about the women's mode of dressing". Two elder women presented a similar critique at the same meeting. The parish meeting agreed with this criticism. Later on, the norms of women's clothing and hairstyles were liberalised and adjusted to the standards of the surrounding community. [Ill. 4.7-4]

In the beginning of the twentieth century, in the early days after the Pentecostal congregation was founded on the island of Åstol in western Sweden, its female members were not allowed to cut and curl their hair or to wear any jewellery. They were reprimanded by the leadership and in some cases even excluded if they had not complied with the

3   Ahlfors, *Julkrubban i Svenska kyrkan*.

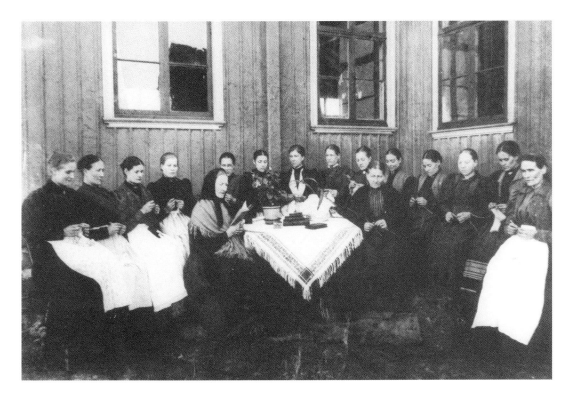

4.7-4 *The women of the Swedish Mission Society sewing group, with smooth hairstyle, in 1894 on the island of Smögen, making items for mission work while one of the older women with the black headscarf reads from the prayer book. [Private collection]*

prevailing standards. However, these standards were gradually adapted to new social conditions in the same way as in the mission church in Smögen. Owing to this change, a younger generation of girls who were baptised in their teens got better opportunities to remain in the congregation when they got further into adolescence as they were able to keep up with trends in clothing fashion.

In the early 1900s, women belonging to the Free Church named 'The Free Friends' in southern Norway could not appear in public without a hat. Neither could they cut their hair. They could not use such a dress novelty as long pants, at least when they attended meetings in the mission house while that was the time when long pants had been quite usual among women in the Norwegian society. Later on, however, such extreme standards for the Free-Friends women disappeared as it was the case in the two above-mentioned Swedish examples from Smögen and Åstol. Thus, the process of adapting to new social conditions was parallel in the Norwegian and Swedish free churches. Firstly, these movements opposed to material novelties but later on they were adapted and applied by a younger generation. In these churches the process of adaptation went slower than in the rest of the society.

Changes in the early 1900s

A phenomenon that contributed to changes in the practice of morning and evening prayers was daily devotions and Sunday services broadcasted by radio, which was introduced in Sweden during the early 1900s. Thus, a farmer's woman told: "At home we read morning and evening prayers with mum and dad. In later years radio came, then we used to enjoy morning prayers and even to worship at the end of the day by radio. Such memorable moments are always a good start for the day and its restful end; they should be more valued." [Ill. 4.7-5]

In the early 1900s, several Swedish free-church movements repudiated films shown at cinema-graphs. It is clearly seen in the protocols of the Mission society congregation on the island of Smögen. It was stated in the minutes of a board meeting: "one of the board members told that he heard a rumour

4.7-5 An elderly woman in the beginning of the twentieth century listening to the radio devotions with her hymnal opened.
[Private collection]

about a woman in the congregation who often associates with non-believers and in all probability goes to the cinema and theatre". One of the board members was to meet and question her. Such a repudiation of cinemagraphs and theatre is also observed among the Home Mission societies at the same time in Norway.[4] Later on such repudiations disappeared, but compared with the rest of the society the new media adaption was slow among revivalists.

Concluding remarks

Changes occurring in the material culture could provoke opposition within the religious revival movements as during the late 1800s and early 1900s these movements strived to guarantee the continuity of traditions. The adaption to changes was slower than in the surrounding society. A significant exception to this was Grundtvigianism in Denmark; this movement was ready to adapt changes from the external life. Exactly the opposite is characteristic of the second great revival movement in Denmark, the Home Mission.

At the same time, changes in piety could also occur. During the 1800s, old church customs such as churching of women after childbirth could disappear owing to the growing industrialism. Certain innovations were also accepted. This applies to advances in medical science and pharmacy. Changes in the use of religious pictures were also observed. Families belonging to the inner church revival movement in western Sweden bought imported new religious pictures and placed them on the walls in spite of the fact that these pictures actually represented Catholic beliefs. On the contrary, members of the free churches bought new mass-produced pictures which focused on citations from religious texts. Memorials in cemeteries changed when the new and durable iron crosses and later granite gravestones replaced the previous wooden crosses. Thanks to this it was possible to inscribe texts on memorials that expressed religious beliefs.

Many standards of the religious life lived on well into the early 1900s, but later on they were in many respects adapted to changes in the surrounding society. The standards for women's clothing at public meetings were liberalised. A technological innovation that was easily accepted in the popular piety of the early 1900s was the radio. It made it possible for listeners at home to participate in the devotions broadcasted on weekdays and Sundays.

4   Seland, *Egdene og "det ellevte bud"*.

BIBLIOGRAPHY

Aagedal, Olaf, and Björg Seland. *Vekkelsesvind. Den norske vekkingskristendomen*. Oslo, 2008.

Ahlfors, Hans. *Julkrubban i Svenska kyrkan. Julkrubbans reception i Stockholms, Göteborgs och Lunds stifts gudstjänstrum fram till 1900-talets slut*. Lund, 2012.

Balle-Petersen, Margareta. "The Holy Danes". *Ethnologia Scandinavica*, 1981, 79-112.

Brander, Hedvig. *Bild och fromhetsliv i 1800-talets Sverige*. Acta Universitatis Upsaliensis. Ars Suetica, 15. Uppsala, 1994.

Bringéus, Nils-Arvid. *Bildlore. Studiet av folkliga bildbudskap*. Stockholm, 1981.

Bringéus, Nils-Arvid. *Folklig fromhet. Studier i religionsetnologi*. Stockholm, 1997.

Brückner, Wolfgang. *Die Bilderfabrik*. Frankfurt am Main, 1973.

Brückner, Wolfgang. *Elfenreigen, Hochzeitstraum. Die Öldruckfabrikation 1880-1940*. Cologne, 1974.

Gustavsson, Anders. *Kyrktagningsseden i Sverige*. Lund, 1972.

Gustavsson, Anders. *Bondeliv på 1800-talet*. Oslo, 2009.

Gustavsson, Anders. *Cultural studies on Folk Religion in Scandinavia*. Oslo, 2012.

Gustavsson, Anders. *Grave Memorials as Cultural Heritage in Western Sweden with Focus on the 1800s*. Oslo, 2014.

Gustavsson Anders. "Folk Culture at the Interface between Emerging Public Health Care and Older Forms of Healing". *Arv. Nordic Yearbook of Folklore*, 2017, 51-90.

Johannesson, Lena. *Den massproducerade bilden. Ur bildindustrialismens historia*. Stockholm, 1978.

Lewis, Katarina. *Schartauansk kvinnofromhet i tjugonde seklet*. Uddevalla, 1997.

Londos, Eva. *Religiös huskonst. Svenskarnas religiösa bilder. Om kristen huskonst*. Jönköping, 1983.

Londos, Eva. *Uppåt vägarna i svenska hem. En etnologisk studie av bildbruk*. Stockholm, 1993.

Rehnberg, Bertil, and Lilian Kullvén. *Julkrubban berättar. Kulturarv och budskap i en helgtradition*. Göteborg, 1995.

Sanders, Hanne. *Bondeväkkelse og sekularisering. En protestantisk folkelig kultur i Danmark og Sverige 1820-1850*. Copenhagen, 1995.

Scharfe, Martin. *Evangelische Andachtsbilder. Studien zu Intention und Funktion des Bildes in der Frömmigkeitsgeschichte vornehmlich des schwäbischen Raumes*. Stuttgart, 1968.

Seland, Bjørg. *Egdene og "det ellevte bud". Kristelig normverk på 18- og 1900-tallet. Egdene og de ti bud*. Kristiansand, 2008.

Slettan, Bjørn. "*O, at jeg kunde min Jesum prise ...*" *Folkelig religiøsitet og vekkelsesliv på Agder på 1800-tallet*. Oslo, 1992.

Ursin, J. *Kristne symboler. En håndbok*. Oslo, 1949.

COLOUR ILLUSTRATIONS

1. *The Queen giving a Testament to a Highland Cottager.* Print published by the Religious Tract Society, c 1850. [London, British Museum: 1870,1210.562]
(Ill. 1.1-1, p. 30)

2. Cover of the Catholic art magazine *Durendal*, 1898.
[Leuven, KADOC-KU Leuven: KYB1702]
(Ill. 1.2-9, p. 62)

3. Fritz von Uhde, *Let the children come to me.* Painting (oil on canvas), 1884. [Leipzig, Museum der bildenden Künste; photo: akg-images nr. AKG97482] *(P. 90)*

4. The Grundtvig Church Copenhagen. Poster (lithograph) by A.W. Jørgensen for the National America Denmark Association, 1942-1945. [Private collection]
(Ill. 1.5-1, p. 94)

5. The Martyrs' Memorial, Oxford, by George Gilbert Scott, 1840.
[London, Royal Institute of British Architects: RIBApix, RIBA31344]
(Ill. 2.1-18, p. 137)

6. Bird's-eye view of the centre of the Gothic Revival village of Vivenkapelle, 1885.
[Marke, Bethune Foundation]
(Ill. 2.2-5, p. 146)

7. Karl Friedrich Schinkel, *Medieval Church by a River*. Painting (oil on canvas), 1815.
[Berlin, Staatlichen Museen zu Berlin, Nationalgalerie; photo: Andres Kilger / bpk]
(P. 160)

8. Interior of the Copenhagen Cathedral (Vor Frue Kirke).
[© Ian Dagnall / Alamy Stock Photo]
(P. 201-202)

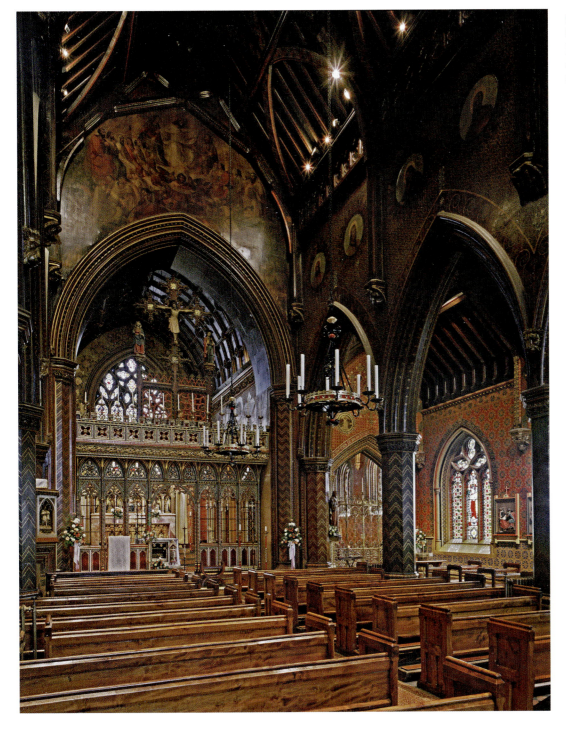

9. The interior of A.W.N. Pugin's St Giles in Cheadle (1841-1846). [London, Royal Institute of British Architects: RIBApix, RIBA105404] *(P. 222)*

10. The church of St Anthony in Pepinster (1893-1899).
[© SPW-AWaP; photo Guy Focant]
(Ill. 3.2-6, p. 253)

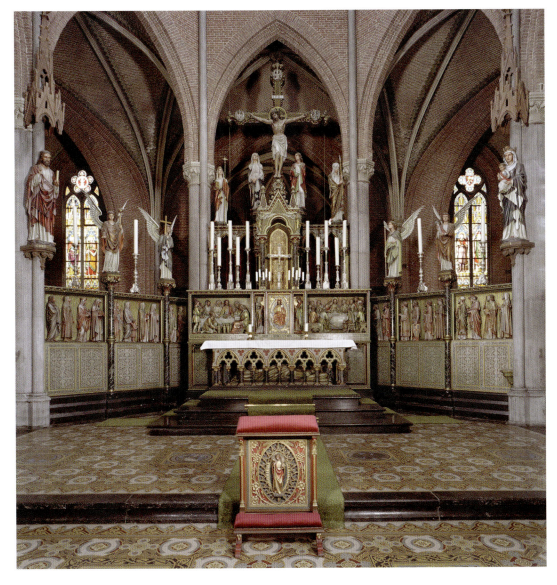

11. Altar in French gothic style in the church of St Lambert in Veghel, designed by Pierre J.H. Cuypers (1862-1863).
[Amersfoort, Rijksdienst Cultureel Erfgoed: 526.512; photo Kris Roderburg, 2007]
(P. 266)

12. Cologne Cathedral, Fourth "Bayernfenster" (The Lamentation of Christ), Königliche Glasmalereianstalt, Munich, 1848.
[© Rheinisches Bildarchiv, Cologne, c001350]
(P. 287)

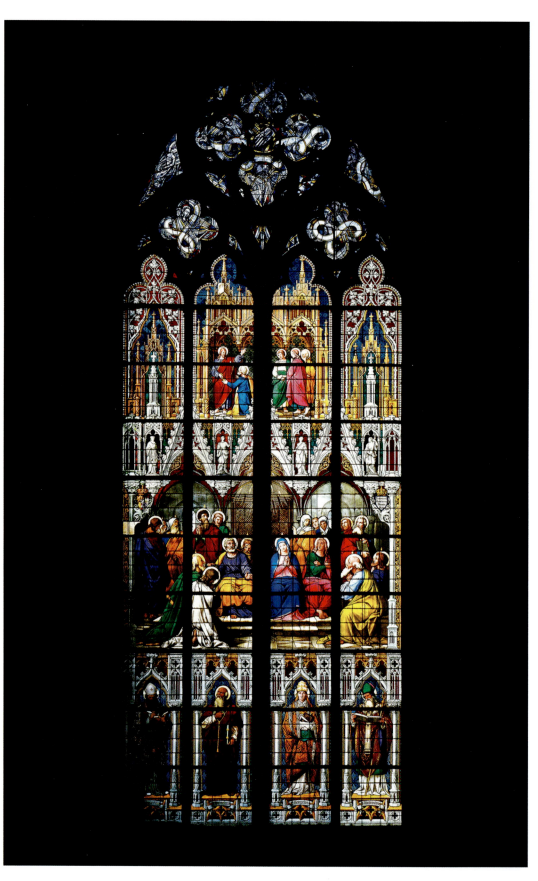

13. *The broad and narrow way.* Popular nineteenth-century lithography. [Private collection] *(P. 319)*

14. Souvenir from the Belgian shrine of Our Lady of Scherpenheuvel: bell-glass with a representation of the statue of Mary in the tree, venerated by the archduke Albert, c 1900.
[Collection P.J. Margry]
(P. 366)

15. Metal Lourdes water container, c 1910.
[Collection P.J. Margry]
(Ill. 4.4-15, p.390)

16. Devotional image of Saint Joseph the Worker.
[Bonn, LVR-Institut für Landeskunde und Regionalgeschichte]
(Ill. 4.6-6, p.410)

AUTHORS

Arne Bugge Amundsen is Professor of Cultural History at the Department of Culture Studies and Oriental Languages, University of Oslo, Norway.

Carsten Bach-Nielsen is retired as Professor of Church History at the University of Aarhus. His field of research is Danish church history in the early modern and modern era. In 2017 he was co-editor of the official three-volume work on the Danish reformation in church and culture. For many years he was editor of *Kirkehistoriske Samlinger*, the leading journal of Danish church history. His latest book is about fiction literature in the former Danish West Indies

Timothy Brittain-Catlin is an historian of nineteenth- and twentieth-century British domestic and religious architecture, and leads the graduate Architecture Apprenticeship course at the University of Cambridge. He was an editor, with Jan de Maeyer and Martin Bressani, of *Gothic Revival Worldwide: A.W.N. Pugin's Global Influence* (2016).

Thomas Coomans is an architectural historian, Professor at the KU Leuven in the Department of Architecture, and program director of the Raymond Lemaire International Centre for Conservation. His teaching includes architectural history, building archaeology, and history and theory of conservation. His research on various aspects of church architecture included medieval churches in the Low Countries, monasteries of religious orders, Gothic Revival, reuse of redundant churches, and Christian church architecture in China from the 1840s to the 1940s.

Wolfgang Cortjaens, PhD in History of Art (Aachen University, 2002), has worked for numerous museums, i.e. the State Museums of Berlin (2006/2007), the Begas Haus - Museum für Kunst und Regionalgeschichte Heinsberg (2011-2015), the Gay Museum in Berlin (2016-2018) and the graphic collection of the Academy of Fine Arts in Vienna (in proxy, 2018/19). In 2020, he was appointed Head of the Applied Arts and Graphics Collections of the German Historical Museum in Berlin. His fields of interest are the nineteenth-century art and architecture.

Jan De Maeyer is Professor emeritus of church history at KU Leuven and honorary director of KADOC-KU Leuven. He is the author of several publications on political and social Catholicism, material Christianity, and the development of religious institutions and congregations. At this moment he is as emeritus with a formal duty Policy advisor for University Archives and Heritage KU Leuven (Rectoral Services)..

Jens Christian Eldal is an art historian, senior researcher emeritus at the Norwegian Institute of Cultural Heritage Research (NIKU), Oslo. He has published several books and many articles, especially about the architectural history of churches and wood as building material during the eighteenth to the twentieth century.

Anders Gustavsson is Professor emeritus in Cultural History at the Department of Culture Studies and Oriental Languages, University of Oslo. His academic research fields are folk religion, cultural contacts, culture of borders, farmers culture, coastal culture, rituals around life cycle, symbols of gravestones, alcohol and temperance movements, folk life painting, field work, history of medicine, and history of tourism.

Dagmar Hänel is a cultural anthropologist / European ethnologist. After finishing her PhD in 2001 she worked in different fields: media, cultural projects and Universities. Since 2018 she is the head of the LVR-Institut for regional studies in Bonn. She works especially on rituals and intangible cultural heritage, regional everyday culture and visual anthropology.

Mary Heimann is Professor of Modern History at Cardiff University, where she also directs the Central and East European Research Group. Her best-known publications are *Catholic Devotion in Victorian England 1850-1914* (1995), "Christianity in Western Europe from the Enlightenment to the Present Day" in Adrian Hastings, *A World History of Christianity* (1999) and *Czechoslovakia: The State that Failed* (2009). She is currently writing a new book on Catholicism behind the Iron Curtain for Yale University Press.

Antoine Jacobs is a freelance historian. He researches and publishes about ecclesiastical art, places of pilgrimage, the Catholic clergy, orders and congregations in the nineteenth and twentieth centuries in the Netherlands.

Wies van Leeuwen is an architectural historian and cultural history researcher. He is particularly interested in the architectural theory of the nineteenth century, church architecture and restoration concepts in the care of monuments. He was policy adviser for cultural history and monuments at the province of North Brabant (the Netherlands) (1979-2015). He is the founder of the Cuypersgenootschap and an expert on the life and work of Pierre Cuypers, about whom he published three books.

Fred van Lieburg is Professor of Religious History in the Faculty of Humanities at the VU Amsterdam. He is Director of History Studies, and co-ordinator of the Amsterdam Centre for Religious History, which is affiliated with the CLUE+ Research Institute for Culture, History and Heritage He has a special interest in the history of Calvinism, Pietism, the Réveil and the Biblebelt.

Patricia Lysaght is Professor emerita of European Ethnology, University College Dublin. She is an elected Member of the Royal Irish Academy, Dublin, and of the Royal Gustavus Adolphus Academy for Swedish Folk Culture, Uppsala, Sweden. She is a former president of The Folklore Society, London (2017-2020) and is currently Vice-President of the Society (2021-2023). She is also a former editor of *Folklore*, London, and of *Béaloideas*, the Journal of the Folklore of Ireland Society.

Peter Jan Margry is Professor of European Ethnology at the University of Amsterdam and senior fellow at the Meertens Institute, a research center of the Royal Netherlands Academy of Arts and Sciences in Amsterdam. His research focus is on modern and contemporary religious cultures, rituals, alternative healing practices, cultural memory, and cultural heritage. He has published various monographs and edited volumes among them *Shrines and Pilgrimage in the Modern World: New Itineraries into the Sacred* (2008) and *Cold War Mary. Ideologies, Politics, and Marian Devotional Culture* (2020).

Caroline M. McGee is an architectural historian specialized in nineteenth- and twentieth-century ecclesiastical architecture and interiors. She has published and lectured on these topics at national and international level. She holds a visiting Research Fellowship at Trinity College Dublin where she earned a PhD for her award-winning study of Hardman and Mayer stained glass in Ireland.

Roderick O'Donnell is an architectural historian currently working as a freelance writer, lecturer and adviser. He is an expert on the works of the English architect A.W.N. Pugin and Roman Catholic church architecture in the UK and Ireland (from the eighteenth to the twentieth century). He was inspector of Historic Buildings at English Heritage (1982-2011) and of Crown Buildings in London (2004-2011). He is an active member of conservation and learned societies.

Tine Van Osselaer is Research Professor in the history of spirituality, devotion and mysticism at the Ruusbroec Institute, University of Antwerp. Her fields of interest are gender and religion; domesticity, family and religion; religion and science/knowledge systems; corporeality and emotions; history of pain; religion and war; celebrity culture, media and religion. Currently, she is the principal investigator of STIGMATICS: 'Between saints and celebrities. The devotion and promotion of stigmatics in Europe, c1800-1950', a project sponsored by the European Research Council (Starting Grant).

William Whyte is Professor of Social and Architectural History and fellow of St John's College, University of Oxford. His publications include *Unlocking the Church: the lost secrets of Victorian sacred space* (2017).

INDEX OF PERSONS

Adam, Robert 246
Adler, Friedrich 165, 167
Alberdingk Thijm, Jozef 59, 65, 68-73, 76-77, 79, 261-262, 266-267
Albermann, Wilhelm 170
Allason, Thomas 134
Allom, Thomas 134-135
Anderson, Robert Rowand 233, 235-237
Appadurai, Arjun 13
Ariëns, Theodore 70
Ark, Friedrich 171
Arnim, Achim von 158
Arnold, Thomas 41
Arrowsmith, Edmund 137
Ashlin, George C. 134, 228-230
Audsley, Georges 232
Audsley, William 232
Augusta Viktoria 14, 83, 88, 177
Aytink van Falkenstein, A. 269

Balat, Alphonse 249
Barnsley, Sidney 240
Barraud, Francis 226
Barthes, Roland 12
Bartholdy, Jakob Salomon 278
Baskett, John 38
Baudri, Friedrich 287
Baudri, Johann Anton 59, 86, 287
Baumann, Povl 103-104
Bayer, August von 164
Beck, Vilhelm 97-98
Becker, Ludwig 178
Bective, Earl of 125
Bedford, Francis 218
Beek, A.J. van 271
Beeton, Isabella 339
Beets, Nicolaas 395
Belanger 161
Bell, Alfred 227, 229
Belloc, Hilaire 136
Benevolo, Leonardo 160
Bennett, Laura 23
Bentley, John Francis 132, 226-227, 213, 234
Beresford Hope, A. J. B. 29, 36
Berlage, H.P. 272
Beskow, Gustaf Emanuel 199, 307
Bethmann-Hollweg, Moritz August von 88
Bethune, Jean-Baptiste 58-59, 73, 146-147, 215, 249-252, 287-288
Beuth, Christian Peter Wilhelm 166
Beyaert, Henri 146
Bickersteth, Edward 327
Bilderdijk, Willem 400
Bindesbøll, Thorvald 101
Bishop, Edmund 231
Bismarck, Otto von 105, 170-172, 414
Blackborn, David 409

Blaeser, Gustav Hermann 175
Blaschke, Olaf 15
Blessing, Werner 406
Bleys, A.C. 264
Blom, Fredrik 202
Bock, Franz 59, 71-72, 86, 290
Bodelschwingh, Friedrich von 98
Bodley, George Frederick 225-228, 236, 240-241
Boeyinga, B.T. 274
Boisserée, Sulpiz 280-281
Boos, Carl 164
Borret, Theodore 72
Børve, Haldor Larsen 196, 305
Bosboom, J. W. 273
Bower, Thomas 233
Bradley, Ian 40
Brakelond, Jocelyn de 128
Brandon, Raphael 233
Brands, J. 261
Brandt, C.J. 101
Brangwyn, Frank 236
Bredée, Marcelis 401
Bremner, Alex 46
Brentano, Clemens von 158
Breunissen Troost, A. 272
Brey, Heinrich 91
Brink, van den H.J. 264
Brinkman, M. 272
Britton, John 219-220
Brodrick, Cuthbert 234
Brom, Gerard Bartel 72, 389
Brom, Jan 268
Brom, Leo 268
Brooks, James 225
Brouwers, Jan Willem 59, 70, 77
Brown, Ford Maddox 338
Brown, Stewart 33
Brunius, Carl Georg 205
Bunyan, John 37
Burges, William 124, 227-228, 240
Burlison, John 227, 229
Burne-Jones, Edward 132, 226, 232, 240
Burns, Robert 330
Busch, Georg 90
Buttel, Friedrich Wilhelm 167
Butterfield, William 131, 224, 240-241
Byrne, W.H. 133

Callenbach, G.F. 399
Callmander, Reinhold 312
Calvin, John 400-401
Capronnier, Jean-Baptiste 229
Carl III/XIV Johan 196
Carlberg, Carl Wilhelm 202
Carlyle, Thomas 128
Caröe, W.D. 233
Carter, John 219

Cartuyvels, Charles 57
Carus, Carl Gustav 158
Caryll (family) 136
Caspar, Karl 90
Cave, James 217
Certeau, Michel de 17
Chadwick, Owen 122
Challoner, Richard 325, 329-330
Chalmers, Thomas 99, 235
Charles II 132
Charles Alexander of Lorraine 245
Charlotte Amalia (Queen) 199
Chateaubriand, François-René de 17
Chateauneuf, Alexis de 302-303
Child, A.E. 230
Christian V 199
Christian VI 188
Christian VII 189
Christian VIII 191
Christian, William 319, 367
Christie, Christian 185, 312
Clarke, Harry 229-230
Clarke, Joshua 229
Clayton, John 227, 229
Clemmensen, Andreas 101, 307
Cloquet, Louis 254
Cockerell, C.R. 228
Coffey, John 345-346
Coleman, Thomas 228
Colley, Thomas 31, 46
Comper, Ninian 241
Cornelius, Peter von 278-279, 281
Costa, Isaac da 400
Croke, Thomas 133
Cromwell, Oliver 347
Crooÿ, Fernand 60
Cubitt, James 36, 232
Cubitt, Thomas 134, 220
Cullen, James 350, 356
Cullen, Paul 124, 134
Cuypers, Joseph 78-79, 264, 268
Cuypers, Pierre J.H. 59, 65, 68, 70-71, 73, 77-79, 195, 215, 261-264, 266-267, 389

Dam, A.W. van 270
Daniels, George 229
Dansdorp, J.J. 260
Davis, H.D. 223
Davison, J.F. 226
Dearmer, Percy 45
Deger, Ernst 279
de Hemptinne, Joseph 144, 250
De Maeyer, Jan 364
Demanet, Charles-Amand 248
De Moerloose, Alphonse 254
Deneumoulin, Jean 142
Denis, Jean-Marie 136

443

Denis, Maurice 61-62
De Ribbe, Charles 366
De Rudder, Pieter 364, 370-371
Desideria (Queen) 196
Dewez, Benoît 246
Dickens, Charles 132, 137, 339
Didron, Adolphe Napoléon 72, 261
Dijck, A. van 266
Dixon, William Francis 229
Döllinger, Ignaz von 106
Donlevy, Andrew 352
Douglas 236
Drake, Friedrich 168
Drewe 233
Drijfhout, B.F. 269
Droste Vischering, Clemens-August von 86
Drummond, Henry 233
Dunn, Archibald Matthias 241
Durand, Jean-Nicolas-Louis 161
Durcan, Patrick 133

Earle, John 234
Earley, Thomas 229
Eastlake, Charles 338
Edelsvärd, Adolf Wilhelm 205
Eliot, George 119
Eliot, Simon 37
Emmanuel, E. 232
Endler, Eduard 90
Erdmannsdorff, Friedrich Wilhelm von 156
Essens, H. 261
Essenwein, August von 283, 288
Esser, Carl 170
Evers, H. 272
Everts, H. 266
Exalto, John 396

Faber, Frederick William 131, 233, 238-239, 334
Fairlie, Reginald 236
Ferstel, Heinrich von 174
Fey, Andreas 290
Firle, Walter 90
Fischer, Antonius 90, 180
Flugel, Gebhard 90
Fog, B.J. 99
Formby, Henry 238
Foucault, Michel 10
Franssen, C. 264
Frederick III 83
Frederick William II 156
Frederick William III 87, 156, 162, 170
Frederick William IV 15, 87, 158-159, 168, 172
Fredrik IV 186, 188
Friedrich, Caspar David 157-158
Frimodt, Rudolf 97
Fritsch, K.E.O. 293
Fuchs, Peter 169

Fuglsang-Damgaard, F. 95
Fürstenberg-Stammheim, Franz Egon von 159

Garlick, Nicholas 137
Garner, Thomas 227-228, 241
Gärtner, Friedrich von 163, 174, 280
Geiges, Fritz 288
Geld, Hendrik van der 267
Georg IV 52
George V 339
George, Henry 103
Georges, Edmond 70
Gerrits, Piet 268
Geuer, Heinrich 72
Gibbs, James 218
Gillberg, Axel 197-198
Gillow (family) 238
Gilly, Friedrich 161
Gisborne, Thomas 327
Giudici, Jan 259
Godefroy, A.N. 271
Goldie, George 228
Gottlob, Kai 106
Goodridge, H.E. 241
Graaf, J.J. 71
Graham, James Gillespie 235
Grauss, G.H. 270
Gray, John 236
Greef, J. de 270
Greuze, Jean-Baptiste 323, 330
Grewen, Joannes (Jan) 74, 388
Gribble, Herbert 131, 233
Groen van Prinsterer, Guillaume 74, 400
Grosch, Christian Heinrich 202-203
Grundtvig, Nikolai Frederik Severin 95, 97, 98,
   100, 101, 102, 103, 104, 105, 106, 107, 108, 109,
   110, 116, 193, 214, 307
Grylls, Thomas John 227, 229
Guinness (family) 124
Gurlitt, Cornelius 178
Gustav Adolf 66, 75, 168, 170, 233

Hadfield, M.E. 133
Hafkenscheid, Bernard 385
Hahn, Hermann 168
Hall, S.C. 349
Hanewinckel, Stephanus 377, 379
Hanno, Wilhelm von 203
Hansen, C.F. 103, 300
Hansom, Charles 225
Hansom, Edward Joseph 241
Hansom, Joseph Aloysius 131-132, 225
Hansom, Joseph Stanislaus 131
Hardman, John 222, 227-230, 238
Hardman Powell, John 238
Harris, Jose 44
Hase, Conrad Wilhelm 155, 164, 167, 283

Hauge, Hans Nielsen 190-191, 194, 299
Haven, Lambert van 188
Haydn, Joseph 291
Healy, Michael 230
Hehl, Christoph 283
Heideloff, Carl Alexander 284
Heimann, Mary 15
Helbig, Jules 55, 58, 288
Hellemans, Staf 10
Hellemons, W. 264
Helleputte, Joris 59, 215, 252-254
Helveg, Ludvig 97
Helweg-Larsen, Povl 104
Hennebique, François 255
Henriksson, Johan 419
Henry VIII 158, 343
Herdewegen, Ilfons 294
Herholdt, Daniel 95
Herres, Jürgen 84
Hertling, Georg von 90
Hesekiel, Georg Christoph 156
Hess, Heinrich M. von 279
Hetsch, Gustav Friedrich 200
Heukelum, Gerard van 65, 71-73, 78-79, 259, 264,
   266
Heylen, Norbertus 361
Hitchcock, Henry-Russell 237
Hjortzberg, Olle 311
Hoffmann, E.T.A. 286, 290
Hoffmann, Josef 61
Hone, Evie 230
Hooykaas, B. 272
Hopkins, Gerard Manley 136
Hove, Bart van 400
Howard, Henry Fitzalan 131
Howard, Philip 131
Hübsch, Heinrich 164
Hucq, E. 151
Hugo, Victor 53
Huijsers, H. 269
Huijsers, P. 260, 270
Hundrieser, Emil 168
Hunt, William Holman 319, 338

Ingraham, Emily Meynell 138
Ittenbach, Franz 279

Jacobsen, J.C. 103
James, John Angell 327-328
Jensen, Ferdinand Vilhelm 200
Jensen, Niels Peder 200
Jensen-Klint, P.V. 95, 103, 106, 108
Jesse, H.J. 271
Jobson, F. J. 36
Joling, Antoon 78
Jones, Griffiths 329
Jong, Servaas de 69

Jonsson, Jakob 418
Jørgensen, Thorvald 108
Joseph II 51, 141, 150, 173
Josephine (Queen) 196
Jungersen, Fredrik 101
Jussow, Heinrich Christoph 162

Kaag, A.H.W. 78
Kalf, Jan 78, 261, 268
Kamperdijk, N. 271
Kampmann, Hack 95, 103, 106
Kane, Paula 370
Kayser, Johann Georg 292
Kayser, Johannes. 264-266
Keble, John 124, 332-334
Keeling, Bassett 229
Kemble, John 137
Kempe, Charles 227
Kendall, H.E. 136
Keppler, Paul Wilhelm von 89
Keuchenius, W.C. 400
Keyser, Hendrick de 271, 275
King, Thomas Harper 58
Kingery, W. David 13
Kirby, Tobias 347
Kleist, Heinrich von 158, 290
Klenze, Leo von 163, 279
Kliefoth, Theodor 303-304
Klimt, Gustav 61
Klopstock, Friedrich G. 38
Knoblauch, Eduard 292
Kohl, Johann 348-349
Kolping, August 85-86
Kopytoff, Igor 13
Korff, Gottfried 413
Korum, Felix Michael 180
Kramm, C. 270
Kühn, Gustav 88
Kuipers, T.E. 274
Kumlien, Axel 1999
Kumlien, Hjalmar 199
Küppers, Alfred 175
Kuyper, Abraham 65, 67-68, 74, 79, 272-273, 400, 402

Laffertée, J.H. 261
Laib, Friedrich 284
Lamb, E.B. 225
Lambert, John 238
Lammers, Gustav Adolf 197
Lancaster, Joseph 42
Lanchester, Henry V. 235
Lange, H.O. 100
Langerock, Pierre 146, 253
Langlois, Claude 370
Lassaulx, Johann Claudius von 157, 176
Lateau, Louise 370

Latour, Bruno 12
Laud, Archbishop 37
Laugier, Marc Antoine 160
Laurent, Joseph 174
Lavers, Nathaniel W. 226
Ledger-Lomas, Michael 43
Ledoux, Claude Nicolas 161
Leeuw, G. van der 272
Lehnert, Adolf 407
Leinster, Duke of 133
Leliman, J.H. 77, 271
Lemaire, Raymond 255
Lenné, Peter Joseph 159, 161, 172
Lenz, Peter (Desiderius) 89
Leo XII 369
Leo XIII 179, 355, 409, 413
Leopold I 52
Leopold II 145, 151, 253
Le Sage ten Broek, Joachim George 68, 73
Lethaby, William 235, 239-241
Levine, Neil 35
Lewandowski, Louis 292
Liebermann, Max 90
Lind, Hans Christian 202-203
Lindgren, Gustav 198
Lingard, John 238
Lingens, Joseph 86, 163
Linssen, Gerard 387
Linstow, Hans Ditlev Frants von 202-203, 310
Lisle, Ambrose Phillipps de 132, 235, 238, 325
Lisle, Edwin de 235
Livingstone, David 45
Lobin, Lucien-Léopold 229
Lom, H. 73
Lorimer, Robert 235-237
Louisa (Queen) 156, 168
Louis Napoleon 14, 66, 269
Ludlam, Robert 137
Ludlow, John Malcolm 99
Ludwig I 162-163, 172, 279-280, 287
Ludwig II 214
Lühr, Waldemar Ferdinand 205
Luther, Martin 18, 116, 168, 170, 192, 320, 400
Lynn, W.H. 228

Maas, J. P. 268
Majerus, Pascal 369
Manning, Henry Edward 132
Marcellis, Charles 248
March, Otto 179
Marès-Joseph (Brother) 141, 250
Margry, Albert 264
Margry, Evert 264, 389
Margry, Jos 390
Margry, Peter Jan 396
Maria Theresa 199, 245
Marnix van St. Aldegonde, Philips 400

Marshall, Hezekiah 231
Marshall, John 226
Martyn, Edward 239
Marx, Peter 180
Mathew, Theobald 348-349, 352
Mattar, Stephan 90
Mayer 229-230
McCarthy, J.J. 123, 134, 228-229
McDannell, Colleen 11, 330
McIntosh Brookes, William 233
Meeûs d'Argenteuil, Anna de 75
Melanchthon, Philipp 18, 116, 168
Melchers, Paul 59
Mengelberg, Friedrich Wilhelm 72, 267
Mercier, Désiré 60, 365, 369
Metternich, Klemens von 155
Miller, Daniel 13
Milner, John 219
Minne, Georges 62
Mirbach, Constable Ernst von 88
Moele, G. 262
Moeller, Henry 60
Moira, Gerald 232-233
Molenaar, N. 263-264
Molkenboer, Th. 262, 264
Moller, Georg 162
Møller, Johannes 98
Montoyer, Louis 246
More, Hannah 327, 329
Moritz, Carl 90
Morris, Joseph 233
Morris, William 61, 108, 226, 240-240
Müller, Carl 279
Müller, Ferdinand 168
Müller, Johann Georg 86, 282, 290
Münzenberger, Franz August 86, 284
Murray, Daniel 352
Murray, John 338
Musgrave, Richard 353
Muthesius, Hermann 180
Muthesius, Stefan 225
Muysken, C. 271

Napoleon 51, 115, 143, 155, 157, 163, 173-174
Neale, John Mason 333-334
Nebel, Ferdinand 164-165
Neergaard (family) 98
Newman, John H. 122, 131, 233, 332-334
Nicholson, Charles 241
Nielsen, Fredrik 98, 106
Nielsen, Magdahl 105
Nissen, Henrik 197
Nixon, James H. 229
Nöggerath, Johann Jacob 164, 175
Nyrop, Martin 95, 105, 108, 110, 308

O'Connell, Daniel 134, 136, 228

445

O'Connor, T.P. ('Tay-Pay') 133
Ohlmüller, Joseph Daniel 164
Oidtmann, Heinrich 312
O'Kelly, Aloysius 356
Oosterman, Jan 268
Orsi, Robert 368
Oscar I 196
Oscar II 199, 312
Otzen, Johannes 293
Overbeck, Friedrich 277-279, 338

Palmstedt, Erik 299
Panofsky, Erwin 12
Paredis, Joannes Augustinus 73, 75
Pearson, John Loughborough 134, 225-227, 232, 240
Peeters, J.J. 260-261
Peeters-Divoort, H. 260
Penrose, F.C. 228
Persius, Ludwig 87, 171-172
Pevsner, Nikolaus 130, 225
Pforr, Franz 277
Phillipps, Ambrose 131-132
Philpot, Glynn 236
Pilkington, Frederick 237
Pinkerton, Robert 396
Pippett, Alphege 227
Pirotte, Jean 365
Pisoni, Gaetano Matteo 245
Pite, A. Beresford 240
Pius VII 143, 369
Pius IX 76, 267, 336, 380, 409
Pius X 239, 268
Plukhooy, P. 260
Poelaert, Joseph 247
Pohl, Wilhelm 170
Polonceau, Camille 248
Pontoppidan, Morten 100
Postumus Meyjes C.B. 271
Prince, H.J. 233
Prior, Edward 240
Pugin, Auguste Charles 219
Pugin, Augustus Welby Northmore 17-19, 35, 58, 69, 72, 116, 121-123, 126-133, 135-137, 213-215, 217, 219-226, 228-229, 231, 233, 235-241, 249-252, 261-262, 281, 302, 331, 334
Pugin, Edward W. 132, 134, 224-225, 227-228, 231, 238
Pugin, Peter Paul 135, 231
Pugin Powell, Sebastian 122
Purser, Sarah 229
Pusey, Edward Bouverie 332-334

Quast, Ferdinand von 281

Raffalovich, Andre 236
Ravené, Peter Louis 175

Reichensperger, August 59, 69, 71-72, 85-86, 167, 178, 214, 261, 281-282, 287
Reiss, Josef Anton 284
Reitsma, Egbert 274
Renard, Heinrich 90
Rendel, H.S. Goodhart 225
Renn, Gottfried 169
Reusens, Edmond 57, 59
Rhind, Ethel 230
Richmond, William Blake 240
Rickards, Edwin A. 235
Riegel, Ernst 91
Riel, Wilhelm Heinrich 411
Riele, G. te 267
Rietschel, Ernst 168
Rijsterborgh, L. 260
Rincklake, August 283
Roberts, William 327
Robinson, J.L. 123
Robson, E. R. 44
Röckerath, Peter Josef 178
Rolfe, Frederick (Baron Corvo) 235
Romein, Th. 270
Rørdam, Skat 98, 103
Roritzer, Matthias 287
Rose, Jonathan 43
Rosenius, Carl Olof 194
Rot, Nicolaas 401
Roth, Miksa 312
Ruskin, John 55, 224, 240, 338
Rossetti, Dante Gabriel 226, 240
Rutten, François Xavier 70-71, 264
Ry, Simon Louis du 162

Sailer, Michael 290
Saint, Andrew 43-44, 134, 217
Saint-Martin, Isabelle 17
Salm, Abraham 274
Salm, Gerlof 274
Salviati, Antonio 288
Sauvage-Vercour, Chevalier de 146
Schadde, Jozef 146
Schadow, Johann Gottfried 168
Schadow, Wilhelm von 84, 278-279
Schaepman, A.I. 72
Schartau, Henric 193-194
Schayes, Antoine 247
Schinkel, Karl Friedrich 87, 158, 160-161, 165-166, 168, 214, 286
Schiøler (family) 98
Schirmer, Heinrich Ernst 203
Schlegel, Friedrich 157-158, 277-279
Schlegel, Frits 96
Schmidt, Christian Wilhelm 169
Schmidt, Friedrich von 167
Schnaase, Karl 88
Schnitzler, Carl 159

Schnorr von Carolsfeld, Julius 88, 278
Schnütgen, Alexander 86, 91
Schraudolph, Johann von 280
Schulze-Naumburg, Paul 109
Schumacher, Fritz 176
Schwarz, Franz-Joseph 284
Schwarzmann, Joseph 279
Schwechten, Franz 283, 289
Scoles, A.J.C. 233
Scoles, J.J. 233-234
Scott, Edmund E. 225-226
Scott, George 194
Scott, George Gilbert 129-130, 135, 137, 164, 214, 223, 225
Scott, George Gilbert (junior) 129-130, 135, 227
Scott, Giles Gilbert 226, 241
Scott, John Oldrid 225, 233
Scott, Walter 324
Scott, William 127
Sedding, John Dando 240
Sellars, James 236
Serrurier-Bovy, Gustave 60
Servaes, Albert 62
's-Gravezande, A. van 269
Shaw, Richard Norman 235, 240
Sherrin, George 234
Shrewsbury (Earl of) 130, 132, 222, 238
Siemering, Rudolf 168
Simons, Menno 400
Sitte, Camillo 178
Sjöberg, Gustaf Erik 199, 307
Skovgaard, Joakim, 101, 107-108, 307, 311-312
Skovgaard, Niels 101, 307
Smit, Judocus 73
Smith, R.G. 234
Soetens, Claude 365
Soffers, P. 264
Soller, August 87
Solomons, Edward 232
Sophia (Queen) 199
Sørensen, H.S. 106
Soubirous, Bernadette 370
Spaans, Joke 369
Spencer, Ignatius 325
Spiegel, Ferdinand August von 408
Sprott, G. W. 45
Spurgeon, Charles H. 36, 199
Statz, Vincenz 87, 163, 169, 281, 283
Staudhammer, Sebastian 90
Stein, Harald 98
Stein, Heinrich Karl Friedrich von 157
Stein, Theodor 171
Steinle, Edward von 168, 279, 281
Steur, A.G. van der 271
Stobbe, Julius 179
Stöcker, Adolf 98-99
Stoclet, Adolph 61

Stokes, Leonard 232
Stoltzenberg, Frans 70, 267, 389
Strack, Johann Heinrich 165, 168, 178
Street, George Edmund 129-130, 223-224, 240
Strobbe, Filip 59
Stübben, Hermann Joseph 177
Stuers, Victor de 65, 75, 77, 79, 264
Stüler, Friedrich August 87, 158-159, 165, 281, 292
Stummel, Friedrich 285
Stupp, Hermann Josef 170
Stuyt, Jan 78-79, 264, 268
Stynen, Herman 54-55
Sutton, John 238
Suys, T.F. 259, 272
Sverre, Ole 195
Swart, Pieter de 259

Tait, A.C. 99
Talbot, John (Earl of Shrewsbury) 130, 132
Taves, Ann 382
Tepe, Alfred 72-73, 259, 263-264, 389
Terry, Richard 239
Thibaut, Anton Friedrich 290
Thiéry, Armand 60
Thoma, Rudolf 177
Thomas Aquinas, 58
Thomson, Alexander 'Greek' 36, 236-237
Thorn Prikker, Jan 289
Thorvaldsen, Bertel 175, 202, 286, 310
Thurah, Laurids 188
Tieck, Ludwig 277
Tite, William 235
Toberentz, Robert 168
Tønnesen, Erik 191-192
Toorop, Jan 268
Trebst, Arthur 286
Treider, Otto 197
Trommius, Abraham 395
Tulder, H. van 263-264

Uhde, Fritz von 90
Umbach, Julius 172
Ungewitter, Georg Gottlob 167, 178
Unna, Simon 401
Ussing, Henry 99-100, 106-107

Vaerwyck, Valentin 254
Vagedes, Adolph von 162
Valk, J. van der 268
Van Assche, Auguste 252, 254
van de Velde, Henry 254
Van de Woestyne, Gustave 62
Van huffel, Albert 255
Van Kerkhove, Pierre 252
Van Overstraeten, Henri 247
Vanvitelli, Luigi 246
Vaughan, Herbert 234, 239

Veesenmeyer, Emil 293
Veggel, A. van 260, 270
Veit, Philipp 278-279, 338
Verhees, Hendrik 269
Verheul, J. 271
Verheyen, Rudolf Wilhelm 179
Verleysen, Cathérine 61
Verriest, Hugo 78
Viaene, Vincent 362
Victoria (Queen) 44, 52, 122, 324, 339
Viérin, Jos 254
Vigeland, Emanuel 311-312
Viollet-le-Duc, Eugène Emmanuel 55, 59, 69, 77, 145, 215, 249, 252, 254, 264
Virgin, Peter 119
Vischer, Peter 286
Voigtel, Richard 164
Voisin, Charles Joseph 59
Vonier, Anscar 241
Vorfeld, Heinrich 91
Vorfeld, Johannes 91
Vorherr, Gustav 174
Vosmaer, Carel 77

Wackenroder, Wilhelm Heinrich 277, 290
Wagner, Arthur 225
Wahlman, Lars Israel 205
Wailes, William 229
Walcker, Friedrich 85, 292
Waldenström, Paul Peter 198
Wallraf, Ferdinand Franz 174
Walsh, Thomas 121
Walters, Frederick Arthur 241
Ward, Thomas 229
Ward, W.G. 334
Wardell, William Wilkinson 132, 137, 225-226, 231
Warnsinck, I. 271-272
Warrington, William 229
Washington, Booker 103
Waterhouse, Alfred 232
Weale, James 55, 58
Webb, Benjamin 333
Webb, Philip 239-240, 240-241
Weber, C. 264
Weightman, John Grey 133
Weil, Johannes Arbo 196
Weinbrenner, Friedrich 162
Weis, Nikolaus 280
Wenck, Heinrich 103
Wennekers, H. 263-264
Wentink, E.G. 274
Wesley, Charles 194
Wesley, John 37, 194, 235, 327
Wessenberg, Ignaz Heinrich von 83-84
Westerberg, Johan August 198
Westlake, N.H.J. 226

Westergaard, Harald 99-102, 107, 109
Weyhe, Maximilian Friedrich 173
Whyte, William 17, 29
Wichern, Johann Heinrich 98, 410
Wied-Runkel, Karl Ludwig Friedrich Alexander zu 157
Wiethase, Heinrich 87, 283
Wilberforce, William 121, 327
Wilde, Oscar 236
Wilhelm I 83, 282
Wilhelm II 83, 88, 288
Wilhelm (Prince) 83
William I 65-66, 361
William II 65-68, 170, 172, 261
William IV 287
William IX 155
William of Orange 170-171
Wilson, Henry 225
Wimmel, Carl Ludwig 171
Wind, H. 269
Wiseman, Nicholas 122, 231, 234, 334-335
Witte, Fritz 91
Wordsworth, William 131, 324
Worthington, Percy 232
Worthington, Thomas 232
Wright, Joseph 38, 40
Wyatt, James 219

Yates, Richard 32-33

Zettervall, Helgo 205, 304
Ziebland, Georg Friedrich 164
Zinzendorf, Nicolas Ludwig 189
Zocher, K.G. 260
Zwijsen, Joannes 262
Zwirner, Ernst Friedrich 159-160, 164-165, 279, 281

447

COLOPHON

Final editing
Luc Vints

Copy editing
Lieve Claes

Layout
Alexis Vermeylen

KADOC
Documentation and Research Centre on
Religion, Culture and Society
KU Leuven
Vlamingenstraat 39
B - 3000 Leuven
http://kadoc.kuleuven.be

Leuven University Press
Minderbroedersstraat 4
B - 3000 Leuven
info@lup.be
www.lup.be